European Union Economies

A Comparative Study

THIRD EDITION

Edited by Drs Frans Somers
International Business School
Hanzehogeschool, Groningen

Contributors

Ian Stone
Richard Bailey
P.J. Drudy
Marisol Esteban
Andrea Fineschi
Milagros García Crespo
Franz Hackl

Markku Kotilainen
Rudi Kurz
Arantza Mendizábal
Carmela Nicosia
Jan-Evert Nilsson
Friedrich Schneider
Kirk Thomson

Addison Wesley Longman Limited
Edinburgh Gate
Harlow
Essex CM20 2JE
United Kingdom
and Associated Companies throughout the world

Published in the United States of America
by Addison Wesley Longman, New York

First published in Great Britain as *European Economies* 1991
Second edition published as *European Community Economies* 1994
Third edition 1998

 ISBN 0 582-30590-X PPR

British Library Cataloguing-in-Publication Data

A catalogue record for this book is available from the British Library.

Library of Congress Cataloging-in-Publication Data

European union economies : a comparative study in economic integration
   / edited by Frans Somers ; contributors Richard Bailey . . . [et al.].
   – 3rd ed.
       p.   cm.
   Rev. ed. of: European economies. 1st ed. 1991.
   Includes bibliographical references and index.
   ISBN 0-582-30590-X (pbk.)
   1. European Union countries–Economic conditions. 2. European
Union countries–Economic policy. 3. Finance–European Union
countries. 4. Comparative economics. I. Somers, Frans.
II. Bailey, Richard.   III. European economies.
HC240.E856   1998
330.94–dc21   97-3194
                                                         CIP

Set by 30 in 10/12 Garamond ITC
Produced by Longman Singapore Publishers (Pte) Ltd
Printed in Singapore

CONTENTS

PREFACE TO THE THIRD EDITION

Since the publication of the second edition of this book three years ago, many developments have taken place. Not only has the former European Community changed its name to European Union, but three new Member States have joined the Union and a definite date for the start of the Economic and Monetary Union has been set.

Naturally, these events have had implications for this new edition of the book. Its name has been changed and it is extended with three new chapters (on Austria, Sweden and Finland). Recent developments in the Union, for instance the latest decisions concerning the EMU and the state of affairs with respect to the enlargements are discussed. The surveys of the economies of the 12 countries belonging to the EU before 1995 have been updated completely.

Compared to the previous edition, the structure of the book has been slightly changed also. The old division in major EU countries (part B) and smaller ones (part C) has been abandoned. Instead, the date of entry is used for grouping countries within the book . Part B discusses the economies of the original six member states (Germany, France, Italy and the Benelux countries); Part C concentrates on the group forming the first enlargement (UK, Ireland and Denmark); Part D deals with the countries of the Mediterranean enlargement (Greece, Spain and Portugal) and Part E with the Nordic countries and Austria (latest enlargement). Furthermore, in every country chapter a specific section on the impact of European integration has been added.

Six new contributors have joined the authors' team: Prof. Friedrich Schneider and Dr Franz Hackl (Linz) prepared the Austrian chapter, Dr Markku Kotilainen (Helsinki) the one on Finland, Jan-Evert Nillson (Stockholm) the one on Sweden and Dr P. J. Drudy (Dublin) the one on Ireland; Carmela Nicosia (Florence) updated the chapter on Italy.

Again, I would like to thank all the contributors, old and new alike, for their great enthusiasm and willingness to cooperate. The publication of the book has been a truly European project, involving 15 authors coming from 11 EU countries.

As with the second edition, I would like to mention Dr Ian Stone in particular for his great help in finding new authors and his language and organisational support.

Frans Somers
Groningen, The Netherlands
January 1997.

PREFACE TO THE SECOND EDITION

For the second edition, this book has been considerably expanded. First, in contrast to the first edition, surveys of the economies of the seven smaller EC countries (the Netherlands, Belgium, Denmark, Portugal, Greece, Ireland and Luxembourg) are included as well. This has been done in order to give a complete overview of all national economies of the European Community. As with the major economies, the analyses of the smaller countries, although less detailed, focus mainly on long-term trends and developments and have the same structure. Naturally, the smaller countries are also incorporated in the part on international comparisons.

Second, the introductory chapter, dealing with the development of the European Community, has also been extended. More attention, not only here but throughout the book, is paid to the discussion of common EC policies and regulations, since their impact on the economies of the individual countries is of growing importance. The common monetary policy, which is aiming at the introduction of one common European currency before the end of the millennium, and the completion of the internal market by the end of 1992, for instance, has far-reaching consequences for the national economies and national economic policies of the Member States. At this moment it is far from certain, that the European Economic and Monetary Union (EMU) will be introduced on schedule as agreed upon in the *Maastricht Treaty on European Union* of 1991. The problems on the currency markets in 1992 and 1993 and the near break-down of the Exchange Rate Mechanism of the EMS in August 1993, do not feed optimism in this respect. Nevertheless, the Maastricht Treaty, and European integration in general, will be of major importance for economic policy and practice of the EC Member States in the coming years. That is why they have been given more stress in this new edition.

Because of the addition of the smaller countries, the structure of the book has been slightly altered. Part A deals with the development of the European Community; Part B discusses the five major EC countries (Germany, France, Italy, the UK and Spain) and Part C the seven smaller ones. Part D is concerned with international comparisons and Part E provided statistical information (in time series) on all twelve economies and in may cases on the US and Japan.

In addition to these extensions, the book has been completely updated. Developments up until July 1993 are included. The events on the currency markets and the changes of the ERM in August 1993 are discussed in a special postscript to Chapter 1 (Part A).

The chapters on the smaller countries are partly written by new contributors: Dr Richard Bailey (Portugal and Denmark) and William Glynn (Ireland). Dr Ian Stone, author of the UK section, prepared the chapters on Greece and Belgium/Luxembourg, and the undersigned the chapter on the Netherlands. From a practical point of view it was not possible to invite a resident from each country involved this time. I would like to express my gratitude to all the old and new contributors, especially for the enthusiasm they showed in the preparation of this book. In particular I would like to thank Dr Ian Stone, who not only wrote three chapters, but also gave invaluable language support in this complicated international project.

Frans Somers
Groningen, The Netherlands
November 1993

PREFACE TO THE FIRST EDITION

This book is concerned with the individual economies of the five major countries of the European Community (EC): Germany, France, the United Kingdom, Italy and Spain. These countries are by far the largest in terms of Gross Domestic Product, area, and population in the EC.

Since the war Western Europe has experienced a strong trend towards economic and political integration. The European Community, founded in 1957 by six countries, nowadays comprises twelve members. Within the EC the progress towards integration has been accelerated by the adoption of Single European Act at the end of 1985, which sets the route for the achievement of a European Single Market before the end of 1992. The final goal of the Act is the foundation of a European Economic and Political Union, mainly based on the principles of a free market economy (*see* part A in this book).

Although Western Europe is moving towards being an economic entity, many differences will remain between individual countries in the Community in terms of economic structure, national policies, labour market, industry, trade patterns, etc.; not to mention distinctions in mentalities, tastes and cultures.

This book is intended to provide a basic understanding, within a limited space, of the economies of the major countries of the Community. It focuses on long-term developments and underlying trends rather than on short-term economic surveys. In this respect it differs greatly from the existing publications from international organisations like the OECD. Special attention is paid to the strengths and weaknesses of each economy, its dominant industries, trade patterns and future perspectives within the emerging common market (part B).

In section C comparisons are made between the countries involved. Differences and similarities in the fields of government involvement, output and growth, productivity and competitiveness and the financial system are mentioned and possible fields of specialisation are identified.

This book concludes with a uniform Statistical Annexe with harmonised data, mainly based on Eurostat and OECD sources (part D). In other parts of this book, referrals to tables in this Annexe are frequently made (prefixed with a D).

At the end of the country chapters in part B the reader will find lists of information on the country concerned can be found (other publications, statistical institutions, government and private agencies).

The book thus serves as an accessible introductory text, giving the reader a basic grasp of the economic structure of the major European countries, as well as a source of information for further investigations. In this sense, it can be used to 'guide' study of the economies of the main EC countries.

The book is aimed at students in business schools, polytechnics and universities. It can be used for business environment studies, EC courses, course offerings focusing on economic policies, preparation for studies abroad.

This publication is the result of a considerable exercise in international co-operation. The chapters on the individual countries are exclusively prepared by contributors living in that particular country: Professor Rudi Kurz from Germany, Professor Andrea Fineschi from Italy, Dr Ian Stone from the UK, Kirk Thomson and Rachel Condon from France and Professor Milagros García Crespo, Dr Marisol Esteban and Professor Arantza Mendizábal from Spain.

The editing, introductory chapter and chapter on international comparisons was done by someone from a 'neutral' country: the Netherlands.

Most of the participants in this project are working for institutions co-operating in international programmes with Hanse Polytechnic Groningen, having its seat in that country.

In total citizens from six EC member states were involved in this project. It did not turn out to be a barrier to a very fruitful co-operation and intensive and interesting discussions.

Frans Somers
Groningen, The Netherlands
January 1991

CONTRIBUTORS

Frans Somers (*Editor*) is a senior Lecturer in Economics at the International Business School of the Hanzehogeschool, Groningen, The Netherlands, and is also manager of International Projects at that institution. Since graduating in 1973, he has worked mainly in the field of higher education and has published several books; among others, one on political economy (1980), two on macroeconomics (1988 and 1990) and two on public finance and government policy in the Netherlands (1990 and 1993). From 1988 to 1990 he was Editor-in-Chief of an economics magazine intended for business students and lecturers. He lectured and was involved in setting up European Studies Programmes at the Budapest University of Economic Sciences (1994 and 1995) and the Prague University of Economics (1995).

Dr Ian Stone is Reader in Economics and Director of the Northern Economic Research Unit at the University of Northumbria, Newcastle upon Tyne. He was educated at the Universities of Leicester, Simon Fraser (Canada) and Cambridge and has previously held lecturing posts at Victoria University of Wellington (New Zealand) and Universities of Newcastle and Sunderland. His research interests are in the field of regional and industrial development. Recent work includes studies on inward investment and labour markets (for the Employment Department), defence industry restructuring (European Parliament and Rowntree), skill shortages in engineering and local impact of universities. His assistants for this book, **Paul Braidford, Charles Jarvis** and **Aidan Oswell** are Researchers in the Northern Economic Research Unit at the University of Northumbria, Newcastle upon Tyne.

Richard Bailey was educated at the London School of Economics and Warwick University. He

is currently Principal Lecturer in the Department of Economics and Government at the University of Northumbria. Research interests and publications in the areas of Comparative Economics and International Political Economy.

Dr P.J. Drudy is Associate Professor of Economics and a Fellow at Trinity College, Dublin. He is also Director of the Centre for Urban and Regional Studies and Bursar at Trinity College. He was formerly a Lecturer at the Department of Land Economy and a Fellow of St Edmund's College at Cambridge University. His main research interests are in urban and regional economics and development and he has written numerous papers on these subjects. He has edited a series of books for Cambridge University Press, including *Ireland: Land, Politics and People, Ireland and the European Community, The Irish in America* and *Ireland and Britain since 1922.*

Dr Marisol Esteban studied at the University of the Basque Country, the London School of Economics and the University of California at Berkeley. She is Head of the Department of Applied Economics of the University of the Basque Country, where she has lectured on Urban and Regional Economics and Contemporary Spanish Economy. Her special fields of interest include labour markets, industrial policies and regional economic development. She has published several books and articles on these topics and has done consultancy work for the public administration.

Andrea Fineschi is Professor of Economics at the University of Flórence. He has also worked at the Universities of Ferrara and Messina after previously teaching in the universities of Siena and Florence (for the first time). His special fields of interest include aspects of economic theory of the classical economists and problems of the Italian economy.

Dr Milagros García Crespo is Professor of Applied Economics at the University of the Basque Country. She was Dean of the Faculty of Economics in Bilbao from 1982 to 1987. Her interest in European issues led her to set up a European Documentation Centre in 1983 at the same university. She established and maintained links with European academic institutions (Kingston Polytechnic in London and the Université de Grenoble). From 1987 to 1989 she was Councillor of Economy to the Basque Government. From 1989 to 1991 she was the First President of the Public Accounts Court of the Basque Country. In 1994 she was appointed President of the Public Accounts Court of Spain, a post that she currently holds. She is the author of many books and articles on economic policy, the Spanish economy and European issues.

Franz Hackl received his doctoral degree in economics at the Johannes Kepler University of Linz. Since 1992 he has been assistant professor and lecturer at the Department of Economics, Institute of Economic Policy. His main research interest is environmental and agricultural economics.

Dr Markku Kotilainen has worked at the Research Institute of the Finnish Economy (ETLA) since 1986, until spring 1996 as a Research Fellow and since then as the Head of Forecasting Group. Before 1986 he worked in the Pellervo Economic Research Institute (PTT) and in the Ministry of Finance. His research interests are mainly in the area of international macroeconomics. His main publications concern exchange rate regimes, European integration and foreign trade. Dr Kotilainen received his doctorate in economics from the University of Helsinki. He has additionally studied economics in Germany (Münster and Kiel) and in Denmark (Copenhagen).

Dr Rudi Kurz worked for ten years as a research fellow and as Deputy Managing Director at the Institute for Applied Economic Research, Tübingen (IAW). He prepared studies and specialist reports for the German Federal Ministry of Commerce and for the Commission of the European Community during that time. He has undertaken research in the United States and was guest scholar at the Brookings Institution, Washington DC. He is Professor of Economics at the Pforzheim Business School and consultant to the IAW since 1988. He published books and articles on technology policy, competition policy and environmental issues.

Dr Arantza Mendizábal is Professor in Economics in the Faculty of Economics and Business Administration of the University of the Basque Country where she has been the Rector of the University. She has considerable experience on economic policy issues and has written widely on the economy of the Basque Country. From 1991 to 1996 she was an elected member of the Central Parliament in Madrid, belonging to the Commissions on Economic and European Issues.

Linti Carmela Nicosia (BA (Law), Messina, Italy; M.Sc (Business Economics) Buckingham, UK), is a Research Associate in Economics at the Universities of Florence and Messina for the Italian National Council of Research (C.N.R.), and Ph.D. Researcher in Economic Organization at the University of Buckingham. She has been a C.N.R. researcher in Economics at the University La Sapienza of Rome. She has published in the areas of Corporate Governance in the Financial Sector and Voting Systems.

Jan-Evert Nilsson is Director at the Nordic School of Planning (Nordplan) in Stockholm and adjunct professor (part time) in Business Economics at the University of Umeå. He was economic advisor to the Swedish Minister of Labour from 1992–1994. His research interests are in the areas of regional and industrial development. He has recently been engaged in a four-year research programme carried out under the aegis of the European Science Foundation concerned with the topic of regional and urban restructuring in Europe. The research work is reported in Jan-Evert Nilsson, Peter Dicken and Jamie Peck (eds) "The Internationalization Process: European Firms in Global Competition."

Friedrich Schneider studied at the University of Konstanz. From 1976 to 1983 he was Visiting Associate Professor at the Carnegie-Mellon-University in Pittsburgh (USA) and afterwards Associate Professor at the University of Aarhus in Denmark (1983 to 1984). Since 1986 he has been Professor of Economics at the Johannes Kepler University of Linz. From 1990 to 1996 he was Dean of the Social Science and Economics Faculty and in 1996 he became Vice-President of the University of Linz. His research fields include general economic policy, taxation, shadow economy, privatisation and deregulation policies.

Kirk Thomson studied at the London School of Economics, the Free University of Berlin and at the Sorbonne. He is now Director of Studies at the Ecole des Practiciens du Commerce International in Paris, where he also lectures in Economics and on aspects of the European Community.

PART A

Introduction

CHAPTER 1

The European Union

Frans Somers

1.1 INTRODUCTION

Since the signing of the Treaty of Rome in 1957 significant progress has been made toward European integration. An internal market is in place and the European Union (EU) is planning to achieve an economic and monetary union before the end of the millennium. In spite of these developments, there are still good reasons to study the national economies within the EU.

In the first place there are still substantial differences between these countries in terms of economic performance as well as in government policies. It is likely that these will narrow in the future; economic convergence and policy harmonisation are prerequisites for further integration.

In addition, there are considerable distinctions in economic structure between the member states. Every country has its own industrial structure and business traditions, reflecting historical circumstances, comparative advantages, government decisions, geographical conditions and chance. These differences will not necessarily disappear. Indeed, even with further integration some features will be reinforced. Integration can lead to more specialisation, because it is to be hoped that full exposure to international competition will lead to a better allocation of factors of production. This reallocation may be realised on the basis of existing trade patterns, comparative advantage, development of new trade relations, etc.

In this book we will examine the economies of the fifteen countries which form the European Union at present: Austria, Belgium, Denmark, Finland, France, Germany, Greece, Ireland, Italy, Luxembourg, The Netherlands, Portugal, Spain, Sweden and the United Kingdom. In 1996 their combined GDP amounted to 6742 billion ECUs[1], roughly 1.17 times that of the USA and 1.84 times that of Japan, the other two large economic blocs in the world.

With a total population of 373 million, as against 265 million for the USA and 125 million for Japan, the EU is the largest economic entity in the world[2].

Within the EU there are substantial differences between countries in terms of GDP and population (see Figure 1.1). Germany is by far the largest country, in 1996 accounting for 27.4% of total Union GDP and some 22% of population. France (18.1% of Union GDP), Italy (14.1%) and UK (13.1%) form a second group. Spain is a middle-sized country, with a GDP 6.9% of the combined Union GDP, while the other seven countries are considerably smaller with a GDP ranging from 4.6% of Union GDP (The Netherlands) to only 0.2% (Luxembourg).

This introductory chapter begins with a discussion of the European integration process: its origins, aims, progress and policies. This will be followed by an assessment of the size, relative

---

[1] ECU stands for *European Currency Unit*, a basket containing fixed amounts of all EU currencies (for more explanation, see par. 1.3.2).

[2] The North American Free Trade Agreement (NAFTA), which came into being in 1993 and is signed by the USA, Canada and Mexico, is a trading bloc and not an economic entity. As a trading bloc it is about equal to the size of the EU in terms of both GDP and population.

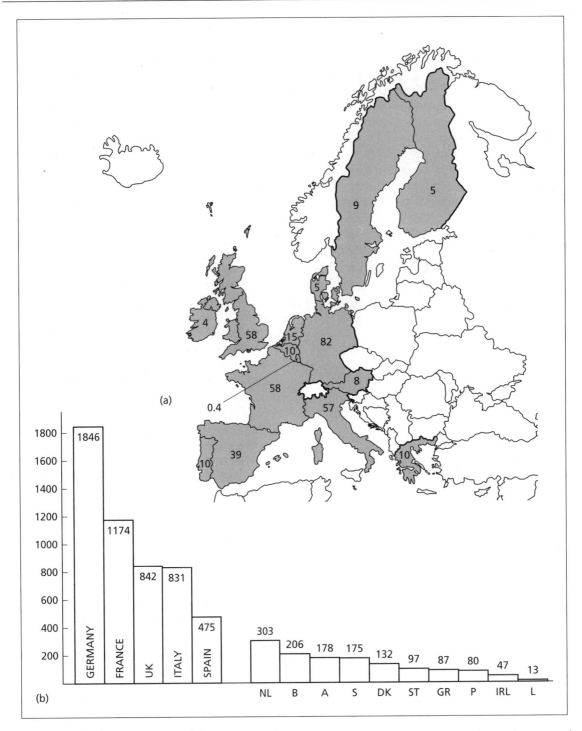

(a)

(b)

Figure 1.1 The European Union in 1996: (a) Population in millions (indicated on map); Total EU population 373 million. (b) GDP at current prices in billions of ECU (European Commission estimates); Total GDP EU15 (fifteen Member States): 6742 ECU

Source: European Commission, *Statistical Annex European Economy*, June 1996.

strength and importance of the European Union. The chapter will end with brief discussion of the main economic indicators of the fifteen economies.

This provides the framework within which the national economies will be studied in more detail in the following chapters of the book. Special attention will be paid in each of the country studies to their institutional and historical background, industrial structure, trade patterns, strengths and weaknesses and problems and prospects within the evolving European economy.

1.2. EUROPEAN INTEGRATION

1.2.1 The origins of the integration process

The aftermath of the Second World War was marked by a pronounced impetus in Europe towards international cooperation. Several factors contributed to this attitude. First of all there were economic considerations. The war left Europe with immense physical destruction, loss of capital goods and an impoverished population. In order to revitalise the European economy the United States introduced the Marshall Plan in 1948 (by means of the Foreign Assistance Act). The initiative was intended to provide Europe with sufficient funds and goods to carry out the necessary recovery programmes. The US aid was granted on a *European* rather than on a *national* basis. A special international institution, the Organisation for European Economic Cooperation (OEEC), was created to distribute the aid among the member countries and to coordinate the assistance programmes. Within the framework of the plan, separate measures were taken to intensify the extent of intra-European trade.

The OEEC, however, was not abolished after the termination of the Marshall Plan in 1950. It continued to promote the liberalisation of international trade and economic cooperation. In 1961 it transformed itself into the Organisation of Economic Co-operation and Development (OECD), an organisation at the service of all

developed industrial countries in the Western World.

A second driving force behind European integration was the Soviet threat and the beginning of the Cold War. By the end of the 1940s the division of Europe into a Western sector and a Soviet-dominated sphere became apparent, after Soviet-inspired Communist take-overs in Romania (1945), Bulgaria (1946), Hungary, Poland (1947) and Czechoslovakia (1948). In response to this development a range of organisations was established, including the West European Union (WEU), NATO (North Atlantic Treaty Organisation) (both in 1948) and the Council of Europe in 1949. The objectives of these organisations were not merely defence against the Soviet threat, but also the protection of values such as freedom, democracy and human rights.

Finally an important incentive for West European integration was the 'German question'. After two world wars, a completely independent Germany was regarded as a potential threat to peace. To link the newly established Federal Republic of Germany as firmly as possible to the other European countries was seen as a solution to this problem.

This question became urgent in the light of what was seen as the increasing Soviet threat to Europe. A strong Europe, both in the military and the economic sense, was thought to be absolutely essential. The German contribution to the strengthening of Western Europe was of great importance, though care had to be taken to avoid allowing Germany the opportunity once more to dominate its neighbours militarily and politically.

For these reasons the French Minister of Foreign Affairs Jean Monnet initiated in 1950 a plan to place the European coal and steel industries under one single supranational authority and to establish a common market in this field. This plan would enable a rapid expansion of these industries, which are of vital importance to the defence industry and overall economic development, without allowing the new West German state full control over them. In addition to France and Germany, other European countries were also invited to participate in this arrangement.

As a result, the European Coal and Steel Community (ECSC) was established (*Treaty of Paris*) in the spring of 1951 by France, the Federal Republic of Germany, Italy, Belgium, the Netherlands and Luxembourg. The foundation for the construction of a much more extensive European Union was laid. For a variety of reasons, major countries like the UK remained outside at this stage.

Attempts by the same six countries to create a common army (the European Defence Community (EDC)) in the early 1950s failed, however. It would have required a supranational political power, which was too advanced a notion at that time. Cooperation was first sought, then, in the economic field on a more modest basis. The Six founded the European Economic Community (EEC) and the European Atomic Energy Commission (Euratom) in 1957 by the *Treaty of Rome*. Euratom was designed for the peaceful development of atomic energy. The treaties came into effect on 1 January 1958.

1.2.2 Towards an economic and monetary union

A major difference between the ECSC and the EEC at that time was that the EEC was only minimally equipped with supranational powers; the main decision-making body within the EEC was the Council of Ministers (of foreign affairs), leaving considerable powers to the national authorities. Important decisions could be taken only by unanimity.

Despite this, the Treaty of Rome envisaged progress towards a kind of economic union. Article 2 of the Treaty of Rome states that:

> The Community shall have as its task, by *establishing a common market* and *progressively approximating the economic policies of the Member States* (author's italics), to promote throughout the Community a harmonious development of economic activities, a continuous and balanced expansion, an increase in stability, an accelerated rise of the standard of living and closer relations between the States belonging to it.

The three Communities (ECSC, Euratom and EEC) duly amalgamated in 1965 to form the European Community (EC).

According to article 8 of the Treaty of Rome the Common Market was to be reached within 12 years (from 1958). A *Common Market* can be defined as an association of nations with free trade among its members, a common external tariff and a free mobility of factors of production. If in addition economic policies are harmonised then the association is called an Economic Union.

The six members failed to meet their original target. By 1970 only the first two of the Common Market criteria had been met: the removal of all internal tariffs and quota restrictions and the erecting of a common external tariff. Free mobility of factors of production and a substantial harmonisation of economic policies were far from being realised by 1970. In fact, it took another twenty years before these goals were met to any extent. A number of factors can be held responsible for the slow progress of the integration process.

First there is the question of national interests. A real Economic Union means that the bulk of national power is transferred to supranational authorities. This implies a substantial loss of national sovereignty for the Member States. From the very beginning of the EEC in 1958, however, individual Member States have been reluctant to accept this idea. The Treaty of Rome envisaged that the decision-making (of the Council of Ministers) by unanimous agreement would be replaced by a qualified majority vote for a wide range of issues in the year 1966. Because of the French opposition, however, Member States kept a right of veto in situations where vital national interests are involved (the Luxembourg compromise of 1966). Subsequently, since its entrance in 1973 it has been mainly the UK which has tried to slow down the integration process for nationalistic reasons.

A second impediment to rapid progress towards a Common Market was the successive enlargements of the Community. The UK, Ireland and Denmark joined the EC in 1973, Greece in 1981 and Spain and Portugal in 1986.

These enlargements shifted the political attention to other questions and made the negotiations on common policies even more complicated.

Finally, the economic crises of the 1970s and early 1980s created an unfavourable climate for free trade. National governments were inclined to return to protectionist policies and to support national industries in order to counter the effects of the international crises upon the domestic economy.

It was during the early 1980s, however, that the drive towards European integration received new impetus. The economic crisis of these years made it clear that the problems in Europe were intensified because producers in the Community were losing ground to their main competitors in Japan and the USA. The fragmented home market of the Community was seen as a major reason for this development, and a call was made for the speeding up of the integration process. A single European market, it was argued, would stimulate economies of scale in production, marketing, research and development and also strengthen competition, enhancing the efficiency and competitiveness of European industry.

A necessary condition for accelerating the creation of the internal market was a change in the Community decision-making procedures, which until then required unanimity in many cases. This condition was met by the adoption of the *Single European Act* in 1985, whereby in matters concerning the internal market the condition of unanimity was replaced by a qualified majority. The Act, which after ratification by all 12 members came into force in 1987, also contained the provision that the internal market should be completed before the end of 1992. In addition to setting a timetable for the creation of an 'internal market without frontiers' the Single Act also amended the original Treaty of Rome by adopting policies in the field of economic and social cohesion, environment, monetary and political cooperation etc. The Single Act can be seen as a major step on the way towards the ultimate goal of an economically united Europe.

Achievement of this goal involves the establishment of an Economic and Monetary Union (EMU), which requires far-reaching coordination of monetary and economic policies among the Member States. Monetary policy, for instance, would be largely transferred from national authorities to an independent European System of Central Banks (a kind of European Fed), led by a European Central Bank (ECB), and national currencies would be replaced by a common currency, managed by the ECB. In the field of fiscal policy, national governments would retain more of their autonomy, but their control would be limited considerably by common policies and restrictions.

At the EC summit meeting of October 1990 broad outlines of a treaty on EMU were set. According to a plan, developed by the European Commission chaired by the Frenchman M. Jacques Delors, EMU should be reached in three stages; the final one to be completed towards the end of the decade. As control has to be substantially surrendered to supranational powers, EMU can only be realised if it is accompanied by a significant degree of *political* integration.

Maastricht and beyond

A final decision was taken during the Maastricht meeting of the European Council of Heads of Government (or State) in December 1991 (the *Maastricht Treaty*). A *Treaty on European Union* was concluded in February 1992, amending the Treaty of Rome substantially. The (Maastricht) Treaty on European Union contains an agreement on an irreversible movement towards *EMU* as well as an agreement on a number of *political* issues. Following the final ratification of the Treaty by all Member States in November 1993, the EC formally became the *European Union* (EU).

According to the Treaty, the Economic and Monetary Union is to be established not later than 1999. By then, the currencies of the individual Member States eligible to EMU will be replaced by a single currency, managed and controlled by an independent European Central Bank. However, without economic convergence, including a certain degree of economic and social cohesion, the introduction of a common currency will not be possible. Hence, convergence programmes are to be adopted to prepare the individual Member States for eligibility.

The term *economic convergence* has two distinct meanings. The first refers to the convergence (i.e gradual decrease in initial differences or disparities over time) of macro-economic variables, which directly influence exchange rate variables, like inflation, budget deficits and interest rates). This is usually called *nominal convergence*. *Real convergence* on the other hand, is the approximation of economic and social conditions (e.g. standards of living, rates of unemployment) throughout the Union; it is commonly measured in terms of the reduction of existing disparities in GDP per capita. Nominal and real convergence are interrelated; in addition nominal convergence is assumed to create the proper conditions for stronger economic growth for the Union as a whole. To be admitted to EMU the Member States should satisfy certain nominal convergence criteria (considered below).

It is envisaged that the Economic and Monetary Union should be reached in three stages:

- *Stage I* (July 1990–31 December 1994): Completion of the internal market, including totally free movement of goods, persons and capital (before 31 December 1992); start of economic convergence programmes of the Member States. All countries are expected to enter the narrow band of the Exchange Rate Mechanism of the EMS.
- *Stage II* (1 January 1994–between 1997 and 1999): Adoption of multi-annual convergence programmes; establishing of a European Monetary Institute which will co-ordinate (but not control) monetary policies and prepare the setting up of the ECB in stage III. Member states must start procedures leading to independence for their central banks.
- *Stage III* (start between 1997 and 1999): Founding of the European System of Central Banks (ECSB) and the European Central Bank (ECB); replacement of national currencies of Member States admitted to EMU by the single

currency. The ECSB will be made up by the ECB and the national central banks, where the latter will be responsible for the implementation of monetary policies set by the (independent) ECB.

The Maastricht Treaty implies an *irrevocable* commitment by the Member State to move to stage III, provided *they satisfy the necessary conditions*. These conditions consist of the following five *nominal convergence criteria*:

1. *Price stability*. The inflation rate should not exceed the average inflation rate of the three countries having the lowest price increases by more than 1.5 percentage points.
2. *Currency stability*. The exchange rate should not have been subject to devaluation within the 'normal' band of the Exchange Rate Mechanism of the European Monetary System for at least two years (see also Section 1.3.2).
3. *Public deficit*. The budget deficit must not exceed 3% of GDP.
4. *National debt*. The public debt must be lower than 60% of GDP, or making 'substantial progress' in that direction.
5. *Interest rates*. The nominal long-term capital interest rates should not be higher than 2 percentage points above the average of the long-term interest rates of the three countries with the lowest inflation rates.

According to the Maastricht Treaty, the European Council will decide before the end of 1996 whether the majority of Member States do satisfy the nominal convergence criteria and at what date EMU can be launched. If no other date has been set, EMU will be instituted on 1 January 1999, but it will be confined to those Member States which fulfil the necessary conditions. The UK and Denmark obtained an 'opting out' clause, meaning that each of these countries was allowed to reserve its decision.

The principle of economic and social cohesion has been stressed in the Treaty. A special Cohesion Fund has been set up to give financial support for environmental and transport projects in Member States with a per capita income of less than 90% of the EU average (Greece, Ireland, Portugal and Spain) over the years 1993–99. Other resources allocated to these countries will be increased as well. These measures are intended to speed up *real convergence* and to ease these countries in meeting the *nominal convergence* criteria by the end of the century.

In addition to EMU the Maastricht Treaty on European Union contained an agreement on *political and social issues*, such as the introduction of a union citizenship, including freedom of movement, the right of free residence and the right to vote and to be eligible for elections at the municipal and European level. The Treaty also includes provisions on a common foreign and security policy which will lead in time to the framing of a common defence policy. In the social field the Treaty provides in an annexed protocol for the consolidation of workers' basic rights, along the path set by the Social Charter of 1989 (a non-binding declaration of principles). The UK, however, opted not to sign this part of the agreement.

The Treaty contains a special provision aimed at ensuring that decisions are taken at the level closest to the ordinary citizen: the so-called *subsidiarity principle* (article 3b). According to this article, the Union should act only if an objective can be better achieved at Union rather than at national level and furthermore the means employed must be proportional to the aimed objectives. The inclusion of this article mainly serves to prevent too great a concentration of political power in 'Brussels'; its object can be seen as the ruling out of an over-centralised federalist approach. In addition, its aim is to reduce the 'democratic deficit' of the Union, i.e. the limited input of Euro-level elected representatives in the decision-making process. The position of the European Parliament, the role of which is mostly advisory, has in fact been strengthened by granting it the power to veto the adoption of a large range of EU rules and regulations. Though the Treaty is a new milestone in the European unification process, it can not be regarded as an unambiguous step towards a federal Europe. The British especially were very keen on dropping the so-called 'F-word'. The EU remains primarily a 'Community of Nations States' for the time being.

It was intended that all twelve EU countries at that time would ratify the Maastricht Treaty on European Union in the course of the year 1992. The Danes, however, rejected the Treaty in a referendum in June 1992. Although the French accepted the terms of the Treaty in their September 1992 referendum, they did so with the smallest possible majority. The British decided to postpone ratification of the Treaty until after a new Danish referendum. After guaranteeing the Danish a number of extra opting out clauses, the latter referendum resulted in a clear 'yes' vote. With British ratification following in the same year, the Treaty was finally approved by the end of 1993.

Soon afterwards it became clear that it would be very unlikely that the *majority of the EU countries* would be able to satisfy all convergence criteria before 1997. In the early 1990s the European economy went into a severe recession. As a result, public deficits and debt for most countries increased sharply to levels well outside the limits set by the Maastricht criteria. In addition, there was turbulence in the currency markets. Rather than moving to more stable exchange rate relationships within the framework of the European Monetary System (EMS), the system came under severe strains. Sustained pressure forced the British government to suspend its participation in the Exchange Rate Mechanism; the Italian government took a similar decision. On top of that, several realignments took place, including the devaluation of the Spanish peseta, the Portuguese escudo and the Irish punt. Sweden and Finland (not Members at that time) could not manage to maintain the unofficial link of their currencies with the system. For the remaining currencies the band was widened in August 1993 from +/– 2.25% to +/– 15% (except for the German mark and the Dutch guilder). This raises the question as to what is considered 'normal' fluctuation margins; the European Council will probably decide that it will be the wider one.

The result of all these developments was that in 1995 not one country satisfied all five criteria (see Table 1.1). Though the European economy clearly recovered in the mid-1990s, it still remains an unrealistic assumption that the majority of Member States would satisfy the criteria before 1997. Therefore it was decided by the European Council in 1995 in Madrid that the EMU will be launched on 1 January 1999. The name of the single currency is to be the *Euro*; the option of using the name ECU has been abandoned. The timetable for the (third stage) of EMU has been set as follows:

- Early 1998: European Council decides which countries will qualify for EMU on the basis of the 1996–97 figures. Establishment of the European System of Central Banks (ECSB) including the European Central Bank (ECB).
- 1 January 1999: Launch of EMU. National currencies of participating countries will be irrevocably linked to the Euro. Euros only used by governments, banks and in the foreign-exchange markets.
- 1 January 2002: Issue of Euro notes and coins and conversion of retail payment systems.
- 31 July 2002: Euro sole legal tender, fully replacing the old national currencies.

At the same summit in Madrid it was also decided that convergence criteria will be strictly maintained. For that reason almost all Member States started or continued rigorous austerity programmes, in an attempt to bring down their public debts and deficits. Severe budget cuts were announced, leading in many countries to strong protest movements by public sector workers, trade unions, oppositional political parties and others. France for example, experienced a large number of strikes and street demonstrations. It is

Table 1.1 Nominal convergence criteria for EMU. Deviation from norm in 1995. European Commission estimates. (Bold figures indicate that the criterion concerned has been met).

	Convergence criteria					
	Inflation rate[1] %	Long-term int. rate %	Budget deficit % of GDP	Public debt % of GDP	Currency score[2]	Number of criteria satisfied
Norm	1.5 + 1.5%	8.2 + 2%	<3%	<60%	+/–	
Luxembourg	4.1	**6.1**	**–0.3[3]**	**5.9**	+	4
France	**1.6**	7.5	5.0	**52.4**	+	4
Denmark	**1.7**	8.3	**1.4**	71.9	+	4
Germany	2.2	**6.8**	3.5	**58.1**	+	4
Ireland	**1.2**	8.3	**2.4**	85.5	+	4
Netherlands	2.1	**6.3**	3.4	79.0	+	3
Belgium	2.0	7.5	4.5	133.7	+	3
United Kingdom	2.4	**8.2**	6.0	**54.1**	–	3
Spain	4.8	11.3	6.2	65.7	–	0
Italy	5.0	11.9	7.1	124.8	–	0
Portugal	5.1	11.5	5.4	71.6	–	0
Greece	9.3	–	9.2	111.7	–	0
Austria	2.1	**7.2**	6.2	69.4	–[4]	3
Finland	**1.6**	**8.8**	5.6	**59.4**	–[4]	3
Sweden	4.1	10.2	8.1	79.9	–[4]	0

[1] Deflator GDP
[2] 15% margins
[3] Surplus
[4] Not participating in the ERM

Source: European Economy, Statistical Annex, June 1996

far from certain whether the targets set by the various governments will be met. Even Germany and France are not certain to satisfy all convergence criteria. If one of these countries fails to do so, EMU will not go ahead or will be at least postponed, because the German–French cooperation is at the heart of European monetary integration.

An alternative would be a relaxation of the criteria. This idea is, however, strongly opposed, especially by the Germans. Weaker criteria might mean a weaker single currency too. Germany is definitely not prepared to give up their solid D-mark by an inflation-prone and unstable Euro. But if economic recovery continues and if the criteria of public debt is interpreted in a flexible way, it may be expected that at least the following countries could qualify for EMU: Germany, France, the Benelux countries, Austria, Finland and Ireland. For countries like Italy, Spain and Portugal a minor miracle is likely to be needed if the criteria are not relaxed. The UK and Denmark might voluntarily decide to stay out.

Fiscal discipline does not stop once countries are admitted to the EMU. At the Dublin summit in December 1996 it was decided to include a 'stability pact', which should guarantee monetary stability. Member States participating in the EMU are obliged to keep their public deficits below 3% of GDP. If a Member State does not succeed in doing so, it has to pay a fine up to 0.5% of GDP, which eventually will contribute to the EU budget. Only in case of a severe recession, defined as decrease of real GDP of more than 2%, is an automatic exemption granted. If GDP goes down by a percentage between 0.75 and 2, the European Council will decide whether the country will be fined or not.

An important question is also what will happen to countries *not* participating in EMU. There are plans to link their currencies to the Euro within a framework similar to the Exchange Rate Mechanism of the EMS (see also Section 1.3.2). Small fluctuations are then still possible, but realignments can take place too. Without such an arrangement the currencies on the non-EMU countries will be floating. In both cases there will be costs and benefits for these countries.

Disadvantages will be higher inflation (probably) and transaction costs and more risk when doing business with these countries. Advantages are the opportunity to implement an independent monetary policy and to protect the economy by means of competitive devaluations or depreciations.

Nevertheless, the cost of non-participation might outweigh the benefits of more international competition and currency stability. For that reason it is sometimes feared that the creation of the EMU might lead to a *two-speed* or even *multi-speed* Europe, increasing the disparities between the countries in the first group and the others. On the other hand a two-speed Europe could also be considered as constituting a convenient solution for countries who want to stay out for the time being because they need a longer period of preparation or even want to opt out. In the latter case a mandatory standard menu would be replaced by a kind of Europe-à-la-carte, leaving Member States to choose the degree to which they would like to participate in common arrangements. This outcome might be especially attractive for countries (e.g. the UK and Denmark) reluctant to move to unification in all its dimensions.

Political complications aside, it seems that support for international integration mostly flourishes in times of economic prosperity; during recessions the enthusiasm for such notions sharply diminishes. In contrast with the second-half of the 1980s, the early 1990s did not really constitute a favourable climate for sustaining the spirit of international integration. In economically hard times short-term self-interest, protectionism and nationalism are inclined to rise. It is thus perhaps not surprising that progress in relation to 'Maastricht' has been slow compared to the Single Act of 1985. Implementation of the latter has turned out to be rather successful. By the end of 1992 almost all (nearly 95%) of the scheduled proposals were adopted by the Council (of Ministers). Frontier checks on goods have been abolished by the adoption of new VAT and excise arrangements and most non-tariff barriers have been removed.

Enlargement of the EU

In addition to the debate on *deepening* there is also an intense continuing discussion with respect to *widening* the European Union. In fact this discussion has been going on ever since the founding of the original EEC in 1958 and has resulted in frequent enlargements (see Table 1.2), the last one being the entry of Austria, Sweden and Finland on 1 January 1995. Because the EU is in principle open to new members, it might well be possible that the EU will be enlarged from 15 to 30 countries in the future (see Figure 1.2).

Table 1.2 Enlargements of the European Union

Year	Entrance of
1958	France, Germany, Italy, Netherlands, Belgium, Luxembourg
1973	UK, Denmark, Ireland
1981	Greece
1986	Spain, Portugal
1995	Austria, Sweden, Finland

Potential candidates: Norway, Switzerland, Poland, Hungary, Czech Republic, Slovakia, Romania, Bulgaria, Estonia, Latvia, Lithuania, Slovenia, Cyprus, Malta, Turkey.

The potential entrants can be split in three groups. The first group consists of countries belonging to what is left of the European Free Trade Organisation (EFTA): Norway and Switzerland (the two other Members of this organisation, Liechtenstein and Iceland, are not interested). The former communist countries in Central and Eastern Europe belong to the second group. A number of countries at the periphery of Europe (Malta, Cyprus and Turkey) form the third group. Not every country is eligible for membership, however. New candidates should generally fulfil the following conditions:

- They should have a European identity, a democratic status and respect for human rights.
- They should not only accept Union laws and regulations (subject to temporary transitional arrangements) but also be able to implement them. This condition presumes

that an applicant has a well-functioning market economy backed by an adequate legal and administrative framework.

On the basis of these criteria the EFTA countries could easily join the EU, while even for the most advanced countries in Central and Eastern Europe (Hungary, the Czech Republic and Poland) a long period of preparation will be required. Other countries, for example Turkey or Slovakia, are not eligible as yet, because, regardless of the fulfilment of the second condition, there are serious doubts about their democratic status and/or respect for human rights, treatment of minorities and such like.

The integration of the EFTA countries into the EU has been taking place since 1973 when the first EFTA members (the UK, Denmark and Ireland) joined the European Union. The next important step was taken in 1992 when the then EU and EFTA countries signed the *European Economic Area (EEA)* agreement, which is intended to extend the internal EU market to the EFTA countries, guaranteeing free movement of goods, services, people and capital across countries of both blocs. The ultimate aim is integration of the economies of all countries involved. The Swiss, however, rejected the agreement by means of a referendum. In the meantime Sweden, Finland, Austria and Norway applied for full EU membership, leading to the entrance of the first three in January 1995. The Norwegians, also by referendum, decided to stay out, but agreed to participate in the EEA. The EEA finally came into force on 1 January 1994, but applies (since 1995) only to the EFTA partners Norway, Iceland and Liechtenstein. Switzerland will stay out and not participate for the time being. Nevertheless, it may well happen that both Norway and Switzerland will apply (again) for full EU membership in the near future. From an economic point of view no fundamental problems are foreseen with respect to enlargement of the EU with former (EFTA) states. The economies of these generally rich countries are similar to the existing EU countries, in both structure and stage of development.

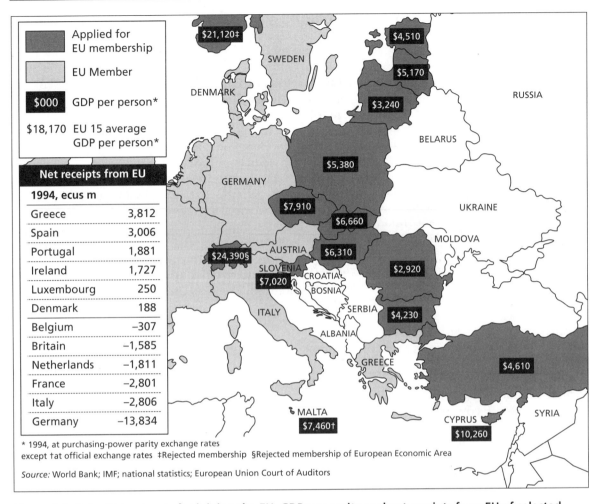

Net receipts from EU	
1994, ecus m	
Greece	3,812
Spain	3,006
Portugal	1,881
Ireland	1,727
Luxembourg	250
Denmark	188
Belgium	–307
Britain	–1,585
Netherlands	–1,811
France	–2,801
Italy	–2,806
Germany	–13,834

* 1994, at purchasing-power parity exchange rates
except †at official exchange rates ‡Rejected membership §Rejected membership of European Economic Area

Source: World Bank; IMF; national statistics; European Union Court of Auditors

Figure 1.2 Potential entrants for joining the EU, GDP per capita and net receipts from EU of selected Member States

Source: © The Economist, London, 3 August 1996

For the former communist countries in Central and Eastern Europe the situation is rather different. As can be seen from Figure 1.2, these countries are far poorer than the rest of the Union and their economies are still in transition. This means that there will be a long way to go for them before they can meet the second criterion of having a well-functioning market economy and consequently being able to implement EU laws and regulations. The integration of the former communist countries in the European economy is, nonetheless, generally viewed as very important. A prospering Central and Eastern Europe will probably result in regional stability and will prevent mass migration and social, political and military conflicts. Enlargement with these countries can therefore be regarded not only as an economic opportunity, but almost also as a political necessity.

For that reason a series of so-called *Europe Agreements* were signed from 1992 on with a number of countries in Central and Eastern Europe: Poland, Hungary, Czech Republic, Slovakia, Romania, Bulgaria, the Baltic States and Slovenia. Most of the agreements came into force in 1995. They include commercial as well as political and cultural elements and are intended to pave the way for the full integration of these countries into the Union. Most of the countries mentioned above have also in the meantime formally applied for full EU membership. Before such a membership can be realised a number of conditions have to be met, however. First, political and economic reform should continue until a full-scale market economy is established. Second, the economies of the countries concerned need to reach a level of development which will enable them to cope when they are fully exposed to international competition. At present, the EU considers these economies too weak to withstand such competition. The agreements provide for a gradual opening of EU markets for all products in a few years time, except for agricultural produce. For their part, Poland, Hungary and the Czech and Slovak Republics have to introduce reciprocal arrangements, though they are granted a longer period of time to do so. With Albania and the Baltic States a less far-going trade and economic cooperation agreement has also been concluded.

For both sides immediate accession for the former communist countries does not make sense. The latter countries would face severe problems in coping with the sudden increase in competition from western Europe. The EU, on the other hand, would face heavy claims on its budget for agricultural expenditure and for regional and cohesion funds and see its monetary policy undermined by weak currencies. This might be to the detriment of the money spent on existing poorer EU countries and might increase the burden for the net contributors of the EU budget (e.g. Germany, Italy and France; see Figure 1.2).

Nevertheless, serious questions can be raised concerning the way the Europe Agreements have been implemented so far. The EU may maintain its tariffs and/or quotas for at least five years (from 1992) on 'sensitive' goods like steel, textiles and meat; for most other agricultural produce they will not be lifted at all. These product just happen to be those in which the East Europeans are assumed to have a competitive advantage. In addition to tariffs and quotas, there are specific clauses enabling the EU to restrict imports from the East, like anti-dumping clauses, animal-disease regulations and rules on state subsidies. Nevertheless, although the EU appears reluctant to liberalise its trade with Eastern Europe, trade with for instance Poland, Hungary and the Czech Republic increased sharply in the beginning of the 1990s. It will be to the general benefit of both parties if this development continues, including an increase in trade in farm products.

Of the third group Turkey is not eligible as a full member at the moment. Instead, an Association Treaty was signed, including the establishment of a customs union, which had come into force by the end of 1995. Malta and Cyprus are in principle accepted as future members and may be among the first countries to join the EU. They are likely to be helped in this by the fact that these countries are too small to constitute a threat to the Union's budget.

An intergovernmental conference dealing with the subject of enlargement is planned for the summer of 1997. Six months later accession negotiations are scheduled to start with Malta and Cyprus, and maybe with the Czech Republic, Hungary and Poland and Slovenia (early 1998 at the earliest). These talks could last several years; therefore it is likely that new enlargements will only take place after the year 2000.

The continuing enlargement of the EU, resulting in a constantly increasing number of Member States, will strongly complicate decision-making in the EU. Every country is represented in the Council of Ministers, the European Commission and a number of other European institutions. In order to speed things up, the rules have to be simplified, e.g. by making more extensive use of majority voting. On the other hand, the large countries in the EU do not want to be overruled by a group of smaller countries, and the smaller countries will not become subordinate to the larger ones. For these reasons the Maastricht Treaty on European Union will be revised in the summer of 1997. The new Treaty should lead to more efficient decision-making, without harming the position of both the larger and the smaller EU countries. To find a solution for this problem will be far from easy.

1.3 MAIN OBJECTIVES AND POLICIES OF THE EUROPEAN UNION

1.3.1 A free and single market

The overall objective of the European Union is, according to article 2 of the Treaty of Rome, the promotion of a harmonious development of economic growth and the accelerated increase of welfare and standard of living in its Member States. Such an objective could be reached in different ways. It is clear, however, that the Union opted for the *free market* as its main instrument to achieve its goals in preference to planning or other state interventionist strategies. A large, free and competitive market is expected to create improved efficiency of production, more economies of scale, an optimal allocation of factors of production and to stimulate research and development. This would, in turn, result in lower unit costs and increased competitiveness of European industry. Government involvement, on the other hand, is generally considered to be detrimental to competition and the optimal allocation of the factors of production. For this reason article 2 focuses on the establishment of a Common Market as the main tool for the achievement of a higher level of welfare. The necessity of approximation of economic policies (also in article 2) is based on the idea that harmonisation of national policies is required to ensure fair competition and also avoid uncertainty in international trade relations. For instance, different tax systems create unequal production costs and profit opportunities and hence discriminate between the producers of different Member States. The same applies to subsidies, environmental policies, social security policies, health and safety standards and quality controls.

The importance of the free market as a method of gaining a higher level of productivity, income and employment and of reducing costs and prices is also embodied in the European Single Act of 1985. According to the so-called Cecchini Report, prepared on behalf of the European Commission, the benefits of the internal market will be derived in a large part from *enhanced competition* within a deregulated internal market. A second factor is the *increased scale* of production. Competition and scale are mutually reinforced by each other. In the medium term, it was estimated that real Union GDP would go up by an extra 5–7% and additional employment of 2–5 million jobs would be created.

Competition in the internal market will be encouraged by:

- the removal of entrance barriers erected by national frontiers;
- the opening up of (national) public procurement markets;
- elimination or reduction of (national) monopolies;
- market deregulation and liberalisation, for instance in the area of financial markets.

This enhanced competition is expected to lead to a fall in production costs, gains in efficiency and price reductions.

In addition to the static effects there are also dynamic effects to be expected from the completion of the internal market.

A more competitive environment is an essential element determining the pace of technological innovation, according to the Cecchini Commission. Pursuit of economies of scale and competition will together encourage the emergence of large, truly European companies, better equipped to compete with their US and Far Eastern counterparts and to command strong market positions. Hence the internal market will eventually affect economic structures which, in turn, will produce an accelerated rate of growth.

Although great emphasis is given to developing market forces, this is not to say there is no role for government in a united Europe. The Treaty of Rome already explicitly identifies a number of common policies to be adopted, e.g. in the fields of competition, agriculture, transport, monetary relations, external trade, taxation and social security. Implicitly it also deals with regional policies. In addition, the European Single Act mentions common policies in the area of environment, scientific and technological development. The Maastricht Treaty on European Union stresses a common monetary and social policy, and makes extra provisions for a (regional) cohesion fund.

Most of these policies are intended to:

- ensure free competition on fair terms;
- guarantee stability and
- provide (quasi) public goods.

Thus, although the Union relies heavily on free market ideas, common policies are not excluded. They are mainly (but not only) meant to compensate for 'market failure' at the EU level.

1.3.2 Common policies

Competition policy

In order to create a more competitive environment, the EU has adopted, for instance, a relatively strict system of *competition rules*. These rules forbid

- restrictive agreements and practices of firms;
- the abuse of a dominant position by firms;
- national government aid to businesses,

but only *in so far as they affect the trade between Member States*. Cartels, operating only at a national level, for instance, are not prohibited by Union laws (although they may be banned by national law). Most of the competition laws are governed by the Treaty of Rome.

Article 85 outlaws *restrictive agreements* and practices between companies affecting trade or leading to distortion of competition within the Union. Examples of such agreements are price-fixing, market-sharing, production restrictions and exclusive purchase and distribution agreements. However, part 3 of the same article grants individual or block exemptions in cases where the reduction in competition will be offset by the likely benefits to the public interest. Examples are joint research and development, patent licensing and motor vehicle dealerships. Research and development, for instance, may have positive external effects or may be too costly to be undertaken by a single firm.

Article 86 prohibits *abuse of a dominant position* within the Common market by firms. A dominant position is identified as the ability of a firm to affect the outcome of the market by exercising monopoly power. It is not the dominant

position as such which is prohibited, but merely the abuse. That is also why this article can seldom be used to prevent mergers or acquisitions. Special regulations dealing with these matters did not come into force until 1990 (see below). It is left to the Commission and eventually to the (European) Court of Justice to define the terms 'abuse' and 'dominant position' (measured in terms of market shares) in individual cases. Their assessment will depend on the product, type of market, market structure and so on.

Articles 92–94 ban national government aid to domestic industries which distorts or threatens to distort competition between firms within the Union. Some exceptions are made, notably development subsidies or regional industry aid.

Articles 87–91 specify the implementation procedures relating to EU competition law. The principal body dealing with this is the *European Commission*, which is delegated by the Council of Ministers to investigate restrictive behaviour and to take appropriate action. This may range from imposing fines or penalty payments to issuing an order to the firm or firms to stop the behaviour. The Commission can start investigations on its own initiative or at the request of injured parties. Those concerned may appeal against Commission decisions at the Court of Justice.

In addition to the Treaty of Rome, regulations with respect to mergers and acquisitions have been developed separately. The need for this kind of regulation became apparent in the run-up to the single market, when many companies were looking for merger or acquisition partners in order to prepare for the enlarged market. Under the *Merger Control Regulation*, which came into force in 1990, mergers or take-overs involving firms with a combined annual turnover of 5 billion ECUs need prior authorisation from the European Commission. Smaller inter-EU mergers are subject to national merger and acquisition regulations, but the Commission may intervene at the request of national governments.

EU competition law has precedence over the national legislation, but it does not replace it. It is mainly intended to secure free competition in an international (inter-Union) context. National regulations are generally much more tolerant, with the clear exceptions of Germany and the UK.

Monetary policy

The EU's monetary policy has been introduced primarily to eliminate uncertainty in international economic relations. Wildly fluctuating currencies have a negative impact on international trade, because they make international transactions more risky. The call for a European stabilisation policy specifically arose after the collapse of the Bretton Woods' fixed exchange rate system in 1971. After some earlier attempts to reach a common arrangement, the *European Monetary System (EMS)* came into force in 1979. All EU countries became members, through the UK did not participate in the *Exchange Rate Mechanism (ERM)* until October 1990. Of the later entrants (Greece, Portugal and Spain) only Greece has thus far not joined the ERM; Spain entered in 1989 and Portugal in the beginning of 1992.

Within the Exchange Rate Mechanism of the EMS, currencies are only allowed to fluctuate within narrow ranges of ± 2.25% ('narrow band') or ± 6% ('wide band') around a central rate. The central rates are calculated on the basis of the *European Currency Unit* (EUC), a basket consisting of fixed quantities of all EU currencies. The quantity of each specific currency in the basket depends on the economic weight of the country concerned in terms of (among others) GDP and intra-EU trade. The quantity is re-assessed every five years or on request. Table 1.3 gives an overview of the composition of the ECU as of September 1989 and the central rates on 1 February 1993.

The ERM forms a *parity grid* of bilateral exchange rates, in which the individual currencies are pegged to each other by means of a fixed relation (within margins) to their ECU central rates. If a currency is inclined to cross its limits set by the margins, the Central Banks of the Member States are obliged to intervene in the currency markets by means of buying (weak) and selling (strong) currencies. The system is adjustable, however. In case of a persistent upwards or downwards pressure on a currency,

Table 1.3 The European Currency Unit (ECU): composition and central rates within the ERM

Currency	Units in ECU[1]	Central ECU rate[2]
Belgian/Lux. franc	3.431	39.39
Danish krone	0.1976	7.28
Deutschmark	0.6242	1.91
Greek drachma[3]	1.440	(292.8)
Spanish peseta	6.885	162.5
French franc	1.332	6.4
Irish punt	0.00852	0.79
Italian lira[4]	151.8	(2106)
Dutch guilder	0.2198	2.15
Austrian schilling		13.7
Portuguese escudo	1.393	192.8
UK pound sterling[5]	0.08784	(0.79)

[1] Composition: as of 1 November 1993
[2] Central rates as of 6 March 1995
[3] Notational central rate
[4] Temporary notational central rate as from 17 September 1992
[5] Notational central rate as from 17 September 1992 (suspension of sterling participation in ERM)

caused by economic fundamentals, it may be decided collectively to devalue or revalue a currency by changing the ECU central rate. Such *realignments* have taken place quite frequently, especially during the early 1980s. So in fact, the ERM is not a system of totally fixed exchange rates; some flexibility is built in by the use of margins and more substantial adjustments are also possible. Even so, its intention at least is to provide short-term exchange rate stability. Until 1992 it did so quite successfully.

Fixed exchange rates have wide-ranging implications for other economic policies. With the exchange rates more or less pegged, it becomes very difficult for Member States to conduct independent economic policies. Exchange rate management and the use of tariffs are no longer available as means of adjusting balance of payments imbalances. This means that inflation, wages and productivity rates, taxes and other factors that determine international competitiveness must be brought into line with each other. Since (within the framework of the internal market) currency controls have been abolished, interest rates cannot diverge significantly either.

The conclusion is that monetary integration can hardly be realised without both economic convergence and harmonisation of economic policies and even political integration. That is also the reason why the EU is attempting to establish an Economic and Monetary Union (EMU) in which the EMS is incorporated. EMU would create an optimal macro-economic framework for intensified competition. The option to protect domestic industries against competition from other EU countries by means of currency depreciation would no longer exist.

The experience with the ERM up until 1992 was quite positive. Though frequent realignments took place, the system nonetheless succeeded in stabilising exchange rate fluctuations, at least in the short term. Moreover it is assumed that the EMS contributed substantially to bringing down inflation in the Member States participating in the ERM. A major explanation for this achievement is that – by pegging them to the ECU – the EU currencies were more or less linked to the German mark. The size of the German economy and the strong commitment of the German monetary authorities to price stability guaranteed a relatively low inflation level, not only in Germany but also in other countries participating in the ERM. The solid German mark acted, in fact, as a monetary anchor in Europe.

So far, so good. The problems in the monetary field emerged, however, in the early 1990s when the economies of the Member States started to diverge, instead of converging as was intended. The UK economy is a clear example in this respect. It probably entered the ERM in 1990 at too high a central rate for the pound in relation to the British competitiveness. The UK position was furthermore undermined as the UK went into recession well ahead of its EU partners. Germany, on the other hand, found itself still in the unification boom, which clearly fuelled inflation. The independent German Central Bank (Bundesbank) responded by adopting tight monetary policies, resulting in relatively high interest rates, in order to bring inflation down. The UK government, in contrast, was inclined to reduce interest rates to boost the weak British economy. These events put heavy strains on the ERM, culminating in the suspension of the UK's ERM membership in September 1992. The example serves to show that a fixed exchange rate without economic policy coordination is an illusion. The UK government reproached the German authorities on the ground that they allowed their national objectives to prevail above Union interests, i.e. currency stability in Europe.

In the same period Italy suspended its participation in the ERM as well, while the Spanish peseta and the Portuguese escudo were similarly forced into devaluations. A year later, in August 1993, the situation worsened. This time it was the French franc which came under attack (together with the Belgian franc and the Danish crown) because of different expectations with respect to the French and German interest rate policies. Speculators assumed that the French authorities would decrease interest rates in order to give the wobbling French economy a boost. When the autonomous German Bundesbank announced that it would leave interest rates unchanged, speculators started a massive attack on the French franc and some other currencies. A devaluation of the French franc would hit monetary cooperation in the EU in the heart, since the link between the Deutschmark and the French franc is at the core of the system.

To deal with this problem, the EU finance ministers decided at the weekend (before the foreign exchange markets opened again) to widen the fluctuation margins of the ERM from 2.25 to 15% on either side of currency's central rates, resulting in total band widths of 30% (except for the D-mark/guilder exchange rate). This way, formal devaluations could be avoided while maintaining the high nominal German interest rates. But of course this was an artificial solution; the EMS hardly *guarantees* monetary stability any more. In that sense, though formally still in place, the system practically broke down. The run-up to the EMU (the Maastricht Treaty came into force a couple of months later) could not have had a worse start. However, in spite of the fact that the EMS was almost set aside, the currency markets nevertheless calmed down after the turbulent events of summer 1993. Most currencies (e.g. the French franc) remained more or less within the old narrow margins, although they were allowed to fluctuate within much wider bands.

This also raises the question as to how the fifth convergence criterion, namely currency stability, should be interpreted. This condition states that the exchange rate should not have been subject to devaluation within the 'normal' band of the Exchange Rate Mechanism of the EMS for at least two years. The European Council still has to decide what is meant by 'normal'. It is expected that it will be ±15%, instead of the old margins of ±2.25%.

The currency crisis of 1992–93 demonstrated that fixed exchange rates are unrealistic and maybe not even advisable if they are not backed up by coordinated economic policies and if the economies concerned diverge too much. Convergence is a prerequisite for monetary integration, though it can also be argued the other way around: convergence may be encouraged by cooperation in the monetary field.

Since the crisis, a debate has started over the implementation of the ERM rules in that period. Instead of treating the ERM as a fixed-rate system, it was argued, the authorities should have regarded it as a fixed-but-adjustable system. Timely and more frequent realignments could have prevented the strains on the system which almost led to its total destruction. Undoubtedly, it does not make sense to act as if Stage 3 of EMU had already been reached. As long as the basic conditions have not been met, the system should be operated much more flexibly. Strictly fixed exchange rates presumes much more convergence than had been realised at that time. Furthermore, if Member States are really determined to realise monetary stability in Europe, they should perhaps give a higher priority to defending (temporarily) weaker currencies. The cost of defending these currencies should be shared, rather than be borne by the weaker states.

Taxation, social and environmental policies

As has been said before (common) taxation, social and environmental policies are adopted principally to guarantee fair competition, because taxes, social security contributions and pollution norms affect costs of production. Harmonisation and standardisation of tax burden, pollution norms, working conditions and so forth are the primary objectives of these policies.

It would have been possible, of course, to leave all these issues to national governments. Every country can then set its own political priorities and economic objectives, for instance, on matters affecting the size of the public sector, government spending and environmental protection. The problem is, however, that distinctive national policies in a single market will distort international competition by creating unfair advantages for companies operating in countries with lower taxes and less strict norms in pollution and worker protection. Not all regulations do affect international trade, however.

Taxation

In the field of tax harmonisation, two approaches are possible: an absolute equalisation with respect to tax bases (the measure of value upon which a tax is levied) and related tax rates and an approach which tries to minimise the externalities of each state's tax systems, especially in the field of competition. The latter approach, which still allows for substantial differentials, has been adopted by the EU. It is based on the principle that differences in the individual tax systems of the member states should not influence the international 'free movement of goods, persons, services and capital' in a single market. Clearly, this requires a certain degree of coordination of tax policies.

Taxes can be classified as *direct* taxes (taxes on wealth and income) and *indirect* taxes (surcharges on prices, which are paid eventually by consumers, like VAT and excise taxes). Since *indirect taxes* are immediately reflected in prices, they should be aligned to a certain degree. Evidence from the United States of America indicates that – in the absence of frontier obstacles – indirect tax differentials between Member States of an Economic Union should not exceed five percentage points in order to avoid tax-induced border trade. There is no case for a complete equalisation, however. That is why the EU decided not to aim at a *harmonisation* of indirect taxes but only at an *approximation*. Value Added Tax (VAT) will be the common sales tax throughout the EU. In line with the above-mentioned principles it was decided by the European Council that, as of 1 January 1993, the minimum standard VAT rate throughout the Union will be 15%, and 5% for (optional) 'necessities'. Zero rates may be maintained for a transitional period for a very limited number of products. It is the intention that the standard VAT rates within the Union will ultimately be found within the range of 15–20%. In that case they will cease to distort trade. In 1996, this aim was still not completely realised, because standard VAT rates in, for example, the Scandinavian countries exceeded 20%.

VAT controls at the internal EU frontiers have disappeared since the establishment of the internal market (as of 1 January 1993). It is the intention that as of 1997 the tax will be collected by the country of origin (the so-called *origin principle*) Importers can reclaim the VAT via the tax authorities in their own countries. Until the new system comes into force, VAT will be collected in the country of final consumption (*destination principle*). The origin principle favours countries with trade surpluses. A common VAT system (with equal structure and rates) is not foreseen in the near future. The present system will be in force until at least the end of 1996.

Plans to harmonise or even to approximate excise duties (levied on fuel, spirits and tobacco) in the foreseeable future have been abandoned, however. Only some rules with respect to inter-country trade have been relaxed. From 1 January 1993 individuals are allowed to purchase in other Member States dutiable products for their personal use at the local applicable rates.

Direct taxes are supposed to affect international competitiveness as well. Personal income taxes and social security contributions increase the costs of production. Corporate taxes and taxes on wealth may influence the movement of factors of production from higher to lower taxed locations. The revenues from taxes, on the other hand, will enable governments to supply a range of public goods and services (e.g. education, infrastructure, health services), which will be beneficial for the inhabitants and also for the business of a country. It can be questioned whether a substantial convergence is needed in the field of fiscal policies. The disadvantage of a high level of taxes can – at least to a certain extent – be compensated by a high level of public provisions. There may occur some policy competition, however, with respect of some taxes (e.g. corporate taxes) and with respect to the efficiency of the public sector in terms of costs and benefits (see also Section 13.2.4).

Apart from these considerations, fiscal policy is pre-eminently accepted as a matter of *national sovereignty.* The provision of social services, health services and education are to be left to national governments. Decision-making with respect to taxation requires unanimity of the Council of Ministers, even after the adoption of the European Single Act. The Member States have been very reluctant to harmonise direct taxes. So far, there has been hardly any progress in this field.

Environmental policy

Environment protection has received greater priority in the last decade, especially since the adoption of the Single Act. There are two main reasons for this. First, pollution does not stop at frontiers and is therefore automatically a matter of common concern. A clean environment can also be considered to be a public good, which probably can be ensured most appropriately through the intervention of a supranational authority. Second, different standards and norms in Member States distort competition. Polluting activities may be moved to those Member States with less strict norms, which in turn benefit from increased production and employment, while other States will eventually be confronted with the resulting pollution too. This clearly offers an unfair advantage.

Environmental policy was not mentioned in the Treaty of Rome. It was launched only in 1972, when it was decided at an Intergovernmental

Conference to develop an EU policy in this respect. Since then a large number of directives, regulations and decisions have been adopted. A milestone, however, was the explicit inclusion of environmental policy in the Single European Act (SEA) of 1987, giving it a legal basis. It was agreed that the most important principles for the common environmental policy from then on should be *prevention* and the *polluter pays principle (PPP)*. The latter means that external costs of pollution (costs not accounted for in the market price) should be 'internalised' (included in the price). The PPP relies on the use of *market forces* to implement environmental policies. In the 1990s even greater emphasis will be put on this kind of approach. Economic instruments like taxes and tradable permits (permits for activities with polluting effects which can be bought and sold) will become of increasing importance in achieving the goals set by the policy makers. An example is the introduction of a combined CO_2/energy tax, proposed by the European Commission in 1992.

Guidelines and objectives for environmental policies are outlined in the so-called *Environmental Action Programmes* (*EAPs*). The first was launched in 1973; normally they have a time horizon of 5 years. The fifth programme, called *Towards Sustainability* was adopted in 1992 by the European Commission and Parliament and covers a longer period: until the year 2000. The programme stresses the concept of sustainable growth which will not compromise the ability of future generations to meet their own needs. It uses a combination of regulation and market-based instruments such as taxes, subsidies and tradable permits. The financial means for these measures come from various EU sources. In order to coordinate this financial support in an effective way, the Fifth Action Programme introduced a new tool: the *Financial Instrument for the Environment (LIFE)*. There remains a lot of work to be done, however. Compared to other economic blocs, the standards set by the EU are generally only minimal. For some issues, e.g. taxation and energy policy, decision-making by unanimity is still required. This affects environmental policy

as well. Due to conflicting views the combined CO_2/ energy tax, for instance, though proposed in 1992, was still not adopted in 1996.

Social policy

The Treaty of Rome explicitly mentions the promotion of the improvement of living and working conditions and close cooperation between Member States in the social field. The latter should be pursued in order to set the same (basic) standards throughout the EU and to avoid 'social dumping' (shift of production to places with minimal social standards). Nevertheless, social policy received only minimal attention in the first decades of the EU. Substantial progress was only made in such areas as the freedom of movement of workers, equal treatment of men and women, and health and safety protection.

The neglect of social policy in the early years of the EU has been heavily criticised. The call for a more comprehensive policy resulted in the adoption of a *Social Action Programme (SAP)* in 1974. The main objectives of this programme were the attainment of full and better employment and the harmonisation of working and living conditions. Social policy gathered momentum, however, with the adoption of the *Social Charter* in 1989 by the European Council of Heads of Government. There were major concerns at that time that the desired internal market, as proposed by the SEA, would lead to a downward pressure on social standards induced by increased competition. The Social Charter is a declaration of principles, which should be transformed into rules and regulations by means of social action programme. It covers for instance the improvement of living and working conditions (e.g. maximum working week), right of freedom of movement, social protection (e.g. establishment of a national minimum wage and the guarantee of social assistance for people without jobs), health protection and safety at the workplace, worker consultations and equal treatment of men and women.

The Social Charter was not signed by the UK. For this reason the UK was also against the proposal to include a Social Chapter in the Maastricht Treaty on European Union. The British opposition resulted in a separate protocol, attached to the treaty, offering the other Members the opportunity to make laws in the social field, based on the Social Charter, without UK involvement. Apart from this problem, it is unlikely that an approximation of social policies will take place very rapidly within the EU. First, different social standards reflect not only differences in attitudes and political priorities but are also caused by economic disparities. Without real convergence it will be very difficult to bring social policies in line with each other. Second, social policy is not on the top of the agenda of the Union. Economic integration is the most important concern. Differences in social policy might lead to unfair competition in the Single Market. For that reason some consensus must be reached on the basic principles of the national social policies; a common supranational EU social policy is not the objective.

Transport policy

For international trade *transport costs* are of vital importance; they form a substantial part of production costs. In many countries, however, elements of the transport sector are heavily subsidised. This is because transportation generates considerable external benefits, e.g. in the field of environment protection, energy conservation, infrastructure, industrial development and employment. Transport can, in fact, be considered as a quasi public good: although the criteria of non-rivalry in consumption and non-excludability of benefits are not applicable in this area, it is nevertheless at least partly provided by government. In most countries transport markets are highly regulated and protected. Without a common policy in this respect, industry's production costs will be substantially distorted by national policies. Such a common policy should aim basically at the removal of discriminating regulations with respect to market entry and the use of national infrastructure, the harmonisation of fiscal, social and technical conditions of operation, and the coordination of the development of a European transport infrastructure.

Until recently progress in this field has been rather limited. The completion of the internal market in 1992 has resulted, however, in a number of new directives which should eventually lead to opening-up of national transport markets to other EU competitors. Transport quotas will be gradually abolished. According to a White Paper, adopted by the Commission in 1992, the freedom to provide services everywhere in the Union will be the ultimate goal. Many conditions still have to be fulfilled, especially in the field of harmonisation and liberalisation, before this goal can be achieved.

In the field of road haulage, complete liberalisation should be realised by 1 July 1998. From that date cabotage (the right to carry out transport services in other member states) will be fully allowed. Until then, a system of quotas will be maintained. There are plans to open up the heavily state controlled and subsidised air transport market as well. A number of reform packages have been adopted by the EU; the last one, which came into effect in 1993, is designed to liberalise civil aviation before the year 2000. Full liberalisation of sea transport started in 1993 and is planned for completion in 2004.

In order to promote an adequate international transport infrastructure, the EU came up with a number of initiatives for the development of Trans-European Networks (TENs). There is room for EU action here because national governments are by nature inclined to favour the domestic transport infrastructure. The TENs include networks not only in the field of traditional transport but also in the field of energy and telecommunications. The EU acts as cofunder; the money is coming from various EU sources (e.g. the budget, the European Investment Fund and the Cohesion Fund).

The conclusion is that most of the common policies mentioned above support the working of the free market rather than hindering it. They create, in fact, the necessary conditions for the operation of the market or are intended to reduce market imperfections. There are some major exceptions, nevertheless, like the agricultural policy and the regional and industrial policies.

Common Agricultural Policy (CAP)

The Common Agricultural Policy (CAP) is very important in the Union; it accounted for about 50% of the Union's Budget expenses in 1996. In the early 1970s these expenses amounted to more than 80% of the Budget. In absolute terms the agricultural spending has constantly risen, but the (still fairly small) Union budget has increased to an even greater extent.

Agriculture is heavily subsidised and protected within the Union; it is certainly not left to the forces of the market. The main reason for this policy is that the EU wants to remain substantially self-sufficient in food production, which is of vital interest for any society. As a consequence of this principle, producers are guaranteed a fair standard of living, mainly through the setting of minimum prices and levying of tariffs on food imports. Other goals of the CAP are the stabilisation of markets, regular supplies and reasonable prices for consumers. The latter would be, however, much lower in many cases if there were no CAP at all. The CAP is heavily criticised, because of its interventionist approach, which causes high costs and excess production (because of the guaranteed prices) and has discriminating effects on non-EU suppliers; but there is also a strong lobby in its favour.

For these reasons, the CAP has come under severe pressure in the last decade. The emphasis has shifted from protection and guaranteed prices to restructuring and output restriction. Quotas have been set (e.g. in the case of milk); guaranteed farm prices have been reduced and price support for most products has been limited to maximum quantities. A set-aside scheme was introduced to compensate farmers prepared to take land out of production. An income support system was set up to prevent a strong fall in farmers' incomes. The last package of reforms, named after Commissioner Macsharry, were implemented in three stages, starting in 1993 and ending in 1995. Though the reforms were rather successful in bringing production under control and reducing surpluses, they did not result in a decrease in EU agricultural spending, mainly because of the built-in income compensations.

In the early 1990s the need to reform the CAP was further increased by pressure from the EU's trading partners (especially the USA) within the framework of the GATT talks. Agriculture was becoming a major obstacle to further trade liberalisation. By the end of 1993, however, a GATT settlement became possible, requiring all parties to reduce average tariffs and subsidies on agricultural produce by about one-third, generally to be realised within six years.

Regional policy

Like agricultural policy, regional policy is not in line with the general market orientation approach of the Union. It is adopted mainly to support weak regions within the Union. These regions consist of

- regions lagging behind in development;
- declining industrial areas;
- regions with high long-term unemployment levels;
- underdeveloped rural areas;
- regions with a low population density.

The latter category of regions were added because of the enlargement of the EU in 1995 with the Scandinavian countries Finland and Sweden. All these regions are generally characterised by low incomes and high unemployment rates. As can be seen in Figure 1.3, there are large regional differences in wealth within the EU.

The *per capita* incomes of Portugal, Greece, Spain and Ireland are far below the EU average for all regions. The poorest regions are situated in Portugal (Alentego), Greece (some islands and Macedonia) and East Germany with *per capita* incomes of between 40 and 50% of the 1992 EU12 average. Among the more wealthy countries considerable regional disparities can be found. The peripheral regions of the UK (including the North of England, Northern Ireland and Wales) and the South and the Islands of Italy are notable for their low levels of income, emigration and low job opportunities compared to the national average. *Per capita* income in Italy's Mezzogiorno is only two-thirds of the EU12 average. In most cases lower income

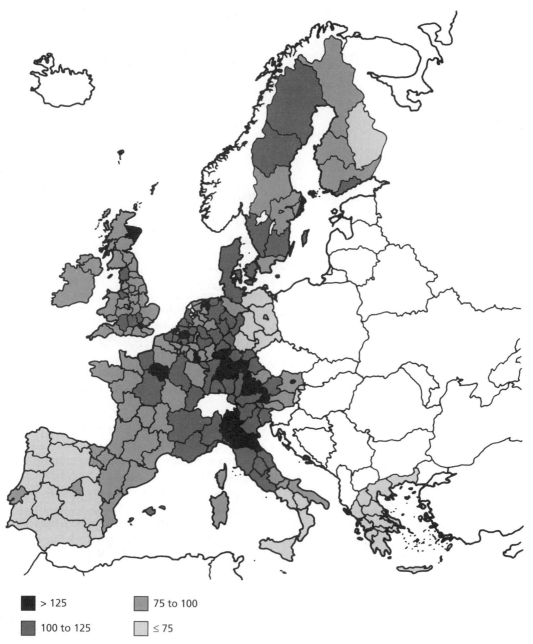

Figure 1.3 GDP in Purchasing Power Standards per region, 1992, EUR15 = 100

Source: Eurostat, Europe in figures, p. 353

regions are less developed rural areas (Portugal, Greece, Spain). Other regions have problems due to decline in the staple industries, such as coal and steel, textiles, shipyards (North of England, Wales, parts of Belgium and North of Spain), or because of an unfavourable geographical position (e.g. too far away from the centres of economic activity).

Wealth is generally concentrated in large urban areas, like the Paris region (Ile de France) with a per capita income of 170% of EU-average (in 1992), the region around Milan (Lombardia, 135%), Hamburg (198%) and Bremen (156%), Greater London (144%), Brussels (175%) and Copenhagen (140%).

The disparities between the different regions are very substantial. The problem is that in practice they have a natural tendency to intensify. The prosperous centres are generally characterised by considerable *external economies of scale*, because of the availability of a developed infrastructure, skilled labour, suppliers, output markets and usually also because of their accessibility. This has led to a very unbalanced development.

Free movement of labour and capital within the EU can worsen this situation, as these factors of production seek the highest returns. The conclusion is that economic integration can even reinforce regional imbalances; and these imbalances in turn can be a (political) threat to further integration. Convergence in economic performance (real convergence) is of great importance for integration. That is also the main reason why the EU is involved in regional policy-making and why this matter is not entirely left to national governments. Another reason is that there is frequently a need to coordinate investments in basic infrastructure, especially if these investments are beneficial for more than one member state (e.g. border crossing transport networks). The policies are intended to counterbalance the unequal development and to support the weaker regions. They are additional to national policies and consist of public aid to local industries, investment in infrastructure, loans for restructuring industries etc.

The regional policies are mainly financed by the EU Structural Funds, which include (among others) the European Regional Development Fund (ERDF) and the European Social Fund (ESF). Funds are also distributed by the European Investment Bank and the Social Cohesion Fund. By far the largest part of the aid of the Structural Funds (about three-quarters) goes to those regions whose development is lagging behind. To qualify for this aid a region must have a per capita income of less than 75% of EU average income. That is why Portugal, Greece, Ireland, Spain, the South of Italy and East Germany (see Figure 1.3) receive by far the bulk of the money (more than 80%). For a country like Greece the EU regional aid is equivalent to about 3% of its GDP. For countries like France and the Netherlands this percentage is generally less than 0.3%. On top of that, countries with a per capita income of less than 90% of EU average (Greece, Ireland, Portugal and Spain) will receive additional aid between 1993 and 1998 from the Cohesion Fund. The setting up of this Fund was provided for in an annexed protocol on economic and social cohesion of the Maastricht Treaty. Such a cohesion, it was argued, is a necessary condition for successful integration. The additional aid package should help the poorer Member States in preparing for the EMU and was an important reason for these states accepting the Maastricht deal.

The effects of EU regional policies should not be overestimated. The total budget for the period 1994–99 amounts to 141 billion ECU, about 0.43% of EU GDP (around 30% of the Union's budget). Although the funds allocated to these policies have been increased substantially, they are still fairly limited, and generally smaller than the national regional funds.

In the last decade some regions managed to catch up (e.g. those regions in Ireland, Spain and Portugal), while other regions lagged even further behind (e.g. those regions in Greece and southern Italy). The European Commission has estimated that the budget required to increase the per capita incomes of the poorest regions to 75% of the EU average would have been at least 1% of EU GDP per year for a number of years. The richer countries have not been prepared to pay for that; especially since they have already enough problems in reducing their public deficits and expenditure.

Industrial policy

Industrial policy (apart from competition policy) can be defined as government actions to influence industry and thus considered as a state interventionist policy. It is a highly debated issue within the EU. On the one hand it used to be heavily supported at a national level by countries with a rich tradition in this respect like France and Italy, while countries like Germany, the Netherlands and the UK were generally more in favour of liberal economic policies.

Industrial policy was not explicitly included in the Treaty of Rome. Within a free market, however, national industrial policies may lead to a distortion of competition if some Member States strongly support their national industries, while others do not. This is the first reason why an a EU-wide industrial policy was set up. Such a policy should coordinate and provide financial support and set common rules for state aid and (possible) restructuring at the national level. In the first decades of the Union industrial policy was mainly used to restructure declining industries like coal, steel, shipyards, textiles and clothing. In terms of money, Union involvement with industry was of limited significance in this period.

In the 1980s a second reason for an EU-wide policy emerged. The economic position of Europe strongly deteriorated at that time, in particular with respect to Japan and the USA. In the field of products with a high technological content especially, Europe was more and more lagging behind. That is why the attention in the 1980s shifted to the more advanced industries such as information technology, telecommunications, nuclear energy, aerospace and bio-technology. EU-wide industrial policy should be more focused on the creation of a *competitive advantage*. Instead of supporting the losers it would be better to help the winners. Several programmes were adopted to promote research and development (R&D) for high-technology industries. The ESPRIT (European Programme for Research and Development in Information Technology) was launched in 1983 to support private joint R&D in the information industry. It was followed by further programmes such as ESPRIT II, RACE, EUREKA and BRITE, supporting private joint R&D in the field of advanced technology.

Since 1984, cooperation between companies in the area of R&D has been granted a 'block exemption' from competition rules. In the Single European Act, the Treaty of Rome was changed in order to give this technology support a legal basis. In so-called 'framework programmes', with a duration of 4 years, goals are defined and budgets assigned. The Fourth Framework Programme of 1994–98 is provided with a budget of 12.3 billion ECU.

Advocates of this policy of technology support argue that there are substantial external benefits and external economies of scale related to R&D. Benefits of R&D financed by certain companies will also accrue to other companies; these market imperfections can be offset by government support to industry in this respect. Opponents stress that state intervention constitutes a potential danger to free international trade, because subsidies distort prices and provoke similar reactions by the governments of trading partners.

Apart from financial aid to specific industries, the EU industrial policy in the last decade focused very strongly on improving the general business environment of EU industry. The creation of the internal market is supposed to be an incentive for industry concentration (by means of mergers, take-overs and expansion) and thus for economies of scale. Technical harmonisation and standardisation (part of the 1992 project) should also contribute to the creation of the right conditions for mass production. This, in turn, should be a stimulus for innovation, because R&D expenses can be spread across more units of production in that case. The improvement of the operation of markets is a basic precondition for increased industrial strength. The priority of the industrial policy in the 1990s is to enhance international competitiveness, as was also stressed in the Commission's White Paper *Growth, Competitiveness, Employment*, published in December 1993.

Conclusion

The European integration process is based on a market-oriented approach. With a few clear exceptions, most of its policies are designed to realise a large, free, internal market characterised by strong and fair competition.

This approach is not very remarkable when put into a historical context. The very start of the integration process was made immediately after the war, with the adoption of the Marshall Plan, which strongly reflected American free market ideas. During the era of the Cold War attempts were made to build up a strong counter-force to the communist threat in Europe and to defend freedom and democracy. Initially the general idea was that this should be a military and political power, as was reflected by the proposals for the European Defence Community and the ECSC during the early 1950s. But in a later stage emphasis shifted to economic power. The large and free market should play an important role in the development of such a power as can be observed in the Treaty of Rome, for instance. The adoption of the European Single Act can be considered as an European attempt to keep up with the USA and Japan; countries with very large and competitive home markets. The Act was brought about in a period in which free market ideologies were generally very dominant. The (Maastricht) Treaty on European Union finally should be the last step towards an economically integrated Europe, also based on free market principles.

The bringing into line of national and EU interests and policies constitutes a major challenge over the coming years. A common currency and common monetary policy, for instance, require a far more nominal and real convergence than realised so far. The lack of nominal convergence (inflation, interest and exchange rates, budget deficits), in turn, partly reflects different views on fiscal and monetary policy, e.g. with respect to recessions. Real convergence (GDP per head) will probably not be realised in the short-term, although three of the four least-favoured economies (Portugal, Spain and Ireland) have made remarkable progress in recent years. Another problem undermining the market-based integration may be the distinct views of Member States on the future role of the nation state and the public sector in the economy. Last but not least: nationalism and the fear of loss of sovereignty constitute major obstacles for further integration. There remains much to

be done before Europe will be truly economically united.

1.4 THE EU: SIZE AND RELATIVE IMPORTANCE

As a single identity, the European Union is one of the three dominant economic blocks in the world. With a GDP of 6440 billion ECU the EU surpassed, in 1995, the USA, which had a GDP of 5294 billion ECU in that year. Japan followed, at some distance, with 3834 billion ECU (see Table 1.4). These figures, however, are strongly dependent on exchange rates of dollar and yen against the ECU.

In terms of population, the EU also leads with 372 million inhabitants compared to 263 million in the USA and 125 million in Japan. United States citizens are still on average the richest of the three blocks. Measured in purchasing power index figures, their average income was 140 in 1995, Japan being second with 114 and the EU third with 100. The EU and Japan are catching up (the latter very rapidly); in 1960 the USA led with 182 against 100 for the EU and only 54 for Japan.

The relative strength of the Japanese economy can also be seen from the very favourable unemployment and inflation figures and the large current account surplus. The negative trend of the double-weighted unit labour costs are not caused by internal factors but largely by the strong appreciation of the yen since the middle of the 1980s.

Worthy of note is also the large proportion spent on investment in Japan and the relative low level of spending on consumption. Gross fixed capital formation amounted to around 30% for the last decade. This reflects the fact that Japan puts heavy stress on technical innovation and the growth of its production capacity. The Japanese position strongly contrasts with that of the USA, where gross investment is relatively low and consumption high. The EU occupies a position in between, but it is closer to that of the USA.

A break-down at industry level shows that the EU, compared with Japan and the USA, has the largest market shares (in terms of value-added)

Table 1.4 Main economic indicators, EU, USA, Japan 1995

	EU	*USA*	*Japan*
Population (millions)	372	263	125
Gross Domestic Product (GDP)			
current market prices (billion ECU)	6,440	5,294	3,834
per head[2], PPS, EU = 100	100	140	114
Unemployment rate[1]	10.9	5.6	3.2
average 1991–1995	10.2	6.5	2.6
Inflation[2]	4.0	2.5	0.8
(average GDP deflator 1991–1995)			
Gross fixed capital formation[2]	19.5	16.2	29.8
(average % of GDP 1991–1995 at current market prices)			
Private consumption	62.1	67.4	58.1
(average % of GDP 1991–1995 at current market prices)			
Nominal unit labour costs			
(relative to 19 industrial countries double export weights			
1991 = 100	91.4[2]	96.7	138.9
1980 = 100	91.4[2]	86.7	160.3
Exports of goods and services[3]	8.9	11.4	9.8
(% of GDP at current market prices)			
Imports of goods and services[3]	8.3	13.1	8.3
(% of GDP at current market prices)			
Balance on current account			
(% of GDP), average	0.5	– 2.1	2.2
1991–1995	– 0.7	– 1.3	2.8

[1] Percentage of civilian labour force
[2] Relative to 6 industrial non member countries; 1991–94: excluding East Germany
[3] EU: External exports/imports; goods only

Source: *European Economy*, June 1996
Figures based on European Commission estimates.

in industrial activities with a moderate or even weak growth in demand. Examples of these industries are: food products, tobacco, beverages, textiles, leather, clothing and metal products. In strong demand sectors like office and data processing machines, electrical and electronic goods and chemical products the EU is clearly surpassed by the United States and, despite its bigger size (in terms of GDP and population), its market share does not deviate very much from that of Japan. The conclusion is that the proportion of EU industry in the strong demand sector in relation to the whole of EU industry is obviously smaller than that of the two other blocks. Products of industries in strong demand sectors generally have a high technological content and require huge R&D investment. They are normally only produced on a very large scale to cover development costs. A large home market is a prerequisite for these products.

The awareness of a growing gap between the EU and its two rivals in the field of fast-growing high-tech industries became a major driving force behind the speeding up of the integration process within the Union at the end of the 1980s. The EU's industries can only keep up if they operate within a large unfragmented internal market, as exists today on completion of the Single Market. Relative backwardness in the technological field also explains the present emphasis on joint R&D research in the EU's industrial policy.

The current account of the EU is normally fairly balanced; in contrast to that of Japan, which over many years has shown a large surplus, and that of the USA, which mainly has a deficit (see Figure 1.4). Exports and imports of goods and services generally constitute about 9% of GDP for both Japan and the EU and around 12% for the USA.

Developing countries and other European OECD (non-EU) countries are by far the most important trading partners for the EU, accounting for, in 1994, respectively 34% and 26% of extra-EU exports and for 30% and 26% of its imports. Exports to the USA and Japan accounted only for 23% of total EU exports and 26% of imports. The trade deficit with Japan reached 26 billion ECU in 1994.

The Japanese trade pattern is completely different. About 51% of its total exports went to the

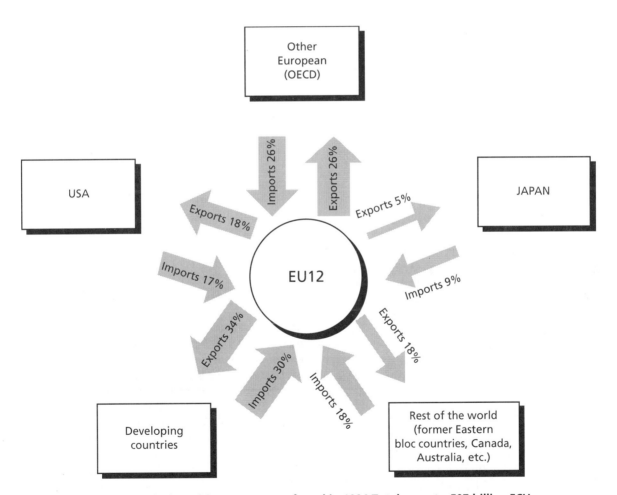

Figure 1.4 Extra-EU trade (EU15) in percentage of total in 1994 Total exports: 507 billion ECU; Total imports: 514 billion ECU

EU and the USA and 37% of its imports originated from these areas (1990).

The trade between the three dominating blocks is clearly out of balance; a problem which has provoked many disputes. The USA reproach the EU for using unfair trade practices like subvention and protection, especially in the field of agriculture. Americans fear that despite its free market rhetoric, the EU might build up a 'Fortress Europe', with little access for foreign exports.

The EU, for its part, complains about limited access to the Japanese market due to non-tariff barriers and feels itself flooded with Japanese high-tech products (electronics, cameras, cars, computers and so on). But the EU's main orientation on less developed countries and neighbouring countries obviously shows a lack of competitiveness in the advanced sectors of strong demand. This structural weakness may, among others, be overcome by a more integrated large single market within an integrated European economy.

1.5 A BRIEF OVERVIEW OF THE FIFTEEN EU COUNTRIES

1.5.1 Germany

Of the fifteen EU countries Germany is by far the largest. With a population of 81.6 million people (including East Germany) it exceeds by far the population in the next largest EU countries: France, Italy and the UK, all having a population of around 58 million (1995, see Table 1.5). Its GDP of 1846 billion ECUs exceeded France, the second country, by 57%.

The western part of Germany is – after Luxembourg – also leading with respect to GDP per head; and it had until recently the lowest inflation and unemployment rates and its competitiveness and export performance were impressive. Its real GDP growth rate in the last decade was only moderate, but until recently it was a very stable and balanced economy.

In the early 1990s this favourable situation changed rather drastically. One reason for this was the integration of the East German economy (after the unification in 1990), which has involved high costs for restructuring, cleaning up the environment, infrastructure, education and social programmes (unemployment, retraining and retirement). As a result, Germany is – after an initial expenditure boom – confronted with serious imbalances in the field of inflation and public deficit and with stagnant growth. This development was reinforced by the recession in the early 1990s.

A second reason is that there are serious concerns about German competitiveness. Costs have risen strongly, mainly due to high wage increases, a real appreciation of the mark, and rising costs of environmental protection, congestion and other factors. The increase in costs is not fully matched by an increase in productivity.

Long-term prospects for the German economy are uncertain. Eventually unification may turn out to be an incentive for the combined German economy in terms of market enlargement and investment opportunities. The problems related to the high costs have to be addressed. Substantial structural reforms will probably be required.

1.5.2 France

Until the early 1980s the French economy was characterised by a heavy degree of state intervention, culminating in an attempt to fight the recession of the early 1980s with Keynesian reflation policies. High inflation rates and repeated depreciations were the main results of these policies.

Since 1982, France has made a major shift in its economic policies towards more liberal and free-market approaches; together with the improving world economy this caused a sound recovery of the French economy in the second half of the 1980s. Austerity policies and its policy of 'competitive disinflation' succeeded in reducing inflation and the budget deficit to very acceptable levels, as well as improving the competitiveness of its export industry and achieving a balanced current account and stable currency. The deep recession of the early 1990s showed that the problems were far from over, however. The public deficit sharply increased again, unemployment rose to unacceptable levels and the franc came under severe attack. The present

Table 1.5 Main economic indicators, 1995

Table 1.5 Main economic indicators, 1995

	Germany	France	Italy	UK	Spain	Nether-lands	Belgium	Austria	Sweden	Denmark	Finland	Greece	Portugal	Ireland	Luxem-bourg
Population (millions)	81.6	58.1	57.3	58.5	39.2	15.4	10.2	8.0	8.9	5.2	5.1	10.5	9.8	3.6	0.4
Gross Domestic Product (GDP) current market prices (Mrd ECU)	1846	1174	831	842	428	303	206	178	175	132	97	87	80	47	13
average real growth in % 1986–95	2.6[1]	2.2	2.1	2.3	2.9	2.5	2.2	2.5	1.2	1.7	1.4	1.5	3.1	4.8	3.5
GDP per head, PPS, EU=100%	109.3	106.7	104.7	98.5	76.2	103.5	103.5	112.6	97.3	114.1	92.3	64.3	69.7	90.0	165.2
Unemployment rate average 1986–95	5.8[1]	10.4	10.0	9.3	20.0	7.0	8.6	3.6	4.8	7.5	9.8	7.5	5.8	15.3	2.1
Inflation (GDP deflator) average 1986–95	2.8[1]	2.8	6.0	4.6	6.4	1.5	3.1	3.1	5.3	2.9	3.9	15.1	11.2	2.6	4.7
Gross Fixed capital formation average 1986–95 (% of GDP at market prices)	19.7[1]	20.0	19.0	17.2	21.8	20.3	18.0	24.3	18.0	17.2	21.3	21.6	26.4	16.3	22.9
Private consumption average 1986–95 (% of GDP at market prices)	61.5[1]	60.2	61.7	63.4	62.8	59.8	62.8	55.7	52.7	53.0	54.8	73.0	64.4	58.7	60.7
Nominal unit labour costs (relative to 19 industr. countries double export weights, 1980=100)	102.3[1]	86.8	92.8	82.3	80.5	87.5	95.2	126.4	78.0	100.1	98.4	107.2	120.7	82.4	89.5
Exports of goods and services (% of GDP at market prices)	23.0	23.5	27.6	28.0	23.7	52.5	74.2	37.6	40.8	33.7	37.6	16.5	29.5	76.3	91.4
Imports of goods and services (% of GDP at market prices)	22.0	21.1	23.4	29.0	23.6	46.7	68.5	38.6	34.5	29.6	30.0	26.9	37.7	61.9	81.4
Current balance (% of GDP at market prices)	–1.0	1.6	2.4	–2.3	4.8	5.0	–3.7	–2.0	2.0	0.4	3.4	–2.7	–0.4	6.6	17.5

[1] West Germany

Source: *Statistical Annex of European Economy*, June 1996

French government is very determined to defend the franc and to bring the deficit down to a level below the Maastricht criteria. Wage moderation, budget cuts, a further liberalisation of the economy and a tight monetary policy will be the most important policy instruments. This is, in the view of the government, the only way to reduce the high level of employment and to generate economic growth.

1.5.3 Italy

Italy, on average, showed rather moderate growth rates in the last decade. A remarkable feature of the Italian economy is the large presence of small and medium-sized companies, which have turned out to be one of the major driving forces behind Italian success. The growth is lacking in terms of balance, however. While the economy of Milan and other northern regions is generally doing fairly well, the economy of the South is rather stagnant and the gap between the two parts of the country is continuing to widen. Full exposure to international competition within a united Europe may even accelerate this trend. Other significant problems are the inefficient public sector, the large budget deficit and debt, the high inflation rates, organised crime and – last but not least – political problems. Political scandals and the revelation of widespread corruption affairs in the early 1990s undermined the credibility of the Italian economy, resulting among other things in a sharp depreciation of the lira on the currency markets. All these problems have to be addressed if Italy wants to maintain confidence in its economy. At present, strong attempts are made to bring the public deficit down from around 10% in the early 1990s to below 3% in 1998.

1.5.4 United Kingdom

The UK has succeeded in the last decade in bringing to an end a long period of poor performance. In the 1960s and 1970s the average UK growth rate was only a meagre 2.5% against an average of 4.0% for the present 15 EU members. But since the early 1980s UK growth rates are generally in line with average EU15 growth; since 1994 even higher. It appears that the UK is on its way back. Partly responsible for this development might be the radical structural change the UK economy has undergone since the first conservative government under Thatcher came into power by the end of 1979. Government involvement has been strongly reduced and the UK economy is at present the most liberalised market economy in Europe. Furthermore, the main focus of economic activity has been shifted from manufacturing to services. The financial service sector, in particular, is very strong: the UK has become the financial centre of Europe. Nevertheless, the UK economy still exhibits important structural weaknesses, such as regional disparities, low investment levels, an underdeveloped infrastructure, and a large current account deficit. The latter can be considered to be a result of a continuing structural weakness in international competitiveness; an aspect which partly explains the UK's hesitation to participate in the EMU and to support other steps leading to the economic unification of Europe.

1.5.5 Spain

The Spanish GDP per head is still far below the EU average; but since 1986, it has been catching up. The Spanish economy has shown a large number of imbalances in the last decades, e.g. high unemployment, interest and inflation rates. Due to the policies of the Franco era it was a rather closed, protected, regulated and monopolised economy. Recent Spanish governments, however, have quite successfully implemented policies to liberalise the economy and prepare Spain for full integration into the EU. The Spanish economy is much more competitive now and has a large growth potential. For instance, a much greater part of the female population could be integrated into the labour force. Investment in the 1980s and 1990s was very high, much of it financed by foreign capital. The Spanish economy succeeded fairly well in recovering from the recession of the early 1990s and managed to reduce sharply a number of imbalances by the mid-1990s (e.g. inflation, public and current account deficit). This could provide a sound base for sustained high growth rates.

1.5.6 The Netherlands

The Netherlands suffered more than any other EU country from the crisis in the early 1980s, chiefly due to the effect of rising labour costs caused by increased social security expenditure. In the last decade rather successful policies have been implemented aiming at reducing labour costs, the size of the public sector and the budget deficit, liberalising the economy and increasing profitability of the private sector. These have resulted in a recovery of economic growth and, very remarkably, in a significant rise in employment. Strong points of the Dutch economy are the low inflation level, international competitiveness, a stable currency and the country's central location within Europe. The still low labour participation rate and high social expenditure level continue to be matters of concern.

1.5.7 Belgium

Belgium has realised only a moderate growth in recent decades. It is an extremely open economy, characterised by low inflation rates, a high degree of competitiveness and a strong currency. Major problems, on the other hand, are the excessive national debt, high public deficits, fast rising labour costs, unemployment and regional disputes and disparities. The central location and international orientation put the country in a favourable position with respect to European integration. Substantial progress has been made with respect to nominal convergence in recent years; the most difficult criterion, relating to EMU, will be the one relating to public debt, which stands at over 130% of GDP (1996 figure).

1.5.8 Austria

The open Austrian economy has been doing fairly well in the last decades. It generally has low inflation and unemployment rates, a GDP growth above the EU average, a strong currency and its per capita income is among the highest of the EU. Important industry sectors are tourism and manufacturing of machinery, steel and metal. A broad consensus on economic policy is guaranteed by the system of 'social partnership', a kind of decision-making in which the government as well as industry and the trade unions are involved. This system provides economic and political stability but may also reduce flexibility, innovation and structural change. Current problems include a fall in demand facing the country's tourist industry and the size of the public deficit. A drastic fiscal consolidation programme has been introduced to address the latter problem.

1.5.9 Sweden

Until 1970, Sweden was one of the richest countries in the industrialised world and a kind of role model for a developed welfare state. It was characterised by an extensive social security system, low income differentials and virtually full employment. Since the oil crises of the early 1970s economic growth has been relatively stagnant. One of the major reasons is probably that Swedish governments stuck too long to Keynesian reflation policies to fight recessions and maintain full employment. These policies resulted in very high levels of public expenditure (generally more than 60% of GDP) and public deficits. This led in turn to sharply increasing costs, necessitating frequent devaluations in order to stay internationally competitive. Since 1990 successive governments – non-socialist as well as socialist – have pursued tight fiscal and monetary policies. After a deep recession in the early 1990s the Swedish economy shows some clear signs of recovery.

1.5.10 Denmark

Until recently, Danish growth was lagging behind the average EU15 growth over the last 35 years. Explanations for this underperformance are the high starting level of economic development in the 1950s and the slow growth of productivity. The latter is mainly due to the high levels of public expenditure and high levels of non-market services employment. Rigidities in the labour market are a constraint as well. The cost competitiveness and international orientation of the Danish economy are strong points. Since 1986, successive Danish governments have tried to decrease public intervention in the economy with increasing success. This might explain – at least in part – the recent improvements of the Danish economic performance.

1.5.11 Portugal

Portugal has shown very high growth rates in the last four decades, though it was more severely hit by the recession in the early l990s than most other EU countries. Its entry into the EU appears to have been beneficial for the country. It is in the process of restructuring, aiming to convert the former highly regulated, state dominated economy into a market-oriented one. Investment is very high, but the high inflation rates and the weak competitiveness remain a matter of concern. Supply-side improvements are of vital importance to withstand increased competition in the open single market and to maintain its favourable long-term growth rates.

1.5.12 Finland

The Finnish economy went through a very deep recession in the early 1990s, resulting in a cumulative decrease in GDP of 12% in the period 1990–93. The government deficit went up to around 6% and unemployment to 18% in 1994–95. The main causes of this development was an overheated economy in the late 1980s resulting from financial liberalisation and the collapse of trade with the former Soviet Union. The recession was followed by strong export-led growth in the mid-1990s, facilitated by a sharp depreciation of the Finnish markka in the early 1990s. The strongest industrial sectors are paper, paper products and printing and telecommunication equipment. The main points of concern on the mid-term remain the public deficit and unemployment.

1.5.13 Greece

Greek economic performance in the last decade has been relatively poor, in spite of substantial aid from the EU structural funds. The most important problems for Greece are fiscal imbalances, public sector inefficiency, lack of competitiveness, underdeveloped infrastructure and low investment. To some extent the difficulties arise from the high degree of state intervention during the 1980s; since 1991 the Greek governments have been trying to address the problems. This has led to an improvement in the fiscal imbalances and a reduction of inflation to below double digits. The new Greek government of Simitis, which came into power in 1996, has stated determination to continue these austerity policies. A further reduction in inflation and interest rates and the public deficit are key elements in fostering sustained economic growth.

1.5.14 Ireland

Ireland has managed to realise impressive growth rates in both the long and the short run. It succeeded in redressing a number of imbalances in the 1980s, especially high inflation rates and budget and current account deficits. It has been quite successful in attracting foreign investors, mainly multinationals, by offering favourable investment conditions. The relatively advanced foreign owned sector is not very well integrated with the more traditional indigenous sectors, however. The main problem remains job creation, which is necessary to accommodate the rapidly increasing work force. Together with Spain, Ireland has the worst unemployment record in the EU.

1.5.15 Luxembourg

Luxembourg has shown an outstanding performance in terms of growth and virtually all other macroeconomic indicators in the last decade. It is the smallest, but also by far the richest country in Europe. It has become a major international financial centre and is also heavily engaged in other international services. The outlook for

Luxembourg is favourable, with no problems in meeting EMU criteria.

1.6 BIBLIOGRAPHY

Artis, L. (1994): *The Economics of the European Union, Policy and Analysis*, Oxford

Barnes, I., Barnes, P.M. (1995): *The Enlarged European Union*, Longman

Church, C.H., Phinnimore, D. (1994): *European Union and European Community, a handbook on the post-Maastricht Treaties*, Harvester Wheatsheaf

Cockfield, L. (1994): *The European Union, Creating a Single Market*, Wiley

Commission of the European Communities, *General Reports on the Activities of the European Communities* (annually)

Commission of the European Communities, *European Economy* (quarterly)

Costin, H. (1996): *The European Union, Managing in the Global Economy*, The Dryden Press

Dyker, D.A. (ed.) (1992): *The European Economy*, Longman

Economist, The (1994) 'European Union, A survey of the European Union', 22 October 1994

El-Agraa, A. (1994): *Economics of the European Community* (4th edn), Harvester Wheatsheaf

Fagerberg, J. (1993): *European Economic Integration, A Nordic Perspective*, Avebury

Gibbs, P. (1994): *Doing Business in the European Union* (3rd edn), Kogan Page

Griffiths, A. (1992): *European Community Survey*, Longman

Hiteris, T. (1994): *European Community Economics* (3rd edn), Harvester Wheatsheaf

McDonald, F., Dearden, S. (eds) (1994): *European Economic Integration* (2nd edn), Longman

Nugent, N. (ed.) (1994): *The Government and Politics of the European Union*, Macmillan

Pinder, J. (1994): *European Community, The Building of a Union*, Opus

PART B

EU6: the six original member states

PART B EU6: THE SIX ORIGINAL MEMBER STATES

In part B the economies of the original six countries, who founded the European Economic Community (EEC) and Euratom in 1957, will be discussed. This group consists of: Germany (chapter 2), France (chapter 3), Italy (chapter 4), The Netherlands (chapter 5) and Belgium and Luxembourg (chapter 6).

As mentioned in the introductory chapter, the main driving forces behind the European integration in the era following the Second World War were

- the revitalisation of the European economy
- the wish to build up a strong Europe against the perceived Soviet threat
- political (especially French) ideas to integrate Germany into the new Europe in order to avoid future conflicts

The foundation of the EEC and Euratom followed the establishment of the ECSC in 1951 by the same six countries; in 1967 the three Communities merged into the European Community (EC).

The movement towards European integration in the participating countries was strongly supported by centrist parties, including those from the centre-right and centre-left. These parties dominated the political scene, in particular in Germany and the Benelux countries. Opposition to the formation of the various European Communities came mostly from parties on the extreme left (like the Communists) and the (extreme) right (e.g. conservatives and nationalists). These parties hold strong minority positions particularly in France and Italy. Communists considered European integration to be not on the interest of the working class. Moreover, they did not like the 'anti-soviet ideas' stance of the supporters of integration. Nationalists feared that their country would face a loss of independence and national influence. After the establishment of the EEC in 1957, the nationalist Gaullist party in France returned to power, leading to a considerable slow-down of the integration process in the 1960s. In Germany and the Benelux the establishment of EEC was supported by a vast majority.

The original six include the three largest countries (in terms of GDP): Germany, France and Italy. The combined GDP of the six founding nations constitute more than two-thirds of the EU's GDP at present. The French-German cooperation is still considered to be at the core of the European integration.

CHAPTER 2

Federal Republic of Germany

Rudi Kurz

2.1 INSTITUTIONAL AND HISTORICAL CONTEXT

2.1.1 Historical overview

Economic development in Germany has been a success story throughout most of the post-war years. Full employment, stable prices, the peaceful resolution of social conflicts, a strong currency and international competitiveness have been the characteristics of German economic performance. During the last years some of these characteristics changed significantly as a consequence of German unification, European integration and increasing global competition. The German economic system had, and still has, considerable difficulties in coping with these challenges. Policies and institutions are adapted only reluctantly. Given the well-organised resistance against innovative solutions and the large number of pending reform projects, Germany's economic perspectives are no longer so bright.

The post-war economic development of Germany may be subdivided into the following four periods:

- 1948–65: A reconstruction period characterised by high growth rates, price stability, increasing employment and the establishment of a strong position in international trade. Distributional and environmental issues caused little concern.

- 1966–79: A state interventionist period characterised by the Keynesian principle of state-guaranteed full employment and an extension of the welfare state. Deficiencies inherent in the basic ideas and two oil price shocks brought this period to an end.

- 1980–90: A period of liberalisation characterised by the withdrawal of the state on all fronts: the policy of full employment was replaced by a policy of long-term growth, government intervention in the market by deregulation and privatisation and the levelling off of increased expenditure on social security and subsidies.

- The 1990s: The focus of this period is on improving the attractivity of Germany as a location for business activity and investment and on economic reconstruction in the new states (*Bundesländer*) in east Germany.

Germany's economic success has been attributed to a large extent to the particular economic system that was established after World War II – the *Soziale Marktwirtschaft* (social market economy). It is essential for anyone who wishes to understand the German economic miracle (*Wirtschaftswunder*) to become acquainted with the major features of this specific system. Anyone planning to do business in Germany should understand how it works, because not only does it grant basic economic freedoms but also it defines the conditions that apply to the use of private resources in business and the obligations that have to be met. The *Soziale Marktwirtschaft* is intended to be both efficient and humane (W. Eucken). It is an attempt to achieve a balance between market efficiency and social interests (A. Müller-Armack). To adapt this system to changing conditions in the process of economic development is a permanent challenge. The next section describes some major characteristics of this system.

Seven years after the beginning of the German unification process it seems to be feasible to describe the German economy as an entity rather than referring to it as two separate worlds. Although the number and significance of differences between east and west have declined, they are still considerable. Therefore throughout the text there are hints on these differences and a special section (2.6.3) is dedicated to the economic results of the unification process.

2.1.2 *Soziale Marktwirtschaft* – some major characteristics

Constitutional principles

The German constitution – the *Grundgesetz* (GG) of 1949 – has been modified in the process of unification but not changed fundamentally. The states of the former German Democratic Republic (GDR) joined the Federal Republic of Germany (*Beitritt* in accordance with article 23 GG); it was not the creation of a new state. The GG does not codify the *Soziale Marktwirtschaft*. It leaves open the possibility of changes in the economic system. However, there are narrow limits to such changes because any economic system has to be compatible with inalienable human rights and the decentralised political structure, i.e. the strong position of the *Bundesländer* and the local communities (*Gemeinden*).

Based on the human right of individual freedom the GG guarantees freedom of press, art and science, the liberty to move within the country, to form labour unions and to conduct labour conflicts. Private property is guaranteed. Its use has to

serve the general welfare of the community. Expropriation and adaptation for social use are possible (article 15 GG) if this benefits the community and if financial compensation is paid. In article 20 GG the FRG is defined as a democratic and social federal state (*demokratischer und sozialer Bundesstaat*). This is to emphasise the significance of social justice for the long-term existence of a market economy and to protect the federal structure of the state (*Föderalismus*). The latter is defined more precisely by attributing specific functions and sources of revenue to every level of state activity. With regard to the vertical division of labour within the government sector the principle of subsidiarity (*Subsidiaritätsprinzip*) applies: federal and state involvement occur only when local communities are unable to cope. Decentralisation creates coordination problems, but experience shows that the advantages of flexibility and autonomy are dominant factors.

As a consequence of European integration (Maastricht Treaty of 1992) and of German unification a constitutional reform added new elements to the GG in 1994. In a new article 20a protection of natural resources is made an explicit aim of the German state. This has a primarily declamatory character and does not directly constitute individual rights. However, it is one step to transforming the social market economy into a ecological–social market economy. Article 23 GG now states the realisation of a European Union as an aim of German policy and allows for that purpose to transfer rights of sovereignty (under certain qualifications regarding e.g. the *Subsidiaritätsprinzip*). Constitutional reform (new articles 87d–f) also provided the fundament for basic reforms in some industries which so far had been defined as part of the public sector (e.g. railways, mail and telecommunication).

Law relating to competition

Competition is perceived as the motor of economic progress and wealth. Competition, especially in the small- and medium-sized enterprises (SME) sector, has always been an important stimulant in the German economy. To protect the freedom of competition, the control and regulation of cartels and monopolies represents a vital part of government policy. The most important law in this field is the *Gesetz gegen Wettbewerbsbeschränkungen (GWB)*. Its major contents are as follows:

- Cartels and concerted actions by groups of firms are in principle forbidden, with some exemptions defined by the law (e.g. to apply common standards or to manage a structural crisis). Some sectors (like transportation, public utilities, agriculture) are not subject to these provisions.
- The conduct of monopolies (*marktbeherrschende Unternehmen*) is controlled in order to prevent them from abusing their market power (e.g. by charging too high prices).
- Large firms are subject to provisions governing mergers. If the cartel authority (*Bundeskartellamt*) rejects a merger, the Minister of Commerce may grant permission if the economic advantages outweigh the disadvantages of restricted competition (e.g. in the case of Daimler-Benz/MBB in 1989).

All three aspects are also covered by EU provisions: Cartels by Art. 85 of the EU treaty, conduct of monopolies by Art. 86 of the EU treaty, mergers of European dimension by the EC Merger Guideline of 1990. In some cases conflicts of competence arise and a consistent competition policy approach has yet to be found. The sixth GWB revision – going to be effective in 1997 – will adapt German law to EU provision (with some exceptions, such as fixing of retail prices for books).

Other important general competition laws are the *Gesetz gegen unlauteren Wettbewerb (UWG)* which formulates rules for fair competition (according to good business practices) outlawing discriminatory and misleading practices as well as certain forms of advertising. Another law (*Rabattgesetz*) rules what regular rebates (a maximum of 3% of sales price) and what special rebates may be granted. In addition, a large number of specific rules (economic regulations) for entry into or competition in various markets exist and have reduced competition to the disadvantage of consumers. However, these regulations

are eroding under an ongoing reform process. This process has been enforced and is driven by new technologies (especially in telecommunication), EU policies (determined to tear down national barriers for European competitors) and poor performance in the regulated sectors (low productivity and high costs being burdened on public budgets and/or on customers). Only a few examples can be given here.

Regulated industries and social regulations

Free competition may not always lead to socially beneficial results and hence limits to competition have to be defined in the political democratic process. Restrictions to free competition refer to certain industries (economic regulations) or to certain characteristics of products and production processes (social regulations). All of these regulations have the side effect that they protect established firms and harm potential competitors. Therefore regulations are often instrumentalised in the political struggle for protected monopolies. Reforming these regulations when economic conditions change always requires the defeat of vested interests tied to the status quo. Considering this, changes in the institutional design during the last years, are remarkable. On the other hand the state has created new monopoly structures in the waste treatment industry where the *Duales System Deutschland GmbH (DSD)* dominates the market.

Transportation. The *Deutsche Bundesbahn* is no longer a public enterprise but became a private profit-oriented company (*Deutsche Bahn AG*) in 1994 and will be split up into several independent companies – and then sold to private investors. Most important, a separate company which owns and sells the use of the rail network is planned for the future. However, the constitution (Article 87e GG) rules that government has to hold the majority of this company. In air transportation from 1997 on airlines based in other EU countries will start to serve national German routes and thus end the quasi-monopoly of *Lufthansa AG*. Lower prices, enlarged choice of destinations and increased range of service options will be the consequence. Surface transportation of goods is liberalised only on a step-by-step basis because foreign carriers profit from more favourable conditions (less taxes and regulations) in their home countries (liberalisation with harmonisation). Rate-setting has been abandoned but controls of market entry (concessions) still exist. Surface transportation of persons is open for EU firms and in some communities and counties public transportation is already provided by foreign firms.

Telecommunication. Until 1989 most segments of the telecommunication markets in Germany were under control of the quasi-authority *Deutsche Bundespost*. With *Postreform I* the business of this authority was separated from the Ministry of Post and Telecommunication and split up into three independent divisions: tele-communication, mail, and banking. *Postreform II* in 1994 converted these divisions into private companies (*Aktiengesellschaften*), a formal privatis- ation because all shares are held by the state. However, in late 1996 a large amount of Telekom shares (several billion ECU) will be offered at the stock markets. The *Telekommunikationsgesetz* of 1996 rules that – as decided by the EU council of ministers in 1994 – in 1998 the telecommunication monopoly will end and the network is open for competitors. This is going to raise difficult questions especially on the terms for using local networks. Meanwhile, Telekom AG engages in international strategic coalitions (with France Télécom and Sprint) to gain strength for the dawning age of competition. Major challengers have already formed (like Mannesmann, allied with AT&T or Viag and RWE allied with British Telecom). Comparable significant changes apply to the mail sector, where only the core of the monopoly – transportation of letters – may prevail until 2004.

Production and distribution of electricity, the most important part of the energy market, is still the domain of a few large private enterprises endowed with territorial monopolies and linked with local distributors and the interests of local communites by a fee (*Konzessionsabgabe*) of about 3 billion ECU for the exclusive right to serve a community and to build a network on their territory (*Wegerecht*). Based on the *Energiewirtschaftsgesetz* of 1935 the activity is not subject to control by cartel authorities but by the ministers for economics of the Bundesländer. The EU directive on electricity of 1996 is going to change this gradually. The *Energiewirtschaftsgesetz* as well as the GWB are going to be reformed in order to open the market according to the EU directive. Especially large industrial customers (licensed customers) will then have the opportunity to buy cheaper electricity from abroad and German utilities are obliged to grant access to their networks for distribution – under fair conditions. Freeing the large customers could force electricity companies to increase prices for SME and for private households. Electricity companies say that they will not be able to succeed in European competition as long as safety and environment standards differ between countries.

There are also some reforms of social regulations, i.e. of regulations directed toward the protection of consumers, employers (occupational health and safety) or the environment. The most prominent example is the law on shop closing hours (*Ladenschlußgesetz*). The reform of this law has become a symbol, a *pars pro toto* for prospects of reforms in German economy and society. After lengthy debate shops are now allowed to open Monday to Friday from 6 a.m. to 8 p.m. and on Saturday from 6 a.m. to 4 p.m. A more comprehensive liberalisation (Sundays, 24 hours) has been blocked by unions and small retailers, who fear advantages for large shopping centres. Unions have negotiated a 20% surplus on wage during the evening and Saturday afternoon hours. No reliable projections of effects on prices, revenues, employment (some project 50 000 additional jobs) and concentration are available. Clearly, consumer's convenience will improve.

Another important deregulation issue, involving an effort to eliminate bureaucratic inefficiency and encourage 'lean government', is the simplification of permission procedures for (potentially dangerous) new industrial plants as well as for new infrastructure (like power plants or roads). Permission procedures are considered to be a serious barrier to investment, although empirical evidence to prove that is sparse. In 1991 a law – with the anti-bureaucratic title *Verkehrswegeplanungsbeschleunigungsgesetz* – was passed to accelerate the modernisation of transportation infrastructure in the new states, in 1993 a *Investitionserleichterungs- und Wohnbaulandgesetz* followed, affecting especially the opening of new industrial areas and permissions for the construction of new plants. The process was reinforced by the results of various commissions (one established by the EU, the Molitor-Commission) and resulted in the *Beschleunigungsgesetz* of 1996 which addresses the permission for plants potentially harmful to air or water quality. In sum, it is much easier and less time-consuming to get permissions for new plants in Germany today than it was a few years ago. In part this is not only due to less bureaucracy but also to a reduction of citizens' participation rights and to lower (environmental and safety) standards. In 1993 a reform of the law on biotechnology (*Gentechnikgesetz*) became effective which replaced permission by notification in cases of low risk and made it easier to get permission for field experiments with new plants. Basically unchanged so far, are the craft codes (*Handwerksordnung*): in order to protect customers, craftsmen have to have special training and a formal qualification (*Meisterprüfung*) if they want to run their own firm. This is one example of a qualification of the principle of freedom for entrepreneurial activity as stated in Section 1 *Gewerbeordnung*.

Financial system

The *Gesetz über die Deutsche Bundesbank* of 1957 rules that the Bundesbank

- is autonomous, i.e. independent from the federal government;
- has only one goal, the stabilisation of the price level and is obliged to support the economic policy of the Federal Government only to the extent that such policy is compatible with this goal;
- may provide credit for public budgets only within exactly defined limits (to bridge liquidity gaps).

The law also defines the available instruments: minimum reserve standards, conditions and quantity of refinancing drafts and securities (discount rate, lending rate) and open-market intervention. The Bundesbank does have the freedom to choose its target monetary indicators (quantity of money concept). The German government has insisted that these features are reflected in the structural rules of the European Central Bank because article 88 GG requires that the Bundesbank's competences may be transferred to the ECB only if it is independent and determined to fight inflation. Decisions on the exchange rate regime are made in the political system, not by the Bundesbank. The FRG is a member of the European Monetary System and hence the Bundesbank is obliged to intervene in order to stabilise exchange rates within margins of fluctuation of ±15% (until August 1993 this was ±2.25%). For all other currencies flexible exchange rates apply.

Because of the great importance of the financial system (banks, insurances, building and loan associations) to the effective operation and stability of the economic system, this industry is subject to specific control by a regulatory authority (*Bundesaufsichtsamt für das Kreditwesen*). Market entry and competitive behaviour are not perfectly free. In order to control new forms of capital market activity and insider trading a new authority (*Bundesaufsichtsamt für den Wertpapierhandel*) was established in 1995.

Legal foundations of labour markets

The freedom to design individual labour contracts is restricted by labour laws and by the existence of collective agreements between unions and employers (*Tarifverträge*) from which individual labour contracts may deviate only if such deviation is to the advantage of the employee (*Günstigkeitsprinzip*). Laws on labour conflicts (strikes and lock-outs) do not exist and so courts have to participate in resolving such conflicts. Collective agreements are negotiated separately for each industry (trade, textile, construction etc.) and for regions which are smaller in size than the *Bundesländer*. All employers –

and all employees organised in unions – are obliged to apply the *Tarifvertrag* as a minimum standard. This constitutes a *de facto* minimum wage – for example, in the construction sector this is as high as 9 ECU. The system leaves little flexibility for adaption to the individual situation of a firm.

Lay-off-protection. No employee who has worked more than six months in a firm may be laid off without good reason. Such a reason can be a crisis of the firm, or reasons may be found in the individual conduct of the employee. The regular notice requirement is 4 weeks and this increases with duration of employment. Firms with less than 10 employees are not subject to the strict lay-off rules and lay-off protection in general will be reduced in the future because it is perceived as an impediment to hiring. To prevent the circumvention of lay-off rules, labour contracts for a limited period of time may last no longer than 18 months. Temporary workers may not be employed in the same firm for more than 6 months. In cases of mass lay-offs and fundamental restructuring of firms, a social plan (*Sozialplan*) has to be negotiated between management and employees to minimise social harm and to compensate those who are laid off. Compensation can amount to the equivalent of several months' pay. The *Sozialplan*, therefore, can be very expensive and may ruin a firm which is already in trouble.

The working time of employees is restricted by various legal rules: Sundays and public holidays are in principle free and only work which is in the public interest may be performed (e.g. in hospitals) and, in rare special cases also for economic reasons (e.g. maintaining continuous production). For juveniles specific restrictions apply (e.g. piecework is not allowed). Women are granted a paid holiday of six weeks before and eight weeks after the birth of a child. Normal working hours should not exceed 8 per day and may not exceed 10 per day. The number of days paid holidays per year must be a minimum of 18. Many of these provisions are of little practical relevance because collective agreements in most cases go far beyond these minimum standards (e.g. as regards working hours per week and paid holidays which are 6 weeks on average).

If an employee becomes sick, the employer is obliged to continue wage payments for 6 weeks. After that period health insurance takes over the payments. No unpaid days (*Karenztage*) exist so far, full payment starts with the first day of sickness. This generous provision is thought to contribute to relatively high rates of illness (on average 5% of personnel) and hence to high costs for firms. Therefore, the law was changed in 1996 and firms may now pay only 80% of income (or reduce holidays to up to 5 days). However, in a fierce struggle unions succeeded in defending most of the former status by including the 100% provisions in collective agreements.

Employees are granted extensive rights of co-operation and codetermination. For all enterprises with more than five employees the *Betriebsverfassungsgesetz* of 1972 applies. This law grants employees and their elected representatives (*Betriebsräte*) comprehensive rights of information and consultation (working hours, breaks, workplace design, etc.). For large corporations (AG, GmbH) with more than 2000 employees – of which there are about 500 – the *Mitbestimmungsgesetz* of 1976 goes far beyond that. It stipulates that half of the members of the board (*Aufsichtsrat*) are elected by the employees. In stalemate situations the vote of the chairman (who is a representative of the capital-owning side) counts twice. This means that we do not have full parity in employees' codetermination.

Social security system

The FRG has built up one of the world's most advanced and most expensive social security systems, which has contributed significantly to the avoidance of social conflicts. Its main elements are as follows.

Pension fund. For all employees with an income of less than 4210 ECU per month (3580 ECU in the east German Bundesländer) membership of the scheme is mandatory. Contributions are paid half by employers and half by employees and amount to 19.2% of gross income – and will increase to 20.3% in 1997. In addition payments come from the federal budget (about 38 billion ECU, i.e. 20% of pension funds' expenditures) to compensate, for example, for pension payments to east German citizens who haven't had a chance to pay any contribution to the system and nevertheless are entitled to receive pensions. Individual pensions depend on the amount of contributions made and the general increase in incomes of the active workforce (*Generationenvertrag*). Pensions are index-linked, that is they increase according to the level of average net wage incomes. The average pension for male persons is about 980 ECU per month (820 in the east German Bundesländer) and 410 ECU for females (530 ECU for east German females).

Health insurance. All employees with less than 3160 ECU (2680 ECU in east Germany) monthly income must have health insurance. Contributions are paid half by employers and half by employees and amount to more than 13% of gross income. Major efforts have been made by the federal government to contain the cost explosion in the health care system – including cost participation of the insured (e.g. for each prescribed medicament) and restrictions for doctors, hospitals and the pharmaceutical industry. The halt to cost escalation was of a temporary nature, because the incentive structure of the system has not been changed. Further restrictions are now under debate.

Unemployment insurance. All employees have to contribute to the scheme regardless of the amount of their income. Contributions amount to 6.5% (from a maximum of 3160 ECU or in east Germany 2680 ECU per month) and are paid half by employers and half by employees. Based on his or her contributions, an employee who becomes unemployed receives up to 67% of his or her last net income (*Arbeitslosengeld*) and contributions for pension fund and health insurance are paid. After one year of unemployment, payments are reduced to a maximum of 57% (*Arbeitslosenhilfe*), paid only if the unemployed has no other sources of income.

Social aid (Sozialhilfe). This aims at enabling all people to live with dignity even if they are without income. It is paid only if no other source of income is available (e.g. from property or family members). Social aid is paid by the local authorities, creating a heavy budget burden associated with increased unemployment.

Insurance against accidents in the workplace: to cover the risks of accidents in the workplace, employers have to pay contributions to an insurance scheme (*Berufsgenossenschaften*) who compensate damages and take care of rehabilitation for injured workers. The rates of contributions depend on the risks in the firms and the employees' incomes.

A new element was added to the social safety net in 1995: a public insurance of nursing-care (*Pflegeversicherung*) mandatory for all employees with monthly incomes less than 3160 ECU (respectively 2680 ECU). Contributions amount to 1.7% of gross income and are paid half by employers and half by employees. However, to make this new element cost-neutral for firms, a paid legal holiday was eliminated. *Pflegeversicherung* pays for nursing of chronically sick and for old-age nursing at home as well as for stationary care in nursing homes. Payments depend on the degree of nursing intensity (up to 1500 ECU per month).

In sum, contributions to the social security system paid by employees and by firms amount to more than 40% of gross labour incomes. Contributions paid by employees may cause a reduction of their income of up to 770 ECU per month. The firms' share of the burden is to a large extent responsible for additional labour costs of more than 80% of wages, which is the highest in the world. In order to avoid a further increase in this burden, a reform of the social welfare system is unavoidable. The challenge is to make the system more effective, granting state protection where individuals would be overcharged hence conserving the contribution of the system to social and political stability of the republic.

2.1.3 Participants in policy formation

Parties and their political power

Political development in the FRG has been dominated by three political parties: the *Christlich Demokratische Union (CDU)* and its affiliated party in Bavaria *Christlich Soziale Union, (CSU)*;

the *Sozialdemokratische Partei Deutschlands (SPD)* and the *Freie Demokratische Partei (FDP)*. CDU/CSU and SPD are *Volksparteien*, trying to address all groups in the electorate. While CDU/CSU have a relatively stable share of the votes of more than 40%, the SPD's share has been declining and is now in the 35% realm. This decline is partly a consequence of the rise of the green party (*Bündnis '90/Die Grünen*) in the 1980s, which has a share of votes of almost 10% now – although it still hasn't got a fully elaborated economic programme. The FDP's following is the upper middle class; as a consequence this party now and again has difficulty in obtaining the minimum of 5% of the votes necessary for representation in federal and state parliaments. However, this small party played an important role because none of the *Volksparteien* had an absolute majority and hence they depended on coalitions with the FDP. The *Partei des Demokratischen Sozialismus (PDS)*, the successor of the communist SED which governed the German Democratic Republic (GDR) for 40 years, is struggling to become an additional left-wing player in the party system – with little success so far in west Germany but with about 20% shares of votes in east Germany where the party articulates the population's discontent with rapidly changing lifestyle and high unemployment. Extreme right-wing parties (*Republikaner, NDP*) had only short-term successes in the past by taking advantage of high immigration (too many 'foreigners') and unemployment rates.

The economic policy of the post-war period has been characterised by stability and continuity. Most of the time Conservatives and Liberals set the course. When Social Democrats participated in the Federal Government from 1966 to 1982 there were no radical changes, partly because they had to compromise with their coalition partners (CDU or FDP). This political continuity has greatly benefited the German economy. In the Social Democrat–Liberal era (with Chancellors W. Brandt and H. Schmidt) the welfare state was expanded and Keynesian strategies of full employment were applied – with the consequences of an increasing public deficit. After 1982 when the FDP formed a new coalition with the CDU/CSU emphasis has been given to eliminating deficits and to improving conditions for long-term economic growth (supply-oriented economic policy). Although German unification made some pragmatic deviations necessary, this basic orientation of economic policy hasn't changed. At the federal level Chancellor H. Kohl and the Conservative-Liberal coalition are elected until 1998. The majority in Länder parliaments and hence in the *Bundesrat* is not in Conservative–Liberal hands. Therefore, in all matters where basic interests of the Länder are involved, federal government has to compromise with the *Bundesrat*, especially with social democratic views.

Major lobby groups and business associations

A large variety of organised groups participate in formulating economic policy employing formal (e.g. hearings) and informal (e.g. financial support and lobbying) methods. Most important are the unions with about 11.5 million members organised by industry groups, 9.5 million of them united in the *Deutsche Gewerkschaftsbund (DGB)*. However, union membership is declining rapidly. Traditionally, unions have had a close relationship to the SPD, but this affinity is declining. Employers organise themselves in industry-specific associations where membership is voluntary. The most important umbrella organisations are the *Bundesverband der Deutschen Industrie (BDI)* and the *Bundesvereinigung der Deutschen Arbeitgeberverbände (BDA)*.

All three million enterprises are required to be members of regional chambers of commerce (*Industrie- und Handelskammer, Handwerkskammer*). These serve as bodies of self-administration, organise examinations on completion of apprenticeship and for qualification as foreman, give consultation to and educate young entrepreneurs, settle internal industry disputes and undertake public relations work. The umbrella organisations are the *Deutsche Industrie- und Handelstag (DIHT)* and the *Deutsche Handwerkskammertag*. Resistance of enterprises against mandatory membership (with fees of about 500 million ECU per annum) is increasing.

2.2 MAIN ECONOMIC CHARACTERISTICS

2.2.1 Population, labour force, employment

Even before unification the FRG had the largest population of all EU countries. The new states added about 16 million so that the total population of Germany is now almost 82 million (see Table G17). Population density is high but has declined somewhat owing to unification (from 247 inhabitants per square kilometre to 229). The population lives in 36.9 million households; the most frequent type of household is the single household (one third of all households). More than 7 million of the population are foreigners, of whom 2.1 million are in employment.

The age structure of the population is changing significantly. The proportion of older people in relation to the active population (i.e. people 65 and older / people 15–64) in the FRG, as in some other European countries, will increase dramatically from the current 25% level to more than 45% in 2040. This will cause serious economic and social problems during the coming decades.

The participation rate of the labour force declined from the mid-1950s to the late 1970s by five percentage points. It then started to increase and is now 49% (see Table G18). The labour force is 39 million, about three million of which are self-employed or work in family businesses.

After years of full employment (unemployment rate less than 1%) unemployment in (West) Germany began to rise in the early 1970s. In 1985 the unemployment rate had risen to 7.2% (see Table G20 and Figure 2.1(c)) it subsequently declined and the 'unity boom'

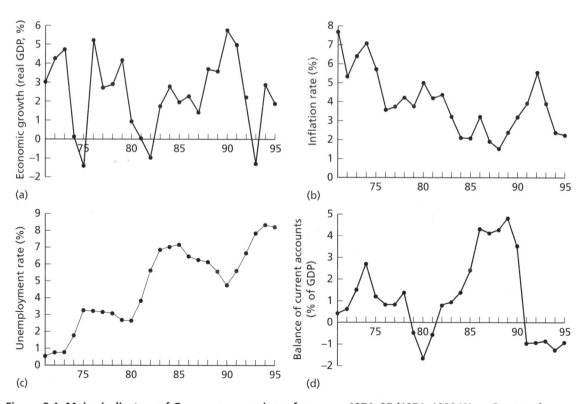

Figure 2.1 Major indicators of German economic performance 1971–95 (1971–1990 West Germany)

Source: Sachverständigenrat (1996, Tables 21*, 26*, 66*, 74*) and author's calculations.

PRODUCTION !

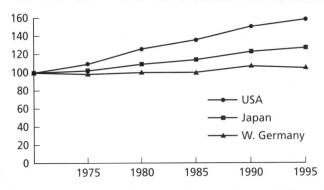

Figure 2.2 Employment in the USA, Japan and West Germany 1970–95 (1970=100)

Source: Sachverständigenrat (1996, Table 1*).

brought it down to 4.2% in 1991 – the same level as ten years before. Within a period of ten years more than 2 million new jobs had been created without significantly affecting unemployment because of the growing labour force. After 1991 the unemployment rate started to increase again and is now 9.3%. About 3.5 million people are registered unemployed – 2.5 million in west and 1 million in east Germany. To that have to be added part-time workers, persons in state-subsidised jobs, persons in qualification and retraining programmes and (in east Germany) persons in early retirement – altogether about 1.5 million additional people who are at least partly unemployed. If, in addition, account is taken of the 'hidden reserve' of people who would like to work but do not apply for jobs under the present hopeless conditions, the actual job gap in Germany is about 6 million. However, compared to the USA or to Japan, Germany has not been successful in creating new jobs (see Figure 2.2).

One third of the registered unemployed is without a job for more than one year. The chances of the long-term unemployed being reintegrated in the production process are very poor. This in turn is one of the factors which make the social security system more and more costly. The cost per unemployed person is estimated at about 15 000 ECU in total (expenditure plus revenue losses). Multiplied by the official number of 3.5 million unemployed, this is a total economic loss of about 50 billion ECU. Of

course, this money amount does not include the harm and the despair experienced by the affected individuals.

There are large regional differences in unemployment rates, ranging from 5% in some districts in the south to 20% in the east, and there is little mobility of labour which could contribute to eliminate these differences. A sectoral break-down (see Table G19) reveals that the percentage of the German labour force employed in industry is still very high at about 38%, i.e. the highest proportion among all EU nations (for comparison: USA 24%). There has been a long-term decline from 44% in 1980 to 49% in 1970 and this trend is continuing. The metal and electrical industries have lost a quarter of all jobs within the last five years (but are still the largest industrial employers with about 3.5 million jobs). Also declining is the proportion employed in agriculture (now 3.5%). Because of the relative low proportion of the service sector it is supposed that an expansion of this sector could significantly contribute to a reduction of unemployment. However, even in parts of the service sector, employment is going to decline in the future, e.g. in the public sector (now about 15% of total employment). With respect to firm size we find 98% of all firms in the industry sector have less than 1000 employees; these SME firms provide two thirds of all industry jobs. The reduction of industrial jobs takes place mainly in large firms

– from 1980 to 1993 they eliminated 700 000 jobs, while only 300 000 were lost in SME.

After two decades of high unemployment, the recognition that the problems cannot be solved without fundamental changes in labour market rules and the social security system has become widely agreed. The subject of the debate is how to reform – what to change and what to preserve. Unit labour costs have become internationally uncompetitive, this is especially so in east Germany where wages approach the west German level much faster than productivity does. Other cost components are not sufficient to compensate for this, and Germany is becoming increasingly unattractive as a business location. Under increased international competition, the annual average productivity growth of about 2% is no longer sufficient to defend high social standards and to resolve the unemployment problem. Unit labour costs must be reduced significantly. Unions already offer industry-wide agreements to renounce wage increases if employers guarantee employment. At the level of individual firms, employers enforce far-reaching concessions like longer and more flexible working hours without additional payment. This is a serious challenge for the traditional system of collective agreements. To relieve firms from legal additional wage costs, major reforms of the social security systems will be necessary during the next few years. Firms have already shown considerable creativity in developing ways to employ people without the burden of high labour costs, e.g. by making their employees self-employed (truck-drivers, waiters etc.), by splitting up full-time jobs into part-time jobs with a maximum payment of 590 DM per month (so no contributions to the social security systems have to be paid), or by (legally and illegally) employing cheap workers from abroad (in conditions of their home country) especially in the construction sector.

These market adjustments could be complemented by government programmes of active labour market policy such as retraining, job creation schemes and wage cost subsidies, to target persons and regions with extraordinary prob-lems. However, in its efforts to save money, the federal government is further restricting active labour market policy.

Even if comprehensive reforms could be implemented, it is doubtful whether full employment in the traditional sense is going to prevail again over the next decades. More realistic is that there will be a rise of new, flexible forms of activity, including work on a contract basis, several jobs at the same time, frequently changing jobs, and activity in private self-help groups (families, political and social initiatives, neighbourhood projects etc.). This can make life a lot more troublesome and uncomfortable; but it could also improve the quality of life. The introduction of a basic income (*Grundeinkommen*, *Bürgergeld*) could contribute to making the second alternative more probable.

2.2.2 Growth and business cycles

The FRG's gross domestic product (GDP) at current prices is 1850 billion ECU (see Table G21), about 90% of this still originates from the old states. Germany's GDP accounts for roughly 28% of the EU's GDP. As a consequence of this salient position, the German business cycle has a crucial impact on other EU economies. The German GDP per capita of 22 600 ECU is, despite its decline as a consequence of unification, among the highest in the EU, still higher than that of France, the UK or Sweden. However, it is surpassed now by Luxembourg, Denmark, Austria and Belgium (see Table G24 and Figure G1).

Long-term growth performance

Real GDP growth rates in (West) Germany have shown a declining trend over the last 40 years. During the *Wirtschaftswunder* in the 1950s the average growth rate had been almost 9%. In the 1960s it was 4.4%, in the 1970s 2.7% and in the 1980s 2.2% (see Table G23); the 1990s have so far brought an average growth rate of 1.4%. However, declining growth rates do not imply economic decline: in 1989, for example, real GDP increased by 30 billion ECU, i.e. by 3.4%; in the early 1960s this would have been an 8% growth rate. Compared to the 1950s German GDP per capita had tripled by the end of the 1990s. Even when the *Wirtschaftswunder* was over, GDP per capita increased by more than 50% in the 1970 to 1990 period, an annual increase of more than 2%. Compared to the EU average, the German growth performance is about the same; Germany has not been an engine of growth but neither has it been retarding economic growth in Europe.

Expressed as purchasing power of wage income earned in one minute the benefits from long-run growth are as shown in Table 2.1 (working time in minutes).

Table 2.1 Growth and purchasing power

	1960	1995
1 kg bread	20	11
250 g coffee	46	13
0.5 Ltr beer	15	3
1 Ltr petrol	14	4
mail (letter)	5	3

Source: Institut der deutschen Wirtschaft (1996, Table 52).

Another result of decades of prosperity are increasing assets. No comprehensive statistical data on size and distribution of individual wealth are available. However, consumers' durables are well documented (e.g. 95% of all four-person households own a car, up from 30% in 1965) and money assets as well: private households own about 2.3 trillion ECU on saving accounts, in building societies, insurance treaties etc. – resulting in 115 billion ECU interest income annually. Market value of real estate property (private homes and apartments) is about 3.4 trillion ECU; about 50% of private households own real estate.

Business cycles

During the postwar period West Germany faced four major recessions: a mild one in 1966/67, two more serious recessions in 1974/75 and 1981/82, and the latest one in the aftermath of the unification boom 1992/1993. After recovery in 1994, economic activity weakened again in the second half of 1995 and real GDP growth in 1996 is projected to be less than 1% (see Figure 2.1(a)). For 25 years – until 1974/75 – the typical pattern of business cycles were growth cycles, i.e. cycles without a decline in real GDP. GDP development during the 1980s has been characterised as *Wellblechkonjunktur*, a continuous expansion with only minor changes in the growth rates. The difference in pattern is related to the change in the principles guiding economic policy. Since the early 1980s the emphasis has been on stimulating long-term growth (supply-oriented policy) rather than on trying to reduce unemployment by means of Keynesian deficit spending. As a consequence there was no spectacular boom. However, the economy became more robust and has been able to absorb shocks such as the stock market crash of 1987. The period of steady growth came to an abrupt end in the early 1990s. First, German unification caused an extraordinary boom in 1990/91 with a real GDP growth rate of 5.7% (1990) – the highest in 20 years. The unification boom was also to the advantage of Germany's European neighbours (especially France) because their exports to Germany increased significantly. This boom ended abruptly in 1992 when the demand-side fireworks were over and old structural problems (international competitiveness) as well as new ones (German unification) became dominant. GDP in west Germany grew by only 1.8% in 1992 (Germany in total 2.2%) and then declined by 1.8% (respectively 1.2%) in 1993. In 1994/95 recovery was weak and the economy was vulnerable to recessionary forces which began to dominate in late 1995. During 1996 the economy recovered somewhat, but with an annual growth rate of less than 1% unemployment further increased. In the east German Bundesländer growth rates have been above average but no self-sustaining growth process has been established. To analyse recent developments in more detail, the components of demand are discussed separately.

Consumption and personal saving. Private consumption is the largest demand factor and amounts to about 58% of aggregate demand in united Germany (west Germany 55%). It hasn't increased much since 1992. This was due to low increases of disposable incomes (1–2% p.a. in real terms), caused primarily by a decline in real net wage incomes (by 8% from 1992 to 1995). A slight decrease of the personal saving rate (personal savings divided by disposable income) to 12.2% (as low as in 1983) couldn't compensate for that. Private consumption isn't going to recover as long as mass incomes do not increase. These depend on the labour market situation and on the tax burden. Both factors will not improve. Even if the announced tax reform should become effective in 1998 or 1999, this will only shift but not reduce the tax burden (see Section 2.3.2).

Government consumption. The share of government consumption in aggregate demand peaked in 1981 (20.7%) and then declined continuously by three percentage points within a decade. Unification pushed it again to the 20% level (for more details see Section 2.3.1).

Investment. Gross fixed capital formation in Germany was about 20% of GDP in the 1980s, i.e. about level with the EU average (see Table G29). During the unification boom in 1991–92 it rose considerably. Investment in equipment was at the core of the boom (with an annual growth rate of 9.5% in 1991). It came to an abrupt end in 1992 and then declined in three subsequent years (by 28 billion ECU in total). Investment in construction was less affected by this decline primarily because of favourable interest rates, housing shortage in the west German states, and low housing quality in the new states. In sum, investment is too weak to stimulate an economic expansion.

Profits. The share of gross labour income in national income is 71.5% (1995). Incomes from entrepreneurial activity and assets (profits) more than doubled in the 1980s while labour incomes (wages) increased only by 50%. In united Germany profits increased by 21%, wages by 16% (1991 to 1995). After a maximum share of wages in 1993, the share of profits has improved in the most recent years. Increases (in percent) were as shown in Table 2.2.

Table 2.2 Profits and wages

	Profits	Wages
1994	11	2
1995	9	3

Source: European Economy, Annual Economic Report

However, in a long-term perspective the profitability of business activity in Germany seems to have declined (see Section 2.6.3).

External trade. The traditional surplus in the west German balance of exports and imports of goods and services was extremely high throughout the 1980s. It peaked in 1989 at 6.4% of GDP (70 billion ECU). Unification changed this pattern dramatically. With a deficit of about 100 billion ECU in their external trade balance, the new states turned the surplus into a deficit (10 billion ECU in 1992). Although this deficit is gradually decreasing, export performance had not been a strong stimulus for economic expansion. Stable prices make German products more competitive abroad while the strong DM has the contrary effect. Real effective exchange rate today is about the same as in 1972.

Inflation

The west German inflation rate has always been much lower than in the other EU states. In fact, until recently, it was only about half the EU average (see Table G31). Since 1989 inflation rates have been rising up to 4.4% in 1992, caused by higher import prices (oil, raw materials), the depreciation of the DM (against the US dollar and the Yen), increases of indirect taxes, fees for government services and sectoral bottlenecks (e.g. in house construction), and higher wage increases. These factors together with the demand pull from the new states generated a wave of price 'hikes'. If the new states are included, the German inflation rate in 1992 was 5.5%, higher than the EU average. The Bundesbank sought to prevent a new price-wage spiral and responded with monetary restraints and higher interest rates – with negative effects on domestic demand. This, and the normalisation of price increases in east Germany, made the inflation rate decline. It is now as low as 1.4%, well below the EU average. The Bundesbank responded to that (and to the strong international position of the DM) with the all-time lowest central bank rates (see also Section 2.4.2) and thus provided a positive element for economic recovery. Despite moderate inflation rates during almost its entire existence, the DM has lost about 70% of its purchasing power from 1948 to 1995.

Perspectives

Prospects for economic growth in Germany over the next few years are gloomy. German economic policy has to deal with an accumulation of different problems:

- economic development of the east German state, costing billions for many more years, and burdening west German consumers and industry;
- consolidation of public budgets and modernisation of state activity;
- increasing international competition (see Section 2.6.3).

The resolution of these interrelated problems requires both solidarity from all groups of society and political leadership. Currently there is a lack of both and therefore the next couple of years will be hard and crucial ones for Germany. To overcome the recession, demand should increase. However, public budgets are highly indebted and hence government expenditure cannot be boosted. For the same reason there is little room to cut taxes in order to stimulate investment and consumer demand. A significant stimulus from the new states is unlikely for various reasons (see Section 2.6.1) although rebuilding infrastructure and industry provides ample opportunities for business activity. Hopes currently focus on lower costs of production (wages, direct taxes, regulation and bureaucracy costs), more innovation (products, production processes, forms of organisation) and stimuli from abroad (e.g. growth of world trade).

2.2.3 Cost of production and productivity growth

West Germany has the highest labour costs in the world. The total cost of about 22 ECU per hour (1995) splits up into two components: wages are about 13 ECU per hour, and additional labour costs (such as social security contributions, paid holidays, bonuses) are more than 9 ECU per hour.

Additional labour costs in industry amount to 80% of wages; in the banking sector they are almost 100%. Less than half of the additional costs are imposed on firms by law, the remainder result from collective and individual agreements. In east Germany wages (9 ECU) as well as additional labour costs (75%) are still considerably lower than in the west.

International comparison shows that it is additional labour cost rather than wages which make labour in (west) Germany so expensive. Wages are higher in Denmark and in Switzerland, but nowhere do we find higher additional labour costs than in west Germany. Total labour costs in the UK are less than half of those in Germany, in Portugal they are only 20% and in the US about 55% of the German level; Japan has lost its status as a cheap labour economy, but its labour costs are still only 78% of those in Germany.

The increasing labour costs are in part compensated for by productivity growth. In the 1980s productivity per employee increased by 1.5% per annum. Productivity increase per employee working hour was 2.3% p.a. This difference results from the reduction in the effective number of working hours to 1500 p.a., i.e. less than 30 per week. During the 1990s hourly productivity increased by 2.9% p.a. Only if hourly real wages had increased faster than that would labour actually have become more expensive in Germany, i.e. real unit labour costs would have increased. However, this has not been the case for years. Therefore, real unit labour costs have been slightly but steadily decreasing since 1981 in west Germany as well as in united Germany (see Table G27). A similar development is reported for the EU average, while in the US and Japan no such decrease appeared. In this respect German competitiveness has actually improved over recent years.

A special problem exists with respect to the new states. Part of their inheritance from the GDR period was low labour productivity. Low wages would represent the obvious way to sustain international competitiveness; however, in these circumstances open borders would have caused a mass emigration of the east German population. For this reason, wages in the east increased faster than productivity – and made it difficult to create jobs without government subsidies. In 1995 labour productivity in east Germany was still less than 60% of that in the west but wages were already at 75% of the west level.

Although empirical evidence does not support the hypothesis of (increasing) labour costs being at the core of Germany's economic problems, a great deal of attention is given to this issue in political discussion. Many firms have already reduced those parts of additional labour costs which are optional. Now the legal and the collective components are the subject of the debate (e.g. unpaid days of illness, working time, pension funds, unemployment insurance). Attempts are being made to reduce direct labour costs by increasing weekly labour hours without additional payment; this allows the employee to keep his income – he loses leisure time, but not his job. This happens on the firm level in many cases and was also negotiated on the industry level ('Alliance for Jobs' in the metal industry). Hence an accelerated decrease of real unit labour costs is probable for the future.

Other costs of production are discussed at other places in this chapter, e.g. taxation (Section 2.3.2), costs of capital (Section 2.4.2), environmental protection (Section 2.7.2). Costs caused by regulation and state bureaucracy have already been mentioned (see Section 2.1.2) and prospects are that, in sum, they are going to decrease. For the effects on international competitiveness see Section 2.7.3.

2.2.4 Economic structure

Sectoral structure

The analysis of economic activity by major sectors reveals that manufacturing – most importantly automobiles, chemicals, machine tools and electrical engineering – still has a dominant position with a share in gross value added of 25.5% (down from 40% in the 1960s). Construction, mining, energy and water supply have a combined share of 9.8% (13% in the 1960s). Agriculture's share is only 1.1% (5.5% in the 1960s). The share of trade and transportation has been declining slightly (to 14%). The government's share increased until the early 1980s, has declined since then and approached 10%. Unification made this share rise again to 11.6% at present. The only sector which has expanded its share markedly is the service sector, including banks, insurances and other services. Within 30 years this share has more than doubled and is now 35%, i.e. about the same as the sum of all industrial sectors. Private households account for 2.8%. In a reduced three-sectoral perspective we have (in 1994): agriculture 1%, industry 35%, services 64% (see *Sachverständigenrat* 1995, S. 376).

Industry structure, concentration and firm size

The investigations of the *Monopolkommission* (1996) reveal no clear trend towards concentration in (west) German industry. While concentration ratios have increased in some branches, in others they have either remained unchanged or have declined. Unification has had no significant effects on concentration so far. The most concentrated industries are (market share of the ten largest firms): tobacco (98%), air and space (95%), oil (94%), computers (89%), mining (88%), cars (74%), iron and steel (74%), ship building (74%), rubber (60%), and pulp and paper (54%). The number of mergers and acquisitions has increased significantly. In 1982/83 the *Bundeskartellamt* registered 1100, in 1992/93 the number was 3250 (3550 in 1990/91). This increase is interpreted as a reaction to the European Single Market, the need to be present in global markets and increasing R&D costs. The sectors with highest R&D activities were chemicals/pharmaceuticals, financial services and trade. In addition to R&D activity, cooperation in various forms (joint ventures, strategic alliances) has become a more and more important phenomenon – often with cartel-like effects.

SME still play an important role in the FRG economy and are crucial to its strength and flexibility. Their position is not endangered, although the interdependence between large enterprises and SME is increasing as a consequence of lean production and just-in-time policies. Large firms (especially in the automobile industry and in machine tools manufacturing) cultivate a more intensive cooperation (e.g. in R&D) with their SME suppliers and, in addition, have reduced the number of suppliers by relying on 'system suppliers' which provide large components of the final product and work with the sub-suppliers. The number of liquidations and insolvencies of firms – mainly SME – is increasing, but is more than compensated for by an increasing number of new firms. The net increase in west Germany alone is about 100 000 firms p.a. – twice as many as fifteen years ago. Therefore, the German weakness in new business formation has somewhat improved.

Regional structure

Article 72 GG states that federal government policy should aim at equivalent conditions of life in all regions of the republic. While the regional disparities within the old FRG were small compared with European standards, this changed significantly with the incorporation of the new states. Disposable income per capita in the new states is only two thirds of that in west Germany, and unemployment rates are twice as high. Lower environment quality and quality of infrastructure (roads, telecommunication, schools) further widen the gap in the quality of life between the two regions. However, these differences are decreasing as a result of major government programmes for regional development and restructuring. In some cases, subsidisation goes beyond the rules that are agreed within the EU (see also Section 2.6).

Within west Germany the southern parts (the states of Baden-Württemberg and Bavaria) for years have been the regions with a good economic performance while economic problems (declining industries, high unemployment) were concentrated at the northern and western periphery. More recently, the restructuring especially in the automobile industry and in machine tools manufacturing has increased the economic problems in the former boom regions. Furthermore, some inherent limitations to development for the booming regions have become apparent, such as high real estate prices and rents, traffic congestion and problems with waste disposal.

2.3 GOVERNMENT INVOLVEMENT IN THE ECONOMY

2.3.1 Government expenditure and the future role of the state

Government expenditure (including social security) as a share of GDP (*Staatsquote*) peaked in 1982 at 49.3%, then steadily declined to 45% in 1989. During the 1980s it was lower than the EU average while it had been higher during the preceding two decades (see Table G32). Unification and weak economic performance (higher unemployment) after 1992 made this share rise to 50%, which is above the EU average. It is one of the explicit goals of the present federal government to reduce the *Staatsquote* to the 45% level by the year 2000.

Total government expenditure is 935 billion ECU (1995). This includes federal, states and local communities' budgets as well as expenditures of the social security system. Public expenditure without the budgets of the social security systems is 640 billion ECU, federal state and Bundesländer spending about 40% each and the rest spent by local communities. The largest part of this money is spent for personnel (31%), paying for 6 million (part- and full-time) employees including 2 million life-time civil servants (*Beamte*). An increasing share goes into interest payment for public debt (11%), only 8% is material investment. The expenditures of all public budgets for social policy are 590 billion ECU (including, for example, pensions, social aid, subsidies for housing and for children), i.e. 7250 ECU per capita; related to GDP (*Sozialleistungsquote*) this is 33%. Despite this high expenditure, there is poverty in the midst of wealth; 5 million people receive social aid resulting in costs of more than 25 billion ECU. The federal budget for defence has been declining but is still 25 billion ECU.

Government subsidies for business activity, according to the official report (*Subventionsbericht*), amount to 62 billion ECU; according to an investigation by German research institutes, the amount is actually more than 100 billion ECU, about 40% of this amount going to east Germany. The largest part of subsidies is used to support industry (15 billion ECU), agriculture, housing and transportation. Public R&D subsidies amount to 16 billion ECU, about 1% of GDP – less than in France and Sweden.

Perspectives. The future development of size (*Staatsquote*) and structure of public expenditure depends on the role of government in economy and society. If government is perceived as an obstacle to economic dynamics and as tutelage of autonomous man, its activities should be reduced. This perception is becoming more influential in Germany and to the extent that it becomes practical politics, the *Staatsquote* will decline especially as a consequence of

- *Privatisation and de-bureaucratisation* (Entbürokratisierung). This implies not only reduction of bureaucracy but goes beyond that to reduce government activity to its core (lean government). Only a few activities like jurisprudence, police and revenue offices are safe from privatisation considerations. The danger is, that under the pressure of budget deficits, privatisation decisions are not dominated by efficiency considerations and valuable public assets (especially real estate) is sold for short-run financial reasons.
- *Reform of the welfare state.* Social security expenditures which constitute additional labour costs for firms are the most important reform target. However, so far no proposals for basic reforms – e.g. reducing public pensions to a basic income (*Grundrente*)

combined with more private insurance – have any chance of being implemented and prospects are that social security expenditures will further increase.

- *Less government intervention and subsidisation.* This would imply less support for old, declining industries as well as for new emerging ones. The latter are best supported by generally favourable economic conditions, especially low taxes. However, contrary to that philosophy, special interest groups so far are very successful in conquering public funds (e.g. aerospace, biotechnology).

2.3.2 Taxation

Total government receipts relative to GDP increased significantly during the 1970s and early 1980s. The trend was then reversed and the gap between the FRG and the EU average became smaller. In 1990 it was as low as in the early 1970s (43.3%). In order to finance German unification, taxes (e.g. personal income tax, mineral oil tax, value added tax, insurance tax) and contributions to social insurances have been increased. Income taxation has been increased temporarily in 1991–92 by a 7.5% surtax (*Solidaritätszuschlag*). From 1995 on, the *Solidaritätszuschlag* has been reintroduced – for an indefinite time. Value-added tax was increased to 15% (reduced rate 7%) as of 1 January 1993. This made government receipts rise to 47% relative to GDP. This is higher than the EU average but is still surpassed by France and the Netherlands. The sum of taxes and compulsory contributions to social security insurances relative to GDP (*Abgabenquote*) is now 43.6% (1995), with taxes making up 24.2% and social insurance contributions 19.4%.

The relation of tax revenues to GDP does not differ much from the one 30 years ago but contributions to the social security system have doubled (from a 10% level in the mid-1960s). Hence, the increasing government burden on the private sector stems primarily from higher costs of the welfare state.

Tax revenues result primarily from income taxes (42%) and from value-added taxes (29%).

Other taxes on incomes and assets (like *Gewerbesteuer, Vermögenssteuer*) provide 12% of tax revenues, other specific taxes on consumption (e.g. on petrol, tobacco, beer, coffee) provide 17%. The major source of income taxes is labour income. The share of this source in total tax revenues has risen constantly from 12% in 1960 to 30% in 1980 and 34% in 1995 (150 billion ECU). During recent years (1989 to 1995) tax revenues from other sources of private income have decreased (from 20 to 14 billion ECU) as well as revenues from corporate income (from 18 to 10 billion ECU). All tax revenues are distributed to federal, state or local level in a complicated scheme for revenue sharing formulated in the constitution and there are additional compensation payments between the public budgets (*Finanzausgleich*).

Although most of the increase in government expenditure burden was caused by the social security system, the political focus is now on tax reform where it might be easier to implement reforms. Many of the tax reforms in the past have made the German tax system more and more complicated, especially income taxation. Most of these complications were implemented for reasons of social justice and to support a large number of other political objectives. However, a complicated system is not necessarily a just system, especially when tax burden increases steadily and the average citizen is no longer able to understand it. Therefore, the main direction of future tax reform is simplification. For income taxation this means to eliminate allowances and to reduce tax rates without changing the size of revenues. A number of different models are under discussion. It is easy to suggest different tariffs (in general with a top marginal rate of less than 40%) but it is much more difficult to propose the elimination of exemptions and allowances than to defend such proposals against the protest of special interest groups. Emphasis in the debate is already shifting towards a proposal to pay for reduced income tax rates by increasing the value-added tax after 1998. This would also serve the object of European tax-harmonisation.

2.3.3 Public debt

Public debt (federal, state and local) amounted to 1 070 billion ECU at the end of 1995. This includes off-budget institutions like the *Erblastentilgungfonds* (debt of *Treuhandanstalt* and *Kreditabwicklungsfonds*, altogether 175 billion ECU), the German Unity Fund (*Fonds Deutsche Einheit*), and the *Bundeseisenbahnvermögen* (i.e. debt of former Bundesbahn and Reichsbahn). This represents 58% of GDP and thus below the 60% level formulated in the Maastricht Treaty. The debt burden per capita amounts to 13 050 ECU – higher than in the USA, but considerably lower than e.g. in Belgium (26 000 ECU). More than half of the public debt is owed to private domestic banks. A significant part of the public debt (300 billion ECU) is foreign debt and involves overseas interest payments of about 20 billion ECU annually. Total interest payments on public debt are 70 billion ECU per annum.

Table 2.3 Public debt

Public debt 1995	%
Federal	38
State	26
Local	10
Other	26
Total	100

Public net borrowing (including social security insurances) as a proportion of GDP was 3.5% in 1995 – and hence beyond the Maastricht Treaty criterion of 3%. The proportion has declined from a maximum of 5.6% in 1975 to almost zero in 1989 (see Table G34). Then German unity brought a new wave of public deficits. Public borrowing absorbs almost half of the annual saving of private households.

The reduction of public deficits is an agreed goal of all political parties, especially in order to fulfill the Maastricht Treaty budget criteria. The main approach of government is to cut expenditure. However, as the economy is still in a recession, public austerity could become a drain on expansion and contribute to further reduction of revenues as well as to increase social security expenditures. Budget consolidation by tax increases is not popular, nevertheless a higher value-added tax or 'eco-taxes' (introduction of a CO_2-/energy-tax) are probable policy initiatives.

2.4 FINANCIAL SYSTEM

2.4.1 Structure of financial institutions

The banking system

A characteristic of the German banking and financial systems is the dominant role of commercial banks which, unlike the specialised banks in other countries, engage in all kinds of bank business: short-term and long-term deposits, short-term and long-term credits, issue of and trade in bonds and stocks (*Universalbanken*). This system has advantages for the customer because firms may rely on only one bank (*Hausbank*). However, it also causes problems because of the concentration of information and economic power. Occasionally there is a revival of the debate on restricting the banks' share of stocks of industrial firms and their participation on boards of competing firms. The close interrelationship between banks and industry also has some drawbacks regarding the development of financial markets, e.g. a very narrow stock market and little information for the public on firms' activities. Today most banks also engage in insurance, building-society and real estate activities (*Allfinanz*). New financial superpowers are emerging but there is also fresh competition, e.g. between giants like Deutsche Bank and Allianz. To meet international competition, R&D activity in the financial sector is increasing and the large German banks aspire to become global players.

The German banking system, with a total business volume of about 3.7 trillion ECU (sum of balance sheet), consists of 3872 independent banks with 48 721 branch offices (end of 1994). Characteristic of the German bank system and dominating in general bank business, are local and regional savings banks and savings and loan associations (*Sparkassen, Genossenschaftsbanken*) and their central institutions (*Girozentralen, DG-Bank*) – with about half of the business volume and a large network of branch offices. The three large banks (Deutsche Bank, Dresdner Bank, Commerzbank) have a share of 9% of business volume, subsidiaries of foreign banks about 1%. About 3.7 billion ECU of money assets are invested with German financial institutions, most of it by private households (more than 60%) and the largest part of it (40%) at banks. Other important players in the financial markets are insurance companies (14%), building societies (2%) and investment funds (5%).

Money and capital markets

Relative to the country's economic strength, German financial markets are underdeveloped. During the last years there have been a number of institutional and legal changes designed to make the German financial market more attractive (e.g. foundation of the *Deutsche Börse AG* and the abolition of the stock exchange tax, *Börsenumsatzsteuer*). Key characteristics of the German financial markets are the importance of the bond market relative to the share market, and a marked long-term orientation. The German bond market with a volume of 1.4 trillion ECU is the third largest in the world (next to the US and Japan). The major issuers of bonds are large banks and the government, primarily the federal government. This is the most common method by which banks refinance the credits they grant to business and the public sector. About 2100 stock corporations exist but less than one third of them are quoted on the stock market. In addition, about 500 foreign stocks are traded in German stock markets. There are eight exchange centres, the main one being Frankfurt/Main. The volume of new issues per annum was 11.5 billion ECU during the first half of the 1990s, this has doubled compared to the 1980s. In 1995 20 firms were admitted to the stock exchange. The exchange turnover in the FRG is the second highest in Europe – however, only about half of that of the UK.

The weakness of the German stock markets has been explained by numerous factors, e.g. favourable conditions (in the tax system) for external finance, a reluctance by both insurance companies and the general public to holding shares, the central role of banks in corporate control and the marked aversion of firm-owners to sharing information with investors. The traditional system has the important disadvantage that it is hard to find capital for fast growing new enterprises with no material assets (venture capital). This has become a serious barrier for the foundation and the growth of new firms in Germany. Considerable political efforts are undertaken to change this and make the stock exchange a more flexible institution for meeting the capital requirements of German business. Specifically, a new stock market will be established in 1997 with less stringent admission conditions than the regular market and tax exemptions will be allowed for profits from sales of shares in successful new ventures. In addition, public funds are provided to improve the risk capital base of SME. Regardless of these changes, German firms are exploring the use of foreign (especially US) capital markets more intensively.

2.4.2 Monetary policy, interest rates, exchange rates

In the 1970s the Bundesbank's monetary policy moved towards monetarism; however, this position never became totally dominant as it did at times in the USA and the UK. From 1974 on, the Bundesbank formulated a target for the expansion of the quantity of money (M3). This intermediate goal is now announced every year in December for the following year. In 1994 and in 1995 the target corridor for the growth of M3 had been 4–6% and in 1996 it is 4–7%. The 1996 target is based on the assumption of a 2.5% growth of real production potential, a maximum tolerable inflation rate of 2% and a decrease in the velocity of money of 1%. During the last twenty years the target was met only in every other year. Consequently, the Bundesbank's strategy has become the subject of a critical debate, the results of which will be relevant for the future policy of the European Central Bank. The Bundesbank perceives monetary targeting as a symbol of the German 'stability culture', a signal of continuity, and a self-commitment of the central bank. The Bundesbank admits that monetary targeting has become more difficult because of financial innovations and an increasing volatility of monetary variables; the response should not be to give up on the concept, but to handle it more flexibly with a mid-term orientation, supplemented by other indicators like M1 and enlarged M3. Another controversial debate – with implications for the policy of the European Central Bank – has been the strategy on minimum reserve requirements for financial institutions. These were reduced significantly (to 1.5% for saving accounts and to 2% for all other assets), but the instrument was not abandoned.

Interest rates in (west) Germany have been relatively low, a favourable side effect of price stability, compared to other European nations and to the USA (see Tables G35, G36). This had changed temporarily in the wake of German unification with higher inflation rates and increasing domestic capital demand. However, recently, interest rates have declined significantly. Short-term interest rates have been 4.5% in 1994 and only 3.5% on average in the first half of 1996. This was made possible by an all-time minimum of central bank rates (discount rate of 2.5%). Because of low inflation rates, the short-term real interest rate is still about 2%. Long-term interest rates have declined to less than 6% – about the US level – and significantly less than the EU average. Real long-term interest rate hence is about 4%, i.e. the same as the average of the past two decades.

The strength of the DM is reflected in its exchange rate. Over the last three decades the DM has been revalued against almost all other currencies – with the exceptions of the Yen and the Swiss Franc. Compared with the currencies of the 19 important industrial countries, the DM has been revalued by about 70% over the last twenty years (see Monthly Reports of the Bundesbank, Table G42) and by 10% over the last five years. However, the DM value in mid 1996 is not much higher than it was three years ago. The US dollar–DM exchange rate had been declining throughout the 1970s, then recovered in the early 1980s and peaked in 1985. Since then the devaluation trend has been dominant, with significant fluctuations. By the end of 1995 the US dollar had been devalued against the DM by about 100% within a decade; while Germans had to pay almost 3 DM per dollar in 1985, it is only about 1.50 DM now. This is good for German tourists but has forced hard decisions on exporters, especially the automobile industry (e.g. the BMW and Mercedes-Benz building plants in the USA). Within the European Monetary System (EMS) the exchange rate of the DM remained almost unchanged until 1992. This was primarily due to the success achieved by the other European countries in coping with inflation. The turmoil in the EMS in 1992 resulted in a revaluation of the DM. After 1992 there have been temporary revaluations of the DM, but today the DM's position is basically the same as in 1993.

Germany's international reserves amount to 60 billion ECU (net), higher than that of Japan or the USA. 60% are in foreign currencies, primarily US dollars. Gold reserves, valued at the low original purchasing costs, amount to 7.2 billion ECU, and their market value is about 25 billion ECU. The DM's role as an international reserve currency increased considerably during the 1980s. Among the international reserve currencies the DM is second to the US dollar with a share of about 20%.

2.5 INTERNATIONAL RELATIONS

2.5.1 Foreign trade by country and by industry

Germany is the world's second largest exporter and importer of goods – next to the USA and followed by Japan. Germany's share in world exports is about 10%, the share in imports less than 9%. Related to GDP; exports (of 385 billion ECU in 1995) were 21.2%, imports 18.5%. The largest part of Germany's foreign trade is European trade, especially EU internal trade. From 1958 to 1994 the share of German exports

to EU countries increased from 37.9% to 48.9% (see Tables G38, G39). Germany's major trading partner is France, taking 12% of exports (44 billion ECU) and providing 11.3% of Germany's imports (36 billion ECU). Other important customers are the UK, Italy, the USA and the Netherlands (each more than 27.5 billion ECU). The position of the USA as a destination of German exports is almost the same as three decades ago. The importance of Asian countries is increasing (e.g. Japan 2.6%, China 1.5%). The most remarkable increase of recent years has been in trade with the transitional economies of eastern and central Europe, which now receive 8% of all German exports, and have become the second most important destination of German exports. There remains a large potential for further increases in this market. After years of decline, the share of exports to developing countries has slightly increased recently. The most important sources of imports to Germany – next to France – are the Netherlands, Italy, Belgium and the UK. Germany shows a trade deficit with only a few countries, such as Japan (8 billion ECU) and China (3 billion ECU). The countries most dependent on German imports are Austria, Switzerland and, to a lesser degree, Denmark, the Netherlands and France (all receiving more than 20% of their imports from Germany).

The new Bundesländer contribute only 2% to Germany's foreign trade (exports and imports of about 7 billion ECU each). The regional structure of their foreign trade is characterised by a high share of the middle and east European reform countries (40% of imports, 35% of exports), but orientation towards western countries is increasing.

Exports are concentrated in four sectors: automobile industry (17%), machinery (15%), chemicals (14%) and electrical and electronic engineering (13%). The most significant change in export structure is the declining share of machinery which was once almost 20%. Imports are less concentrated: electrical and electronic engineering amounts to 12% of imports, automobiles to 11%, chemicals to 10%, textiles to 8%, oil, gas and petroleum products to 6%, food to 6% and agricultural products to 5%.

Other notable features of international trade which do not apply the traditional sectoral categories include:

- *Technology-intensity*. Germany's share in world trade of technology intensive goods is about 20%, comparable to that of the USA and of Japan.
- *Environmental technology* (filters, waste treatment, measurement and control technology). Germany has lost its position as a world market leader and is now number three (next to the USA and Japan) in this rapidly growing field (with a market share of less than 20%).

As Germany depends heavily on open foreign markets, German trade policy has always favoured free trade and opposed all forms of protectionism. However, protectionist elements still exist in various forms in the German economic system: old ones (like subsidies for coal mining, agriculture, aerospace technology, nuclear energy) and new ones, especially those associated with rebuilding the economy in the New States (see Section 2.7.1). A major area of concern is the application of 'fair trade' with regard to ecological issues. Germany is pushing to define (European and world-wide) social and ecological minimum standards in order to have a clear orientation for identifying social and ecological dumping practices. The German government fosters exports e.g. by granting credits with special conditions (development aid for building a subway in Shanghai), by an export credit insurance scheme (*Hermes Bürgschaften*), by negotiating investment protection agreements, and by organising trade fairs. On the other hand there is a range of export controls (e.g. for weapons).

2.5.2 Balance of payments

From 1982 to 1990 Germany's current balance was in permanent surplus, reaching a peak in 1989 at almost 57 billion ECU, i.e. 4.8% of GDP. German unification changed this situation. Within two years the surplus changed to a 17 billion ECU deficit (in 1991). This deficit continued and is still present, although it is somewhat smaller now (13 billion ECU in 1995, less than 1% of GDP).

The main reason for the switch in the balance of payments was in the trade balance. This balance always had surpluses with a maximum of 70 billion ECU in 1989. However, in 1990 imports increased by more than 10% and in 1991 by a further 16%. At the same time growth rates for exports were 3% and 0.5% respectively. Hence the high surplus in the trade balance contracted to only 11.5 billion ECU in 1991. During the following years the trade balance recovered and the surplus in 1995 was 48 billion ECU.

The service balance sector has traditionally been in deficit – primarily because Germans spent about 30 billion ECU per year as tourists abroad. The German preference for travelling abroad has been reinforced after unification because people in the new states haven't had this option before. A small contribution to the deficit in the service balance comes from a negative balance in revenues from patents and licences (2 billion ECU).

In the past a considerable positive contribution to the balance of payments came from a surplus of investment income. This surplus decreased to less than 2 billion ECU in 1995 because of high German capital imports and because of a low level of interest rates world-wide.

The balance of unrequited transfers (transfers by foreign workers, payments for international organisations and grants) always showed significant deficits. The amount of deficit declined slightly in the 1990s and is now about 30 billion ECU.

To compensate for the deficits in the balance of payments, increasing capital imports to Germany were necessary. Within a period of only three years, Germany changed from a net capital exporting nation to a capital import nation: from 71 billion ECU capital export in 1989, to 47 billion ECU capital import in 1992, and a further 30 billion ECU capital imports in 1995. Most of the capital import resulted from foreign portfolio investment, especially in government bonds, i.e. a (gross) amount of 124 billion ECU in 1993. However, Germany remains the world's second largest creditor nation (next to Japan) with net foreign assets of about 150 billion ECU – although this is only half the amount of 1991. Gross German assets abroad are about 1.2 trillion ECU.

Much attention has been given to the relatively small item foreign direct investment (FDI). German FDI abroad increased to 26 billion ECU in 1995 and was more than 50 billion ECU over the three-year period 1993–95. FDI investment in Germany was less than 10 billion ECU during that period. In total, German direct investment abroad amounted to 125 billion ECU by the end of 1995, the largest part of which (about 40%) was in the USA. It has been calculated that this investment created about one million jobs abroad. The questions arising are why this investment was not made in Germany and whether the increasingly negative balance of direct investment signals a general decline of Germany for international investors (see Section 2.7.3).

2.6 IMPACT OF EUROPEAN INTEGRATION

From its beginnings in the 1950s, Germany has always been an active proponent of European integration, based on the French–German reconciliation. The strong German commitment to the European idea made it much easier to find international acceptance for German unification because it cushioned resentments and fears of a revival of German nationalism. Hence progress in European integration is, for Germany, not only economically but also politically of vital importance. Nevertheless, there are debates on how the integration process should best proceed and how some of the deficiencies of European institutions could be eliminated. In the following some potential sources of conflict are discussed.

2.6.1 European Economic and Monetary Union (EMU)

This is currently the most important issue, emotionally loaded because it is accompanied by the end of the DM and of an autonomous monetary stabilisation policy. Hence Germany has made considerable efforts to influence the design of the European Central Bank, its instruments (e.g. the minimum reserve) and its monetary policy concept (making the quantity of money a central

indicator). Germany will have problems to fulfill the deficit criteria (deficits in public budgets less than 3% of GNP) and the debt criteria (less than 60% of GNP) of the Maastricht Treaty in 1997 but article 104c of the Treaty is flexible enough to make sure that Germany will pass the examination in early 1998 and the beginning of EMU has not to be postponed. Germany insists on the introduction of a mechanism which sanctions high public deficits in the EMU in order to guarantee a minimum of convergence in fiscal policy. For those EU members who cannot join EMU in 1999 ('outs'), a credible mechanism to reduce currency fluctuations should be established (EMS II).

While economic integration proceeds, political integration (Maastricht II) makes little progress. On the agenda should be subjects such as enlarging versus deepening of the union, the role of regions (and the subsidiarity principle), autonomous financial resources for EU, environmental union (e.g. a trans-European net of biotopes), and the *Leitbild* (vision) of an advanced free trade area versus the 'United States of Europe'. Additionally, no significant progress has been made in the area of economic policy coordination, a necessary complement to the EMU requirement for a uniform monetary policy.

2.6.2 Subsidiarity versus centralisation and uniformity

Subsidiarity is an idea which stems from the federal tradition of states like Germany. It is formulated in article 3b of the EU treaty and guarantees that no problems are addressed at the EU level which could be solved at lower levels. This article counters fears of a centralistic and bureaucratic Europe and it limits tendencies to harmonise and standardise. While it is easy to agree on these rather general formulations, disputes arise in concrete cases. For example, is the idea of trans-European transportation networks a sound one? To what extent are European guidelines or directives necessary on tourism statistics, on balance sheets or on systems to protect financial investors? No doubt, a minimum of uniformity is necessary but there must also be room for alternative institutional solutions to be tested. Otherwise Europe would give away one of its strengths and lose approval of citizens which want to conserve regional identity.

2.6.3 Competition policy

The EU has provided important impulses for deregulation in sectors like transportation, energy, banking, insurance and telecommunication, and thus stimulated competition. The forthcoming reform of German competition law (GWB) is going to adapt German provisions to the European ones (articles 85, 86 of the EU treaty). Prohibition of cartels will be reformulated and sectoral exemptions abolished. A general formulation for exemptions from the prohibition of cartels and the (European) instrument of group exemptions (e.g. for R&D cartels) is controversial. A conflict emerges in merger control: while the EU commission and parts of German industry would like to lower threshold values and hence to enlarge the scope of the EU merger guideline at the cost of national merger control, German antitrust experts oppose this. More competition for Brussels could reduce costs and uncertainty of firms and guarantee level conditions throughout the EU. German refusal is based on past practice (out of 350 cases the Commission rejected only 4 and demanded significant changes in 24 cases) and on doubts concerning the institutional construction. Final decisions made in the EU commission do not reflect competition principles 'purely' but are subject to regional and industrial policy considerations. Only an independent antitrust authority could resolve this problem. With globalisation of economic activity, an EU initiative is required to form a global antitrust institution.

2.6.4 Subsidies and east German reconstruction

In the past Germany always supported the EU commission actions in restricting government subsidies to enterprises in order not to distort competition. In its efforts to modernise east German industry, the German government is now providing investment grants in sectors where overcapacities already exist (e.g. for Eko-Stahl in Eisenhüttenstadt) and subsidising enterprises beyond any economic justifications (e.g. Dow Chemical in Buna-Leuna). The EU commission has tolerated this as a practice based on article 92 IIc which exempts grants to overcome German separation. However, the commission is now trying to define limits to that practice (in the case of VW plants in Saxonia). There is a danger that this 'subsidy mentality' will increase and affect other EU countries – to the disadvantage of all.

2.6.5 Trade policy

EU trade policy follows the rules defined by WTO. EU antidumping policy hence is applied only if an importer charges significantly lower prices than in other parts of the world market – and if this is to the disadvantage of the EU. The commission then charges antidumping duties. Less than 1% of EU imports are affected by such antidumping measures (primarily in the chemical, the textile and the machine industries). This does not include cases in which importers 'voluntarily' increase their prices and thus collect extra profits instead of paying duties. Antidumping policy is always in danger of becoming an instrument of protectionism and of serving special interest groups. In general, Germany opposes all protectionist efforts. But Germany is also one of those EU members who call for social and ecological minimum standards to restrict child work and the destruction of global commons (like tropical rain forests). Low prices based on violating these standards would then cause antidumping measures.

A major dispute between Germany and the EU arose over the import of bananas when the European single market came into existence in 1993. Until then EC members had different import conditions. Bananas from Latin America could be imported duty free to Germany. Britain, France and Spain protected banana producers in their former colonies from the competition of the Latin American bananas. With the single market this protection was no longer possible and Latin American bananas could influx, for example, via Germany. Therefore, the quantity of Latin American banana imports was restricted. Consumers, especially in Belgium, Denmark and Germany had to pay for this protection by higher banana prices. In order to protect special interest groups another complicated and expensive system of market intervention has been created which confirms many negative prejudices on EU policy.

2.6.6 Environmental effects

EU policy is widely perceived as an obstacle to sustainable development rather than a positive contribution – as it should be according to the EU treaty (articles 2, 3 lit.k, 130 r-t) and the fifth environmental action programme (1993–97). In many fields German environmental policy is ahead of EU policy (e.g. in air quality, waste management, goal for reduction of CO_2 emissions). However, there are other fields where Germany is not in compliance with EU guidelines (e.g. drinking water and the protection of birds). Hence an undifferentiated critique of EU policies is not adequate.

EU policy contributed considerably to the dramatic increase of air and road transportation with its negative impacts on the environment. Liberalisation and deregulation (eliminating of price controls and barriers to entry) were not accompanied by provisions to adapt traffic flows to infrastructural and environmental limits. By applying a narrow definition of cost, the EU commission blockades effective pricing strategies (e.g. the toll for the Brenner Autobahn may include only direct costs of sustaining the road but not external costs like noise and air pollution). EU agricultural policy is still dominated by the idea of intensifying production – despite existing overproduction. This continuously causes high environmental damage (soil, ground water, diversity of species) and reduces the quality of products. Production of tobacco is subsidised by more than one billion ECU annually, and at the same time ministers of health warn of the risks of cancer from smoking. In energy policy, support for nuclear energy is still dominating and renewable energies are neglected. Some of the regional

and structural programmes and projects (cohesion fund, trans-European networks) generate long-term environmental and economic disadvantages (e.g. subsidies for more effective fish trawlers, without provisions to limit catches to the reproduction rate of fish populations). No significant contributions to reduce global warming have been made, CO_2/energy tax has not been implemented. EC directive 1836/93 on voluntary eco-audits (EMAS) has stimulated environmental awareness in the industrial sector. However, so far the voluntary activity does not justify the retreat of public policy. The opportunity to adapt some European environmental standards to the higher level of the new members Austria, Finland and Sweden have not been taken so far. Further steps of European integration should also consider chances for 'greening the treaty' (e.g. by including environment protection in articles B and 2).

2.6.7 Financial contributions

Germany contributes about one third to the EU budget, a contribution larger than that of France and the UK combined. The net contribution amounts to more than 10 billion ECU annually. After unification German per capita income is close to EU average but German per capita net contributions are still the highest. Based on an agreement dating back to 1992 this will not change until 1998, although high German financial support for central and east European countries (CEEC) and for refugees could be an argument to modify this. After 1998 Germany will insist on a new scheme of burden sharing (oriented at GDP/capita rather than GDP).

2.7 SPECIAL ISSUES

2.7.1 German unification – a preliminary résumé

When the communist systems in CEEC broke down, no elaborated theories or guidelines were available on how to reform or to transform a centrally-planned economic system with state ownership most efficiently. Academic disputes arose whether transformation to a market economy should proceed rapidly or gradually and what positive elements of the old system might be worth preserving. Actually, the transformation process was not and still is not ruled by theoretical design but rather is a search process determined by the interplay of short-run political interests.

The transformation process in east Germany is very specific, not comparable to any of the other CEEC. Its speed and direction was to a large extent dictated by the desire of the east German people to enjoy the amenities of the west German system as fast as possible. Solidarity combined with the widespread overestimation of the potentials of the east German economy – and resulting from that the underestimation of transformation costs – made rapid transformation agreeable for the west German population.

Six years after the GDR joined the FRG in accordance with Article 23 GG in October 1990, Germany is still struggling hard to cope with the challenge of unification. It is clear today that the challenge has widely been underestimated, that the process of integration requires more time and more money than expected. The prospering landscapes (*blühende Landschaften*) which were expected within a few years (according to a promise of Chancellor Kohl in 1991) have not materialised so far. Hopes for a second *Wirtschaftswunder* have been disappointed. Decisions made in the past have put the integration process on a development path which could hardly be corrected today. The crucial decisions and their consequences will be outlined in the following sections.

Currency union

The currency union which came into being on 1 July 1990 was based on a conversion rate for GDR Mark into DM of 1:1 for wages, pensions and bank deposits of up to 4000 Mark (all other assets and debt 2:1). This political decision meant an enormous revaluation of the Mark. Although the official exchange rate (enforced by GDR authorities) had been 1:1, based on economic facts it would have been in the range of 4:1 (some say 10:1). What seemed to be a political gift to east German citizens turned out to have fatal consequences. The revaluation shock made east German products extremely expensive and unaffordable especially for traditional customers in the CEEC. While the east German people were granted 'fair' conversion conditions for money assets and wages, these conditions contributed to deprive them of their jobs and to devalue the industrial assets.

Property rights

Restoring private property rights has been and still is painfully slow. This is in part the consequence of a political decision and in part caused by an overburdened administration and jurisdiction which was not in a workable condition during the first integration years. The crucial political decision had been to give restitution priority over financial compensation. All private property which was expropriated after 1949 has to be returned to the former owners if they claim it. This procedure considerably delayed and blocked investment, especially in city centres. In early 1993 only 15% of the more than two million restitution claims had been settled, and in 1995 one million cases were still unsettled. The property of the former agricultural production cooperatives (LPGs) to a large extent ended up in corporations under the control of the former directors who influenced and took advantage of the low evaluation of LPG assets. The majority of LPG members were degraded to rural workers or unemployed.

Industrial assets and activity of *Treuhandanstalt* (THA)

In the first step of privatising the state enterprises – which made up 90% of the economic activity of the GDR – ownership has been transferred to a huge public institution, the *Treuhandanstalt* (THA). The THA was given the political directive to privatise rapidly instead of trying to redevelop and to modernise the firms. However, the sometimes disastrous (technical, safety and environmental) condition of the firms combined with the prospect of increasing wages made the industrial assets unattractive for private investors. Only at very low prices and with partial shutdowns and high numbers of lay-offs could the THA sell some of the firms. In many cases privatisation succeeded only after huge public subsidies were granted (e.g. 5 billion ECU for Dow Chemical to sustain chemical production in Buna-Leuna with 3000 workers). This in turn led to an increasing conflict with EU subsidy codes – culminating in the VW case in 1996. The new, highly productive factories (e.g. the Opel factory in Eisenach is the most productive of all GM factories worldwide) provide only few jobs. The very few large firms which have survived or have invested in east Germany are exceptions and cannot compensate for the fact that within a very short period of time most of the east German industry disappeared. Today only 500 000 of the former 3.4 million industrial jobs are left. Even innovative east German firms like Foron (first CFC-free refrigerator) were finally forced out of the market by more powerful competitors. The east German economy is characterised by much higher shares of the construction sector (16% of value added compared to 5%) and the public sector (20% compared to 13%) than the west German states. Because of the weak industrial base, chances for self-sustaining growth are poor.

THA activity ended in 1994. By then 14 500 firms had been sold, activating private investment of more than 100 billion ECU and conserving 1.5 million jobs. In sum, the east German industrial and agricultural assets (estimated at about 300 billion ECU by THA president Rohwedder in 1990) were sold with no surplus at all; instead THA left a deficit of 140 billion ECU. A huge amount of assets have been destroyed – and redistributed to small groups (e.g. to already wealthy people from west Germany and to clever former directors of LPGs) instead of distributing shares to the people. Billions of DM have been wasted because of fraud, corruption, incompetence and a lack of control.

Wage policy

In 1990 average wages in the GDR were 1200 Mark per month (FRG 3500 DM per month) and productivity was 30–40% of that in the FRG. Therefore, with an exchange rate of 1:1 the east German states had no advantage in labour unit costs compared to west Germany. This initial situation deteriorated as a consequence of collective wage agreements negotiated by (west German) unions and employer organisations. Within a few years wages were to increase to the west German level (e.g. in the metal industry by 1996). These agreements were the result of a misperception of the prospects of the east German economy and of a unfortunate constellation of interests. Labour unions wanted to be attractive for new east German members (by formulating high wage demands) and they wanted no cheap labour competition which could threaten jobs in west Germany. Employers did not resist because they were interested in the purchasing power of the east German population, not in new competitors – and low labour costs were and are offered in the MEEC in abundance. Furthermore, any deterioration of the labour market situation improved prospects for benefiting from additional government subsidies. In 1994 the average wage was 71.5% of the west German while productivity was only 51.8%. Given these data, high unemployment was unavoidable. About one fifth of the labour force of 8.8 million people is un- or underemployed today. This caused at least as much migration of qualified personnel to west Germany as larger wage differences would have done. Many firms already pay less than the collectively agreed wages – and although this is illegal employees agree to save their jobs.

Perspectives

An evaluation of the perspectives should not only focus on the deficiencies but also sum up the successes, which are:

● *Monetary stability*. The rapid decline of temporarily high inflation rates (20% in 1991, 8% in 1992) made low interest rates possible and despite that, German bonds are still attractive for foreign investors (compensating for the deficits in the balance of current accounts), i.e. basically international confidence in the potency of the German economy has not suffered.

- *Modernisation*. After the old (labour-intensive) equipment and assets had become obsolete, the formation of new, modern equipment and public infrastructure has made considerable progress (investment rates in the new states being higher than in west Germany).
- *The environmental situation* (air and water quality) has improved considerably as a consequence of factory shut-downs and building of cleaning facilities. However, hundreds of square kilometres of nature have been sacrificed to industrial areas (creating a large supply not met by demand), traffic infrastructure, and shopping malls outside the cities. Almost none of the hazardous waste deposits have been cleaned up – chances for demonstration projects with considerable international market opportunities (unlike the prestigious Transrapid project) have been missed.
- *Quality of life* has improved because more than three million apartments and houses have been repaired and modernised, and the financial situation of the large group of retired persons improved significantly.

Most important will be to improve the attractiveness as a business location, to attract outside know-how and capital and to mobilise internal entrepreneurial potentials. A modern infrastructure, high qualification and more flexible labour contracts could support this. One proposal is to form a coalition of unions, employers and government to tie future transfer payments to a freeze of wages for several years and to grant east German citizens shares in the remaining public assets. Conditions for the foundation of new firms, training and consultation for founders will have to be improved. 700 000 new firms were founded after 1990 (providing three million jobs). Many of them did not survive under unfriendly structural and cyclical conditions. Recession in early 1996 made closures and

bankruptcies increase dramatically (from 1000 in 1992 to 7500 in 1996). Today 500 000 firms exist, primarily SME (less than 50 firms with more than 1000 employees).

Gross transfer payments from west to east Germany amounted to about 500 billion ECU over the last six years – and there is no prospect that they could be reduced significantly below an annual 100 billion ECU level (6% of GDP) during the next years. Two-thirds of the money comes from the federal budget, the rest from the pension fund, unemployment insurance, the Bundesländer and the EU. Some reforms in the numerous subsidy programmes will be made and a maximum of 35% will apply to all investment subsidies.

How many more years will approaching west German standards take? Under plausible conditions (2% growth in west and 5% in east Germany) BIP per capita in east Germany will approach the level of some of the weaker west German states (i.e. about 80% of the west German average) within ten years. Until then probably another 500 billion ECU of subsidies will be necessary. During recent years the idea of convergence based on higher growth has not been very successful (Figure 2.3).

Political stability is still fragile. Many east German citizens feel that they are the losers of unification because of unemployment and dependency on west German money. Less than 5% of the east German property ended up with east German citizens – a second and final wave of expropriation made possible by the conditions of integration. Although there is an abundance of consumer goods and no one lives in misery, the overwhelming change was widely perceived as a loss, a loss of social contacts, of participation and of familiar structures, rules and opportunities. As the people's movement (*Bürgerbewegung*) which played a crucial role in 1989 did not succeed in becoming a political organisation, no authentic east German reform force exists to change unsatisfactory conditions (only PDS tries to fill in this gap).

Insights from the German transformation process may benefit debates on extending EU by integrating some of the MEEC. The message of

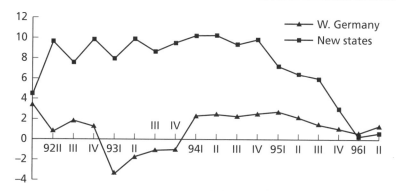

Figure 2.3 Real GDP growth in west Germany and in the new states (quarterly percent change at annual rates)

Source: Sachverständigenrat (1996, Table 27*) and author's calculations.

the German experience is to proceed slowly, support reforms, political and economic convergence without formal integration. Premature integration could become quite expensive.

2.7.2 The ecological challenge – towards sustainable development

Environmental policy has been an important issue with considerable impact on the German economy for more than 25 years. During this period quite a number of acute ecological problems have been resolved. Pollution of rivers and lakes has been reduced, air quality improved, waste management is organised in a sophisticated manner, toxic substances are handled with more care. The number and extent of environmental regulations have increased on all levels of state legislation, for example, on emission control, solid waste, waste water, chemicals, noise and biotechnology.

German industry spends about 10 billion ECU each year, more than 120 billion ECU during the last 20 years, on environment protection. An even larger amount of money has been spent by government. But even combined, the expenditures of government and industry amount to less than 2% of GDP.

Despite these expenditures, even in traditional fields of environment policy a lot of problems are still unresolved. NO$_x$ emissions have not been reduced, during summer months

ozone concentration exceeds the standards, millions of Germans are drinking water which doesn't comply with EU standards, most toxic dumps remain to be redeveloped. Management of solid waste ended up in a complicated and expensive recycling, or rather, down-cycling, system. Nature is in retreat (120 hectares are lost each day to land settlement), woodlands continue to die (*Waldsterben*) and the list of endangered species grows longer.

In addition to the unsolved 'traditional' environmental problems, new global challenges demand more attention: climate change and depletion of the ozone layer. As the 1992 UNCED conference in Rio made clear, all highly industrialised countries will have to change their patterns of production and consumption and have to find a less resource-intensive path for sustainable development, i.e. stop satisfying the needs of the present at the cost of future generations. With respect to the Rio conference the German government formulated the goal to reduce CO$_2$ emissions by 25% until 2005 (base 1990). While official government statements still stick to that goal, no active policy measures have been implemented so far. The CO$_2$ emissions of united Germany have declined because of economic crisis and the substitution of coal by natural gas (Figure 2.4). Chances for significant increases in energy efficiency have not been taken, e.g. in insulation of buildings, the transportation system, and co-generation of energy and heat.

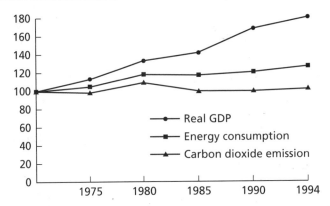

Figure 2.4 GDP, energy consumption and carbon dioxide emission (west Germany)

Source: Sachverständigenrat (1996, Tables 26*, 80*, 82*) and author's calculations.

It is often argued that a more consequent environment policy would endanger the international competitiveness of German industry and would increase unemployment. While this is true for some sectors (like iron and steel, non-iron metals, and parts of the chemical industry), the total macro-economic effects are positive: about one million people are employed in producing environmental goods and services and Germany has a share of 20% in the growing world market for environmental technology. Investment in environmental quality is a necessary condition for the success of sectors like tourism, food production and even microchip production. Highly qualified personnel in high-tech industries demand environmental quality as a part of quality of life. Because of its low share in the total production cost (on average less than one percent) it is unlikely that firms will move out of Germany just because of this cost factor.

Of course, the level of environmental quality could be obtained at lower costs if a more efficient mix of instruments were applied. German environmental policy is still very much dominated by the command-and-control approach, i.e. government dictating adaptation strategies (e.g. a certain technology like scrubbers for power plants). No significant steps have been taken to replace this instrument by more efficient economic instruments like taxes and duties, tort law, tradable emission permits. All political parties favour the idea of an ecological tax reform –

taxing the consumption of natural resources and spending the revenues to reduce additional wage costs – and yet it has not been implemented because potential structural and distributional effects mobilise too much resistance of special interest groups. The inability of the political system to implement reforms has given way to a 'new approach' based on voluntary solutions negotiated between industry and administration (e.g. on CO_2 intensity, fuel standards of cars, and recycling of waste). Environmentalists perceive this as the capitulation of environmental policy.

In conclusion, German environmental policy has neither resolved the domestic problems nor adequately responded to global challenges. Coping with the economic crisis seems to be more important today. In consumers' and voters' opinion, environmental issues no longer have the highest priority. Enterprises are still in the process of catching up with the environmental consciousness of consumers and with government regulations. However, more and more enterprises accept the responsibility for their products from 'cradle to grave' and restructure the production process and the product portfolio. The EC directive 1836/93 on voluntary eco-audits contributed to improving environment management systems. More international solutions, for example an EU energy tax, could help to overcome the standstill in German environmental policy.

2.7.3 Improving Germany's attractivity as a business location

Under conditions of global competition even large countries like Germany are nothing but a region which has to compete for international mobile capital and entrepreneurs. It is the primary task of economic policy in this new environment to provide an overall attractive, favourable, well-balanced set of framework conditions (infrastructure, taxation, labour force, institutions etc.) and to develop the internal potentials of the region, in order to form a unique network. Regional economic systems compete which each other and the challenge for economic policy is to take an active role in creating, designing, improving and innovating these systems. It becomes more important to invest in the immobile factors than to invest in 'national champions' because there are no 'German' or 'Bavarian' firms. Loyalty to a certain location has become a luxury which firms can afford only within narrow limits.

Years of high surpluses in the trade balance and in the balance of current accounts suggested that there is no need to worry about the attractivity of Germany as a business location. The state of self-confidence has been disturbed by a number of facts:

- Germany's share in world exports of R&D intensive goods declined (to 16% in 1993; Japan 21%, USA 19%).
- Direct investment (see Section 2.5.2). While the high direct investment of German firms abroad might be interpreted as a necessary complement to exports (most German direct investment is in the USA and in other industrial nations, only a small part is directed to countries with cheap labour), the low direct investment of foreign firms in Germany needs explanation. Is Germany just an expensive place for investment – a problem which competitive processes and exchange rates can resolve – or are there other (legal and cultural) barriers to entry? Which of these barriers could be eliminated and which are deliberate and worth defending against global pressure (like environmental and social standards)?

- Total R&D spending in (west) Germany declined from 2.9% of GDP in 1989 to 2.4% in 1994 (about 40 billion ECU). The ratio is now lower than in Japan (2.9%) and in the USA (2.5%). The relative decline is primarily due to a stagnation of private R&D spending in Germany. Public R&D spending is widely spread over a variety of areas, not targeted on specific technologies or industries.
- The ratio of corporate net profits to sales (as published by the Bundesbank for west German corporations) declined from 2.63% in the 1970s, 1.93% in the 1980s to 1.66% in the 1990s. However, this decline is at least in part caused by the profit and reserve policy of corporations (building up hidden reserves instead of distributing it to shareholders) and by favourable tax deductions (e.g. special depreciation rules in the new states) which reduce taxable profits.

These facts and observations provide the basis for an intensive and continuing analysis of the strengths–deficiencies–profile of Germany and political reforms to reinforce strengths and to reduce deficiencies. The most important strengths of the German economic system may be summarised in the following three points:

- a qualified labour force at all levels of employment with a unique work ethic and know-how;
- a highly developed infrastructure–making mobility, communication and distribution easy;
- social, political, and monetary stability reducing the uncertainty in calculating the return on investments.

The main problems of the economic system contributing to unattractiveness of Germany as a business location seem to be:

- rigid institutions defended by well-organised interest groups (in part the other side of the stability coin);
- high costs of labour, social safety, energy, environment protection and high taxes – in sum, costs which are higher than justified by the advantages of the system (when the proportion of unit labour costs is, for example,

4:1 compared with Poland or Hungary, it is hard to compensate this);

- diseconomies resulting from agglomeration (e.g. real estate and housing costs, traffic congestion).

All of the problems are closely related to the strengths of the system. Therefore any reforms must be careful to retain these strengths while correcting the weaknesses. It is quite clear which issues should be on the political agenda: a redefinition of government activity, deregulation and privatisation to give more opportunities to entrepreneurial activity; a simplification of the complicated tax system and reduction of the tax burden on labour and entrepreneurial activity; reduction of social safety costs; and a strengthening of social consensus mechanisms (informal groups of conflict resolution, technology assessment etc.). Some reforms are currently being implemented – such as regulatory reform in sectors like telecommunication, transportation, banking and public utilities; others, such as reform of the social security system, will take more time. Improvements during recent years have had some positive results, for example, in the automobile industry where Mercedes-Benz and VW made location decisions for new factories in Germany – although considerable amounts of public money and concessions of unions were necessary to get these results. Even biotechnology seems to have a future in Germany, because acceptance of the population has increased, critics take a more differentiated position (no general rejection) and participate in stakeholder dialogues, and duration of appliance procedures declined. Highly qualified scientists who founded biotechnology firms which are now prospering small- and medium-sized enterprises (SMEs) have proved the attractiveness of Germany for biotechnology research and production; now the large companies (like Bayer and Hoechst) are following and are investing in Germany.

2.8 FUTURE PROSPECTS

Germany faces a period of accelerating structural change and of hard choices. For years to come the German economy will be dominated by the efforts to adapt to a new international division of labour caused by the revolution in East Europe and the rise of new economic centres especially in southeast Asia. The process of German unification will add more problems than stimulating effects to German economic development over the next years. Not only EU stability criteria but also the high tax burdens will dictate further cuts of public budgets. The political challenge is not to sacrifice important investments in the future, such as R&D, education and environment protection, but to redefine priorities. In the longer term Germany's role as a bridgehead in East–West relations may contribute to prosperity.

Germany must find its place in the new international division of labour by implementing an active strategy beyond mere cost reduction. Measured by global standards, Germany as a nation – or rather as a region within the global economy – will remain at the high-quality high-price end of the market spectrum. In this position cost reduction is not sufficient – and could even be dangerous if it causes an international race for lower costs (deflationary process) in which all would lose. Therefore, Germany is condemned to innovation. It not only has to become a place where new technologies emerge and are introduced in the market place but also one where social innovations prosper, i.e. new forms of the organisation of economic and social processes. Major social innovations are required to redefine the role of labour (more flexibility, retraining, participation) and of social security (more private initiative), to find sustainable consumption and settlement patterns, as well as a culture of social dialogue (e.g. on the consequences of new technologies). In this respect economic policy in other EU countries, such as Denmark or the Netherlands, is more 'modern' than in Germany. So far, the political system in Germany seems to be unable to provide for basic institutional reforms. The stalemate results from well-organised special interest groups who defend their privileges as well as from a public mood which is characterised by pessimism, the impression of an unavoidable decline in wealth, resignation and retreat to individual niches.

Germany has always played an active role in the European integration process and was among the major proponents of the Maastricht Treaty. However, there are serious objections to this step in further integration. First, there is the fear of sacrificing the stable DM. Then there is an uneasy feeling about delegating more and more decision-making powers to an anonymous bureaucracy in Brussels. The gap between decision-making and democratic control gets wider and people are not willing to accept this. And finally, it has yet to be shown how the principle of subsidiarity can contribute to preserving regional identity. While there is a broad consensus that European integration is still a good idea, there is considerable doubt on how to proceed further (e.g. deepening versus widening).

German economic development and lifestyle is not sustainable. High economic performance is still based on burdening future generations by a high consumption of non-renewable materials and energy sources, by emissions which exceed the carrying capacity of eco-systems and by patterns of land use which destroy the living space of non-human species. Environmental problems have added a new dimension to the 'big trade-off' (A. M. Okun) between economic efficiency and social justice (equality). Sustainable patterns of development will have to address a new 'magic triangle' of efficiency, equality, sustainability. Solutions will come neither from defending obsolete structures nor from a free-market dogmatism without respect for traditions and values. The debate on a transformation of the German economic system into a social–ecological market economy lost priority when problems with German unification increased. But it remains the single most ambitious project on the political agenda in which Germany could take a pioneering role.

2.9 BIBLIOGRAPHY AND SOURCES OF INFORMATION

Literature

Biedenkopf, K. (1990): 'The Federal Republic of Germany: Old Structures and New Challenges', in Calleo, D.P, Morgenstern, C. (eds) *Recasting Europe's Economies: National Strategies in the 1980s*, Lanham, NY/London, 79–99

BUND (Bund für Umwelt and Naturschutz Deutschland e.V.) Misereor (eds) (1996): *Zukunftsfähiges Deutschland. Ein Beitrag zu einer global nachhaltigen Entwicklung*. Studie des Wuppertal Instituts für Klima, Umwelt, Energie, Basel etc.

Bundesminister für Wirtschaft (various years): *Jahreswirtschaftsbericht der Bundesregierung*, Bonn

Deutsche Bundesbank (various years): *Geschäftsbericht* (Annual Report), Frankfurt am Main.

Fels, G., Furstenberg, G.M. v. (eds) (1989): *A Supply-side Agenda for Germany*, Springer, Berlin

Giersch, H., Papué, K.-H., Schmieding, H. (1992): *The Fading Miracle: Four Decades of Market Economy in Germany*, Cambridge

Graskamp, R. *et al.* (1992): *Umweltschutz, Strukturwandel und Wirtschaftswachstum*, Westfälisches Institut für Wirtschaftsforschung (RWI), Essen

Härtel, H.-H. *et al.* (1995): *Grenzüberschreitende Produktion und Strukturwandel. Globalisierung der deutschen Wirtschaft*, HWWA Institut für Wirtschaftsforschung. Hamburg

Heilemann, U., Reinicke, W.H. (1995): *Welcome to Hard Times. The Fiscal Consequences of German Unity*, American Institute for Contemporary German Studies at the Johns Hopkins University, Washington, DC

Institut der deutschen Wirtschaft (1996): *Zahlen zur wirtschaftlichen Entwicklung der Bundesrepublik Deutschland*, Köln

Lampert, H. (1995): *Die Wirtschafts- und Sozialordnung der Bundesrepublik Deutschland*, (12th edn), Olzog, München

Monopolkommission (1996): *Elftes Hauptgutachten 1994/1995*, Nomos, Baden-Baden

OECD (various years): *Economic Survey Germany*, Paris

OECD (1993): *Environmental Performance Reviews: Germany*, Paris

Ottnad, A., Wahl, S., Grünewald, R. (1995): *Risse im Fundament*. Die deutsche Wirtschaft bis 2005, Springer, Berlin

Rat von Sachverständigen für Umweltfragen (1996): *Zur Umsetzung einer dauerhaft-umweltgerechten Entwicklung*. Umweltgutachten 1996, Bundestagsdrucksache, Wiesbaden

Sachverständigenrat zur Begutachtung der gesamtwirtschaftlichen Entwicklung/Council of Economic Experts (various years): *Jahresgutachten* (Annual Report), BundestagsdrucksacheWiesbaden

Sinn, G., Sinn, H.-W. (1993): *Kaltstart. Volkswirtschaftliche Aspekte der deutschen Vereinigung*, (3rd edn), Deutscher Taschenbuch Verlag (dtv), München

Smith, E.O. (1994): *The German Economy*, Routledge, London/New York

Statistisches Bundesamt (various years): *Statistisches Jahrbuch für die Bundesrepublik Deutschland*, Metzler-Poeschel, Stuttgart/Mainz

Welfens, P.J.J. (ed.) (1996): *Economic Aspects of German Unification. Expectations, Transition Dynamics and International Perspectives*, (2nd edn), Springer, Berlin

Sources of information

Arbeitsgemeinschaft deutscher wirtschaftswissenschaftlicher Forschungsinstitute e.V. (ARGE), Königin-Luise-Str. 5, 14195 Berlin

Bundesanstalt für Arbeit, Regensburger Str. 104, 90478 Nürnberg

Bundesministerium der Finanzen, Graurheindorfer Str. 108, 53117 Bonn

Bundesministerium für Wirtschaft, Villemombler Str. 76, 53123 Bonn

Bundesverband der Deutschen Industrie (BDI), Gustav-Heinemann-Ufer 84, 50968 Köln

Deutsche Bundesbank, Wilhelm-Epstein-Str. 14, 60431 Frankfurt

Deutscher Gewerkschaftsbund (DGB), Hans-Böckler-Str. 39, 40476 Düsseldorf

Deutscher Industrie- und Handelstag (DIHT), Adenauer Allee 148, 53113 Bonn

Presse- und Informationsamt der Bundesregierung, Welckerstr. 11, 53133 Bonn

Statistisches Bundesamt, Gustav-Stresemann-Ring 11, 65189 Wiesbaden 1

Umweltbundesamt, Bismarckplatz 1, 14193 Berlin

CHAPTER 3

France

Kirk Thomson

3.1 INSTITUTIONAL AND HISTORICAL CONTEXT

3.1.1 Introduction

It is worth, even if we are concerned principally with the economy, giving some attention to relevant aspects of the political and social environment. France, like its neighbours, can be regarded as a stable democracy. Nevertheless, it should be remembered that the present constitution, the so-called Fifth Republic, dates from as recently as 1958, and was modified in 1962 to provide for a directly elected President with considerable powers. The crisis which led to these constitutional changes, associated with the war of independence in Algeria, shook French democracy to its roots. If such major upheaval seems unlikely to repeat itself in the near future, there remains the general danger that industrial disputes and social problems can easily degenerate into violence, whether it concerns farmers, fishermen, students, civil servants, or other disgruntled groups.

The French political system remains highly centralised. The President wields considerable power as elected head of state. He alone appoints the Prime Minister and defines the general line of policy. The Prime Minister is responsible for supervising the day-to-day implementation of policy, managing the Government, and seeing that appropriate legislation is passed by the separately elected legislature. He can be dismissed and replaced whenever the President sees fit. Since the presidential and the legislative elections do not normally coincide, situations can easily arise where the legislative majority is in opposition to the President. This occurred recently in the periods 1986–88 and 1993–95. In both periods, President Mitterand recognised democratic principles rather than constitutional obligation, and appointed a Prime Minister from the right-wing opposition. In neither period did party difference lead to political crisis. Indeed, the experience tended to reveal the surprising degree of consensus on economic and foreign policy which exists amongst mainstream French politicians.

Until the victory of François Mitterand, the socialist candidate, in the 1981 presidential election, French politics had been marked by a high degree of ideological division. As far as the mainstream parties of the democratic right and left are concerned, this has largely disappeared. More recently, observers have pointed to a general feeling in the population that political leaders are powerless to deal with social and economic difficulties, such as low growth and unemployment. A growing minority support extremist parties such as the *Front National*, while at the other end of the political spectrum the *Parti Communiste Français* and the far left retain considerable working-class loyalty. A worrying cleavage is seen to exist between the opinions of the Parisian political establishment and many sections of the population. The narrow approval given to the 'Maastricht' referendum in 1992, and not only the widespread public sector strikes of late 1995, caused by proposed social security reforms, but also the surprising sympathy shown to the strikers by a majority of the private sector work-force, can be taken to indicate that the political and economic costs of European integration will be paid, at best, with the utmost reluctance.

3.1.2 The 'dirigiste' tradition

One of the features of the French economy has long been the intimate relationship between the business world, in particular the nation's industrial and financial leaders, on the one hand, and the political and administrative élite, on the other. In a somewhat simplistic manner, two explanations for this intimacy, which is rivalled only in Japan, can be put forward.

France has a long tradition of highly centralised administration going back to the time of Colbert and Louis XIV. The liberal economic philosophy which spread among France's neighbours never took hold in Paris, where the state remains the guarantor of freedom rather than a threat to it. State intervention in economic life has seldom been a source of controversy, and the development of indicative planning after 1945 was more a continuation of existing reflexes than an exciting innovation. Recent pressure from Brussels to limit the role, and the advantages, of public enterprises is seen more as a threat to sovereignty than a necessary and legitimate encouragement of competition. It is difficult, in this respect, to distinguish clearly between attitudes of the parties of the right, and those of the left.

Associated with this tradition has been the development of an industrial and administrative élite recruited from the system of *grandes écoles*.

These highly selective graduate schools, which exist outside the normal university structure, attract the best students. A limited number of their graduates go on to study at the *Ecole Nationale de l'Administration*. Students from these schools fill the top positions in the civil service, run many if not most of France's large businesses and have dominated successive governments of both right and left. Individuals will shift regularly and easily between government, public administration, public enterprise and private enterprise.

It is a phenomenon which has both strengths and weaknesses. The economic, political, and administrative élite of France is highly trained and competent. It shares common values, and a common social and educational background. Many will have had a professional life involving both public service and business leadership, tending to reduce the mutual ignorance which often bedevils cooperation between public administration and industry in other countries. On the other hand, there has been a tendency to have businesses and financial institutions run by top managers without any direct experience. Leaders of public, and large private, enterprises in France will be nominated from outside rather than promoted from within. Also, some attribute the country's recent corruption scandals, in part, to an imprecise definition of the frontier between public and private interest.

3.1.3 The background to economic policy

The broad lines of economic policy in France meet with a wide degree of consensus from the leaders of business and the political establishment. This consensus is based on a firm commitment to European integration, and the perceived need to achieve integration in conjunction with Germany. If this is more a strategic or diplomatic objective than an economic one, it is, nonetheless, one of the main constraints limiting the freedom of action of successive French governments when confronting the two key problems of growth and employment within the Maastricht context. Over the past 15 years,

French economic policy has been remarkably consistent, certainly since the major policy change in 1983.

In 1981 the presidential elections ushered in the 14 years of the Mitterand presidency. The 1981 socialist platform committed the new government to a range of radical measures, such as widespread nationalisations, social security and retirement improvements, a shorter working week, longer paid holidays, and substantial increases in the level of the minimum wage. Partly ideological, but also partly pragmatic with the avowed aim of reducing unemployment through reflation, the net effect of these measures was twofold. Growth was increased marginally (Table G23) with a beneficial effect on unemployment, but, on the other hand, France was out of step with its EU and OECD partners who were applying restrictive measures to deal with the effects of the oil price increases in 1980–81. As a result, a rapidly worsening trade deficit was caused (Table G37), accompanied by a series of exchange rate crises, with the French franc being devalued three times in eighteen months.

March 1983 saw a fundamental reappraisal of policy, and the decision to anchor France to the European Monetary System, and hence to currency stability, rather than to maintain a more risky but more independent push for growth. From this date, short-term and long-term measures were introduced to bring French rates of inflation down to those in Germany, to bring under control public spending and deficits, to slow salary increases, and to restore business confidence and profitability. This policy came to be known as competitive disinflation, an expression which suggests the multiple objective of bringing down French inflation rates within a zone of stable currencies, achieving gains in competitivity for French exports, and thus improving market share in export markets.

Although developments in European integration, the Single Market, Maastricht and EMU, have changed the environment in which this policy is to be applied, successive governments have remained firmly committed to its success. The policy of competitive disinflation can be said to have melded imperceptibly into the effort to satisfy the so-called Maastricht criteria, which the present Chirac/Juppe government are determined to meet by 1998. Other key areas where the impact of integration has been perceptible over recent years are the reform of the banking and finance system, agriculture (the battle over reforms to the CAP and the Uruguay Round), and the question of government support for public enterprise and deregulation.

3.2 MAIN ECONOMIC CHARACTERISTICS

3.2.1 Population and labour

Latest estimates put the total population of metropolitan (excluding overseas territories and *départements*) France at 58 million (Table G17). France has similar population trends to those of its neighbours. The 'baby boom' of 1945 which followed the Second World War was followed by declining fertility rates, and from the early 1970s the population was no longer fully replacing itself. With latest fertility rates at 1.7 per woman there is no reason to suppose that the trend to a slowly ageing population will change. The precision of future estimates depends on unpredictable social variables, but with an estimated rate of 1.8 per woman it can be assumed that the French population will be in decline by 2045. The impact of ageing, however, will increase rapidly in the near future. The population over 85, for example, will increase from roughly 1 million to 1.5 million by the year 2010. From the year 2005 the over-60 population will begin to increase rapidly as the 'baby-boomers' reach retirement age.

The question of the size of the immigrant population is social rather than economic. The classification itself depends on rules governing the acquisition of nationality. The foreign population was estimated at 6.4% in 1993, with a net annual immigration of some 60 000 per year. Nearly one half of the immigrants come from Africa, of which the large majority are from the Mahgreb. Of the foreign population at present in

France 35% are from the three countries of the Mahgreb, 38% from Italy, Spain and Portugal, and 5% from Turkey. Of these, the largest number, 38% lived in the Paris region.

In terms of geographical distribution there are three main zones of population increase – Île de France (Paris region), Rhones-Alpes (Lyon) and the Mediterranean coastal area (Provence-Alpes-Côte d'Azur and Languedoc-Roussillon). Nearly 19% of the total are concentrated in the Île de France.

Working population

The total working population in 1994 was 25.5 million (Table G18). The number employed, however, was 22.1 million, which can be compared with the figure of 21.7 million in 1980. The French economy has failed to generate sufficient employment for the annual demographic increase, with a result shown in high and stable levels of unemployment. It has been estimated by one research unit (OFCE) that from 1996 to 2000 the working population will continue to increase by some 150 000 per year for demographic reasons, but changes in activity rates will increase the required number of new jobs to 200 000 per year at least.

Activity rates have varied for several reasons. Firstly, there has been a marked increase in female activity, which (25–49 years) has increased from a little over 50% in 1968 to more than 80% in 1995. On the other hand the rate for males in the 15–24 year group dropped from 61% to 34%, as more and more remained in full-time education. Young people of both sexes have been continuing in education partly to improve their chances in the labour market, but also to avoid unemployment. The rate for males over 50 dropped from 54% to 32%, under the impact of early retirement schemes and frustrated unemployed workers leaving the labour market entirely.

3.2.2 Employment structure

The main changes in employment in France have taken place progressively as the economy has adjusted structurally. In the period 1970 to 1991 employment in agriculture and fishing fell from 13.3% to 5.7%. This figure is likely to fall sharply in the near future in view of the disproportionately high numbers of farmers close to retirement. Manufacturing employment peaked at 24% in 1974, but had fallen to 17.3% by 1991. Dramatic falls in employment took place in the 1980s in traditional sectors such as iron and steel, and shipbuilding. Employment in the service sector increased from 49% (1970) to 66% (1991), with particularly large increases in education, health, and public administration. Within market services, the largest increase over recent years has been in the supply of services to industry, explained by the trend to contract out for work previously done by full-time employees.

A striking development in recent years has been the increase in part-time employment, even if, at a level of 15.6% of jobs in March 1995, the proportion is lower than other comparable economies.

3.2.3 Output and growth

Following the Second World War, output grew rapidly in France, and the 1945–74 period is often referred to as the 'trente glorieuses'. From 1969 to 1973 real GDP was growing at around 6% per year. The quadrupling of oil prices in 1973 checked this hectic expansion and led to a period of growing unemployment, stubbornly high inflation, and lower growth rates. Despite an already worrying tendency for French inflation rates to remain higher than those in Germany, giving rise to tensions in the foreign exchange markets, the economy appeared to be moving back into equilibrium when the second oil crisis caused another external shock.

The Mitterand victory ensured that the French response to the shock was markedly different from that of other industrialised nations. Thanks to the fiscal expansion engineered by the Mauroy government, French policy was out of step with its competitors. Domestic demand expanded by 4% in 1982, but the trade deficit and the foreign exchange difficulties were such that the March 1983 devaluation was linked to a range of deflationary accompanying measures of some severity. Growth dipped to a new low of 0.7% in 1983, and did not pick up until the second half of 1987, stimulated by improved rates of investment and lower energy prices. If growth was satisfactory in 1988 and 1989, the situation changed for the worse after 1990. Despite the stimulus represented by German reunification and the improved export performance of French industry, growth faltered in the 1990s, culminating in recession in 1993.

The reasons for France's lacklustre performance in recent years are manifold, but most observers pick out the impact of restrictive monetary policies (high real interest rates and low inflation), and the inability of the government to stimulate demand through fiscal measures. Both difficulties are linked to the determination to meet the Maastricht criteria.

3.2.4 Labour market

The virtual stagnation of French employment in recent years has already been referred to. Between 1980 and 1993 the number of jobs increased by less than half a million, with an average of 37 200 per year. Under the impact of the 1983 austerity programme employment declined in the early 1980s, increased timidly in the period 1985–87, and increased more vigorously with faster growth from 1987 to 1990. Employment peaked at 22.5 million in 1991, but declined again in the two following years. Increases in 1994 and 1995 were not sufficient to reduce unemployment. According to certain estimates (INSEE) employment only increased in the period 1974–90 when GDP growth was over 2.3%, because of the underlying improvement in productivity. Another estimate (OFCE) claims that in order to reduce unemployment the economy needs to generate between 300 000 and 350 000 new jobs every year, taking into account the demographic increase in the working population and the modification in activity rates brought about by economic growth. In other words to reduce unemployment by 100, there must be an increase in employment of between 130 and 150. In 1995, as an indication, employment increased by 155 000 with a growth of GDP

of 2.2%. In view of the rather pessimistic forecasts regarding growth at present in vogue, there seems little immediate hope of seeing unemployment substantially reduced.

Unemployment in France shares many of its characteristics with that in other member states of the European Union. Seen historically, it has grown inexorably since 1974, stabilising at times then increasing again. Clearly, the labour market in France is not functioning as it should.

The question of unemployment is the source of many misunderstandings. Firstly, like any market it is the scene of a multitude of movements. In 1991, for example, 3.7 million people found jobs. Of these 1.9 million simply changed jobs without being registered as unemployed. One million had never before been employed (students etc.), and only the remaining 800 000 had at any time passed through the unemployment statistics. It must also be remembered that measuring unemployment is in some ways an almost impossible task. The interface between work and non-work is difficult to measure in any but a purely arbitrary manner. On the margin of those who fall into the category labelled unemployed there is a wider group of those who are working part-time but would prefer a full-time occupation, those who have abandoned the attempt to find work entirely, those on sponsored training schemes, those who have never been employed but would like to work provided jobs in the vicinity exist, etc.

With such reservations regarding the statistics, it can be said that the 1995 average, according to INSEE, was 11.6% (using the ILO definition). For men the figure was 9.8%, and for women in the same category, 29%. Looking at unemployment in terms of qualifications it is important to note that the lower the level of education, the greater is the risk of being jobless. The rate for unskilled manual workers fluctuates around 20%. The rate for North African immigrants is around 30%. The figure in the summer of 1996 was 12.6%, and rising.

The imbalance between the supply of labour and the demand is most obvious in the case of new entrants. In a study in 1992 the OECD highlighted this particular aspect of the problem. In 1989, for example, despite an activity rate in France which was significantly lower for the 15–24 age group than elsewhere in Europe (27.5% as opposed to 36.6%), the French unemployment rate was two points higher. Another area of difficulty concerns the long-term unemployed (more than one year) who approach 34% of the total.

What are the causes of high and lasting unemployment? Firstly, there is the 'liberal' market-orientated approach which suggests that the problem in France is closely linked to the administrative regulations which surround the labour market and prevent it from functioning freely. One of these barriers is the minimum wage (known in France as the SMIC, the *salaire minimum interprofessionel de croissance*). Since the minimum wage in France is relatively high in relation to average rates it is often singled out as an impediment to employment to the least productive, particularly the young. A related problem is the relatively high 'tax wedge' created by high levels of social security contributions paid by employees and employers. Unemployment and related benefits, it is argued, provide high replacement ratios and act as a disincentive to look for employment. For those earning the SMIC, for example, the ratio is as high as 84%.

Another argument concentrates not on the need for a more deregulated labour market, but on economic policy, in particular the monetary policy which has led to historically high real interest rates. Low rates of inflation, it is argued, are in themselves desirable, but not if the cost of maintaining them is high unemployment. The government should, therefore, be prepared to take the risk of letting the exchange rate slide as a result of bringing down interest rates in order to stimulate demand and investment.

Government policy has evolved over the past twenty years. Ever since 1977, various governments have felt the need to be seen to be doing something about the unemployment problem. The result is a bewildering series of measures which change frequently, and are of uncertain effectiveness. In 1994 total expenditure on unemployment came to 4.03% of GDP, of which 41% was used to pay unemployment benefits. Expenditure on so-called active measures is

concentrated on two types – training courses for the unemployed and new entrants to the labour market, on the one hand, and direct subsidies aiming at reducing the cost of certain types of labour, on the other. Some 2.4 million people benefited from active measures in 1994, although the Ministry of Labour estimated that the macroeconomic effect in terms of the reduction of unemployment was 80 000. Recent measures concentrating on the long-term unemployed (the 'initiative-employment contract') have proved successful in bringing numbers of this category back into employment, but for 150 000 contracts signed the total effect on unemployment was only 20 000. Once again, active measures seem to be rearranging the queue of unemployed rather than reducing the total number.

3.2.5 Consumption, savings, and investment

Consumer spending, the largest part of domestic expenditure (Table G28), has remained at slightly over 60% of GDP throughout the 1980s and 1990s. During the 1980s household consumption was increasing at an annual rate much the same as in other EU member states, 2.4%. The rate of increase dropped sharply with the onset of the economic slowdown from mid-1990, and in the period 1992–95 the annual rates of increase were 1.3%, 0.1%, 1.4%, and 1.7%. This lower rate of increase is explained by the lower rate of income rise and consumer pessimism in an uncertain environment.

A more subtle approach to the consumption/saving trade-off can be made by looking at household saving as a percentage of gross disposable income. During the 1970s high rates of inflation were associated with a savings rate fluctuating around 20% of gross disposable income. The savings rate fell from 20% in 1978 to 11% in 1988. From 1988 the savings rate increased again. The most widely accepted explanation of this phenomenon is that consumers reacted to a lower rate of increase of their real disposable income in the years up to 1983, and the drop in savings represented a desire to maintain consumption. From 1983, however, the lower rates of inflation meant that less savings were required to maintain the desired levels of real money balances. Improvements in purchasing power counteracted this trend from 1988. The increase in the savings rate to between 13% and 14% in the 1990s is attributed principally to interest rate sensitivity (OECD) in the current deregulated financial environment, and to the precautionary motive (INSEE) as fear of unemployment becomes widespread.

The level of industrial fixed investment is influenced by anticipations of future profits and the cost and availability of long-term capital. The period of rapid growth in France before the first oil shock was accompanied by high rates of investment and high gross profits. The annual growth of investment dropped from nearly 8% to 0.1% after 1973, and further to an annual fall of 1.2% from 1980 to 1984. With the change in economic policy in 1983, the share of salaries in industrial added value began to fall and that of profits (from 25.8% in 1980 to 32.6% in 1992) to rise. It took two years after 1983 for the restriction in salaries to feed through into investment, but in the period 1985–91 investment increased at an annual rate of 6.7%. But already by 1991 high real rates of interest led to a fall in investment, which was amplified by the general business slowdown. Business investment dropped by 6.7% in 1993 (21% in 1993 in manufacturing), and only improved slightly in the two following years. Despite continuing high profits in the 1990s, businesses preferred to reduce debt rather than invest, thanks to the effect of prevailing high real interest rates.

Investment by French industry in research and development still lags somewhat in comparison to the main competitors. Total expenditure on research and development had risen from 1.8% of GDP in 1980 to 2.4% in 1990, according to the Raynaud report on the French economy (1993). The German figures were 2.4% and 2.9%, and the UK figures were 2.25% and 2.3%. In terms of high technology products market share, France had 6.5%, Germany 12% and the UK 7.7% (Raynaud report). Industrial research expenditure remains concentrated in certain sectors (aeronautics, electronics, energy, pharmaceuticals), and publicly financed research is largely defence orientated.

3.2.6 Inflation

France has had a historical tendency to be more inflation prone than many of her neighbours, particularly Germany (Table G31). Measures, such as indexing, and price controls, as well as tightly regulated money markets, lessened its impact, but the establishment of the European Monetary System was to necessitate the convergence of German and French inflation rates. Without convergence, regular, and politically humiliating, devaluations were unavoidable (e.g. 1981–83).

The policy of bringing down inflation to below levels prevailing in Germany and other EMS partners, applied without compromise after the crisis years of 1981 and 1982, was to be known as competitive disinflation. The main aim was to restore a competitive edge to the French economy, after the difficult period of the early 1980s, and there were four principal pillars. A tight monetary policy was to reduce general inflation, budgetary policy was to stabilise and reduce public borrowing requirements, salary increases were to be brought down to ensure competitive costs, and structural reforms were to be implemented to create a dynamic and competitive business environment.

In so far as inflation rates can be considered as an indicator of the policy's success there is no doubt that the results were satisfying. The France–Germany differential fell from 6.4% in 1983 to –0.2% in 1991. Since that year French inflation has remained below that in Germany. In addition, low increases in nominal labour costs in a stable exchange rate zone have meant that unit labour costs have been increasing more slowly in France than elsewhere in the EU. In the period 1987–91, for example, unit wage costs were increasing at roughly one half the EU average. Improved competitiveness helps explain the improvement in France's foreign trade balance, and the increase in export market share in the EU from 15.5% in 1987 to 17% in 1992.

3.2.7 Production and market structure

Changes in output

As in most developed economies, France has witnessed significant changes in the structure of production over the past twenty-five years. Production in agriculture and manufacturing industry both make up a noticeably smaller percentage of added value, while the share of services, both private and public sector, has increased. The general trends can be seen in Table 3.1.

French farming has benefited from the effects of the Common Agricultural Policy. France is the world's second largest exporter of food products behind the USA, and, together with the processing industry, agricultural products make a major contribution to the French balance of trade. On the other hand, the number of full-time farm units has declined (582 000 in 1990), and the number will probably stabilise at approximately one half the present figure at the beginning of the next century. Associated with this movement, the average farm size increased from 31.8 hectares in 1979 to 43.6 in 1990.

Size of firms

In 1991, production of goods and services in France came from just over two million industrial, commercial, and service enterprises, one million farms (full- and part-time), around 40 000 financial institutions, and 250 000 establishments, both public and private, providing non-market services.

Of the various enterprises in the market sector, the vast majority (over 90%) had fewer than 10 employees. These micro-enterprises were con-

centrated in the market service, construction, and commercial sectors. Those in the industrial sector were to be found in activities requiring specialised knowledge rather than capital such as skilled craft workers. They provided 32% of total employment, and 21% of added value.

Half the small and medium enterprises (classified as having 10 to 499 employees in France) operate in the tertiary sector. Another 16% are to be found in construction. As a general rule, where considerable capital is required for cost effective output, the degree of concentration tends to increase. In the armaments industry, the four leading enterprises are responsible for 89% of production, whereas in textiles the share of the four leaders is only 7.5%.

Small businesses suffer from a number of handicaps – high levels of expensive short-term debt, and an obligation to provide longer customer credit, for example – but are seen as an important element in the economy, especially as a source of employment. As a result, successive governments have put together a tissue of fiscal and administrative measures to support them.

3.2.8 Productivity and growth potential

The relationship between productivity trends, levels of employment, and potential growth is complex, but merits attention. Employment will expand more rapidly when there is a gap between productivity growth and that of GDP. Between 1981 and 1990 French GDP was expanding at an average of 2.4% per year and productivity at 2.0%. Between 1991 and 1995 the figures were 1.3% per year in both areas. Other European countries were not substantially different. The main contrast is between Europe

Table 3.1 Changes in the structure of production

	% Total added value		% Total employment	
	1970	1992	1970	1992
Agriculture	7.6	3.1	13.3	5.1
Industry	32.4	25.2	28.0	20.7
Services	51.4	58.4	48.8	67.0

Source: INSEE

and the USA. Employment expanded at 1.4% per year in the USA between 1980 and 1993, whereas the rate in Europe was 0.2%. Since a greater proportion of added value generated by growth goes towards salaries in France (as in the rest of Europe) than it does in the USA, it follows that the rate of growth required to generate employment is higher.

Analysis of growth trends and potential GDP is an exercise fraught with statistical difficulties. Recently, INSEE has estimated the long-term growth trend of GDP in the 1980s and 1990s to be 2.2% per year. Various methods exist for calculating potential GDP, and the results estimate the output gap for the French economy in 1994 to be between –2.0% and –3.1%. A reasonable estimate for potential annual growth would be 2.9%. It is the failure to achieve growth at this rate which is the underlying explanation for the growth in unemployment over the past 20 years.

3.3 GOVERNMENT INVOLVEMENT IN THE ECONOMY

The role of the state has expanded significantly since the Second World War, as elsewhere. Nevertheless, attitudes to state intervention in France have long differed to those in similar countries. It has always been considered quite natural for the state to take an active role in managing the economy. This role has been exercised not only through appropriate fiscal and monetary policies, but also through a large public sector, including significant sections of the financial services, public utilities, manufacturing, transport, energy, and, in addition, a government sponsored system of planning. State intervention has been on the defensive over recent years, under the double attack of liberal economic theory, and the pressure of the European Commission.

3.3.1 Indicative planning

The French system of indicative planning has attracted much attention over the years, since it was first set up by Jean Monnet in 1946. The history of French planning can be roughly divided into three periods.

In the first period from 1947 to 1961, France was undergoing the experience of post-war reconstruction. The magnitude of the task lent itself to some degree of centralisation as long-term priorities had to be established, and the government had at its disposal a range of instruments of direct control. In the second period, 1962 to 1975, parliamentary control over the establishment of the plan was established, the scope of the plan extended to include social questions, and the indicative nature of the plan became more evident. As the economy passed from a period of managing shortages to one of managing the abundance of rapid growth, the laying down of objectives could no longer depend only on the state and its experts. In other words, the quantification of objectives gave way to a more subtle approach in which the plan became the centre of a prolonged national debate designed to make the various partners in the economy aware of the need for mutually compatible medium-term objectives. In the third period, subsequent to the first oil shock, from 1975 to the present day, the growing difficulty in forecasting in an economy increasingly open to the world economy threw the planning process into some disrepute. The objectives of the plans were either overtaken by external events, or rendered irrelevant by internal political changes.

At the present time, planning survives in two respects. The work of the General Commissariat of the Plan continues as a centre for the discussion and analysis of the coherence of the government's macroeconomic objectives. But today its work is simply one of many similar institutes of economic and social analysis. The planning activity itself has been integrated into the relationship between state and region. Following the Decentralisation Law of 1982, in which new powers were given to directly elected regional bodies, a series of planning contracts have been drawn up between central government and the regions which make it possible for regional ambitions to be realised in a manner which is coherent with central macroeconomic objectives.

3.3.2 Fiscal policy

The increasing role of the government in the economy explains the steady increase in public expenditure since the Second World War. Between 1950 and 1990, public expenditure rose from 33.3% of GDP to 51%. Over the same period tax and social security contributions rose from 28.3% of GDP to 43.8%.

The general level of government expenditure (Table G32) can be said to have risen in three steps in recent years, subsequent to the two oil price shocks of 1973 and 1980, and with the onset of the 1991 crisis. Each shock has had a ratchet effect on public spending as higher levels of unemployment have worked through into the system of social support. Of even greater importance than the level of expenditure, particularly in the post-Maastricht era, has been the general government borrowing requirement (Table G34). The reflation introduced by the Mauroy government in 1981 quickly led to an alarming increase in the government deficit, and, from 1982 to 1986, the socialist governments set out successfully to bring the deficit down to 3% of GDP. The boom years saw a stabilisation of the deficit at a tolerable level, but from 1991 the situation worsened. In 1992 and 1993 the deficit was allowed to widen in the hope that the automatic stabiliser effect of government spending would compensate growing unemployment.

By 1994, at 5.8% of GDP, and with the EMU timetable setting a tightening constraint it was considered that additional restraint was required. This coincided, in 1995, with a change of president (Chirac) and a new prime minister (Juppé). The new government, confronted by a worsening budgetary situation, introduced, after a period of hesitation, new taxes, announced restrictions on spending, and committed itself to reducing general net borrowing from 5% in 1995 to 3% of GDP in 1997. Nevertheless, it has proved extremely difficult to rein in public expenditure in the past, and the medium-term fiscal policy of the government depends very much on its ability to control social security spending.

One element in the budgetary puzzle which significantly hampers the government is the growing public debt and the associated servicing charges. The 1995 debt/GDP ratio of 52% was still within the Maastricht criteria, and (according to OECD estimates) the level of debt will remain below the 60% limit by 1997.

The international finance markets were concerned, in the summer of 1995, that the new government appeared to be compensating a widening gap between revenues and expenditure by increasing the former, rather than limiting the latter. Indeed, both the level of government expenditure, and that of taxes and social security contributions remain high by international standards. In 1995 the total tax and social security contributions came to 44.5% of GDP. Despite the efforts of a succession of governments of left and right, this figure has remained stable since the early 1980s. As a point of comparison, in 1993 the figure for France was 43.9% of GDP, Germany 39%, and the UK 33.6%. Of the French total 25.2% represents taxation, and 19.3% social contributions (against a European average of 12.2%).

Taxation in France presents a number of peculiarities. Personal income taxes are relatively unimportant (in 1987 they represented 12.7% of tax revenues as against a European average of 26.3%). Half the households in France pay no income tax, but on the other hand 5% of taxpayers pay half the income tax revenue of the state. The system is highly progressive with considerable allowances for children and dependents. Income tax reform has been declared to be a priority of the present government, but the difficulties in the face of reform are considerable. One problem, for example, is that tax is paid in the year following that when the income was earned. It would be desirable to move towards a 'pay as you earn' system, but what would be the solution for the period of transition? As things stand, the solution has been to introduce income-based taxes similar to an income tax, such as the *contribution sociale généralisée* (CSG), which supplement government revenues, and leave the political hot potato of income tax reform untouched. The other area requiring reform is the manner in which the social security expenditure is financed, since this falls largely on employer and employee contributions (up to 21.8% of GDP in 1995). It is now widely accepted that these payments at such a level act as a disincentive to employment. As a response to the deficits in the social security budget, two new taxes have recently been introduced which are based on income rather than employment. The first, introduced in 1991, the CSG, was raised to 2.4% of all incomes in 1994 and is currently planned to replace a growing proportion of social expenditure. The second, the *remboursement de la dette sociale* (RDS), is levied at 0.5% of all income and is intended to repay the accumulated social security debt over the coming 13 years. Indirect taxes are a major source of tax revenue. The basic rate of the value-added tax was raised to 20.6% in the summer of 1995 as part of the deficit stabilisation measures.

3.3.3 Regional policy

Despite France's cultural and geographic diversity, the problem of regional variations in employment prospects has not been as acute as in other countries in Europe. In 1994, for example, unemployment in Languedoc-Roussillon was 16.1%, and that in the Nord-Pas-de-Calais was 15.4%, compared with the then national average of 11.7%. Amongst the most favoured regions, unemployment in Alsace was 7.1%, and in the Rhône–Alpes 10.8%.

Since 1963, the *délégation à l'aménagement du territoire* (DATAR) has been the agency responsible for implementing policies designed to deal with the two main regional problems, helping backward rural areas and those hit by structural industrial change (iron and steel, shipbuilding). This regional role of DATAR has been modified, on the one hand, by the growth in funds available through the regional and agricultural policies of the EU, and the new powers given to the elected regional assemblies by the Law of Decentralisation in 1982. The regional authorities are now, for example, responsible for stimulating the regional economy through aid to private industry, the creation of public services and improvements in transport. To some extent,

the newly voted law on regional policy (February 1995) will return power to the centre, since the government once again becomes the final arbiter in regional policy, despite the existence of a 'National Council' for regional policy, composed of local and national delegates, with an advisory rôle. In order to reduce differences in per capita incomes, redistribution of incomes between regions will be increased with the aim of reducing differences to a range of 80–120% of the national average by 1997. At present, concern is concentrated on the plight of those rural regions undergoing depopulation, either because of their inhospitable climate and terrain, or because of declining employment and income in farming. In the debate about the reforms to the Common Agricultural Policy in 1992, fears that a reduction in farm support would worsen the situation in rural France and intensify regional differences were commonly expressed.

3.3.4 Industrial policy

Industrial policy in France has seen a fundamental change over the past twenty years. Before the 1981 change of government French policy deliberately set out to favour 'national champions', and to encourage branches with rapidly developing technologies. The decisions to concentrate on nuclear energy for electricity production, and to set up the high-speed train network date from this period. Despite undoubted successes, one disadvantage of this policy was that the technological innovations were slow to diffuse in industry as a whole and research spending remained rather low. The interventionist industrial policy of the socialists in 1981 was as much aimed at modernising French industry as it was at fulfilling ideological commitments. The sweeping nationalisations of 1982 were accompanied by major investment programmes, and industrial restructuring. This radical approach proved shortlived, and in 1983 began the return to management autonomy, even in the nationalised enterprises. By the 1990s, industrial policy had become limited to the creation of a competitive environment conducive to industrial efficiency. Direct aid to industry as a whole declined, and aid to nationalised industries and enterprises was designed either to absorb operating deficits, or to prepare them for privatisation. Only in the reorganisation of the defence industry would the present government appear ready to indulge in an active role in industrial planning. What might be described as the traditional French interventionist approach to industrial policy is largely a thing of the past.

Apart from privatisation, active industrial policy is now limited to encouragement given to small businesses. A number of measures introduced by the government in 1995 were aimed at facilitating their access to the stock exchange, to help them improve their equity position, and the establishment of a new bank specialising in funding for small business. Policy in France today seems to coincide with the prevailing mood in Brussels regarding state intervention in industry.

3.3.5 Public enterprise and privatisations

In three successive waves, the Popular Front period of 1936, the post-liberation reorganisation, and 1982, large sections of the French economy passed into public control. The post-war nationalisations involved mainly transport, energy, banking and insurance. Renault was the only major manufacturing enterprise involved. The common theme at the time of post-war reconstruction was to control those sectors where substantial investment was necessary, and to ensure that the state could direct to those sectors the capital required. The 1982 nationalisations were strategic in character, and gave the state the means to intervene directly in the industrial choices of France's economy. Five major industrial groups were involved (CGE, Pechiney, Rhône-Poulenc, Saint-Gobain and Thomson), as were 41 banks and finance houses. The steel industry (Usinor and Sacilor) was already in state ownership. Major shareholdings were taken in advanced technology enterprises such as Matra, Dassault, Bull, and ITT France. Precise estimates vary, but by 1985 some 24% of the French economy was under state control, the highest proportion in the OECD.

This state sector, larger than in any other comparable economy, was rolled back firstly by the right-wing government between 1986 and 1988. The privatisations concerned notably the industrial enterprises Saint-Gobain, CGE and Matra, in communications Havas and TF1, and in banking the Société Générale, Paribas and Suez. The privatisation programme was relaunched in 1993 by the Balladur government, which provided for the selling off of 21 publicly owned groups. In the next two years the Banque Nationale de Paris, Rhône-Poulenc, Elf, the UAP (insurance), the Seita (tobacco), Usinor-Sacilor and Pechiney were removed from public control.

Few contest the privatisations undertaken so far from the point of view of industrial efficiency. But a number of questions have been raised which relate to the financial environment of French industry. Some fear that control of French industry could easily fall into the hands of foreign investors. French industrial enterprises remain relatively small compared to their German and British competitors. There is also a lack of long-term capital available in the French capital markets where the value of stock exchange valuation represents some 26% of GDP as against around 91% at the London Stock Exchange, due in large part to the method of financing pensions. Associated with this is the weakness of institutional investors on the Paris bourse. Others fear that if the logic of private enterprise is extended beyond the traditionally competitive sector into what has always been considered in France as the sector of public service – energy, transport, telecommunications – there will be a decline in public welfare.

3.3.6 Competition policy

Until the early 1980s, a generally interventionist approach to economic policy had not attributed great importance to encouraging effective competition in French economic life. Nevertheless, the decision in December 1986 to remove virtually all remaining price controls was counterbalanced by setting up the *Conseil de Concurrence*. This competition council has wide powers to investigate market structures and corporate behaviour, to make recommendations, and to deal with complaints addressed to it by businesses, the administration, or by private and professional associations. A number of restrictive practices are forbidden such as collusion in price-fixing, and tendering for public contracts, and restrictions on access to markets. Mergers, which may lead to a dominant position, can be investigated if they reach certain thresholds (defined in terms of turnover or 25% of market share). In 1994, the Council was asked to deal with 140 complaints and requests for an opinion.

In a larger sense policy regarding competition also involves the official response to Community directives concerning the deregulation of markets dominated by public enterprises. Implementation has been described by the OECD as 'very gradual'. No deregulation has taken place in the energy sector. Little has been done regarding the position of the SNCF in rail travel, and, despite the planned liberalisation of telephone services in 1997, France Télécom has not yet announced any timetable for privatisation.

3.4 FINANCIAL SYSTEM

Prior to the 1980s the French financial system was highly regulated. Recent changes to a more market-orientated approach have taken place for several reasons – the government's borrowing requirement increased substantially in the early 1980s, technical innovations and internationalisation changed the banking environment, there was a growing desire to see Paris evolve into a leading world financial centre, and the implications of the Single Market and EMU meant that liberalisation, already under way, had to be extended.

3.4.1 The banking system

In 1984 a new law reformed the legal environment of the French banking system. It marked a fundamental change in that all institutions exercising banking activities were placed under the same legal definition, ending the previous multitude of different statutes, and banks were henceforth allowed to engage in any banking activities instead of being limited to defined areas. A series of supervisory bodies was set up amongst which the *Commission Bancaire*, under the supervision of the Banque de France, ensures that banking regulations are respected.

The vast bulk of commercial banking in France is carried out by the three 'national' banks, (Crédit Lyonnais, BNP, the Société Générale, and their subsidiaries), and a number of general banks specialising more in business customers (Banque Indosuez, Banque Paribas, the Crédit Commercial de France and the Crédit Industriel et Commercial), but retaining a network of branches and the networks of mutual banks (in particular the Crédit Agricole, the Banques Populaires, and the Crédit Mutuel). Banking, despite its diversity, is highly concentrated. In 1992, the five leading institutions covered nearly 60% of deposits. The commercial banking system in France suffers from several difficulties caused by a failure to adapt to changes in the market environment. Profitability is low, there is an oversupply of branches and therefore relatively high costs, and there is an excess of labour. The crisis of the Crédit Lyonnais is not typical of French banking as a whole, but seems rather to be the result of poor management controls and unsatisfactory supervision.

Alongside the commercial banks, there are a number of similar institutions, offering more specialised services – savings banks, finance houses, and specialised agencies such as the Caisse de Depôts et Consignations (which centralises the deposits of the savings banks), the Crédit Foncier, and others.

The Banque de France

Set up in 1800 and nationalised at the end of the Second World War, the Banque de France is the central bank, carrying out all the traditional functions this implies. Since 1994, the Banque de France has enjoyed independence from the government of the day regarding its main function of defining and implementing monetary policy. This change in statute was part of the commitments undertaken within the framework of the Maastricht treaty. The first article of the new statutes of the central bank states quite clearly that the first priority is to maintain price stability. It is true that this mission is to be fullfilled within the framework of the general economic policy of the government. A Council of Monetary Policy, comprising six members, apart from the Governor of the Banque de France and the two Assistant Governors, was established to deliberate on monetary policy. All members are independent and have irrevocable mandates of nine years. Such independence, however, is not beyond all contestation as recent tension between the government and the present Governor, Mr Trichet, has implied. In addition, the central bank is responsible for supervising the banking system, for managing the foreign currency reserves of the state, and for carrying out the necessary foreign exchange transactions which the government's exchange rate policy implies.

3.4.2 Monetary policy

Following independence in 1994, the Banque de France announced numerical inflation objectives, for the short and medium term. Prices should not rise by more than 2% in the year. In order to achieve this final objective, two intermediate objectives have been stated, one internal and the other external. The franc should remain stable within the exchange rate mechanism of the European Monetary System, and the annual increase in M3 should be compatible with a medium-term trend of no more than 5%.

Since the abolition of domestic monetary controls in 1987, and the foreign exchange controls in 1990, the most commonly employed instruments to achieve these objectives have been the use of the interest rates on the money markets. Short-term interest rates on the money markets are allowed to fluctuate within a band defined by the lower tender (*appels d'offres*) rate and the higher repurchase (*pensions de 5 à 10 jours*) rate. The Bank also has the possibility of influencing liquidity by means of open market operations in the secondary market for Treasury Bills (*Bons du Trésor*), and by calling on the

banks to maintain special deposits (*réserves obligatoires*). This latter instrument is not used at the moment, but could be reactivated when deemed necessary.

Questions of interest rates (Tables G35 and G36) are intimately linked to the franc exchange rate (Table G42), and to the repeated speculative attacks launched on currencies in the exchange rate mechanism since the crisis of September 1992. One of the major problems facing the French economy has been the rise in real interest rates in the 1980s. Since the more recent count-down towards EMU, the French rates have had to remain rather higher than those imposed by the Bundesbank, despite a lower rate of inflation. The main reason for this, of course, is the so-called risk premium applying to the French franc. The markets have not yet been convinced by the stability of the French franc to the same extent as they have been convinced of the stability of the deutschmark. Any suggestion of a relaxation of French monetary policy, which would imply lower interest rates and the toleration of a relative depreciation of the franc as against the deutschmark, has sparked off a wave of speculation, which the Banque de France has had to counter by interest rate increases. Nevertheless, and despite the speculative crisis of July 1993, which led to the widening of the exchange rate mechanism fluctuation bands to ±15%, the franc has remained aligned to its deutschmark rate. In the first semester of 1995, the OECD calculated French real short-term rates at 5.1% and long-term at 5.9%. The German rates were, at this time, 2.9% and 4.5%. In addition, the effective exchange rate had appreciated by 8%, as compared with the first semester of 1992. In the short run, these interest rate differentials and exchange rate strength act as a brake on economic growth. French businesses are encouraged to reduce the burden of their debt rather than to invest, and the cost of financing inventories increases. Conscious of this problem, the Banque de France has slowly and prudently reduced its intervention rates during 1995.

3.5 INTERNATIONAL RELATIONS

3.5.1 Foreign trade

Seen over the long run, it can be said that after the first oil shock it has taken France almost 20 years to return to the stable trade surpluses it enjoyed in the 1960s and early 1970s. The most worrying period was 1986–91, when there was a noticeable deficit in manufactured goods.

A first impression of the situation, and recent changes, can be gained by looking at Table 3.2. The first item on the list, food and agricultural products, has been regularly in surplus, thanks to French exports of cereals, fruit and vegetables, AOC wines, champagne and cognac. The exports of cereals benefited from higher world prices and a resumption of exports to China.

The drop in the energy deficit stems from the depreciation of the franc against the dollar (oil imports are billed in US dollars), and an increase in the exports of electricity, which is a result of French investment in nuclear power.

Manufactured goods cover a wide range of different sectors. Those where France has been particularly successful recently include perfumery, motor vehicles, and aircraft. In many sectors where there is no surplus there has been a noticeable drop in the deficit.

France is now the world's second largest exporter of services, transport, insurance, consultancy, as well as one of the world's leading tourist destinations. The slight fall in the tourist surplus reflects the appreciation of the franc, and security concerns in 1995 (the wave of terrorist attacks centred on Paris in the summer).

The present position represents a steady improvement which has been going on for five years. The reasons for the improvement, however, have changed with the state of the French economy, and its international environment. As early as 1990, French exports benefited from the impetus of German reunification. With moderate levels of imports into France this stimulus lasted until mid-1992. As France then slipped into recession, imports fell back faster than exports, while from mid-1993, exports began to rise again, some months before imports. The excellent figures for 1995, a difficult year when European markets were stagnant and the franc was appreciating, were in large part due to exceptional items such as the export of aircraft. On the other hand, it must be admitted that, even if the atony of domestic demand has helped keep down imports, French exporters have been able to improve competitiveness thanks to low salary increases and to the improvements in productivity provided by higher recent rates of investment in manufacturing (prior to 1993). Differences in inflation and pressure on profit margins have enabled French exporters to reduce the full impact of the appreciation of the franc.

The geographical distribution of French foreign trade (see Tables G38 and G39) shows, firstly, a marked and growing concentration on intra-EU trade. With the membership of Austria, Sweden, and Finland, this now amounts to 63% of the total. Trade is also rather concentrated among a limited number of partners. The top twenty partners share 84% of French imports and 80% of the exports. The leading suppliers of

Table 3.2 Foreign trade balance (goods and services) – billion FF

	1992	1993	1994	1995
Food and agricultural products	53.2	56.9	44.9	51.5
Energy	−78.6	−68.6	−65.7	−59.5
Manufactured goods	3.8	43.1	47.3	56.4
Services (exc. tourism)	57.8	60.8	75.2	80.2
Tourism	58.5	59.5	59.4	54.3
Total goods and services	94.5	151.6	161.1	182.9

Source: Comptes de la Nation, 1995

France remain Germany (18%), Italy (10%), and Belgium–Luxemburg (9%). Leading destinations of French exports are Germany (18%), Italy and the UK (9% each), followed by Belgium and Spain. The second largest group of trading partners are the non-EU OECD countries, particularly the USA, Japan and Switzerland. The pattern of trade has changed elsewhere. In 1995 there was an increase of 28% in French exports to the rapidly developing Asian economies (particularly Malaysia, Thailand and Hong Kong), and a large increase in trade with the eastern European economies.

3.5.2 Balance of payments

Over the past twenty years the French balance of payments has undergone several fundamental changes as the economy has become increasingly integrated into world trade and world capital flows. The total flows recorded in the balance of payments represented 30% of GDP in 1973, and 140% in 1993. International trade increased in the same period from 18.6% of GDP to 24.2%. Until 1988, current transactions represented the bulk of these flows, but now flows associated with portfolio investments represent 70% of the total.

Having been in deficit throughout the 1980s (with the exception of a slight surplus in 1986), the current account (Table G37) went into surplus in 1992 and, by 1995, had reached 1.6% of GDP. France is now the world's second exporter of services, and is one of the world's leading tourist markets. The trade balance has been irregular over the past 20 years. A period of deficits, following the first oil price shock, lasted from 1974 to 1980. A large deficit, caused by the effects of the Mauroy reflation policy, in 1982 had been gradually reabsorbed by 1986, but the trade deficit worsened again up to 1990. From this year the situation improved.

During the 1970s, and in the first half of the 1980s, foreign direct investments in France and French direct investments abroad were modest. However, the position changed from 1987, and French direct investments grew rapidly to peak at FF150 billion in 1990. Similarly foreign direct investment in France grew, but more slowly, and peaked in 1992. The two flows are now close to balance with deficits of only FF4 billion in 1993 and FF5 billion in 1994. In 1995 foreign direct investment was FF61 billion and French direct investment was FF48 billion. France would seem to have overcome its difficulty in attracting foreign investment interest.

Portfolio investment increased during the 1980s with the selling of government securities abroad from 1982, the reopening of the Eurofrance market in 1985, and the general improvement in confidence in the franc. Financing the deficits in the basic balance, particularly from 1989 to 1992, was largely done through attracting foreign portfolio investment in the form of government securities. These funds tend to be rather unstable. The years 1992 and 1993 saw net inflows of FF187 billion and FF17 billion, followed in 1994 and 1995 by net outflows of FF308 billion and FF60 billion.

3.6 SPECIAL ISSUES

3.6.1 Social security reform

Few in France would be ready to deny that the social security system is in need of reform, but any attempt to introduce real improvement creates hostility rather than consensus. The public sector strikes, which broke out following the reforms announced in November 1995, are a good example of the dangers reformers are likely to meet. The problem of expenditure on social protection is far from unique to France. The problems are demographic, macroeconomic, and institutional. Demographic, in the sense that the ageing population of France is creating an ever larger number of citizens of retirement age, who live longer than their predecessors, and expect higher standards of health care. The demographic problem will become rapidly more serious when the generations born in the immediate post-war period reach retirement age, around the year 2010. In 1990, the ratio of contributors to retired persons was 2.03, in 2010, the ratio will have fallen to 1.41.

The problem is macroeconomic, at least in France, because some 70% of the revenues of the social security system come from employer and employee contributions, and are based directly on salary levels. As unemployment increases, or to put it another way, since the total level of employment in France has hardly risen over recent years, the revenues of the system do not keep pace with the growth in expenditure. The result has been, in recent years, a growing deficit (FF54.8 billion in 1994, FF64.5 billion in 1995, and an accumulated debt of FF250 billion), which contributes to the general public deficit at a time when the government is trying to meet the Maastricht criteria. But in addition, it is argued, financing the social security budget by what is essentially a tax on employment discourages job creation (see Table 3.3).

Table 3.3 Social security contributions (average worker 1991)

	Employers	Wage earner
	as % of average wage	
France	43.8	17.1
Germany	18.2	18.2
Italy	50.1	9.0
United Kingdom	10.4	7.6
EU	24.2	10.2

© OECD, 1994, *Economic Survey France.*
Reproduced with permission of the OECD.

In France, the problem is also institutional, because reforming the social security system involves reforming a complex organisation, which brings together many conflicting interests. The system covers several aspects of social protection; unemployment assistance, retirement pensions, family assistance, and sickness benefit. In the latter category, for example, there are 19 different systems of medical insurance. There are 538 different arrangements for retirement pensions. In addition, the system has been managed by commissions which represent employers and trade unions. With trade union membership declining the unions have had a direct interest in maintaining the status quo in the social security which assures them status and power.

The reform of the retirement arrangements for the vast bulk of private sector workers (the *régime général*) was carried out by the Balladur government in July 1993. The pension arrangements in France are relatively generous. A worker receiving the minimum wage will retire on 90% of his former income. Higher income earners can expect some 65%. The essence of the reform consisted in slightly prolonging the period of time required to qualify for a full pension from 37.5 to 40 years. Whilst not preventing retirement at 60, the reform does mean that many will have to work beyond 60 to qualify for full rights. The reform also modified calculation of the salary of reference on which the pension is based. The calculation changed from using the last 10 years of salary to using the last 25 years. In this way, it was hoped that enough had been done to ensure that this section of the social security system would remain in balance until the year 2010.

The question of changing the system of retirement pensions from one of income transfer to one of capitalisation was put to one side. There are several arguments against a system of capitalisation. Firstly, the generation of wage earners who had to live through the period of changeover would have to pay double for the new system and for the old one which still depended on them. Again, the pensions would depend on the outcome of an uncertain economic future.

Nor was the question of the special retirement arrangements for the public sector workers dealt with. These were left intact for the next prime minister.

In November 1995, Mr Juppé announced a global reform of the social security system. His proposals were far-ranging. One of the key elements was to widen the role of the special income tax used to finance, in part, the social security expenditure, the *contribution sociale centralisée* (CSG), with a view to replacing some of the employee contributions. He also called for a special tax, the *remboursement de la dette sociale* (RDS), which is to last for 13 years, and will repay the accumulated social security debt. This will be a tax on all revenues levied at the rate of 0.5%. One sickness insurance scheme is ultimately to be installed for all categories, in replacement of the various schemes at present. A variety of cost-cutting measures were to be introduced in hospitals and various aspects of the health system. Finally, two proposals which antagonised the unions were announced. The special retirement schemes for civil servants and other special categories were to be reformed, and Parliament was to be given the right to vote annually on the social security budget. The major part of the reform was pushed through, even if in the face of the strikes Juppé backed down over the reform of the special pension schemes. On the other hand, like all reforms of the social security structure, the future remains unclear. The deficit, which Juppé claimed would be brought down to FF17 billion as a result of the reform, now looks likely to be around FF46 billion for 1996.

3.7 FUTURE PROSPECTS

After an unexpectedly sharp recession in 1993 (GDP −1.5%), and a recovery in 1994 (GDP +2.8%), which did not follow through into 1995 (GDP +2.2%), commentators seem unsure and apprehensive in the summer of 1996. Official forecasts suggest moderate growth of 1.3% for the year 1996, but there seem to be few grounds for certainty. Indeed, a series of indicators showing falling prices give real cause for concern.

Ever since France opted for economic orthodoxy in 1983, and turned its back on a Keynesian reflation which, if continued, would have led France into protectionism rather than European integration, similar economic policies have been followed. The policy of 'austerity' (1983–85) became the policy of 'competitive disinflation' (1985–90), which in turn became the policy of the 'strong franc' (1990–93). The term used to describe the policy changed, but the policy remained intact. From 1993 the Balladur government continued these policies, and despite what was said in the presidential election campaign, the new President, Chirac, in October 1995, reaffirmed his determination to give priority to the respect of the EMU timetable, and the Maastricht criteria. French economic policy has been dominated, then, by three themes: building an inflation-free environment; the retreat of the state from an active role in the economy; and the maintenance of the franc/deutschmark exchange rate parity.

Within this framework many structural reforms have been undertaken with some notable successes. Important changes have been introduced into the labour market and the social security system, Paris is now an important international financial centre, and French industry is performing well in export markets. The public sector has been substantially cut back through widespread privatisations. The efficiency of French industry and commerce can be seen in the foreign trade surpluses.

On the other hand, no real solution has been found to the major problem of unemployment, and none seems at hand. In view of the fiscal consolidation now under way, there is no reason to suppose that growth will accelerate to the level needed to substantially reduce unemployment in the near future. Indeed, preliminary estimates for 1996 suggest that growth will be around 1%, in a conjuncture marked by stable or even falling prices and rapidly growing unemployment.

The machinery required for a more impressive economic performance is in place. What is required is the injection of fuel to get the machinery working at a high speed over a long period.

3.8 BIBLIOGRAPHY AND SOURCES OF INFORMATION

INSEE (monthly): *Economie et Statistique*
INSEE (annual): *Tableaux de l'Economie Française*
INSEE (annual): *L'Economie Française – Rapport sur les Comptes de la Nation*
INSEE (March, July, December): *Note de Conjoncture de l'INSEE*
Ministère de l'Economie (monthly): *Les Notes Bleues de Bercy*
Observatoire Français des Conjonctures Economiques (1995, 1996): *L'économie française*
OECD: *Economic Surveys*, France 1994–95

La Découverte/Credoc (1996–97): *L'Etat de la France*

La Documentation Française (June, 1993): *Evaluation de la situation sociale, économique et financière de la France,* Rapport Raynaud

Le Monde (1995): *L'année économique et sociale*

Useful Sources of Information

Banque de France, 39, rue Croix-des-Petits-Champs, 75001, Paris tel 01-42-92-42-92

Centre Français du Commerce Extérieur, 10 avenue d'Iéna 75783, Paris tel 01-40-73-30-00

Chambre de Commerce et d'Industrie de Paris, 2 rue de Viarmes, 75001 Paris tel 01-45-08-39-20

INSEE, 18 boulevard Adolphe Pinard, 75675 Paris tel 01-41-17-50-50

OFCE, 69 Quai d'Orsay, 75340 Paris tel 01-44-18-54-00

OECD, 2 rue André Pascal, 75775 Paris tel 01-45-24-82-00

CHAPTER 4

Italy

Andrea Fineschi
Carmela Nicosia

4.1 INSTITUTIONAL AND HISTORICAL CONTEXT

4.1.1 Institutional framework

Italy is a parliamentary democracy, with the government chosen not directly by the electorate, but requiring the support of Parliament (the Chamber of Deputies and the Senate). With the exception of the 1948–53 period immediately following the approval of the Constitution and during which the Christian Democratic Party has had an absolute majority in Parliament, Italy had a succession of coalition governments for the entire post-war period. These governments have been very unstable mainly because of the proportional electoral rule which, in its previous pure form (before the recent introduction of a mixed electoral system), allowed the continual presence of many political parties in Parliament.

The first important changes in the political structure occurred in the early 1960s and the second half of the 1970s. In the first period, the Socialist Party participated for the first time in a coalition government in which its majority partner was the Christian Democratic Party. In the second half of the 1970s, a national unity government was formed with the support of the Communist Party.

The instability of the political system has had several economic consequences. It has resulted in a preference for monetary policy, carried out by the more stable financial institutions. Fiscal policy has been used as a short-term expedient but rarely practiced in a 'radical way' (as it was used by other countries after the oil crisis). It is only since 1992 that fiscal policy has been systematically used as tool of macroeconomic policy.

The need to reconcile differing, and often contradictory, political interests has been a major determinant of policy choice in post-war Italy. Thus, in the early 1950s, whereas economic policy was clearly oriented towards market deregulation and refusal of Keynesian policies, large-scale state enterprises were developed in several essential sectors of the economy. Nor is it fortuitous that in recent years, despite the official support to the free market economic policy, the size of the state enterprise sector has only been slightly reduced. These contradictions emerge out of political compromise.

In addition, the Italian administrative structure is a fragmented system of self-governing local units (regions, provinces and boroughs) whose finance is controlled by the central government. This power structure makes both the day-to-day running of the local authorities and the implementation of new government policy measures particularly complex. In order to increase the efficiency of local government administration, a proposal of institutional reform provides for the introduction of an 'administrative federalism', implying a simplification of the tax system and a transfer of powers and responsibility to different levels of local government (municipal, provincial and regional).

The proportional electoral system, and the consequent coalition governments, have been major contributory factors to the serious state of public debt in recent decades. For example, though a strict control of public expenditure would have been an obvious policy choice in the face of economic difficulties following the oil shocks of 1973–74 and 1979–80, it would have destroyed coalition governments in which component parties represented different social interests and different regions of the country.

In spite of the instability of coalition governments Italy has, until recently, experienced a relatively stable political majority supporting the government. Electoral results after the Second World War and the emergence of the 'Cold War' were influenced by the so-called 'factor K' – a *conventio ad excludendum* from government of the Communist Party, which was the most representative of the Italian working class. The 'factor K' disappeared with the end of the 'Cold War' and the disintegration of the Soviet Union. The 1992 parliamentary elections and the following local elections overturned the traditional majority. In the last election in 1996 the centre-left parties' coalition ('The Olive') prevailed and led for the first time to a left-oriented government. Political scientists defined the Italian democratic system before 1992 as a 'locked' democracy, because of the lack of alternating governments. However, this opinion must be reviewed in the light of the latest 'left turn' of the Italian government.

In recent years a structural revolution occurred in the political composition as a consequence of two main events. First, the division of the Communist Party has led to two separate left parties, one more moderate and the other going back to the old Communist Party. Second, the judicial operation 'clean hands', aimed to investigate on the transparency and fairness of the conduction of public affairs, has led to the disappearance of the Socialist and Christian Democratic Parties, both turned upside down by the inquiries which laid their last decade's illegal activities bare. The inquiries of 'clean hands' against political corruption, which has been unfortunately one of the most typical features of Italian governments (particularly in the 1980s), have been quite numerous and effective. Apart from some sceptic views, the general feeling is that the 'clean hands' operation could lead to the legal prosecution of corrupt politicians and to a 'cleaner' public administration in the future.

The most significant change in the Italian political structure, however, was the abolition in 1993, by means of a public referendum, of the proportional electoral system in its pure form, and the parliamentary passage of a new electoral law. The introduction of this new mixed electoral structure – a plurality system with some seats awarded according to proportional rule – gave origin to the current political bipolarism characterised by two large groups, one of centre-right and the other of centre-left. This change could imply a poorer representation of different views and a weaker impact of voter behaviour on the electoral outcome. However, it made possible a reduction of party fragmentation which has been leading to collusive behaviour between electorate and representatives, political corruption inside and among parties, and high 'positional rents' reaped by politicians (Mudambi *et al.* 1996; Nicosia 1996).

It is too early to draw definitive conclusions and judgements about both the political result of the new electoral law and the last government's conduct. The expectation, however, is that different political forces alternating in the government of the country, under the new electoral system, could reduce political 'corruption'. The process of institutional change has been also determined by the pressure of an enormous public debt. The hope, well supported by international economic research in the field (Alesina and Tabellini, 1987), is that Italy will be successful in reducing public debt in a context of more stable and authoritative governments. This thesis would seem to be supported by the actual government's conduct, strictly oriented towards restrictive economic policies in order to keep inflation low and to reduce public debt. However, as we have already pointed out, any definitive judgement at this point in time would be premature.

4.1.2 Political structure and the trade unions

The nature of the political structure of Italian democracy has also had repercussions on relationships among workers' organisations and the relationship between workers' organisations and the government. The organisations representing workers and employers' interests certainly have a strong influence on the economy, as is often the case in countries with liberal–democratic political structures.

Organised labour in Italy is represented by three main trade unions (*Confederazione Generale Italiana dei Lavoratori, CGIL; Confederazione Italiana Sindacale dei Lavoratori, CISL;* and *Unione Italiana dei Lavoratori, UIL*) organised according to productive sector, rather than by occupation. However, in recent years, a number of small unions have emerged which are occupationally based and independent of the three major unions.

The origin of the main trade unions can be traced back to the various political parties to which they were linked. For example, the CGIL was linked to the Communist and Socialist parties and the CISL to the Christian Democratic Party. The link between unions and political parties, made more complex by inter-party relationships, and the exclusion of the Communist Party from government, though its supporters and members formed a majority in the largest union CGIL, explain the reluctance of the unions to assume a unified position with regard to government policy. This was especially true when large-scale social agreements were proposed by the government. Because of the influence of the latest political upheaval (see Section 4.1.1) government–unions relationships have changed and trade unions' independence from political parties seems to have increased significantly. The agreement of July 1993 between industry and unions about the cost of labour has provided for a limitation of nominal wages growth to the level of inflation. This is important because of the obvious positive effects in controlling price inflation. Finally, as in all industrialised countries, the strength of the unions and their ability to represent Italian workers depends to a large extent on the stage of economic development, the level of unemployment, the political climate, firm size and ownership, whether private or state.

4.1.3 Social policy

The influence of the European Union social policy on the evaluation of national objectives and the discussion about the social dimension of state intervention have led to the need to redefine the limits of the Italian Welfare State. It is not only a political problem but also involves ethical and moral aspects. The question concerns all the areas of public intervention in relation to social policy: health care, workers' pension schemes and workers' insurance against accidents.

The national health system provides free assistance for both Italian citizens and foreign residents who demand its services. Established during the 1970s, it operates through a system of local health centres (*Unita' Sanitarie Locali, USL*) and it is financed by transfers from the State to the Regions, and then from the Regions to each centre. This structure of the health system, and the increasing costs of health assistance, have led to a significant rise of public expenditure on health services from the mid-1970s, creating serious financial difficulties. In the 1980s, the increasing demand for health services (associated with higher national income) and technological development in the medical field led to a rationing of health care publicly provided and to the development of competition between the public and private system. The reorganisation of the health system must be viewed in the wider context of the policies to balance public accounts. With the legal revision of the health service system, the previous principle of universality has been redefined. Whereas the dimension of universal and unconditional access to the health service has not been modified, the aspect of financial contribution has been modulated according to the user's income.

Istituto Nazionale per l'Assicurazione contro gli Infortuni sul Lavoro (INAIL), is the public institution financed by workers and employers, providing for employees in case of accident at work. In this regard, a recent regulation (1995) about workers' safety obliges staff training against the risk of accidents at work.

In the Italian pension scheme, pensions are paid through *Istituto Nazionale per la Previdenza Sociale (INPS)*, an institute also financed by the compulsory contributions of workers and employers. In the context of the above-mentioned reorganisation of the Welfare State, the pension system has been recently modified by a law of social security reform which will become effective as from 2001 after a long period of provisional regulation. The new regulations abolish retirement pensions (obtainable after 35 years of duty and contribution, without age limits), and provide for a single form of 'old age pension' (obtainable only at retirement age and with a minimum period of contribution fixed by law), and for pensions' harmonisation in the public and private sectors. The previous pay-based system of pensions' calculation (on the basis of a salary assessment over recent working years) has been replaced with a new contribution-based system, on the basis of contributions proportional to the salary paid during the workers' active life. The new form of social security guarantees a balance between revenue and expenditure, thus limiting the effect of revenue expansion associated with the previous system.

The state system for the unemployed operates differently from those in the countries of northern and central Europe. There are varying levels of assistance for workers. Because of the social and political importance of mass dismissals, workers in large firms are specifically protected by the *cassa integrazione guadagni* scheme, that is a wage-related unemployment benefit scheme which applies both in ordinary cases of temporary lay-off, and in case of much longer periods of unemployment. Workers dismissed by small firms and people looking for their first jobs are given much less protection. If they are registered as unemployed, they are eligible for only a small benefit for a comparatively short period.

4.1.4 Market regulations

European Union competition law does not replace national anti-trust legislation which can co-exist as parallel law at the internal level in so far as it does not hinder the uniform application throughout the European rules on cartels. In the case of Italy, the first organic body of domestic rules on competition came into force only in 1990. As a consequence, anti-trust rules are less developed in Italy in comparison with other member countries (such as the UK and Germany) with older traditions in this field.

Three different institutions supervise market competition in the Italian economy: the *Autorita' garante della concorrenza e del mercato* has general responsibility for ensuring markets are competitive; the *Autorita' garante per l'editoria* supervises market competition in the specific field of the media; the Bank of Italy is responsible for overseeing competition in the banking and insurance sector.

The country's anti-trust law is not based on the old (neo-) classical model of perfect competition; in accordance with EU anti-trust rules applying to anti-competitive behaviour and governing the control of concentrations within the European market (articles 85, 86 and 90 of the Treaty of Rome, see Chapter 1 about competition policy), the assessment as to whether competition rules are infringed is dictated not simply by company size but rather on the basis of the actual market power that a company (or group of companies) possesses. For example, though FIAT produces almost all Italian cars, it is not considered to abuse a dominant market position, affecting the market's outcome by exercising monopoly power, unless it does so by colluding with foreign companies.

The level of competition in the manufacturing sector is quite satisfactory when compared to that prevailing in other European countries, largely due to the liberalisation of foreign trade. Nevertheless, protected sectors continue to exist, especially in the service sector, and this is one of the major causes of the higher level of inflation frequently experienced by the Italian economy.

The law limiting firms in the field of the media regulates the television market, divided between the State (*Radio Televisione Italiana, RAI*) and the private corporation *Fininvest*, and the press (mostly daily papers), controlled by a handful of large publishing groups, often owned by the important industrial groups. The main function of this law is to consider simultaneously the two kinds of information and to limit the market power of the companies in the whole market. In order to guarantee pluralism, an important judgement of the Constitutional Court (December 1994) established that any private subject is not allowed to control more than 20% of the national networks. The new anti-trust law in the field of the media, likely to be passed by 1997, and the *Stet* (public telecommunications) privatisation should promote the development of the telecommunications' sector.

The extent of market competition in the banking sector is limited. Nevertheless, the objective of achieving more competition needs to be reconciled with the fact that banks have to be large in order to compete in the European market. A boost to the expansion of Italian credit institutions is also coming from the recent process of radical reorganisation which is occurring in the Italian banking system after the introduction of the 'universal bank' model in 1993 (see Section 4.4.2).

4.1.5 Historical context

During the late 1960s and early 1970s western economies were characterised by a significant level of social conflict in relation to both the distribution of income and industrial relations. In Italy, compared with other western countries, this was a long-lasting and deep-rooted conflict, especially in the 1970s, when a rediscovered sense of trade union unity gave workers' organisations a strong negotiating position.

The prices of raw materials began to increase at the end of the 1960s, followed by an unexpected and sudden rise in the price of oil (1973–74). Inflation hit the Italian economy when it was already suffering deep social conflict. The 1975 agreement between trade unions and the main employers' organisation (*Confindustria*) on linking

wages to the rate of inflation – the wage indexation scale (*scala mobile*), later abolished by public referendum – was considered by the *Confindustria* to be an instrument for lessening the conflict over the distribution of income and for improving industrial relations. It was also welcomed by the trade unions as it gave automatic protection to real wages against sharp price increases (including those of imported goods affected by the constant devaluation of the lira). Exchange rate depreciation and expansion of public spending simply dampened down the bitter social conflict of the 1970s and postponed resolution of the problem to a later date. The sharp rise in public spending, due to the social security and health legislation in the mid-1970s, (at a time when there was a loss of potential revenue due to delays in introducing tax reform), considerably increased the negative difference between fiscal revenues and current expenditure, and made public debt progressively grow. The systematic devaluation of the lira also helped to reduce social conflict since it meant that the vicious circle of price and salary increases did not halt economic growth.

From 1977, trade unions became less aggressive (during the period of the national unity government, 1976–79). This, together with a foreign exchange policy oriented towards a strong national currency *vis-à-vis* the dollar (the currency in which raw materials and energy supplies were paid for), yet floating in regard to other European currencies, meant that in the late 1970s, there was less inflation, a recovery in investment and an improvement in the foreign trade balance.

The second wave of oil price increases (1979–80) hit Italy when its economy was in a phase of strong growth. This continued until the second half of 1980 making it difficult to control inflation, and accentuating the trade deficit. The delay in adjusting to the international economic cycle worsened the problem of inflation and foreign debt.

In the late 1970s and early 1980s there were significant changes in Italian monetary, financial and foreign exchange policy, reflecting changes which had occurred in the world economy. In 1979, Italy's entry into the EMS constrained

Italian economic policy and removed a great deal of its discretionary power to influence the currency's value. Although Italy suffered a worsening of its foreign commercial accounts, the government's indication to the employers and unions that price increases would not be accompanied by devaluation exerted a downward influence on the inflation rate.

In 1982, the 'divorce' of the Central Bank from the Treasury relieved the Bank of Italy of the obligation to act as 'buyer of last resort' at the auctions of public debt bonds. This measure changed the policy of financing the public debt, which shifted from issuing public debt bonds (outside the market) through the banking system, to financing the debt largely through the market itself. As a consequence of both the above-mentioned 'divorce' and the entry to the EMS, Italian real interest rates rose sharply in the early 1980s (reaching levels above those of the 1970s and indeed of other countries in the industrialised world) so increasing the cost of servicing public debt.

In the early 1980s the major companies, helped by the white-collar work-force, took action (dismissals of workers who were members of extremist organisations, movement of employees from one place to another, measures to lay workers off) to reduce the negotiating power of trade unions inside the factories. During the 1980s, however, according to all the indicators (see Figure 4.1) social conflict diminished, thus leading to a recovery of the major companies' profitability.

The period of growth came to an end in the early 1990s when the effects of the world economic depression began to impact on Italy. The devaluation of the national currency inside the EMS in September 1992, immediately followed by the lira's exit from the European Exchange Rate Mechanism (ERM) left the currency freely floating in the market and brought an end to the exchange rate policy started in the late 1970s. The impact of devaluation was immediately positive in terms of the current balance and, because of the low level of domestic aggregate demand, it did not immediately result in increases in prices. The economic situation in Italy since 1993 has been characterised by GDP growth and relatively low inflation. Output increased rapidly owing to the

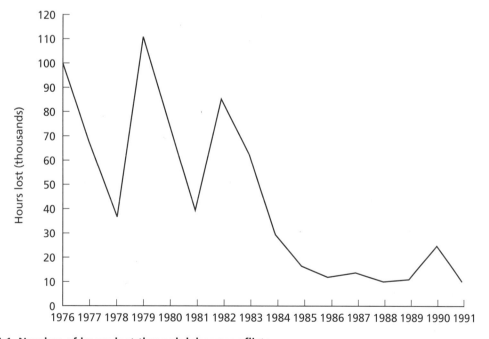

Figure 4.1 Number of hours lost through labour conflicts

Source: ISTAT.

greater competitiveness of Italian exports, productive investments, and profit margins. However, the rate of unemployment has remained fairly stable at about 11%. From the end of 1995, a new phase of decreasing production started. As a consequence of restrictive policies designed to achieve the convergence criteria set by the Maastricht Treaty, a drop in domestic demand for consumption and investment resulted in a decline of GDP growth (1.8% in 1996, data of May, Table G23) coupled with still very high unemployment. Although the Italian economy is currently showing a slowdown, some important improvements can be noticed in terms of exchange rate appreciation and stability, low inflation (which is back to the levels of late 1960s), a favourable balance of trade and a permanent primary surplus in the public accounts (public revenues surplus on public expenditure net of interests on public debt).

4.2 MAIN ECONOMIC CHARACTERISTICS

4.2.1 Gross domestic product

The estimation of gross domestic product (GDP) is especially difficult in the case of Italy because of the significant quantity of products and services traded within the 'black economy' which escape measurement by *Istituto Centrale di Statistica (ISTAT)*. Examples include people having several jobs but officially registered only in one, people who are not legally employed, and people working at home so to avoid paying taxes. However, more recent ISTAT's estimates of national income, with black market activity taken into consideration, can be considered fairly reliable.

From 1983 to 1988 Italy experienced a phase of relatively high growth (see Figure 4.2). It is interesting to note the time lag by which the Italian economy experienced the effects of the second oil shock which was responsible for the delay in recovery in the early 1980s. Thus, the average rate of growth of 2.2% in the period 1981–90 is a relatively favourable result when we consider the extremely poor performance of the economy in the 1981–82 period.

The trend moved clearly downwards at the end of the 1980s to reach the worst performance in 1993, in line with other European countries like France and the United Kingdom (see Table G23). The years 1994 and 1995 have been characterised by fast productive growth, one of the highest in the most industrialised countries (see Table G23 and Figure 4.2), and mainly due to the compo-

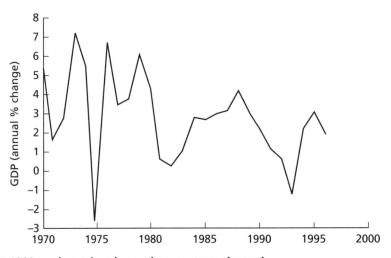

Figure 4.2 GDP at 1990 market prices (annual percentage change)

Source: Statistical Annexe of European Economy, Eurostat, Table G23.

nents of exports and domestic investments. If we consider the value in 1995 of per capita GDP (see Table G24) measured in PPS (Eur15=100), the Italian level of 104.7 should be interpreted as a very good performance by central and northern Italy, given the marked difference in per capita income existing between the south and the centre–north (see Section 4.6.1). Italian industry (mainly chemical, iron and steel) has benefited by favourable economic trends, such as the lira's devaluation, increase in exports and lower labour cost. However, this did not contribute to an increase in employment. From the end of 1995, a decline in economic activity occurred once more. The 1.8% percentage increase in GDP in 1995 (at 1990 market prices) is a significant slow-down in comparison with the two previous years. The restrictive policies of the last four years, coupled with a general lack of confidence, have led to a decline in consumption demand. Overall investments have decreased by 1.7% (see Table G30), and mainly in the public sector. The margins of productive capacity, although subject to a relative reduction in all the sectors, have shown different trends in different areas of the country. Whereas in the centre–north regions there has been a relative expansion due to the strong presence of export firms, the recovery has been very weak in the south regions.

4.2.2 Employment and unemployment

The high rate of unemployment is currently one of the most serious economic problems, not only in Italy but in all the EU countries.

The phases of upturn in GDP during the 1980s and 1990s have failed to alleviate the problem of unemployment in Italy as a whole. While most of the north and the centre of the country have experienced almost full employment, the south and the islands (Sicily and Sardinia) have continued to suffer high and rising unemployment. Since the mid-1970s the Italian working population (due to the post-war birth explosion and the increase in active population which typically follows a phase of intense urbanisation) has grown faster than new jobs have been created, leading to a steady increase in unemployment over the period since the mid-1970s (see Figure 4.3).

In the late 1980s, data relating to Italy as a whole show that the level of unemployment fell slightly (see Section 4.6.1 on the trends of unemployment in the different regions). The onset of recession from 1990, however, saw unemployment resuming its upward path, reflecting the world recession and the restrictive fiscal policy necessitated by the huge public debt. As in other EU countries, young people,

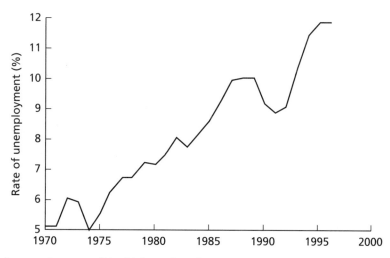

Figure 4.3 Rate of unemployment (% of labour force)

Source: Statistical Annexe of European Economy, Eurostat, Table G20.

women and less qualified people are the most likely groups to be affected by unemployment. The level of unemployment in the north of the country is low even compared with the best performing European economies. The worsening of unemployment levels in recent years (mainly linked to deficits in public finances) has concerned the Mezzogiorno of Italy where the current unemployment rate is 21% compared with 7.8% in the centre–north regions. Moreover, the tendency for large companies (with over 500 employees) to implement a policy of almost continuous reduction in the size of their work-force has been counteracted by job creation in small- and medium-sized firms which are more numerous in the north and central areas. This helps to account for the contrast in unemployment levels between these areas and the south.

The employment structure in terms of the relative shares of the three traditional productive sectors (agriculture, industry and services) has broadly followed the usual patterns for industrialising economies. Table 4.1 shows the evolution through time of the various sectors of employment, indicating the speed with which the structure of the Italian economy has been transformed from a largely agricultural economy in the early 1950s to a mature industrial economy (in 1988 less than 10% of work-force was employed in the primary sector). It is interesting to note that the proportion of people currently employed in industry is much lower than at its peak at the end of the 1960s. This reflects a distinct feature of the more recently industrialised economies, which have quickly adopted modern labour-saving techniques. Moreover, according to the latest figures, the proportion of agricultural workers in Italy is progressively declining and is not so high as it was in comparison with most industrialised countries. This fact could be explained, on the one hand, by the decreasing importance of the agricultural sector relatively to the industry and services sectors and, on the other, by the process of decreasing labour-intensity of agricultural cultivation in Italy.

Table 4.1 Employment by sector

Sector	1954	1966	1981	1988	1995
Agriculture	39.9	24.9	13.4	9.9	3.9
Industry	32.8	40.7	37.5	32.5	32.4
Services	27.3	34.4	49.1	57.5	63.7
Total	100	100	100	100	100

Source: ISTAT.

4.2.3 Consumption and savings

Consumption has been a fairly stable component in aggregate demand, although the items consumed have changed a great deal in the post-war period and especially in the last two decades. There has been a reduction in the share of spending devoted to foodstuffs and an increase in that going to services. This development, as well as changes in the composition and type of products consumed, followed the same pattern as those of countries experiencing industrialisation at an earlier date.

In recent years a change in consumption demand occurred. The increase in consumer expenditure, even if positive in nominal value, started to become weaker than the growth of GDP. Consumer expenditure as a percentage of GDP has shown a decrease of 0.6% from 1993 to 1995 (from 62% to 61.4%, see Table G28). According to ISTAT estimates about families' consumption, a serious gap emerged between the north and the south of the country where the percentage of families living under the poverty threshold (22%) is double that of the north. The slowdown in consumer expenditure is concerning almost all the industrial sectors, even in the textile–clothing industry, which is generally experiencing demand for exports, and in the foodstuffs sector whose demand is relatively inelastic by definition. Such an unfavourable trend of consumption expenditure is a consequence of different factors. It is partly the effect of a restrictive fiscal policy and income stagnation, and is also a consequence of structural factors like negative expectations (uncertainty about future perspectives for employment and income, price slowdowns and expectations of further price reductions induce to postponement of consumption expenditure).

The level of total savings as a proportion of income is particularly high in Italy. The share of total savings accumulated by families reached the level of two thirds at the beginning of the 1990s (from one third at the end of the 1970s), including a high proportion of government bonds. In the future, however, the gradual balancing of public accounts will probably lower this proportion in the financial portfolio of Italian families.

Among other industrialised countries, Japan is the only country which has a higher savings/income ratio. Family savings are especially high in comparison with other countries also because both Italy and Japan have a large number of family firms whose savings are counted as family and not company savings. Company savings increased during the 1980s and 1990s as a consequence of higher profits, and the generally high levels of self-financing among firms has been restored. A high rate of company profits has always been the policy of the central bank, not only because it is an extremely strong stimulus to investment but also because a high level of self-financing means greater flexibility in the firm decision-making.

4.2.4 Investment

In order to evaluate the Italian investment trends in the 1980s it is necessary to consider the various investment items and leave aside investment in real estate, as trends in the latter depend on very specific factors which are usually dissimilar to the motivations for other types of investment. Investment in plant and machinery is particularly significant in terms of industrial performance. This item has been consistently positive in the period since 1982, particularly in the second half of the 1980s, owing to the growing proportions of investment expenditure devoted to expanding productive capacity. The company investment trend in the 1980s (plant and machinery) has been especially impressive. If total investment as a proportion of GDP for the 1980s is less than that of the 1950s or the early 1960s, this is largely due to the fact that there has been less invest-

ment in the housing sector and by the State. The total investment trend, excluding investment in real estate, is more in line with other industrialised countries. Moreover, breaking down the figures for investment in the construction sector, we see that investment by industry in new factories has returned to a high level in the late 1980s and the modest overall figure is due to public investment spending (roads, ports, drains etc.) restricted by financial constraints. After decreasing at the end of 1980s and the early 1990s, as is clearly shown in Figure 4.4, investment has been the most dynamic component of internal demand in 1994 and 1995, favoured by external demand and fiscal incentives. The gross fixed capital investment (mainly plant and machinery) has grown by 5.9% at constant 1990 prices, one of the highest rates among the major European countries (see Table G30). In a context of high long-term interest rates (see Table G36), the financing of this intense investment activity has been easily satisfied by having recourse to self-financing, made possible by a very good profitability. From the end of 1995, a decline of confidence regarding the future internal and international economy has caused (not only in Italy but in some of the major European economies) a slowdown in investment activity.

4.2.5 Inflation

Inflation in Italy, in the 1970s and the 1980s, has been closely related to the oil price trend as well as to the negotiating strength of the trade unions. The inflation rate, particularly high during the major increases in oil prices (1973–74 and 1979–80), gradually reduced during the second half of the 1970s and the downward trend continued in the 1980s as a result of the large reduction in the oil price and the sharp fall of the dollar in 1985 (see Figure 4.5). A further downward influence on the rate of increase in prices in the 1980s came from the forced abandonment of the practice of systematically devaluing the lira, following Italy's entry into the European Monetary System in 1979.

In the period following the oil shocks, price rises were experienced by most countries in the

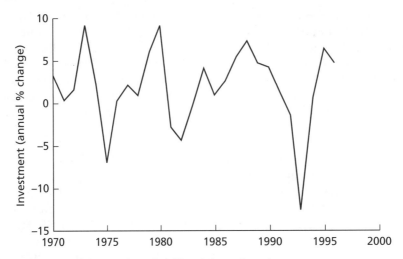

Figure 4.4 Investment: annual change (% of civilian labour force)

Source: Statistical Annexe of European Economy, Eurostat, Table G30.

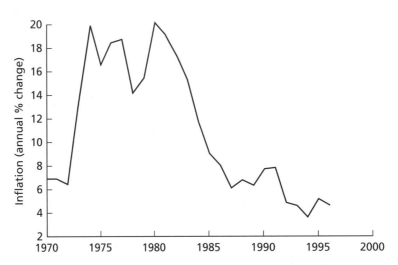

Figure 4.5 Inflation (price deflator GDP) (at market prices, annual % change)

Source: Statistical Annexe of European Economy, Eurostat, Table G31.

western world, but the level of Italian inflation was particularly high in comparison with other industrialised countries. The inflation rate differential between Italy and other major economies decreased significantly during the second half of the 1980s. In 1993, in spite of a significant devaluation of the Italian lira against the major currencies, Italian inflation (4.4%, Table G31) was in line with that of its major European trading partners.

After an increase of 1.5% in 1994–95 (the effect of both the exchange rate depreciation and rise in consumer price) which widened the gap with respect to German and French inflation rates more than 3%, many external factors have contributed to a further reduction in inflation rate. Some of these factors are typically structural, like the adoption of a restrictive monetary policy, the abolition of the automatic system of wage indexation and the achievement of a permanent primary surplus in the public accounts (excess of public revenues over expenditure net of the interest on public debt). Some other factors are relating to the economic situation, like the lira appreciation, the slow-down in consumer expenditure and the high unemployment rate. Exchange rate trend and business cycle have effectively worked to the decline of inflation rate to less than 4% during 1996.

Growth and low inflation are not necessarily incompatible. A low inflation rate tends to reduce nominal interest rate, thus decreasing government spending for debt payments and providing incentives for economic growth.

4.2.6 Market structure

Until recently, before the change in the ownership and control structure of some large companies (like Ferruzzi and Olivetti), Italian market structure has tended to be dominated by the presence of a small group of families owning a significant proportion of the largest private companies. This ownership characteristic has resulted in a substantial concentration of economic power and it has also restricted the development of the Italian stock-exchange market.

Before the recent privatisation, State-owned firms constituted a considerable element in many industrial sectors. The extent of Italian state-ownership can be partly explained by state intervention to save a number of banks (and firms owned by those banks, see also Section 4.4.1) from collapse in the years of the great depression after 1929. In addition, a large number of firms were established or purchased by the state in recent decades to create or maintain employment, especially in the south. The process of privatisation is now changing the internal allocation of ownership and control of some state holdings and state-controlled enterprises, thus transforming the structure of the Italian market.

The Italian organisational structure, when analysed according to firm size, is characterised by a large number of small firms, which is an unusual characteristic for an industrialised economy (see Section 4.6.2). In recent decades, the output of 'modern' sectors with high rates of technological development has come to account for an increasing proportion of the total. However, still important are the 'mature' or 'traditional' industrial sectors in which technology appears to have reached the point where further improvement is limited. Although it is easy for countries in earlier phases of industrialisation to enter these sectors, the Italian experience shows that product differentiation, design and flexibility, play so important a role in a number of 'traditional industries' that it is entirely possible for countries with relatively high labour costs (like Italy) to compete successfully against those with low labour costs.

4.2.7 Income distribution

The pattern of income distribution changed during the 1980s as a result of an increase in the profits of major companies and a reduced rate of increase in wages. Because of the public debt 'demonetarisation' policy (following the separation of the Bank of Italy from the treasury), the state paid a much higher volume of interest on public debt bonds. Since most of the bonds are owned by the relatively well-off sections of the population, the change in public debt financing redistributed incomes towards the higher income classes. Increasing profits and decreasing wages also characterise income distribution in recent years. The increase of the profit share in the domestic income is explained by the higher average labour productivity; the decrease in wages is partly due to the government policy aimed to put an end to increases in public sector wages.

From the geographical point of view, in the last two decades there has been a progressive increase in the per capita income gap between the centre–north and the south of the country, where the concentration of poor families (whose consumption expenditure is lower than the half of the domestic average) is much higher. This kind of territorial income redistribution is analysed in greater depth in Section 4.6.1.

4.3 GOVERNMENT INVOLVEMENT IN THE ECONOMY

4.3.1 Expenditure, revenues and public debt

During the last two decades, public expenditure has increased at an average annual rate above the

EU average, reaching its peak in 1993 (see Table G32). However, this level of expenditure has not been accompanied by the required improvement in the services offered to the public and industry. This trend of increasing public spending has been reversed since 1993 because of the influence of both the poor productivity of the public service sector and the reduction in expenditure on social services and state investment. Public expenditure on transfers and interest paid on public debt (whose trend is shown in Figure 4.6) account for most of the public expenditure budget. According to the last figures (May 1996), the percentage of total government expenditure as a component of GDP is 52%.

Looking back at the last twenty years, a sharp increase in the state expenditure occurred from the second half of the 1970s until the early 1980s. It was mainly due to transfers to families and firms as well as payments of interest on the state debt bonds. A large part of the growth in public debt in the 1970s is explained by the lag between increase in expenditure and corresponding rise in revenues, due to a delay in putting tax reforms into practice. The accumulation of an extremely high level of public debt has been accompanied by an increasing burden to service the debt, especially from the early 1980s when the rates of

interest naturally rose sharply as debt was serviced in the market (as a consequence of the 'divorce' of the Bank of Italy from Treasury).

From 1992, and for the first time in the post-war period, fiscal policy has been systematically adopted by the Italian government. In the period 1992–96 the government action to rebalance public accounts has been considerable compared to other European countries. A restrictive fiscal policy conducted both by cutting government expenditure for health and national insurance and by interventions on the tax-revenues side, together with the privatisation of national state enterprises, have reduced budget deficit/GDP and public debt/GDP ratios. The extent of the public deficit (measured as a percentage of GDP) for 1996 is around 4%, close to the fixed European standard of 3%, whereas the total gross public debt represents the most negative characteristic of the Italian economy. Although slightly declining (after 15 years of progressive growth) in consequence of the above-mentioned policies, public debt/GDP ratio (124.5%, data of May 1996, see Table G9 and Figure 4.7) is very high compared with the convergence criterion of 60% fixed by the Maastricht Treaty.

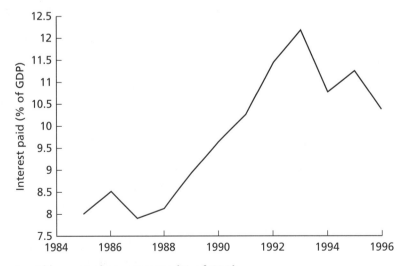

Figure 4.6 Interest paid by central government (% of GDP)

Source: Statistical Annexe of European Economy, Eurostat, Table G9.

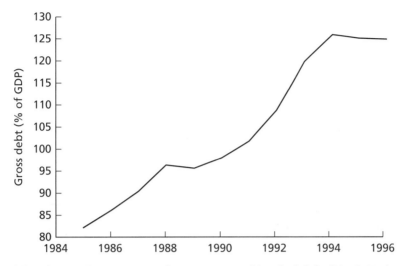

Figure 4.7 Gross debt of central government (average annual level of debt (% of GDP)

Source: Statistical Annexe of European Economy, Eurostat, Table G9.

4.3.2 Industrial policy

During the 1980s Italian industrial policy has been mainly concentrated on promoting the process of 'restructuring' among the major industrial companies (see Section 4.5.1), especially those which were the focus of the bitter social conflict in the 1970s. State enterprise like *Istituto per la Ricostruzione Industriale (IRI)*, *Ente Nazionale Idrocarburi (ENI)* and *Ente partecipazione e Finanziamento Industrie Manifatturiere (EFIM)* suffered serious financial losses. The state facilitated the recovery of profits and investment by transferring financial resources to industries (through subsidies to production, payments for workers laid off for short/long periods, and support for technological innovations). These measures have eased the social conflict which often accompanies a policy of industrial restructuring.

Privatisation of state-owned firms is one of the most important targets of the 1990s government policy directed to redefining the nature of government intervention in the economy – from producer state to regulating state. In the first place it offers a means of reducing the size of financial resources transferred from the state to state-owned enterprises for purposes of covering operating losses. Secondly, it should help

government regain the confidence of the most relevant 'rating houses' and international finance companies who consider privatisation as a means of achieving a recovery in Italian public finances. Finally, the process of privatisation is considered a way of both improving efficiency in managing the privatised companies and reducing the risk of corruption. On the other hand, achieving privatisation is made more difficult due to the extent of the financial problems afflicting the major private Italian companies and the reluctance of foreign industrial groups to purchase some Italian state-owned assets, given the unstable economic and political environment. From the perspective of the seller (the state), the problem is one of how to sell the heavily loss-making industrial companies as well as those with budget surpluses and at the same time avoid the risk of being left with the financially weak companies, having lost the possibility of cross-subsidising these via profits from stronger companies.

The way of conducting privatisation of state holdings – telecommunications Stet, oil group *Ente Nazionale Idrocarburi (ENI)*, electric energy *Ente Nazionale per Energia Elettrica (ENEL)* and banking – is going to affect the economic structure of the Italian system. The main criticism about the first phase of privatisation (1993–96) does not concern the amount of sales realised (30 000 billions of liras, not very different from the values realised in similar periods of time in other major European economies) but rather the lack of a precise institutional plan of reform. A general plan, involving the structure of the financial system, the level of competition in public utilities' markets and the rules of corporate governance of privatised companies, is the prerequisite to conduct privatisations as a route to growth and not simply as a reallocation of control from a public to a private monopolistic administration. In the specific case of Stet privatisation, the telecommunications holding, the process of privatisation will take place under the supervision of a control authority with the power to regulate the tariffs discipline, promote market liberalisation and define the future structure of the sector. Telecommunications is characterised by significant economies of scale and scope (advantage of supplying different products) producing high barriers to entry and highly concentrated industrial structures. This makes important a regulatory activity of an authority of experts which protects and promotes competition. A possible limitation of the plan for Stet privatisation is the association of golden share (a special right of veto given to the government on some decisions) potentially *sine die*, plus a 'stable ownership group', since the presence of a golden share would actually make sense only in the case of 'public companies' whose ownership is typically dispersed. The question of ownership and control allocation is particularly relevant for the case of Stet (more than ENI and ENEL) because it operates in a sector where the rapid technological development and the high level of investment activity require more guarantees that shareholders will exercise their role as owners and not only as cash-flows takers.

The banking privatisations must be considered particularly important because of the interaction of financial institutions with the industrial system through shareholdings (even under precise constraints). Intimately linked to the process of privatisations, the question of corporate governance involves both the aspects of monitoring management of the privatised companies and the problem to define administrative and accounting responsibilities of managers and auditors. The objective of privatisation – more efficiency and competition, higher profits and market value – cannot be fully reached if the process of privatisation does not lead to a new control and ownership structure, maximising the convergence of interests between managers and shareholders and the final performance of the privatised companies. Empirical estimates for British financial institutions indicate that a high ownership dispersion is not always associated with a situation of insufficient control upon managerial conduct and therefore with a worse performance (Mudambi and Nicosia, 1997). However, the Anglo-Saxon model of the 'public company' characterised by highly dispersed ownership, (although offering the advantage of not involving just one controlling group to which management must be responsible for its administration), does not allow an effective monitoring of managerial choices unless there are efficient external mechanisms (like the threat of take-overs) and institutional investors for managerial control, which require a well-developed stock exchange market. In this regard, the low level of competition in the 'market for corporate control' (where it is possible to get information or to buy shares with the specific purpose of acquiring control over companies, typically the stock exchange market) has been the main obstacle to the managerial and strategic renewal of the banking sector. The lack of an efficient system for managerial control is the main reason why an 'intermediate' model (linking dispersed ownership to a stable holding group) seems to be, at least in the short run, the ownership structure to be preferred in order to optimise the performance of the Italian privatised financial institutions (Nicosia, 1996).

4.3.3 Environmental policy

The causes of environmental pollution in Italy are those typical of any industrialised country:

industrial processes, the use of chemicals in agriculture and the expansion in both the quantity and quality of consumer commodities. The level of environmental pollution depends on the ability of public administration to face the problem and, from this point of view, Italy has room for improvement. Different types of pollution characterise the different regions of Italy. In contrast to the north and the industrialised parts of the country (especially in the Po valley), the south does not suffer the consequences of intensive industrialisation but experiences pollution problems related to ineffective urban and land planning, overuse of soil resources and inadequate arrangements for dealing with waste materials. Air pollution in the towns and cities is a general problem, resulting from the excessive use of private cars, which, in turn, reflects the inadequacy of public transport.

Italy's environmental regulation has emerged only in the last ten years as an independent set of regulations which comply with the EU objectives in the field of environmental protection. The establishment in 1986 of the Ministry of the Environment, and the introduction of a specific administrative centre responsible for the national environmental policy, represent a turning point in the Italian legal system concerning this area. The guidelines of environmental policy involve the identification of environmental problems in specific areas (the environmental triennial plan operates in eleven fields and/or projects) and the selection of appropriate policy instruments to achieve planned targets, consistent with the EU environmental interests and objectives.

The economic effect of environmental pollution is obviously higher when the value of what is damaged is higher. This is certainly the case in Italy, where architectural, artistic and natural patrimony is enormous. On the other hand, firms do not welcome charges and taxes on polluting activities because of their effect of increasing production costs. Thus, government efforts in this direction receive only limited support in parliament in the face of intense lobbying against such measures. A serious policy of reducing environmental pollution through economic incentives has still to be implemented in Italy.

4.4 FINANCIAL SYSTEM

4.4.1 The general system

In order to understand the Italian financial system we need to bear in mind the savings patterns in the various sectors of the economy (families, firms, the state and the foreign sector). In net terms, the household sector has traditionally been largely in credit, firms in deficit, and the state sector also increasingly in deficit since the beginning of the 1970s.

The structure of the financial system, as outlined in the 1936 Banking Law, was based on the separation of banks and companies, essentially designed to avoid the possibility of collapses of the major banks caused by the bankruptcy of key companies (as happened in the early 1930s).

In brief, the financial system has operated until recently in the following way. Company financing has been both direct, by means of shares and debentures, and indirect, by means of banks (short-term credit) or by credit institutions (*Istituti speciali di Credito*) (medium–long term credit). The *Istituti speciali di Credito* have had the specific institutional role of financing companies in the medium–long term, obtaining their funds by selling bonds mainly to the major banking institutions and, to a lesser extent, to insurance and finance companies. The Italian stock exchange has had a limited role in the financing of industry, owing to the relative lack of institutional investors and the large proportion of small firms which, by their very nature, are not dependent on stock-exchange financing. The main cause of the limited number of institutional investors has to be found in the structure – almost exclusively public – of the national insurance system. This explains the modest flow of savings coming on to the stock market.

The public deficit has been mainly financed by issuing public debt bonds and by drawing upon a special Treasury current account held with the central bank in accordance with strict legal limits. The public debt bonds can be bought by the general public and the central bank which, as already mentioned, is no longer obliged to act as a 'buyer of last resort' at the auctions of public debt bonds. Local public administrations have financed their own investment through a Deposits and Loans Institute (*Cassa Depositi e Prestiti*), a financial institution (derived from the French financial experience) which is a section of the Treasury using deposits collected by the Italian Post Office. However, its role in financing local authorities diminished as savers showed a preference for holding their savings in banks rather than the Post Office. The system has allowed only occasional exceptions to the 'separation rule' between banks and companies. An example is *Mediobanca*, a medium- and long-term credit institution operating also as a merchant bank for major companies.

In the 1990s, the structure of the financial system has been transformed either by the process of liberalisation of the EMS or by the 1993 Banking Law (see next section). The introduction of the 'universal bank' has abolished the principle of specialisation in short- or medium–long-term credit, and the rule of separation between banks and companies has been revised. Finally, it should be expected that the process of privatisation and the presence of institutional investors (pension funds will start to be operating very soon) will gradually increase the dimension and the role of the Italian Stock Exchange.

4.4.2 Banking system

Banks obtain funds through customers' deposits and pay interest both on deposit and current accounts. Before the privatisation of *Istituto mobiliare italiano (Imi)* and of two banks of national interest (*Comit* and *Credit*), most of the major banks were state-owned, a situation which arose because of the direct state intervention to save a number of private banks involved in the bankruptcy of companies in the early 1930s. The development of the banking system has involved a significant reduction in the differences between the various types of banks, in terms of how they operate to collect funds and by the type of financing in which they specialised. A network of banking services throughout the country is guaranteed by local credit institutions

as large banks are generally located in the major towns.

The banks became the centre of the financial system which grew out of the 1936 Banking Law; a position that has been consolidated over the post-war period. The reasons for this central role of the banks were different: the progressive marginalisation of the Post Office as a means of saving; the increase in the number of banks throughout Italy; the growth of local banks; the progressive growth of the public debt; the increasing placement of bonds and shares in the banks' portfolios (from the state, state organisations and special credit institutions); the marginal role undertaken by the stock exchange in financing industry.

Between the mid-1960s and the end of the 1970s – due either to the indirect pressure known as 'moral suasion' from the Bank of Italy or to a 'pegging' policy to maintain low interest rates, and directly because of the administrative measures of the monetary authorities – banks progressively acquired more of both government bonds and bonds issued by the special credit institutions. In particular, the monetary authorities laid down minimum proportions of bank deposits to be held in the form of bonds. On the other hand, banks were performing well as their interest rates on deposits were above those of the other short- and medium-term financial institutions, so that families preferred bank deposits to other ways of saving. Thus, the central role of banks in the financial system is explained both by the fact that they were the direct or indirect source of more or less every kind of loan operation, and by the fact that the bulk of family savings took the form of bank deposits.

The differentiation of credit institutions according to the terms of time deposits and periods of loans was the reasoning behind the Banking Law of 1936 in order to guarantee the stability of the banking system. In practice, however, banks were involved extensively in the provision of medium- and long-term loans (by buying bonds issued by the *Istituti speciali di Credito* and a large number of state-issued bonds) and the stability of the system was mainly based on the control exerted by the Bank of Italy.

This situation was considerably modified at the beginning of the 1980s. The separation of the Central Bank from the Treasury, associated with the government decision to finance its deficit through the market, implied a weakening of the banks' role as mediators in the savings market, which can be easily understood in quantitative terms by looking at the composition of family portfolios showing a sharp increase in the amount of public debt bonds (yielding high net returns), and a decrease in bank deposits.

The most significant stage in the process of structural and institutional reorganisation of the Italian banking system is represented by the 1993 Banking Law which introduces two main changes. It modifies the previous system of banking specialisation by lowering the gap between banking, financial and insurance markets, and provides for a structural transformation of public banks as limited companies or cooperative societies.

As far as the principle of credit specialisation is concerned, the model of the 'universal bank' allows all the credit institutions to do short-, medium- and long-term credit and loan operations, providing they observe Central Bank rules relating to 'prudent' conduct of their operations. As a consequence, the major banks are extending the spectrum of their activities. Moreover, the delegated law Eurosim of July 1966, following the EU directives about investment services' liberalisation, allows banks to deal directly into the markets without the intermediary activity of the *societa' di intermediazione mobiliare* (SIM) (stock brokerage companies which were the only subject allowed by the Italian law to deal in listed securities in the stock exchange market). This change towards 'mixed groups' strategies in the banking sector should bring about economies of scale and scope while still gaining economies of specialisation.

The features of Italian banking activity and particularly the low level of market competition in business finance services and shareholdings can be traced back to the principle of separation between bank and industry (Trequattrini, 1994). Moreover, because of the lack of competition in the 'market for corporate control', the recent decrease in banks' profitability has not been followed, as it had to be, by a change in the strategies and management (Barca, 1994). With the new 1993 regulation, the traditional prohibition of banks participating in the ownership of firms (a requirement of monetary authorities rather than a rule established by law), has been reconsidered. A wider use by monetary authorities of the power to authorise cross-holdings relationships between bank and industry, together with the promotion of mergers and acquisitions aimed at creating fewer big banking groups, and the process of financial innovation, should lead to an improvement in the efficiency and competitiveness in the Italian banking system at European level.

4.4.3 Monetary policy

Italian monetary policy during the 1980s can be regarded as both a cause and a consequence of the main economic policy choices made in Italy during the late 1970s and early 1980s: the membership of the EMS and the demonetarisation of the public debt. Joining the EMS involved the imposition of a more rigorous monetary policy in order to contain the exchange rate fluctuations within internationally fixed constraints. The demonetarisation of the public debt (following the 'divorce' between the Central Bank and the government) allowed the Central Bank to recover its autonomy in controlling the money supply. As a consequence, the Bank of Italy was able to follow a more restrictive policy on money supply, as shown in Figure 4.8, presenting the annual percentage change of M2 (including savings deposits which have a high degree of liquidity in Italy). To better understand Figure 4.8 it is necessary to bear in mind that in the first years of EMS the 'central parities' of European currencies changed frequently and not marginally, and that monetary policy was allowed to become restrictive in nominal terms over a number of years in accordance with the decrease in the rate of inflation. The higher real interest rates caused by restrictive monetary policy and by public debt demonetarisation have had uneven effects on different business sectors;

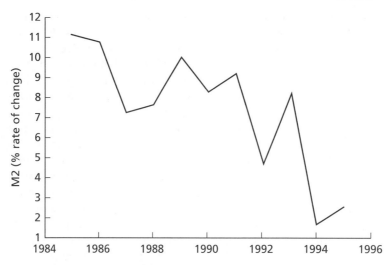

Figure 4.8 Money supply (M2) (annual % rate of change)

Source: Statistical Annexe of European Economy, Eurostat, Table G9.

mainly large firms took advantage of the lower level of the 'prime rate' and of the ease of access to international financial markets characterised by lower interest rates. The higher interest rates were also supposed to operate positively in limiting public expenditure because of the higher cost of financing public debt.

Because of the permanent inflationary gap with the other European countries, due to both the high demand in some productive sectors and to the exchange rate depreciation, the more recent monetary policy of the Bank of Italy (aligning to those already implemented in the past by the central banks of Germany, England, Spain, Sweden, Finland and others), has been mainly directed to maintain price stability, according to the strategy of inflation targeting. The adoption of a restrictive line in liquidity control can be regarded as a natural consequence of a move towards more autonomy for the Bank of Italy from the Treasury, and it has been mainly implemented by increasing the official discount rate and through open-market operations. Although a slowdown in the growth of monetary aggregates (a negative growth in real terms) and in the credit expansion have been the direct consequences of this political line (Figure 4.8), it has contributed to containing inflationary

expectations, leading to a progressive exchange rate appreciation and a reduced differential rate of yield on long-term government bonds between Italy and Germany.

4.5 INTERNATIONAL RELATIONS

4.5.1 General remarks

At the beginning of the 1950s Italy radically changed its international economic policy, transforming itself, in a very short space of time, from a highly protected to a relatively free economy, at least in regard to trade in products and services. Entry into the Common Market accelerated this process. The lack of natural resources, and the fact that Italy began to industrialise at a later date than many other countries, have had a dual effect on the economy. On the one hand, these factors have created a strong stimulus for technological innovation but, at the same time, they have acted as a permanent brake on the expansion of the economy. As Italy does not have much in the way of natural resources, any expansion in production must, by definition, be accompanied by an increase in the imports of raw materials, and as a consequence, every expansionary phase must be accompanied by an increase in the exports of goods and services or by inflows of capital.

The first phase of industrialisation after the Second World War was characterised by a surplus in the balance of payments including services: exports increased rather more than imports owing to the low level of Italian wages and to the adoption of modern technology in a number of industrial sectors, other contributory factors were the receipts from tourism and the remittances sent home by emigrants. Apart from a brief period (1963–64), this trend generally continued until the end of the 1960s. The first oil crisis worsened the problem of the balance on international accounts but the policy of continually devaluing the lira, which started at the beginning of the 1970s and was pursued until 1979 when Italy joined the EMS, allowed Italian industrial products to maintain competitiveness in the international market.

4.5.2 Recent trends

Membership of the European Monetary System brought a halt to the policy of adjusting the rate of exchange to internal price rises, constantly practised between 1972 and 1979. If the new policy had positive effects in terms of containing inflation (through lower prices of import of raw materials and foreign commodities), it also adversely affected the Italian trade balance, especially in comparison with the German D-Mark area countries. In the 1980s the balance of trade was continually in deficit and the current account worsened (see Figure 4.9). The positive balance on invisible items was insufficient to compensate for the deficit in the balance of trade. Tourism, which in the past contributed in a major way to balancing the current account, is gradually becoming less and less important because the rise in per capita income in Italy has influenced more Italians to travel abroad, while the higher cost of living in Italy, compared to the earlier period, has deterred foreign visitors.

In most of the 1980s, the balance of payments became dependent on the net inflow of capital, attracted by the high interest rates in Italy. The rates have been generally above the EU and international averages. The need to have interest rates at a sufficiently high level to permit an overall balance in foreign accounts comes as a direct consequence of the use of exchange rate policy as an instrument for controlling inflation (something very close to the policy of the USA).

It seems likely that trade deficits during the 1980s were largely caused by the worsening of

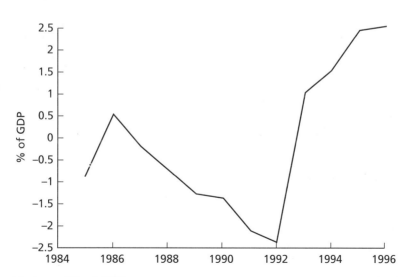

Figure 4.9 Current balance (% of GDP)

Source: Statistical Annexe of European Economy, Eurostat, Table G9.

trade with the German D-Mark area and especially Germany itself. The German mark, and the currencies linked with it, have been undervalued inside the EMS with respect to most European currencies, including the Italian lira. Moreover, the rules established within the EMS have significantly reduced room for discretion in exchange rate policy on the part of national governments.

In 1992, the turbulence in world financial markets had a marked influence on a number of currencies and especially on the Italian lira. After a devaluation of lira inside the EMS (and an unsuccessful attempt to maintain the new parity) both the Italian and British governments opted to remove their currencies from the EMS. As a consequence, the lira's value fell substantially in comparison with the major world currencies and, as expected, the Italian economy (as well as the British economy) enjoyed the virtuous circle of growth, buoyant exports and low inflation. The current balance between Italy and the rest of the world (EU and extra-EU countries) after a short lag has been in constant and increasing surplus (also due to a decrease in imports because of a low GDP growth), which has allowed a considerable reduction of the net external debt accumulated during the 1980s (see Figure 4.9). The re-entry of the lira into the ERM (in November 1996), although favouring imports (especially raw materials), could result in a decline in exports (no longer favoured by competitive devaluations), and also delay the cut in interest rates necessary to revive growth and relieve the financial burden of the government.

4.6 IMPACT OF EUROPEAN INTEGRATION

The process of European integration – the fully open European market, the regulative action of European political authorities, the introduction of a common monetary system – has involved radical changes in the national systems of the member countries, both on the economic and political side. The effects of this integrative process on particular countries have constituted some political–economic benefits and costs which are the result of both 'common' and 'country-specific' factors. The purpose of this section is to evaluate some aspects of these advantages and disadvantages in the case of Italy.

4.6.1 The impact of EC integration on the macroeconomic performance and political and legal system in Italy

The evaluation of the Italian performance after the involvement with the EMS is not unequivocal. It is unquestionable that, at least until 1992, the exchange rate mechanism of the EMS has had a positive effect of discipline in the implementation of macroeconomic policies, although the constraint of a 'quasi-fixed' exchange rate adversely affected the Italian balance of trade (exports no longer favoured by the systematic practice of competitive devaluations). GDP growth rate has shown different trends: a phase of stagnation occurred after joining the EMS (1979–82), followed by a recovery in the period 1983–88; then a new phase of slowdown in production occurred in 1989–93; in the years 1994–95, following the lira's exit from ERM, there was a new recovery, followed by a fall in 1996. Growth, although improving, has not been sufficient to absorb the high unemployment which has been rising almost continuously. On the other hand, the inflation rate has shown a decreasing trend during the 1980s and, after periods of slightly rising prices in 1990–91, 1992 and 1995, it settled at 3.5% (proxy data for 1996) so as to reduce the differential with Germany and France to around 2 points. Italy's performance appears satisfactory in terms of GDP growth rate and inflation rate, but less so when considering public debt/GDP ratio. The Treasury-bills rise caused a progressive increase in the cost of debt service. Public debt currently amounts to more than 120% of the GDP; although slightly decreasing recently as a consequence of deflation, it is still very distant from the standard of 60% fixed by the Maastricht Treaty.

It is a difficult task to determine the direct effects of the EMS on the Italian macroeconomic performance in the period 1979–92, and in fact there are different interpretations concerning the declining inflation rate and productive growth as a possible benefit of the EMS, and the increasing public debt and unemployment rate as a possible cost of it (Fratianni and Von Hagen, 1990; Giavazzi and Pagano, 1985). The introduction of the EMS in 1979 has involved the need for all the members to choose their monetary targets and inflation rates in accordance with the fixed standards, which has produced benefits in terms of price control and the output–inflation trade-off in Europe. There is no doubt that a non-cooperative game modelled between strong currency countries (like Germany whose currency is 'strong' not only because it is perceived as more likely to rise in value rather than to devalue against other units, but also because of the low interest rates reflecting the absence of risk associated with it) and weak currency countries (like Spain, Italy or even France, where the stability of the franc over the past decade has been maintained through abnormally high interest rates) ends up in a competitive deflation, with output losses larger than in the case of a currency agreement (Collins, 1988). On the other hand, however, it has been argued that fixed currency arrangements allowed Germany to sustain a non-inflationary growth at the expense of the growth rates of the other EMS countries (De Cecco, 1989). In the case of Italy, this would have implied a higher deflation than that autonomously planned by the Bank of Italy which, in turn, might have caused a slower GDP growth rate and a lower employment level.

The proposed monetary union of 1999, involving the introduction of a single currency (the 'euro') and a single European central bank, will imply substantial changes for all the involved economies. The economic benefits deriving from being part of the same market and having a single currency are not very different from those associated with a system of fixed exchange rates. They are mainly in terms of saving in currency transaction costs, exchange risk and uncertainty in trading, which favour economic integration and development of trade among countries. Advantages could also accrue from creating a single European monetary area,

vis-à-vis the US dollar and Japanese yen, since a strong euro, associated with low interest rates, could result in a considerable supply of capital for Europe, thus encouraging investment and innovative activity. However, it is important to distinguish between the 'natural' role played by a currency because of its strength and stability within a given monetary area, like the deutschmark, chosen by the market as 'anchor-currency' in the European ERM, and the 'legal' status of a currency, like the euro, officially determined as the single currency of the monetary union. Whereas the 'natural anchor' is replaceable by another currency if it becomes unstable, in the case of a 'legal anchor' this option is not available. This difference is important to the extent that any economic instability of the EU area does have the effect of diminishing the stability and increasing the degree of risk associated with the 'legal anchor' against the other major currency areas (dollar and yen). It follows that high costs could derive, and not only to Italy, from an imperfect convergence of the fundamentals among member countries. Moreover, monetary union will not allow national sovereignty in controlling fiscal and monetary policies in order to solve problems of internal equilibrium. This will imply a loss of control on internal interest rates and the impossibility of taking advantage of the currency devaluation. The probability of success of the single currency, and the probability for Italy of receiving benefits, is therefore strictly dependent both on the degree of economic convergence in the trend of fundamentals and, above all, on the ability of maintaining a high degree of economic convergence in the long run.

The process of European integration has involved not only constraints upon the conduct of macroeconomic policy but also changes in the political and legal system of the member countries. The Italian government has always been in favour of European integration, showing a very high rate of support for increasing the powers of European institutions when compared with the attitudes of other member countries (Merusi *et al.*, 1987; Bardi, 1989). It is also true, however, that Italy has often been blamed for being late in applying European regulations or for violating European directives. This indicates that, if there is agreement about the net benefits of European integration, these are not achieved without costs. The production of European regulations with direct legal effects has influenced the internal hierarchy of norms in each member country. In the case of Italy this has produced additional elements without evident change in the jurisdiction of national organs. All the European norms of harmonisation, coordination and coexistence, however, have implicitly led to a supranational control over some internal legislative decisions. As for the European jurisdictional system of human rights protection, the action of the European Court has constrained the national jurisdictional powers in areas covered by European laws. These constraints may involve some costs on the Italian legal system in terms of lost control by the Constitutional Court. However, despite the possible restriction on domestic legislation about fundamental rights, stemming from the need to serve the 'general interest' of the EU, it is unquestionable that an advantage accrues to Italy from being part of a supranational and integrated system which operates for human rights protection at European level. Finally, a positive evaluation of the political benefits of European integration derives from the consideration of the strengthening of Italian political stability and position in the international context (Cotta, 1992).

4.7 SPECIAL ISSUES

4.7.1 Economic dualism

Every European economy has specific characteristics, although there is a tendency for differences to diminish. Territorial dualism and the special role played by the small- and medium-sized firms in the production system are two special characteristics of the Italian economy.

The Italian economy has experienced two phases of intense industrialisation, the first at the turn of the century and the second in the period since the Second World War. The first phase concerned a small area, almost exclusively the industrial 'triangle' of Milan, Turin and Genova. The second, although more widespread, still did not include part of the south of Italy and the Islands. A case study by the research office of the Bank of Italy (Banca d'Italia, 1996) makes a systematic comparison of the south's economic performance with that of the centre–north in the period 1950–1995. Territorial dualism is obvious in terms of differences in per capita income between the most and the least advanced regions. The period 1952–72 has been characterised by a clear tendency in the south's performance to converge towards the better performance of the centre–north regions. However, statistical measures show that from the mid-1980s the north–south divide has once more begun to widen (Figure 4.10). In recent years, the growth of income in the south of the country, the *Mezzogiorno*, has been markedly lower than in the north. Figure 4.10 clearly shows the sharp reduction which recently occurred in the south GDP/centre–north GDP ratio which goes back to the value of thirty years ago (56.7%). The widening of the gap can be partly due to the different demographic dynamic, and mainly to the lower productive growth of the south. Moreover, the contraction of investment activity and the modified regime of subsidies to the depressed areas have considerably weakened the policies for Mezzogiorno, with negative effects on the still low competitiveness of the south industry.

Employment in the south also fell from the mid-1980s, progressively widening the gap with respect to the centre–north. From 1984 there has been a slight reduction in the south's share of the total number of people employed in the nation as a whole, associated with a larger overall increase in the population at working age in the south. Figure 4.11 shows that, while employment (especially male) in the centre–north has increased in the period 1984–90, it has fallen rapidly in the south during the same period. In the period 1990–94, although the employment rate has shown a strong reduction both in the south and centre–north regions (where the increase in the number of employed people has

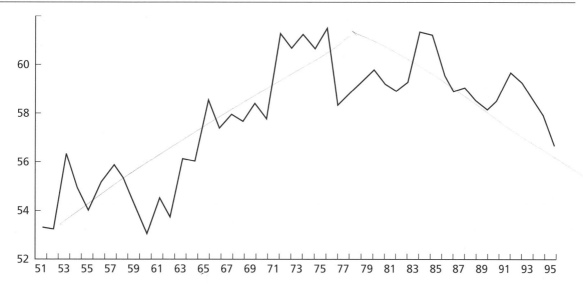

Figure 4.10 Relative GDP south/centre–north (% ratio at current prices)

Source: Bank of Italy on ISTAT and SVIMEZ data.

concerned mainly the female component), the drop of employment rate in the south has been much stronger.

In many respects the economic situation of the south is contradictory. Family consumption in the Mezzogiorno has increased continuously. The value of investment in the construction sector (excluding housing) has grown in absolute terms in the south and relatively more than in the north. Moreover, investment in machinery has not been less than in the centre–north. The individual productive sectors are more capital-intensive in the south, partly because of the presence of state-owned heavy industry. The phenomenon suggesting that capital-intensive production tends to locate in less developed countries is known in economic literature as the *Leontieff paradox*. Public spending is distributed in Italy largely according to the population distribution and so per capita public spending in the south (both for state investment expenditure and state expenditure on services) continues to be higher than revenues.

As far as the banking system is concerned, a strong gap exists between the south and centre–north performance, although the average rate of growth of bank deposits, post office sav-

ings and banks investments is higher in the south than in the centre–north. In the south, bank investments have fallen as a proportion of bank deposits, but this has been due to an increase in bank deposits (the role of the banks in the south has maintained its primary importance) rather than a fall in bank loans. From the mid-1980s, the Bank of Italy favoured acquisitions of capital shares, take-overs of some credit institutions by bigger and more efficient financial institutions, and the opening of new branches in order to improve the performance and competitiveness of the system. However, the banking sector in the south still shows less efficiency in resource allocation, costs of intermediary activity and development. The reasons for such gaps between north and south banking performance are both structural and related to the market mechanism. First, the gap reflects the different level of risks of credit activities in different geographical areas of the countries. Southern banks' customers are generally more fragile and risky and this increases the expected costs of the banks. Second, because of the credit market structure, higher rates can be applied in those local markets where competition is weaker, and the banks' capability for clientele

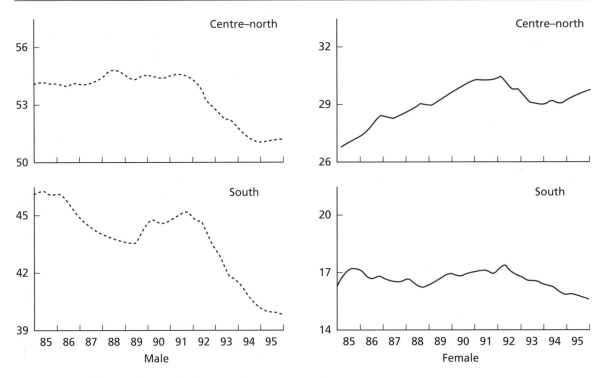

Figure 4.11 Percentages of total population employed, by sex and geographical areas

Source: Bank of Italy on ISTAT data.

selection is lessened. The objective should be to allow the weak, risky and small agents to get credit necessary for local growth, without disturbing the economic equilibrium of the banks. Although the cost of labour (as well as the cost of indebtedness) is lower in the south, the efficiency of industrial production in the Mezzogiorno is inferior to that of the centre–north. There is no one definitive explanation for this phenomenon and the various theories are often contradictory. Some scholars take the view that the gap is widening because of the government assistance to the southern industries which, through credit and tax benefits, allows them to survive, even if they are not really competitive. Others believe that the total amount of services offered by the government to the industrial sector (infrastructure and administrative services) is so low that the industrial costs in the south are decidedly higher. Yet others believe that there are environmental dis-

economies, that is higher costs associated with the fact that the industrial sector is not well integrated and lacks important links. Although the above factors are important, they do not give a complete explanation of the lower productivity in the south. In fact, many other regions of Italy have experienced industrialisation in the last few decades and have experienced similar difficulties. Those economists who believe that the problems of the economy in the Mezzogiorno are not purely of economic nature, but can be largely attributed to social and political causes, would seem to have a case. The lower productivity of some firms can be put down to the lack of competition. In some southern areas, the presence of the public sector in the running of companies often implies that management is more concerned with maintaining employment levels, filling the jobs with people of the same political or social background, rather than efficiently managing the company. Finally, it is

crime

argued that the economic grounds for the running of a company are not the same in the south as in the rest of Italy as many companies are exploited by 'organised criminal groups' and not infrequently controlled by these groups. This discourages potential competition and entrepreneurial activity. High unemployment is considered to be one of the reasons why there is an extremely high level of organised crime in Campania, Calabria and Sicily, although it would be an overstatement to attribute a direct cause–effect relationship to these variables. The strong economic control of criminal organisations in the above-mentioned areas of the south of Italy is also associated with significant illegal revenues coming from traffic in drugs. On the basis of economic analysis of this phenomenon, the legalisation of drugs (associated with effective state action against organised criminality) has been supported as a way to reduce the negative influence of criminal power on the economic development of the 'controlled' areas (Fineschi, 1993). The difficulty of working in the south also leads to the so-called phenomenon of 'exit' of entrepreneurs and managers, as well as of the more skilled workers. This point is a particularly serious factor as those who do 'exit' are often the most talented, skilful and enterprising people, those more likely to change the existing state of things. The process of European integration could accentuate difficulties which already exist in the weakest parts of the Italian economy. The outcome of the process of integration depends on the growth potential of the most backward areas to absorb workers from the poorest regions. The present rate of unemployment in a large part of Europe (especially of the young and women) does not allow us to be optimistic about the possibility of absorbing workers from the south of Italy into other EU countries and/or the north of Italy. At the same time, the type of economic development in the most advanced Italian and European industrial areas requires a specialised workforce. If this were to come from the south of Italy, it would result in a further impoverishment of the area as well as a worsening in its prospects for future growth. We

still need to assess whether the south of Italy will be able to offer investment opportunities for companies from the most advanced areas of Europe and in what measure the southern Italian companies will be affected by the increased integration of the European market. The answer to the first question involves assessing whether the companies from the advanced European countries will be more able to exploit the development opportunities in the south of Italy than those from the north of Italy have done in the past. The most realistic answer seems to be a negative one, if we reflect upon the comments on the Mezzogiorno economy made above. The potential for economic development in a large part of the south is limited by the existing conditions (widespread organised crime and inefficiency in the public administration system) which hampers the development of entrepreneurial ability. It is doubtful that the European companies will be able to do any better than the entrepreneurs from the south and the north–centre regions have done up till now. Ex-communist bloc countries of eastern Europe offer better investment opportunities (especially lower wages) than many regions of the south of Italy. With regard to the second question, the effect of European integration on southern Italian companies is not different from that produced by the intense competition during the 1980s. Like the latter phenomenon, it is widening the gap between the south and the north. Moreover, with monetary union, exchange rate devaluation will be ruled out. The problem of closing the gap between the south and the north has to be resolved, above all, by the south of Italy itself, by removing the factors which have for so long hindered development. These problems are beyond the scope of economics and their answer can only be found in institutional and political policies.

Investment by EU firms

4.7.2 The role of small firms

The second aspect of the Italian economy worthy of assessment is the important role that very small and small companies have played (and continue to play) in the development of Italian industry. A large number of small- and medium-sized firms were created during the Italian industrial boom in the 1950s. In the 1960s it seemed that the 'natural' development of the industrialisation process would have been associated with an increase in company size as well as a movement from the traditional sector to industries which are, on the basis of historical experience, more typical of an advanced industrial society. However, the 1970s were characterised by a proliferation of small firms (accompanied by the fact that many large companies ran into difficulty) and by a particular vitality of the more traditional industrial sectors (ones in which the technology is assumed to be 'mature' and amenable only to slow improvement).

The contribution that small companies have made to the development of the Italian economy is multi-faceted and includes income and employment creation as well as a significant addition to exports. The contribution they have given to employment in manufacturing industry can be seen considering the very high number of people employed in small-sized firms (with less than 50 employees) compared to the number of employees in medium-sized and in large plants (more than 500 employees).

From the geographical point of view, whereas in the centre–north the very small and small plants have developed much faster than the medium-sized and large plants, in the south and Islands the number of employees has decreased in very small companies and increased in large companies.

The phenomenon described above has given rise to a lively and prolonged academic debate. There are two main positions. The first interpretation suggests that the economic development and the particular prominence of small companies can be linked to a single pattern of growth that originates from the regions which have a key role in Italian capitalism. This line of thought has two sub-theories. The first underlines the difficulty experienced by large companies in adapting to conditions of increased change and instability which have affected the national and international markets in the 1970s. The second indicates a defensive strategy against organised labour (adopted in the 1970s by large companies) which is based on the decentralisation of the production to smaller factories which are less unionised, have lower labour costs and more flexible work practices. Both the explanatory positions underline, however, the dominant role of major companies with respect to small firms.

The second interpretation gives importance to the autonomous aspect of the development of the small companies. This is based on a number of theories. The best known is the theory captured in the title of Schumacher and Doglio (1973, 'Small is beautiful', used as slogan in the 1970s and 1980s when small organisations proposed themselves as a more efficient alternative to the large enterprises. More useful, perhaps, is the theory which stresses the inherent strength in an integrated system of small companies which operate in a restricted industrial area ('industrial districts' in the terminology of Alfred Marshall) and benefit from economies of scale, external to the single firm but internal to the group of firms which constitute the industrial district.

There is no single adequate explanation for the fact that there are so many small and very small companies in Italian manufacturing industry. Decentralisation of production capacity from large- to small-scale units and the persistence of small companies in areas which have experienced a slower process of industrialisation are part of an international phenomenon, but the integrated system of small companies in delimited industrial districts are a typically Italian phenomenon. This type of organisation of production certainly does not seem to be transitory or cyclical but rather it is a special and persistent characteristic in the development of Italian industrialisation.

4.8 CONCLUSIONS AND FUTURE PROSPECTS

The Italian economic growth has recently come to a halt. It is timely to consider whether we can expect a phase of growth in the near future. As the Italian economy is closely linked to international markets, the performance of the other major economies, especially the USA, Japan and Germany, severely affects the Italian performance. This is not the place to consider the possible developments in the world economy, but it is important to consider the possible consequences of the further integration of the Italian economy into Europe in the 1990s.

On the basis of the experience of steady liberalisation of the economy during the post-war period (liberalisation in the early 1950s, entry into the Common Market, progressive liberalisation of capital movements with foreign countries and the acceptance of a single European market), one could argue that it has generally brought positive results: stimulating innovation in production processes and forcing Italian companies to learn how to operate in international markets. Without underestimating the possible difficulties of adaptation for some sectors (especially credit and finance companies) to the 1993 liberalisation process, it is possible to assert that a more extensive liberalisation is positively affecting many sectors of the Italian economy which are gaining competitiveness from a freer market environment with respect to a protected one. Moreover, a marked phase of modernisation will be the result of the privatisation process which is gradually reducing the presence of the state sector in the market. The coordination of fiscal and monetary policies necessary for European integration is leading the state to act in a more prudent way, given that harmonisation is needed for integrating the European market.

The monetary union of 1999 offers the prospect of a different scenario. A forced effort to reach monetary union may turn out to be a disaster for the weaker countries and for European integration itself. For the Italian economy two main difficulties emerge: the external constraints and limits on the government's ability to reduce the public debt.

The phase of European integration starting with the creation of the European Monetary System (and culminating in the Maastricht agreement) has produced contradictory effects on the Italian economy. The positive effects were, in the early 1980s, the positive impact of the external limits on price determination and a stricter discipline in determining internal and external relations. The tendency of EMS to limit the extent and frequency of changing parities between European currencies has resulted, on the other hand, in unsustainable external limit being imposed on the Italian economy (as well as on other weaker economies outside the D-Mark area). One of the most noticeable features of the development of the Italian economy in the 1980s was certainly the strength of the lira in international markets (due to the high rates of interest) which created inflows of foreign capital, and the search for finance on foreign financial markets by Italian operators. The capital account surplus allowed the economic system to operate at a high level of activity even though the current account was in deficit. As for the government's ability to reduce public debt, which is the most serious problem of the Italian economy, the restrictive fiscal policy of the last few years is leading to a reduction in the net rates of interest which, coupled with a process of deflation, seems to be one important way (though not the only one) to balance public sector accounts.

Economic policies for dealing with the difficulties of the Italian economy at the end of 1980s were influenced significantly by the international context. The growth in the German economy has, for most of the 1980s, been slower than that of the Italian economy as the German authorities have taken special care to keep inflation at a low level (this policy is usually traced back to the consequences of high inflation in the period immediately after the First World War). Given the higher inflation rate in the Italian economy in the 1980s, German policy, together with the exchange rate stability maintained by the EMS among European currencies, caused a large deficit for Italy in its trade with Germany. In this context, the steps agreed at Maastricht could not be in the interests of economic growth in Italy and in other weaker European economies. The choice made by the Italian government to temporarily leave the EMS, prompted by the wish to avoid the dissipation of the country's foreign currency reserves, was a sensible decision. Although economists of both the monetarist and Keynesian schools argued that the lira's withdrawal from the EMS could be regarded as a long-term position, rather than a short-term expedient, the intention of Italy to participate in the monetary union in 1999 has been clearly expressed by the Italian government. Italy is actually still very distant from achieving the convergence criterion of 60% in public debt/GDP ratio, although not so distant from the 3% of budget deficit/GDP ratio; the other criteria of interest rates, price and currency stability are not impossible to achieve. The greater stability of the lira's exchange rate has led to the re-entry in the ERM, and both the fiscal intervention of the Italian government (mainly directed to control public expenditure) and the restrictive line adopted by the Bank of Italy are currently operating to maximise the possibility for Italy to enter the European monetary union. However, the success of the EMU, and the possibility for the Italian economy to receive its benefits, requires high and stable economic convergence of fundamentals in the EU, and this seems to be not yet achieved.

4.9 BIBLIOGRAPHY AND SOURCES OF INFORMATION

Alesina, A., Tabellini, G. (1987): A Political Theory of Fiscal Deficits and Government Debt in a Democracy, NBER Working Paper No. 2308

Bagnasco, A. (1977): *Tre Italie: la problematica territoriale dello sviluppo italiano*, Il Mulino, Bologna

Banca d'Italia (1990): 'Il sistema finanziario nel Mezzogiorno', numero speciale dei *Contributi all'analisi economica*, Rome

Banca d'Italia (1993): *Relazione annuale del Governatore alla assemblea generale ordinaria dei partecipanti*, May, Rome

Banca d'Italia (1996a): *Bollettino Economico*, February, n.26

Banca d'Italia (1996b): *Relazione annuale del Governatore alla assemblea generale ordinaria dei partecipanti*, May, Rome

Barca, F. (1994): 'Allocazione e Riallocazione della Proprietà e del Controllo delle Imprese: Ostacoli, Intermediari, Regole', in *Il Mercato della Proprietà e del Controllo delle Imprese: Aspetti Teorici e Istituzionali*, Banca d'Italia

Bardi, L. (1989): *Il Parlamento della Comunita' Europea*, Il Mulino, Bologna.

Becattini, G. (ed.) (1987): *Mercato e forze locali: il distretto industriale*, Il Mulino, Bologna

Cavazzuti, F. (1986): *Debito pubblico e ricchezza privata*, Il Mulino, Bologna

Collins, S.M. (1988): 'Inflation and the European Monetary System', in F. Giavazzi, S. Micossi and M. Miller (eds.), *The European Monetary System*, Cambridge University Press, Cambridge

Confindustria (1990): *Rapporto annuale a cura del Centro Studi Confindustria*, May

Commissione CEE (1987): *Le regioni della Comunità allargata*. Terza relazione periodica sulla situazione socio-economica e sullo sviluppo delle Regioni della Comunità, Luxemburg

Cotta, M. (1992): 'European integration and the Italian political system', in Francioni, F. (ed.), *Italy and EC Membership Evaluated*, St Martin's Press, New York

De Cecco, M. (1989): 'The European Monetary System and national interests' in P. Guerrieri and P.C. Padoan (eds) *The Political Economy of European Integration*, Hemel Hempstead, Harvester Wheatsheaf

Fineschi, A. (1991): 'Alcune osservazioni sulla politica monetaria e sul tasso di cambio in Italia negli anni ottanta', *Quaderni di economia, statistica e analisi del territorio*, Messina

Fineschi, A. (1993): 'Introduzione ad una analisi dei costi e dei benefici della legalizzazione della droga', in *La Criminalita' in Toscana*, Ricerche e contributi/1, Regione Toscana, Giunta Regionale, pp. 144–177

Fratianni, M. and Von Hagen, J. (1990) 'The European Monetary System ten years after', in Meltzer, A.H. and Plossers, C. (eds), *Carnegie-Rochester Conference Series on Public Policy*, vol. 32 North Holland, Amsterdam

Fuà, G., Zacchia, C. (eds) (1983): *Industrializzazione senza fratture*, Il Mulino, Bologna

Giavazzi, F. and Pagano, M. (1985): 'The advantage of tying one's hands', *European Economic Review*, **32**, 1055–74

ISTAT (1992): *Annuario di contabilità nazionale*

Istituto Nazionale per il Commercio Estero (1989): *Rapporto sul commercio estero*, Rome

Ministro del lavoro e della Previdenza Sociale (1989): *Rapporto 1988. Lavoro e politiche della occupazione in Italia*, Rome

Mediocredito Centrale (1989): *Indagine sulle imprese manifatturiere*, Rome

Merusi, F., Padoan, P.C., Colasanti, F. and Vilella, G.C. (1987): *L'integrazione monetaria dell'Europa*, Il Mulino, Bologna

Mudambi, R., Nicosia, C. (1997): 'Ownership structure and firm performance: Evidence from the UK financial service industry', *Applied Financial Economics*, forthcoming

Mudambi, R., Navarra, P. and Nicosia, C. (1996): 'Plurality versus proportional representation: An analysis of Sicilian elections', *Public Choice*, **86**, 341–57

Nicosia, C. (1996): 'The effect of rules on voter's behaviour: A comparison betweem electoral systems', *Quaderni di Economia, Statistica ed Analisi del Territorio* no. 21, Universita' degli Studi di Messina

Nicosia, C. (1996): 'Allocazione proprietaria e controllo nelle societa' di intermediazione finanziaria', *L'Industria*, no. 2, pp. 251–76

Schumacher, E.F. and Doglio, D. (1977): *Il piccolo e' bello: una tecnologia dal volto umano*, Moizzi, Milano.

SVIMEZ (1990): *Rapporto sul Mezzogiorno*

Sylos, Labini P. (1986): *Le classi sociali negli anni '80*, Laterza, Bari

Trequattrini, A. (1994): 'Da banche pubbliche a banche del pubblico: il testo unico e il processo di privatizzazione', in *Bancaria*, no. 3

Valli, V. (1988): *Politica economica. I modelli, gli strumenti, l'economia italiana*, La Nuova Italia Scientifica, Rome

CHAPTER 5

The Netherlands

Frans Somers

5.1 INSTITUTIONAL AND HISTORICAL CONTEXT

In terms of income and number of inhabitants, the Kingdom of the Netherlands is the largest of the smaller EU countries. The country is a 'constitutional monarchy', meaning that the powers of the monarch are clearly limited by the constitution. The function of the King or the Queen as head of state is more or less symbolic; in fact, a system of parliamentary democracy clearly prevails. The most important body of the Parliament, the Lower House (Second Chamber), is elected by a direct proportional system, with a relatively low electoral threshold for political parties. The government, headed by a prime minister, is appointed by the parties in the Lower House who after elections manage to form a coalition, which (normally) will command a majority.

5.1.1 Political fragmentation

As in Italy, there are numerous parties represented in Parliament, reflecting the highly fragmented nature of Dutch society. In the past, political differences were determined not only by socio-economic interests but also by religious distinctions between Roman Catholics and the various Protestant denominations.

Throughout the present century, the Dutch have coped with the religious differences by dividing society into a number of strictly separated blocs, capable of peaceful coexistence with each other. Every group – religious or ideological – had its own (publicly financed) educational establishments, clubs, newspapers, trade unions and political party. This way, dangerous confrontations between religious groups were avoided and class conflicts reduced as well. Socio-economic antitheses were partly replaced by religious ones.

The significance of religion in Dutch society has diminished sharply since the 1960s. This development has been reflected in the decreasing size of the religion-based political parties. The most important ones merged in 1980 to form one united Christian Democratic party (*Christen Democratisch Appel, CDA*). Nevertheless, it is generally the case that no single party has an absolute majority in Parliament, which means that all governments are based on coalitions of at least two parties. Dutch society, consisting of *minorities* only, is a very pluralistic one. Major parties represented in Parliament – apart from the centrist Christian Democrats – are the left wing Social Democrats (*PvdA*) and (liberal) Democrats (*D'66*) and the right-wing Liberal Party (*VVD*). The Christian Democrats have usually been in power, governing on the basis of a coalition with either left-wing or right-wing parties. The new coalition government, made up of PvdA, D'66 and VVD, which took office in 1994, was, however, the first one this century not supported by a religious party.

5.1.2 Welfare state

Religion is probably also one of the major factors that contributed to the strong expansion of the *welfare state* in the Netherlands. Parties based on religion, which were (until 1994) always in the centre of political power, had to reconcile the conflicting social and economic interests of their members, of employers and employees alike. One way of dealing with conflicts is to develop a wide variety of social security provisions, which protect workers against the hardships of a market economy. Although, therefore, direct government intervention in the Dutch economy is fairly limited, government involvement is nonetheless quite high because of the very extensive social security system. This system provides generous benefits for many groups in society, including the unemployed, pensioners, disabled and (until recently) sick workers and in general for every person without means of subsistence. Virtually no-one without adequate means of subsistence is excluded from the Dutch welfare system which provides 'care from cradle to grave'. It is the main reason why an underclass and social exclusion has not emerged in the Netherlands. The Dutch welfare state has contributed significantly to an integrated society without extreme social tensions and extreme crime rates. It is assumed to be a major explanation for the social and political stability in the country. The latter can be considered as a positive element for the business environment as well.

The social security system clearly has its price too, however. It has given rise to a huge public sector, which may be argued to have negative effects in terms of restraining development of the business sector, economic growth and employment. The problems became especially noticeable in the early 1980s, when the economy was in crisis, and the system was overburdened with claims. In 1983, total government expenditure amounted to almost 61% of GDP, a higher share than for all other EU countries (Table G32). Since then, successive Dutch governments have implemented strict austerity policies, aimed at reducing the size of the public sector and the overall burden of taxes and social security contributions. Scaling down the size of the public sector will remain a major issue for governments in the coming years, particularly as high taxes have a negative

impact on Dutch competitiveness within the rapidly developing European internal market.

5.1.3 Trading nation

Another characteristic of the Netherlands, deeply rooted in its history, is the dominant position of trade and its related services in the economy. The central location of the Netherlands in western Europe, at the mouth of the rivers Rhine, Meuse and Schelde, and surrounded by countries like the UK, Germany and France, created the optimal conditions for developing a trading nation. In its 'golden age' in the 17th century, Holland was one of the most important maritime nations. Nowadays, the seaport of Rotterdam is the biggest in the world, and is not only of importance for the Netherlands but also for the adjacent parts of Germany and generally as a transshipment harbour for bulk products and container transport. Schiphol (Amsterdam) Airport is one of the top five European Airports in terms of passenger and freight traffic handling. International distribution and transport services are thus prominent industries. In addition, the country has long been an international centre for financial and other trade-related services.

Because of the fertile soil and the favourable climate, Dutch agriculture has always been a successful part of the economy. This sector has been developed by a unique blend of private farming, cooperation between producers, scientific research institutes and the government, and a good educational system. Manufacturing industry, on the other hand, has never played a dominant role in the Dutch economy.

5.1.4 Open economy

Because of its strong orientation to trade the Dutch economy is one of the most open economies in the world. Exports and imports of goods and services amount to about 53% of GDP. Within the EU this figure is only surpassed by Belgium and Luxembourg. This openness, however, makes the Dutch economy very vulnerable to external developments such as recessions and especially protectionism. That is why the country keenly supports free trade and has always strongly advocated economic integration. Together with Belgium and Luxembourg it established a customs union in 1944 (the Benelux) and it has been a member of the European Communities (EEC and Euratom) right from the start in 1958. Its main competitive advantage lies in its geographical position, which can be best exploited in a Europe without frontiers.

5.2 MAIN ECONOMIC CHARACTERISTICS

5.2.1 Gross domestic product

Dutch performance in the field of growth in recent decades has not been particularly impressive. Before the first oil shock of 1973 real growth rates were on average about 5% per year, slightly ahead of the average of the fifteen countries, which nowadays form the European Community. During the stagnation period 1974–83 the real GDP growth rate dropped to 1.7%, which was considerably below the EU15 average of 2.7%. In the phase of economic recovery from 1984 to 1990 the average growth rate of 3.1% was largely in line with the average EU rate. The Dutch economy was, however, less affected by the recession in the early 1990s than most other Member States and has shown a faster than expected recovery. During 1991–95 the average Dutch economic growth of 1.9% was clearly above the average EU15 growth of 1.4% (Table G23 and Figure 5.1, panel A). It would appear that a number of measures to improve the economy taken by successive Dutch governments since the early 1980s started to show results (for more detail see Section 5.2.4).

Dutch population growth rates, on the other hand, are generally far above European average. Between 1973 and 1991 for instance, a period of weak to moderate economic growth, the Dutch population increased by 12.1% – almost double the rate of growth for the EU15 as a whole (6.6%). The combined result of these developments was that the Netherlands has been losing its place as one of the richest EU countries. GDP per head of population (average EU15 = 100) fell from 110.8 in 1971 (fifth highest) to only 99.5 in 1991 (ninth place; Table G24). The country has been overtaken by countries like Belgium, Italy and Austria. Figure 5.1, panel b, clearly illustrates this relative decline. Since 1991 the Dutch position has slightly improved.

The main reasons for the deterioration of the Dutch position in the 1980s were the vulnerability of the economy with respect to international disturbances and the inability of the highly developed welfare state to cope with economic crises and mass unemployment and to generate enough jobs.

This subject will be discussed in more detail in Section 5.7.

5.2.2 Population and employment

The Netherlands is a very crowded country with 15.5 million people in 1996 living on 42 000 km². The population density of 369 inhabitants per square kilometre – the highest within the EU – puts great pressure on natural resources and the environment. Land is very scarce and the country is confronted with a serious pollution problem.

Although the figure for the labour force as a percentage of total population is in line with the EU average (see Table G19), the participation rate is rather low if measured in terms of full-time job equivalents.

The employment rate (employment as a percentage of the population aged 15–65 years) in terms of full-time equivalents is low. In 1995 it was equal to around 50% in the Netherlands, 55% in Germany, 56% in France, 58% in the United Kingdom and 66% in Denmark. Only countries like Ireland, Spain and Greece show lower or similar levels of employment. Labour participation is clearly an issue of concern in the Netherlands. The difference between the figures in terms of persons and those in full-time equivalents is caused by the high degree of part-time employment, especially among women.

Important factors contributing to the low employment rate (in terms of full-time equivalents) are:

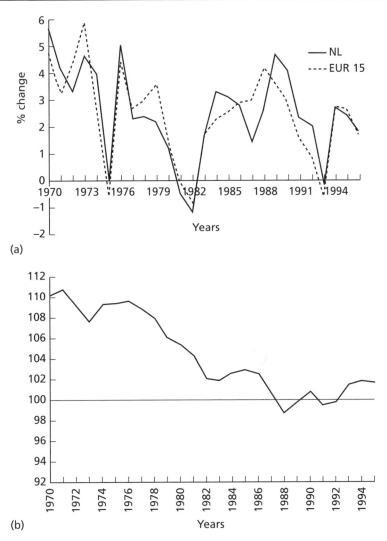

Figure 5.1 Real GDP growth per head, 1970–95: (a) at 1990 market prices; (b) at current market prices (PPS: EUR15 = 100)

- The (still) *low participation rate of women*. Until the 1960s Holland was a relatively conservative country, with clear distinctions between the role of both sexes. Since then, many cultural changes have taken place, which have resulted in more and more women taking paid (mostly part-time) jobs. The process is continuing; women still have some way to go before they have catch up with males and also with women in other EU countries.

- The relatively high number of (long-term) *unemployed* and – even more important – the large number of *disabled workers*. Holland is striking for the sheer size of its disabled population; particularly given that it is one of the world's best performers in terms of health indicators. The way the social security system is operated (considered in Section 5.7) provides a major explanation for this phenomenon.

- The *rapid increase of the population at working age*. The population between 15 and 65 years in the Netherlands has been increasing much faster than in the surrounding countries. This development is caused by the high birth rate and the immigration of mostly younger people. Until the early 1980s, the Dutch economy did not generate enough additional jobs to absorb these large numbers of new entrants on the labour market. Only since 1982 has employment creation exceeded labour supply growth, leading to a decrease in unemployment and a slightly increased employment rate.

One side of the problem is that the Dutch economy obviously did not create enough jobs to absorb the (rapidly increasing) labour supply. The reasons for this will be discussed in Section 5.7.

5.2.3 Consumption, savings and investment

Private and collective consumption (in terms of GDP) in the Netherlands have been below the EU average for a considerable time (see Tables G26 and G28). Investment, however, has been generally in line with the EU average during the last decade (Table G29). The difference in the use of GDP is made up by the high export surplus of the Netherlands (equivalent to 5% of GDP, see Table G26), indicating that the Dutch economy normally has a high national savings surplus.

Business investment recovered strongly in the 1980s, averaging around 20% over the decade. Although this rate seems unexceptional by international standards, there are nevertheless some worries about this figure. First, compared to Japan (more than 30% in the beginning of the 1990s) and other fast developing east Asian countries, this proportion is rather low. Second, because of its extreme openness, international competitiveness is of vital importance to the Dutch economy. One of the strongest features of the Netherlands is its high labour productivity, which is expected to offset high labour costs. Investment should be a major instrument in achieving this goal.

Government involvement in the economy is considered to have been unhelpful in this

respect. Too large a part of government expenditure has been used for consumption. These expenses have been financed in a substantial part by revenues from natural gas, which alternatively could have been used to finance government spending on infrastructure for instance, or on support for research and development. The last two Dutch governments have decided, in fact, to give more priority to investments in infrastructure, which will partly be financed by means of a special 'Natural Gas Fund'.

Finally, it should be noted that massive government borrowing to finance the public deficit may have caused the 'crowding out' of private investment.

Another factor contributing to the moderate investment ratio is the large and persistent national savings surplus. According to the Dutch Central Bank, net outward investment in 1994 represented 5.4% of GDP, the highest proportion among all OECD countries. The Netherlands has become an important foreign investor, with a net creditor position of around 30% of GDP in 1994. With the exchange rate firmly pegged to the Deutschmark, no correction can be expected from a strong appreciation of the guilder. However, it would be much more beneficial for the Dutch economy if part of the national savings surplus was invested in the domestic economy, especially in light of the fact that a substantial part of the labour force is unemployed. In response, over the last decade or so successive Dutch governments have pursued policies designed to improve the general investment climate (e.g. promoting wage moderation, reducing taxes, deregulation etc – see below).

5.2.4 Wages and prices

The level of wages and prices is of crucial importance for the competitiveness of the Dutch economy. Since the economic crisis in the early 1980s, Dutch governments have given priority to policies aimed at *moderating wage increases*. Part of this approach was an attempt to decrease the collective burden of taxes and social security contributions. In line with these policies, employers and unions agreed in 1982 to give job creation priority over wage increases. In addition, more room was created for decentralised wage negotiations and wage differentiation at branch and company level.

These policies appear to have been quite effective. In the 1980s productivity rose at a faster rate than real wages, resulting in a reduction in real unit labour costs. This reduction was more marked than in most other EU countries, Japan and the US. Holland was surpassed by only Portugal, Ireland and Spain in this respect (see Table G27). The decrease of unit labour costs came to an end in the early 1990s, due to a sharp increase in the non-wage labour costs and a slowing down of productivity growth.

The wage share in value-added of the (non-energy) business sector decreased from 94.7% in 1981 to reach a low of 80.2% in 1990 (see Figure 5.2 (a)), leading to a significant recovery of the capital share in value-added and the profitability of firms. During the mild recession of the early 1990s, the wage share in value-added temporarily increased and profitability dropped, but the recovery of the mid-1990s is expected to lead to a significant improvement in both indicators. Overall, the hourly labour costs in industry are still very high; in 1993 Holland was surpassed by only Denmark and Germany in the EU. On the other hand, the country is the best performer in terms of labour productivity (defined as GDP/hour) in the EU (see also OECD, 1996, 76–80 and Melkert, 1996).

In relation to the *reduction in inflation* the Netherlands has been very successful (see Figure 5.2 (b) and Table G31). The country had the lowest average inflation in the 1980s and the early 1990s, even surpassing Germany. The gain in competitiveness resulting from decreasing unit labour costs and a negative inflation differential *vis-à-vis* other industrialised countries has

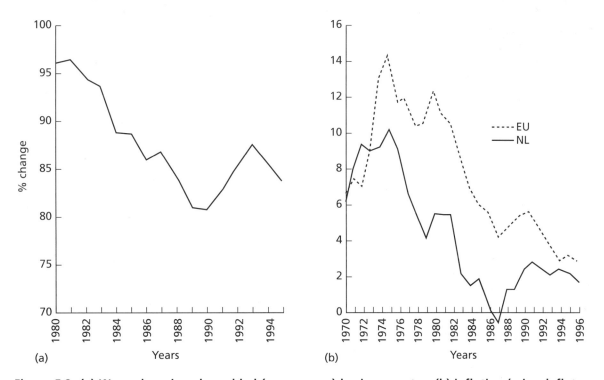

(a) Years (b) Years

Figure 5.2 (a) Wage share in value-added (non-energy) business sector; (b) inflation (price deflator private consumption)

Source: (a) CPB, *Macroeconomische Verkenning*, 1996; (b) Eurostat 1996.

been partly offset, however, by repeated revaluations of the guilder. Especially since the currency crises of 1992 and 1993 the guilder has been appreciated in real terms against most other European currencies. It is expected that inflation will remain low in the mid-term. If the European currencies stabilise, then this may result in a renewed improvement of the Dutch position, since competitive devaluations of other currencies will not take place in that case.

5.2.5 Economic structure

As can be seen from Table 5.1, services (market and non-market) are by far the most important economic activity in the Netherlands. In terms of employment, Holland has proportionately the largest service sector of all EU countries (see Table G19).

The relative size of the service sector is a reflection of the importance of the Netherlands as a trading nation and distribution centre and of the fact that a relatively large proportion of national income is devoted to non-market services like health care, education and social services.

Figure 5.3 illustrates the prominent role of the Netherlands as a distribution centre and transit port. The port of Rotterdam and Schiphol

Table 5.1 Structure of output, 1994

	Share of value added	Share of employment
Agriculture, forestry and fishing	3.7	4.8
Industry (incl. construction)	29.5	24.7
Services and general government	66.8	70.5
Total	100	100

Source: Central Bureau of Statistics, National Accounts, Statistics Netherlands.

airport play a crucial role in this transit trade. The Netherlands likes to present itself as 'the' *Gateway to Europe*, as part of an effort to attract investors from outside the EU. Almost half of the American and Japanese multinationals have located their main European distribution centres in the Netherlands. Apart from direct trade services, like harbour facilities, transport and communication, the country has obtained a strong position in other business services, e.g. financial services and information technology. A comparative advantage of the Netherlands, apart from its geographical location, is its strong international orientation. Most Dutch people speak

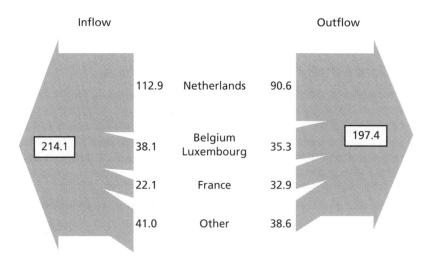

Inflow		Outflow
112.9	Netherlands	90.6
214.1 38.1	Belgium Luxembourg	35.3 197.4
22.1	France	32.9
41.0	Other	38.6

Figure 5.3 Flows of transit goods in the EU, 1987 (millions of tons)

Source: Miljoenennota 1993/CPB *Ondersoeksmemorandum* 97.

several foreign languages and are used to international contacts. With the growing internationalisation of the world economy this is clearly an advantage. On top of that, services like distribution, transport, communication and finance are characterised by a higher level of productivity than the economy as whole. The strong presence of these services is also one of the major explanations for the outstanding productivity performance of the Dutch economy (OECD 1996).

Though parts of the service sector are very strong, *agriculture* and the related *food industry* are normally regarded as a success story of the Dutch economy. The Netherlands occupies second position as a world exporter of agricultural products, after the USA. The food industry is by far the biggest industry and food products contribute around 18% of total exports of goods – the second largest export category (1994 figures). Several factors have contributed to the impressive performance of Dutch agriculture. Natural conditions are quite favourable and private family farming guarantees a high degree of competition and motivation. On the other hand, there is traditionally an extensive cooperation between Dutch farmers. For instance in the field of milk processing, banking, purchasing and selling, farmers operate cooperatives to promote their common interests. Furthermore, with government sponsorship, research and educational institutes, information services and farmers cooperate closely.

There are, though, clear threats currently facing Dutch agriculture. First, there are environmental constraints. The pressure on the environment from the intensely industrialised agriculture concentrated on a small area are enormous. The sector is for instance confronted with a huge manure waste problem, one of the major sources of acidification. Second, there are overcapacity problems, which could persist given EU policies. Changes in the CAP, induced by GATT-talks, are likely in the near future, however. Prospects for cattle breeding and grain farming look somewhat gloomy, although forecasts relating to horticulture are more optimistic.

Apart from the food industry, the role of *manufacturing industry* is rather modest in the Netherlands. The most important (non-food) industries are chemicals and electrical, metal and mechanical engineering.

The chemical sector, the biggest one in terms of value added, is heavily involved in bulk products and very much internationally oriented. In addition, oil refineries are found around the port of Rotterdam. The geographical location of the Netherlands and its efficient transport facilities (e.g. its waterways) explain to a great extent the development of these industries. Major Dutch firms in this field with headquarters in the Netherlands are AKZO and DSM (Chemicals) and Royal Dutch/Shell (oil). Electrical engineering is the second largest branch of manufacturing industry. It is dominated by Philips, one of the world's biggest producers in this field, which has its headquarters in the Netherlands. The metal and metal articles industry occupy the third place (in terms of value-added). The latter is dominated by small and medium-sized companies.

Generally, it is considered that the technological level of Dutch manufacturing industry is not high enough (see also Section 5.5). In the field of research and development (R&D) the Netherlands is clearly more and more an underachiever. The country spent in 1993 only 1.8% of GDP on R&D (down from 2.3% in 1987), compared to an average of 2.5% in the surrounding major West European countries and 3% in the USA. While public expenditure on R&D is similar to that in other developed countries, private spending seriously lags behind levels elsewhere (Ministry of Economic Affairs, 1995c). Most of the private R&D spending (55% in 1993) is initiated by 'the big five' Dutch multinationals (Shell, Unilever, Philips, AKZO and DSM), though their share is sharply decreasing, leading to an overall downward trend in private R&D spending. Although the Dutch performance does not differ so much from other smaller countries and is partly compensated by strong imports of technology, there are some fears that the competitiveness of the manufacturing industry might be negatively affected in the long run.

Until recently the *market structure* was not characterised by a high degree of concentration in most industries. Although a handful of large multinationals originated from the Netherlands, small- and medium-sized enterprises (SMEs) prevailed. Only in industries like steel, electrical engineering, chemicals, mining and quarrying, aircraft and food and drink does big business dominate. European integration, however, has resulted in a strong impulse towards concentration. Many mergers have resulted, for instance in the banking and insurance sector.

Nonetheless, large parts of Dutch industry have remained relatively unaffected by these developments so far; small and medium enterprises are still an important feature of the Dutch economy. The total number of enterprises increased from 460 000 in 1985 to 650 000 in 1995; 558 000 of them employing less than five workers and only 4900 more than 100 workers. SMEs still dominate the commercial and non-commercial services, construction, transport and communication, hotel and catering and parts of manufacturing.

The high proportion of SMEs does not mean, however, that competition in the Netherlands is particularly fierce. Collusive behaviour and high entry barriers are widespread (Commission of the European Communities, 1995). Until recently, cooperation agreements between firms were allowed as long as they were judged to be without harmful effects. Even price agreements were permitted, but there was evidence of abuse. On top of that, existing firms were protected against new entrants by all kinds of regulations, varying from legal entrance requirements to zoning and licences. The Dutch government could not prevent mergers and acquisitions, even those leading to a share of, for example, more than 50% on the domestic market. EU legislation is, of course, much stricter; but it is only applicable if restrictive behaviour is affecting international trade.

Especially since the early 1990s it has been generally recognised that the above microeconomic rigidities might have led to effects such as price increases, lower quality, lack of flexibility and reductions in output. Moreover, with the increasing internationalisation of the economy, Dutch practices more and more came into conflict with EU competition law, leading to a number of investigations by the European Commission. For these reasons competition policy in the Netherlands has become gradually much stricter. Horizontal price agreements are in principle forbidden (since 1993), unless it can be proven that they are in the public interest. Market sharing agreements were banned in 1994. Entrance requirements have been simplified and shopping hours extended, within the framework of a more general deregulation. These measures are assumed to result in increased competition and greater economic efficiency and international competitiveness.

5.3 GOVERNMENT INVOLVEMENT IN THE ECONOMY

The Netherlands does not have a tradition of direct state intervention in the economy. The country has never possessed a large state enterprise sector and the government's involvement with industrial and regional policies has always been relatively limited. There are two areas, however, where the government has played a very explicit role, namely in the fields of wage determination and social security provision.

5.3.1 Wage determination

The wage negotiation process in the Netherlands is initially conducted at a central level, where employers' associations, trade unions and the government participate in the bargaining process. Sometimes these negotiations result in central agreements. Such agreements contain general guidelines for the subsequent negotiations between employers and employees at industry, branch or (large) company level. The collective labour agreements concluded on this level can be (and normally are) declared binding for all firms by the Minister of Social Affairs and Employment.

The whole process of decision-making is based on a neo-corporatist model of tripartite consultation. In fact, cooperation and mutual consultation prevail over conflicts and strikes as a method of decision-making. The government influences the bargaining process by means of persuasion and also by manipulating, for example, the rates of payroll taxes and social security contributions. The outcome of the process is intended to be consistent with the actual government policy, particularly as the government will be confronted directly with the results, since many benefits are related to the wage level. This means that the level of public expenditure is evidently affected by the outcome of the bargains.

Cooperation between the social partners and government is not only limited to wage negotiations. There are numerous administrative bodies and councils which are run on a tripartite basis. The most important is the *Social Economic Council (Sociaal Economische Raad – SER)*, consisting of representatives of employers, employees and independent experts assigned by the government. The government has legal obligations to consult this council before taking any decision in the socio-economic field.

The above system of industrial relations was largely established immediately after the Second World War, although its roots stem from even earlier. The dominance of religion in the social and political field offers a major explanation for the emergence of this neo-corporatist system. In recent decades it has weakened, however. The major advantage of the system is that it is a method of bargaining, which allows class conflicts and devastating strikes to be avoided. Moreover, it offers the government a clear instrument for influencing the economy. On the other hand, it lacks flexibility and does not always produce results with are in line with the prevailing market conditions. It is expected that, over the coming years, the system will weaken so as to give more room for flexibility and decentralisation.

5.3.2 The social security system and the public sector

As mentioned above, the core of the Dutch welfare state is a comprehensive statutory system of social security. The construction of this system took place largely during the 1950s and 1960s: a time of high economic growth and virtually no unemployment. The high birth rates resulted in a favourable demographic composition, with relatively few pensioners. The population was assumed to be pretty healthy. It was not foreseen at that time that the system would have to cope with mass unemployment and an ageing population. On the contrary, it was anticipated that the number of persons entitled to social security benefits would be limited. For instance, when the *Disablement Benefit Act* came into force in 1968, it was only expected that at most 100 000 persons (in the long run) would be eligible for an allowance.

From the moment that the economic crisis of the 1970s set in, it became clear, however, that the system would be overburdened with claims. As a result, the total expenditure of general government went up very rapidly (see Figure 5.4). Almost all the rise from 42% of GDP in 1970 to 61% in 1983 can be explained by the rise in transfer incomes (including interest payments). Current receipts increased, though by a smaller amount, causing the public deficit to rise (to 6.6% of GDP in 1982).

Payroll taxes, social security contributions (and other taxes) had to be substantially increased in order to fill the gap. This in turn

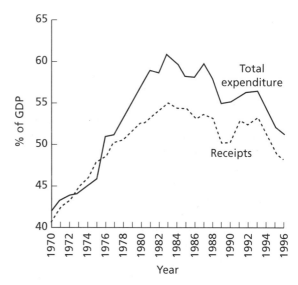

Figure 5.4 Total expenditure, current receipts and net borrowing of central government, 1970–94 (1995, 1996 estimates)

Source: Eurostat (see also Tables G32–34).

drove up labour costs, undermining Dutch competitiveness and the profitability of firms, causing further unemployment and so on. Although the origins of the recession were mostly external in the beginning (the oil shock, international monetary and trade problems), the problems were made much worse by the structure of the Dutch economy. It is understandable, therefore, why successive governments, since the first centrist–right government under prime minister Lubbers came into power in 1982, have made budget cuts, reductions in taxes, social security expenditures and public deficits their first priority. Changes of the make-up of the coalition on which the government was based in 1989 and 1994 (including the participation of left-wing social democrats) did not make any substantial difference in this respect.

Until 1994 the first priority was to *reduce the public deficit*, for which yearly targets were set. Apart from internal objectives, this was also required in order to meet the EMU convergence criteria of a maximum of 3% for the public deficit and 60% of the public debt. This policy turned out to be broadly successful; the public deficit (general government net borrowing) has been brought down to 3.2% in 1993 and is expected to remain below 3% from 1996 on.

Since 1994, when the new coalition government of the liberal party (VVD), socialist party (PvdA) and social liberals (D66) took office, the objectives have been slightly changed. The central target is a *planned reduction on public expenditure*, while a ceiling of 3% has been set on the public deficit. If this target is met without exceeding the limit for the deficit, there will be room for a reduction in the collective burden of taxes and social security payments. One of the reasons why this more *structural approach to the budgetary policy* was chosen is that this way the pro-cyclical effects of a policy purely focused on the deficit can be avoided. During a recession the deficit will normally go up, giving rise to the need for additional budget cuts. This might have a negative impact on domestic demand, intensifying recessionary forces. The opposite might happen during an upturn of the economy. Furthermore, the new policy could only be adopted *after* the public deficit was brought down to an acceptable level.

Nonetheless, since public expenditure and collective burden in the Netherlands are still considered to be too high, public finance is and will remain a matter of concern for Dutch governments.

5.4 FINANCIAL SYSTEM

5.4.1 Financial markets

Traditionally, Amsterdam has been an important financial centre. Although its stock market is rather small compared with London, Paris or Frankfurt, it is quite large in relation to the size of the country. By the end of 1994 the capitalisation of shares amounted to more than 60% of the Dutch GDP, while bonds added to another two-thirds of GDP. After the UK (with a total stock market capitalization of around 110% in 1994) the Netherlands has by far the highest proportion of investment financed through the stock market. In France, Germany, Italy and Spain (with respective stock market capitalisations of 33%, 23%, 18%, 34% in that period) financing through the banking sector is much more important.

On the demand side, the stock market is strongly dominated by a limited number of large international firms. The four largest companies (Royal Dutch Shell, Unilever, ING and ABN AMRO) account for about 56% of total share turnover (1994). The bond market is dominated by the government, which usually absorbs more than three-quarters of net bond lending. Trading in government bonds accounted for 93% of total bond turnover in that year (Commission of the European Communities, 1995).

On the supply side of the capital market, institutional investors like insurance companies, pension funds and social insurance funds are the biggest actors, accounting for 45% of total net supply in 1991. The banking (23%), foreign (15%), and household and business sector (14%) are far less important. The dominant position of the institutional investors stems partly from the high degree of contractual savings in the Netherlands. This is also a major reason why the Netherlands has a very high savings ratio (see Sections 5.2 and 5.5). In addition to the stock market there is a parallel market providing access to venture capital for smaller firms.

In the early 1980s the city lost a considerable part of the available business to its competitors, mainly to London. Compared to its main competitors the Amsterdam Stock Exchange was small and expensive, with too much of its business dominated by large, internationally operating parties who are very sensitive to trading costs. Starting in 1986, however, measures have been taken to deregulate the market, increase efficiency and reduce the costs of financial intermediation. In 1994 radical reforms of the trading system were introduced, splitting the market into fully computerised wholesale and retail segments. As a result, part of the trade has returned in recent years.

Although the banking sector is not the most prominent participant in the capital market it is nevertheless quite well developed. It shows a high degree of concentration. The two largest banks (in terms of balance sheet total), the *Algemene Bank Nederland (ABN)* and the *Amsterdam–Rotterdam Bank (AMRO)* merged in 1991 to form the new giant *ABN AMRO*. In 1990, the so-called 'structure policy' rule forbidding mergers between banks and insurance companies was liberalised. Henceforth only a declaration of 'no objection' from the Central Bank (*De Nederlandsche Bank – DNB*) is required. This change enabled a merger in 1991 between the second largest bank, *NMB-Postbank*, with a large insurance group, the *Nationale Nederlanden*, into a new financial conglomerate called *Internationale Nederlanden Groep bv (ING-bank)*. The third bank, *RABO*, obtained a large stake in another big insurance group. The top three banks (*ABN AMRO, ING* and *RABO*) nowadays have between them well over 80% of the combined balance sheet total of the country's banking sector. Compared with other banks in the EU they still are only middle-sized.

5.4.2 Monetary policy

The main objective of monetary policy in the Netherlands is the maintenance of internal and external stability of the national currency, the guilder. In the last decade the stress has shifted more and more toward exchange rate stability, however. There are two basic reasons for this. First, external relations are of major importance for the Dutch economy. A stable guilder, strictly pegged to the Deutschmark, is an absolute condition for stable trade relations. Second, the ability to control inflation by monetary policy has been diminished very significantly in the last decade. The liberalisation of capital markets and the marked increase international capital mobility loosened the grip of the monetary authorities on the money supply, especially the external component of it. Besides, it would appear that a substantial increase during the second half of the 1980s in the national liquidity ratio (M2/net national income), which was the old target variable of monetary policy, did not really result in an upward pressure on inflation. The business sector used the newly created liquidity mainly to increase its financial soundness. The relation between the money supply (M2) and inflation seems, therefore, rather weak.

In fact, the Netherlands has already had a *de facto* monetary union with Germany for more than a decade, with the guilder firmly pegged within a margin of ±1% to the Deutschmark. The justification for this policy is twofold. First, Germany is by far the most important trading partner for the Netherlands, counting for almost 30% of its total exports. Second, the German authorities have a very strong commitment to price stability. This guarantees – via a stable guilder-mark exchange rate – a stable price level in the Netherlands as well. The exchange rate policy is backed up by a policy which aims to control domestic money creation. This policy should prevent problems of excessive money growth, leading to large capital outflows and hence downward pressure on the exchange rate. Last but not least, the Treasury and the central bank agreed in 1981 to avoid monetary financing of the public deficit.

The main policy instrument used for exchange rate stability is the interest rate. The Dutch central bank (*De Nederlandsche Bank, DNB*) closely follows the German interest rate policy. Only in special circumstances, e.g. in 1995 and 1996 when the guilder was very strong, does the central bank alter the interest rates independently of the *Bundesbank*. In addition to changes in the official interest rates (e.g. discount rates), *DNB* mostly uses open market operations to influence market interest rates. Open market operations in combination with mandatory cash reserve requirements and mandatory deposits at the central bank can also be used to squeeze the monetary base of the banking sector, which will prevent excessive domestic money creation.

To conclude this section, it can be seen that the Dutch monetary authorities have been very successful with respect to both external and internal price stability. Inflation in the Netherlands has been the lowest of all EU countries in the last decade, even lower than Germany. The Dutch guilder is – together with the mark – the strongest currency in the EU. The country will probably easily satisfy the EMU criteria in this respect.

5.5 INTERNATIONAL RELATIONS

As has been noted, the Netherlands has an extreme open economy. The average (goods and services) export rate (exports/GDP) amounted to 47% in the 1970s and went up to 56% in the 1980s. The corresponding figures for the average import rates (imports/GDP) were 46% and 51%. As a result, the country normally has a large and persistent current account surplus (see Figure 5.5).

Part of the current account surplus is due to the extraction of natural gas, which is an important export good and also a substitute for energy imports. But even when energy is excluded, there usually remains an impressive trade and current account surplus. Although the latter surplus is usually substantially offset by a huge capital account balance deficit (meaning an out-

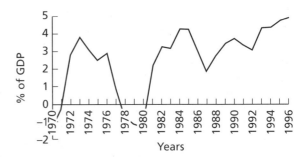

Figure 5.5 The Dutch current account balance 1970–96. Surplus (+) or deficit (–) as a percentage of GDP (1995, 1996 estimates)

Source: Eurostat. Table G34

flow of money), the overall balance of payments in most years shows a surplus. That is one of the reasons why the Dutch currency, the guilder, has over time tended to revalue against the ECU.

The traditionally low inflation rate together with high productivity are the main causes of the competitiveness of Dutch industry. The Dutch position was, however, strongly affected by the steep increase of labour costs in the early 1980s, caused by the combination of an economic depression and rather generous social security provisions (see Section 5.3). Since then, Dutch competitiveness has improved substantially, especially in the second half of the 1980s. The Netherlands was most successful of all EU countries in bringing its relative unit labour costs down (measured in 1991 dollars): from 114.2 in 1980 to 100 in 1991 (index figures). Government austerity policies and wage moderation are the major explanations for this achievement. Dutch unit labour costs remain a matter of concern, though, because unit labour costs (in a common currency) once again showed a tendency to increase during the recession in the early 1990s to reach a (estimated) level of 108.5 in 1996 (European Commission figures of 1996).

5.5.1 Geographical orientation and composition of trade

The bulk of Dutch exports is directed to other EU countries. For instance, in 1994 75% went to the eleven countries, which (together with the Netherlands) made up the EU in that year. European integration had a clear effect on the direction of trade: in 1958 only 58% of total exports went to these other eleven member states. The neighbouring countries are by far the most important trading partners: 29% of total exports went to Germany, 13.9% Belgium/Luxembourg, 11% France and 10% the UK (see Table G38). The same holds, more or less, for imports, although the percentage of imports originating from EU countries (55% in 1994) does not match the export figure (75%). Germany is the largest exporter to the Netherlands (21%) followed by Belgium/Luxembourg (11%), the UK (8.5%) and France (7%; 1994 figures; see Table G39).

The composition of the Dutch commodity exports is as follows: 24% machinery and transport equipment, 18% food and drink, 16% chemicals, 12% manufactured goods, 7% energy, 5% raw materials and 18% other goods (1994). A notable feature is the high proportion of food, drink, energy and raw materials; together these account for 30% in total exports. In addition, a substantial part of the chemicals output consists of basic bulk products. There are, in fact, some serious concerns about the specialisation of Dutch industry, e.g. that is too focused on primary products with a rather low technological content. If Dutch industry wants to maintain its strong export position, it needs to shift towards more knowledge-intensive, high-tech production. Investment (among others in R&D) would be a key factor in this process. In this manner the Netherlands would be able to keep its strong international competitiveness. According to the *World Competitiveness Report* of 1995, Holland ranks in seventh position in the world.

5.6 IMPACT OF EUROPEAN INTEGRATION

The Netherlands has been a Member State of the European Union and its predecessors right from the beginning. The exact impact of this membership on the economy are, of course, difficult to assess. Other factors might have played an important role as well. Nevertheless, it can be argued that European integration has had a substantial influence in relation to the following:

- Trade has been diverted away from non-EU to EU countries. This applies especially to exports. Total trade of goods and services (as a percentage of GDP) has risen only slightly compared to 1958.

- Competition and efficiency have been increased. European integration, rules and regulations might be considered as factors contributing to the creation of a more competitive environment in the Netherlands. The adoption of more stringent competition laws, the trend towards deregulation and privatisation of public utilities might be favoured by European factors.

- The social security system has been reformed. Social security is still considered a matter of national sovereignty within the EU. Nonetheless, no country can afford an inefficient and excessively costly social security system. The increased competition in the EU has been one of the factors forcing Dutch governments to reduce social security spending and bring it more in line with the European average.

- The public deficit has been reduced. The need to bring the deficit down is clearly reinforced by the EMU requirements.

- Public investment. Within the Single Market a more fierce 'policy competition' is emerging. There is a greater pressure on governments to create an adequate infrastructure in order to support a favourable business environment. The stress in the Netherlands so far has been for investments in transport infrastructure like airports, harbours, roads and railways, as well as in education and training.

5.7 SPECIAL ISSUES: EMPLOYMENT AND INACTIVITY

The low employment rate (in terms of full-time equivalents) is generally considered to be the biggest problem for the Dutch economy. For every two persons of working age there is only one job available. It is the main reason why the Netherlands lost its position as one of the richest European countries. The economy is, in fact, operating below its potential. The Dutch economy has not been generating a sufficient number of jobs, although the situation has started to improve recently. There are a number of explanations for this disappointing performance. The most important are:

- *Structural problems*. The profitability of the Dutch business sector has been relatively low for a long period. Labour costs have been high, mainly due to the generous social security system, leading to high taxes and social security contributions. Although profitability recovered strongly during the upswing in the second half of the 1980s, it still remains a matter of concern. New recessions can easily result once more in upward pressures on labour costs via increasing social security contributions. This way, recessions might be self-reinforcing.
- *The social security system*. The social security system offers little incentives for people to re-enter the labour market. Most of the unemployed receive benefits – if they have to maintain a family – on the net social assistance (welfare) level, which is practically the same as the net minimum wage. Until the recent reforms, disablement schemes were frequently used as an alternative to unemployment benefit programmes. The programme offered an easy route for firms wishing to reduce the size of their work-force; poorly performing workers could – if they were prepared to cooperate and after a period of sickness – be declared partially or totally disabled. The advantage for workers was that the scheme offered more generous and permanent benefits.

The origins of disablement do not necessary have to be related to the work-place itself: sport accidents, psychological problems or a deterioration of general health equally qualify. So, in contrast to general practice in most other countries, both professional and social risks are covered by the disability insurance laws. The number of disabled persons peaked in 1993, when 917 000 persons received benefits, compared to a total work-force of 6.5 million and a population of 15.2 million. In reality the disablement programme contains a huge unemployment component.

Moreover, especially until a couple of years ago, unemployment and disablement programmes hardly encouraged people to either search for new jobs or participate in (re)training schemes. There is a strong incentive for such people to stay for a long time, or even permanently, in the social security system (a phenomenon known as the 'social security trap').

- *Rigidities on the labour market*. The Dutch labour market does not work very efficiently. Reasons for this are:
  - The high level of minimum wage, preventing the labour market from clearing on the lower side. This means that an excess supply of low-skilled workers will not be eliminated by decreasing wages to levels appropriate for these categories.
  - The strongly centralised collective bargaining system, in which employers' associations, trade unions and the government participate, results in relatively inflexible wage levels which adapt only slowly to new market conditions.
  - Lay-off restrictions, allowing firing of employees by employers only in case of 'economic necessity' and only after prior approval of the Public Employment Service.

The lack of efficiency of the labour market is also indicated by the relatively pronounced sectoral mismatch. Persistent unemployment exists alongside a substantial number of vacancies.

A low employment rate does not necessarily mean that the official *un*employment rate is high. In the Netherlands, it is clearly below the average EU level of the early 1990s (6.5% versus 10.2% for EU15). For a better understanding of the real problem it makes sense to use the concept of *broad unemployment* (OECD, 1996, p. 46), which includes all unemployed and inactive persons of working age receiving a social security benefit and persons enrolled in special job creation programmes. Measured in full-time equivalents broad unemployment is over 25% for more than a decade. On the one hand this might be an overestimate of the real slack in the labour market, since most of the disabled are not available for work. Earlier estimates of the hidden unemployment component in the scheme vary between 10 and 50%. On the other hand, the concept of broad unemployment does not include discouraged and involuntary part-time workers. It can be concluded that inactivity of persons of working age (in full-time equivalents) in the Netherlands is considerably higher than in most other countries.

Since 1982 successive Dutch governments have introduced a number of measures in order to address the problems of the labour market and to promote employment creation. These include: (1) wage moderation, (2) reform of the social security system and (3) specific measures addressed at the labour market.

Wage moderation, including the reduction of non-wage costs (taxes and social security contributions) has been discussed above. The *reform of the social security system* is meant to make the system less expensive and is indirectly linked to the objective of wage moderation. But on top of that, it is also meant to remove the disincentives for beneficiaries to look for a job. The reforms have been focused especially on the disability and sickness schemes. For instance, in 1993 the duration of disability benefits for new entrants was reduced and made dependent on the number of years they worked previously. A much more stringent definition of disability has been introduced and all current disabled below 50 years old are gradually being re-examined according to this new definition. In 1996 the sickness insurance was privatised. In the last decade, the number of benefits has been gradually decreased. Persons living on welfare are (since 1996) confronted with stricter obligations to accept a job. In a number of cases, the measures clearly have had the desired effects: for instance, from 1994 onwards the number of disabled persons has dropped by more than 25 000 persons per year.

Measures addressed at the labour market have consisted, among others, of fiscal measures to reduce the cost for employers of hiring workers at a minimum wage and a number of special employment programmes in the public sector for low-skilled workers. Most measures focused especially on the lower end of the labour market.

These government policies have proved to be quite successful. In the last decade the Dutch economy managed to create more than 100 000 new jobs a year. Nowhere in Europe is employment growing that fast. On the other hand, the labour supply increased at about the same pace (see Section 5.2.2). Although not everybody wants to have or manages to find a full-time job, unemployment has nevertheless been decreasing. This trend might be reinforced during the expected upswing of the economy in the late 1990s; moreover, it is assumed that the labour supply growth will decelerate in the near future. This might result in a rather low unemployment rate. Nonetheless, the Dutch economy still has a long way to go before the employment rate reaches an acceptable level.

5.8 FUTURE PROSPECTS

In the last decade a number of favourable developments with respect to the Dutch economy have taken place. Employment is rapidly increasing and public expenditure, the collective burden and the public deficit are decreasing. Reforms of the social security system have taken effect, making the system less expensive and removing the disincentives to work. This means that some important structural imbalances are diminishing.

This adds to the strong points, such as political stability, a low inflation record, the current account surplus, the strong and stable currency and the international orientation of the economy. The country is likely to be one of the first candidates to enter the EMU (though its national debt is still too high).

Nonetheless, there is still room for improvement. The problems of the Dutch economy are particularly found at the microeconomic level. Matters of concern are the technological level of the Dutch industry, rigidities on the labour market and some goods and services markets, public finances and especially the employment rate. Recent governments, however, have shown their determination to address these problems. Most important, arguably, is the employment rate. If it could be raised to the average European level, the Netherlands could regain its position among the richest countries of the Union.

5.9 BIBLIOGRAPHY AND SOURCES OF INFORMATION

Official publications

Central Planning Bureau (annually) *Macro Economische Verkenning*

Central Planning Bureau (annually) *Centraal Economisch Plan*

Central Planning Bureau (1992), *Scanning the Future, a Long-term Scenario Study of the World Economy 1990–2015*

De Nederlandsche Bank (annually): *Jaarverslag*

Central Statistical Office (annually): *Statistisch Jaarboek*

Commission of the European Communities (1992): Country Studies, *The Netherlands*

Commission of the European Communities (1995): *The Economic and Financial Situation in the Netherlands*, European Economy No. 1

Ministry of Economic Affairs (1995a): *Benchmarking the Netherlands – a test of Dutch competitiveness*

Ministry of Economic Affairs (1995b): *Economy with Open Frontiers*

Ministry of Economic Affairs (1995c): *Knowledge in Action*

Ministry of Finance (annually): *Miljoenennota*

Netherlands Scientific Council for Government Policy (1993): *Shaping Factors for the Business Environment in the Netherlands after 1992*

OECD (annually, latest edition 1996): *Economic Surveys, The Netherlands*

Other publications

Artis, M. and Lee, N. (1994): *The Economics of the European Union, Policy and Analysis*, Oxford

Barnes, I. and Barnes, P. (1995): *The Enlarged European Union*, Longman

Buunk, H. (1995): *De economie in Nederland* (3rd edn), Wolters-Noordhoff, Groningen

Central Planning Bureau (1992): *FKSEC, a Macro-Econometric Model for The Netherlands*, Stenferd Kroese, Leiden

Church, C. and Phinnimore, D. (1994): *European Union & European Community, A Handbook on the Post-Maastricht Treaties*, Harvester Wheatsheaf

Cockfield, Lord (1994): *The European Union, Creating a Single Market*, Wiley

Compaijen, B., Butter, F.A.G.den, (1991/1992): *De Nederlandse economie* (four volumes), Wolters-Noordhoff, Groningen

Dyker, D. (ed.) (1992): *The European Economy*, Longman

Geest, L. van der and Sinderen, J. van (1995): *Kracht en Zwakte van de Nederlandse economie*, Barjesteh, Meeuwes & Co, Syntax Publishers, Rotterdam

Hirtiris, T. (1994): *European Community Economics*, 3rd edn, Harvester Wheatsheaf

Koopmans, L., Wellink, A.H.E.M., Woltjer, H.J., Kam, C.A. de (1996): *Overheidsfinanciën* (8th edn), Stenferd Kroese, Leiden/Antwerpen

McDonald, F. and Dearden, S. (1994): *European Economic Integration*, 2nd edn, Longman

Melkert, A. (1996): *De verzorgingsstaat in internationaal perspectief*, ESB no 4066

Sinderen, J. van *et al.* (1994): *De kosten van economisch verstarring op macro-niveau*, ESB 3954

Somers, F.J.L., Sinderen, J. van, (1996): *De economie van het overheidsbeleid* (2nd edn), Wolters-Noordhoff, Groningen

CHAPTER 6

Belgium and Luxembourg

Ian Stone
Charles Jarvis

6.1 INSTITUTIONAL AND HISTORICAL CONTEXT

6.1.1 Political background

Belgium was formed as a European nation in 1830, when Dutch-speaking Flemings and French-speaking Walloons forged an alliance in opposition to Dutch (William I's) autocratic rule. The new buffer state kingdom was supported by other European powers and its neutrality guaranteed under the Treaty of London (1839). In spite of the understanding that the government should be made up of identical numbers of French and Flemish-speaking ministers, governance has been rendered complex by a regional and linguistic split between the two large regions of Flanders and Wallonia, superimposed upon a conventional left–right span of views (Socialists, Christian Democrats, Liberals) in both communities. Belgium today remains an uneasy union of linguistically distinct regions to which power is being devolved by stages.

Political difficulties arising out of communal differences between the Flemings in the north of the country and Walloons in the south – and the particular interests of Brussels (the French-speaking enclave in Flemish territory) – lay behind the process of devolution. The period since 1970 has seen the effective dismantling of Belgium's unitary state. How far this process will go is still unclear. The Minister-President of the Flemish government, Mr Van den Brande, has argued that the reform of the Belgian state should evolve from a federation of regions and communities into two states within a confederal system. Yet there are powerful voices opposed to even taking federalism too far and recent years have seen a number of large anti-separatist demonstrations. While conflicts between separatist and nationalist politicians continue, among the Belgian people there is a clear majority in favour of federalism.

The 1980 regionalisation laws, which came into effect in 1982, involved the splitting of the country into three communities (French, Flemish and German-speaking) with responsibility over matters relating to the individual (education and culture), and into three spatially defined regions (Flanders, Wallonia and Brussels), each with powers relating to their specific territory. The third phase of constitutional reform, drawn up in 1988, transferred further spending powers to the Regions and Communities, including public works, research, communications, environmental protection, local economic development and energy; while Brussels attained its own directly elected assembly and executive. The executives of these entities are autonomous in that they have the power to prepare bills which, if they are passed by the assembly, become law.

The fourth constitutional change occurred in 1993 and came into effect after the 1995 election, when a further dissolution of the Chamber of Deputies and the Senate took place. The number of seats in each has been reduced from 212 to 150, and from 174 to 71, respectively. Further to this, both the Flanders and Wallonia regional parliaments were brought into line with the Brussels assembly; all members of regional parliaments are now directly elected. The constitutional changes of 1970, 1980, 1988 and 1993 have progressively pared away central government responsibilities, leaving just fiscal policy, defence, and law and order. It seems unlikely that the 1993 constitutional changes will be the last; a review of the effects of administrative autonomy upon the three regions is scheduled to take place in 1999.

Central government is under increasing pressure from Flanders nationalist politicians for further devolution due to suggestions that Flemish money is subsidising Wallonia's increasing welfare and social security payments. Prime Minister Dehaene seems unlikely to push for further constitutional change, as time is needed to allow Belgium's institutions to settle into their new roles, and for the development of interregional cooperation.

For the purposes of this chapter, it is not possible to identify a consistent grouping of regions, since various forms of economic union exist with neighbouring states. Apart from being an EU member since the inception of the Community, Belgium is a signatory to a 1944 treaty of economic union with the Netherlands and Luxembourg (Benelux), which came into force in 1948. Particularly close relations exist with Luxembourg. These are formalised through the Belgium and Luxembourg Economic Union (BLEU), involving parity of currencies, integrated foreign trade and payments and a joint central bank. In keeping with common practice, therefore, this country study incorporates Luxembourg – both as a separate section and within the section on trade and payments (where its statistics are integrated with those of Belgium).

6.1.2 Economic background

Belgium's central position within the EU, together with its well-developed transport network, skilled labour force, open economy and government investment incentives, has made the country an attractive location for inward investment by multinational companies. Its industrial structure is notable for its concentration on a limited number of sectors and specialisation in standardised semi-finished goods as part of a wider integrated production system involving economies of neighbouring countries.

A high dependence upon imported energy (80% in the early 1970s) resulted in a sharp deterioration of the country's terms of trade following the oil price shocks of the 1970s. International competitiveness fell sharply as wage costs rose due to continued indexation, high pay awards and increased social security contributions. The public sector deficit rose as revenues declined and spending to combat unemployment – including the subsidisation of declining sectors – escalated. The government's attempt to hold purchasing power at an artificially high level caused the balance of payments to move sharply into the red.

When, in 1982, the Socialists in the coalition were replaced by the Liberals, it was formally recognised that consumption-supporting policies had become unsustainable. The whole thrust of economic policy was changed, with special emphasis given to encouraging enterprise. The restoration of competitiveness through devaluation (by 8.5% within the ERM) of the Belgian franc was central to the new strategy. To limit the impact of this upon inflation, devaluation of the currency was combined with the introduction of an incomes policy and price controls. Public spending was reduced and the corporate tax burden eased. The austerity programme gave rise to a significant improvement in investment and profit levels and generally improved economic performance during the later part of the 1980s. However, while most of the indicators have bounced back robustly since the mid-1980s, the economy still seems to be dogged by a stubbornly high rate of unemployment and by the level of public spending and indebtedness – problems exacerbated by the recession of the early 1990s.

The effects of the early 1990s recession upon the Belgian economy were made more severe by the policy of making the B-Franc closely track the D-Mark. Since the 1993 low-point of the business cycle growth in the economy has resumed, though it is still dogged by structural difficulties and high unemployment. The 2% annual average growth in real GDP during 1985–94, has been sufficient only to sustain existing jobs; the Belgian record in respect of creating new jobs is relatively poor.

Explanations for this largely focus upon labour costs. There is awareness in Belgium that price competitiveness has been eroded in the 1990s: (1) During 1990–95, relative unit labour costs expressed in a common currency deteriorated by nearly 13% against a group of 19 competitor countries (*EU Annual Report*, 1996); (2) In a 1993 international league table of hourly labour costs for blue collar workers in manufacturing, Belgium was placed fourth (DM36.3 per hour), behind West Germany (DM42.7), Switzerland (DM39.5) and Japan (DM37.3); the UK was sixteenth (DM22.2), while Portugal, which came twenty-first, had total hourly labour costs amounting to DM7.8 (Institut der deutschen Wirtschaft, Köln). The Belgium Federation of Enterprise has argued that high direct and indirect labour costs (social security payments, and the complicated and expensive redundancy procedures) result in the economy facing a 10% competitive disadvantage over neighbouring economies. It points out that these costs hamper job creation directed at the lower skilled members of the labour force, and encourage firms generally to replace labour through adopting capital intensive modes of production (*Financial Times*, 1995).

6.1.3 The global plan

To combat the high costs of labour the socialist coalition government implemented in 1993 a 'global plan' for employment, competitiveness and social security. Its main aim is to reduce the relative cost of labour, through the dilution of the wage index by excluding tobacco, alcohol, and fuel prices from the 'cost of living basket'. The plan has the added advantage of making wages less responsive to increases in indirect taxation. Although the old wage negotiation system was fairly successful in terms of preserving social harmony, it tended to work against employment creation; hence the government also introduced a real wage freeze (covering 1994–96). Its hope is that the social partners (employers and unions) will review their negotiating practices and establish a framework which – without requiring further intervention – will ensure satisfactory employment and labour costs.

Implementing the Global Plan also entails reducing the burden of direct taxation and social security costs. Direct taxation on labour in Belgium accounts for around 30% of GDP, which is six percentage points above the EUR15 average. To attain this gradual reduction in direct taxation, the government has selectively reduced employer costs (e.g. social security payments) for those sectors of the economy that are most open to foreign competition and employ young or low skilled people. The Global Plan measures have been restrained by Belgium's need to balance budgets in line with the European Monetary Union target. Thus the reductions in direct taxes have been offset by increases in indirect and corporation taxes.

It is too early to assess the effectiveness of the Global Plan, but it is unlikely that such measures will provide a lasting solution to the long-term structural problems faced by the Belgian economy. Job creation in 1994 amounted to 16 000, which is only half the level achieved during the second half of the 1980s. The wage freeze is time-limited and catch-up wage rises might well follow the expiry of the measure (the OECD predict that wages will rise by 4% in 1997). Government has stated that the cuts in social security and other indirect labour costs are once-and-for-all changes but employers are calling for further measures to reduce labour costs (including subsidies). Such measures are unlikely to be forthcoming in the light of Belgium's need to satisfy the budgetary criteria for Monetary Union.

6.2 MAIN ECONOMIC CHARACTERISTICS

6.2.1 Gross domestic product

Over the period 1975–87, there were only three years in which the Belgian economy grew at the EUR15 rate or above, and the overall average for these years was below 1.5% per year. This period encompasses the 1980s austerity measures which paved the way for a stronger growth performance during 1988–90, when growth (annual rate 4.1%) ran ahead of the EUR15 average for the first time since the 1960s. Recession in its main export markets has contributed to slower expansion in the 1990s; average real growth rate was 1.3% during 1991–95 compared with 1.4% for EUR15. Although there has been some improvement in the rate of GDP growth since 1993, Belgium is still finding it hard to match growth performances achieved elsewhere in the EU (Table G23). Nevertheless, helped by its relatively slow population growth (see below), GDP per head is comfortably above the EU average, by around 12% in 1994 and 1995 (Table G24). Belgium's average income is similar to that of Austria and Denmark and bettered only by Luxembourg and (west) Germany.

6.2.2 Labour market and unemployment

Belgium is a small country, with an area of 30 500 km², a population of 10 million and a density of 328 persons per km². The population is divided unevenly between the different regions, with the largest share in Flanders (58%), followed by Wallonia (33%) and Brussels (9%). It has one of the lowest birth rates in the EU and, with a low rate of immigration since the mid-1960s, numbers have risen only slowly (about 0.1% per annum since 1980). These considerations, together with a declining labour participation rate, mean that the labour force has grown slowly over the past two decades (e.g. 0.11% per year during the 1980s).

The civilian workforce of 4.01 million is relatively small in proportion to the total population (41% in 1993 compared to EUR12 average of 45%) and very substantially below the levels found in Denmark, the UK and Germany in particular (Table G18). Male participation rates, which have long been below other EU countries, fell faster than elsewhere in the 1980s; at 71% in 1994 the figure for Belgium is some five percentage points below the EU average (European Commission, 1995). Rising female participation rates have not fully compensated for this, and the 61% figure overall (males and females) in 1994 was still some five percentage points below the EU average (and 12 points lower than the participation rate in the UK).

Out of a total civilian employment in 1993 of 3.72 million, only a small proportion (2.4%, second only to the UK and Germany within the EU) is engaged in agriculture, forestry and fishing. Industry accounted for nearly 27% of the total, of which nearly three-quarters of a million workers are in manufacturing (a fifth of total employment). While industry in general is a smaller employer in Belgium than in the EU as a whole (28.7% compared with 32.5%), the employment share of services (68.5%) is among the highest in the Community and well above the EUR15 average of 62.5% (Table G19). Belgian public sector employment, although falling back slightly in recent years, is up by 40% compared with 1970 and stands at 0.9 million, or just under one-quarter of total employment.

The trends in participation rates reflect both structural changes in the economy and labour market policies. The decline in industrial employment and expansion of job opportunities in services – many of them for part-timers – has favoured women. Indeed, the growth in total employment in the 1980s was entirely due to an increase in part-time employment (which doubled between 1975 and the end of the 1980s). Legislation giving part-time workers the same rights (e.g. social security) as full-time workers has encouraged growth of part-time working. At the same time, other government policies had the effect of containing labour supply growth in the 1980s, e.g. compulsory education (up to the age of 18) and early retirement schemes; the latter were particularly important in encouraging males to withdraw from the labour force.

In spite of the slow growth in the labour force, unemployment is a persistent problem, reflecting the low rate of growth of employment since the mid-1970s (ascribed by the OECD to the discouragement to job creation of taxes and problems of labour market rigidity). Belgium's unemployment rate of 10.7% during the 1980s was slightly higher than the average for EUR12 (9.6%). However, the rate fell during the course of the 1980s from its post-oil shock peak of 12.5% in 1984 down to 7.8% in 1990. The economy's relatively strong performance over these years (with an estimated 161 000 jobs created over 1984–89), combined with the impact of government schemes designed to encourage early retirement, enabled Belgium to finish the decade with a jobless rate officially below the EUR15 figure of 8.3% (Table G20). This situation still applies, although the rate crept up to over 9% by late 1992 with the onset of recession; post-recession the economy has yet to create many new jobs and in 1994 the unemployment rate increased to 10%. These are, of course, standardised EU rates; Belgian official statistics put unemployment somewhat higher, at 13.5% in early 1995.

The unemployment level is strikingly uneven spatially (see Section 6.6) and includes a large proportion of long-term unemployed. The number of unemployed who had been without work for over a year fell from its 1988 peak (78%) to 59% in 1993. Long-term unemployment gives rise to problems of workers being cut off from the labour market and erosion of their skills. The problem is particularly acute among females, who made up 59% of the unemployed in 1994; a notably large proportion (by EU standards) of these are long-term unemployed married women. Female unemployment (13% in 1994) is exactly equal to the EUR12 average, while – chiefly due to the withdrawal schemes – unemployment among males is more than two percentage points below the Community average (8% as against 10%) (European Commission, 1995).

In recent years government has given increasing attention to eliminating rigidities in the labour market. This has included the introduction of a system whereby each unemployed person under the age of 46 who has been out of work for nine months is given a 'guidance plan' involving vocational training and employment schemes. Belgian unemployment programmes had previously tended to be generous and easily accessible; there are now tighter checks on the availability for work of unemployed persons, as part of a policy of introducing more stringent entitlement criteria. Concern that early retirement policies encouraged experienced employees to leave the labour force at a time when there are fewer new entrants (with not only budgetary, but possibly supply-side implications for the economy) led the authorities to institute a gradual rise in the early retirement age. These measures have been supplemented by the reductions in social security payments for specific types of employers described in the discussion of the global plan (Section 1).

6.2.3 Consumption and investment

Private consumption as a percentage of GDP increased in the decade up to 1985, from 60% to 65.5%. Since that time it has been cut back, and averaged 62.5% during 1990–94; a figure which is only slightly above the long-standing EUR15 average (Table G28) The fall in consumption's share in Belgium has resulted from government's austerity policies aimed at redistributing income from the personal to the corporate sector in order to redress the balance between investment and consumption.

Investment (gross fixed capital formation) fell sharply in the recession of the early 1980s, reaching a low point of 15.6% in 1985, compared with 22% in the 1960s and 1970s. During the late 1980s, however, Belgium recorded the largest proportional gains in investment achieved anywhere in the EU and by 1990, when the annual overall investment rate peaked, it was once more above 20% of GDP. This performance was widely held to reflect the impact of wage restraint and improved terms of trade upon corporate profitability, combined with reductions in the company tax burden. The situation proved short-lived and investment levels have since dipped once more. They have yet to fully recover from the effects of the 1991–93 recession. Investment was below the EUR15 average for the period 1990–94, hovering at around 17.5% of GDP in 1994 and 1995.

6.2.4 Wages and prices

To safeguard competitiveness and jobs, the government has on occasions stepped in to suspend wage indexation and free wage negotiations. Thus, such arrangements were suspended for a number of years following the 1982 devaluation. Restraint of pay levels in the public sector has also been exercised, with the effect of limiting earnings growth to half the levels achieved in the private sector. Real unit labour costs, which increased markedly in the 1970s, fell sharply in the years following 1982, and for the 1980s as a whole exhibited a greater fall than that recorded in EUR15 (see Figure 6.1), USA or Japan. Concern to maintain international competitiveness is built into Belgium's institutional framework relating to pay settlements. Under the terms of legislation introduced in 1989, the bipartite Central Economic Council has to monitor the economy's competitiveness against its main competitors. If the situation is deemed to have deteriorated, and the social partners (employers and unions) cannot agree on remedial action, then the government may take action (ultimately intervening in the wage indexation system).

The wage freeze introduced recently as part of the global plan is consistent with the 1980s attempt to give priority in policy to maintaining the competitiveness of Belgium's open economy. A slight upward movement in real unit labour costs occurred at the end of the 1980s (Table G27), and the recent measures would appear to have contributed to the steady downward trend in real unit labour costs in the period since 1992. The freeze on wages has, however, caused political conflict and sparked industrial action. Strikes occurred in the rail and airline industries during 1995. This industrial action has spread throughout the public sector following the collapse of the accord between government, unions and employers in May 1996, when it was proposed that post-freeze wage increases should be kept in line with those of Germany, Holland and France.

Wage controls have contributed to the achievement of low inflation levels (and vice versa). Tight economic policies in the period following the 1982 devaluation brought the annual

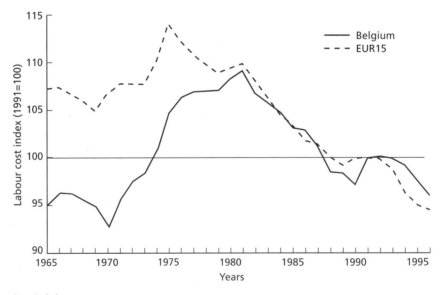

Figure 6.1 Real unit labour costs

Source: Eurostat, Table G27.

rate of increase in prices down from a level of around 8% – broadly in line with the EU average – to very low rates of just over 1% per annum during 1986–88 which, among EU countries, was shared only by West Germany, the Netherlands and Luxembourg. Inflation subsequently rose in the early 1990s, reaching 3% before falling back to 1.5% in 1995 (CPI figures in *EU Annual Report*, 1996), partly in response to the tight rein placed by the central bank upon monetary and credit aggregates. This 1.5% figure, which has continued into 1996, is comfortably amongst the lowest in the Union.

6.2.5 Market structure

The agriculture sector accounts for just over 2% of total employment (1.8% of total GDP) in the economy, the smallest in the EU next to the UK (Figure G2). The average size of holding is small (70% are under 20 hectares), and there is concentration on livestock products and horticulture. Industry (including construction) accounts for just over 31% of gross value-added. No significant mining activity is undertaken, following the closure of the remaining loss-making coal mines at the beginning of the 1990s. The contribution of services to output in Belgium (67% in 1992, Table G25) is higher proportionally than anywhere in the EU apart from Denmark, and reflects in part the country's central role within EU, NATO and multinational company administration, as well as significant levels of activity in areas of finance and transport/distribution.

Manufacturing in 1993 accounted for 22% of GDP. Traditional industries such as iron and steel, non-ferrous metals, textiles and heavy engineering nowadays make a relatively small contribution to industrial output. The sectors which now dominate manufacturing are chemicals (including bio-technology and pharmaceuticals), light engineering and food and drink. Belgian producers have increasingly concentrated upon the processing of raw materials and the production of semi-finished goods. The country has relatively limited capability in areas of electronics (including computers), robotics and instrument engineering.

Belgium's strategic location and open economy – together with equal treatment accorded nationals and foreigners alike with respect to investment incentives, taxes and business laws – have encouraged significant levels of direct investment from overseas. Foreign corporations operating in Belgium account for one-third of all employment, with US companies accounting for around two-fifths of the stock of assets. As well as petrochemicals and chemicals, a notable target of inward investors has been car assembly; and factories set up by leading multinational car producers have led to a disproportionate share of Europe's car industry employment being located in Belgium. The development of Brussels as an important financial centre has also attracted foreign operators. A little over half of the recent inflow of foreign direct investment is in the services sector, much of it connected with the setting up of 'coordination centres' by foreign-based companies.

The economy is dominated by a small number of relatively large companies which, by means of an elaborate structure of holding companies and operational units, play a major role in almost every sector of industry finance and trade. Groupe Bruxelles Lambert (GBL) and Société Générale de Belgique are examples of such organisations; the latter is the country's largest with interests in almost a third of corporate sector. Although the commercial banks are legally prevented from holding investments directly, they are closely involved with industrial and finance corporations through a system of interlocking shareholdings.

6.3 GOVERNMENT INVOLVEMENT IN THE ECONOMY

In Belgium, as in other countries, total expenditure by general government has risen as a proportion of GDP over time. Expenditure rose particularly sharply after the oil shocks, when the state tried to maintain the level of consumption despite a decline in real income, resulting in expenditure rising to 63% of GDP in 1981. It has since been progressively reduced to around

54% in 1995, which is only two percentage points above the EUR15 average (Table G32). This reduction in expenditure has enabled the government to consistently pare down its net borrowing requirement, which had risen sharply at the end of the 1970s to a peak of 13.1% of GDP in 1981 (see below). Belgium's 1995 level of borrowing is equivalent to over 4.5% of GDP. Significantly, after a long period when the net borrowing requirement of the government was proportionately larger than the average for other EU countries, 1994–95 marks the point at which the borrowing requirement in Belgium fell below the average level among other Union members (Table G34; Figure 6.2).

Belgium faces a considerable problem of accumulated public debt which, at 136% of GDP in 1994, is more than double the average debt of EU members. Not all of the threefold rise in gross debt since 1970 is due to spending itself; the OECD estimates that around half of the gross debt is attributable to the 'snowball effect', i.e. the self-sustained rise in the debt/GDP ratio due to the burden of interest charges on the cumulative deficit. As shown above, the primary balance of government has been transformed since the early 1980s. More recently, as Table G1 shows,

the net financing requirement (excluding interest charges) of government has fallen to around 5% in recent years. However, average annual interest payments have been equivalent to over 10% of Belgium's GDP during the period 1991–95, resulting in the government being left with a large net financing requirement and making government bond issues a major factor within the Belgian capital market. Government is aware of the need to bring the public deficit down to below 3.5% of GDP, in order to ensure the continuous reduction of the gross debt to GDP ratio and to escape from the situation where the burden of the stock of debt crowds out other public expenditure.

There is limited scope for reducing the net borrowing requirement to meet the 3% Maastricht target through increasing taxes. Although the comparatively low revenue contribution from indirect taxes (including VAT, 27% of GDP) suggests opportunities for raising revenue, Belgium's overall tax burden is quite high with a larger proportion of GDP taken as tax (46% in 1993) than the EU on average (42%). In particular, taxes on household incomes and employers' social security contributions are both high by EU standards. Taxes on capital (corpo-

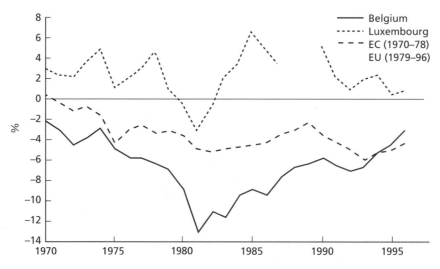

Figure 6.2 Net government lending/borrowing as a percentage of GDP. (Data not available for Luxembourg, 1988–89)

Source: Eurostat, Table G34.

rate profits, property, estates) are more moderate when allowance is made for exemptions and deductions (which has the effect of almost halving the effective tax rate of 39%). However, given that the exemptions and reductions are specific instruments of policy (i.e. to encourage employment creation, investment, regional development and the attraction of headquarters functions of international companies), government is reluctant to interfere with these incentives. High marginal tax rates – the maximum personal rate is 55% – and inefficient administration has led to evasion and a substantial black economy. This helps explain why tax revenues over the last decade or so have tended not to keep pace with income growth.

Cutting expenditure is also difficult. A significant reduction in public investment occurred over the course of the 1980s. However, the scale of this fall – from 3.6% of GDP in 1980 down to 1.4% in 1990s – made only a relatively small contribution to solving the problem at the expense of threatening the quality of the country's public infrastructure. Substantial reductions in subsidies to business were pushed through in the 1980s, particularly in relation to steel and shipbuilding. Operating and investment subsidies have also been reduced in respect of railways and ceased in relation to coal following the final closure of the mines. The bulk of remaining subsidies are confined to the Walloon region, where most of the traditional industry is to be found; the newer industries of the Flemish region receive little in the way of subsidy. Efforts to achieve further expenditure savings are likely to focus on (1) improving efficiency of public administration and (2) increasing budgetary discipline in local authorities (European Commission, 1996).

Social expenditure in Belgium has shown a tendency to rise at a faster rate than the EU average, due to rapid increases in expenditure on unemployment benefits, pensions and health. OECD figures show that during 1970–83 social expenditures rose from 13% to nearly 22% of GDP, with the subsidy (i.e. allowing for contributions) to the social security system increasing from 3% to over 8% of GDP. Spending on social benefits as a percentage of public expenditure

(excluding interest), at around 55% in the first half of the 1990s, was still much higher than in countries like the United Kingdom, west Germany, and the Netherlands, the equivalent figures for which were in the range 33–40% in the early 1990s.

Like other major EU economies, the government has found it especially difficult to curb health care spending. This is publicly financed and is not subject to market constraints; demand has increased due to pressure from both suppliers and consumers and its share of GDP rose during 1988–92 from 5.7% to 6.5%. Despite the rise, however, as a proportion of GDP, health care expenditure in Belgium remains somewhat below the level in most of its EU neighbours.

6.4 FINANCIAL SYSTEM

Belgium and Luxembourg are joined in a monetary union; the currencies have parity and circulate freely in both states. The central bank, the Banque Nationale de Belgique (50% state-owned), is responsible for conducting monetary policy on behalf of government. It administers interest rate policy largely through the manipulation of interest on Treasury certificates and, following a new banking law introduced in 1988, can require private banks to deposit with it compulsory reserves as circumstances dictate.

Reflecting its position as the location of the EU Commission headquarters, as well as numerous other public and private headquarters functions, Brussels has become a major financial centre within Europe. In particular, it has developed as the principal banking centre for private sector use of the ECU. Many foreign financial institutions have been attracted to the city, especially by the absence of regulations on capital movements. The Belgian banking sector is the most internationalised in the EU, after Luxembourg and the UK. Nearly half the total assets of the banking system – and two-thirds of the interbank business – is in the hands of foreign operators. In 1960, 67 out of 83 banks were domestically owned and controlled; in the early 1990s only 21 out of 86 were entirely in the hands of nationals. Belgian banks are not large in international terms; the biggest (Générale Banque) only just figures in the world's top 100.

During the early 1990s the Brussels stock exchange was deregulated in an attempt to enhance competition and additional protection for the financial consumer was provided through a new regulatory framework. The stock exchange was expanded by bringing on board off-market and foreign transactions. Brokerage charges became partially liberalised and the reporting requirements of transactions were strengthened. In 1991, the Belgian futures and options market, Belfox, was established and commenced trading initially on the basis of a notional government bonds. Further to these changes, the Belgian banking system in general was also overhauled; following the liberalisation of credit institutions, there are no longer any legal distinctions between the respective 'banks'.

Deregulating the country's financial markets was intended to help reduce government's debt service costs and bring monetary policy mechanisms into line with practices elsewhere in the Community. This has been done essentially by putting tight limits on the government's direct access to Banque Nationale credits and by enhancing competition in the market for public debt. Previously, Belgian banks effectively had the monopoly over the market for government debt, since non-residents and resident non-financial businesses have not been allowed to buy Treasury certificates. The 1991 reforms have made Treasury certificates available for purchase by others besides Belgian and Luxembourg financial intermediaries, thus boosting competition for government debt and encouraging the development of a more active secondary market in public short-term debt. Deregulation, the introduction of new financial instruments, and reductions in the withholding tax on bonds and dividends have been designed to attract foreign savers and increase the volume of business carried out on the Brussels stock exchange, thus increasing the importance of Brussels as a financial centre within Europe.

6.5 INTERNATIONAL RELATIONS

6.5.1 Foreign trade

Due to the customs and economic union (BLEU), trade and payment accounts are amalgamated with those of Luxembourg. The economy is an extremely open one, with exports of goods and services in 1995 equivalent to no less than 75% of GDP (a substantially higher proportion than for any other country within the EU and well above the OECD average of around 25%). The high level of integration with other EU economies is reflected in the fact that 72% of exports from BLEU in 1994 were to other member states. The main trading partners are the neighbouring continental countries of Germany, France and Netherlands, which accounted for 53% of Belgium–Luxembourg's exports and 51% of imports in 1994 (Tables G38/39). Raw materials, energy and intermediate products make up a significant share of the imports, with an estimated 40% import content in exported items. There is still a significant proportion of relatively low value-added items (non-ferrous metals and iron and steel products). Predictably, for a relatively small economy, imports of finished manufactures and capital goods (machinery and equipment) are also significant.

6.5.2 Balance of payments

Increased competitiveness has been the basis of an improvement in Belgium's current account position since 1980, when the deficit on visible and invisible trade reached 4% of GDP. The deficit was eliminated by the mid-1980s, when the economy recorded its first current account surplus since 1976. The surplus in 1994 was equivalent to nearly 6% of GDP. As Table G40 shows, trade in goods makes a marginally smaller contribution to this surplus compared with that in services. Although smaller in aggregate value (around a quarter of that involved in merchandise trade), the services account has consistently been in surplus over the period since 1980. Freight and insurance in particular are important net earners of service income.

The capital account should benefit from the financial reforms aimed at modernising and opening up the markets. The holding of franc assets has been made more attractive, reversing the previous pattern of large outflows of investment in securities. Incoming foreign direct investment, including inflows connected with take-overs of Belgian companies, make a substantial net contribution to the country's capital account.

6.5.3 The exchange rate

Pegging the Belgian franc to the D-mark has been central to the anti-inflation policy, which has been aided by small upward realignments within the ERM since devaluation in 1982. The National Bank of Belgium maintains a 'hard currency' stance designed to meet the EMU exchange rate target. (Since 1990 it has applied a narrower fluctuation band than that formally required by ERM rules.) While this looks like being successful in terms of meeting the Maastricht criteria, it does mean that independent use of monetary policy within the country is prevented, since interest rates have to be set so as to maintain exchange rates within the defined range regardless of the implications for domestic monetary growth. This helps explain the government's emphasis upon maintaining international competitiveness through supply-side measures and its institutionalised approach to wage determination. The tight association between currencies also gives rise to a close relationship in terms of short-term interest rates. Since the adoption of the hard franc, short-term interest rates have been more or less on a par with the D-mark, although because of the scale of government debt, longer-term interest rates include a risk premium over D-mark bonds.

6.6 SPECIAL ISSUES: PROBLEMS OF DEVOLVED REGIONAL ECONOMIES

The process of gradual devolution of powers from national to sub-national units was outlined in Section 6.1. This section outlines the nature of the two main regions, and draws attention to the structural characteristics and problems confronting the respective governments of the new political and economic entities.

6.6.1 Flanders

The Flemish-speaking region of Flanders – the upper-half of Belgium minus a small pocket carved out of its southern flank by Brussels – is the dominant region in modern Belgium. It has 58% of the country's population, 60% of the output, and 68% of both industry and exports (1994 figures). Annual output growth in the 1980s (2.9%) outstripped both national and EC rates; following a 30% increase in industrial production during 1984–90, growth of industrial output has remained above that of the country as a whole in the period 1992–95. Industrial conversion of the textile and coalmining areas in this region has been relatively successful; Flanders has thus acquired a large proportion of Belgium's new jobs during the 1980s and 1990s, which helps account for the fact that the region's unemployment rate (officially 7.4% in mid-1994) is notably lower than that in Wallonia and Brussels (both around 13%).

Flanders' regional structure is simpler than Wallonia's, due to the fusing of responsibilities relating to 'region' (local economic planning and development, agriculture, energy, environment, transport, public works and housing) and those of 'community' (education, culture, broadcasting), which remain separate in Wallonia. Central government has turned over to the regional authorities responsibility for the 'national' sectors, so-called because they have tended to rely on subsidies. Flanders benefited from the fact that the expensive process of restructuring the textiles sector was undertaken before the transfer of responsibility, though the regional government itself undertook the closure of remaining coal mines in Limburg, preferring to use the resources tied up in subsidies to diversify the local economy.

Support for new enterprise is a feature of the industrial policy, and is reflected in the activities of the Flemish Investment Company (GIMV), which concentrates its assistance on helping successful companies to grow through interest rebates, seed money for investment and provision of equity capital. Among other development initiatives, the regional government has established the Inter-University Micro-Electronics Centre (IMEC), to link universities and business in diffusing ideas and know-how into industry.

The growth performance of recent years is only partly the result of such initiatives and support. Its populace, by EU standards, is noted for being disciplined, well-educated, multi-lingual and enterprising. Flanders has also benefited from its diverse spread of industries – including chemicals, carpets, food processing, mechanical engineering, non-ferrous metals and the larger part of Belgium's car assembly capacity. The share of industry in terms of contribution to output (31% in 1994) and employment (26%) is significantly higher than the national average. Services accounted for just 66% of employment (57% of output) in 1994. Particularly important within this is transport and communications, revolving significantly around Antwerp (Europe's second largest port) and nearby Ghent and Zeebrugge.

6.6.2 Wallonia

The French-speaking region of Wallonia is smaller in population (3.3 million) and less successful economically than its northern neighbour. Traditional industries of steel, glass, coal, electrical engineering, textiles and metalworking were proportionately more important in this part of Belgium, and their steady decline has hit the region hard. Industry's contribution to total employment, which amounted to 52% in 1961, had fallen to a quarter by the early 1990s. No longer are the majority of the workforce employed in a small number of large companies; small- and medium-sized enterprises are much more in evidence today. The coal mines have closed and the largely state-owned steel industry has been slimmed down. The legacy of the past lives on, however – for example, in the low new firm formation rates often found in old industrial areas.

There are developments in new industries – including biotechnology, aerospace, new materials and pharmaceuticals – and the region has strengths in other sectors (notably chemicals, and paper, printing and publishing), but with inward investment favouring Flanders, new job creation in industry has been slow. Indeed, large firms in the traditional sectors still provide the overwhelming bulk of the region's exports. Service sector employment has increased sharply and contributed around 70% of Wallonia's jobs in the early 1990s. The number of these new jobs, however, has not been sufficient to fully replace the 103 000 industrial jobs lost during the 1980s; in contrast to the situation in Flanders, Wallonia's economy recorded an overall fall in employment during the decade. During 1991–95 the region has lagged behind Flanders in terms of the rate of increase in industrial production. Thus, in spite of a virtually static population over the period since before the war, the registered unemployment rate (12.9% in 1994) is nearly double that in Flanders. Moreover, there are local black spots, mainly the former mining areas, with significantly higher rates than the average for the region. Inter-regional migration (and even inter-regional commuting) between Wallonia and Flanders is restrained by linguistic barriers among other factors – another rigidity affecting the labour market.

Walloons see regionalisation as an opportunity to remedy the decline of their economy. They feel that national policies – for example relating to industrial subsidies – have not allowed them to benefit from their position at the heart of the 'industrial triangle' of western Europe. The region's industrial strategy is thus directed at developing the region's technological base and diversifying its industries. Inward investment is encouraged, and the Walloon Regional Investment Company (SRIW) provides start-up funds and equity capital for new firms on a selective basis, whilst also propping-up existing loss-making companies of strategic value so they can restructure their activities. An important aspect of the industrial strategy is the attempt to increase the degree of processing of the region's basic commodities (steel and agricultural products) in Wallonia itself; the pattern hitherto has been for firms in Flanders to add this value.

Wallonia's GDP per head in the early 1990s was around a fifth below the level for Belgium as a whole (and the EUR15 average). Regional autonomy is likely to have the effect of worsening the position of Wallonia *vis-à-vis* its richer neighbours to the north, since the redistributionist role of the central government is to be at least reduced and possibly phased out altogether. Indeed, one of the forces behind the constitutional reforms has been the political dissatisfaction in Flanders over the extent to which it subsidises its poorer neighbour. A transitional arrangement on central funding will be of help until the late 1990s, providing for a modest transfer of resources from Flanders and Brussels to Wallonia. Even after that time, it is currently envisaged that social security will remain a national responsibility.

6.7 BELGIUM'S FUTURE PROSPECTS

Belgium has performed relatively well in terms of meeting the convergence criteria established at Maastricht. In sharp contrast to the UK and Denmark, both of which are close to meeting the criteria, Belgium has expressed unequivocally its intention to be one of the founding members of EMU. Meeting the convergence criteria has become the defining issue economically and politically within Belgium and all policies and goals are subservient to this objective. The 1995 election was brought forward by six months to allow the incoming government time to draft an austerity budget (global plan), providing the government with the political mandate to strive towards European integration. EMU is playing a pivotal role within the Belgian psyche, holding the political consensus together, while tough fiscal policy is being applied to tackle the crisis of public debt. Prime Minister Jean-Luc Dehaene has forced three laws through the senate giving his government the right to bypass parliament when drawing up the 1997 budget. Such measures are usually reserved for national emergencies.

While its neighbour Luxembourg meets fully all of the criteria, Belgium has a problem over meeting the dual criterion on public finances. Given the huge size of its cumulative debt, the Belgian government is focusing upon reducing its net borrowing requirement to around 3%; hence the 1995 budget cuts of Bfr 105 billion across a whole range of federal government, social security and regional authorities. Certainly, there will continue to be great internal budgetary pressure on its level of social security provision, made especially difficult given the relatively high level of unemployment. It would undoubtedly be to Belgium's advantage if social security provision were generally raised throughout the EU (via acceptance of the social chapter), since the country operates with comparatively high indirect labour costs but low direct labour costs.

While the Belgian economy's openness and integration with its larger neighbouring states makes it vulnerable in the face of economic downturn, the fact that the country's producers are already exposed to international competition should leave the economy well placed to benefit from further integration among EU states (and enlargement of the Community). For such opportunities to be fully exploited unit labour costs will need to be kept under tight control, especially since maintaining cost competitiveness via manipulation of the exchange rate is largely ruled out. Recent OECD projections of Belgian labour cost increases above those in neighbouring economies raise questions about the economy's future competitiveness and ability to attract vital inward investment. It is likely that improving the functioning of the labour market will be a particularly important aspect of economic policy in the coming years.

6.8 LUXEMBOURG

Created as an independent state in 1815, the Grand Duchy of Luxembourg is a constitutional monarchy with legislative power vested in its elected Chamber of Deputies and executive power delegated by the monarch to chosen ministers. The population of this tiny country is close-knit, with a fierce national pride. It has been a partner in the economic union with Belgium since 1921, and was an original member of the Common Market. The smallest member state in population terms, with just 410 000 inhabitants (of whom approximately a third are foreign nationals), Luxembourg is highly dependent upon trade, with 92% of its GDP exported in 1995. It is very successful economically. The country's GDP growth rate in the 1980s (3.6%) was equal highest in the EC, and rates of over 3% in 1994 and 1995 were ahead of most EU member states (Table G23); GDP per head is by far the highest in the EU (65% above the EUR15 average in 1995, Table G24); and unemployment at 3% is the lowest of all member states and well below the EU average of 11% (Table G20). The Luxembourg government, alone among those in the EU, does not need to borrow to cover expenditures – for many years it has been a net *lender* (Table G10). The country meets fully the criteria for monetary union.

Important structural shifts in the productive base made during the 1980s lie behind this performance. The industrial sector, which accounted for some 45% of GDP in 1970, has declined in importance; industry and energy combined contributed only 22% of total output by 1993 (OECD, 1995). Within industry, iron and steel – long the mainstay of the economy and accounting for a quarter of GDP and 15% of employment in 1973 – has steadily diminished in size and by 1995 accounted for just 6% of GDP and 7 000 jobs out of total civilian employment of 203 000. Tax exemptions and investment subsidies have been used since the 1960s to encourage a diversified industrial structure, and new areas of activity have been developed, notably chemicals, engineering, plastics, glass, aluminium and food processing. Luxembourg has attracted relatively few manufacturing foreign investment projects in recent years, but in line with its policy of economic diversification, the government has recently developed a more active industrial policy (founded on infrastructural investment and financial incentives) designed to attract manufacturing investment.

The main development over the past three decades has been the growth of the service sector which accounted for just under 70% of employment in 1993 (Figure G2). Apart from the increase in employment in services associated with rising incomes, the sector has expanded on the basis of more outward-oriented activities including the Euro institutions (Parliament, Investment Bank and Court of Auditors), media and communications developments (broadcasting and film-making), shipping registration, and finance.

Banking and insurance now accounts for one-quarter of GDP – though only 10% of employment (OECD, 1995). Since the 1970s, Luxembourg has established a leading role in Eurocurrency markets and in offshore D-mark deposits. A liberal legislative and regulatory system – including lenient reserve requirements, an absence of stamp duty on security transactions, the lack of a withholding tax on dividend or interest payments for non-residents and rigorous banking secrecy – have been important factors in the emergence of the Duchy as a major financial centre. Location and facility with languages are the natural advantages offered to investors. In 1991 it had over a thousand registered financial institutions – nearly 200 of them foreign – employing between them over 20 000 people. While Luxembourg's share of Eurocurrency transactions declined in the 1980s, new areas of business, including private client banking and investment fund management, have emerged to take its place.

Policy-makers are cautious about the country becoming as dependent upon financial services as it was previously upon steel. They are concerned that harmonisation within the EU may undermine Luxembourg's competitive advantage and are well aware of the Commission's disapproval of the prized secrecy laws. Active encouragement of technologically based industries is part of a conscious effort to diversify the economic base. The healthy state of the public accounts (a reflection of high incomes and low unemployment) has allowed the government to carry out improvements in infrastructure and to bring down the rates of personal income tax and corporation tax, both of which have been somewhat above EU levels in general. The government is, as ever, careful in its handling of revenue, recognising that its ageing population will increasingly impose demands in the form of pensions, healthcare and social security.

Skilled labour shortages should not constrain production potential; foreign labour is not discouraged from settling in the country (29% of the resident population is foreign) and there is an increasing number of 'frontaliers' (the 30 000 Belgians, French and Germans who daily commute into the Duchy). Indeed, with a fertility rate only three-quarters of that needed to maintain the population, such inflows have more significance in Luxembourg than for any other European state. This is simply the labour market dimension of a more general feature of the Benelux zone; namely, that the local components are extensively involved in broader functional regions which are spread across national boundaries. As such, this part of Europe offers insights into the concept of a 'Europe of regions' and how it might evolve.

6.9 BIBLIOGRAPHY

Barclays Bank (1994, 1995): *Belgium*, Periodic Country Reports, Economics Department, London

Barclays Bank (1996): *Luxembourg*, Periodic Country Report, Economics Department, London

Bughin, J., (1992): 'Benelux' in Dyker, D. (ed.), *The National Economies of Europe*, Longman, London, pp. 126–59

Economist, (1995): 'Belgium' and 'Luxembourg' in *Economist Country Profiles*, London

European Commission (1993): *Portrait of the Regions*, Dir-Gen for Regional Policy/Statistical Office, Luxembourg

European Commission (1995): *Employment in Europe, 1995*, Luxembourg

European Commission (1996): *European Economy: Annual Economic Report for 1996*, Dir-Gen for Economic & Financial Affairs, Luxembourg

Financial Times (1995): 'Survey of Belgium', 28 June; 'Survey of Luxembourg', 24 October

Ministry of Flemish Community (1996): *Flanders in Figures*, Planning & Statistics Administration, Brussels

National Bank of Belgium (1996): *Report 1995*, Brussels (annual)

OECD (1994–95): *Belgium/Luxembourg Economic Surveys*, Paris

OECD (1995): 'Belgium' and 'Luxembourg' in *Economic Outlook 1995*, Paris

EU9: first enlargement – UK, Ireland, Denmark

PART C EU9 FIRST ENLARGEMENT: UK, IRELAND, DENMARK

In Part C the economies of the group of countries, who formed the first enlargement in 1973, will be surveyed. In terms of GDP, the UK's economy (Chapter 7) ranks fourth in the present EU, after the German, French and Italian one. The Danish (tenth in size; Chapter 8) and Irish economy (fourteenth in size; Chapter 9) belong to the smaller ones.

The UK declined to participate in 1958, since it had strong trade interest outside Europe (especially with its former colonies and the USA); moreover, it did not want to give up too much of its sovereignty. Participating in the EEC was only supported by the smaller centre Liberal Party, while the major parties, Conservatives and Labour, were strongly opposed to the UK's membership at that time.

In order to avoid exclusion it initiated the establishment in 1960 of the European Free Trade Association (EFTA), a much looser trade block of the UK and six smaller European countries not participating in the EEC. One year later, the UK government had already changed its position, arguing that EFTA was not large enough to serve its trade interests. Together with (former) EFTA countries Ireland, Denmark and Norway it applied in 1961 for full membership, though it wanted many concessions from the Community. Only after long and difficult negotiations and repeated vetos of the French president De Gaulle (who retired from office in 1969), the UK finally became a member of the Community in 1973.

The close trading links of Ireland and Denmark with the UK put considerable pressure on these countries to become members of the EC as well. Both countries accepted accession in popular referenda with vast majorities of, respectively, 83% and 63% of the votes. The Norwegians, however, also by referendum, rejected accession; they would do the same in 1994.

Though the UK and Denmark became full members of the EC in 1973, they have remained fairly reluctant towards (further) European integration.

CHAPTER 7

The United Kingdom

Ian Stone
Paul Braidford

7.1 INSTITUTIONAL AND HISTORICAL CONTEXT

7.1.1 Political background

The United Kingdom consists of the countries which make up Great Britain (England, Scotland and Wales) together with the province of Northern Ireland. It is a constitutional monarchy of long standing, so the constitution itself is not a written one; instead it is formed by elements of statute, common law and convention. Nowadays, supreme legislative authority resides in Parliament, which is divided into two Houses, the Lords and Commons. The former, which consists of a mixture of senior Church of England bishops and hereditary and appointed life peers of the realm, revises and amends laws emanating from the democratically elected Commons. Although the Lords can make a useful contribution to the process of law-making, its power is restricted to delaying enactment of legislation.

The UK electoral system is based on the principle of 'first past the post'. Each of the country's 650 constituencies returns one member to the Commons, and the leader of the party with the largest number of Members of Parliament at a general election is by tradition asked by the monarch to form a government. A clear majority for any one party gives substantial powers to the executive of government to pursue its legislative

programme during its parliamentary term of up to five years. Since 1945, the government has been formed by one of two parties, Labour and Conservative. The fact that smaller parties with a significant proportion of the vote are, under this system, poorly represented in terms of Parliamentary seats has led to increasing pressure for a change in the electoral system to one of proportional representation. However, parties are usually more inclined to pursue this idea when in opposition than when they themselves are in power, with the result that the UK system continues to stand in contrast to many of the systems of political representation existing elsewhere in the EC.

The present (Conservative) Government is divided over the issue of EU membership – the 'Eurosceptics' see Europe primarily in its economic dimension; there is resistance to the idea of political union and no commitment to the concept of 'Social Europe'. Indeed the latter is seen as interfering with the free operation of markets (while also giving the UK possible competitive advantage through non-participation, although it should be noted that many of the Social Chapter's provisions have effectively been imposed via legal challenges in the UK courts). Perhaps because of the 'island mentality' and the UK's historical development – particularly the 'special relationship' with the USA – there is a strong nationalist outlook which is sensitive to loss of sovereignty. 'Subsidiarity', however, is a concept the government is more keen to employ in relation to Europe than domestically, where the principle runs against its inclination to centralise power and to resist any devolutionary pressures, whether from Scotland and Wales, the English regions, or local authorities, which have steadily lost their autonomy in decision-making.

7.1.2 Economic background

The post-war period up to the late 1970s was characterised by a consensus between the two main political parties over economic policy. Both adhered to the notion of a mixed economy of private and public enterprises, with regulation of markets, the use of Keynesian demand-management policies, and the maintenance of the welfare state. The election of a Conservative government led by Margaret Thatcher in 1979 marked a departure from this well-established pattern as the government introduced a radical policy programme aimed at reversing Britain's economic decline. The high degree of centralisation of power helped the Thatcher governments in particular to make sweeping changes in respect of economic policy and institutions during the 1980s.

The economy had functioned poorly by OECD standards during the 1960s and the problems of the 1970s were appreciably worse. Although it retained (through the Commonwealth) special links with its former colonies, Britain's post-war economic interests moved increasingly towards Europe, culminating in membership of the European Community in 1973. This opened the economy to increased competition, which, combined with the OPEC oil shocks, led to rising unemployment, serious balance of payments difficulties and high inflation. The interventionist policies deployed with apparent effectiveness during much of the post-war period – aggregate demand management mainly through fiscal adjustments, backed up by a prices and incomes policy – became less effective in the face of structural changes occurring in the international economy.

The Conservative governments led by Margaret Thatcher and (from 1990) by John Major, have pursued policies founded on an economic and political philosophy of free enterprise, emphasising market-based allocation of resources and a rejection of the notion that government should act as a prime mover in the economy. The principal focus of stabilisation policy during this period has been inflation, the main weapon against which has been monetary policy. This was pursued initially through controlling the money supply, and subsequently by reliance upon the interest rate policy and exchange rate targeting (including entry into the European Exchange Rate Mechanism (ERM)). Fiscal policy has aimed at balancing the budget at a reduced level of government spending. Creating scope for tax incentives to encourage enterprise has been an element of the economic strategy to improve the output responsiveness ('supply-side') of the economy. In addition to reductions in rates of income tax to stimulate work effort, successive social security reforms have sought to reduce the disincentive effect of benefits on willingness to accept low-paid jobs, and legislation has been passed to limit the activities of trade unions and thus their power to increase real wages. Other supply-side measures include reducing taxes on business, 'liberalisation' of markets through the abolition of controls, reduction in subsidies to industry and privatisation.

Over-expansion of the economy in the second-half of the 1980s led to deflationary measures (higher interest rates) resulting in a prolonged recession. In 1992, with inflation reduced to minimal levels and faced with rapidly rising unemployment, the government gave priority in policy to promoting recovery; in contrast to the policy in the recession of the early 1980s, it ran a significant counter-cyclical budget deficit, while the pound's forced exit from the ERM in 1992 allowed a substantial reduction in both the value of the pound and interest rates. The economy subsequently has experienced a prolonged period of relative stability, with minimal intervention in the economy via monetary policy, and no attempt made to rejoin the ERM, or to achieve the convergence criteria as a policy objective. Interest rates, inflation and (once it settled after exit from the ERM) the exchange rate, have all fluctuated within a small range, while GDP growth has been unimpressive, but steady. The large budget deficit which emerged in the early 1990s has persisted, in spite of repeated efforts to reduce government borrowing.

7.2 MAIN ECONOMIC CHARACTERISTICS

7.2.1 Population and labour supply

As in other EC countries, the rate of population growth in the UK has fallen markedly over the post-war period. The size of the population has risen by only 5% (to 58.7 million) during 1971–96 (Table G17). The UK civilian labour force (i.e. those in work and the unemployed) has been increasing at a faster rate than the population, rising from 24.9 to 28.2 million during 1971–93 (+13%). This growth, combined with a rise in female activity rates, has more than compensated for the labour force effects of the fall in the male participation rate caused by rising numbers staying on in education, early retirements and the increased number of 'discouraged workers' (i.e. those who have dropped out of the labour force on losing hopes of finding employment). The male activity rate (81% in 1971) was down to 73% in 1995, but this still represented 15.7 million workers (down only slightly from 15.9 million in 1971). In contrast, female participation rates have risen, from 44% to 54% over the same period (12.2 million workers, up from 8.9 million in 1971), reflecting the impact of smaller family size, labour-saving household devices, the structural shift from manufacturing to services and changing social attitudes.

The civilian working population is relatively high in the UK. At 49% of total population in 1993, it was joint second highest among member states (average 45%) (Table G18). This reflects the high activity rates for both males and females compared with those in other EU countries. A further rise in the female participation rate is expected; combined with a continuing rise in the population of working age, it is anticipated that this will lead to a further expansion in the UK civilian workforce.

The rise in both the number and proportion of females in the labour force reflects a significant increase in part-time working. Almost a quarter of all jobs fall into this category. In 1993, 42% of female workers were part-time, compared with 6% among males (*Labour Market Trends,* 1994). The particularly rapid growth of service sector employment in the UK over the 1980s was a major factor in this development, since it is in this sector (notably distribution, hotels and catering) that many of the part-time jobs were created. During 1981–93 the increase in the number of part-time jobs (1.3 million) was exactly the same as the number of full-time jobs lost. Thus, while males in the UK work significantly longer hours than their European counterparts, working hours among women are at the lower end of the EU spectrum. There has also been a shift among employers towards more use of temporary contracts, and thus a larger 'casualised' element in the work-force.

7.2.2 GDP and output growth

The 1980s real growth performance was noticeably better than that of the 1970s which, following the expansionary boom of 1970–73, subsequently averaged below 1% per annum. During 1981–90 the average real rate of GDP growth was 2.6%, above the average of the EUR15 economies (2.4%), though behind both the USA (2.9%) and Japan (4.2%) (Table G23). Indeed, the UK average of 3.7% growth in real terms over 1983–88 represented the highest sustained rate of increase for 30 years; a dramatic turnaround in economic performance, given that the UK had by far the lowest real rate of growth among the European member states in both the 1960s (EUR12 average 4.8%, UK 2.9%) 1970s (EUR12 3%, UK 1.9%). The UK emerged from the early 1990s recession somewhat earlier than its European partners, and has subsequently grown at a relatively brisk rate (1993–95 average 2.8%) compared to the EUR15 (1.6%).

There is debate, however, as to whether the long-term growth trajectory of the UK economy has significantly improved. Periods of relatively rapid growth have been accompanied by years of low or negative growth when (excessive) deflationary measures were applied. In the recession of the early 1990s (as in the one of the early 1980s) UK output fell more than in the rest of Europe. Only Sweden and Finland registered greater output falls in the early 1990s (Table G23). The overall growth rate since 1979 turns out to be just 1.9%; very much what might be expected given the priority assigned to inflation control.

The UK's relative international position in terms of per capita GDP has fallen (from 13th in 1979 to 18th in 1994 according to the OECD), having been overtaken by some Far Eastern states. Even before the latest recession, UK output per head was significantly behind not only that of the USA and Japan, but also the other major economies of West Germany and France; while being roughly on a par with Italy. However, UK per capita output is in line with the EUR15 average, the same relative position as in both the late 1970s and 1990 (Table G24).

7.2.3 Employment structure

In terms of labour demand, the main change since the 1970s has been the dramatic fall in manufacturing employment. Employment in this sector fell almost by half during 1971–94, from 8.2 million to 4.6 million, and stands at less than 20% of total employment. This contraction has been more than balanced in aggregate terms by the expansion in service employment, which grew over 1971–94 from 13.5 to 18 million (although many of the new jobs in this sector have been part-time). A substantial proportion of the growth in service jobs was created in the finance and business services sector, which doubled its employment over the period, adding two million jobs. The proportion of employment in the service sector (68%) is among the highest in the EU, and significantly above the EUR15 average of 62.5% (Table G19). While construction has remained a fairly steady proportion of total employment (6–7%), agriculture (2.2% of employment in 1994) has contracted slightly since 1971, as has mining and quarrying (1.7 down to 0.4%) and energy and water (1.5 to 0.9%) (*Labour Market Trends*, 1995).

7.2.4 Unemployment

In the UK, as in the EC in general, the average rate of unemployment during the 1980s was more than double that of the 1970s. Unemployment rose steadily from under 2% in the 1960s to 3.8% in the 1970s, and 9.8% in the 1980s (Table G20). This latter figure was similar to that for EUR12, though above that for the USA and nearly four times the total in Japan. Unemployment in the UK rose especially rapidly in the recession of the early 1980s: from 1.1 million in 1979 it moved upwards until 1986, when 3.1 million people (11.4%) were registered unemployed, a proportion markedly higher than that in other EC countries. With restructuring and strong recovery of output, the rate subsequently came down to below the EUR15 level, reaching 7% in 1990 (Table G20), before the onset of yet another deep recession saw the rate rise again to a peak of 2.9 million (10.4%) in late 1992. The earlier and stronger recovery compared with that in Europe, combined with labour market measures designed to reduce the cost of labour and maximise its flexibility (described in Section 7.1), helped bring down UK unemployment to just over 7.6% (2.1 million) in mid-1996, compared to a European average of over 11% (Figure 7.1).

The official rate of unemployment is normally substantially higher for men than for women (e.g. 10.9% and 4.3% respectively in June 1995). Gender differences in unemployment are exaggerated in UK statistics, however, because the unemployment count includes only those successfully claiming unemployment benefit, and married women make up a significant proportion of those seeking work but not eligible for benefit. Labour Force Survey estimates of unemployment based on international (ILO) definitions – counting persons who are without work but available for employment and who have actively sought work recently – put the rates for men and women at 10% and 6.9% respectively for 1995. Moreover, comparisons of UK official unemployment rates over time are misleading due to a number of changes in the official definition of unemployment during the

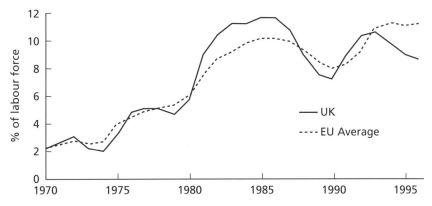

Figure 7.1 Unemployment rate 1970–96
Source: Eurostat, Table G20.

1980s, most of which have had the effect of reducing the official unemployed total.

7.2.5 Productivity and wages

The productivity performance of the UK economy during the 1980s was hailed by supporters of 'Thatcherite' polices as vindicating the government's approach to economic management and particularly its emphasis on supply-side policies. In fact, there is considerable debate as to the nature and longer-term significance of the productivity 'miracle'. The UK had a long history of lagging behind OECD countries in productivity growth: real output growth per employed worker in the UK (1.3% in the 1970s) was about half of that for the EC as a whole. The leap to 2.5% per annum growth for the whole economy in 1980–88 went against the trend in the rest of the OECD, as shown in Table 7.1, with only Japan (2.9%) doing better. The performance of manufacturing was even more dramatic, averaging over 5% in the 1980s and around 3.6% for the period 1990–95; again, clearly above the levels in competitor nations.

This performance is, in part, a reflection of the shake-out of labour in the recession of the early 1980s, when the least productive firms were squeezed out of existence and those which survived did so only by tackling over-manning, restrictive labour practices and inefficient forms of work organisation. Privatisation of nation-

Table 7.1 Output per person employed in major industrialised countries (av. annual % change)

	Manufacturing				Whole economy			
	1960–70	*1970–80*	*1980–88*	*1989–93*	*1960–70*	*1970–80*	*1980–88*	*1989–93*
UK	3.0	1.6	5.2	3.3	2.4	1.3	2.5	1.1
USA	3.5	3.0	4.0	2.4	2.0	0.4	1.2	1.0
Japan	8.8	5.3	3.1	3.1	8.9	3.8	2.9	1.5
FRG	4.1	2.9	2.2	1.9	4.4	2.8	1.8	1.6
France	5.4	3.2	3.1	1.5	4.6	2.8	2.0	1.4
Italy	5.4	3.0	3.5	NA	6.3	2.6	2.0	1.5
Canada	3.4	3.0	3.6	NA	2.4	1.5	1.4	
G7 Av.	**4.5**	**3.3**	**3.6**	**2.4**[1]	**1.7**	**1.8**	**2.0**	**1.35**[2]

[1] G5 average
[2] G6 average
Sources: HM Treasury, *Economic Progress Report*, April 1989; UK White Paper on Competitiveness, 1995; European Economy

alised industries – in manufacturing, such as steel manufacture and shipbuilding, and the utilities and transport – has also been followed by rationalisation and eradication of overstaffing. Another important influence upon this productivity performance has been the growth of new sectors – specialist chemicals, electronics, financial and business services – with high productivity based on substantial inputs of human and physical capital.

Despite UK manufacturing productivity growth continuing to outstrip its competitors, there remains a gap between the UK and Germany and Japan, which are up to 30% ahead in terms of output per person employed (White Paper on Competitiveness, 1994). Furthermore, the impact of the 1980s productivity increases upon the UK's international competitiveness has been restricted by the continuing high level of British wage and salary increases. The economy has long been characterised by upward pressure from wage and salary costs, and the trend was steeper in the 1980s than the 1970s. The faster rate of earnings growth was the result of buoyant profit levels, improved productivity and shortages in skilled labour, rather than union militancy. From 1982 through to 1990 the growth of average annual earnings was steady at 7–9%, responding little to either reductions in the inflation rate or slackening of the labour market. While earnings growth was offset to an extent by the productivity gains – so that real unit labour costs rose only slightly in the 1980s – this was in contrast to the falling costs of most trading partners (see Table G27). Competitiveness was maintained only by virtue of reductions in the value of sterling. The recession of the early 1990s reduced earnings rises to a 25-year low; however, they have continued to increase at a rate in excess of inflation, especially in manufacturing; it is the fall in the value of the currency which is mainly behind the reduction in UK unit labour costs since 1992.

7.2.6 Inflation

The UK economy suffered relatively high rates of inflation in comparison with its trading partners

during the 1970s, but steadily improved during the 1980s and – apart from a brief bout of inflation accompanying the boom of the late 1980s – has remained a relatively low-inflation economy since then. Following the shocks of the 1970s, which saw an average inflation rate of 13.5% (compared to the EUR15 average of 10.9%), the incoming Conservative government's principal aim was to reduce inflation by controlling the money supply. The tight monetary growth did assist the process of reducing inflation from over 16% in 1980 to 5% by 1984 (see Table G31), but also brought about a deep recession and high unemployment, which simultaneously reduced inflationary expectations and (in conjunction with trade union reform) weakened the power of labour. The subsequent recovery helped push inflation back up to over 7% in 1990, but deflationary measures employed from 1988 brought the Retail Price Index (RPI) down sharply to below 3% in the period since 1993 (just below the EUR15 average; see Figure 7.2). In August 1996 the rate for the UK was 2.1%; while this is below the average in Europe (2.3%), there were no fewer than nine member states with rates lower than 2%.

7.2.7 Consumption, savings and investment

Consumer spending is by far the largest component of UK total expenditure; bigger, proportionately, than in all the EU economies apart from the notable case of Greece (Portugal and re-united Germany have similar levels). As a proportion of GDP, it began the 1980s at around 60%, jumping in 1986 to 62.5%, and then rising slowly to 64% in the mid-1990s (Table G28). The trend is, in part, explained by the real growth in personal sector incomes (mainly wages and salaries) aided by reductions in the rates of income tax which have produced high real rates of post-tax income growth, particularly during the boom of the late 1980s. The real contrast between the UK and other member states is not so much the *proportion* of GDP going to consumption (the EUR15 figure is 62%), as the fact that the majority of countries have either main-

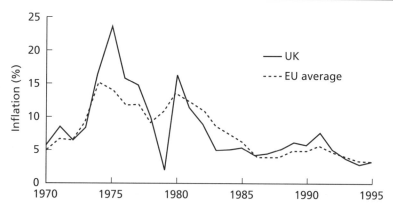

Figure 7.2 UK consumer inflation 1970–95

Source: European Economy, 1995.

tained a steady proportion over the period since 1980 or recorded a reduction in that share.

The rise in consumer spending has been accompanied by a steady fall in the *personal savings ratio* (saving as a percentage of personal disposable income). From 14% in 1980 the personal savings ratio fell sharply to a low of 4% in 1989, reflecting the expansion of credit due to relaxation of monetary restrictions and lower expected rates of inflation (households feel less need to replenish money reserves when savings are not being rapidly eroded by inflation). The trend to reduced saving has also been ascribed to the 'wealth effect', whereby, as property prices and shares values rose faster than inflation over the 1980s, people with such assets felt wealthier and thus less inclined to convert income into wealth through saving. The late 1980s saw a particularly rapid rise in house prices. In comparison with other member countries the UK has a high proportion (around 70%) of households in owner-occupation, which has been encouraged by devices such as tax relief on mortgage interest and exemption from capital gains tax. As house-owners saw the value of their chief asset rise significantly, the general response was to use this equity as security for further loans to finance further consumption.

This helps explain why consumer expenditure over the period 1984–90 grew faster than personal disposable income, contributing to over-heating of the economy in the late 1980s. Since then, the situation has gone into reverse. Deflationary measures (higher interest rates) have had a particularly sharp effect upon the housing market, and falling house prices have left many home-owners with a problem of 'negative equity', where the value of the property is below that of the mortgage outstanding (estimated in 1996 to still apply to 750 000 households). Falling assets values, together with uncertainty over employment after the recent recession, has led to consumer reluctance to spend, reflected in the upward trend since 1990 in the personal savings ratio.

National saving is, of course, the sum of private (personal and company) and public saving, and the decline in personal saving in the 1980s was offset by an increase in company saving and a steady fall in the level of dis-saving by the public sector (e.g. it recorded a positive level of savings in 1988). Thus, *total* savings as a percentage of GDP turn out to be relatively stable over the 1980s (Table 7.2). Although personal savings have risen in the 1990s, the level of dis-saving by government has also increased substantially, causing a significant overall fall in gross national saving as a percentage of GDP. The savings level in the UK is now, like that of the USA, markedly lower than in the other major economies and only two-thirds of the EU average.

Table 7.2 Comparisons of national saving as a percentage of GDP (annual averages)

	USA	Japan	Germany	France	Italy	UK
1980–1984	19.0	30.8	21.0	20.5	22.7	17.0
1985–1989	16.6	32.9	23.9	20.4	20.9	16.1
1990–1994	15.4	33.5	21.7	19.9	18.4	13.3

Source: © OECD, June 1996 *Economic Outlook.*
Reproduced with permission of the OECD

Investment, gross domestic fixed capital formation (GDFCF), increased proportionately more over the 1980s than consumer spending; its share of GDP rose from around 16% during the first half of the 1980s to around 20% at the end of the decade (near to the EUR15 average of over 21% (Table G29). This welcome convergence with EU rates has not been sustained; the rate in the 1991–95 period has been barely above 15%, compared with a EUR15 average of around 19%.

'Total business investment' involves the trading sector of the economy, including nationalised industries but excluding private investment in dwellings and general government investment. This vital aspect of investment, accounting for two-thirds of GDFCF, reached levels in the late 1980s which (as a proportion of GDP) were the highest for almost two decades (i.e. from 11% of GDP in 1977 to nearly 17% in 1989). The performance has not been sustained, however, and private sector investment has since fallen back to its 1977 level (*Economic Trends*, 1995).

Manufacturing is a relatively small part of total business investment – a fifth in 1995 compared to over a third in 1970 (*Economic Trends*, 1995). This level reflects ongoing structural changes within the economy in favour of the financial sector and distribution, and provides support for the argument that improvement in the productivity performance since the early 1980s is largely the result of labour intensification.

General government investment and public corporation investment over the period 1977–90 fell from a combined total of 6% to 2.6% of GDP, reflecting the impact of privatisation and government attempts to reduce public spending. Since 1989 government investment spending has grown in line with GDP at around 2.5%.

7.2.8 Income distribution

Income in capitalist societies is generally unevenly distributed, and it takes a combination of progressive income taxes and welfare benefits to reduce the inequality. In practice, UK post-war experience indicates that redistribution of post-tax incomes via direct taxes has tended to be more from the top towards the middle income groups, rather than towards the bottom; it is effectively left to the welfare benefits to effect an improvement in post-tax position of the poorer groups.

Since 1979, however, Conservative governments have sought to reform taxation and reduce the burden of direct taxes in line with its supply-side strategy. This has been done by a combination of increased tax thresholds and cuts in marginal tax rates. By 1988, the standard rate of income tax had been cut from 33% to 25% (with the subsequent introduction of a rate of 20% for those on very low incomes), while the maximum rate on earned income came down from over 80% to 40%. Such changes are of little assistance, however, to those either below the tax threshold or paying little tax, while being of considerable benefit to the better-off groups previously in high tax brackets. Furthermore, VAT (a purchase tax) has risen substantially, and been extended into areas not previously covered (notably energy charges), which has placed an added burden on poorer households. Benefit changes, by comparison, have been modest; most were indexed in line with prices, which for state retirement pensions meant a shift away from the previous practice of linking pension increases to the rise in the higher of prices and earnings.

Recent research on income distribution has shown that the distribution of pre-tax earnings of full-time employees widened over 1979–92 (Johnson, 1996). While the overall rise in earnings (after housing costs) was 36%, the 5th percentile saw a *decrease* of 18% in income (and a rise in expenditure of 18%), and the 95th percentile saw an increase of 61% (with spending increasing by only 45%). The share of income going to each of the lowest three quintiles of households thus fell between 1979 and 1991 (taken together, from 42% to 36%), while that of the top one-fifth of households rose from 35% to over 41%. The combined tax and benefit changes are calculated to have caused the top 10% of earners to be £80 per week better off in 1992 than they would have been under the 1979 tax and benefit regime; the bottom 10% actually paid more in tax and received less in benefits than would have been the case in 1979. This picture should be seen in the context also of a uneven distribution of wealth, where the top 5% own over a third of total wealth.

The incidence of poverty in the UK is relatively high compared with similar EU economies. Adopting the European definition (expenditure of household less than 50% of the EU average) gives a percentage below the poverty line of 16%, which is just on the average for the EU as a whole (excluding Luxembourg) in the second-half of the 1980s, when the UK was ahead of Greece, Ireland, Spain and Portugal, but well behind both the smaller EU economies of Belgium, Denmark, Netherlands (average 3%) and the larger economies of West Germany (7%), France (12%) and Italy (14%). This measure can be distorted due to large rises in the incomes of the better-off, which would 'increase' the incidence of poverty without appreciable changes at the bottom end of the scale. However, looking at numbers on benefit (a democratically accepted minimum level) produces much the same picture: in 1994, 9.9 million individuals in 5.7 million families were dependent on Income Support (a minimum means-tested benefit), compared to 4.4 million individuals in 2.9 million families receiving the equivalent in 1979. The incidence of poverty in the UK has thus more than doubled, and become more concentrated among non-pensioner groups, over the last 15 years.

7.3 PRODUCTION AND MARKET STRUCTURE

7.3.1 Output structure

The contribution of individual sectors to overall growth in output has changed as the economy has evolved structurally. The largest change involves the contraction of the output share of manufacturing and the rise in that of services, which now makes up nearly 67% of GDP. Finance-related activity has been the main contributor to the expansion in the service sector, with an output (excluding net interest receipts) equivalent to over 21% of GDP in 1994. The figures for energy and in Table 7.3 reflect the declining importance to the economy of North Sea oil and gas.

Table 7.3 Contribution to UK GDP by industry (%)

Industry	1984	1987	1990	1994
Agriculture	2.4	2.0	1.9	2.0
Energy and water supply	10.3	6.5	4.6	5.0
Manufacturing	24.5	24.9	23.2	20.9
Construction	6.2	6.4	7.2	5.4
Financial services[1]	14.4	17.2	19.3	21.5
Other services	41.9	43.2	43.8	45.3

[1] Excluding net interest receipts
Source: UK National Accounts, *Blue Book*, CSO, various years.

7.3.2 Industrial structure by firm size

In the early 1990s there were 2.5 million firms in the UK, employing just under 20 million persons. Some 92% of these firms employ fewer than ten people and account for 28% of total employment. The number of manufacturing enterprises has increased since 1980, from around 90 000 to 130 000 in 1992. Of these, 126 000 employed less than 100 workers, contributing 27% of all employment and one-fifth of output. The 437 manufacturing enterprises with 1000–5000 employees contributed 20% of total manufacturing employment, and the 93 enterprises with greater than 5000 employees a further 27% (*Census of Production*, 1992).

The structure has changed over the last decade in favour of smaller enterprises. The share of employment in manufacturing accounted for by firms with fewer than 200 employees increased from 25% to 35% during 1980–92; while in firms with less than 100 employees the share increased from 19% to 28%.

During the 1960s and 1970s large enterprises were favoured by government and mergers were encouraged in the interests of achieving scale economies. Since 1979 the official position has shifted and emphasis given to promoting the formation and growth of small firms. A range of support measures were introduced, including payments to the unemployed who started their own business, better access to finance, and special tax relief for investors in small firms. These measures, in combination with changes in markets, technology and business organisation, have undoubtedly contributed to a significant change in the size structure of UK enterprises.

The last decade has seen a large rise in the number of new businesses, while the incidence of self-employment increased from 2 million in the late 1970s to 3.2 million in 1993. Self-employment as a proportion of total employment rose steadily from around 8% in the 1970s to 12.5% in 1993, although this is still slightly below the EU average of 15%. In keeping with broader structural trends, the vast majority of these businesses are engaged in services (distribution, catering and repairs) and construction, rather than manufacturing. Around 48% of the self-employed are found in agriculture, construction and the distributive trades (below the European average figure of 55% in those sectors), with a further 14% in banking, business services, renting and real estate.

7.3.3 Production specialisation

UK competitive strengths are characterised by their breadth rather than their depth, with the top 50 industries accounting for a low proportion of total exports in comparison with other leading industrial nations. In industry, strengths are found in chemicals, petroleum, pharmaceuticals, paints, engines, defence goods, electrical generation equipment, aircraft and textile fibres – together with consumer packaged goods (food and drink, household products and cosmetics) and household furnishings (porcelain, ceramic products and carpets). The UK is, as a result of foreign investment, also competitive in the manufacture of semiconductors and computers, cars, and electrical and electronic consumer goods including televisions. UK industry is less strong in office products, textiles/clothing, mechanically based consumer products, and most machinery industries. Beyond manufacturing, there are significant clusters of activity in publishing, recording, information products and software, as well as in finance and trade-related activities (money management, retailing, auctioneering and global trading, international legal and insurance activities). Many of the industries which enjoy a competitive advantage are related to luxury, leisure, entertainment and wealth, and often involve niche market or high technology products and services. The character of car production illustrates this: apart from Rolls Royce and Jaguar, British firms lead in the racing car market; competitiveness in production models increasingly relies upon foreign companies including Nissan and Toyota, both of whom have established major plants in the UK in the last decade.

7.3.4 Multinational business

Most large firms operating in the UK are multinational enterprises, with extensive activities overseas. The British economy is more internationalised than its EU neighbours: in the 1980s it was second only to the USA as the source of overseas investment by multinational companies and is exceeded only by the USA and Canada in terms of the stock of foreign investment. The inward stock of foreign direct investment (FDI) from non-EU countries in 1993 stood at $120 billion, compared with $60 billion in Germany, the next largest total within the Union (OECD). Altogether, in 1992, over 1500 manufacturing enterprises – just over 1% of the total, but accounting for 27% of total sales and a fifth of employment – were in foreign ownership. Half of the foreign sector's manufacturing employment was American, though the balance has shifted to some extent in recent years, with expanded direct investment by Japan (over half of its European investment has come to the UK) and the Far East, and by the former EFTA countries seeking access to the Single Market.

FDI tends to be concentrated in the medium and high research-intensive sectors, with proportionately high representation in chemicals, mechanical engineering, electrical and electronic engineering, motor vehicles, instruments and office machinery. In some sectors (notably computers, consumer electrical and electronic goods, cars, and North Sea oil) foreign producers are dominant – and have been crucial in the turnaround in UK trading performance in relation to these items. New foreign manufacturing investment has been much encouraged since 1980 (see Section 7.4.6) and the government has been keen to avoid jeopardising the inflow; hence its refusal to sign up for the Social Chapter. FDI is regarded by government not only as a means by which manufacturing capacity lost since the 1970s can be replaced, but also as a mechanism for introducing into the economy new work practices and manufacturing techniques. While strong foreign interest is found in some non-manufacturing sectors such as banking (see below), most service sector areas of activity are domestically owned.

7.4 GOVERNMENT INVOLVEMENT IN THE ECONOMY

7.4.1 Public expenditure

The Thatcher governments set out in 1979 to 'roll back the frontiers of the state'. High state spending was portrayed as a burden on private sector business (e.g. through 'crowding out' private sector investment) and an interference with the consumer's freedom to choose. Policies were introduced aimed at progressive reduction of spending, both in absolute terms and as a share of GDP. This involved tighter controls on spending, together with the adoption of a policy of extensive privatisation. The medium-term financial strategy, entailing the annual preparation of four-year cash expenditure plans, has since 1980 provided the framework for both monetary and fiscal policy, with monetary control being supported by a tight fiscal stance. Individual government departments have had to operate within cash limits which have exerted downward pressure on public sector wages and the number

of public employees. The 1992 introduction of the 'new control total' for non-cyclical expenditure – whereby the level of real expenditure is set below the underlying real rate of growth – now covers 80% of government spending (it excludes social security spending, which is related to the level of unemployment). Within this system, ministers from each department have to argue for their share of the set total.

Around a quarter of general government expenditure is undertaken by local authorities using revenue from the local tax supplemented by central government grants. Central government has attempted to exert control over this spending through the concept of total standard spending. This is the amount that central government considers appropriate for each local authority to spend on the main services, based on an assessment of its needs. Since 1984, local governments have been prevented from increasing the level of their spending through raising local rates by 'capping' (the placing of limits on expenditure). It was first applied selectively to the 'excessive spenders' – provoking charges that this was politically motivated, since these authorities tended to be Labour-controlled councils in areas (major urban centres) with significant economic and social problems. Since 1992 it has been applied universally, further weakening local governments in relation to the centre so that they have little power to influence the local economic environment; a situation which stands in contrast to that in most EU member states.

While government spending has proved stubbornly resistant to attempts at pruning, the UK has been more successful than most EU economies in bringing down government expenditure as a proportion of GDP (see Table G32). Expenditure (including net lending less privatisation receipts), which was equivalent to 45% of GDP in the first half of the 1980s, subsequently fell to below 40% of GDP in the late 1980s. Given that it was only *after* economic recovery (and falling unemployment) that the ratio of general government spending to GDP fell below its level of 1979, it may be that the fall was due more to rapid economic growth than to curbs on falling expenditure; clearly, however, the rate would be higher but for the tight controls on spending. Since the late 1980s, the impact of the recession on unemployment and social security benefits (demand-led elements of spending) has pushed public expenditure back up to around 43–44% of GDP, where it is currently hovering. In spite of the considerable efforts by government to hold back spending on welfare, since 1979 this has increased as a proportion of GDP (from 23% to 26%). The rise also reflects, to some extent, a modification in government's attitude towards public expenditure as a counter-cyclical device. UK central government spending is, as a proportion of GDP, among the lowest in the EU, where the average was around 49% in the 1980s and has since risen to over 50% (Table G32).

The composition of public spending has been relatively stable over the decade to 1994. Two-thirds of spending occurs under four headings – social security, health, education and defence. Expenditure on social security (mainly transfers) increased from 13% of GDP in 1983 to nearly 15% in 1994. Health spending, which stood at 5% in 1983, has increased only marginally. The level of expenditure in both departments is influenced by rising numbers of elderly in the population. Of the other large departments, Defence has seen its budget decrease from 5% to 3.6% of GDP, mainly as a consequence of the ending of the Cold War. Education and Science has remained more or less unchanged at 5%. Of the smaller departments, Law and Order (6%) grew faster than any other department, Transport spending remained unchanged, while the budgets of Trade and Industry, Housing and Energy all fell in real terms, reflecting reduced state subsidies to industry and the shift of public assets (including nationalised industries and council houses) into private hands.

The government is finding it difficult to make further reductions in the face of the high current deficit. Social security spending cuts are difficult given high unemployment and increasing numbers of pensioners; rising numbers of children and students (and the awareness of its current failings) makes education a hard target; and the

nature of demand and supply conditions relating to health makes it peculiarly difficult to make cuts in the National Health Service. Overall spending on health in the UK is, in any case, lower as a share of GDP (6.7% in 1994) than in other major economies. A backlog of necessary capital spending (which was reduced as part of cuts in state spending in the 1980s) add to the government's problems in reducing its expenditure in the 1990s.

7.4.2 Revenue sources

In spite of the avowed intention of successive Conservative governments to reduce the burden of taxation, it has remained persistently at or above its 1979 level, reflecting the difficulties in reducing spending. However, the burden is relatively modest by international standards; as, indeed, was actually the case in 1979. Recent Eurostat figures show that, with total tax revenues (including social security contributions) equivalent to 35% of GDP in 1995, the UK share was, along with Spain, the lowest in the Union (average 42%) – well below Germany (42%) and France (44%), and closer to the traditionally low-tax economies such as the USA (29%) and Japan (30%). This share has remained fairly constant for over a decade, and it is clear that Britain is not overtaxed compared to other countries. The UK differs from other OECD countries in that *income tax* as a share of GDP has tended to fall. This partly reflects the government's wish to shift tax from a direct to an indirect basis. Income tax and social security contributions in 1993 amounted to 48% of tax revenues, compared to 61% in France and 64% in Germany. Top marginal rates of income tax have been substantially reduced since 1979, and in 1990 were below those in all other major economies, though the highest rate applies at a comparatively low income in the UK. The standard tax rate, however, is relatively high by international standards, while the tax threshold is low in comparison. It remains the government's objective – PSBR permitting – to reduce the standard rate from 24% (following the 1996 budget) to 20%, which it has introduced for very low earners.

The reduction in the higher rates of tax and the relative shift away from direct taxation is part of a programme of tax reform, a principal aim of which is to stimulate work effort and entrepreneurial activity. It is thus not surprising that in terms of equity the changes are regressive (see Section 7.2.7). It has yet to be convincingly demonstrated that reducing tax for the higher income earners has actually resulted in greater work effort.

Another justification given for reducing taxes is the effect of high rates upon actions of individuals and firms which result in a contraction in the size of the tax base. This was felt to apply particularly in the case of the company sector. Certainly, many large companies paid very little tax in the UK as high marginal tax rates and extensive deductible investment allowances encouraged corporate accountants to manipulate balance sheets. Corporation tax has thus been simplified, with many allowances phased out, and a reduction in the tax rate, in stages, from 52% to 33% (25% for companies earning less than £300 000 per annum) was introduced in the 1980s. UK company taxation is now attractively low compared with other countries, though the phasing-out of capital allowances has made the 33% figure a deceptively modest one. In 1995–96, corporation tax contributed 10% of total revenue.

The UK, like other countries, has placed increased emphasis upon National Insurance contributions as a source of revenue. Although this is technically not a tax, it has the same effect upon disposable income as income tax. The contribution of NI is noticeably smaller as a proportion of the GDP than its equivalents in either Scandinavia or France and Germany, but it still accounts for just over 18% of government revenue. Indirect taxes have increased in importance, and are the second largest component of government revenues (43%), the second highest figure in the EU. VAT, the rate of which was raised from 8% to 15% in 1979, and then to 17.5% in 1991, currently contributes 20% of revenue, compared to 14% in 1983, the largest rise in the EU. Zero-rating applies to most food, reading matter, public transport, children's clothing and footwear, and medicines. Excise duties (on petrol and fuel oils, tobacco, alcohol, betting and gambling), principally aimed at raising revenue, contribute a further 14% to revenue (among the highest in the EU).

7.4.3 The PSBR and the National Debt

The Public Sector Borrowing Requirement (PSBR), or difference between revenue and expenditure, which rose sharply during the early 1970s from 1.3% of GDP to 5% in 1976, subsequently fell back steadily during the 1980s, although it is currently proving difficult to push down following its rise during the recession of the early 1990s (see Figure 7.3).

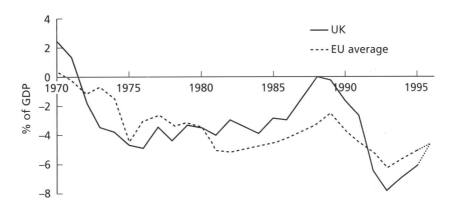

Figure 7.3 Net lending (+) or borrowing (–) of central government

Source: Eurostat, Table G34.

The average annual net borrowing figure in the UK during the 1980s – helped by better economic performance, tight fiscal management and a comparatively low level of government spending overall – was substantially below the EC average for 1981–90 (2.3% of GDP compared with 4.2% for EUR11); the UK was second only in the EC to Luxembourg (Table G34). Indeed, aided by substantial privatisation proceeds ('negative spending') and unexpectedly high tax receipts, the PSBR itself (briefly) became negative in the late 1980s. This was the first time this had occurred since 1971, and it meant that the PSBR was converted to the PSDR (Public Sector Debt Repayment). The PSDR, which was £15 billion in 1988–89, was used to reduce the National Debt, which, allowing for liquid assets of the public sector, was down to £150 billion (28% of GDP) in 1991 – a reduction of the National Debt rivalled in scale only by Luxembourg among EC member states. The PSDR rapidly evaporated as expenditure increased due to rising unemployment and the PSBR was up to nearly 8% of GDP by 1993. It has since fallen back to 6% (1995), and although it is projected to fall further, a recent EU survey noted that the deficit should still be a cause for concern, since at this stage in the recovery it should be substantially lower and falling, if not emerging into debt repayment.

7.4.4 Industrial policy

Radical changes have occurred since the 1970s in UK policy towards industry. The Labour Government of 1974–79 emphasised interventionism; its industrial strategy attempted to bring together employers, the unions and government to plan for industrial growth. It established a National Enterprise Board, extended state ownership through nationalisation, instituted planning agreements with industry, sought to develop industrial democracy, and introduced a range of financial subsidies for firms, sectors and problem regions. During the 1960s and 1970s, expenditure on subsidies increased substantially;

by 1975 these amounted to 4% of GDP and 8% of government expenditure.

The interventionist approach was replaced in the 1980s by a policy of increased reliance upon markets. Supply-side policies, aimed at reducing the level of dependence upon the state and encouraging an 'enterprise culture', have included denationalisation of publicly owned industries (privatisation), deregulation (removal of restrictions on the supply of particular goods and services), contracting-out of public services to private firms, reductions in the range and levels of sectoral and regional subsidies to industry, and support for new and small businesses (see Sections 7.3.2 and 7.4.5/6). Corporatist institutions of economic management have been closed down or downgraded, at least in the national economy (see Section 7.4.6). In accordance with this strategy, since 1979 the annual level of real spending on subsidies to industry has fallen, and in 1990 was equivalent to just 1% of GDP and 3% of public expenditure.

7.4.5 Privatisation

Following the privatisation and deregulation since the beginning of the 1980s, the UK is now the most market-oriented economy in the EU. In 1979, the state sector of industry, the public corporations, accounted for 9% of GDP and over 7% of employment. While the major programme of nationalisation occurred in the early post-war years, when coalmining, railways, gas and electricity were taken into public ownership, further (less systematic) nationalisation took place in the 1960s and 1970s, largely of industries in long-term decline (steel, shipbuilding) and individual firms facing bankruptcy, such as British Leyland and Rolls Royce. Since 1979, the trend has reversed, with ownership of virtually all of these industries reverting to the private sector – either as private sales to companies (e.g. Rover Group, Vickers shipbuilding), sales by share offer (e.g. British Gas, British Telecom, the Central Electricity Generating Board, local electricity boards and the water companies, and non-utilities such as British Steel, British Airways and British Rail), or flotations of government holdings (e.g. in British Petroleum, British Aerospace).

Although the state assets were often sold at prices significantly below their market value, cumulatively during 1979–92 proceeds amounted to £42 billion (not counting those from the sale of council houses, worth over £17 billion during 1979–89). They thus had a significant impact upon government finances – reducing the PSBR in the late 1980s by around 1.5% of GDP – though at the expense of a future contribution to revenue from income streams of profitable industries. There is some doubt, however, over the extent to which privatisation has widened the private shareholding base through its sales by share offer; many people purchased shares only because short-term capital gains were virtually guaranteed by undervaluation.

However, the privatised firms have not been subjected to full market forces. Many are still effectively monopolies, or face strong competitive forces only in certain parts of their business (usually the business sector, especially among large users, with typically much less choice facing ordinary consumers). Hence, regulatory agencies (such as OFGAS for British Gas, OFTEL for British Telecom) have been established, employing pricing formulas such as RPI-X (inflation minus a constant) and overseeing quality. Many companies still face criticism over excessive profits. While the privatised companies have been able to improve the efficiency of their operations (e.g. British Steel, now highly competitive within the EU), and have been given an advantage over state-controlled counterparts elsewhere in the EU in diversifying their activities and developing new products (e.g. British Telecom's new global networks), overall strategy has been lacking in the piecemeal, gradual programme – for example, electricity privatisation impacted severely upon UK coalmining, since the privatised generators switched to cheaper feedstocks (gas and imported coal).

Other types of privatisation can be identified. One is 'contracting-out', whereby provision to public bodies (e.g. local authorities, central government departments, publicly owned schools and hospitals) of certain goods and services is switched from the public bodies themselves to private firms through competitive tendering. Examples include catering, refuse collection, maintenance functions, and even prison services. Another involves the removal of restrictions on competition, or 'deregulation' of markets. The ending of legal monopolies granted to suppliers of particular services – e.g. the legislation limiting competition in the provision of bus and coach passenger transport – has been seen as an aspect of privatisation in the 1980s, as has deregulation of the Stock Exchange (examined below). Elsewhere, 'internal' or 'quasi' markets have been introduced. In health, General Practitioners 'buy' services from competing hospitals for their patients, with hospitals encouraged to opt out of direct control of the District Health Authorities to become semi-independent.

7.4.6 Regional policy

Regional policy was an important element of industrial policy in the 1960s and 1970s. As a proportion of public expenditure, regional spending in the late 1970s was double that in most other European countries. It focused on diversifying the economies of peripheral regions – Scotland, Wales, northern England and Northern Ireland – where the traditional industries of coalmining, shipbuilding, steel and textiles, were in decline. Companies were encouraged to establish factories in 'development areas' by means of investment grants, subsidies and tax concessions and by restricting development in the south and midlands, resulting in convergence between peripheral and core regions in employment and income. Regional policy was criticised, however, for the high cost per job created, its lack of selectivity (e.g. supporting investments which would have occurred anyway), its relative neglect of services and indigenous enterprise, and for encouraging the establishment of 'branch plant economies', largely restricted to assembly activities and prone to closure during company rationalisations.

The policy has been radically reformed since 1980. The budget has been slashed to less than one-sixth of the level in the 1970s; automatic investment grants have been phased out in favour of discretionary aid linked to employment creation or retention. Emphasis is given to attracting foreign investment and assisting the 'indigenous sector' – SMEs – through investment grants, innovation support, and subsidies for marketing, design and manufacturing systems. The area eligible for regional assistance has been radically reduced. Apart from Northern Ireland (for which there are special provisions), policies focus on sub-regions – mainly major conurbations in the north and west – plus under-developed rural areas such as the Scottish Highlands and Islands. A substantial proportion of assisted areas have 'intermediate' status, and are not eligible for the full range of assistance, though they do qualify for EU (ERDF) aid.

Although the revisions may make regional intervention more cost-effective, the 'north–south divide' in the UK intensified in the 1980s following the adoption of a more market-oriented approach to regional economies. Job loss through manufacturing decline mainly hit the north and west (even extending down to the west Midlands, centre of the engineering industry), while the services-based expansion of the 1980s was located disproportionately in the south, particularly around London. The north–south employment gap widened from the mid-1970s through to the late 1980s, when unemployment rates in the regions of the 'north' were more than double those in the 'south'. Although in the recent recession the south experienced faster rises in unemployment than nationally, this reflects the fact that the rise and fall in house prices was most marked in the south, and its prominent part in fuelling the consumer boom (see Section 7.2.6) was mirrored in the subsequent collapse in asset values and spending. In fact, the south still has significant structural advantages, e.g. a skilled and educated population, a favourable industry mix, the higher-order functions (e.g. head-offices) it undertakes within the UK productive system, a high rate of new firm formation and a favourable location in relation to the EU's economic core.

The period since 1980 has also seen a diversion of assistance towards the inner cities. Manufacturing contraction in (particularly inner) urban areas prompted a range of targeted initiatives as urban spending tripled in the decade to 1993. These include enterprise zones (offering tax advantages and reduced planning controls in run-down areas), urban development corporations (which approach urban renewal in their defined areas through infrastructure investments, site assembly, and by 'levering in' private development money). These initiatives have been criticised for concentrating on property development, for their limited impact in providing jobs for those living in the vicinity, and for the fact that the specific agencies established to undertake regeneration activity have displaced local authorities in this role. Policy in the 1990s has shifted its focus towards combining public and private funding on business *projects*. The 'city challenge' allocates public funds to only a selection of the projects submitted, based on those which most effectively combine public and private sector funding and cooperation, thus forcing local authorities and locally based quangos to work together with private industry. The challenge approach was extended in 1994 with the launch of the single regeneration budget for England which funds projects which are 'underpinned by a strong local partnership and will enhance the quality of life and competitiveness in an area'.

7.4.7 Competition policy

For purposes of national competition policy, monopoly is defined as one firm (or group of firms acting in concert) accounting for 25% or more of the relevant regional or national market. Mergers involving this share, or (since 1994) assets of £70m or above, may be referred to the Monopolies and Mergers Commission (MMC) for investigation into whether the merger is against the 'public interest' (encompassing not only price and quality, but also technical progress and international competitiveness). The policy has been extended to include such anti-competitive practices as favouring some firms at the expense of others through discriminatory pricing and the supplying of retail outlets only if it agrees not to sell competitor's goods. In contrast to practice in the USA and elsewhere, UK policy is not based on the presumption that monopoly is undesirable; it recognises that there are potential benefits (e.g. scale economies and technical progress) to set against the costs of reduced competition, and accordingly each case is examined on its merits. Finally, legislation has been used to prohibit producers from fixing minimum retail prices for their goods; this has proved particularly effective and fixed prices for goods in all UK shops have now virtually disappeared.

UK monopoly policy, however, has been criticised for being slow and ineffective. Investigations can take several years, and governments have been reluctant to impose formal conditions, usually preferring to accept voluntary assurances from the companies involved. This, plus the fact that relatively few monopoly and oligopoly industries have actually been subjected to investigation, leads to the conclusion that the policy has not modified significantly either the structure or conduct of these industries. Similar conclusions apply to mergers. During the 1980s merger boom, very few takeovers were referred to the MMC. Indeed, since the legislation was introduced, a very small proportion of mergers have actually been investigated, although the possibility of referral has undoubtedly modified behaviour, particularly in relation to horizontal mergers. The government has generally stuck to the line that capital markets function generally in an efficient manner, transferring assets to the companies and management best equipped to make use of them, and that merger decisions are thus best left to the market.

National competition policy is increasingly influenced by the EU. The Union's policy relating to cross-border mergers, which came into force in 1990, means that large mergers will increasingly fall within the ambit of European competition policy (Articles 85 and 86). The Commission and UK merger policy has come into conflict, e.g. concerning the takeover by British Airways of British Caledonian. Although the deal was previously granted approval by the MMC, the Commission insisted that, in the interests of European competition, conditions (the selling-off of particular routes) should be attached to the takeover. The Commission also intervened to reduce the amount of state aid offered as part of the deal by which British Aerospace acquired the state-owned Rover Group (now owned by BMW).

7.5 FINANCIAL SYSTEM

7.5.1 Financial institutions and markets

The UK financial sector comprises banks (retail and wholesale), discount houses and non-bank financial intermediaries (deposit-takers such as building societies and the National Savings Bank, together with insurance companies, pension funds, investment trusts and unit trusts). The system has undergone radical structural change as a result of extensive deregulation, concentration (via mergers), functional 'de-specialisation', and internationalisation, resulting in more competition between institutions over a wider range of financial activities.

The banking sector

The Bank of England, a public sector body since 1946, is central to the financial system. Its banking department functions as banker to government and to banks in general. The Bank's role includes implementing monetary policy through influencing interest rates in the bill market, using direct controls and restricting bank credit; it regulates the issues of notes and coins, manages the issue of government stock, and intervenes for government in the foreign exchange market; and it also exercises general supervision over the banking system and acts as 'lender of last resort' to banks. Its supervisory role has recently been strengthened so that it acts to ensure adequacy of banks' capital reserves, that an acceptable ratio of primary liquid assets to deposit liabilities is maintained, and that each bank's exposure to risk of loss on foreign exchange markets is in line with its capital base. Since the UK's withdrawal from the ERM in 1992, the Bank's role in relation to the control of inflation has been strengthened. Unlike the Bundesbank, however, it still cannot act independently in relation to maintaining currency stability, although is now able to openly criticise government policies, making it more difficult for governments to pursue party political objectives through monetary policy.

Banking in terms of lending and depositing in sterling is dominated by the 'retail banks', which deal mainly in individually small transactions and accounted for just over half the sterling liabilities of the banking sector as a whole. Merchant banks have diversified their activities away from guaranteeing repayment of commercial bills into provision of advice for businesses, financial reconstructions and portfolio management. While many have acquired firms of stockbrokers since 1986, allowing them to become market makers in securities, some smaller merchant banks have themselves been acquired by domestic or foreign banks and now operate as subsidiaries. Foreign banks – 336 of which were operating in the UK in early 1995 – have grown with the development of the international banking system over recent decades. They have risen to prominence with the development of the Euro-currency markets for which London is the key centre, and their main business is in wholesale banking in foreign currencies. The number of banks from both Europe and Japan increased substantially during the 1980s, and the position of London as a major financial centre (with a quarter of international bank lending in 1990) depends crucially upon their contribution.

Non-bank financial institutions (NBFI)

These include pension funds, building societies, unit and investment trusts and insurance companies, and fulfil a range of specialist functions. The largest category is building societies, total sterling deposits of which in 1990 was equivalent to three-quarters of that of banks (a proportion which has fallen in recent years as a number of the societies have converted to bank

status). Their main function is taking deposits and lending money for house purchase (via mortgage), but deregulation has seen them generally move closer to banks. The 1986 Building Societies Act freed them from many of the previous restrictions on their activities, and allowed them to offer a greater range of financial services (e.g. insurance, pension fund management, and investment), as well as offering chequing accounts, credit cards, and other facilities previously associated with banks.

Insurance companies are important within the non-bank sector because of the vast sums – particularly for life insurance – accumulated over long periods and invested so as to meet claims and earn profits. In 1995, estimated long-term funds were put at £483 billion, around half of which is in UK commercial and industrial shares. Pension funds have increased at an even faster rate, and now account for £519 billion; again, half of this is in the form of ordinary shares, giving them a large ownership stake in UK industry. With merchant banks, the NBFIs owned in the late 1980s more than three-quarters of ordinary shares by value, compared to under 40% in 1963, when individuals held the majority of shares. The portfolio decisions of the NBFIs thus considerably affect the share prices, and on balance add to their volatility.

The main development in the UK capital market in the 1980s was the 'Big Bang', which swept away most of the restrictions in the markets and saw the introduction of new technology. The ending of restrictions governing ownership and capital resources of member firms, strict separation of functions within the market and the level of commissions which were charged, resulted in large financial corporations moving into the stock market. A number of these were international firms and half London's brokers are now foreign-owned. The market has become more competitive, with much lower commissions on large deals. The new technology has enabled London to participate fully in the trading on global securities, allowing a unified market for dealing in international shares. This has been important in maintaining London's position, alongside New York and Japan, in the 'golden triangle' of security dealing. The UK financial sector currently has comparative advantages in that institutions and markets elsewhere in Europe are more regulated and less developed; in the longer-term competition from the latter is likely to increase significantly.

7.5.2 Banks and industrial finance

It is a long-standing criticism of the UK banking sector that it has failed to provide adequate finance for industry. In the bank-based systems of France and west Germany, the banking sector plays a major part in the financing of industry, while the securities market is poorly developed and has a relatively minor role. Bank-based systems foster close relations between banks and their large customers; the former often have a substantial equity stake in the company and are well placed to provide financial support for new products and expansion. The UK financial system, like that of the US, is basically a market-based one; its securities market is active and provides a major part of the finance for industry, while the banking sector role is less prominent. UK banks do not generally buy shares in companies; institutions are the major holders of industrial equities. UK companies thus meet long-term capital needs mainly by selling shares, or through the sale of fixed interest securities to individuals or NBFIs; UK banks provide mainly short-term (working) capital.

There are important implications arising out of UK financing arrangements. Reliance on the equity and securities market for long-term finance results in a preoccupation, on the part of companies, with short-term profit and dividend goals. This is because poor performance can lead to a fall in the share price (and thus value) of the company, making it vulnerable to takeover by predators. The encouragement towards short-term rather than long-term decision-making can undermine a company's development. Moreover, while institutional shareholders have been criticised for not using their influence to ensure firms are managed efficiently and enterprisingly, industrial restructuring within the bank-based system is often

initiated and orchestrated by the banks, and 'constructive' mergers are more common as a result.

A trend towards closer links between banks and industry is under way in the UK, with greater use of industrial experts by banks, and greater willingness to take equity in promising companies. The growing influence of foreign banks has been important in this process, as has the integration of banking and the securities business. The gaps in the UK market in the provision of funds for risky ventures and smaller firms have to some extent been filled in recent years by initiatives such as the Unlisted Securities Market, the Third Market and the Business Expansion Scheme, and an increase in the number of private companies specialising in the provision of venture capital.

7.5.3 Monetary policy and the money supply

It was the government's view in the 1980s that excessive monetary growth (i.e. exceeding that of real output) was the primary cause of inflation and the medium-term financial strategy provided the framework for monetary policy. The aim was to keep money growth broadly in line with growth in nominal output and income. Interest rates and net government borrowing levels were used to control monetary growth as measured by £M3 (stock of cash and sterling bank deposits – interest and non-interest bearing – held by UK residents). Higher interest rates were used both to restrain private sector lending and enable the funding of the PSBR by selling government debt to the non-bank public. Banks were thus unable to increase their holdings of public sector assets, restricting their ability to create deposits and thus expand the money stock. Reductions in the PSBR were necessary because of its direct impact on the growth of £M3 and because the monetary target would put upward pressure on interest rates and tend to 'crowd out' private investment unless the demand for funds from elsewhere in the system was reduced .

However, by 1988 monetarism was effectively dead after repeatedly overshooting monetary growth targets (monetary growth was twice the EUR12 rate) and changes in the targets themselves. In 1986 it was recognised that the £M3 target variable had an unstable velocity of circulation, prompting a switch to M0 (notes, coins and bankers' balances) which was too narrow a concept of money stock to be strategically significant. The difficulty in achieving monetary targets stemmed partly from the existence of a range of substitutable monetary assets, so that control over one form of 'money' led institutions and individuals to make increased use of forms not subject to control. It was also due to structural changes occurring within the financial sector, which reduced differences between banks and building societies, and competition between them, resulting in increased holdings of assets in interest-bearing deposit accounts. Changes in behaviour also had an impact; in particular the increased insensitivity of private sector borrowing to interest rates.

When inflation returned as a problem in the late 1980s, following the consumer boom, concern shifted away from using interest rates to target the stock of money towards influencing the level of demand *via* the exchange rate and interest rates themselves. It was recognised, in the words of one commentator, that 'the crucial variable in controlling inflation was the pressure of demand . . . If this is set right, the money stock will tend to look after itself' (Kennedy in Artis, 1996).

7.6 INTERNATIONAL RELATIONS

7.6.1 Balance of payments

The current account

The UK is an open economy, with exports of goods and services equivalent to 26% of GDP in 1994 and imports 27%. Next to (west) Germany (average 30% during 1981–90) this is the highest among the large EU economies (France 23%, Italy 21%, and Spain 20%), although it is some way behind the smaller economies. Over the post-war period, an increasing proportion of UK output has been traded overseas, with a particu-

larly sharp rise occurring in the years immediately following EEC entry in 1973. UK trade has in recent decades reversed its historical dependence upon sales in developing countries (the share of which fell from 37% to 16% over 1955–90) and the former major Commonwealth nations (Australia, New Zealand and Canada), in favour of trade with advanced non-Commonwealth industrialised economies, and especially those of the EU. Thus, while the general trend within the Union states has been for intra-community trade to take up an increasing share of the total imports and exports, this is most dramatic in the case of the UK. In 1958 only 22% of UK trade (exports and imports) was with EUR12 countries; the 1994 figure is around 54% for exports and 50% for imports, although this is still proportionally among the lowest within EUR12 (average=58%) (Tables G38/39).

The commodity composition of UK trade has also changed radically. In the 1950s the UK was essentially an importer of primary products (77% of imports in 1955 consisted of food, basic materials and oil) and an exporter of manufactures (80% of total exports). A massive deterioration in the non-manufacturing side of the balance of payments resulting from the Second World War made it necessary for the UK to run a substantial manufacturing trade surplus (equivalent to 11% of GDP in 1951). The non-manufacturing visibles account moved, however, from deficit in the early 1950s (over 13% of GDP) to a virtual balance in the 1981–85 period, followed by a return to a deficit of around 1% of GDP (Table 7.3). This transformation reflects factors such as falling real costs of food and raw material imports, increased domestic food production due to technical advances and subsidies, the switch from natural to synthetic production materials, and changing output composition in the economy as a whole. Nonetheless, though falling as a proportion of GDP, foodstuffs and raw materials have remained in overall deficit, and it was the exploitation of North Sea oil which most improved the non-manufacturing visible account, mainly through turning a £4 billion oil trade deficit in the mid-1970s into a *surplus* of £8 billion in 1985. The oil surplus has since diminished dramatically – from 21% of exports in 1985 down to 6% in 1994 – but the surplus of £4 billion is by far the largest positive contribution to the balance of payments.

UK trade in manufactures has also undergone significant change. The share of finished and semi-finished manufactures in total exports has remained around its 1955 level of just above 80%, but the share of these goods in imports has increased from 23% to 82% in 1994. UK trade is now characterised by the exchange of manufacturing goods and services with other advanced industrial nations. The economy is thus more exposed than previously to overseas competition, and this has been linked to the other major trend, the gradual disappearance of the manufacturing surplus. From the massive surpluses of the 1950s, the surplus fell to 5.6% of GDP in the 1960s, and then 3.4% in the 1970s, before vanishing altogether in 1982. By 1988, the deficit (£14 billion) on manufacturing trade was equivalent to nearly 4% of GDP, before it improved relatively to 1.5% in 1993 (Table 7.4). While in 1960 the UK accounted for 17% of world manufacturing exports – similar to west Germany (19%), but well above France (10%) and Italy (5%) – in 1991 the figure was down to just 9% (compared to west Germany 20%, France 10% and Italy 8%).

The UK has traditionally had a current account surplus, with the positive balance on invisible items (earnings from sale of services, together with interest, profits and dividends from overseas assets) more than sufficient to offset visible trade deficits. The period since 1970 has seen a departure from this pattern. Poor export performance combined with oil price rises to push the current balance into deficit during the mid-1970s. When North Sea oil came on stream shortly afterwards, the current account moved sharply back into surplus (+£7 billion in 1981); even the visible balance was positive during 1980–84. Subsequently the situation went into reverse. With a growing manufacturing deficit, and a fall in the oil surplus, a domestic consumer boom made matters worse by sucking in imports. In 1989, the visible trade deficit reached £25 billion. The surplus on invisibles has been insufficient since 1986 to cover the visibles deficit, and in 1989 – allowing for an invisibles surplus of over £2.3 billion – the current account was still £22.5 billion in the red. This has fallen since (the visibles deficit was £11 billion in 1994 and current account deficit £2 billion), but in the context of a slow recovery this represents a problem. Whereas previously recession has tended to move the current account back into surplus; this did not happen in the early 1990s. However, invisible earnings are growing – they were at their strongest for a decade in 1994, with a balance of some £9 billion – while the deficit in the visibles account was at least showing signs of falling (figures from '*The Pink Book*', 1995).

Table 7.4 UK visible trade balances by main categories (% of GDP)

	Manufactures	Food, drink, tobacco	Basic materials	Fuels	Total non-manufg	Visible balance
1951–60	+8.4	−5.6	−4.6	-0.7	−10.8	−2.4
1961–70	+5.6	−3.4	−2.0	−1.0	−6.4	−0.8
1971–80	+3.4	−2.2	−1.5	−1.8	−5.4	−2.1
1981–85	−0.2	−1.1	−0.9	+1.9	−0.1	−0.2
1986–90	−2.6	−1.0	−0.7	+0.5	−1.2	−3.6
1991	−0.7	−0.8	−0.5	0	−1.3	−2.1
1992	−1.4	−0.8	−0.5	+0.1	−1.4	−2.5
1993	−1.5	−0.8	−0.5	+0.3	−1.0	−2.4
1994	−1.3	−0.7	−0.5	+0.6	−0.6	−1.8

Source: NIESR, *The UK Economy* (1990); updated using 'The Pink Book' (CSO).

Capital account

Following the ending of exchange controls in 1979, major asset holders sought to increase their rate of return and diversify their portfolios by the acquisition of foreign securities. Outward flows of portfolio investment by UK residents increased sharply in the 1980s and they exceeded inflows by around a half during 1980–91. Direct investment overseas grew dramatically during the second half of the 1980s (from £5 billion in 1983 to over £20 billion by the end of the decade) causing a significant rise in the gross stock of UK-owned foreign assets, which globally stands second only to that of the USA. Direct inward investment into the UK also surged over this period reaching £19 billion in 1990 before being choked back by the recession. The inflow reflects attempts by US and Far Eastern companies to gain a foothold in the post-1992 single European market; in recent years 60% of US and 40% of Japanese investment into the EU has come to the UK.

Net borrowing via the capital account has bridged the deficit on the current account which has been a feature of UK external relations since the 1970s. In keeping with its traditional international banker role, the UK is a net borrower short-term and net lender long-term. The long-term lending is predominantly in the form of portfolio and direct investment, which has increased steadily in value over the years. This has permitted the UK to run a current account deficit without necessarily giving rise to greater net foreign indebtedness. However, it should be noted that net flows are tiny relative to *gross* capital flows, making the UK balance of payments vulnerable to speculative movements of money and necessitating a greater degree of interest rate and exchange rate flexibility than in countries which do not perform this role within international money markets.

7.6.2 The exchange rate

Since the move from fixed exchange rates to a 'managed' float in 1972, the general trend in the value of sterling has been downwards (although periodic upward movements have occurred). Four phases can be identified for the period since 1979. The effective exchange rate (EER), based on a basket of currencies weighted by share of UK trade, rose sharply between 1979 and early 1981, when the index moved from 104 (1985=100) to 133. The UK's petro-currency status at a time of rising oil price was a major factor in this upward movement, which was also influenced by high UK short-term interest rates and the effects of the deep recession in terms of improving the current account. This was followed by a fall in the EER in the period to 1986, partly induced by a fall in oil prices, when the index reached 86. The third period, 1986–92, saw the EER index rise once more (to 99), reflecting a policy switch towards using interest rates as a means of managing the exchange rate (i.e. keeping the value of the currency within a target range), rather than to control money supply. The rationale was that tying the value of sterling to a low inflation economy (west Germany's) would – by emphasising the government's commitment to low inflation – influence expectations and thus help to control price rises. From 1985, interest rates were used to ensure sterling 'shadowed' the German D-mark, initially at £1:DM3, later increased to DM3.20. This was an unofficial exchange rate target, but nonetheless represented a return to a fixed rate regime, and paved the way for the UK to join the ERM in October 1990.

Hindsight suggests that the UK joined the ERM at too high a rate (£1:DM2.95) – estimates suggest around 10% too high – given the size of the current account deficit. With German interest rates enhanced as a result of re-unification borrowing, the UK found itself during the early 1990s in a position of needing to reduce interest rates to promote recovery, while being unable to do so and remain within the ERM band of 6% around the central rate. The UK government was reluctant to devalue sterling within the ERM so soon after joining. In the event, the turmoil in European exchange markets in late 1992 led to the pound being withdrawn from the ERM and allowed once more to float. After an immediate sharp fall, the exchange rate in this fourth phase has been relatively stable but drifting downwards (EER index at 76 at the end of 1995), before strengthening somewhat in 1996.

During the 1980s, the exchange value of sterling – whether boosted by the effects of domestic oil production or by subsequent government attempts to squeeze inflation levels through cheaper imports – was frequently such as to damage the manufacturing sector for which government appeared to have scant regard. The macroeconomic environment of the early 1980s in particular, and especially the sudden and sharp increase in the exchange rate, led to uncompetitiveness and the loss of sections of manufacturing which would have been perfectly viable at exchange rates which subsequently applied. The value of manufacturing has been positively affirmed since 1992, as growth via exports rather than consumption has been pursued. The onus for the response by manufacturing to the opportunities arising from a competitive pound rests with the private sector, which has to prevent price competitiveness being eroded by wage and salary increases. The long-term downward trend of the value of sterling against other currencies is a reflection of the relative inability of UK producers to maintain competitiveness through productivity improvements and control over wages; living standards have fallen behind trading partners as a result.

7.7 SPECIAL ISSUES

Government's willingness to intervene on industry's behalf is minimal and its opportunities for doing so have in any case been reduced in recent years by privatisation and by EU rules. It has frequently been argued, however, that revenue from Britain's oil proceeds (now very much diminished) could have been directed systematically towards a programme of infrastructure investment (communications, education and training), with positive long-term effects on industrial competitiveness, instead of fuelling a consumer boom and covering the benefit costs of high unemployment. Certainly, price competitiveness achieved through exchange rate

depreciation is not the main route to success as far as many traded products are concerned, and developments in the skills base and product innovation are vital elements of economic competitiveness. The following 'special issues' thus relate to elements needed to underpin a strategy for improving international competitiveness.

7.7.1 Investment in research and development

One area crucially affecting future industrial competitiveness is research and development (R&D). The UK has been falling behind its trading partners in this form of investment, reflected in the fact that the UK firms, compared with their major competitors, tend to export lower-value, less R&D-intensive products ('mature' technology), and to import high-value new technology items. Many of the country's exports are thus in areas where world demand is growing relatively slowly, as well as being more open to competition from newly industrialising countries.

In terms of industrial structure and specialisation, the UK should be an R&D-intensive economy, comparable to the USA, Japan, Germany and Sweden. Yet, in 1994, UK R&D investment was equivalent to 2.2% of GDP, below the level in Germany and France (both 2.4%), the USA (2.5%), Japan (2.9%) and Sweden (3.1%). The UK real rate of growth of industrial R&D was the second lowest in Europe during 1985–1991, falling by 6.2%, while real expenditure has been virtually static since then. It has been suggested that the comparatively poor performance is linked to 'short-termism' (see Section 7.5.2) and the relatively higher cost of capital for long-term R&D projects in the UK (Crafts, 1992).

The situation is not helped by the relatively high concentration of R&D effort on defence industries. While the total government-funded R&D spending as a share of GDP was in 1993 higher than in many EU countries, a relatively large proportion (around 45%) goes on defence-related projects. While this is equivalent (as a proportion of GDP) to that devoted to defence-related R&D in France, it is far higher than the figure for Italy, Germany and Japan (all in the range 6–9%) (OECD, 1995). The problem is that while 30% of the UK's highly qualified scientists are employed in the defence sector, the spin-off to the wider industrial economy from defence R&D expenditure is limited, due to the specialised nature of defence products, and security-related restrictions on the diffusion of resulting technological developments.

Civilian R&D was fairly static in Europe as a whole in the second-half of the 1980s, but this masks a wide range of variation between countries, while research in the Higher Education sector increased fairly rapidly. In both these areas, the UK lagged behind the average among EU states. The UK still has a relative strength in R&D within the Higher Education sector, but this capacity has been undermined by spending cuts. Continuing weakness in this area will restrict UK participation in the growth of trade in high-technology products.

7.7.2 Education and training

The observed tendency for the UK, compared with leading industrial countries, to concentrate on lower technology products is also linked to the comparatively poor performance in education and training. R&D is unlikely to be fully exploited unless management and work-force have the appropriate skills; it has been argued that the UK is caught in a vicious circle, whereby low skill levels within the work-force and low technology activities reinforce one another. Compared to most other advanced industrial nations, in the early 1990s Britain produced fewer graduates overall, had a smaller stock of scientists relative to the population, and a lower output of engineers and technologists. In 1991, the percentage of relevant age groups entering full-time tertiary education was 28% in the UK, compared with 43% in France and 44% in Germany. Moreover, British pupils' attainment at maths and science is significantly lower than that of its competitors, and the rate of participation in education or training among 16–17-year-olds, though improving over the past decade, remains lower than in most other European countries. The low level of educational attainment is not offset by higher levels of work-based training: UK firms devote on average a smaller proportion of their turnover to training compared to Japan, Germany and France.

Government has taken action in relation to these shortcomings, introducing a National Curriculum in schools (supplemented by regular testing of standards and assessments of teaching quality). Recent years have also witnessed a change from the previous position whereby the UK focused its higher education investment towards producing a relatively small number of high-quality graduates. Higher education expanded significantly during the early 1990s, so that roughly one-third of young people now continue education at university or the equivalent. This expansion has been accompanied, however, by a significant reduction in expenditure per student and thus pressure for cost savings within the expanded university network, threatening the quality of provision. The attempt to hold back government spending has temporarily halted the expansion in student numbers, as well as contributing to moves for a further shifting of the costs of higher education onto the students themselves (through initiatives such as the proposed 'graduate tax').

In respect of training a number of important initiatives have been taken over the course of the last decade. A network of local training and enterprise councils (TECs) has been established, which gives the private sector a central role in the identification of skill requirements and the provision of appropriate training. A system of National Vocational Qualifications (NVQs) has also been developed, facilitating accreditation within a standardised framework of vocational qualifications in line with practices elsewhere in the EC. Within this overall framework, however, the emphasis in terms of skills formation is still based upon the market. Unlike in Germany, where the type and amount of training is regulated collectively by employers (supported by works councils and unions), training in the UK is a matter for individual firms, and there is an incentive for companies to act as free riders and 'poach' skills from other employers. This discourages companies from investing in apprenticeships and other forms of general training, as does the relatively narrow wage differential in the UK between adult workers and apprentices. In such an environment, the relatively low level of public financial support for training – and for vocational training for 16–18-year-olds in particular – makes it unlikely that initiatives such as the TECs will bring about the major expansion in private training required.

In education and training – as in other important areas, such as transport infrastructure – the preference over the last decade or so for private market-based decisions over collectivist solutions has limited spending in areas where competitor states have been prepared to commit public resources towards the achievement of long-term strategic advantage. The contrast between Britain and France in the quality of rail links to the Chunnel is a prime example. It is, of course, true that 'government failure' can lead to misplaced investment which is wasteful of resources and that problems cannot always be solved by throwing money at them. But the government's reliance on the market in key areas of resource allocation has frequently caused too short-term a view to be taken, resulting in structural weaknesses and the loss of long-term opportunities for growth and development. The fact that education and training have moved centre stage within policy debates should ensure an improved flow of resources into these areas. In the event of a change of government (see below) this would occur within the context of a more pragmatic, less market-driven approach to human capital accumulation.

7.8 EUROPEAN INTEGRATION

The imminent decisions concerning the relationship of the UK to the European Union will have a crucial impact on the nature and direction of the economy into the new millennium, and the focus of this final section is thus upon this crucial issue. Despite widespread scepticism within the UK government about the process of integra-

tion in recent years – most recently manifested in the BSE ('mad cow disease') furore – all political parties support the continuation of EU membership, with varying degrees of commitment to different aspects of integration. Ambivalence towards Europe within the Conservative government means that meeting convergence targets do not figure as a formal target of policy. (The government's 1996 position on Monetary Union is that it will participate in the discussions, but reserves the right not to join.) If the Conservatives remain in power, there is likely to be little change in this stance, unless the particular configuration of power following the 1997 general election gives the Eurosceptics more leverage on policy.

Opinion polls strongly suggest that the next government will be formed by Labour, and this is likely to result in a more pro-European stance, involving the implementation of the Social Chapter, more economic policy coordination (as a prelude to full economic union), support for reform of the CAP and increased accountability of EU institutions. Labour would be likely to firmly resist a move towards federalism and any increased European control over taxation or security matters. Broadly speaking, with the exception of the Social Chapter, this is also what the Conservatives are committed to; but Labour appears to be less divided over these issues and is more likely to be able to reach agreement with other members of the Union. It should also be remembered that whatever the public pronouncements, integration is proceeding via a number of mechanisms: for example, foreign plants operating in the UK and British firms with subsidiaries abroad both tend to comply with social policy rules on works councils and worker participation in spite of the official UK opt-out from the Social Chapter.

An assessment of the UK economy shows that it is now reasonably well placed in terms of meeting the convergence criteria. The transition to a low-inflation economy seems to have been accomplished and the prevailing rate of just over 2% is well within two percentage points of the best performers; the debt/GDP ratio (54% in 1995) is among the best in the EU, and below the 60% target (although it is rising steadily, and OECD projections are that this will continue); both long-term and short-term interest rates are relatively low, and although some increase is anticipated in response to the upwards tendency in process, they are not expected to rise significantly. While the government deficit/GDP ratio, currently 5.5%, is still fairly high, it is projected to decrease slowly towards the 3% Maastricht target. More generally, European legislation has been embraced, with most directives on health and safety and product standards being rapidly incorporated into the relevant British legislation.

Britain has been prominent in arguing for extended membership of the EU (particularly where, as with the latest enlargement, the new entrants are likely to be net contributors to the budget). Attempts at deepening its involvement have been less welcome, and the concerns about the likely economic impact of EMU are a good example of this. Apart from the political issues involved, the benefits of a single currency (removal of transactions costs involved in changing currencies and removal of exchange rate uncertainty leading to more efficient location of industry within Europe) have to be set against the costs of not being able to use an independent monetary/exchange rate policy to deal with economic shocks. In particular, it has been argued that the UK economy's cycle is not closely synchronised to that of Germany and the core countries of the Union and thus a common monetary policy may not suit its needs.

Can Britain afford to be left out of monetary union? There is a real possibility of a 'two-tier' system, in which EMU is established by an initial core of countries, joined later by a second tier of peripheral states. First-tier countries would plainly be in a position to influence MU development to their advantage (as indeed happened when the Common Market was formed, with the UK finding in 1973 that policies had been instituted which effectively increased the cost of entry). Among the important issues for Britain are: (1) whether the City of London would be able, if the UK were outside the core MU, fully to participate in 'Euro'-denominated business; it is possible that its position in relation to rival financial centres in Frankfurt and Paris would be undermined; and (2) the kind of arrangements which might emerge to regulate the exchange rate relationship between those inside and those outside of the MU system. Would the peripheral states be free to enhance their competitiveness by devaluing their currencies *vis-à-vis* those of the core MU states? The latter question is important, from the UK perspective, not least because of its potential impact on the country's ability to continue attracting a large share of the foreign investment coming into the EU.

7.9 FUTURE PROSPECTS

The UK economy since the late 1970s has undergone significant change. It is no longer the 'sick man of Europe' as far as a range of economic indicators are concerned. It leads its fellow member states in terms of opening its markets to competition and allowing market-determined resource allocation. Its flexible labour markets and general business climate make it the preferred location within the Union as far as inward investors are concerned. There is still debate, however, as to whether the 1980s saw Britain's relative decline *permanently* reversed. Some commentators insist that the reforms of the 1980s simply allowed the economy to catch up, taking advantage of gains which were foregone in the previous period; others argue that the dynamism of the economy has been affected positively by reforms which have made it more flexible and increased its capacity to respond to change. Whichever view proves to be correct, it is vital for the future performance of the UK economy that weaknesses in the education, training and technology fields are corrected.

Economic policy is unlikely to change radically in the foreseeable future. The alternative political party to the Conservatives, Labour, has radically changed its approach to economic management over the past decade – to the extent that the bulk of the institutional reforms implemented since 1979 (including those relating to trade unions) will be retained when, as seems likely at the time of writing, the party is returned to power. Labour would introduce a degree of political decentralisation, but otherwise the changes would be marginal in character. For example, tackling unemployment would be given higher priority, but not at the expense of controlling inflation; Labour insists it will operate tight budgetary controls. Plainly, Labour has come to terms with the restricted policy environment created by globalisation and European integration.

7.10 BIBLIOGRAPHY AND SOURCES OF INFORMATION

UK government/official publications

Bank of England: *Quarterly Bulletin*
Central Statistical Office: *Census of Production*
Central Statistical Office: *Economic Briefing*
Central Statistical Office: *Economic Trends*
Central Statistical Office: *Financial Statistics*
Central Statistical Office: *Labour Market Trends*
Central Statistical Office: *UK Balance of Payments ('The Pink Book')*
Central Statistical Office: *UK in Figures*
Central Statistical Office: *UK National Accounts ('The Blue Book')*
OECD (1995): *Main Science and Technology Indicators*
OECD (1995): *Economic Outlook*
OECD (1995): *The UK Economy*, Economic Surveys, Paris
UK Government White Paper (1995), *Competitiveness: Forging Ahead*, Cmd. 2867, HMSO, May 1995

General books/articles on the UK economy

Allen, S., and Jones, G. (1995): *UK Business in Europe: a Statistical Comparison*, HMSO
Artis, M. (ed.) (1996): *The UK Economy* (14th edn), Oxford University Press
Barrell, R. (1994): *The UK Labour Market: Comparative Aspects and Institutional Developments*, Cambridge University Press
Crafts, N. (1992): 'Institutions and economic growth: recent British experience in an international context', *West European Politics*, **15**(4), 16–38
Curwen, P. (ed.) (1994): *Understanding the UK Economy* (3rd edn), MacMillan Education
Economist, The (1996): 'Britain's New Politics', 21 September
Griffiths, A. and Wall, S. (eds) (1995): *Applied Economics* (6th edn), Longman
Hutton, W. (1996): *The State We're In* (2nd edn), Vintage
Johnson, P. (1996): 'The assessment: inequality', *Oxford Review of Economic Policy*, **12**(1)
Smith, D. (1992): *From Boom to Bust: Trial and Error in Economic Policy*, Penguin.

Journals

British Economy Survey (Longman)
Business Briefing (Chambers of Commerce)
The Economic Review (Philip Allan)
Economics (The Economics Association)
Lloyds Bank Economic Bulletin
National Institute Economic Review

CHAPTER 8

Ireland

P. J. Drudy

8.1 INSTITUTIONAL AND HISTORICAL CONTEXT

Ireland is a small peripheral island economy on the edge of Europe. One viewpoint suggests that it is a good example of an economy characterised by 'dependency' of various kinds over several centuries. Thus, it was dependent on its larger island neighbour, Great Britain, for centuries up to 1921 when it achieved a measure of independence. Even then, however, strong economic linkages remained, particularly in relation to trade. After several decades of protectionism from the 1930s, Ireland began in the 1960s to adopt strong 'outward-looking' policies which included the attraction of foreign industrial investment. It can be argued that the country became, and remains, heavily dependent on such investment. In 1973, Ireland joined the European Community, now the European Union. Since then its trade links with continental Europe and elsewhere have increased significantly while those with Britain have reduced. Those supporting the dependency view would argue, however, that Ireland's earlier dependence on Britain has been largely replaced by a wider reliance on economic developments and policies forged in the European Union and elsewhere (Seers *et al.*, 1979).

A second viewpoint suggests that since the 1950s Ireland has gone through a process of 'modernisation', with increased industrialisation, urbanisation and demographic patterns similar to developed Europe and the United States. This modernisation process has been facilitated and assisted by such factors as mass communications, associations with and membership of international organisations and by foreign investment. It has been generally welcomed by all political parties and by the brunt of the population.

Ireland's dependency on its larger island neighbour, Great Britain, goes back at least to the twelfth century. However, it was during the sixteenth and seventeenth centuries that much of the country was colonised by British planters. The Act of Union of 1801 ensured that Ireland was administered from London and, in effect, became a region of Britain. This situation held until 26 counties of Ireland achieved independence in 1921. The long era of dependency on Britain has been the subject of much debate. Some writers have argued that the 'imposed' relationship with Britain (including free trade) was the primary reason for Ireland's failure to develop over a long period of time. This was undoubtedly an important factor but the explanation is likely to be more complex. For example, Ireland lacked significant iron and coal resources which would have enabled it to benefit from the industrial revolution. Its peripheral location away from the main raw materials and markets was a possible inhibiting factor. Its rapidly growing population up to the 1820s was also a relevant concern. Whatever the reasons, Ireland lagged behind Britain and most European countries in relation to industrial development throughout most of the nineteenth and into the twentieth century. The vast majority of the nineteenth-century Irish population, largely rural-based, existed at a subsistence level and were heavily dependent for their survival on an undeveloped agricultural industry and, in particular, on the potato crop. A series of famines over the decades 1822 to 1842 and the Great Famine of 1845–49 (when the potato crop failed) were indicative of the wretched conditions in which the population lived. During the Great Famine, it is estimated that about one million people died from malnutrition and a further million emigrated, mainly to the United States. By 1921 a further 3 million had left. The Great Famine marked a fundamental change in Irish demographic history when the population, previously increasing significantly, commenced to decline. During the century after the Famine, the population declined by 50%. The losses were most severe in the rural and least urbanised areas of the west and north-west. In a situation where much of the land was owned by plantation landlords, many of whom did not reside in Ireland, the land was operated by tenant farmers and farm labourers. This latter category suffered most during this difficult period. As we shall see, emigration has remained a fundamental difficulty in Ireland right up to the present day.

In December 1921, a Treaty was signed which gave independence to 26 counties of Ireland with a land area of 70 280 km². This is now called the Republic of Ireland. The other six counties, Northern Ireland, were to remain part of Britain with limited devolved government. This 'partition' of Ireland was a contentious issue and remains highly problematic.

In the post-independence decades and up to the present day, two major political parties, Fine Gael and Fianna Fáil, have dominated the political scene. It is difficult to identify significant differences in philosophy and approach between these two parties. Both have applauded private enterprise; yet they have consistently encouraged and supported state intervention in economic and social affairs. The Progressive Democrats (a small party founded in recent years) is the only political grouping to argue strongly against state intervention in economic matters. However, the Labour Party and Democratic Left (a further new party) have always espoused and supported state involvement and best represent those with socialist viewpoints in Irish society. The willingness of both the Fine Gael and Fianna Fáil parties to join in coalition governments in recent years with the Labour Party and Democratic Left is indicative of an avoidance of extreme ideological positions. In any case, state involvement has been a consistent element in Irish affairs since independence.

8.2 GOVERNMENT INVOLVEMENT IN THE ECONOMY

8.2.1 Post-independence: from protectionism to export orientation

The Treaty of 1921 was not accepted by all and a bitter Civil War took place between 1921 and 1923. The new elected government, led by Cumann na nGael (later re-named Fine Gael) remained in office up to 1932. During this period, the emphasis was on establishing a framework for democratic government. The previous policy of free trade with Britain continued and, despite the desire for greater self-sufficiency, tariff protection was limited. In the post-independence decade, the Irish economy remained firmly linked to Britain, with 97% of exports going to, and 76% of imports coming from Britain. It seemed logical, therefore, that, when an Irish currency was established in 1927, the Irish pound (amalgamated with sterling in 1826) should have parity with sterling. This one-to-one basis was to remain until 1979 when the Republic joined the European Monetary System (EMS).

At independence Ireland was heavily dependent on the agricultural industry. Two-thirds of the holdings were less than 12 hectares and, despite various Land Reform Acts towards the end of the nineteenth century which had given ownership to the native Irish, agriculture was in an undeveloped state. Much of the land, particularly in the western half of the country, was poor and holdings were fragmented. There had been little in the way of technical advances and incomes were low. Therefore, the primary aim of economic policy during the early years of independence was to raise agricultural productivity and incomes and to encourage the export of agricultural products. This emphasis was seen as important since 32% of GDP and 54% of all employment was provided by agriculture at that time. Free trade was regarded as essential if the costs of farm inputs were to be kept low. On the other hand, price support for agricultural products became a consistent feature of policy from the early 1930s (Matthews, 1982; Kennedy *et al.*, 1988). Little attention was given to industrial development during the 1920s and 1930s and, reflecting the limited development of industry and industrial policy, output and employment growth were weak. Despite the emphasis on agriculture, farm incomes remained static, unemployment was rising and emigration, expected by some to decline after Independence, was greater than in either of the previous two decades.

A new government, led by Fianna Fáil, took office in 1932 at a time when the Great Depression influenced most countries to erect tariff barriers. The government immediately embarked on a strong protectionist policy. The motivation was partly to reduce economic dependence on Britain and to encourage self-sufficiency, but was also aimed at increasing employment and reducing emigration. Duties ranging from 15 to 75% were imposed on a wide range of goods. At the same time, an 'Economic War' with Britain commenced due to the unwillingness of the new government to pay land annuities agreed a decade earlier on behalf of tenants who had purchased their land from the landlords under various land reform Acts. Britain reacted by imposing duties on imports of Ireland's main agricultural exports. The Irish government in turn imposed duties on a further range of goods. By 1937, almost 2000 articles imported to Ireland were subject to import controls. The ending of the Economic War with Britain in 1938 was, however, followed by the Second World War and the Irish high tariffic regime remained in force for several further decades. One further important protectionist measure may also be noted. This was the

Control of Manufactures Acts of 1932 and 1934 which placed considerable constraints on foreign ownership of Irish manufacturing industry. This control lasted, with the exception of the World War period, right up to the 1960s.

These various policies proved effective in protecting and developing new industries as well as expanding older ones and helped Ireland to secure substantial growth of employment during particular periods. Thus, manufacturing employment grew by 40 000 between 1931 and 1939 and by a further 41 000 by 1953. However, employment growth was to be short-lived and the numbers employed in manufacturing fell between 1953 and 1958. Furthermore, the new firms tended to be small-scale units, lacking specialisation, research and development and marketing skills. A strong import propensity, accompanied by little attention to exports (despite the small home market) and a poor export performance, also resulted in recurrent balance of payments difficulties in the late 1940s and 1950s (O'Hagan and McStay, 1981).

Even from the late 1940s there had been a recognition of the difficulties of relying unduly on the protectionist and self-sufficiency policies which characterised the post-independence decades. Whatever the advantages of such policies, they were not creating sufficient jobs to stem the tide of emigration. An export orientation, invariably required in a small open economy, was not being achieved. Therefore, a number of agencies, which were to assume significant roles in later years, were established at this time. These were the Industrial Development Authority, An Foras Tionscal (the Industrial Agency), Coras Trachtala (the Export Agency) and Bord Failte (the Tourist Board). The Capital Investment Advisory Committee, appointed in 1956, strongly argued for a change of direction and laid particular emphasis on productive capital investment which encouraged exports. One of the most important measures introduced in 1956 was the Export Profits Tax Relief Scheme, whereby manufacturing firms were to be freed from taxation on profits earned on export sales. In 1957 Ireland joined the International Monetary Fund and the World

Bank. The White Paper on *Economic Development* in 1958 and, arising from this, the *First Programme for Economic Expansion* (1959–64) emphasised again the need for productive investment. It favoured the dismantling of tariffs and incentives to promote industrial development. The emphasis in the future was to be on outward-looking and export-oriented policies which attempted to attract foreign companies to Ireland and abandoned protectionism. During subsequent decades, this approach was to continue and included the cutting of tariffs, the repeal of the Control of Manufactures Acts, the signing of an Anglo-Irish Free Trade Agreement, joining GATT and the European Community. Later, in 1979, the Republic was to join the European Monetary System. It strongly supported the Single European Act in a referendum in 1986 and the Treaty on European Union in 1992.

8.2.2 Towards industrialisation and regional development

It will be clear from the foregoing that since independence successive Irish governments became actively involved in economic matters. This was particularly the case in relation to the development of industrial policy which we examine in this section. Although the previous emphasis on agriculture was to continue in Ireland and a combination of price support and structural policies was pursued, it was recognised from the 1950s that more serious attention to the development of industry was required in order to provide employment for those leaving agriculture. The Undeveloped Areas Act of 1952 established 'designated areas' in the western half of the country. These areas were to receive special capital grants to persuade Irish industrial concerns to locate there. This Act established an industrial agency, An Foras Tionscal, to administer the grants for land, buildings and machinery and for the training of workers. This agency was to be joined later in the 1950s by two further agencies in the west of Ireland. These were Shannon Free Airport Development Company (now re-named Shannon Development) and Gaeltarra Eireann (now

Udaras Na Gaeltachta), designed to support manufacturing and other initiatives at Shannon Airport and the Irish-speaking areas respectively. During the 1960s these agencies were supplemented by the establishment of county development teams in the designated areas and regional development organisations; the latter were reconstituted in 1994 as Regional Authorities. The concern to give special assistance to the designated areas was well justified in view of the range of special difficulties in agriculture in these areas and the failure to provide sufficient alternative employment opportunities to counteract losses from that industry. This 'regional orientation' of industrial policy was to continue in the years ahead.

As mentioned above, one of the most important measures introduced during the 1950s was the Export Profits Tax Relief Scheme, under which manufacturers exporting their products were freed from taxation on the profits from export sales. While this was not a major incentive to indigenous firms concentrating on the local market, it was especially attractive to foreign firms with an export orientation. During this period, therefore, a range of British firms serving the British and other markets located branch plants in the Republic. They were to be joined by considerable numbers of firms from the United States, West Germany, Japan and elsewhere in the decades ahead.

The 1969 Industrial Development Act merged An Foras Tionscal with the Industrial Development Authority (IDA), established in 1949 as an industrial promotion agency, but now vested with wide-ranging powers and covering all of the Republic. The IDA could give grants towards the purchase of fixed assets of up to 60% of the cost in the designated areas and up to 45% elsewhere, although grants were to be given only if the Authority was satisfied that 'employment of a reasonably permanent nature' would be provided. In addition, the Authority could give grants towards re-equipment, modernisation, improvements or expansion of up to 35% in the designated areas and 25% elsewhere. It had powers to give grants towards the reduction of interest on loans, towards loan guarantees, training, and reduction of factory rents. It could also purchase or construct buildings and industrial estates. The powers granted to the IDA under the legislation were thus extensive.

There were however a number of serious criticisms of the 1969 Industrial Development Act. For example, the policy could be argued to have a 'capital bias' in that it emphasised – and the vast brunt of its expenditure went to fund – investment in land, buildings and machinery. This was of course in line with the philosophy that such investment would increase output and that employment growth would inevitably follow – a philosophy which was prevalent in many countries. In retrospect, we know that the association between output and employment is weak. In addition to this, it could be contended that insufficient 'conditions' had been attached to the disbursement of scarce state funds over an extended period up to 1986 when new legislation was introduced. A wide range of enterprises, whether promising or not, were eligible for assistance. Despite the best intentions of the IDA, not all 'promised targets' for employment could be met. In such cases, there were few real powers to retrieve substantial grants. Finally, there was criticism of the alleged 'regional bias' of the policy towards the designated areas in the west of the country in the face of emerging difficulties (and especially job losses in the industrial sector) in the east, especially in the Dublin area.

By the 1980s there were serious concerns that, despite the extensive range of incentives available, industrial policy was not having a significant impact in creating sufficient new employment or in reducing unemployment. A major *Review of Industrial Policy*, commissioned by the government, was published in 1982. This called for a significant reduction in the level of grant aid to foreign firms, a re-allocation of expenditure in favour of internationally trading indigenous industry and sub-supply firms and a far greater 'control' over the process of industrial development by the government and relevant agencies (National Economic and Social Council, 1982). The *Review* was particularly critical of the nature of the foreign investment and argued that few firms had a truly stand-alone operation in

Ireland. The vast majority of electronics firms were, it was contended, 'manufacturing satellites' performing only partial steps in the manufacturing process such as assembly, test, packaging or simple machining or coating functions. Chemical and pharamaceutical firms were criticised for their failure to carry on research and development in Ireland. The *Review* laid considerable emphasis on the development of indigenous industry and urged that such industry must be re-organised to emphasise the building of structurally strong Irish companies.

The study received some recognition in a White Paper on *Industrial Policy* in 1984 and in a new Industrial Development Act in 1986. The Industrial Development Act of 1986 introduced a range of fundamental changes to the earlier approaches. Henceforth, there was to be much more emphasis on the requirements of the market. First, the criteria for eligibility for grants were tightened up considerably. In future, there would be an increased emphasis on exports, appropriate products and ability to compete on an international scale. Supported firms would require an adequate equity base; they must provide new employment and increase local value-added. Second, incentives were introduced for internationally traded services. This was a new and important departure. Third, the legislation shifted the emphasis somewhat from funding fixed assets towards developing export markets, the acquisition of technology and research and development. Ireland's past record in relation to research and development had been particularly poor and this latter move was overdue. Fourth, employment grants were introduced. In a country where labour surplus was a recurring issue, it may seem surprising that capital subsidies were favoured over labour for so long. This 'factor-price distortion' was now being addressed to some extent. Fifth, the legislation specified that more careful monitoring of public expenditure would be required. Thus, the cost per job, the viability of the employment and the 'spin-off' effects would be assessed in regular 'reviews'. Sixth, more rigorous regulations were introduced regarding the repayment of grants by enterprises which failed to meet employment targets. Finally, the distinction between the grant levels for large industrial enterprises in the designated and non-designated areas was terminated. This latter measure was introduced in view of the heavy orientation of previous policies towards the western half of the country, despite the fact that serious manufacturing losses had been evident for some time in other parts of the country and especially in the Dublin area (Drudy and MacLaran, 1994).

Under the new legislation, the IDA administered a range of new measures to reflect the requirements given above. In the case of 'large' industry, these included a reduction in capital grants to a maximum of 25%, product development grants and management development grants. As regards 'small' industry, employment grants were introduced, as well as management and product development grants and a range of incentives for firms in an 'enterprise development programme'. Prior to this, it could be argued that small companies had received little attention. They were apparently being 'crowded out' by the large ones with more political and financial clout, despite the growing literature indicating the significance of the former in terms of employment, linkages with indigenous and overseas firms, skill development and regional dispersal (see O'Farrell, 1986). A special 'International Services Programme' was also initiated which included grants for employment, management, feasibility studies, training, research and development and the purchase of computers, equipment and buildings. Separate legislation established an International Financial Services Centre in the Custom House Docks area of Dublin where generous incentives were to be available in the form of rates remission as well as tax and rent allowances.

8.2.3 Government finances: fiscal, monetary and exchange-rate policy

Apart from agricultural and industrial policy, successive governments in the Republic of Ireland have intervened in relation to a range of economic and social issues. Thus, since the 1960s expenditure on health, education, social welfare

and housing has increased significantly. The state also either owns or has a share in over 100 enterprises, ranging from transport to electricity. In view of the relatively small tax base to fund expenditure, this has caused serious difficulties during some periods. Prior to the 1970s, Irish governments had aimed to balance current revenue and expenditure and borrowing was used primarily to finance capital programmes. However, the escalation of oil prices in 1973 influenced the government to introduce a current budget deficit in order to counteract the deflationary effects of the crisis. Borrowing increased significantly and the PSBR rose from 9% of GNP in 1972 to 18% in 1975. By the early 1980s it had risen to 20% and the current budget deficit reached 7% per cent of GNP (see Table 8.1). See also Table G34 for details of 'net borrowing' as a percentage of gross domestic product (GDP).

Table 8.1 Current budget deficit, capital borrowing and the PSBR as % of GNP

	Current budget deficit	Capital borrowing	PSBR
1977	3.6	6.1	12.5
1981	7.3	8.4	20.1
1985	7.7	4.4	14.7
1989	1.2	1.0	3.0
1993	1.3	1.1	2.4
1995	1.1	0.7	1.8

Source: Department of Finance, Dublin, various years.

Table 8.2 National debt and interest payments

	Debt £IR m	% of GNP	Interest £IR m	% of GNP
1977	4 229	75.2	279	5.0
1981	10 195	93.2	796	7.3
1985	18 502	111.4	1827	11.0
1989	24 828	112.0	1956	8.8
1993	29 932	106.2	2159	7.6
1995	31 186	91.9	2317	6.8

Source: Department of Finance, Dublin, various years.

By this time, it was recognised that government borrowing was at an unduly high level but little progress was made in dealing with the problem until 1987 when the level of national debt became unsustainable. In 1977 the national debt was £IR4229 million or 75% of GNP (see Table 8.2). By 1987 it had increased sixfold to stand at £IR23694 million or 125% of GNP. Interest payments over the same period increased from £IR279 million (5% of GNP) to £IR1935 million (10% of GNP).

Government expenditure was cut back as from 1987 and an attempt was made to widen the tax base. Borrowing for capital purposes was also reduced significantly. While spending cuts are never popular, there was a general public acceptance of the need to take action. Interest rate reductions also helped. The nominal interest rate on exchequer borrowing had been 10% in 1985. By 1994 it was down to 7%. Interest payments as a proportion of GNP fell accordingly. A number of wage agreements, negotiated amicably between the government and the 'social partners' (employers, farmers and trade unions) also played a critical role in curtailing expenditure. One such agreement was the Programme for Economic and Social Progress, agreed in 1991 and covering the period 1991–93. A second agreement, the Programme for Competitiveness and Work, covered the period 1994–96 while a further agreement, Partnership 2000 for Inclusion, Employment and Competitiveness, covering the period up to 1999, was concluded in late 1996. All of these agreements accepted wage increases broadly in line with expectations on inflation.

The effects of the reduction in public expenditure and interest rates are obvious from Table 8.1 where the current budget deficit, capital borrowing and the PSBR all declined significantly as a proportion of GNP. It is clear that the debt/GNP ratio also fell sharply during the 1990s (see Table 8.2). This 'fiscal stance' is broadly in accordance with that specified in the Maastricht Treaty and the Irish public finances now compare favourably with that in most other EU member states.

There was until recently little prospect of pursuing an independent monetary policy in Ireland. With a fixed exchange rate between sterling and the Irish currency up to 1979, an Irish money market did not develop. A Central Bank had been established in 1942 'to safeguard the

integrity of the currency', but its powers were limited to such things as the issuing of 'credit guidelines'. Recent legislation (e.g. the Central Bank Act and the Building Society Act of 1989) gave much more power to the Central Bank to control the commercial banks, money brokers, financial futures traders, companies in the International Financial Services Centre and the building societies. Due to the openness and smallness of the economy, however, it is still difficult to envisage how the Irish Central Bank could pursue an independent monetary policy. It can and does attempt to influence the Irish exchange rate by buying and selling foreign exchange and it exercises some control over the commercial banks by open market operations. However, it is constrained by external influences and flows across foreign exchanges (Leddin and Walsh, 1995). If European Monetary Union is eventually achieved, the power of the Central Bank in Ireland (as well as in other EU states) will of course be further diminished.

As mentioned earlier, there was, in effect, a monetary union between Ireland and Britain from 1826 and the one-to-one basis between the Irish pound and sterling continued after independence up to 1979. As long as there is such a fixed exchange rate, it could be expected that – in line with the theory of purchasing power parity – the price level in the small Irish economy would be closely linked to, and largely determined by, the price level in Britain. Domestic factors were important, but the impact of 'imported' inflation was regarded as much more important and Irish and British inflation rates had been remarkably similar for long periods. For example, during the 1960s and 1970s the divergence in the two rates was less than 0.5%. However, the divergence between British inflation and the West German one was about 6% over the same period. This resulted in a significant depreciation of sterling and the Irish pound against the Deutschmark. The Irish government had therefore decided to accept the invitation to join the European Monetary System in 1979 in the hope that, if the Irish exchange rate were tied to the Deutschmark, Irish inflation would fall to the German level. This did not in fact happen as quickly as was envisaged. The strong existing trade patterns between Ireland and Britain remained and real appreciation of sterling affected Irish prices. Therefore, in the early stages of EMS, Ireland continued to 'import' inflation from Britain. It was not until the late 1980s that Irish inflation reduced to the German rate and Ireland was able to gain the benefit of EMS. Inflation has remained low since then (see Table G8).

8.3 THE PERFORMANCE OF THE IRISH ECONOMY

We have summarised above a range of policies pursued by governments in Ireland over several decades. What impact had these in terms of the objectives set? It is of course very difficult to separate out the impact of government policy from a range of 'market' factors on both a domestic and international scale. Bearing in mind this caveat, we examine a number of variables which were regarded as significant by successive governments over the last few decades. We examine in turn Ireland's export performance, its record in relation to GDP, the pattern of emigration and changes in employment and unemployment.

8.3.1 Export performance and balance of payments

The composition of Irish trade has changed significantly in recent decades. For example, in 1961 live animals and food accounted for 61% of exports. By 1995 this figure had dropped to 20%. At the same time, the exports of manufactured goods has increased significantly from 18% to 68%. About three-quarters of these exports are accounted for by foreign firms which, on average, export about 86% of their production in comparison with 33% for indigenous Irish firms. The foreign firms export primarily 'high technology' products and account for about 40% of European PC software production (McAleese and Hayes, 1995).

The geographical destination of exports has also altered significantly over recent decades. As mentioned earlier, the vast brunt of Irish trade was with the UK at the time of independence and, even by 1960, the UK took 75% of Irish exports. By 1995, however, this proportion had dropped to 28%. Over the same period, the proportion of exports going to other EU countries increased from 7% to 40%. Exports to other non-EU countries likewise increased. The main influence on the diversification of trade has been the role of foreign firms with marketing strategies designed to capture markets in Europe and further afield. Ireland has also managed in recent years to establish strong trade links with the Middle East and a number of less developed countries, particularly for food. It may be noted too that the export of services, though currently small, is likely to grow significantly. The establishment of an International Financial Services Centre in Dublin, the increase in Irish data processing for export, the activities of medical and consultancy firms, and links with Eastern Europe, point to the increasing importance of services in Irish trade. The proportion of imports from the UK have also declined while the EU figure has increased, although the changes are not as significant as in the case of exports.

Ireland now enjoys a large overall balance of trade surplus, and has done so since 1985. The country is a large net exporter of food, chemicals and electronic data-processing machines and large surpluses are earned in trade with France and Germany. On the other hand, trade deficits occur with the United States and Japan. The most significant positive change in recent years has been the transformation in relation to the current account, from a deficit on the balance of payments of 15% of GNP in 1981 to a surplus of over 8% in 1993. Ireland's 'balance on current transactions with the rest of the world' shows a similar trend (see Table G37). This has been accounted for largely by the strong export performance, particularly among foreign firms. The exploitation of natural gas which reduced energy import requirements and relatively low oil and commodity prices from the mid-1980s have also helped. Positive transfers from the European Union Common Agricultural Policy and Structural Funds (which are examined below) have also played an important role in improving Ireland's balance of payments position. Furthermore, this improvement has occurred despite significant profit repatriation by foreign firms and interest payments on foreign debt – these two items alone accounted for an outflow of £IR 4.6 billion in 1995.

8.3.2 Gross domestic product

The growth of Irish GDP in the 1960s at 4.2% per annum was relatively poor by European standards when growth rates reached unprecedented levels (Table G23). However, Ireland performed better than most countries in Europe during the 1970s. During the 1980s, although growth fell off (to an average of 3.6% per annum), the Irish rate again compared favourably with the rest of Europe. Finally, Ireland has recorded exceptional growth rates during the 1990s and especially during the last few years. It is noteworthy that the Republic's growth rate has far exceeded that of its nearest neighbour, the UK, in most years since 1960. During these three decades, the sectoral composition of GDP also changed significantly. In 1960 (using 1994 constant prices), agriculture accounted for 25%, industry 30% and services 45% of total GDP. By 1994, these proportions had changed to 9%, 38% and 53% respectively, indicating the structural alterations by sector over the period.

GDP per head compared unfavourably to the European average over a period of three decades from the 1960s. GDP remained at about 60% of Europe up to 1980 and was less than two thirds for the 1980s. However, significant changes have occurred in recent years and by 1995, Ireland had reached 90% of the European norm (Table G24). There are many reasons for this improvement. For example, policies which facilitated low inflation, low interest rates and modest wage settlements were critical to an improvement in Ireland's competitive position. Significant progress in relation to cost competitiveness has also been made in relation to essential 'infrastructure' such as telecommunications and electricity supply. The attraction of international mobile investment is heavily dependent on the availability of such infrastructure at a competitive price. There is little doubt too that foreign firms have made a significant difference to Ireland's economic performance in relation to output and productivity. The annual growth rates of output and productivity in excess

of 10% during the 1980s (and slightly less impressive growth rates during the 1990s) can be largely attributed to foreign firms.

On the basis of the GDP figures given above, Ireland has fared better than some other EU members, such as Spain, Portugal and Greece on the 'periphery'. However, it still lags far behind the other relatively well-off 'core' countries. Whether Ireland's improvement can be sustained in the years ahead remains to be seen. In any case, it should be noted that GDP is not an entirely acceptable measure of economic and social well-being and tells us nothing about the *distribution* of income. As in other countries, Ireland has significant pockets of low income groups in both urban and rural areas. These blackspots have above average rates of unemployment, poor levels of educational attainment and indeed suffer 'multiple deprivation'. GDP obviously fails to capture such realities and it would therefore be unwise to rely unduly on this concept as a measure of success.

8.3.3 Population, migration and the labour force

We noted earlier the significant change in the direction of policy from the late 1950s. Had this any effect in counteracting the significant losses of population through migration which characterised the previous decades? Interestingly, the year 1961 marked the beginning of a period of population growth after more than a century of decline and the population increased from 2.8 million in 1961 to 3.6 million in 1996 (see Table G17). Much of this growth has been concentrated in the east of the country and, in particular, in the Dublin conurbation, which now contains 1.1 million or 29% of the national population. The adjoining areas within commuting distance of Dublin have also experienced significant increases since 1961. Despite this growth of population (due to natural increase), net emigration continued, though at a relatively low rate of 13 000 persons per annum during the 1960s. During most of the 1970s, this was replaced by a net immigration of 13 600 per annum, but net emigration resumed as from 1979, reaching 27 000 per annum during the period 1986–91. Despite the positive position since 1991, it is clear that, during almost four decades since independence, emigration has remained a consistent difficulty for the Irish economy and society. Over the 70-year period there were only two short periods when inward flows exceeded outward ones (see Table 8.2). It may be noted too that, since the early 1980s, the birth rate has fallen significantly and is now close to the European norm. This is reflected in the fall in the natural increase shown in Table 8.3. It seems unlikely therefore that significant population growth will occur during the coming decades.

Despite this, policy makers are currently faced with significant numbers of entrants to the labour force due to past demographic trends and the relatively young age structure. The Irish labour force has grown by 304 000 persons, or 27%, over the period 1971–95 and, while all regions have increased, the growth has been heavily concentrated in the Dublin area. Dublin accounted for 43% (130 000) of the total labour force growth during this period, and by 1995 composed almost one third of the nation's labour force. The extent of the employment challenge depends, of course, on participation rates. The Irish male participation rate (at 82% in 1993) is similar to many European countries; however, the female rate (at 40%) is significantly

below the European norm and can be expected to increase in the years ahead. In any case, the extent of the labour force growth indicates a major requirement for employment provision over the next decade.

8.3.4 Employment and unemployment

Table 8.4 sets out the changing pattern of employment in the three main sectors since 1971. The numbers in agriculture have declined consistently and the proportion employed in that industry is now little over 11% of the total. Industry (including building, gas, water, electricity as well as manufacturing) performed well during the 1970s but fell off significantly during the recession of the 1980s. Some recovery appears to have occurred since 1991, but total industrial employment in 1995 was only about 6% above what it was in 1971 and was less than it was in 1981. While this compares favourably with other European countries, it poses particular difficulties for Ireland in view of the need to employ the continuing losses from agriculture.

Since the manufacturing industry has constituted about two thirds of industry and, as shown earlier, has been the central focus of policy for an extended period, it is instructive to examine

Table 8.3 Natural increase, net migration and population change, 1926–96

Period	Average annual natural increase	Average annual net emigration (inward less outward)	Average annual population change
1926–35	16 318	−16 675	− 357
1936–46	17 380	−18 712	−1 332
1946–51	25 595	−24 498	1 097
1951–56	26 887	−39 353	−12 466
1956–61	26 416	−42 401	− 15 985
1961–66	29 253	−16 121	13 132
1966–71	29 630	−10 781	18 849
1971–79	35 129	13 617	48 746
1979–81	40 117	−2 523	37 594
1981–86	33 824	−14 377	19 447
1986–91	23 849	−26 834	−2 985
1991–96	18 426	637	19 063

Source: *Census of Population*, Central Statistics Office, Dublin, various years.

Table 8.4 Employment and the labour force, 1971–95 (000s)

	1971	1981	1991	1995
Agriculture	273.1 (25.9)	188.6 (16.5)	158.2 (13.8)	139.8 (11.3)
Industry	322.7 (30.6)	365.9 (32.2)	313.3 (27.3)	343.3 (27.8)
Services	459.0 (43.5)	583.3 (51.3)	677.6 (58.9)	750.5 (60.9)
Total employed	1054.8 (100.0)	1137.8 (100.0)	1149.1 (100.0)	1233.6 (100.0)
Labour force	1119.5	1271.1	1382.9	1423.5

Source: Census of Population, 1971–91, and *Labour Force Survey* 1995, Central Statistics Office, Dublin.

the pattern of manufacturing activity in recent decades. Data for the two decades since 1975 are provided in Table 8.5. First, it will be noted that the number employed in Irish firms has fallen by 26 700 over the two decades (from 143 400 to 116 700). On the other hand, foreign firms increased in employment by over 21 200 (from 74 900 to 96 100) – resulting in an overall net loss for all manufacturing of 5500. Foreign

firms now account for 45% of total manufacturing jobs compared with 34% 20 years ago. In some regions, such as the west and mid-west, foreign firms account for more than half the manufacturing jobs (Drudy, 1991). Out of the ten sectors in Table 8.4, foreign firms dominate in terms of size in four of these and are particularly strong in the two 'growing' sectors of chemicals and metals/engineering. The relatively low level of 'linkages' of such firms with the Irish economy is a matter of concern.

It may be noted that the above results were achieved as a result of an enormous job creation effort and at considerable expense. Thus, in the case of Irish manufacturing firms, gross job creation of 212 000 was offset by gross losses of 238 700. Gross gains of 152 600 were achieved in the case of foreign firms, but losses amounted to 131 500. The performance in creating *new* jobs was therefore impressive; the record in maintaining *existing* jobs was, however, very poor. The cost involved was considerable. Annual expenditure in the early 1990s on industrial grants was estimated to be about IR£460 million per annum. An additional cost of about IR£150 million was incurred in the provision of

Table 8.5 Foreign and Irish manufacturing employment by sector, 1975–95

	1975				1995			
	Foreign	Irish	Total	Sectoral % 1975	Foreign	Irish	Total	Sectoral % 1995
Non-metallic minerals	4 108	12 342	16 450	7.5	2 279	7 572	9 851	4.6
Chemicals	7 487	4 466	11 953	5.5	14 663	3 848	18 511	8.7
Metals and engineering	25 946	23 944	49 890	22.8	51 411	31 013	82 424	38.7
Food	10 215	40 816	51 031	23.4	7 642	31 923	39 565	18.6
Drink and tobacco	7 892	3 919	11 811	5.4	4 073	2 035	6 108	2.9
Textiles	6 602	10 217	16 819	7.7	5 752	3 671	9 423	4.4
Clothing, footwear and leather	5 860	19 320	25 180	11.5	3 017	7 933	10 950	5.2
Timber and furniture	542	10 056	10 598	4.9	432	8 973	9 405	4.4
Paper and printing	2 319	13 537	15 856	7.3	2 044	11 610	13 654	6.4
Miscellaneous	3 973	4 784	8 757	4.0	4 787	8 141	12 928	6.1
Total	74 944	143 401	218 345	100.0	96 100	116 719	212 819	100.0

Source: Industrial Development Authority, Dublin, 1975 and 1995.

tax relief to manufacturing firms. The total cost of industrial policy (almost exclusively aimed at manufacturing) was therefore in excess of £IR600 million per annum.

The sectoral composition of Irish manufacturing has undergone significant change over the two decades. The metals and engineering sector has now replaced food as the largest contributor to employment and accounted for 39% of total employment in 1995. Chemicals (including pharmaceuticals) also increased its share. On the other hand, there were serious declines in the numbers employed in food, drinks and tobacco, textiles, clothing and footwear. Thus, the 'traditional' sectors of manufacturing activity are being replaced by modern 'high-tech' ones. The latter are dominated by foreign firms; the former by Irish indigenous firms. This heavy dependence on foreign firms and the low 'linkages' with the local economy has prompted policy-makers to devote far more attention to the development of indigenous firms in recent years. The overall conclusion must be that, for a modest net gain in manufacturing employment by foreign firms and a significant net loss in such employment by Irish firms, a significant effort and cost has been involved. In line with international trends, it can be expected that employment growth in manufacturing will be modest, if not static or in decline, in the years ahead.

In contrast to industrial employment, services have shown reasonable growth over the past few decades (see Table 8.3). The total number employed in services grew by 12 000 per annum during the 1970s, 9000 per annum during the 1980s and 18 000 per annum between 1991 and 1995. Much of the growth has been accounted for by increased opportunities in commerce, insurance, finance and business services. Professional and personal services, including tourism, also displayed significant change. The rate of growth has, however, lagged well behind most other European countries and the United States. Dublin is the predominant service employer and contains 40% of the national total. It has secured 37% of the national growth in services and has grown by 58% since 1971. However,

growth rates exceeding this have been achieved in the west and north-west of the country, indicating a dispersal of services in recent years.

While the increase in services is to be warmly welcomed, a number of points may be made. First, the increase compares unfavourably with most other European countries and has been insufficient to cater for new labour force growth as well as counteracting the consistent decline in the numbers in agriculture and the modest performance of industry. Second, there is increasing concern regarding the 'quality' of some service-type jobs. Many of these jobs, and in particular those held by females, are part-time and poorly paid. They offer minimal training and poor career prospects (O'Donovan, 1996).

The overall net increase in employment since 1971 (179 000) has fallen far short of the growth in the labour force (304 000). As a result of the relatively poor employment creation record in relation to requirements, the numbers unemployed trebled in the Republic since 1971 (from 64 700 to 189 800). The rate of unemployment similarly deteriorated from 6% in 1971 to 14.4% in 1995 (see Table 8.6 and Table G20). The Republic has been well above the European average for more than 30 years and is now exceeded only by Spain and Finland. Furthermore, it may be recalled that the Republic has been characterised by a high rate of emigration over many years. In the absence of this, unemployment would be even more problematic. In addition, it can be argued that the current unemployment rate is maintained artificially 'low' by a range of Government employment and training schemes initiated in recent years. These schemes accounted for 115 000 'jobs' in 1995. If

Table 8.6 Numbers and percentage unemployed, 1975–95

	1971	1981	1991	1995
Number	64 692	133 295	233 790	189 900
Percentage of labour force	6.0	10.8	14.8	14.4

Source: Census of Population, 1971–91, Labour Force Survey, 1995 and EUROSTAT.

such schemes had not been available, unemployment emigration would have increased further. Finally, it should be noted that more than half the unemployment in the Republic can be classified as long-term, i.e. unemployed for more than one year. Indeed, the rate of long-term unemployment is higher than the *overall* unemployment rate in most OECD countries (O'Hagan, 1995). This is a matter of growing concern.

8.4 IMPACT OF EUROPEAN INTEGRATION

In view of its new outward-looking approach from the late 1950s, it was to be expected that Ireland would seek membership of the then European Community as soon as the opportunity arose and, together with the United Kingdom, it sought to join in 1961. The simultaneous application to join made sense in view of the close economic links between the two countries. When the United Kingdom's application was vetoed, Ireland therefore decided to remain outside. Ten years later, membership was more firmly on the agenda and both countries, together with Denmark, joined the Community in 1973. At the time, the Irish government placed considerable hope on the positive benefits of membership and stressed the role the Community could play in 'regional development' (Government of Ireland, 1972). A special 'Protocol', included in the Irish Treaty of Accession, referred specifically to the need to reduce regional imbalances. The aim of reducing disparities between the regions had of course been set out in the Preamble to the Treaty of Rome in 1957. However, this was given new impetus by Ireland and the United Kingdom in 1972 and that year can probably be regarded as a turning point in the evolution of a Common Regional Policy.

The official mood of optimism was reflected in the results of the May 1972 referendum which recorded a remarkable 83% of the voting population in favour of entry to the Community. Of the three acceding members at the time, it seems that Ireland was by far the most enthusiastic. It

was, in a sense, a coming of age of the Irish state. Furthermore, Ireland was renewing cultural and economic links which had existed with varying degrees of intensity for centuries (Drudy and McAleese, 1984).

Two decades later, the mood is more sober and circumspect. There still appears to be a widespread, if not universal, belief that if things are difficult for Ireland within the European Union, they would be worse outside. Ireland has been affected by many factors outside the control of the Union, but a range of queries can also be raised concerning the adequacy or otherwise of European policies in resolving the difficulties outlined earlier. We turn now to examine the main European Union policies which have affected Ireland over the last two decades and attempt to assess their impact.

8.4.1 Agricultural and structural policies

The Common Agricultural Policy (CAP), was forged at a time when the Community had over 20% of its work-force in agriculture and low incomes of those in that industry were a matter of particular concern. The *Guarantee Section* of the CAP was designed to support or 'guarantee' the prices of a range of agricultural products, while the *Guidance Section* was intended to bring about improvements in the 'structure' of agriculture. A variety of changes have been introduced to the CAP over the years, but the price support element still occupies more than half the overall budget, despite the fact that the numbers occupied in agriculture have declined significantly in recent decades. Furthermore, the support for agricultural prices has resulted in significant surpluses of agricultural products which must be stored at high cost and subsequently sold on world markets with the aid of subsidies. The 1992 reform of the CAP, designed to control production by reducing guaranteed prices, coupled with compensation payments to farmers, and the GATT agreement under which the Union is committed to reducing the volume of subsidised exports have, to some extent, addressed these problems. Whether the growth in agricultural spending will be more strictly controlled in the years ahead remains to be seen.

The *Guidance Section* of the CAP, together with the Community's social and regional policies, have been given the title 'structural' policies, since they are all designed to improve the structure of the Community's industries and regions. With the accession of Ireland and the United Kingdom in 1973, structural problems and, in particular, regional disparities began to assume considerable significance. In the case of Ireland, the special Protocol included in the Treaty of Accession referred specifically to the need to reduce regional imbalances and by 1975 the Commission had established the European Regional Development Fund (ERDF) to tackle this problem.

The need for social policy was also recognised in the EEC Treaty which established the European Social Fund. At that time, the policy placed particular emphasis on training and retraining as a measure to alleviate the difficulties of workers facing redundancy and the problem of unemployment. New social policy provisions were introduced in 1987 and a Social Charter was signed in 1989 by eleven member states. A special Protocol reaffirming the commitment to social policy (including new provisions on working and safety conditions, equality in the workplace, social security and protection of workers) was added to the Union Treaty in 1992. The Treaty placed a new emphasis on policies relating to education, exchange of ideas, training, youth, public health, cultural heritage and citizens' rights. Environmental policies also assumed a critical significance in aiming at a more 'sustainable' development. In recent years, therefore, rather more attention has been paid to structural, regional, social and environmental policies. However, the overall European budget is still heavily devoted to price support for agricultural products and 54% of the total budget was expended in this category during 1993 (European Commission,1993).

8.4.2 Transfers between the European Union and Ireland

Receipts from and contributions to the European Union in selected years are set out in Table 8.7. It is clear that Irish gross receipts each year have

Table 8.7 Irish receipts from and contributions to the EU, 1985–95 (IR£ millions current prices)

	1985	*1990*	*1995*
Agriculture (Guarantee)	837	1287	1150
Agriculture (Guidance)	56	94	143
ESF	141	128	256
ERDF	76	225	358
Cohesion Fund	–	–	102
Other	18	7	14
Total receipts	1128	1741	2023
Irish contributions	214	284	543
Net receipts	914	1457	1480
As % of Irish GNP	5.8	6.4	4.4

Source: European Commission, 1985, 1990 and 1995.

been many times greater than contributions, resulting in net receipts of IR£14 billion over the period 1985–95. These net receipts represented almost 6% of Irish GNP during this period. The agricultural industry in particular has received significant transfers from the *Guarantee Section* of the CAP, amounting to well over 70% of total EU expenditure in Ireland throughout the 1980s. In line with CAP reform, this had reduced to 57% of the total by 1995.

The *Guidance Section* of the CAP occupied less than 5% of total receipts in the early 1980s, although it increased slightly since the reform of the Structural Funds in 1988. The ERDF has assumed increasing importance in recent years. In Ireland the ERDF is primarily concerned with the development of a range of infrastructure, industry and tourism. Receipts from this Fund increased from 7% of the total in 1985 to 18% in 1995. The ESF is spent mainly on training and retraining in an effort to tackle Ireland's unemployment problem. This Fund showed only a modest increase in its share of the total (from 12% to 13%) over the period 1985–95. It may be noted that receipts from the new Cohesion Fund have also increased in recent years.

Various questions can be raised regarding these various policies, especially those relating to agricultural expenditure. One must, for example, have serious reservations concerning the size of the Guarantee Section of the CAP which continues to account for a disproportionate share of total receipts at a time when only 11% of the Irish population is employed in agriculture. Although Ireland's share of European agricultural output is relatively small, this policy still exacerbates the agricultural surplus problem mentioned earlier. Furthermore, as in other European countries, the receipts from that Section have been overwhelmingly concentrated in the relatively prosperous farming areas in Ireland, and among larger farmers concentrating on 'highly-supported' products. (See, for example, Drudy and McAleese, 1984 and O'Donnell *et al.*, 1989). In effect, therefore, this expenditure widens rather than narrows the gap between the commercial group of farmers and those in the more numerous 'marginal' category.

The Guidance Section of the CAP, on the other hand, has shown little increase. Its share of the total in 1985 was 5%; by 1995 it represented only 7%. Given that agricultural structure in a wide sense is accepted as a fundamental difficulty in countries such as Ireland, the division of expenditure on agriculture seems seriously out of line with requirements.

The Single European Act had called for the reform of the Structural Funds in order to improve their effectiveness in reducing disparities. The reform, introduced in 1988, re-defined the objectives of the Structural Funds and in particular gave priority to promoting the development of less prosperous regions by doubling the level of EU funding for the period 1989–93. Five 'objectives' were set out in the new policy and the less prosperous regions, including Ireland, Northern Ireland, Portugal, Greece and parts of Spain and Italy were classified as 'Objective 1' regions. A recent study estimated that the increased resources from the Structural Funds over the period 1989–93 increased GDP in Ireland by 2.5% in 1993. The investment is also estimated to have generated an extra 30 000 jobs in Ireland in the same year (Economic and Social Research Institute, 1993). A further study argued that significant long-term 'supply-side' effects could accrue in terms of productive capacity, improved work-force skills, new infrastructure and technological development (Matthews, 1994).

While significant positive benefits have been attached to Ireland's membership of the European Union, there have also been some disadvantages. For example, the Union's competition policy means that some measures which formerly gave Ireland a competitive advantage came under scrutiny and were eliminated. Thus, the Export Profits Tax Relief Scheme (which was central in attracting foreign firms to Ireland) was seen to be anti-competitive and was replaced in 1981 by a less generous tax allowance. Membership of the Union has also exposed indigenous Irish firms to the rigours of the market and, while this is reasonable and justified from an efficiency viewpoint, many jobs have been lost in the process. On balance, however, it can be concluded that the benefits of membership outweigh the costs and Ireland remains strongly committed to the further development of the Union.

Looking to the future, it seems that the European Union's Structural and Cohesion Funds could play an important role in raising living standards, reducing unemployment and exploiting more fully Ireland's economic potential. The *National Development Plan*, 1994–99, produced by the Irish government as part of its negotiations for EU funding, has been approved by the European Commission. This *Development Plan* first places a major emphasis on increasing output, economic potential and the provision of new viable employment opportunities. Second, it has the central objective of reintegrating the long-term unemployed into the job market. A range of measures are proposed to improve the productive capacity of the economy; to improve competitiveness and efficiency; to exploit the development potential of local initiatives, including area-based approaches targeted at disadvantaged areas; to develop skills and aptitudes of both those at work and those seeking work; and to integrate those who are marginalised and disadvantaged into the workforce.

The proposed measures include:

- an extension of existing programmes of investment in transport networks, industry, agriculture, forestry, fisheries, tourism, water and sanitary services, education and training;

- an increased emphasis on local development programmes aimed at the long-term unemployed;
- greater emphasis on the development of indigenous industry;
- increased investment in the food industry;
- new initiatives in tourism, including those related to culture and heritage, as well as tourism, angling and marketing;
- upgrading of the national rail network, investment in regional and county roads and the implementation of the Dublin Transport Initiative, designed to improve traffic management in Ireland's capital city;
- increased investment in energy and communications.

Planned expenditure over the period 1994–99 includes IR£6200 million from Union Structural Funds, IR£638 million from Community Initiatives and IR£1150 million from the new Cohesion Fund in constant 1993 prices. Irish government expenditure is expected to be IR£8500 million, while the private sector is predicted to spend IR£3700 million over the period. Total expenditure over the period of the Development Plan is thus expected to be about IR£20 billion. This substantial funding should help to achieve some or all of the above objectives outlined above, but its precise impact remains to be seen.

8.5 CONCLUSIONS

The Republic of Ireland changed from a largely inward-looking protectionist approach to a set of export-oriented and industrialisation policies from the late 1950s. This presented enormous attractions to multinational companies, mostly from the United States and West Germany. Membership of the European Union further confirmed Ireland as an industrial location – an ideal base from which to export on a low tax rate to the lucrative European markets. Export levels increased significantly and Ireland reduced its dependence on the British market. GDP has increased significantly. After a period of severe fiscal and debt difficulties during the late 1970s and 1980s, the public finances compare favourably with our European counterparts.

Despite these positive indicators, a number of serious difficulties remain. Emigration, which was a significant problem for Ireland during the late nineteenth century, has continued with little abatement up to the present time. The decline in agricultural employment continues. Overall employment in manufacturing has also fallen over the past few decades and, although employment in foreign firms has shown a modest net increase, the costs in terms of capital incentives and tax relief given to such firms have been very high. Furthermore, foreign firms have weak 'linkages' with the Irish economy, their investment in Research and Development in Ireland has been modest and the level of profit repatriation is significant, suggesting a relatively low level of long-term commitment. It is widely agreed that a more competitive indigenous employment sector must now become an essential feature of the future Irish economy.

While employment in the service sector has risen, the scale of the increase compares unfavourably with most European countries. The Irish unemployment rate is among the highest in Europe and there is particular concern about the persistence of long-term unemployment. In the absence of various state employment schemes of a short-term nature, the real unemployment rate would be even higher. Despite the range of positive features and improvements in the Irish economy in recent years, it would be wise to face up to the fact that Ireland will continue to remain heavily influenced by international events and trends. The fact that the country is currently well placed and enthusiastic about participating in European Monetary Union should not disguise the fact that such participation could put Ireland at a severe disadvantage unless its structural, locational and unemployment difficulties *vis-à-vis* the core countries of Europe can be overcome.

How does Ireland conform to the dependency and modernisation theories mentioned in the introduction to this chapter? There is little doubt that Ireland is heavily dependent on trade with the outside world and is quickly affected by and dependent on international developments. This is of course the case with all small open economies. Membership of the European Union has significantly lessened Ireland's dependence on one single trading partner. Trade has diversified and membership has brought other significant benefits. However, the country remains heavily dependent on foreign investment.

As regards the modernisation theory, Ireland has undoubtedly changed in a relatively short period of time from being a relatively undeveloped agricultural economy to a 'modern' urbanised one where manufacturing and services play a major role. However, 'modernisation' is largely attributable to foreign investment, including EU funding, and it is only in recent years that serious efforts have been made to develop a competitive indigenous industry. The rationale for these efforts stem from the realisation that multinational companies operate on a global scale. While making an important contribution to Ireland's development effort, it would be unwise to rely unduly on them to resolve the most important problem of unemployment. The provision of adequate and viable employment and a significant reduction in the level of unemployment remain fundamental difficulties to be resolved as a matter of urgency.

8.6 BIBLIOGRAPHY

Drudy, P.J. (1991): 'The regional impact of overseas industry', in Foley, A. and McAleese, D. (eds) *Overseas Industry in Ireland*, Gill and Macmillan, Dublin, pp. 152–69

Drudy, P.J., MacLaran, A. (1994): *Dublin: Social and Economic Trends*, Centre for Urban and Regional Studies, Dublin

Drudy, P.J., McAleese, D. (eds) (1984): *Ireland and the European Community*, Cambridge University Press, Cambridge

Economic and Social Research Institute (1993): *EC Structural Funds: The Community Support Framework*, Stationery Offices, Dublin

European Commission (1993): *European Economy* No. 53

Government of Ireland (1972): *The Accession of Ireland to the European Communities*, Stationery Office, Dublin, p. 38

Government of Ireland (1993): *Ireland: National Development Plan, 1994–99*, Stationery Office, pp. 7–8

Kennedy, K. *et al.* (1988): *The Economic Development of Ireland in the Twentieth Century*, Harvester

Leddin, A., Walsh, B. (1995): *The Macroeconomy of Ireland*, Gill and Macmillan, Dublin

McAleese, D., Hayes, F. (1995): 'European Integration, the Balance of Payments and Inflation', in O'Hagan, J. (ed.) *The Economy of Ireland: Policy and Performance*, Gill and Macmillan, Dublin, pp. 265–94

Matthews, A. (1982): 'The state and Irish agriculture' in Drudy, P.J. (ed.) *Ireland: Land, Politics and People*, Cambridge University Press, Cambridge

Matthews, A. (1994): *The Impact of the Structural Funds in Ireland*, Cork University Press

National Economic and Social Council, (1982): *A Review of Industrial Policy*, Dublin

O'Donnell, R., Danaher, G, McCashin, T. (1989): *Ireland in the European Community*, National Economic and Social Council Report, No. 89, Dublin

O'Donovan, P. (1996): Minimum Standards and Atypical Work, Irish Congress of Trade Unions, Dublin

O'Farrell, P.N. (1986): *Enterpreneurs and Industrial Change*, Irish Management Institute, Dublin

O'Hagan, J. (1995): 'Employment and unemployment', in O'Hagan, J. (ed.) *The Economy of Ireland: Policy and Performance*, Gill and Macmillan, Dublin, pp. 228–64

O'Hagan, J., McStay, K. (1981): *The Evolution of Manufacturing Industry in Ireland*, Confederation of Irish Industry, Dublin

Seers, D., Schaffer, B., Kiljunen, M. (eds), (1979): *Underdeveloped Europe; Studies in Core–Peripherey Relations*, Harvester, Sussex

CHAPTER 9

Denmark

Richard Bailey

9.1 REGIONAL CONTEXT

There is a common tendency in post-war economic writing to treat Sweden, Norway and Denmark, together with Finland, as parts of the same 'Scandinavian experience'. This is justified by reference to important common features – political characteristics, social ideas and economic institutions – deriving, in part at least, from the common experience of a shared history. Perhaps the single feature which identifies these countries as a 'group' is the particular form of institutional structures and policies identified with *welfare capitalism*.

In the course of the 20th century, European countries have been continuously exploring alternative structures of socio-economic organisation to deal with the intractable problems of conflict and coordination between the 'social', 'political' and 'economic' spheres of human activity. The outcome, in post-war Europe, was the emergence of a number of variations on the theme of the mixed economy. In this context, Scandinavia developed a socio-economic discourse and an institutional structure which was quite sharply differentiated from those of other economies – this has become known as the *negotiated economy*. The policy approach emphasised the formulation of a flexible strategy for socio-economic development based on consensual agreement derived from a continuous dialogue between firms, governments, local authorities and interest organisations.

In the current Danish context, this is illustrated in the recent evolution of industrial policy.

From the mid-1980s there emerged a network of institutional investors, public authorities, private firms and trade unions – a loosely articulated grouping known as the Forum for Industrial Development. This became a central actor in a number of restructuring initiatives during the late 1980s and early 1990s (see Pedersen, 1992 and Christiansen, 1994). These semi-formal structures of private policymaking also exist in the labour market where collective agreements established in the leading sectors of the economy become the accepted norm, or the determining framework, for general arrangements in the labour market as a whole.

While there are important features of commonality in institutional structures and policy priorities within Scandinavia, the Nordic countries do exhibit important variations. Subtle political differences and widely varying factor endowments have combined to produce differential policy responses to both internal and external circumstances.

9.2 STRUCTURES AND INSTITUTIONS OF THE DANISH ECONOMY

With a land area of 43 000 km^2 and a population of just over 5 million, Denmark is one of the smallest countries of the European Community. Geographically, the country consists of the peninsula of Jutland and 500 islands located between the peninsula and Sweden. The two main islands are Funen and Zealand; the capital city, Copenhagen, is located on the latter and has historically held a vital strategic position controlling access to the Baltic sea-route.

The natural resources of the country consist of little more than productive farm land and an extended coastline. In this situation, it is not surprising that farming and fishing have long been primary occupations of the local population. In spite of this there has been a strong trend of urbanisation, with 86% of the population currently classified as living in urban areas.

Over a quarter of Danish citizens live in the Copenhagen conurbation, the remaining urban centres being relatively small with no towns in excess of 200 000 population. With the exception of Copenhagen, most of the centres of urban population are located on the peninsula.

International openness, measured by a high trade/GNP ratio, has been a characteristic feature of the Danish economy since the 19th century when agricultural production became increasingly orientated toward the needs of the UK market. Throughout the first half of the 20th century Denmark experienced only modest industrial development, based largely on the increasing commercialisation of agriculture. However, as may be seen from the employment statistics in Table 9.1, rapid changes from the late 1950s onward radically reshaped the structures of the Danish economy.

Table 9.1 Changing structure of employment

Sector/Year	1955	1973	1981	1994
Agriculture	21.8	9.5	7.2	5.1
Industry	34.9	33.8	29.3	26.8
Services	43.3	56.7	63.3	68.1

Source: © OECD 1955–1994 Labour Statistics.
Reproduced with permission of the OECD.

The Golden Age of the 1950s and 1960s represents a 'second industrial revolution'. There was an impressive expansion in the traditional sectors of textiles, shipbuilding and food-processing, together with the emergence of a group of medium-sized, high value-added niche market producers in areas such as furniture, electrical engineering and pharmaceuticals. The industrial expansion in the 1960s led to a dispersal of manufacturing away from Copenhagen to south and west Jutland, and this, together with the emergence of agricultural cooperatives in the food processing industry, contributed to the increasing urbanisation of the population.

While social and political realignments reflected these developments, traditional interest groups of agriculture and industrial labour remained strongly represented in political life. As a consequence, economic strategy reflected a series of social compromises and was geared to ensuring that the distributional consequences of structural change were politically acceptable. The expanding role of the state, a high level of commitment to full employment and the development of increasingly comprehensive welfare provision, were essential features of this process.

The industrial dimension involved a regulative and redistributory role for the state which ensured that some sheltered sectors of the economy absorbed a large share of available resources. The small industrial base and high productivity growth in manufacturing meant that the resource shift from agriculture was mainly to the service sector (see Table 9.1). During the 1960s and early 1970s full employment was maintained through state-financed infrastructure investment, plus rapid growth in construction and state employment. As a consequence, taxation to finance the expansion of state activity, transfer payments and sectoral support policies, rose steeply during this period.

In general the 1960s was characterised by rapid growth, low unemployment and rising real incomes. Very high levels of taxation remained politically acceptable so long as they were accompanied by sustained income growth. The combination of high private and public consumption, however, meant that continued growth of the manufacturing export sector became increasingly dependent on external finance. The net effect of this was the emergence of a chronic structural deficit on the balance of payments, which, by 1972, produced a foreign debt equal to 56% of annual exports and 13% of GNP.

The structural vulnerability of the Danish economy was cruelly exposed by the events of the early 1970s. The impressive industrial development of the 1960s had been accompanied by an increasing dependence on energy, and by 1973 over 88% of fuel consumed was imported oil. The deterioration of the terms of trade occasioned by OPEC policies faced the government with serious adjustment problems. The institutional structures of the welfare economy and the political commitment to full employment led to severe inflationary problems.

With the exception of agriculture, productivity growth in the 'tradable' sector of the economy experienced a decline in the 1970s and 1980s compared with the pre-1973 period (OECD *Economic Survey*, 1990–91, Table K). Macroeconomic polices geared to maintaining levels of employment, combined with a high degree of wage rigidity, resulted in high inflation rates, declining international competitiveness and periodic currency devaluation. During 1973–80 the Krona depreciated against the D-mark from 2.27 to 3.1 (K to Dm); this, combined with a degree of appreciation against the pound and dollar, contributed to the shifting geographical pattern of Danish trade described below.

9.3 MAIN ECONOMIC CHARACTERISTICS

9.3.1 Human resources and the labour market

Denmark has a slow-growing population currently standing at 5.2 million. The changing pattern of civilian employment has been outlined above and shows an increasing concentration of employment in public and private sector service activity.

As in other Nordic countries labour participation rates are very high. In Denmark these have risen strongly in the last two decades from 60% to 80% of the working age group, and currently (1995) stand 10% above the OECD average. The growth in labour participation has been the primary source of labour supply growth at a time of low population growth and limited labour migration. All of this growth is accounted for by

increased female participation and may be largely explained by the nature of the welfare state which provides both positive support for female employment and expanding job opportunities in traditional areas of female employment. This is also reflected in the level of part-time employment – currently standing at just over 23% of total employment.

9.3.2 Output and productivity growth

In the two decades following the oil shock GDP growth was marginally below the EC average; however, there has been a significant improvement in growth performance in the mid-1990s (Table G23). During the earlier period the problem appears to have been the slow growth in labour productivity. Explanations of productivity slow-down are complex and problematic; in part, this may have been a natural consequence of convergence and structural evolution in a country which had already attained high levels of real income. One element explaining slow growth of overall labour productivity is to be found in the explosion of public sector/service sector employment in the 1970s and early 1980s (see Pedersen 1996).

Since 1993 there has been a marked upturn in output growth. This originated from a demand-led expansion stimulated initially by growth in public and private consumption and sustained by subsequent growth in investment. Exports have also contributed to the expansion, benefiting from the international recovery. Productivity growth has been strong and unit labour costs declined in 1993–94, the downside of this was that unemployment did not show any significant decline until 1995. It is difficult to predict how long this high growth will be sustained but the government is implementing policies to improve labour market structures in order to create the microeconomic conditions for sustained growth (see Section 9.4 below).

9.3.3 Prices, wages and unemployment

Denmark, together with other EU countries, has experienced an almost uninterrupted rise in unemployment levels since the early 1970s, annual average unemployment for each of the last three decades being 1.0%, 3.7% and 7.5%. This compares not unfavourably with the average for the other EU countries (see Figure 9.1); however, inter-country statistical comparisons of this sort are notoriously unreliable and at best offer only indications of broad trends.

Ostensibly, wages are determined by central bargaining between trade union and employer organisations. National agreements are negotiated biannually and cover about 30% of manual workers; however, these agreements tend to have an extended impact on general wage negotiations. This can be most clearly seen in the process of establishing reductions in working hours. Unlike the majority of European countries Denmark does not have a statutory maximum working week; however, collectively bargained maximum hours (currently 37 hours per week) have become established as a 'norm' for both union and non-unionised employees. More generally, trade union bargaining has been based on a 'solidarity wage policy'; this has had the objective of securing higher relative increases for the low-paid workers. The result of this has been a considerable compression of wage differentials to a level which is currently amongst the lowest in the OECD area. Market forces intrude into this structure and modify outcomes via decentralised negotiation at the firm level; this has generated substantial 'wage drift', through which skilled workers seek to protect differentials by bargaining for increases above the central norm.

The institutional structures of the labour market have produced a set of working conditions and a system of unemployment compensation, which together have contributed to severe problems of market inflexibility resulting in structural unemployment. Average replacement ratios (the ratio of unemployment benefit to wages) rose rapidly through to the mid-1970s and, although it has fallen slightly since, remains high by international standards. The net effect has been to produce an uncomfortable unemployment/inflation trade-off, with an OECD estimate for NAIRU (non-accelerating inflation rate of unemployment) of 8%. The government is currently addressing this problem of structural unemployment by means of active labour market policies embodied in a 'medium-term strategy' covering the period 1994–98; measures include enhanced training opportunities, limitations on unemployment benefits and income tax reforms aimed at reducing marginal tax rates by 6–9% (OECD *Economic Survey*, 1996, Pt.IV).

Price inflation has been progressively reduced during the 1980s and 1990s, falling from 12% in 1981 to a predicted 2% for 1996. While this compares favourably with the other core EU

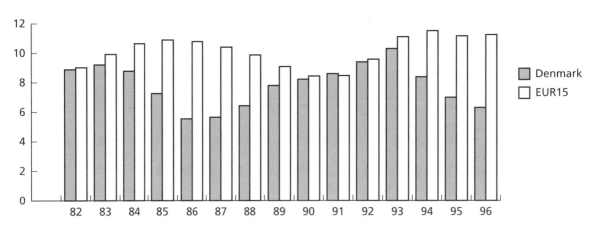

Figure 9.1 Comparative rates of unemployment, Denmark and EUR15.

Source: Eurostat, Tables G1 and G2.

countries (see Figure 9.2), it has been achieved at the cost of high and rising levels of unemployment. Government commitment to a 'hard currency' and the associated financial restraint has provided the essential background for the successful anti-inflation policy, which has also combined a number of supply-side measures to increase labour market flexibility.

9.3.4 Production, firm size and market structure

Some reference has already been made to changes in the pattern of production in the post-war years. Since the 1960s, changes in the distribution of economic activity within the private sector have been influenced by a number of factors, most notably energy price changes, membership of the EC and the increasing social concern with environmental issues. During 1966–93 agriculture's share of value-added fell from 10.2% to 4.4%, while that of manufacturing contracted slightly from 25 to 24%; in compensation, the non-tradeable sector, including construction, utilities and services, expanded from 64% to over 70%. Within these broad categories, the main sectoral expansion has been in financial and business services which grew from 11% to 24% of value-added (OECD *Economic Survey*, 1994, Table K).

The impression that the country has moved from 'pre-industrial to post-industrial' society

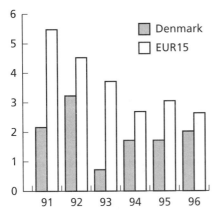

Figure 9.2 Comparative inflation (Denmark and EUR15 GDP deflator)

Source: Eurostat, Tables G1 and G3.

while missing out the intermediate stage is perhaps somewhat misleading, in view of the fact that Denmark has, since the 19th century, had a commercially orientated agricultural sector. However, the small and relatively narrow industrial sector combined with a large market and non-market service sector does represent a uniquely Danish response to the changing global environment.

Manufacturing industry has been, and continues to be, dominated by the small/medium size firm. In 1991 only 20% of business sector employment was in firms employing 500 or more persons, and 40% were employed in firms having less than 20 workers. In comparison, Germany employed 40% of business sector workers in firms employing 500+ workers and only 26% in firms with less than 20 employees (OECD, *Economic Survey*, 1994, Table 21).

Danish industry is frequently described as being 'niche-orientated', that is to say firms and groups of firms focus on specialised sectors within global industries – establishing leading positions in the global market. An illustration is pharmaceuticals, where *Novo Nordisk* is one of only three producers of insulin and is also a world leader in the production of industrial enzymes. A further instance, from the building industry, is *Rockwool* – one of the four leading world producers of mineral wool and a dominant player in the market for building insulation. Similar examples can be found in food-processing, where Danish firms account for 43% of world exports of bacon and 16% of exports of frozen fish fillets. Shipping and ship-building represent another area in which careful targeting on specialist products has enabled the six major Danish yards to position the country as the third largest shipbuilding nation after Japan and Korea.

There has been a rapid growth of mergers and acquisitions during the late 1980s and early 1990s as Danish industry became more internationally orientated in preparation for the enhanced opportunities of the 'single market', and this has marginally reduced the predominance of small firms in the industrial sector. There has also been an increase in the overseas presence of Danish firms – Danish corporations being part of the small band of non-German capitalists making acquisitions through the *Treuhand*. On the other hand, foreign inward investment in the Danish economy has been very limited; few multinational corporations have located in the country – with the exception of Swedish investment in the financial services sector.

9.3.5 Consumption and investment

The share of private consumption in GDP is low by EU standards and is, in part, a reflection of the nature and extent of welfare provision (see Section 9.7.1), this is mirrored by high levels of public consumption and the associated high levels of forced savings (taxation). The falling trend observable since the 1960s seems to have settled at around 52.3% of GDP during the 1990s; this, however, is still 10 points below the European average (see Table G28).

Gross Fixed Capital Formation (GFCF) fell below trend during the 1980s; at least part of this may be explained by fluctuating levels of residential construction and the generally high interest rates throughout the period. In the last years of the 1980s the increase in profit share contributed to investment stability in the face of low levels of capacity utilisation. GFCF as a percentage of GDP fell between 1990 and 1994 mainly as a result of declining levels of public investment by local authorities; however, there is evidence of strong growth in business sector investment in 1994/5 associated with the rising level of profits during the current expansion. In the past, the ratio of GFCF to GDP has fluctuated around 15%, which is below the average for the 'core' EU countries, this may be explained in part by the nature of the Danish manufacturing sector – in particular, the dominance of the small firm sector.

9.4 GOVERNMENT INVOLVEMENT IN THE ECONOMY

A broad measure of the extent of government involvement in the economy is indicated by the government expenditure/GDP ratio. In the 1950s this ratio was one of the lowest of the European countries, but between 1953 and 1973 public consumption and transfer payments grew more rapidly than in any other European state. By the mid-1970s, employment in the public sector exceeded that of the manufacturing sector and Danish citizens became the most heavily taxed of the western world.

The 1980s witnessed political changes commonly described as a 'welfare backlash'. In 1982 a conservative-led coalition government was elected with a 'medium-term economic strategy' which combined policies to reign back welfare spending, reduce direct taxes and restore competitiveness in the manufacturing sector. The return of the Social Democrats to power in 1993 has not significantly altered economic strategy. Fiscal policy became somewhat more accommodating and stimulated a modest expansion of aggregate demand but macroeconomic policy has remained constrained by the all-party commitment to currency stability. While continuing to operate active counter-cyclical policies, the government's medium-term strategy, promulgated in 1993, aims to improve public finances through a reduction in public expenditure relative to GDP. Major continuing reforms of the income tax system have reduced the maximum rate from 73% to 68% and at the same time removed allowances which had enabled a range of interest costs associated with consumer loans to be set against taxable income. In the last two years an active programme of expenditure reduction combined with the beneficial effects of strong GDP growth has led to a fall in government expenditure from 64% of GDP in 1993 to 60% in 1995. In spite of these efforts, government expenditure as a percentage of GDP, and the associated level of public consumption, remain the highest of all the EU countries – 10 points higher than the European average and only exceeded by Sweden (see Table G32). State control of public expenditure is made more difficult because of the high degree of administrative devolution to counties and municipalities. Much of the social expenditure on 'merit goods' such as education, health, social services and public transport is under the control of local authorities, who collectively account for 56% of final government expenditure.

9.4.1 Prices and incomes policies

In the short run, the problem of inflation may be viewed in terms of two interrelated dimensions – the management of aggregate demand and the institutional structures of the labour market which determine the relationship between wages and productivity growth. Danish governments have periodically sought to contain the cost-push pressures by intervening in the centralised wage negotiation process. The 1980s saw a strategic shift in the government approach to the wage bargaining process with the imposition of statutory ceilings, but in recent years this has given way to a more informal system of influence on the key collective agreement, negotiated biannually between the employers' organisation (Dansk Industri) and the industrial union cartel (CO Industri). There is some evidence that this intervention has had an impact in moderating wage increases. The impact of recent wage agreements appears to have halted the compression of skill differentials and thus marginally reduced the structural element in unemployment.

9.4.2 Industrial policy

Danish governments may be regarded as having a 'light touch' in terms of industrial intervention. In manufacturing, the only sector gaining significant financial support has been shipbuilding and even here direct subsidy is being eliminated. Government subsidy to private industry is less than 1% of GDP and is one of the lowest in the EU countries. During the 1980s there had been a shift away from the traditional defensive strategy of supporting vulnerable sectors towards export promotion and technological development. The 1990s have seen the development of a more interventionist industrial strategy, orchestrated by the Ministry for Business Policy Co-ordination (merged with the Ministry of Industry in 1994). The objective has been to identify a series of 'national strongholds' including food processing, transport/telecommunications, tourism/ leisure and environment/energy, and offer government support for these industrial networks. According to an OECD report such support is likely to involve 'an increased emphasis on higher-education and communication facilities, as well as more extensive and direct public involvement in research and product development in the favoured areas' (OECD *Economic Survey*, 1994).

The nature of Danish manufacturing industry is such that success depends on being close to the technological frontier of product and process development; this in turn requires that firms sustain in-house or networked research and development activity. Government encouragement has come in the form a 'technology development programme' which provides consultative support and financial assistance for high-risk capital projects in small firms. The general aim has been to provide incentives for firms to introduce new technology more rapidly and ensure long-term competitiveness in export markets.

Other than the above, the main beneficiaries of government subsidy and support have been the public utilities, especially the social infrastructure activities of housing and public transport. Rent controls and subsidies for housing associations combine with tax relief for owner-occupiers to produce a highly regulated and subsidised housing sector. As in the case of the UK, this, it is argued, results in significant mis-allocation of resources and inhibits geographical mobility.

Direct subsidy for public transport amounts to some 9% of the sector's value-added; additionally, VAT exemption and officially approved competition and price-fixing agreements provide further support for the sector. In the energy sector, natural gas is subsidised by the granting of exemptions from the high-energy taxes imposed on other energy sources. Justification for this sectoral support is that it represents an essential part of the government's comprehensive strategy of environmental protection (see Section 9.7.2).

9.4.3 Regional policy

Changes in the spatial distribution of employment during the 1970s, which involved a relocation of industrial expansion into the Jutland peninsula at the expense of the urban conglomeration on Zealand (Copenhagen), was facilitated by a series of administrative reforms and financial incentives. Local Government reform, together with the *National and Regional Planning Act* (1973), established a framework for the development of regional planning and public service provision based on the 'Counties'. This political and financial devolution facilitated the shift away from the metropolitan 'growth pole' towards a more balanced pattern of industrial development.

Regional balance has not been an important political issue in the 1980s and active regional policies, in the form of soft loans for industrial location, have been gradually phased out. However, there still remain some incentives in the form of capital and training grants for firms locating in areas of high unemployment. The *Small Islands Assistance Act* (1983) addressed the problem of depopulation of the small islands and the government transport subsidy supports ferry communication links which facilitate mainland commuting.

9.5 BANKING AND FINANCIAL STRUCTURES

The post-war years witnessed an extended process of consolidation within the commercial banking system as local banks were increasingly absorbed into nationally and regionally based branch networks. A similar process took place with regard to the savings banks and mortgage credit institutions.

The financial markets remain compartmentalised although there has been some movement towards integration via cooperation and mergers between banks, insurance companies and mortgage institutions. The bond market is extremely large and is a unique feature of the Danish financial system. This market is the primary source of funds for mortgage refinance and public borrowing. Bond issues are the equivalent of 120–130% of GDP, much higher than other EU countries. In contrast, the stock market is small and only limited corporate finance is raised through equity issues.

Nationalbank (the Central Bank) exercises control over the commercial banking system with the traditional instruments of bank rate and open market operations. Historically, these were supplemented by a variety of 'deposit agreements' and credit ceilings. As in other western economies, the inflationary experience of the 1970s led to a review of the relaxed attitude taken to money supply growth. Control of liquidity has not been an easy task in an open economy where there has been a progressive relaxation of controls on capital account transactions. However, a series of changes since 1985 have led to improved mechanisms of credit control through the switch from lending ceilings to formal deposit arrangements. Banks are now required to maintain a credit balance with the Central Bank which in turn issues 'certificates of deposit'. Banks can obtain loans against such certificates up to 90% of their nominal value at an interest rate fixed by the Central Bank. Growth of bank deposits can now be controlled by varying the placement requirements.

The overriding objective of monetary policy has been to keep the exchange rate within its ERM limits and interest rates have been directed towards this end. In essence, current and future monetary policy stance crucially depends on the international environment and the actions of its immediate neighbour, Germany.

9.6 INTERNATIONAL RELATIONS

For Denmark, both history and geography have for long dictated an internationally orientated economic strategy. Since the early 1970s, trade as a share of GDP has grown quite slowly; however, there has been significant expansion in the last six years and merchandise exports and imports currently represent 29% and 25% of GDP respectively (OECD *Country Survey* 1996). Although there has been continued growth in agricultural exports, manufacturing exports have become an increasingly important element of the trade account. In 1991 manufactures represented 67% of merchandise exports compared to 15% for agricultural products.

The other Nordic countries, the United Kingdom and Germany have traditionally been the primary focus for Danish exporters. However, the nature of the evolution of Danish manufacturing has led to an increased dispersal of exports throughout the richer markets of the developed world while agriculture has found expanding markets in the Middle East. In 1958 53% of exports went to three countries, UK, Germany and Sweden, but by 1994 this total had fallen to 40%. The largest decline has been in trade to the UK which fell from 25% to 8% of total exports. Although the German share of exports has increased and now represents by far the largest single market for Danish goods (22%), membership of the EU has not resulted in any trade diversion. In the period 1982–88 Denmark's intra-EU exports grew by 4.2% p.a. while extra-EU trade grew by 5%. Denmark has the distinction of being the only EU country for which intra-community trade has actually decreased as a proportion of total trade – from 59 to 51% between 1958 and 1994 (see Tables G38/9). This picture will be modified by the inclusion of Sweden and Finland within the EU single market.

9.6.1 Balance of payments, external debt and exchange rate policy

A major policy concern of the 1980s has been the intractable problem of Denmark's external debt. It is something of a puzzle that one of the richest countries in the industrialised world should have a debt profile more normally associated with a developing third world country. This situation stems from 26 years of continuous current account deficits, which produced, in 1988, a debt/GDP ratio of 48%. The 1990s have witnessed a significant improvement in the trade position, with a strong growth in exports contributing to a surplus on trade and on the current account. This has been achieved through a modest growth in private saving and the virtual elimination of the government deficit. The current account surpluses produced a decline in foreign debt (27% of GDP in 1994) and a consequent reduction in debt-service costs; however,

domestic growth has resulted in a decline in the current account surplus in 1995, as export growth failed to match the growth in imports. Current government strategy aims at sustaining the strong external position and there is an expectation that the net foreign debt will be eliminated by the end of the decade.

An important dimension of Danish economic policy has been the strict adherence to 'hard currency stance' implied by the government's commitment, effective since 1984, to maintain the krona as a 'core currency' within the narrow band of the EMS/ERM currency grid. This, together with supportive fiscal and monetary policies, contributed to the progressive reduction in inflation illustrated above. However, in spite of strong economic fundamentals (as measured by the Maastricht criteria) the krona was subject to a number of speculative attacks during the period of exchange market instability in 1992–93. The exit of sterling and the lira from the ERM, the subsequent float of the Swedish and Norwegian currencies, together with the devaluation of the Irish punt and Spanish peseta, caused a significant appreciation of the Danish currency against the currencies of some of its major trading partners. In spite of this the Danish authorities have persisted with a policy of maintaining a stable nominal exchange rate with regard to the core European currencies and after some initial depreciation against the deutschmark, the krona moved back to within the old narrow band limits. The success of this policy and the commitment of the government to the maintenance of this policy stance has resulted in a gradual narrowing of the short term interest rate differential between Denmark and Germany (see Table G35).

9.7 SPECIAL ISSUES

9.7.1 The welfare state

Historically, the Nordic countries have developed welfare systems characterised by wide coverage and egalitarian objectives. The political support for these egalitarian aims both derive from, and are reinforced by, the high degree of social solidarity within the national communities. A predictable outcome is a very low degree of wage dispersion compared with other EU countries and a highly redistributive tax and social security system. The system offers generous replacement rates in the event of temporary or permanent loss of income. In addition, considerable stress is placed on the provision of 'services in kind', and, as part of a policy of ensuring that citizens can participate fully in the labour market, subsidised child care and support for the elderly are widely available – provided by municipal authorities.

In a recent OECD study of the Danish welfare system the author summarises the findings as follows:

> ... the Danish welfare model has been very effective in alleviating relative poverty. This is welfare-enhancing and has undoubtedly contributed to the stability of social and industrial relations ... On a more negative side, however, high social insurance replacement rates for certain groups in the labour market seem to have raised reservation wages and thereby discouraged wage flexibility, and raised structural unemployment.
>
> (OECD Survey 1996, p. 78)

In spite of these concerns, Denmark remains committed to a comprehensive and redistributive welfare policy. The associated high levels of personal taxation have been a subject of political concern in recent years and provide the basis for the current measures to shift the burden of the financing of welfare towards labour market taxes based on flat-rate contributions and to a widening of the indirect tax base by the inclusion of environmental taxes (see below).

9.7.2 Environment

Environmental issues have for some time held a high position on the Danish political agenda. In areas such as air pollution, hazardous waste and nature conservancy, Denmark has led the way in setting standards and implementing regulatory controls. Drinking water pollution, in part a consequence of the fertiliser and pesticide use stimulated by CAP incentives, has been tackled by the 1987 Aquatic Environment Plan which set progressive abatement targets on nutrient emissions into water. Energy conservation measures are implemented via a combination of regulation, high energy taxation and financial support for energy-saving investment. There is increasing awareness that environmental quality is simply a matter of domestic policy. International linkages mean that environmental quality is an international public good, and as such, can only be effectively addressed at an international level. Danish initiatives in pollution control have resulted in levels of regulation and taxation which weaken the cost competitiveness of domestic firms. This has led some Danish companies to locate overseas, action which has encouraged the government to advance the case for common environmental policies within the EU. Recent tax reforms have incorporated 'green' taxes, which, in addition to energy taxes, include taxes on waste disposal, water and shopping bags!

9.7.3 Energy

The heavy reliance on oil as a primary energy source has been progressively reduced over the last two decades. However, owing to the Danish rejection of the use of nuclear power, this has involved the substitution of imported coal for oil as a means of electricity generation, with a consequent impact on levels of air pollution. This conflict with environmental objectives produced policy responses which emphasised energy-saving measures and the rapid development of indigenous sources of oil and natural gas. Danish oil and gas extraction from the North Sea expanded rapidly in the 1980s and gas is gradually substituting for coal in electricity generation as well as being used as a direct energy source. As a result of this, Denmark has now become western Europe's third largest producer of gas and oil, and has achieved a net energy surplus. At current production levels oil should last for 20 years and gas reserves for up to 45 years (Barclays Bank, 1995, p. 3).

The success of energy-saving policies combined with the nature of Danish industry has resulted in the country achieving a low level of energy intensity in total output. Between 1972 and 1989 energy use per unit of GDP declined by 30%, giving Denmark one of the lowest energy/GDP ratios of the OECD countries.

9.8 IMPACT OF EUROPEAN INTEGRATION

It is 20 years since Denmark made its somewhat reluctant entry to the EC. The virtual demise of the European Free Trade Area (EFTA) and Denmark's close trading links with the UK left the country with little option. When Norway and Sweden failed to follow the Danish lead, the traditional Nordic political and economic linkages appeared to be under threat. Subsequently the trading pattern, which obliged Denmark to move with Britain, changed radically as Germany became the principal focus for the country's exports. In spite of the EC entry split, the Nordic connection has remained strong, with expanding levels of trade flows, cross-border inter-firm mergers and intergovernmental cooperation.

Danish citizens, like their British counterparts, have always had ambivalent views regarding European integration. Politically, this is reflected in the frequent referendums deemed necessary to provide political legitimacy for any steps toward further integration. While business and agricultural interests remain broadly committed to EU membership, popular suspicion of the EU as an undemocratic decision-making institution, combined with the realisation that Danish political priorities regarding the environment and social welfare are not necessarily shared by other EU countries, produce a pervasive scepticism regarding the benefits of EU membership (see Lyck, 1992).

Following the somewhat unexpected 'No' vote in the Maastricht referendum, the Government worked hard to overturn the decision and, with the help of concessions negotiated at the Edinburgh Summit in December 1992, achieved a reversal of the vote in a subsequent referendum in May 1993. However, the lack of affinity with the south of Europe and an underlying fear of German domination are likely to continue to colour Danish attitudes toward further EU integration. The recent accession of Sweden and Finland to the Union should modify some of the concerns previously expressed. Such a widening of EU membership has shifted the decision-making axis to the north, and is likely to alter the development priorities and political agenda of the Union as it enters the 21st century.

The government faces something of a problem with the rapidly approaching prospect of European Monetary Union. It is one of the few states already qualified to participate in EMU, but the government is tied by its Maastricht opt-out clause and would require a further referendum to reverse this position. At present, government policy envisages a 'very tight exchange arrangement' involving a narrow-band link to the Euro currency; paradoxically, this is likely to require a stricter adherence to the Maastricht rules than for those countries who actually participate in the single currency.

9.9 BIBLIOGRAPHY

Barclays Bank (1995): *Country Report – Denmark*

Christiansen, P.M. (1994): A negotiated economy – public regulation of the manufacturing sector in Denmark, *Scandinavian Political Studies*, **17**(4) 305

Economic Intelligence Unit (1992): 'Denmark' in *European Community: Economic Structure and Analysis* (Regional Reference Series)

Johansen, H.C. (1987): *The Danish Economy in the 20th. Century*, Croom Helm

Lyck, L. (1992): *Denmark and EC Membership Evaluated*, Pinder

Milner, H. (1994): *Social Democracy and Rational Choice: The Scandinavian Experience*, Routledge

OECD (1989–96): *Economic Surveys – Denmark*

Pedersen, O.K *et al*. (1992): 'Private policy and the autonomy of enterprise', *Journal of Economic Issues*, **76**(4)

Pedersen, P.J. (1996): 'Post-war growth in the Danish economy', in Crafts, N., Toniolo, G., *Economic Growth in Europe since 1945*, Cambridge University Press

EU12: Mediterranean enlargement: Greece, Spain and Portugal

PART D EU12 MEDITERRANEAN ENLARGEMENT: GREECE, SPAIN AND PORTUGAL

Greece (Chapter 10), Spain (Chapter 11) and Portugal (Chapter 12) were only accepted as candidates after the removal of the dictatorships in these countries and the restoration of democracy. This took place in the 1970s, paving the way for the entry of Greece in 1981 and Spain and Portugal in 1986.

Greece already concluded an Association Agreement with the EEC as early as 1961 (coming into force in 1962); the Agreement was intended as a first step towards full membership. The army coup in 1967, bringing a group of Colonels into power, prevented further steps towards accession. In 1974, a year after the resignation of the Colonels, the newly elected democratic government applied for membership. The Accession Treaty was concluded in 1979 and came into force in 1981.

In 1975, after a rule of 36 years, the Spanish dictator, General Franco, died. During his reign Spain was totally isolated from the rest of Western Europe. In 1961, a Spanish proposal for an Association Treaty was turned down by the EEC. The economy was highly centralised and protected. After Franco's death a process of political transformation towards democracy began. At the same time Spain made a start with the elimination of state controls and the return to a market economy. A new constitution, based on democratic principles and adopting a market economy model, came into force in 1978. At about the same time Spain applied for full EC membership. After long negotiations about agricultural issues, the free movement of workers and other problems, the Association Treaty was signed in 1985 and came into force on 1 January 1986. At the same time an extensive programme was implemented to prepare Spain for integration in the European economy.

The authoritarian Portuguese regime was removed in 1974 by an army coup. As in Spain, this lead to a restoration of democracy, a strong reduction of state interventionism and a return to a market economy model. About three years later Portugal started negotiations for EC Membership. Together with Spain and under similar conditions it became a member on 1 January 1986.

From the EU point of view political arguments played an important role in accepting the poorer Mediterranean States. It was generally recognised that by accepting Greece, Spain and Portugal, democracy in these countries would be strengthened and stability increased. Though membership of the Southern European states offered new trading opportunities, it also brought with it high costs related to structural aid and increased expenditure within the framework of the Common Agricultural and Fishery Policies. It is not the only case of integration, however, in which political arguments play a major role.

CHAPTER 10

Greece

Ian Stone
Aidan Oswell

10.1 POLITICAL AND HISTORICAL CONTEXT

Once the ancient centre of European civilisation, Greece is now on the economic and political periphery of Europe. It is the only EU country which does not share a frontier with another member state, and in many respects it more closely resembles its Balkan neighbours than its European partners. Psychologically it is part of the west and for decades has looked in that direction for its military and economic support; yet geographically it is in the east and significant elements in the society are ambivalent to the western state and its institutions. Communism's collapse has presented a challenge to the nation's social and political cohesiveness in terms of the fragmentation of neighbouring states and the reassertion of cross-border ethnic divisions, most notably relating to Macedonia. It also, however, deprives Greece of much of its strategic importance for the west, thus undermining its eligibility for special treatment and support enjoyed throughout the post-war era. It is within this context that the present government is attempting to bring the Greek economy – in terms of its structures, management and performance – into line with that of other EU member states.

The USA exerted considerable influence in the quarter century following the Second World War, by virtue of its loans, foreign investment and political support for the only non-communist country in Europe east of Austria. In the period following the 1967–74 dictatorship by 'The Colonels', however, European influence increasingly displaced that of the USA. Democracy was restored in 1974, when the centre-right New Democracy Party was elected to power, and it was out of a concern to nurture the fledgling democracy that Greece (after a period as an associate) was admitted as a full member of the Economic Community in the second enlargement of 1981. The year of entry coincided with the election of the Panhellenic Socialist Movement (PASOK) under Andreas Papandreou.

Having been excluded from power for three decades, the Socialist governments of the 1980s were keen to institute radical change. They adopted an extensive programme of nationalisation, adding the role of entrepreneur to the traditional indirect forms of state influence on the economy based on subsidies, licensing, and price and income controls. The use of increased public spending and an enlarged public sector to redistribute income and employment in favour of PASOK supporters was a marked feature of the early 1980s. At the very point when – learning from experiences in the 1970s – other states in the EC were turning away from such policies as nationalisation, maintaining employment through supporting 'lame duck' industries and by fiscal expansion, Greece embraced them. The inefficiency of state enterprises together with intensified external competition associated with full EC membership combined to produce low real growth and declining investment. The economy ended the 1980s with significant macroeconomic imbalances and widespread structural problems.

The poor economic performance, together with state corruption scandals, precipitated a swing back to the liberal–conservative New Democracy (ND) party in 1990, which formed a government with the barest majority in terms of parliamentary seats. With foreign creditors' increasingly reluctant to finance the ailing consumer-oriented economy, the ND government introduced stabilisation measures, together with a wide-ranging package of liberalising reforms (including deregulation and privatisation) designed to alter expectations and economic behaviour. The Medium Term Adjustment Programme, covering 1991–93 and supported by an EC loan of 2.2 billion ECU, was aimed at reducing the size of the public sector (and the PSBR), bringing down inflation and improving the balance of payments. Short-term deflation was to be combined with medium-term growth through improving the economy's supply-responsiveness.

The ND government collapsed in 1993 and in the subsequent election, the socialists regained power in a landslide victory. Greece also subsequently ratified the Maastricht Treaty with 57% of voters favouring the agreement and only 12% voting against. New Democracy's defeat led to an abandonment of the more radical (in Greek terms) privatisation and public sector contraction initiatives by the incoming PASOK administration. The key elements of continuing fiscal and banking reform were maintained, however, largely due to increasing pressure to squeeze out inefficiencies in an attempt to meet the EMU convergence criteria.

Governments in the 1990s, including the re-elected PASOK administration under Mr Costas Simitis, have been broadly committed to ending the accommodating policies of the 1980s, although PASOK has modified somewhat the approach adopted by its New Democracy predecessor in order to reduce conflict with some of the most influential pressure groups within the economy. The external constraints of attempting to meet the initial EMU convergence criteria mean that businesses now have to rely for their success on efficiency gains (rather than subsidies, low-interest bank loans and devaluations) and that labour has to accept wages in line with its productivity.

10.2 STRUCTURAL CHARACTERISTICS AND TRENDS

10.2.1 Population and labour market

The population of Greece stands at 10.4 million. Whilst population is rising in all of the member states, increases in Greece are more marked than in most. The *rate* of increase has fallen since the 1970s, however, from over 9% in the 1970s as a whole, to only half that rate in the 1980s. The yearly growth rate during 1990–95 was 0.75% compared to an EU average of 0.25%. Projections indicate a rise of over 14% for 1990–2020 compared with a figure of around 4% for the EU as a whole. The Greek labour force growth has fallen slightly over recent years to around 0.8% for the period 1990–95 and forecasts suggest that the work-force will reach five million by 2020.

Currently, the labour force in Greece amounts to 4.1 million with 3.7 million officially employed in 1995. At 41% of total population, Greece's participation rate is well below the EU average of 45%. The country has a history of substantial emigration during the post-war period, particularly during the 1960s. In the 1970s, 9% of the work-force was working abroad (mainly in Germany, but also the UK), providing remittances sufficient to purchase almost a quarter of imports, but depriving the economy of skills. This in turn has hampered recent efforts at restructuring, especially in key sectors such as the financial services and engineering industries. Migration has since fallen away considerably, with the changed labour market conditions in host economies. One estimate for the 1980s put the number of those working abroad at 150 000 (around 3% of the labour force), although there are some four million people living outside the country who are Greek-speaking or think of themselves as Greek.

The previously rapid transformation from a rural to industrial economy slowed dramatically in the 1980s, reflecting attempts to decentralise administration and industry and increased investment and support for the farm sector. Some 21% of jobs were still in agriculture in 1993 which is markedly above the figure of around 5% for the EU as a whole (see Figure G2). At 54% of the employed population, the number of people working in services in Greece in 1993 was significantly less than the proportion across the EU as a whole (62%), further reinforcing the suggestion that the Greek economy is significantly less developed than its European counterparts. Industrial employment, at 24%, is also below the EU average of 31%; reflecting a relatively weak performance by the manufacturing sector, with less than 20% of employment.

The official figure for unemployment in Greece tends to be relatively low by European standards. The unemployment rate for 1986–90, at 6.6%, compares with 9% for EUR15; during 1991–95 the gap was slightly closer, but the pattern is the same – 8.3% compared with 10.2% (Tables G1 and G5). A small rise is detectable during the 1990s, reflecting lay-offs in the state-controlled sector and reduced hoarding of labour among private sector firms. The region of Attiki (Attica) which includes Athens and contains 35% of the national population, recorded a higher than average rate of unemployment in 1995 (11%) whilst the region of Notio Aigaio (which includes many of the main tourist destinations) recorded the lowest level of unemployment for the year at 3.5%. It should be remembered that Greek unemployment figures are comparatively low by EU standards for a combination of reasons, including the method of statistics collection and availability of casual employment in agriculture and the urban informal sector. There is a large difference between these administrative measures and those based on Labour Force Surveys. The latter suggest that the true level of unemployment is double the official figure.

10.2.2 Gross domestic product

In economic terms Greece performed well in the 25 years leading up to 1980, recording a rate of economic growth for the period second only to that of Japan among OECD nations. In the 1960s, real growth in GDP averaged 7.6% per annum; the lower rate of growth of 4.6% between 1971 and 1980 was actually slightly greater than the rate recorded by Japan (and considerably above the average of 3% in the EC). This achievement was based on investment by Greeks and US companies, encouraged by a package of financing arrangements, export incentives and protectionism.

This performance was not maintained, however. In the 1980s the economy suffered from exposure to international competition (as a result of full EC membership), capital flight by Greek nationals (in response to the policies of the Socialist government such as amendments to the taxation of activities like shipping) and a diminished supply of funds from western banks. Real GDP annual growth averaged only 1.6% during 1981–90, a noticeably lower rate than in any other member state (the EC average was around 2.3%). Greece, the high performer of the 1960s and 70s, fell to the bottom of the OECD growth league. Over the period 1991–95, the country's GDP (at 1990 market prices) rose by an average of 1.2% – slightly less than the EU figure of 1.4% for this recession-affected period.

In 1989, when Greece was overtaken by Portugal in terms of GDP per head, it became the poorest EC state. The country's GDP per head is equivalent to only 64% of the EUR15 average for 1995, trailing behind the other low-income countries, Portugal (70%) and Spain (76%) (Table G24). While it has been pointed out that the size of the 'black market' means that the published figures do not fully reflect the level of Greek average income, it is clear that the country's relative position has deteriorated due to its poor recent growth record.

10.2.3 Consumption and investment

Government policy during the 1980s contributed significantly to the situation where an increasing share of output was devoted to consumption (private and collective consumption of general government), partly at the expense of investment. Private consumption rose from 67% of GDP in 1980 to 73% in 1990 and just short of 75% during 1993–95. Given that the current average for the EU is 62% and the next highest total is 64% (in Portugal, Germany and the UK), Greece is well out on its own in terms of the share of output devoted to private consumption (Table G28). Greek governments have also been responsible for consuming large proportions of the nation's output; in 1990 the collective consumption of general government, at 21% of GDP, was the second highest proportion in the EUR12. This level has since moderated somewhat and in 1993 general government expenditure accounted for 15% of GDP – below the EUR15 average of 17% – and putting Greece in the median position among the fifteen member states (Table G26).

This emphasis upon consumption does not appear especially to have restricted investment in the Greek economy. Between 1991 and 1995, gross fixed capital formation at current prices stood at around 21% of GDP, or more than 2% above the EU average for the same period and, among the less developed countries within Europe, lagging behind only Portugal (around 26%). However, the actual level of both consumption and investment has only been sustained by the EU's highest proportional net inflows of goods and services from abroad (equivalent, in 1993, to nearly 13% of GDP) (Table G26).

10.2.4 Wages and prices

The Greek economy's performance in relation to inflation was noticeably poor alongside that of its EC partners in the 1980s. High wage demands following the end of dictatorship forced up real wages at rates twice the improvement in productivity. Inflation indexation of pay, introduced in 1982, subsequently added to the wage–price spiral. During 1981–90, annual inflation averaged over 18% (EUR12=6.5%). The only other EC economy with average 1980s inflation significantly above 10% was Portugal, though it performed markedly better than its Greek counterpart over the second half of the decade. More restrictive fiscal, monetary and exchange-rate policies, plus collective agreements on private sector pay and a pay freeze for public sector workers, has helped to decelerate sharply the rate of increase in compensation per head over the recent period. Although inflation still averaged 14% between 1991 and 1995, policies instituted by the New Democracy administration were instrumental in the fall of inflation to single figures by 1995 – the first time this happened in 22 years (Table G31; see also Section 10.5).

10.2.5 Industry and market structure

Greece remains markedly more dependent on the agricultural sector than any other EU member state. Agriculture, forestry and fishing contributes 17% to output alongside a EUR15 average of just 2.8% (Table G25) and accounts for 34% of Greece's exports. Industry (including construction) accounts for 27% and services 56% of gross value-added respectively. The agricultural sector, with a quarter of the labour force, is characterised by generally low productivity, while the reverse is the case in relation to much of the services sector, a substantial contribution of which is closely associated with the importance of shipping and tourism.

Agriculture's low productivity reflects the fact that some 70% of farms are less than five hectares in size. Some regions, such as Macedonia–Thrace in the north and Thessaly in central Greece, are reasonably well-suited to agricultural development. These zones have higher than average farm sizes, a substantial share of the country's irrigated land and agricultural mechanisation, relatively fertile soil, and access to consumer markets for their tobacco, wheat and cotton crops. The regions have also reaped many benefits from the various EU financial initiatives linked to agriculture, and from the Common Agricultural Policy in particular. Agriculture is much less developed in mountainous and island areas, which make up respectively three quarters and one fifth of the land area. In such areas, farms are generally small and fragmented, soil fertility is poor and transport costs high. Greek meat and dairy producers find it hard to compete at home with northern EU competitors, while 'Mediterranean' crops like olives and vines have been exposed to market competition from Spain and Portugal. Considerable investment was made in the agricultural sector during the 1980s – both by the Greek government and through the EC's Integrated Mediterranean Programmes – including marketing (establishment of cooperatives), storage facilities and irrigation extension.

Mining makes a relatively small contribution to output. Apart from bauxite and magnesite, accessible non-energy natural resources are not especially abundant. Energy resources, however, are hardly more substantial. Production of lignite, which in the 1970s supplied two-thirds of thermal energy, has been in decline, and oil and gas production makes only a meagre contribution, leading to an increasing dependence upon imported oil, coal and direct imports of electricity from Albania (for peak requirements). Imports of crude oil currently account for 5% of all import expenditures. In recent years, schemes such as a gas pipeline from Russia, shipment of liquid petroleum gas from Algeria and natural petroleum gas from Iran have all figured in energy plans. While Greece's overall energy requirement is low by EU standards (12% of household expenditure goes on housing and energy, as opposed to 17% in the UK), it is growing faster than elsewhere in the Union; yet the government has invested very little in projects to develop hydro, thermal, solar or windpower sources. The substantial – and largely unexploited – hydro potential is likely to become more significant in overall energy production. Similarly, there is considerable potential for development of solar power; Greece is the EU's most active market for solar installations, mainly for water heating.

Manufacturing – the output of which has grown only slowly over the past decade or so – accounted for a smaller share of GDP in 1990 than it did in 1960. The sector has never really developed in high technology areas such as electronics and aerospace; its main areas of specialisation have been in labour-intensive and resource-processing activities, including textile, clothing and shoe manufacture; food processing (canned, frozen and dehydrated fruits and vegetables) and drinks (wine and Metaxa brandy); cement production; metal manufacture (nickel, steel and aluminium); chemicals and petrochemicals, including fertilisers; and plastic household articles. Many of these sectors were built up during the period of protection, frequently by foreign companies, though Greek families – particularly those engaged in shipping – have diversified into shipbuilding, oil refining and other industrial activities, just as they have into airlines and tourism.

The 1980s saw many manufacturing plants struggling to survive in a more competitive environment. The nationalisation of a substantial number of large enterprises was not helpful in terms of achieving the efficiency improvements required for international competitiveness. This applies particularly to heavier industries affected by energy supply problems: in spite of plentiful bauxite reserves, production of aluminium continues only because its electricity is subsidised (the same situation applies in relation to nickel production). Cement, which is successfully sold overseas (mainly to the Middle East), is something of an exception to the general pattern, the coastal location of limestone being a major advantage. Some advances might be expected, given the changing political landscape, and Greek industry would certainly benefit from the extra funding the EU will make available through its various funding and development bodies, but much depends on Greece meeting the EMU convergence criteria.

Apart from the state-owned enterprises, larger plants are in the hands of foreign companies and Greek entrepreneurs; the only Greek-based multinational, as such, is Petzetakis, engaged in making plastic tubing products. Beyond this sector of industry, Greek manufacturing is characterised by a multiplicity of small- and medium-sized family-owned companies. This applies particularly in relation to food processing and clothing, and the expanding sub-contract sector, where nationals returning from overseas have established factories making components for larger companies located elsewhere in Europe. Less than 1% of industrial establishments employ more than 50 people and 94% employ fewer than ten. Typically, firms tend to be under-capitalised, over-reliant on bank lending for their financial resources and limited in their adoption of modern business techniques.

Within services, shipping and tourism are of major importance. Shipping has been built up in the post-war period and the fleet largely consists of general cargo and container ships, tankers and cruise ships owned by shipping families such as Onassis, Niarchos, Vardinoyannis and Carras. Government tax policies in the 1980s led some owners to register their ships outside the country; only around half the fleet now fly the Greek flag (although in 1993 this was still equal to around 40% of EU tonnage, and constituted the world's third largest merchant fleet after Liberia and Panama).

Tourism has also grown significantly in recent decades, as modern communications and rising European incomes allowed the country to capitalise on its climate, beaches, islands and archaeological sites. Investment in tourist facilities has more or less kept pace with demand, and a significant increase in the numbers of marinas, golf courses and casinos is in process. Some sections of the industry are however in need of investment, especially the first and second wave of Greek hotels, which are in need of refurbishment. Foreign companies have been active in this sector; they possess considerable advantages in terms of their multinational networks of agencies and airline links. Their chief means of access is through purchasing existing hotels and facilities – a strategy which reflects the extent of the bureaucratic obstacles confronting those wishing to establish greenfield ventures. A host of private family-run hotels cater for the cheaper end of the market and the Greek tourist sector has performed well over recent years. The industry is comparatively efficient, partly due to the lower levels of labour hoarding in the sector (linked to its seasonal nature), and partly due to the absence of patronage appointees and more efficient management techniques.

Elsewhere in the service sector small firms dominate. There are no really large trading companies in Greece; instead, a large number of medium–small firms operate, often on a fairly local scale. This is partly a reflection of the fact that bank credit to commerce has been discouraged for many years by the central bank; credit for wholesalers usually comes from manufacturers, who have better access to bank credit. While some supermarket chains have emerged in recent years, most retailing is in the hands of small independent traders.

10.3 GOVERNMENT INVOLVEMENT IN THE ECONOMY

10.3.1 Government spending

In contrast to the situation in the EU overall, where general government expenditure as a percentage of GDP remained constant at around 48% during the 1980s, a dramatic increase in the size of government spending took place in Greece (from 32% in 1981 to 48% in 1990). Following the changes since the New Democracy government came to power in 1990, spending fell back to 46% of GDP by 1995 (Table G32), which is roughly the same proportion as in Portugal (the nearest comparative economy in terms of stage of development) and below the figure for EUR15 (51%).

These developments have been accompanied by a diminishing government deficit and a stabilisation of the government's debt position. During the 1970s, the general government financial deficit, though increasing, was in line with OECD trends and magnitudes, averaging around 1.7% of the GDP for the decade. Government accounts sharply deteriorated with the oil price shock in 1980, and the situation worsened over the decade. Net borrowing rose to a peak of 16% in 1990 (compared to an EUR12 average of only 4%). This figure had been reduced to 9% of GDP by 1995 (EUR15 = 5%, Table G34). The general government debt stood at 111% of GDP in 1995 (up from 99% in 1992). (On a wider measure of government activity, the public sector's debt has been put at around 130%.) Debt servicing is clearly a problem from a budgetary perspective: while the primary balance of government has recorded surpluses since 1992 (*European Economy*, 1995), large interest payments – amounting in 1995 to over 13% of GDP and 35% of government revenue – have to be made on the public debt.

In an effort to reduce spending the government has in recent years introduced a wage freeze for public sector employees, as well as applying a policy of replacing only one out of every two members of staff leaving public sector jobs and taking steps to reduce spending on pensions (Greece spends relatively 50% more on pensions than the average OECD country, measured against national income). This approach has caused some friction between employers and workers, since it conflicts with the concept of 'jobs for life' which had developed in Greece since the 1950s. The policy is essential in view of the convergence criteria, however. Spending on defence, at over 5.5% of GDP, is also high by EU standards, but it is difficult for government to reduce given the political uncertainty in the region. The Macedonia question continues to be a prominent issue in Greek politics and general Balkan instability requires a continuing, if economically undesirable, investment in defence.

10.3.2 Revenue sources

The growth in the public sector deficit during the 1980s reflected, on the one hand, growth of government subsidies, generous welfare policies and the poor performance of many of the public enterprises, and on the other, the erosion of the tax base. The latter problem is associated with the large size of the unofficial or 'black' economy in Greece, which estimates put at 30–50% of the GDP. Despite the success of recent government initiatives, there remains a culture of tax evasion within Greece and the revenue losses to the state from such activities has been estimated at around 10% of GDP. Although the problem is thought to be worst among the wealthy, professionals, small entrepreneurs and farmers, it is in Greek society in general consid-

ered almost a matter of *philotimo* (honour) to avoid taxes wherever possible.

This problem prompted the New Democracy government's reform of the tax system, which included penalties for evasion, incentives for inspectors, and computerisation of tax records. The government backed away from introducing a notional income tax based on lifestyle in the face of determined resistance from professional groups; tax inspectors do have the power, however, to inspect financial papers and credit card accounts where they find inconsistencies between declared incomes and lifestyle. The compulsory introduction of cash registers has apparently not prevented the practice among the self-employed and partnerships to offer regular clients two prices, one with and one without a receipt. Lower rates for most taxpayers, introduced in 1992, were balanced to some extent by increases in indirect taxes (e.g. on petrol). These changes are reported to have had a positive effect on the revenue collection gap (*European Economy*, 1995). They have also influenced the supply side of the economy, as the incentive structure becomes more related to productivity than political allegiance.

10.3.3 Industrial policy

Recent policy towards industry has differed sharply from that which applied in the 1980s, when nationalisation was central to the strategy for industrial development. This policy failed for a number of reasons, including a shortage of appropriate managerial personnel, lack of effective and independent supervision, immoderate recruitment on political criteria (i.e. buying support through public sector jobs or 'patronage appointments'), promotions based on political connections rather than ability, and the priority given to pay increases over investment. The nationalised concerns became increasing loss-makers as the 1980s proceeded and, as part of a reorientation of policy in favour of the private sector, privatisation has been a key issue for government in the 1990s (see Section 10.3.4).

As in the past, the government operates low interest loans to small- and medium-sized manufacturers, though the earmarked proportion of bank deposits for this purpose has been reduced. Increased competition in the banking sector has substantially pushed down rates for commercial borrowing (see below) and this has had a positive effect on the capital-raising capabilities of Greek entrepreneurs. The rate of corporation tax was also reduced as part of the 1992 tax reforms to a uniform 35% (from its previous range of 42–50%), with distributed profits not taxed again as personal income. This has acted as a stimulant to the supply side of the economy.

10.3.4 Privatisation

The nationalised sector of the Greek economy grew in phases over the post-war period. Foreign-owned utilities and oil production facilities were taken into public ownership after the withdrawal of the Axis powers in 1944; the right-wing government in the mid-1970s nationalised various enterprises, among them banks, shipyards, chemical fertiliser plants, ammunitions works and Olympic Airways; and there was a further round of state acquisitions of private productive commercial and industrial enterprises in the early 1980s.

A programme of privatisation was launched in 1990, with the aims of both confronting the budgetary problem and dismantling a long-standing system and mentality of statism, which had become even more entrenched in the 1980s. Initially, the list included 27 debt-burdened companies which had come under state control in the 1980s. The programme subsequently grew in size, however, and eventually included government asset holdings in the state-controlled banks, shipyards, mines, hotels and insurance companies; the final list of companies for privatisation extended to over 200. In addition, the New Democracy government stated its intention to sell stakes of up to 49% in state-owned utilities, transport companies (including Olympic airways) and some defence industries, and drew up plans for the disposal of some 300 public entities attached to various ministries ('quangos'), many of which had survived only because (like the utilities) they were a useful outlet for patronage appointments.

Progress in carrying through the programme was slow, however, and by 1991 only 19 companies had been privatised (or liquidated), almost all of these small. Subsequent to this, the sale was finalised of AGET-Heracles (Europe's largest cement exporter). A number of obstacles contributed to delays in achieving privatisation, including legal claims by previous owners, problems in coordinating the different public bodies involved, disagreements over the market value of firms and strong political and labour union opposition based on fears of job loss in subsequent rationalisation. Such resistance subsequently choked the programme, and although some restructuring was achieved when a number of ailing firms were brought under the auspices of the Industrial Reconstruction Organisation, the overall impact of the policy has been limited. In 1993, the proposed privatisation of the state-owned telecommunications monopoly, OTE, led to downfall of the New Democracy administration, when a group of former trade unionists in parliament refused to support the government because of their worries about the implications of the privatisation. The subsequent re-election of PASOK (which has even stronger links with the unions) has shifted the issue of privatisation to a lower priority within the political agenda.

10.3.5 Regional policy

Over 50% of industrial capacity is to be found in the Athens–Port Piraeus conurbation, where 30% of the country's population is located. The noticeable concentration of economic activity in the conurbation relative to the rest of the country has attracted the concern of government, as population movement towards the urban areas drain the regions of skilled workers (Sapelli, 1995). The other significant manufacturing centre is Thessaloniki. Efforts have been made by the authorities to decentralise manufacturing from Athens to the provinces and islands, but success has been limited by high transport costs and the difficulty of creating external economies outside the main centres; manufacturing has tended to develop near to an established market.

Since 1983, the proportion of state grant available for a project has been determined by a combination of factors, including location and type of investment (KPMG, 1995). Crudely, in defined zones around Athens and Thessaloniki, schemes only qualify for aid if they meet environmental, energy saving or technological criteria. A series of four further zones have been defined in which progressively higher grant awards apply. The highest awards – up to 55% of project costs – have been available in the northern frontier areas and the islands on the eastern border. Tourism is a valuable source of employment to islands without significant development alternatives, and development of tourist infrastructure (e.g. marinas, golf courses, conference centres) is, *de facto*, an important element of regional policy.

10.3.6 Markets and competition policy

Greek citizens have long been used to government intervention in markets. The Ministry of Commerce exercised extensive discretionary powers to control prices, grant licences, establish marketing boards and allow monopolies for some products. The historically tight regulation related to financial markets is a good example of the state's role (see Section 10.4). Gradual liberalisation from the late 1960s was reversed in the 1980s, with the re-imposition of price controls; deregulation resumed in the late 1980s and accelerated with the change of government in 1990. By 1992, excluding EU-determined agricultural prices, fixed or controlled prices remained on products and services equivalent to 13% of consumers' expenditure (most notably, rents, electricity and petrol). In general, however, price levels on the controlled items do not deviate significantly from a market level. The general aim of the ND government's competition policy was to free up controls within the economy; this approach was taken on board by the subsequent PASOK administration, although the freeing up of controls has slowed dramatically since 1993.

Apart from state-controlled areas, a large number of organised trades and professions

enjoy privileged status in the sense that regulations on competition allow incomes which are in large part economic rent rather than payment for productive work. Moreover, due to effective lobbying, this power increased in the 1980s, when laws were passed to further increase barriers to entry. Public sector trade unions, as well as professional groups and trades, were notable beneficiaries of such legislation during this period. Thus, for example, there are regulations in force which prevent the establishment of a bakery near to another (and restrictions on the sale of bread from other shops), while competition between petrol station operators is practically non-existent, allowing the operation of a system of restrictive opening hours.

Deregulation has not resulted in significantly greater competition, although in certain key markets – and in particular the financial services sector (considered below) – deregulation has led fairly rapidly to increased competition. In a country where the dominant firms and organised trades exert considerable influence, the authorities responsible for ensuring competition have made few inroads. Procedurally, the Competition Committee makes rulings on cases forwarded to it by the Directorate of Market Research and Competition and advises the Ministry of Commerce on sanctions. For a number of reasons, the system does not function effectively, however. There is a shortage of qualified personnel to analyse firms' accounts, consumer associations are weak, and the Ministry has tended to treat organised interests with great leniency.

10.4 FINANCIAL SYSTEM

The financial system in Greece is poorly developed and inefficient by EU standards, although it is slowly improving. Traditionally, Greek business has been a family activity and securities accounted for barely 1% of finance to private companies in the late 1980s. State-owned institutions accounted for 80% of loans made in 1992: 70% of the total by the National Bank and Commercial Bank; and the rest via the

Agricultural Bank, Mortgage Bank and Industrial Development Bank. The clearing system is so slow, inefficient and costly that individuals often prefer to withdraw sums from one bank and manually redeposit them elsewhere. State banks still operate a pass book system, rather than cheque books; and only a small number offer credit card facilities.

Changes have been occurring, however, as banking regulations have been liberalised and Greek legislation has been harmonised in line with the second EU Banking Council Directive. Within an increasingly deregulated environment, competition has expanded dramatically over recent years, resulting in improved delivery and lower pricing of bank loans. Attracted by the large interest rate spread established by the state banks, new banks have entered the market. These include a number of foreign institutions, bringing the total number of overseas-owned banks operating in Greece to more than 20 (out of a total of just 45). Greater competition has reduced the ability of individual banks to fix loan prices and promoted improvements in operational efficiency (e.g. through discouraging overmanning). Like other public institutions, the banks have long been a target for patronage appointments, and exposure to greater competition should undermine this practice as well as making strictly financial criteria more generally the basis of lending decisions.

With lower operating costs, the new banks have been profitable, while gradually building up their market position *via* new and specialised financial products (shipping, lending, mortgage loans, consumer credit) and the quality of the service they offer. However, the shortage of skilled personnel able to develop new financial products and the time it takes to build up a network of branches – together with the absence of a cheap and efficient clearing system – are for the time being undoubtedly to the competitive advantage of the established major banks relative to private and foreign institutions. Thus, the former have so far been able to survive and lenders and borrowers alike continue to be penalised by the relatively high costs of banking (rates for working capital, including taxes and commissions, reached 33% in 1991, although recent increases in competition have squeezed down this figure by around 7 percentage points). The large spread between interest rates and deposits on loans (11 percentage points in 1991) has fallen rapidly and inefficiency has been reduced.

The Greek financial system as a whole has been affected by changes introduced in recent years. The Bank of Greece has become increasingly independent of the government, reflecting in substantial part Union pressure on national governments to meet 'qualitative' as well as quantitative convergence criteria. The Bank has been active in trying to improve the functioning of the country's financial markets, putting pressure on government to reduce its deficits by paring back its access to privileged sources of funding. This has involved the phasing-out of the system whereby banks were obliged to hold an investment ratio of treasury bills equivalent to 40% of the increment of deposits, while banks have also been allowed to convert their stock of obligatory bill holdings into negotiable bonds of varying maturity. The Banks' obligation to earmark 9% of the increment on deposits to finance public enterprises has also been abolished. Structural weaknesses within the financial sector persist, however: in particular, the capital market (centred upon the *Bourse* or Athens Stock Exchange), which, although expanding in recent years, remains small in scale, forcing industry and commerce to rely primarily upon banks for their finance.

10.4.1 Monetary policy

Although efforts to achieve market determination of lending rates continues to be hampered by the high PSBR, which is the principal influence over the cost of credit and the money supply, the changes outlined above have allowed banks to diversify their portfolios and open up the possibility of using open market operations (previously rendered impossible by the narrowness of the government securities market which forced the Bank to rely on more direct controls such as investment rationing). Increasingly, both banks and non-bank residents are holding a more diversified portfolio of assets, and thus are becoming more receptive to changes in the relative prices of these assets. Monetary policy has also been facilitated by the imposition of greater central bank control over sources of bank liquidity (for example, overdrafts on accounts held with the Bank).

Monetary policy in the recent period has been primarily directed at the reduction of inflation. Interest rates are the mechanism for maintaining a 'hard drachma' exchange rate (described in the following section), which is at the heart of the convergence programme in Greece.

10.5 INTERNATIONAL RELATIONS

The EU provided a market for 54% of total Greek exports in 1994 and over 65% of its imports. Manufactured goods (mainly textiles and clothing and metals) currently account for 53% of all exports, with foodstuffs (34%) and fuels (5%) making up the bulk of the remainder. Germany is the principal market for Greek exports (21% of all exports in 1994), followed by Italy (14%), the UK (6%) and France (5%) (Table G38). Imports are dominated by manufactured goods, including machinery and transport equipment, which comprise 62% of all incoming items, with food, drink and tobacco and edible oils accounting for a further 19%. Germany (16%), Italy (17%), France and the Netherlands (both 8%) are the main sources of imported items (Table G39).

During the 1960s and 1970s the pattern of Greek exports shifted from minerals and agricultural products to finished manufactured products and semi-processed goods. This trend reflected the emphasis then placed upon industrial development and was assisted by a barter trade agreement with Eastern bloc states and by the use of a 1% levy on bank loans to subsidise exports. These trade-assisting devices disappeared when Greece joined the EC, contributing to the sharp decline in manufacturing performance since 1980. At the same time, Greeks showed an increasing appetite for imported consumer and manufactured goods; they now buy three times as many goods from the outside world as they manage to sell to it (exports in 1995 were $6 billion, compared to imports of $20 billion; the trade gap has grown from around $10 billion in the early 1990s to over $14 billion) (Barclays Bank, 1996). While imports as a percentage of GDP are just a couple of percentage points below the EU average of 27%, exports amount to barely 10%, the lowest of all the member states.

It is normal, given this weakness in terms of merchandise exporting, for the balance of payments to show a substantial deficit in its visible trade and a sizeable surplus on invisibles (see below). Even so, the net position is one of substantial and long-running deficit on current account. The average annual deficit was equivalent to around 5% of GDP during the period 1980–91; it is currently running at $3 billion, or over 2% of GDP. The size of the external debt, however, has risen substantially since 1981 (when it stood at 22% of GDP) and in 1995 stood at $53 billion, equivalent to 48% of GDP (Barclays Bank, 1996). Interest payments on the external debt amounted to over 10% of the aggregate earnings from exports of goods and services and remittances from workers abroad.

Invisibles are a particularly important element in Greece's current account, reflecting the significance of migrant remittances, tourism and shipping in the economy. Tourism is a major activity and the main foreign currency earner. The number of visitors has risen steadily from around 5 million in 1983 to 11.3 million in 1994 (contributing over $4.5 billion in overseas earnings). Money remitted home by Greeks living abroad contributed a further $2.5 billion to the invisible account in 1994 and earnings from shipping amounted to over $2 billion. The invisibles trade, at around 11% of the GDP, is proportionately twice as large as the average for the EU states as a whole.

Transfers from the EU are another important means by which the deficit on the trade account is covered. These amounted in 1992 to $6 billion ($4 billion in structural aid, farm support, etc, and a further $2 billion in 'cohesion' money). The scale of such transfers is large and important not only for its balance of payments contribution, but also in terms of infrastructural developments (such as underground railway systems in Athens and Salonika and a tourist oriented park and culture zone in Athens) and the government's budgetary situation, although Greece has not always been able to fully take-up allocated funds due to administrative inefficiency. Around $20 billion of EU cohesion funds have been earmarked for Greece – subject to its meeting of the convergence criteria – and these payments will constitute around 5% of GDP per annum over the next 5 years (Barclays Bank, 1996).

10.5.1 Exchange rate

Greece is not a member of the Exchange Rate Mechanism, although the drachma is included in the currency basket of the ECU. It was thus possible, during the 1980s, for the authorities to allow the exchange rate to depreciate to reflect, among other things, Greece's higher rate of inflation relative to trading partners. The extent of depreciation in the 1980s was consequently very significant, rivalled in extent within the EC only by Portugal (Table G41). The drachma's value (relative to both the dollar and the currencies of 19 industrial countries) has depreciated at a distinctly lower rate in recent years (Table G42), reflecting a shift in government policy towards maintaining a rate of currency depreciation which is less than the adverse inflation differential against trading partners. This policy – the pursuit of a 'hard drachma' – is designed to assist with the central bank's primary objective, the reduction of inflation. The currency is more open to speculative pressure following the removal of the remaining restrictions on capital movements in 1995–96. A major devaluation has so far been avoided, however, although the changes mean that the room for manoeuvre on domestic interest rate policy has been reduced.

10.6 SPECIAL ISSUES

10.6.1 The need for improved economic infrastructure

This need was highlighted when the inadequacy of transport and telecommunications facilities was cited as a factor in the failure of the Greek bid for the 1996 Olympic Games. The country's railway system is badly in need of modernisation; road links, particularly north–south, are inadequate; and the telephone system is lacking in standardisation and there are long waiting times for new connections. A number of key projects have been held up in the past as a result of short-term political horizons, including an extension to the Athens underground system (badly needed given the problems of congestion and pollution in the capital city), the new city airport, and water supply improvements. These investments, and others in a substantial infrastructure modernisation programme, are important in the context of attempts to develop Greece as an up-market tourist destination, particularly given the increasing competitiveness of neighbouring Turkish resorts across the Aegean. They are also important in that they are substantially funded by the EU, helping the balance of payments as well as providing a source of employment.

The European Investment Bank made resources available for 1996 to fund the development of the Athens Metro extension, the extension to the container terminal in the port of Athens–Piraeus and the installation of various mobile phone networks throughout Greece. As well as providing much needed support for the tourist industry, planners have estimated that the Metro extension will reduce the traffic congestion in the capital and thereby improve environmental conditions (EIB, 1996)

10.6.2 Public sector inefficiency

This is another area of concern, not least because of the fiscal pressures facing the government. The sector's inefficiency has given rise to wasteful duplication. The low quality of education and health means that these services are widely supplemented with private provision; defective public transport encourages the use of cars and contributes to widespread external costs in the form of congestion and pollution.

Attempts are being made to change the philosophy and culture of the public sector, towards an emphasis upon efficiency and effectiveness and pursuit of national rather than sectional objectives. Achieving efficiency is hampered by the fact that many branches of the public sector posts are filled by political appointments; a practice which has also contributed to overmanning. (Although a target was set of trimming 50 000 (10%) from the civil service payroll by 1993, an EU report noted that the numbers actually *increased* in the early 1990s.) Recognising that failure to make progress on such structural reforms will make it increasingly difficult for Greece to obtain further instalments of European funding – given the stiff terms attached to loans – the government is monitoring closely public sector recruitment and insisting on one replacement only for every two retirees. It has established an independent body to oversee public sector recruitment; the Higher Recruitment Council will act to recruit civil servants on the basis of competence rather than political affiliation. If successful, some progress should be made with regard to civil service inefficiency, and skilled individuals who currently leave Greece to work overseas might be encouraged to stay (OECD, 1995).

10.6.3 Political uncertainty relating to the developments in surrounding countries

This is also an important issue facing Greece. The break-up of the Soviet bloc has exacerbated Greek fears over the territorial ambitions of its neighbours. In particular, it has been concerned at the recognition of Macedonia, the former Yugoslav republic adjoining northern Greece, which has led to nationalistic tendencies resurfacing inside Greece itself. While developments in neighbouring former communist bloc countries raise the possibility that Greece may in the future be bur-

dened by immigration from strife-torn areas, on a broader scale the forms of economic association between such low labour cost countries and the EU may undermine the attractiveness of Greece as a target for inward investment. Equally, of course, the changes affecting the Balkans potentially give Greece a new political and economic focus, for example trade and investment in neighbouring states, especially Bulgaria and Albania. This may alter the Greek perspective on the EU, since membership of the Community would no longer be the country's sole means of combating isolation. There is now the possibility of Greece finding a distinctive role in the south-east corner of a more homogenous Europe.

10.7 IMPACT OF EUROPEAN INTEGRATION AND FUTURE PROSPECTS

Greece has benefited more than most member states from the European Union, in terms of easy loans and monetary transfers, but future flows may be jeopardised if the country is unable to meet the EMU convergence targets. As has been shown, current Greek economic policy is strongly influenced by these constraints, given the fast-approaching deadline for commitment to the single currency. The country has clearly made substantial progress in relation to the key indicators, which are showing clear trends of convergence towards levels prevailing in other member states.

The inflation target for member countries is a rate which is within 1.5% of the best three performing states. While inflation in the Greek economy has declined steadily since 1993 (see Figure 10.1), the current level of around 9% is well outside the target based on the best three performers (Belgium, France and Finland) with rates of just over 1%. Greece is thus highly unlikely to meet the inflation target by 1997. The requirement that either the government deficit should be no more than 3% of GDP or gross government debt should be less than 60% of GDP is also beyond reach. In 1995, the gross debt to

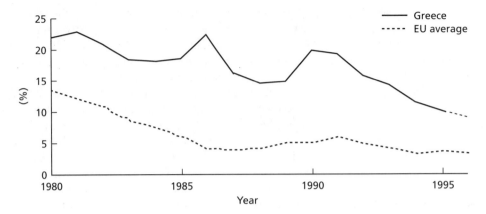

Figure 10.1 Consumer inflation rates 1980–96 (1996 forecast)

Source: Eurostat, private consumption GDP deflator.

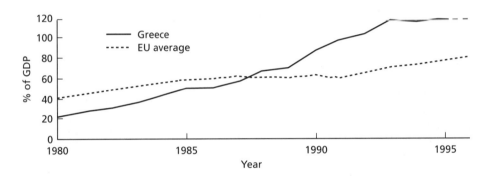

Figure 10.2 Central government gross debt (% of GDP) (1996 forecast)

Source: © OECD 1996 Economic Outlook, based on gross central government financial liabilities. Reproduced with permission of the OECD.

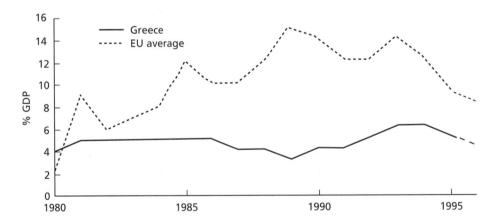

Figure 10.3 Net lending (–) and borrowing (+) (% of GDP) (1996 forecast)

Source: Eurostat, Table G34.

GDP ratio, though it was no longer rising year by year, stood at 111% – nearly double the EU average and the third highest in the EU behind Belgium and Italy (see Figure 10.2). The deficit to GDP ratio has been nearly halved since 1990 (see Figure 10.3), but at 9% is also substantially in excess of the required ceiling.

Governments are also expected to deliver converging nominal long-term interest rates. Accurate long-term nominal rate data is not widely available for Greece after 1988, but we might expect rates to overshoot the targets. Rates in the Netherlands, Austria and Luxembourg are all comparatively low (at around 7–9%), giving a low target rate. Assuming an average of 8% for the best three performers, Greek rates would need to be no higher than 10% to fulfil the criteria. Given that Greek inflation is still comparatively high and thus continuing to exert upward pressure on interest rates, it must be concluded that the target in relation to this indicator is also unrealistic.

The Treaty also incorporates qualitative criteria designed to indicate overall suitability of a given economy for monetary union, including: integration of markets, unit labour cost, various price indices, independence of central bank, the development of the ECU and current account balances. In spite of recent improvements, the Greek economy is, compared with other EU countries, still comparatively poorly developed and inefficient and currently falls well short of the quantitative and qualitative convergence requirements.

Since the country joined the EC, it has been clear that for Greece to properly become a western-style economy, a sustained effort to bring about structural change and performance improvement was needed, involving far-reaching changes in expectations and behaviour in both political and economic spheres. Spurred on by external pressures, governments in the 1990s have undoubtedly been trying to reform the economy in line with the European model. They have faced difficulties in attempting to eliminate outdated regulations and to introduce

free markets into a context which lacks a modern institutional environment and appropriate rules of conduct. However, the policy convergence since the 1980s among the respective political forces within Greece has undoubtedly helped to set the country on the path of convergence with its European partners. EU support should continue to be forthcoming for the reform and restructuring process, although Eastern European application countries may be competing with Greece for financial assistance by the turn of the century. As things stand, however, unless the plans for EMU are rescheduled (or the entry criteria are modified), Greece is unlikely to be in the first group of countries to proceed towards economic and monetary union in 1999.

10.8 BIBLIOGRAPHY

Barclays Bank (1996): 'Greece', in *Periodic Country Reports*, May, Economics Department, London

Central Intelligence Agency (1995): 'Greece', in *CIA World Fact Book*, Washington

EIB, 1996, *European Investment Bank, Annual Report 1995*, Jouve S.A., Paris

Economist (1993): 'Survey of Greece', 22 May

Economist (1995): 'Greece', in *Economist Pocket Guide Book*, Country Profiles, London

European Commission (1995), *European Economy: Annual Economic Report for 1995*, Dir-Gen for Economic and Financial Affairs, Luxembourg

European Commission (1996): 'Annual Economic Report for 1996', *European Economy*, Brussels

Financial Times (1995): 'Survey of Greece', 14 November

Jouganatos, G. (1992): *Development of the Greek Economy, 1950–91*, Greenwood Press, London

KPMG (1995): *Investment in Greece*, London

OECD (1994): *Economic Surveys 1993/94: Greece*, Paris

OECD (1995): *Economic Surveys 1995: Greece*, Paris

Sapelli, G. (1995): *Transition and Modernity in Spain, Portugal, Italy, Greece and Turkey*, Longman, London

Tsaliki, P. (1991): *Greek Economy: Sources of Growth in the Post-war Era*, Praeger

CHAPTER 11

Spain

Milagros García Crespo
Arantza Mendizábal
Marisol Esteban

11.1 INSTITUTIONAL AND HISTORICAL CONTEXT

In analysing the institutional framework and historical context of the Spanish economy there are two years which are of great importance.

- In 1978 the Constitution was approved and the democratic system, suspended since the 1936–9 Civil War, was re-established. Two aspects of the Constitution are specially relevant: first, the adoption of the market economy model in the context of an *état de droit*, and second, the transition from a very centralised economic and political system towards a high degree of decentralisation. The Spanish territory was divided up into 17 autonomous communities responsible for many aspects of local economic activity.
- The year of 1986 is significant since it marks the recognition of Spain as a member of the European Community. This relatively late entry is being compensated for by the determination of Spain to catch up in the European integration process. Nowadays Spain appears to be one of the EU countries most committed to 'Europe'.
- EC integration required the Spanish government to eliminate, over a transitional period of six years, the complicated system of protectionism which historically had influenced and condi-

tioned the evolution of the Spanish industry. Entry into the EC coincided with a period of economic growth which seemed to offer the prospect of reducing the high levels of unemployment which had prevailed in the Spanish economy since mid-1979. Unfortunately, the current recession has increased the unemployment rate, once again, to the dangerous level of 20%.

11.1.1 The Franco period

The new economic model embodied in the Constitution substantially modified the economic management system which prevailed during the 40 years of Franco's dictatorship. The Franco period falls into two main periods, from 1939 to 1959 and from 1959 to 1975.

The 1939–59 period was characterised by (a) the creation of an autarchic economic system, (b) extensive public intervention in the economy, (c) the international black-out, and (d) the relatively minor importance of international trade activities. During this period, basic goods were rationed, productivity levels and per capita income decreased significantly, and there were no institutional channels through which working-class claims could be negotiated. The civil war and its aftermath meant that the production levels of 1936 were not regained until 1951, when US financial assistance flowed in following the installation of US military bases in

Spain. In 1955 Spain was accepted as a member of the United Nations.

The beginning of the second period (1959–75) was marked by the '1959 Stabilisation Plan'. This Plan signalled a new economic approach involving greater use of the market mechanism and thus initiated a slow and somewhat belated process towards liberalisation of both internal activities and external relations. In the event, it proved easier to replace strict state control of the economy with a more liberal approach than to give up the authoritarianism and centralism so entrenched in post-war Spain. The liberalisation process involved the entry of the Spanish economy into the OECD as well as the devaluation of the peseta and the acceptance of foreign investment into the Spanish economic system.

This liberalisation process made limited progress due to entrenched protectionist interests and privileged financial circles for several industrial sectors. Pressure for protectionism was exerted by the main enterprise groups, and as late as 1968 the average customs duty for industrial goods reached 31%. Customs duties were high for an extensive range of imports.

Alongside the rise of protectionism and the preservation of the national market for home production, a period of economic growth commenced in 1960, with sharp increases in real GDP growth rates (averaging 8.6% during 1960–65). Simultaneously, the period saw fixed capital investment increase at a rate of 14% per year. This growth was underpinned by migrant-worker remittances and revenue from tourism which provided the necessary foreign currency to pay for the structural trade deficit and generated surpluses in the balance of payments.

During this period a contradiction manifested itself between the economic evolution, characterised by growth and capitalist concentration, and the politics of the Franco regime. A distinct socio-economic change occurred since the sharp economic growth (in terms of GDP increases) was not followed by the development of a welfare state and a democratic political system.

In 1964, indicative planning was initiated inspired by the French model. The three 'four-year plans' (1964–75) consisted basically of macroeconomic forecasts, which were compulsory for the public sector and indicative for the private sector. These plans introduced a certain rationalisation into public sector activities. However, as the 1960s progressed and the protectionist system was erected and extended, GDP increases weakened, with an average annual growth rate of 5.9% between 1968 and 1973 (see Table G23), and a lower rate of fixed capital investment (7.4%) (see Table G30). At the same time, inflation, which had been under control in the 1960s, was allowed to increase, reaching 11% in 1973 (see Table G31). The period of expansion was artificially prolonged throughout 1974, even though there was an international economic crisis and most industrial countries had already adopted restrictive measures in their economies to counteract the effects of the sharp increases in oil prices.

With the death of Franco in 1975 the period of economic growth came to an end and the process of political transition towards democracy began, even though the country was in the middle of serious economic problems.

11.1.2 The transition towards democracy

The 1973 oil crisis did not modify the economic strategy pursued by the Spanish government. Not only did the government fail to adapt to the recession, but it continued to implement an expansive policy relying on currency reserves and borrowing capacity in anticipation of eventual international recovery. Thus, the Spanish economic cycle ran counter to international trends; GDP increased by 5.6% in 1974 (see Table G23), but there was a pronounced trade deficit and the rate of inflation rose to 16% (see Table G31). Neither output (by using restrictive policies) nor the level of prices (by modifying the exchange rate) were adjusted. On the contrary, an excess of production capacity was generated leading to reductions in productivity levels and an associated increase in average costs and prices. As a consequence, external debt rose and foreign reserves were significantly reduced.

These trends in the major economic indicators continued and even worsened through the following years, so that by the end of 1977 the inflation rate had risen to 35%. The government was eventually forced to undertake a set of corrective short-run economic measures, together with others of a structural and institutional nature.

Inflation was brought under control by the management of public sector expenditure, liquid assets in the hands of the private sector and controls over wage increases. Simultaneously, unemployment levels began to rise (see Table G20). In 1978, GDP increased by 1.5% (see Table G23) while unemployment rose by a further 300 000.

The adoption of the market economy model in the context of an *état de droit* in 1978 meant at last the recognition of political parties as the expression of political pluralism together with the acceptance that both trade unions and employers' associations had a legitimate contribution to make to the defence and promotion of their economic and social interests. This late development explains the limited role of trade unions in economic life and the difficulties encountered when negotiating with the employers' associations who lost the privileges enjoyed in Franco's dictatorship. This is an expression of the fact that Spain is a country only recently introduced into democratic practice.

In addition, the 1978 Constitution led to a new territorial organisation of the state, since it recognised the right of historical nations and regions to autonomy. This has resulted in a high degree of political decentralisation.

The public sector has a significant presence in the economy, accounting for 49.5% of GDP by 1993, a level from which it has been decreasing over the last 3 years (the expected level for 1996 is 45.2%) (see Table G32). Not all the activities generated by public expenditure are carried out by central administration, however. In this context, it is necessary to differentiate at least two levels of administration: 'central administration', i.e. the administration of the central state, other autonomous public organisations and the social security system (whose budgets are approved and operations controlled by the central Parliament) and the 'territorial administrations', which are made up of 17 autonomous communities and the

local administrations (local and provincial authorities). The autonomous parliaments of the autonomous communities and governing bodies of local administrations are responsible for establishing their own budgets and activities.

The decentralisation of public expenditure, measured in terms of the amount administered by the autonomous communities, has significantly increased in the last decade, as a consequence of the transfer of responsibilities from central administrations and the increasing role of local authorities in the Spanish political system.

The responsibilities transferred to the autonomous communities range from health, culture and education to housing, urban planning, roads and other infrastructures, several elements of industrial policy and training programmes, and even tax control in some communities (e.g. Navarre and the Basque Country). In this context, a reform is under discussion to modify the financial system of the autonomous communities by widening their control over personal taxation.

11.1.3 Spain's entry into the EC

Although Spain had been trying over a long period of time to integrate itself into the EC, it was not until 1978, with the transition towards democracy, that its candidacy was taken seriously into consideration by Brussels. The first and very important consequence of entry into the EC was the need to dismantle the protectionist system behind which Spanish industry had traditionally sheltered. From that moment onwards, the need to improve the competitiveness of Spanish production and the urgent need to carry out the restructuring of many industrial sectors became a priority for economic leaders.

This need to undertake a restructuring of the production system came at a time of recession lasting from 1979 to 1985. During this period GDP grew at an average annual rate of only 1.5%, with a positive contribution from the foreign sector, a stable level of internal consumption and a negative rate of investment (see Tables G23 and G30). This demand and production crisis led to the loss of over 1 million jobs –

over 3 million people unemployed, equal to an unemployment rate of more than 20%, by 1985 (see Table G20). Furthermore, the inflation rate remained close to 10% (see Table G31). The weak economic activity together with an increased demand for social services affected both the income and the expenditure of the public sector, public deficit thus reaching 6% of GDP by the mid-1980s.

While experiencing these severe economic difficulties Spain became a member of the EC in 1986. Right from the start, the Spanish economy embarked on a period of expansion that gradually seemed to overcome the most important economic problems. Yet, the economic cycle turned again by 1990, along with international economic activity, and all major economic indicators showed a negative trend between 1991 and 1994 (see Table G6). Unemployment was maintained at 24.1% in 1994. Similarly, attempts to control the public deficit (7.5% of GDP in 1993) and the deficit of the balance of trade (3.6% of GDP in 1992) failed dramatically. Finally, inflation showed no sign of falling and remained over 6% in mid-1993, even though reducing inflation had become the major objective of economic policy. During the last two years a slow recovery has taken place and major economic indicators are coming under control, especially inflation and the public deficit (forecast values for 1996 are 3.6% and 4.4% respectively; see Table G6).

11.2 MAIN ECONOMIC CHARACTERISTICS

11.2.1 Human resources

Population

The Spanish population in 1995 amounted to 39 million (see Table G17). The country experienced the process of *demographic transition* (the shift from high death and high fertility rates to low death and high fertility rates) later than northern European countries. This has pro-

duced a radical change in the age pyramid which has gradually become narrower at the base and wider at the peak.

While birth rates in the 1960s and early 1970s were relatively high in the context of a process of intense economic growth, they dropped drastically over the late 1970s and 1980s. Nowadays, Spanish demographic trends mirror general trends in northern and central Europe. The reasons for this change are not clear; while the economic crisis and the subsequent insecurity have had an impact, other changes in society and attitudes are also considered important. Nevertheless, the major economic consequences of this change will only be noticeable in 15 years' time.

Although low in numbers, a steady flow of immigration was observed during the 1980s, mainly from South American and North African countries. This development is in contrast with the traditional emigration trends.

Previous trends towards concentration of the population in the large metropolitan areas (Madrid, Barcelona, Valencia) have continued at the expense of central rural areas. At the same time, traditional areas of population growth, such as Bilbao, in the Basque Country, have lost population due to the crisis in their industrial base. The regions where population has grown at the fastest rate are located in the triangle between Madrid and the Mediterranean coast.

Active population

During the 1960s there was a significant increase in the active population, approximately one million people over the decade, representing 38% of the total population by the end of the period. This increase in the active population, however, was not accompanied by the generation of a sufficient number of jobs, which in turn provoked a slight increase in unemployment.

The industrialisation process of the 1960s caused a shift of the labour force from the agricultural sector towards industry and service activities. However, these sectors were unable to absorb the workers flowing from agriculture. The alternative and effective safety valve for the

Spanish economy was the constant emigration to northern and central European countries. This process continued until 1974 when the international economic crisis brought this process to an end (see Table 11.1).

Table 11.1 Spanish migration to Europe (1959–74) (number of migrants)

Year	Emigration	Immigration	Balance
1960–64	658 848	254 068	+404 780
1965–69	324 784	216 584	+108 200
1970–74	462 276	396 400	+65 876
1975–79	69 089	336 500	–267 411
1980–85	99 246	91 006	+8 240

Source: Instituto Español de Emigración, 1987.

Throughout the recession, the entire industrial sector was seriously affected. This was exacerbated by the closure of foreign labour markets to Spanish workers, leading to a severe increase of unemployment levels and a stabilisation in labour-market participation rates. Although the economic recovery of 1985 together with demographic factors (the baby-boom of the 1960s) have resulted in a steady increase in the numbers of the active population, Spanish levels remain lower than the EU average, especially for women (below 30%). Recently, major institutional changes have been introduced to facilitate the integration of women into the labour market.

Employment

Throughout the 1975–85 crisis period, employment decreased by more than 2 million jobs, falling to 10.5 million jobs in 1985. Between 1985 and 1991, alongside economic recovery, 1.8 million net jobs were generated, even though with the return of the recession jobs disappeared again, with a slight recovery in 1995 and, probably, in 1996 (see the annual percentage change in Table G6).

Ongoing structural change means that employment in agriculture continues to fall (10.2% of total employment in 1993; see Table G19), even though the contribution of agriculture is still significant compared to EU average levels.

Industrial employment (30.8% of total employment in 1993), on the other hand, dropped drastically during the late 1970s and early 1980s, but during the period 1987–90 experienced a relative recovery. Between 1991 and 1993, however, all industrial sectors lost employment in varying degrees.

The service sector has made the greatest contribution to employment generation in the economy and, in 1993, accounted for 58.9% of total employment. Throughout the 1980s and early 1990s service employment, both in market and non-market sectors, steadily increased, though at a slower pace than in the recent past.

Unemployment

The fact that the post-war demographic explosion took place in Spain in the 1955–65 period (ten years later than in the rest of Europe) has meant that the entry of a large number of young people into the labour market together with the late integration of women into the labour market intensified the effects of employment loss during the decade from 1975 to 1985. Unemployment levels reached a peak of 3 million people (21.6%) in 1985 (see Table G20). With the economic recovery of the late 1980s, unemployment levels steadily fell but by the early 1990s the unemployment rate surpassed again the psychological barrier of 20% (24.1% in 1994 to decrease slowly in 1995 and 1996), bringing the issue of unemployment to the centre of the political debate.

Unemployment figures show an irregular distribution by age and sex. The rate for women (30.2% in 1995) is significantly higher than that for men (18.1% in 1995). There is discrimination in the labour market against women, not only in terms of the number of jobs available but also in terms of salary levels and working conditions. By age group, youth unemployment is by far the most acute, even though in relative terms it is the group which showed the fastest recovery. Better employment opportunities offered by the labour market as well as the trend to remain longer in the educational system are responsible for this development. This high unemployment rate for young people may be due to both the fact that, in periods of crisis, starters are in a very unfavorable position and the fact that, due to neglect in the public sector, employment programmes specially oriented to the young are not very developed in Spain. The relatively lower rate of unemployment among the older age groups is due to an extensive use of early retirement practices.

11.2.2 Major production indicators

Gross domestic product (GDP)

The economic crisis beginning in the mid-1970s seriously affected the entire economic system as can be seen from GDP performance (see Table G23). Between 1975 and 1980, Spanish GDP grew at rates significantly lower than other developed countries. However, in the 1981–84 period, a time of general recession, GDP increased at comparable rates. From 1986 to 1990, the Spanish economy grew again at the

highest rates among the EU countries. There was intense growth in terms of per capita GDP, not seen since the Spanish economic boom of the 1960s. In recent years, low rates of GDP growth have been dominant, even negative for some years (–1.2% in 1993).

During the 1955–74 period, when the Spanish economy underwent the fastest economic growth of its history, employment and production structure changed drastically. The importance of the primary sector diminished in favour of industry, and more especially in favour of construction and service activities.

Later on, the proportionate loss of agriculture and industry was significant, as the service sector expanded to account, by 1985, for over 50% of total employment and more than 55% of GDP. While the reduction of the primary sector in relative terms may be seen as part of the process of modernisation of the economy, the fall in industrial activity can be explained both by the crisis in the sector and a restructuring of production. The contribution to GDP of the secondary sector fell by more than five percentage points.

Table 11.2 Structure of industrial value added by sector (1975–94) (%)

Sector	1975	1985	1994
Strong demand sector	5.3	8.5	9.8
1 Office equipment, computer and precision instruments	0.8	1.8	1.4
2 Electrical equipment and electronic material	4.5	6.7	8.4
Medium demand sectors	25.4	27.3	27.5
3 Chemistry	7.3	9.2	9.9
4 Rubber and plastics	4.6	4.1	4.8
5 Machinery and mechanical equipment	4.9	4.9	4.0
6 Transport equipment	8.6	9.1	8.8
Weak demand sectors	69.3	64.2	62.7
7 Basic metal products	6.2	6.3	5.1
8 Metallic products	10.5	8.1	7.7
9 Non-metallic mineral products	10.4	8.1	8.7
10 Foodstuffs, drinks and tobacco	11.5	18.8	20.8
11 Paper	7.9	6.0	7.0
12 Textile, leather, clothing and shoes	14.8	11.8	8.5
13 Wood, furniture and other	8.0	5.1	4.9
Total industrial sectors	100.0	100.0	100.0

Source: Myro, R., Gandoy, R. (1995): 'Sector industrial', in García Delgado, J.L. (ed.), *Lecciones de Economía Española*, Civitas, Madrid.

There were also important changes in the structure of industrial production. Table 11.2 analyses this transformation, breaking up industrial activities into 13 industrial sectors and classifying them into three main groups: strong, medium and weak demand at the international level. According to this classification, Spanish industrial structure in 1975, and in the most recent past, presents the characteristics of a developed country of intermediate level, with a reduced proportion of strong-demand industries, an important presence of medium-demand activities and still a significant number of weak-demand industries.

However, the evolution of the recent past shows an increase in strong-demand sectors (over 4 percentage points between 1975 and 1994) with the growing presence of new activities – office equipment and computers and electronic material. The group of medium-demand sectors has increased its share in total production by 2.1 percentage points in the same period. This increase is due mainly to the automobile sector and oil refineries. The group of weak-demand sectors has lost its share, falling by 6.6 percentage points since 1975. This fall is general with the exception of steel activities and foodstuffs, and relates especially to shipbuilding, leather, clothing and shoes.

This restructuring of industrial structure mirrors a similar change in internal consumption and demand, even though the concentration of industrial production in traditional activities is not only a consequence of the concentration of demand around them but also the result of a specialisation strategy which does not seem to be the most appropriate from the point of view of industrial competitiveness. Thus, the analysis of the ratio of exports over imports for different industrial sectors (see Table 11.3) shows that for all types of production, imports have traditionally been higher than exports. What needs to be highlighted is not only the low level reached by advanced industrial activities but, more importantly, the difficulties faced by traditional industries to compete in a more open environment since the entry into the EU. The progressive dynamism shown by some of the

Table 11.3 Industrial specialisation and foreign trade (1975–94) (%)

	1975	1985	1994
Production / internal consumption			
Strong-demand sectors	78.2	77.4	67.6
Medium-demand sectors	91.8	103.3	90.5
Weak-demand sectors	99.1	105.6	95.1
Total	95.9	102.5	91.0
Cover rate of foreign trade			
Strong-demand sectors	30.1	43.4	53.3
Medium-demand sectors	56.0	111.7	82.1
Weak-demand sectors	85.2	155.4	77.3
Total	65.1	115.1	75.4

Source: Myro, R., Gandoy, R. (1995): 'Sector industrial', in García Delgado, J.L. (ed.), *Lecciones de Economía Española*, Civitas, Madrid.

advanced sectors is a positive development which has also to be appreciated.

The service sector exhibits three main characteristics in Spain:

- It has been the most dynamic in terms of employment generation and production growth.
- It is the main sector in terms of its share of GDP and total employment.
- Little is known about its main structural characteristics since any study on service activities in Spain encounters countless limits imposed by the available statistics.

A detailed analysis of the contribution of different service activities to the generation of gross value-added can be found in Table 11.4. According to this division, the most important sectors by 1990 were: commerce, maintenance and repairs; credit and insurance; renting of buildings; and restaurants, hotels and bars.

The activity branches with the highest growth rates during the late 1980s and early 1990s were: air transport, communications and public administration services, each increasing by over 4% per annum at constant prices. At the same time, there are some branches which remained fairly stable, such as commerce, maintenance and repairs, railway transport and passenger transport by road. A small number of activities

Table 11.4 Contribution of service activities to the generation of gross value-added (1975–90) (%)

Branches	1975	1985	1990
Commerce, maintenance and repairs	24.22	19.92	19.05
Restaurants, hotels and bars	8.22	8.68	8.53
Road transport	5.56	5.27	4.72
Other transport	5.15	4.00	3.81
Communications	2.23	2.51	2.48
Credit and insurance	8.18	10.10	11.65
Renting of buildings	9.78	9.75	9.31
Market education and health	4.89	3.80	3.27
Other market services	14.37	13.45	14.35
Domestic services	1.60	1.55	1.68
Public services	15.80	20.97	21.15

Source: Martínez Serrano, J.A., Muñoz, C. (1995): 'Sector servicios', in García Delgado, J.L. (ed.), *Lecciones de Economía Española*, Civitas, Madrid.

contracted during the period, such as marine transport, and the private activities of education and health, which contrast with the significant increase in public activities in these areas. In conclusion, it should be noted that the economy's dependence on the service sector is not caused by public services financed through the public budget (the relative weight of which is four percentage points lower in terms of GDP than the EC average), but rather that the importance of the service sector is derived mainly from the key role of tourist activity and the relative weakness of the industrial sector.

Consumption and saving

In the last two decades private consumption has exhibited considerable stability; from initially high levels, it increased its share of GDP by two percentage points during 1981–84. From 1985, however, private consumption has gradually declined as a proportion of GDP towards EU average levels – thus liberating resources for saving. Public consumption has shown a steady upwards trend, and thus has had a moderately counter-cyclical effect, though it has not reached the levels experienced by other European countries.

The level of savings has developed according to consumption requirements. Thus the savings level is depressed during the hardest years of the crisis, since lower levels of production and employment loss made it necessary to dedicate a higher percentage of resources to consumption. Since the economic recovery of the late 1980s economic measures have been taken by the government to encourage internal saving and restrict consumption, both to control inflation and reduce the deficit in the balance of trade.

Gross fixed capital formation

The development of gross fixed capital formation appears to be very different from that of most EU countries. This aggregate, in Spain, fell in the period 1975–84 with a sharp recovery after 1985. Since the mid-1970s public investment has worked in a counter-cyclical way, maintaining its share of the GDP in the critical years. Undoubtedly, private investment has been critically influenced by macroeconomic conditions.

Table G30 shows some interesting results. The average annual increase in gross fixed capital formation during the 1961–70 period reached 11%, almost double the average rate of the EC countries. Subsequently, in the depression of 1975–85, it experienced a sharp decline, rising again to the highest in the EC by 1989 (13.6% against an EC average of 7.2%). The possibility of Spanish economic growth approaching average European levels depends crucially upon this capacity to generate investment. In fact, investment growth after 1985 was linked to a great extent to the expectations generated by the entry into the Community, and was assisted both by fiscal measures and a significant increase in foreign investment.

Nevertheless, as can be seen in Table G30, investment growth rate has been declining since 1990, reaching its lowest level in 1993 (–10.6%). The reasons behind this development have to do with current financial conditions and negative expectations on the part of investors linked to the international economic recession of the 1990s.

In sum, there has been a narrow cause–effect relationship between investment effort and effective growth of the Spanish economy.

Income distribution

The distribution of national income is important because of its effects upon social welfare and also because it affects the dynamics of growth itself. In Spain, the change in income levels and distribution has been rapid and far-reaching.

The per capita income of the Spanish population increased from 337 US dollars in 1960 to 2275 US dollars in 1974. During the recession of the early 1980s, real income grew very slowly at an annual average rate of 1.2%, and real per capita income at 1.16%. This situation has changed markedly since 1985, and in 1995 per capita income in Spain amounted to 76.2% of the EU average. The income expansion and the radical change of the productive structure were accompanied by particular problems. In the first place, economic growth did not generate enough employment, thus resulting in the migration of over two million people in search of work abroad. Another feature was the lack of a modern public sector able to satisfy the collective needs of the country and to correct the uneven distribution of rent and wealth.

While per capita income is important, a key question is how it has been distributed among different social groups. The limited information available in Spain (see Table 11.5), shows that despite a gradual but constant trend towards greater equality between 1980 and 1990, the Spanish income distribution model is still characterised by great income inequalities between social groups. In 1990, the share of the bottom 20% amounted to only 8.2% of the total household income as against 39.7% of the top 20%.

Table 11.5 Cumulative distribution of final household income (1974–87)

	1980	*1990*
Top 20%	41.3	39.7
Top 40%	63.7	62.0
Top 60%	36.1	38.0
Bottom 40%	19.5	21.1
Bottom 20%	7.2	8.2

Source: Ayala, L. *et al.* (1993): 'La distribución de la renta en España, una perspectiva comparada', in *La distribución de la Renta*, vol. II, F. Argentaria, Madrid.

11.2.3 Wages and productivity

Real labour costs rose from 1970, especially from 1974 until 1980. This was primarily the result of the performance of wages and salaries. Net real wages over the 1970s grew constantly because of the strength of trade unions throughout the political transition. During the 1980s, however, the rate of increase was systematically reduced. However, a factor which has prevented labour costs falling further is the growth of social security contributions which have gradually accounted for a bigger share of total labour costs. The further increase in social security contributions at the end of 1992 reinforced this trend even though since 1994 they have once again decreased (see Table G27).

As far as productivity is concerned, during the 1960s, a sharp increase in labour productivity took place, mostly in the industrial sector. Since 1975, the increases in productivity are mainly due to employment reduction, as firms have attempted to offset wage increases.

Until 1973, the performance of labour costs and productivity ran a parallel course while in the 1973–79 period a pronounced gap developed as a consequence of the sharp increases in real labour costs and the stagnation of productivity. Since 1980, the gap between the performance of labour costs and productivity has been reduced enabling the recovery of working profits. On the one hand, labour costs have decreased due to a lower rate of wage increase; on the other, the increases in productivity of industrial activities have also made their contribution. However, productivity increases have not been the result of an increase in production levels, which have remained stagnated, but the outcome of a reduction in industrial employment and the closing down of a large number of unproductive firms. It was only as recently as 1985 that a real economic recovery took place with increases in production without significant reductions in employment levels.

Nevertheless, the competitiveness of the Spanish economy in the European market, in terms of relative unit labour costs, remains problematic if one takes into consideration the range of labour-intensive sectors which are still predominant in the economy.

11.3 GOVERNMENT INVOLVEMENT IN THE ECONOMY

11.3.1 Fiscal policy

The public sector inherited from Franco's dictatorship was small, centralised and extremely interventionist. The welfare state as known in most European countries never existed, and thus health, education, social benefits or the provision of infrastructures were, and still are, undeveloped.

In the first two years of the political transition, until 1977, economic policy in general was not a concern for the political leaders, even less budgetary policy. Between 1977 and 1982 an expansive fiscal policy was carried out, manifested in a sharp increase in public expenditure (see Table G32). It must be remembered that the crisis provoked the adjustment of many private and public firms, with the transfer of costs from the private to the public sector through subsidies and other financial transfers to firms. Simultaneously, there were major increases in taxes and social security charges in order to finance unemployment benefits to an increasing number of unemployed workers. As a result of this passive adaptation to the crisis, the necessary fiscal and financial reform process was postponed, financing public expenditure via increasing deficits, mostly covered directly by the Bank of Spain (see Table G6).

Thus, when the Socialist party came to office in 1982 the budgetary situation was characterised by a large public deficit (5.6% of GDP), caused by the absence of fiscal reform, the demographic and financial crisis of the social security system, the costs of economic restructuring and the outburst of wage and social demands which had been suppressed during the dictatorship's period.

It was necessary to re-establish the basis for future economic growth, the only way to create new employment. In order to attain this, the entire economic system had to be stabilised and modernised. Briefly, the major tasks were: (a) to restructure public firms, (b) to balance the social security budget, and (c) to decentralise public income and public expenditure, as ordered by the 1978 Constitution.

The 1984–87 *Medium-term Economic Programme* put forward a general reduction in real wages, a very restrictive monetary policy, and a budgetary policy designed to reduce public deficit at a time when industrial restructuring was to have important effects on the budget. The income raised through the tax system was to be primarily directed at the objective of deficit reduction. Fiscal policy was to take second place behind wage control policy and the demands of monetary policy.

Throughout the 1977–82 period, public expenditure increased ten percentage points, going from 27% to 37% of GDP (see Table G32). Between 1982 and 1993 public expenditure continued to rise slowly to peak at 49.5% of GDP to decrease thereafter to 46% in 1995.

This contrasts clearly with that of other EU countries. Despite this sharp increase in public expenditure, Spanish levels are still low compared to EU average levels. Moreover, while most of the other countries built up the welfare state during the period of economic expansion after the war, Spain has had to attempt this task in the middle of economic recession.

Public income has experienced a clear boost, going from below 25% of GDP in 1975 to over 40% in the 1990s. The factor which explains this behaviour is the evolution of tax income that went from 25% of GDP in 1982 to over 35% in the 1990s after a much needed tax reform. Yet, it still remains five percentage points below EU average.

The performance of the public deficit (see Table G34), can be divided into four different periods:

1. Between 1977 and 1982, the public deficit went from 0.6% to 5.6% of GDP.
2. Between 1982 and 1985, the efforts to control it were unsuccessful, and it reached a maximum of 6.9% of GDP.
3. Between 1985 and 1989, the public deficit dropped constantly until it was 2.8% in 1989.

4. Since 1989 the public deficit began to increase again to peak at 7.5% in 1993 to diminish slowly thereafter, in line with the EU average.

Analysis of the evolution of the three most important budgetary variables shows that the stabilisation objective has not been attained to a great extent. If integration in the Community requires the coordination and convergence of economic policies, Spanish budgetary policy should be directed at selectively increasing the dimension of the public sector and improving the financial position of the tax system by combating tax evasion in order to reduce the structural deficit.

The deficits registered in the recent past have considerably increased the size of the public debt and interest payments by the government (see Table G6). The level of public debt in Spain (if measured in per capita terms) is not high compared with the rest of EU countries, and only a small part is financed on the international financial markets.

Every international economic organisation evaluated positively the evolution of Spanish public budget in the 1980s. On the income side, fiscal pressure was increased avoiding, however, significant increases of per capita fiscal pressure. In addition, entry into the European Community in 1986 obliged Spain to introduce a VAT system which subsequently entailed a radical reform of the entire indirect tax system. The growth of public expenditure was restrained while the number of people who benefited from social services was augmented by increasing the efficiency of the system. Moreover, this general appraisal appears to be even more favourable if one considers that during the period restructuring and re-industrialisation measures absorbed more than one billion pesetas.

Spanish economic recovery started in 1985 when the public deficit reached 7% of GDP. This level of deficit was justified by the need to finance a public expenditure dominated by transfers to families and firms, with investment just reaching 5% of total expenditure. The key factor that explains the reduction of the deficit to 2.8% of GDP in 1989 was the economic recovery which allowed the expenditure related to the economic restructuring of the 1980s (subsidies and benefits) to diminish and the income via taxes to increase. The recession in the early 1990s brought the opposite effect and control of the public deficit is proving difficult for the government, even though it is one of the main priorities for economic policy.

The above developments partially explain the Spanish gap in terms of public facilities and services, as in Italy, where there is a clear contrast with most European countries. Nevertheless, the increase in public expenditure does not enter the political agenda as reducing public deficit is the priority, even if it may be argued that differences in the level of infrastructures, public facilities and services that exist between Spain and their competitors may hinder Spanish development in the future.

11.3.2 Industrial policy

It is common nowadays to describe the economic crisis experienced by all developed countries after 1974 as a structural crisis, especially affecting industrial systems and strategies. Sectors such as shipbuilding, steel or household equipment, characterised by standardised and unsophisticated technology and a less highly qualified work force and labour intensive processes, faced a substantial excess capacity in all industrialised countries.

The crisis focused, in general terms, on those sectors in which the Spanish economy had specialised during the 1960s and where most of the efforts had been concentrated. As a consequence of increasing costs resulting from oil price increases, among other things, together with the emergence of the so-called 'newly industrialised countries' (NICs) in the international context, Spain lost the relative advantage in those sectors.

In this context, while most of the countries affected by the crisis reacted rapidly adapting their productive structures to new market demands by reducing productive capacity and channelling resources towards new activities, Spain reacted slowly. This contributed to further losses of competitiveness at the international level. This situation notwithstanding, industrial policy, between 1975 and 1982, was aimed at stimulating export activities and supporting foreign investment as a way of combating the excess capacity and the shortage of internal investment, without paying any attention to technological issues. Moreover, the absence of an adequate macroeconomic policy together with the passivity of most of the economic agents – directly affected trade unions and entrepreneurs – made the implementation of a determined strategy of industrial restructuring even more difficult. The measures adopted during this period were merely defensive, in an attempt to adapt to the crisis and, therefore, to freeze the sectors most directly affected. This was based on the belief in the soundness of the industrial structure prior to the crisis as an adequate foundation for the future recovery of the Spanish economy.

Clearly in contrast with the strategy just described (which, nevertheless, comprised some measures to solve the most acute problems of certain big firms), industrial policy from 1982 was primarily aimed at facilitating industrial restructuring. This policy was carried out in the context of the 'Restructuring and Re-industrialisation Law' of July 1984, aimed at the so-called 'mature' or 'traditional' sectors. These sectors were: steel, shipbuilding, textiles, electronic components, shoes, electrical equipment for the automobile sector, fertilisers, iron-alloys, foundry products, cooper products, etc. The main objectives of this law and strategy were:

1. to adapt industrial supply to the new market conditions, with a subsequent reduction in excess capacity in order to secure an adequate level;
2. to rationalise production processes, which implied both technology modernisation and a shift in production specialisation;
3. to correct the financial structure of the different firms affected; and
4. to halt the de-industrialisation process undergone by the Spanish economy since the beginning of the crisis, i.e., to introduce a programme of re-industrialisation.

Behind these objectives lies an attempt to raise the competitive level of these firms to meet European standards and re-establish Spain's position in the new international market that emerges from the crisis.

The most relevant instruments which support this restructuring process are:

1. *labour measures*: mainly early retirement facilities and improved unemployment benefits and conditions for people made redundant by restructuring firms;
2. *financial measures*: grants and subsidised credits to firms, equity participation by the public sector;
3. *regional measures*: appropriate regional incentives to mitigate the geographical impact of the restructuring process since the firms affected presented a high degree of geographical concentration. Thus the 'urgent re-industrialisation areas' were created to enhance the re-employment opportunities of redundant workers;
4. *measures to support technology development*: the provision of finance and other services to generate R&D activities among industrial firms; and
5. *measures to support small- and medium-sized enterprises*: assistance by providing long-term finance and stimulating the emergence of joint strategies (e.g. common marketing or R&D strategies).

By 1989, restructuring plans had almost been completed, with generally satisfactory results. 792 firms had been included within these plans (683 in the textile sector alone, but one must take into consideration the varying sizes of firms in different sectors), with a total investment of 650 billion pesetas and an employment reduction of approximately 84 000 jobs (out of an original work-force of 281 000 workers). Most of the restructured sectors show a clear recovery trend (productivity increases, financial soundness, profits), even if for some sectors, e.g. steel or shipbuilding, the results fall short of the objectives.

Now that the restructuring process of traditional sectors has officially come to an end, the

'White Paper for the Industrial Sector' of 1995 summarises the current industrial policy designed to respond to the challenges faced by the Spanish industry: the integration into the European Union, the new agreements of the GATT signed in Uruguay and competition intensification derived from a global international context. In this context, the policy develops along the following lines of action:

1. the promotion of a more open, self-sustained and competitive industrial model. This implies the concentration of efforts on high value-added sectors and high-range products with a great strategic development potential;
2. an active science and technology policy aimed at increasing the level of human, technical and economic resources assigned to the development and integration of technology within industrial firms with the final objective of upgrading the technological level of the Spanish economy and reducing the differences with major competitors in Europe;
3. development of a specific programme directed at the small- and medium-sized enterprises in order to improve their competitiveness, based on the promotion of joint technology activities, the diffusion of modern management techniques and strategies and the integration into national and international networks;
4. to enhance the efficiency of public firms, adapting them to the on-going process of market liberalisation in order to operate in similar conditions to private firms. At the same time, a reduction in the size of the public industrial sector is sought actively through a determined policy of privatisations.

11.3.3 Social policy

As discussed above, there are close links between fiscal policy and the expansion of social expenditure. The aim of this section is to discuss the structural reform of the social security system in Spain. This process has resulted partially by fiscal difficulties but also by the obvious need to build up a welfare system.

Before covering a survey of the reform process, it seems appropriate to explain briefly the main features of the social security system before the crisis. This analysis will highlight sharp differences between Spain and most countries within Europe, which in turn will allow us to understand the relevance and difficulties of the current reform.

The creation of the social security system

The 1964 Social Security Law and related developments in 1967 marked the beginnings of the social security structure which is now under reform. The aim of this law was to build up a fee-based social security network which would guarantee a package of retirement pensions, health services, unemployment and disablement benefits, following the German model. The beneficiaries, according to the chosen system, were the wage-earning population, and, through special schemes, several other working groups on account of the particular characteristics of the sector or working conditions (e.g., miners).

From the financial viewpoint, the system had to meet its needs through social contributions paid by workers and employers (mainly the first group) and state contributions. Nevertheless, the system was financed up to 95% through social contributions.

Until 1972 when a legal reform took place, the level of protection was fairly weak because the system's financial resources were insufficient. More importantly, and despite this financial shortage, the system was obliged to generate an important volume of savings to finance other activities apart from those to do with social assistance.

The 1972 reform aimed at a radical change. An improvement in the level of protection was to be provided through better management of the available income and an increase in state contributions. This would generate sufficient resources to finance the desired expansion of social expenditure. However, these objectives were not achieved because of the impact of the economic crisis. As early as 1977, the policy response to the crisis imposed serious restrictions on the expansion of social expenditure. The reform of the social security system was to be implemented on the basis of an immature social security structure in which, for example, the guaranteed average retirement pension was below the average official minimum wage.

The 1977–85 transition period

Until the Social Security Reform Law of 1985, governments tried to solve the financial problems of the system by working on three different fronts. On the income side, a general reduction in employers' contributions, consistent with a more general strategy of wage restriction, was undertaken together with an increase of state transfers to sustain the system. On the expenditure side, the strategy focused on two lines of action. On the one hand, attempts were made to improve the management of the system, thus cutting down current expenditure levels. On the other, social expenditure was simply frozen. Between 1977 and 1986, with the exception of the expenditure linked to unemployment, total expenditure of the social security system increased by less than 1% of GDP. In 1976, the social expenditure/GDP ratio was 12.3%, while in 1985 this figure had dropped to 11.8%. This development is especially relevant since it took place at a time when a significant restructuring process was taking place in the economy with the subsequent increase of social needs and demands.

The issue of unemployment benefits deserves special attention because of the sharp increase in unemployment levels as we have already seen. Legal changes to the system sought to diminish the level of expenditure by making it harder to access the unemployment benefits. As a result of these legal changes, it is estimated that since 1985 only 30% of the unemployed have been entitled to get unemployment benefits. This situation can only be understood if one remembers the role played by the family as a protection network in Spanish society.

The current reform

The 1985 Reform Law contemplated a whole range of legal changes with the objective of con-

trolling the expansion of social expenditure on retirement pensions. It was an explicit recognition that the financial crisis of the social security system could not be solved by larger state contributions and was reinforced by general government concern with the size of the public sector deficit.

The next step of the reform came with the 1987 Budget Law. From this moment, state transfers to the social security system were to be used to finance health expenditure. Pensions were to be financed exclusively from social contributions. A complementary step had already been taken in 1985 with the regulation of pension funds, thus allowing the private sector to enter into a sector previously reserved for the state.

A further step came in 1991. It refers to what in Spain are called 'not paid for' pensions or welfare pensions, that is the pensions received by those people who are not entitled, for different reasons, to get a pension from the traditional system.

Despite these reforms, the system came under pressure again in 1992, because of the increase in the level of unemployment, which obliged the government to increase employers' contributions to the social security system and to restrict considerably the access to unemployment benefits. These changes, known in Spain as the *decretazo* met with tough opposition on the part of both trade unions and employers' associations.

The debate over the feasibility of the pension system of Social Security lies at the centre of political and social attention. The general concern over the financial situation of Social Security led the Parliament to set up a Commission to analyse the financing of the system and make recommendations for change. The conclusions, known in 1995 by the name of *Pacto de Toledo* (Toledo Pact) are extremely general and inconcrete and do not shed any light on current and future financial problems. The Commission only suggests not making drastic changes to the system but introducing minor reforms to guarantee the financial balance. In the context of a tough political and social debate, the government signed an agreement, after the summer of 1996, with trade unions which guarantees that pensions will increase in line with the performance of the Consumer price index, which arouse, enormous discontent on the part of employers' representatives.

11.3.4 Labour policy

Developments in the labour market during the 1980s/early 1990s can be split into three clearly defined periods: 1980–85, with a massive reduction of jobs; 1985–91, with a distinct recovery in employment, and the period from mid-1992 in which employment began to fall again, to recover after 1995, as we have already discussed. Thus, employment levels and general economic performance have run parallel to each other over the entire period. Improvement in employment and economic recovery seem to go hand-in-hand, despite the labour policies implemented to improve employment conditions. An analysis of the labour market, however, would be incomplete without mentioning the significant changes in labour force management that have taken place over these years, especially those changes aimed at increasing the flexibility of the labour market. There are also structural changes which bring the Spanish labour market more into line with those of most European countries, even though the common problems appear to be more severe, given the specific features of Spain's economic development model.

The emergence of a democratic system in the late 1970s brought major changes to labour management strategies such as the recognition of the right of trade unions and employers' organisations to sign collective labour agreements within the different sectors of the economy. However, the real basis of labour policy in Spain is defined by the 1980 Employment Law and the 1980 Workers' Statute, which developed the general rights written down in the Constitution. Both laws modified significantly the previous legal network, through the introduction of a considerable degree of flexibility into labour relations management by allowing the option of signing part-time contracts and contracts for a limited time period in all sectors of the economy and for any worker.

The result of these changes has been the design of a whole range of flexible contracts, which have given the Spanish labour market the highest degree of flexibility in the entire Community. The reform helped in the process of employment creation, but by the end of 1989, 26% of all jobs were carried out under a part-time contract and almost all the jobs linked to the recovery were associated with the different forms of temporary contracts. In 1992 only 8% of the new contracts were signed on a permanent basis. An increase of this degree of flexibility is difficult to foresee, due to the serious macroeconomic consequences, in terms of demand, that an economic recession would bring if such an important group of workers were sent to unemployment. In fact, in late 1993/early 1994, with recession at home and the rate of unemployment over 20%, the government modified the legislation, extending the length of the temporary contracts from three to four years, in an attempt to reduce the rate of increase of unemployment, and introduced a new type of contract – a training contract – in an attempt to facilitate the entry into the labour market to young unqualified workers (one of the groups most seriously affected by unemployment). Anyway, the issue of the need to reform labour market legislation to diminish labour costs and promote employment growth is again in the political arena, and both the government and employers' associations seem to share similar views even if no clear proposal has yet been presented. Trade unions, as one might expect, have announced their total opposition to such a strategy.

Finally, it is necessary to mention here those labour policies aimed at adapting labour force qualifications to new job requirements. This strategy has been designed by the 'General Council of Occupational Training' made up of representatives of workers, employers and the administration. It is been carried out through 'national training programmes' financed by the administration and compulsory contributions from employers, and other programmes implemented by the autonomous governments financed through their own budgets. The expansion of occupational training activities after 1986 has been a consequence of both the availability of the financial resources of the European Social Fund and the internal concern over labour qualification levels. The issue of 'training' is becoming a central topic of concern, as it is recognised that the qualification shortage faced by many sectors may hinder future economic growth and employment generation.

11.4 FINANCIAL SYSTEM

11.4.1 Banking system

The Spanish financial market has undergone constant change since 1975. Its major characteristics have become very similar to those of other national markets within the European Union.

In the traditional system, the presence of public institutions in the market was led by the Central Bank, *Banco de España*, and the *Instituto de Crédito Official (ICO)* which oversaw several (state-owned) banking institutions, each one specialising in financial transactions for specific economic activities such as industry, shipbuilding, agriculture, etc. Their importance was due to the fact that they distributed the public resources earmarked for investment.

By the early 1960s, the private banks were legally divided into two groups, commercial and industrial. The purpose of the authorities was then to encourage bank specialisation (industrial or business banks – commercial or deposit banks), which, as a matter of fact, never occurred. In this sense, private bank lending to companies, mainly for investment plans, constitutes an important feature of Spanish economy for it also took place in the form of banks acquiring majority interests in many of those firms. This close involvement in industrial management and financing is not found in the Anglo-Saxon world, unlike Spain or Germany.

Competition was very restricted and it was not until 1978 when foreign banks were allowed to create branches under strongly restrictive regulation. Thereafter, conditions of entrance and restrictions to the activities of foreign banks have been relaxed, preparing the transition to the liberalisation of capital flows at the beginning of 1993.

As the industrial crisis deepened throughout the late 1970s, a bank crisis occurred in Spain. From 1978 to 1985, 58 private banks failed – representing 27% of total bank liabilities. According to experts, the major causes of this crisis have to be found in the real system crisis and in management errors ranging from unorthodox practices to general undervaluation of financial assets due to high inflation rates and failures of enterprises.

Also remarkable was the lack of legal devices to enable the *Banco de España* to supervise banking activities. The very first measures were taken by 1978, when the problem arose. Since then, there have been several initiatives extending Central Bank control and power over dubious institutions. Simultaneously, a number of banking institutions have been created through cooperation of the Central Bank and private banks (*Corporación Bancaria*) to prevent financial crisis and instability.

During the 1980s the Spanish financial institutions underwent several major changes. In the private banking system, as a consequence of the crisis and other inter-bank relations, a process of mergers began with total support from the public authorities in order to increase their size to promote competitiveness in the sector within the context of increased liberalisation of financial activities. The banking crisis, resulting in a higher degree of concentration, has also induced a debate on the effects for the banking system of the traditional relationship with industry. In fact, and despite the positive and negative arguments considered, a trend away from direct industrial involvement can be observed for the major banks. The causes may be found in the industrial and banking crises themselves as well as the so-called European *Second Directive* (Directive 89/646) which imposes limits on these types of banking practices.

The *Cajas de Ahorros*, owned by local authorities, have evolved from their ancient savings-bank financial activity to their present fully banking business; the volume of their deposit liabilities now represents more than 40%

of the entire system. The merger of the two major *Cajas de Ahorros*, the *Caixa de Barcelona* and the *Caixa de Pensiones* has resulted in the first credit institution in Spain in terms of the volume of deposits. The *Cooperativas de Crédito*, operating locally, are private institutions initially created for aiding regional development and presently operating as banks.

Finally, other financial intermediaries have to be considered as well, like insurance, leasing and factoring companies or pension funds, which have grown, in many cases, under the control of private banks. They are playing an increasing role in the Spanish financial market.

Since 1993 especially the competition conditions have been modified to a great extent and many foreign banks and other financial institutions have initiated full operations throughout Spain. In this sense, usual comparisons between domestic and foreign institutions based on absolute figures are not relevant and other references like business profitability or growth ratios per employee tend to reflect a certain superiority of foreign competitors. Moreover, the Cechini Report pointed out that the cost of Spanish financial services ranked first in the European Community, representing 34% more than the average for those four countries which were more efficient.

Nevertheless the increased competition has had so far only a slight effect on the level of profits of Spanish financial institutions and Spanish banks still present the highest profitability levels in the EU, which explains the desire of foreign financial institutions to enter into the Spanish market. The factors which explain this situation are related to lack of real competition in many segments of the market and high differentials between offered and asked rates.

The stock exchange market had been underdeveloped in Spain because of traditional interrelations between financial and industrial capital. Similarly, capital markets were restricted to long-term credit institution loans. The relative low levels of revenues and savings and the role of financial mediation performed by banking institutions were causes of the limited importance of the stock exchange market in the Spanish economy until the 1980s. Since 1985, capital inflows from abroad and the change in Treasury deficit funding have been contributing to the strengthening of the stock exchange market. Nevertheless, this has not been achieved easily because of the problems created by the antiquated market.

Unlike London, with its famed 'Big-Bang' approach to the technological *aggiornamento* of the stock exchange, the Spanish government favoured a gradualist approach to modernise their operations and promote their activities.

The main financial assets traded on the market are short-term treasury bills (*Pagarés* and *Letras del Tesoro*), commercial paper issued by major firms and various bonds and mortgage securities offered by credit institutions. The large inflow of foreign investment since 1985 into the Spanish economy has helped in the consolidation of the stock exchange market.

The reform of the financial system has also affected the public sector. In 1991 the *Corporación Bancaria Argentaria* was created as a publicly owned share company to compete in the market with the rest of the financial institutions. It has integrated the *Banco Exterior de España* and the three traditional public banking institutions (*Banco Hipotecario*, *Banco de Crédito Agrícola*, and *Banco de Crédito Local*) that have belonged to the ICO since 1988. On the other hand, a 'financial agency for development' has been set up within the ICO to carry out government's economic policy.

As a result of the reform, the public sector carries out its activities through *Argentaria*, a financial holding which aims at becoming one of the major financial groups, while the ICO works as the governmental agency. Nevertheless it has to be remembered that the traditional state financial flows to these banks ceased on Spain's entry into the EC. Since 1986, public banks have continued to carry out long-term investments, but have financed them in the market, for state financing is no longer allowed. In order to carry out their activities, public financial institutions need to be able to generate profits. With this in mind *Argentaria* is involved in a process of privatisation.

11.4.2 Monetary policy

In 1992 the Bank of Spain was given full autonomy by the government to draw up and carry out monetary policy, anticipating, thus, the full autonomy of Central Banks agreed by those countries willing to participate in the third stage of the European Monetary Union.

Monetary policy in Spain started in 1973 with the major aim of controlling the pace of money supply growth. Similarly to most industrialised countries, the Spanish government established a two-tier system of control by defining an intermediate objective (in recent years the M4, also called liquid assets in the hands of the private sector, ALP) and the relevant instruments related either to Central Bank activity in the money market (i.e. leading to increases or decreases of reserve balances of credit institutions), or to different legal devices of credit control called *coeficientes*, obligatory rates to be maintained between different parts of their balance sheet by domestic banking institutions. This system has been usually described as a fractional reserves system.

Since the mid-1980s monetary policy faced countless difficulties to control the growth of money supply, due to a number of different factors: interest rate liberalisation, financial innovations which increased the range of financial assets, foreign capital inflows or the high rate of economic growth. Nevertheless, the strength of monetary growth and the relative inefficiency of short-term fiscal policies, given the public sector deficit, induced the authorities to use restrictive monetary policy as the most important anti-inflationary instrument.

A number of subsequent reforms were introduced in the instruments applied by the Bank of Spain in order to make their operations more efficient. This process of reform resulted in a substantial change in the way in which the Bank of Spain operates monetary policy. Intermediate targets (such as the M4 defined above) have been substituted by a final objective – the inflation rate – and the mid-term price stability objective has also been set up – until 1998 the consumer price index should be under 3% per annum. All monetary intervention instruments are applied to attain this overriding objective.

11.5 INTERNATIONAL RELATIONS

11.5.1 Trade policy

Unlike other countries in western Europe, Spain did not undertake a rapid process of liberalisation in foreign trade after the end of the Second World War. It was not until 1959 that the Stabilisation Plan initiated a slow process of foreign liberalisation, after twenty years of 'economic autarchy'. This fact and the absence of political democratic liberties until the end of the 1970s excluded Spain from the process of European integration. Thus, and despite the fact that in 1970 a preferential agreement was signed with the Community, Spain did not become a member until 1986. It is, therefore, necessary to analyse first the main characteristics of Spanish trade policy until the end of the 1970s, and then to discuss the major changes caused by the integration into the EC.

The most important feature of the tariff protection system of the Spanish economy was its complexity, due to continuous modifications of the 1960 tariff system. In spite of this, the liberalisation process resulted in a significant decrease in tariff barriers, which went from an average of 16% in 1960 to 7% in 1974, to increase slightly in the second half of the 1970s, and decrease again during the 1980s to reach 5.5% just before the integration of Spain into the EC.

In addition to the tariff system, several 'trade regimes' co-existed (trade of state, bilateral, global and exempted) which made distinctions between imports depending on the type of goods or their origin, establishing import quotas and restrictions. In 1960, only 40% of total imports came under the category of 'exempted trade', but in 1974 this percentage had increased to 85%, while the 'trade of state' (the most restrictive category) had become marginal by 1965.

This protectionist network was complemented by the '*Impuesto de Compensación de Gravámenes Interiores'* (ICGI) (Tax to Compensate for Internal Taxation), theoretically introduced to tax import products as home products, but which in practice meant a protection level of 2 or 3%.

At the same time, Spanish authorities designed several instruments to support export activities, which in many cases concealed dumping practices. Thus, together with special tariffs for goods in transit, credits to exports, export insurance and other instruments, a very special form of tax reduction for exports was at work. This reduction was an adjustment at the border in line with the ICGI. While this tax overestimated Spanish indirect tax levels, it also overestimated tax reductions. So, in fact, it was a concealed subsidy to exports. Hence, some fiscal adjustment at the border, theoretically neutral, became in practice a very important instrument of Spanish trade policy over the years.

The integration of Spain in the EU has introduced many changes in the regulations of Spanish trade policy. In essence, this has involved the substitution of the general regime in force in the EU for the complex web of fiscal and tariff protection previously in place. This has resulted in a reduction in the level of protection available to much of Spanish production and a significant loss in competitiveness in several industrial sectors such as steel or shipbuilding. The Common Tariff System with countries outside the EU and the progressive elimination of tariff barriers in relation to other Union members represents a most important innovation for the Spanish economy. Thus, at the end of the transitory period, the end of 1992 according to the Accession Treaty, Spain became a full member of the tariff union.

Taking into account the structure of Spanish foreign trade, this means that more than 75% of total imports, which come from Community countries or other countries with which the Community has signed preferential agreements, will enter into Spain exempted from any tariffs or duties. Moreover, tariff barriers have been significantly diminished for the remaining 25% of imports, because Spanish tariffs prior to the integration were three points above Union levels on

average. In sum, the full integration has resulted in a substantial reduction in the level of protection of the Spanish economy. The first effects of this end in tariff barriers are already noticeable, in the form of a significant increase in imports. In the 1986–90 period imports grew at an average annual rate of 17.5% in volume terms. Throughout the 1990s, the growth rates of imports have stabilised at a lower level (6.6% for the period 1990–93) while exports have known a significant increase (10.8% for the same period against an increase rate of 4% between 1986–89). Nevertheless, the positive export performance has lost momentum as the impact of 1992–93 devaluations disappears.

11.5.2 The structure of foreign trade

The territorial structure of foreign trade

Western Europe has always been the most important market for Spanish exports and, in a smaller proportion, it has been the major supplier of the Spanish economy (see Tables G38 and G39). This fact has been reinforced during the 1980s, especially as a consequence of the integration into the EU. Thus, in 1995, 72.4% (52.3% in 1985) of total exports went to other countries within the Union, while a slightly lower percentage of total imports came from them (65.1% in 1995; 36.8% in 1985). The rest of the countries of western Europe account for only 5% of total Spanish exports and 6% of its imports. These percentages are surpassed by the USA which ranks first in both cases among non-European developed countries, despite the fast increase in imports from Japan. Yet, exports to Japan account for only 1.6% of total exports in 1995.

During the 1980s, among developing countries, in terms of both imports and exports, a clear downward tendency can be observed in the participation of OPEC countries, due to the fall in oil prices which has reduced its buying capacity. The loss of importance of the Latin-American countries is also significant. This traditional market fell from accounting for 8% of total exports in 1980 to 3% at the end of the decade. The foreign debt crisis is the origin of this development since it has limited their opportunities to pay in any foreign currency. Nevertheless, in the early 1990s a revival of exports has taken place (trade with Latin-America represented 6% of total foreign trade in 1995) due to favourable economic conditions in several countries of the Latin-American region. Imports arriving from Latin-America have been reduced in percentage terms, mainly because they are energy goods. On the other hand, the newly industrialised countries (NICs) of the Asian Coast still account for a small part of Spanish imports and exports (2% and 1.8% respectively in 1995), even though its growth rate has been very high in recent years.

The volume of trade with Eastern European countries is unimportant in the Spanish economy. In fact, the weight of both imports and exports has decreased in the last decade: exports have gone from 2.9% in 1985 to 1.2% in 1993, while imports have moved from 2.4% to 1.5% for the same period.

The concentration of Spanish foreign trade in the EU market is so pronounced that the largest four countries (France, Germany, Italy and the UK) accounted in 1995 for 52.4% of total Spanish exports and 49.3% of its imports. France ranks first, as far as sales are concerned, while Germany is in first position in relation to purchases. Portugal, Spain's neighbour, deserves special attention since, despite its relatively small economic potential, it receives more than 8.1% of total Spanish exports. Thus, Spain is Portugal's second most important trading partner, just behind the powerful German economy. In fact, Portugal is the only country in the European Community for which imports from Spain become relevant at all.

The sectorial structure of foreign trade

With regard to imports, Spain has always had three major sources of foreign trade dependence: energy products, intermediate products and capital goods. In the first group, the lack of oil resources leaves a clear imprint on Spanish imports. In 1981, energy imports represented 42% of total imports, having risen steadily from 1974 onwards, when they doubled in value compared to the previous year (25% against 13% in 1973). After 1981 a noticeable fall took place, and although in 1985 they still amounted to 36% of the total, in 1995 they were only 9%. Obviously, this evolution has been clearly influenced by oil price levels.

Intermediate products, in contrast to energy products, represented 40% of total Spanish imports in 1981, steadily increasing their share throughout the decade to reach a peak of 47% in 1988 and decrease again to 37.7% in 1990 and 23.6% in 1995. The fact that a sizeable part of imported intermediate products are of an agricultural nature needs to be highlighted. In the industrial sector, almost every sector shows a high level of dependence from foreign intermediate goods.

Capital goods have significantly increased their presence in the structure of Spanish imports in the last years. In 1981, they represented just over 9% of total purchases to foreign markets; in 1985 this became 11%, in 1990 38.1%, decreasing again in 1995 to 22.5%. This is a good indicator of the high level of technological dependence of Spanish industry.

Finally, consumer goods show a very stable behaviour accounting during the period 1990–95 for 12.5% of total imports. It is interesting to highlight the rapid increase in the pace of purchases from abroad for direct consumption since the integration in the European Union, especially in the automobile sector.

On the exports side, intermediate goods, other than energy products, play the major role in the Spanish trade, since they represented in 1981 almost 49% of total exports, and they were still 43% in 1990. The other main export sector until 1988, consumer goods (37% of total exports), account in 1990 for only 12%. Within this group, foods gradually lost their share, while durable consumer goods increased their importance. The automobile sector is responsible for over 75% of durable consumer goods' exports. As far as capital goods are concerned, a change in the trend can be observed from 1988 onwards. They represented just below 12% of total exports during the decade but in the 1990s exports of capital goods amounted to 38% of the total.

The joint analysis of foreign trade by geographic area and type of product shows that the trade pattern with industrialised countries is very different to that with developing countries. Spain exports in relative terms more consumer goods to the OECD countries and capital goods and intermediate products to developing countries. Among exports to the EU countries, durable consumer goods (especially cars) dominate: non-durable consumer goods constitute the most important item of exports to the USA; and food items are the major component of sales to Japan. Among developing countries, the export of capital goods becomes more relevant for the Latin-American countries than other markets.

With regard to imports the Spanish economy gets capital goods from OECD countries, from whom it buys most of the durable consumer goods. From the developing countries, Spain purchases raw materials, especially energy products, with the exception of the NICs from whom durable consumer goods are mostly obtained.

Nevertheless, different studies on the impact of EU integration on Spanish exports show a decrease in the traditional comparative advantage of Spanish industry in natural-resource or labour-intensive products, in favour of products with high economies of scale and to a lesser extent product differentiation or scientific knowledge. This evolution, together with the high concentration of trade in the OECD area, must be taken into account to develop an export policy in the future based not so much on competition via prices, but on aspects such as design, higher quality and better marketing services.

11.5.3 The balance of payments

Despite the fact that the openness of the Spanish economy is still below the European Union average, the growth rate of goods and service exports was surpassed during the 1980s by only two other countries in the EU, Ireland and Portugal. However, Spain endures a lasting trade deficit (see Table G40), that traditionally was covered by surpluses of the balances of services and trans-

fers. During the 1980s this trade deficit reached problematic levels between 1980 and 1983, due to the oil bill, and from 1988 as a consequence of the integration in the EU together with the economic recovery. The recession starting at the end of 1992 has again decreased this deficit in recent years due to a lower level of imports.

The positive results of the balance of services derive mainly from the income from tourist activities, that represents over 60% of total income from services. On the other hand, investment income and technical assistance have always displayed a negative balance, because of the dependence of the industry on foreign technology and investment.

The balance of transfers always shows a positive result, due to emigrants' remittances. The presence of more than a million Spanish people in Europe contributed to compensating the deficit in the balance of trade, even if it was in a smaller proportion to the receipts from services.

Because of this compensatory effect of services and transfers, the current account balance occasionally displays surpluses, and, in any case, significantly smaller deficits than the balance of trade. In fact, once the impact of oil price increases in the early 1980s had been overcome in 1984, 1985 and 1986, Spain showed a surplus in its current account balance. However, in 1988 (see Table G6), the deficit on the current account represented approximately 1% of GDP, rising continuously afterwards to reach a level of 3.6% in 1992. From this year onwards, the economic recession together with speculative attacks against the peseta forced several devaluations (see Table 11.6) which have contributed

Table 11.6 Exchange rate of the peseta (1989–95)

Date	Devaluation %	Exchange rate (pesetas/ECU)
19 June 1989	–	133.8
17 October 1992	5	139.1
21 November 1992	6	143.3
13 May 1993	8	154.2
5 March 1995	5	162.4

Source: Donoso, V. (1995): 'Balanza de Pagos y Equilibrio Exterior', in García Delgado, J.L. (ed.), *Lecciones de Economía Española*, Civitas, Madrid.

again to a reduction in the current account deficit in recent years.

Previous examples of this situation can only be found in the mid-1970s, after the first oil crisis. However, in the last few years, the evolution of the oil market cannot be better. The increasing trade deficit is associated with a declining surplus on services. It is difficult to ascertain the extent to which the worsening situation in the balance of trade was the consequence of the economic recovery in the late 1980s, the integration in the European Union, or other factors. In any case, the last evolutions have proved that it was not possible to continue with this situation in the long term.

A positive assessment of the deficit on the current account suggests that the foreign debt supports the financing of the investment process which in the medium term will improve the production system which, in turn, will enhance the competitive position of Spanish products. A negative view, however, considers that this deficit may generate foreign payment difficulties in the long run, strangling future economic growth.

In any case, the inflow of long-term capital, especially abundant since 1987, is financing the deficit on the current account. Thus, the balance on current account and long-term capital has been positive since 1983.

While direct investment is reasonably stable, portfolio investment is highly volatile. Moreover, it does not seem possible, in the context of the monetary convergence process introduced by the Treaty of Maastricht, that the Spanish economy can maintain for a long period a significant differential of interest rates, with the subsequent loss of attractiveness for long-term capital. Therefore, and without unnecessary alarm, even if the current trade deficit does not cause problems in the short run, it must be considered as one of the major concerns for future economic strategy.

The increase in currency reserves led to the strengthening of the peseta after 1987 even though it is not a hard currency – this did not prove helpful for Spanish exports. This position of the peseta was consolidated by the integration of the Spanish currency into the European Monetary System in mid-1989. Since this coincided with the

large trade deficit, this decision was controversial. On the one hand, it helped to finance the deficit since it guaranteed profitability levels. On the other, it did not support the reduction in the trade deficit, which lies at the root of the deficit on the current account. In addition, the interest rate differential necessary to attract foreign capital and maintain the exchange rate imposed severe deflationary pressure on the domestic economy.

In fact, in the context of the 'crisis in the European Monetary System' starting in 1992/3, and despite serious attempts by the Central Bank to support the peseta by reducing currency reserves significantly, the peseta has been devalued four times by a total of more than 25%. Most analysts argue that the current exchange rate of the peseta corresponds to the relative competitive position of the Spanish economy and welcome a more realistic economic approach.

11.6 IMPACT OF EUROPEAN INTEGRATION

Three elements commit Spain to a future as an integrated member of the European Union: the *Treaty of Accession*, signed in Madrid in June 1985, the *European Single Act*, signed in Luxembourg in February 1986, and the integration of the peseta into the European Monetary System in June 1989.

By signing the Treaty of Accession Spain accepted the European Community's rules and practices. However, this was to be accomplished over a transition period of seven years, so that full integration was achieved at the end of 1992. This process of integration of Spain into the European Community was soon affected by the signing of the European Single Act, and reached its full momentum with the entry of the peseta into the Monetary System in the summer of 1989. An exchange rate of 65 peseta/1 mark was fixed, with a 6% fluctuation band, similar to that of the Italian lira, in recognition of the inflationary pressures within the Spanish economy. The rapid decisions adopted by the Spanish government were undoubtedly eased by the favourable attitude of Spanish society as shown by the polls on European issues.

As already stated, the economic liberalisation of the 1960s made it possible for Spain to enjoy the benefits of economic growth. However, the pace of this liberalisation was constrained by political priorities and was very dependent upon favourable internal conditions. By contrast, economic liberalisation in the 1980s was driven by the requirements of integration into the European single market. This obliged Spain to accept a very precise timetable and to implement it without hesitation or failure. Participation in the construction of the European Union requires Spain to be rigorous both in the process of opening up to external markets and the maintenance of the internal equilibrium, in coordination with the rest of the European economies.

The desire of Spain to become a European country, in the sense of a modern liberal economy, compels the entire society to accept substantial social and economic effort in order to close the development gap between it and the richer members of the EU.

The best indicator of the major changes occurred in the Spanish economy as a consequence of the integration into the EU is undoubtedly the evolution of foreign trade. The first consequence was an increasing trade deficit, which went from 3.6% of GDP before the integration to 6.1% in 1992, just after the end of the transitional period, due mainly to an increase in imports, which have stabilised in later years.

This performance of imports which exerted a contractive effect on the GDP was compensated by the dynamism of internal demand during the late 1980s, which in turn was halted at the early 1990s by a severe fall in investment. This made the trade deficit problem apparent.

In sum, this evolution is the expression of the trade cost that the Spanish economy had to pay as part of the integration process, because after the entry into the EU trade balances deteriorated for all trade items, even for those, such as textiles, for which Spain had traditionally enjoyed a comparative advantage.

Despite the fact that foreign trade is always the major element in an integration process, its effects are better observed by analysing the evo-lution of Spanish per capita income in relation to the EU average during the integration process, as an indicator of real convergence. From this analysis four major points may be concluded:

1. Between 1985 and 1990 average per capita income rose from 70.5% to 75.5% of the European average, due to a sustained expansion of the Spanish economy, with an annual cumulative rate of increase of GDP of 4%.
2. This expansion was interrupted after 1990, with periods of acceleration and decrease in economic activity, which has contributed to the maintenance of the development gap with the richer members of the EU.
3. By 1996 the peak reached in 1975 (77.8%) had not yet been attained.
4. The periods of economic expansion (recession) coincided with those of convergence (divergence) from the EU average.

This 'cyclical determinism' should not be seen as a critique of the integration process since the liberalisation process induced works as an incentive for competitiveness and efficiency and is helping in the overcoming of the 'traditional gap' of the Spanish economy, due to its recent political history.

11.7 SPECIAL ISSUES

11.7.1 The future of agriculture

The future of Spanish agriculture within the EU is still full of uncertainties, despite the apparent popularity of Spanish products among other EU members. Spain has the greatest agricultural potential of the southern European countries, but severe natural deficiencies (climate, altitude) working hand-in-hand with structural problems, related to the distribution and the size of agricultural firms (too small in the north, too large in the south and centre), combine to make the problem of integration a difficult one. These issues may limit future competitiveness of several sectors and regions of Spanish agriculture since other EU countries do not suffer from these problems, as the difficulties faced by many agricultural firms after the full integration in the EU in 1993 seem to demonstrate.

Differences in the main production structures explain the contrast between Spanish areas of specialisation in agriculture and those of other EU countries. EU agriculture is primarily oriented towards cattle raising while vegetable production is dominant in Spanish agriculture. Moreover, Spanish productivity is significantly lower for most products (1.5 times less than EU average and 4 times less than those countries with the highest levels of productivity – Belgium and the Netherlands – in 1992). Nevertheless, it has to be acknowledged that differences in productivity are less significant in agriculture than in other sectors, since products are highly distinctive. Thus, competitiveness depends less on prices than on quality and services offered by products of different origins. In sum, Spanish agriculture appears to be specialised, in the context of the EU, in vegetable and fruit production and sheep, goats and pigs raising, while maintaining a high competitive level against Mediterranean products (olive-oil, fruits and vegetables).

The integration into the EU has accelerated a thorough and yet unfinished restructuring process of modernisation and the merging of small firms in order to enable them to compete with the more powerful European companies. Over the period 1980–95, the sector has gone from operating in a traditional environment to coping with a general liberalisation of frontiers and markets, with a resulting loss of one million jobs. As an outcome of this restructuring process, Spain appears to be the EU country which has undergone the fastest growth in productivity levels, since it has increased by three times over the period. However, the constant increases in production have resulted in short increases in real income per job (even more so if European subsidies and grants are excluded) together with a downward trend in real agricultural income.

The new Common Agricultural Policy (CAP) will have diverse effects upon Spanish agriculture depending on the specialisation and level of development of different regions, but it will generally intensify the need for restructuring to enable Spanish agriculture to reach the necessary size to become competitive and to participate in the production–distribution–industrialisation process at EU level.

The agro-industrial sector in Spain is limited in size, even though a high and increasing percentage of total sales in the sector is concentrated in the hands of a small number of firms. However, the average firm, by volume of sales, differs greatly from the average firm operating in the EU market.

Among big firms, the level of direct foreign investment has increased over the recent past, covering most activities. The employment and productive structure of these Spanish subsidiaries is similar to those of national companies, but their strategies in terms of foreign trade and technological innovation differ greatly. From a geographical perspective, the location of Spanish agro-industry seems to favour demand factors, which works against less developed traditional agricultural regions.

11.7.2 Tourist trade

The tourist trade represents a major source of economic wealth in Spain, resulting both from internal but mainly external demand. By the mid-1980s, foreign visitors to Spain exceeded 40 million per year. Estimates in 1995 show that this sector accounts for over 9.3% of GDP and 10% of total employment. Moreover, since the 1960s, income from tourism has been a crucial feature in the Spanish economy, for it has worked as a counterbalance in the balance of payments, compensating for the traditional deficits in the balance of trade necessary to undertake the process of industrialisation and modernisation of the economy.

Geographically, this sector is highly concentrated in a number of the Spanish regions – the Balearic Isles, the Mediterranean Coast and the Canary Isles – where it has been a driving force of economic development. Spanish tourism originates primarily from the EU, France, Portugal, the United Kingdom and Germany being the most important countries (in the mid-1980s tourists from these four countries accounted for over 70% of total foreign tourists).

The development of the Spanish tourist sector has been highly dependent upon the standards of living of EU citizens. Thus, this sector grew steadily from the 1960s (when the Liberalisation Plan and some political changes made Spain a more attractive country for tourists) until 1973, due to the effects of the international crisis. The economic recovery of the 1980s resulted in a period of strong growth in terms of number of visitors, income, employment, etc. However, by 1989–90 the sector experienced a substantial reduction in its activities linked, it seems, not to an absolute decrease in demand but to a shift of the demand away from Spain and directed to other Mediterranean countries. In this respect, the military and political crisis faced by some traditional competitors in East Europe and North Africa in the recent past have worked in Spain's favour. The tourist industry recovered in 1992 and this expansion continues nowadays.

Despite this development, the tourist trade in Spain is in the midst of a severe crisis and in need of a profound restructuring. This situation is influenced by changes in demand but it is mainly the result of the way in which the sector has been developed since the 1960s.

The sector developed, without any special attention from the public sector, in accordance with the desire of the private sector both to increase supply and to attract demand. This growth focused on short-term benefits without any clear long-term strategy. It was not until 1990 that the government recognised the need to undertake a reform of the sector and initiated the preparation of the 'White Paper of Tourism' which eventually defined the major strategies to be undertaken by both the public and private sector to adapt Spanish tourist industry to the challenges it faces.

The major issues which should be confronted:

- a high concentration of tourist activities in some months of the year, mainly in the summer;
- 'sun and beach' tourism, accounting for over 80% of total demand with a clear underdevelopment of other types of tourism (cultural, professional) despite the existing clear potential;
- the comparative low quality/price relationship of tourist services in Spain (hotels, restaurants, leisure facilities);
- the environmental disasters in many tourist areas and the underdevelopment of public services and facilities;
- the lack of a clear and coordinated policy between central and autonomous governments together with the lack of adequate marketing abroad of Spanish tourist attractions.

Despite these major problems for the trade, the prospects for the sector seem to be positive because of the obvious Spanish potential for tourism and the well-developed structures and tradition of the industry. Following the advice contained in the 'White Paper', there are already indications of a shift towards diversification, entrepreneurial management and co-ordination of public and private strategies to improve the quality of services, with extended training schemes and capital investment.

11.8 CONCLUSION AND FUTURE PROSPECTS

The Spanish economy has followed a similar trend to that of other European economies. The recovery initiated in the second half of 1993 has led to significant economic growth, with an increase rate of GDP of 3% in 1995. Simultaneously, significant progress has been made in the correction of the most important economic disequilibria: with regard to inflation, the gap between Spanish and EU levels has been reduced; public deficit performance appears to be equally satisfactory, but the most relevant feature of Spanish economic development in the recent past has been the improvement of the labour market.

The labour market reform and the control over salary increases have allowed the economic recovery to have an impact, at last, on the labour market. In contrast with 1994 performance, when economic growth did not have a significant effect on employment, during the recent past there has been an important increase in labour supply in relation to production growth rates. Thus, the rate of employment growth in Spain is higher than the EU average.

In this context, the integration process, if it includes a process of convergence towards average EU welfare standards, requires the continuation of the process of economic growth. With this objective in mind, the centre of Spanish economic policy has been the Convergence Programme focused on the reduction of the inflation rate and the correction of public deficit, to enable the Spanish economy to fulfill by the end of 1997 the conditions established by the Treaty on European Union in Maastricht.

Inflation rate by mid-1996 reached 3.8%, just less than a percentage point above the reference level of the Treaty. This is a low level of inflation, if Spanish historic trends are taken into consideration, but constant efforts are still needed if this condition is to be achieved. Some of the new economic developments which make this further decrease in the rate of inflation possible are:

- the emergence of a model of economic growth with consumption growing at a lower rate than production levels;
- the autonomy of the Bank of Spain, which, by making price stability its main objective, contributes to the credibility of the anti-inflationary strategy of monetary policy;
- the liberalisation of a number of markets (labour, finance sector, telecommunications, air transport, private insurance, etc.). These reforms will undoubtedly have an impact on the evolution of prices and will improve the efficiency and growth capacity of the Spanish economy.

The overriding fiscal aim of the Convergence Programme is the control and reduction of the government deficit since it affects inflation rates and interest rates in the long term. The objective is to reduce the public deficit to 4.4% of GDP by 1996, to reach a level of 3% in 1997.

The performance of the public deficit in Spain was particularly marked by developments in 1993, when economic recession increased the deficit level to 7.5% of GDP. Since then, fiscal policy has been oriented primarily by the need to reduce public deficit. This decrease is to be achieved by a reduction in the growth rate of public expenditure, which would increase less than the GDP, since it is believed that any increase in public income has only temporary effects on the deficit as it is easily absorbed by greater expenditure. Besides, it has to be taken into account that even if individual fiscal burdens in Spain remain one of the lowest in the EU, they have increased at a fast rate in the recent past, so that there is a commitment to maintain the 1993 levels, when the reform of direct and indirect taxation became fully operative.

During 1994 and 1995 the public deficit decreased by 1.6% of GDP, mainly through a sharp reduction in expenditure, which decreased from 49.2% of GDP in 1993 to 46.8% in 1995 while public income decreased only from 42.1% to 40.8% for the same years.

The political change brought about by general elections in mid-1996, with the Conservative Party coming to power, has brought a little uncertainty until the public budget for 1997 is known. So far, the economic measures adopted by the incoming government are very heterogeneous and range from liberalisation measures which intensify the strategy followed by the previous government to a number of fiscal measures (changes in personal and capital taxation) which may have a negative impact over public deficit control. They may be counterbalanced, however, by other complementary changes in a number of indirect taxes such as alcohol, tobacco, etc. Moreover, the government has announced a very unpopular measure in an attempt to ensure that the convergence conditions are met: the freeze of the salaries of civil servants at all levels of government, which has aroused strong public discontent.

Nevertheless, there is no doubt that the objective of Spain being in the group of countries that will implement the third stage of European Union remains a major priority for the new government, and its economic strategy will continue that carried out by the Socialist government: a mix of restrictive fiscal policy that allows a more flexible monetary policy, enabling a reduction in interest rates – thus helping in the process of economic recovery.

Are there any alternatives to this policy of convergence? There is no obvious alternative to the structural microeconomic measures directed at improving competition and flexibility levels of labour, capital and technology markets. And this is the most urgent task, since major divergences with European competitors are to be found in these areas, rather than the features of major macroeconomic imbalances. Therefore, the answer has to focus on these last measures.

Supporters of the Convergence Programme, major political and economic forces, highlight the benefits derived from full integration and tend to underestimate its costs. Trade unions do not consider the 'nominal convergence' as a priority but they have not succeeded in generating an effective opposition to the mainstream economic strategy. It has only been recently that some voices have been heard among prestigious economic experts pointing to some major concerns for the Spanish economy incorporated by the future single market. Earlier in this chapter we characterised Spain as an intermediate economy whose competitiveness has been based primarily upon a comparative advantage in terms of labour costs. Thus, and despite the positive prospects, the concerns arise from the lower technological level of many Spanish firms, which may endanger external equilibrium, as well as from the process of fiscal harmonisation and the prospect of higher wage and social demands. This may result in greater fiscal pressure or an increase in public deficit, as a consequence of rising expenditure levels. With full integration and the absence of 'autonomous' fiscal and monetary policy, the Spanish government will lack the means to correct these imbalances, which may have a very negative effect on firms' feasibility and jobs.

Nevertheless past experience suggests that liberalisation has always produced very positive effects on the Spanish economy, and this encourages in most observers an *a priori* optimistic attitude towards the impact of European integration – even if it means an increase in competition for Spanish sectors and firms.

11.9 BIBLIOGRAPHY AND SOURCES OF INFORMATION

Bibliography

The following books provide more information on the issues discussed in this chapter as well as a very complete bibliography on each section.

Alcaide, J. *et al.* (1995): *Problemas Económicos Españoles en la Década de los 90*, Galaxia Gutenberg – Círculo de Lectores, Madrid

García Delgado, J.L. (ed.) (1993): *España. Economía*, Espasa Calpe, Madrid

García Delgado, J.L. (ed.) (1995): *Lecciones de Economía Española*, Editorial Civitas, Madrid

Tamames, R. (1995): *La Economía Española*, Ediciones Temas de Hoy, Madrid

VV.AA. (1995): *La Economía Española en un Escenario Abierto*, Fundación Argentaria – Visor Distribuciones, Madrid

Among the periodicals that provide up-to-date information on Spanish economic issues the following may be recommended:

Economía Industrial, published by the 'Ministerio de Industria y Energía', Castellana, 160, 28046 Madrid, Tl. 34-1-4588010

Información Comercial Española, published by the 'Ministerio de Comercio', Madrid

Papeles de Economía Española, published by the 'Confederación Española de Cajas de Ahorros', Padre Damián, 48, Madrid,Tl. 34-1-4586158

Sources of information

Banco de España, Servicio de Publicaciones, Alcalá 50, Madrid, Tl. 34-1-4469055

Consejo Superior de las Cámaras Oficiales de Comercio, Industria y Navegación de España, Claudio Boello, 19, 28001 Madrid, Tl. 34-1-2752307

Dirección General de Aduanas, Guzmán el Bueno, 137, Madrid, Tl. 34-1-2543200

Instituto Nacional de Estadística (INE), Paseo de la Castellana, 183, 28071 Madrid, Tl. 34-1-2799300

Ministerio de Economía y Hacienda, Paseo de la Castellana, 162, 28046 Madrid, Tl. 34-1-4588664

CHAPTER 12

Portugal

Richard Bailey

12.1 INSTITUTIONAL AND HISTORICAL CONTEXT

A brief history of this small but long-established European state is necessary in order to understand and appreciate its current economic condition and circumstance. For a short period in the late 15th and early 16th centuries Portugal was the centre for the pioneering 'voyages of discovery' which led to the great expansion of European economic power in the centuries which followed. The protracted conflict over the establishment of trading empires, which characterised the 300 years following the discovery of the Americas, crucially influenced Portugal's subsequent development.

The country was established as an independent kingdom in 1140, but Phillip II of Spain reunited the crowns in 1580 with the practical objective of consolidating the vast empires of the two countries. However, the reverses experienced by Spain during the Thirty Years' War created the opportunity for Portugal to re-establish its independence in 1640. There followed a period of pre-industrial capitalist development, under the leadership of the Duke of Erceira, but this was cut short by the Methuen Treaty of 1703. This Anglo-Portuguese treaty, while providing Portugal with valuable political support in struggles with her continental neighbours, had the effect of locking the country into a relationship of political and economic dependence on Britain for the next 200 years.

For much of the 20th century (1928–68) Portuguese development was dominated by the pro-feudalist and anti-liberal vision of one man – Antonio de Olivera Salazar. Salazar's dictatorship was profoundly anti-developmental and ardently nationalistic; consequently, throughout the 'Golden Age' of post-war development Portugal remained in semi-isolation. Although the country was a founder member of NATO and subsequently became a member of EFTA, economic and industrial development was narrowly focused on strengthening and sustaining linkages with her remaining colonies. Until the mid-1970s, industrial development proceeded within the context of a hierarchical, autocratic social structure, and the main focus of economic development was on the traditional sectors of textiles, clothing, ceramics, and agricultural process industry.

The country experienced some modest output growth in the 1960s and 1970s but infrastructure investment and welfare services were largely neglected. There was no convergence with the richer more developed economies of continental Europe and per capita incomes remained at around a quarter of the EC average. This contrasts with Spain, its immediate neighbour, which achieved some significant convergence, with per capita income growing from 33% to 58% of EC average. In summary, during the two decades of the 1960s and 1970s Portugal remained a semi-detached peripheral economy of western Europe.

Following Salazar's withdrawal from public life in 1968 the dictatorship lost much if its direction and, more importantly, the support of the military. An army coup in April 1974, backed by widespread popular support, set Portugal on a path of modernisation. Initially this ushered in a decade of political confusion and radical economic change. The 1970s saw the nationalisation of vast swathes of industry, business and financial services, the collectivisation of significant sections of agriculture, and the granting of independence to all the remaining colonies of the empire. Somewhat surprisingly, this period also saw the enactment of a Parliamentary Constitution and stumbling progress towards a democratic multi-party system.

The inherent difficulties of structural modernisation have, until the last decade, been exacerbated by the political instabilities associated with frequently changing minority governments. The needs of social and political modernisation were given particular urgency by Portugal's application and subsequent entry to the European Community in November 1985. The mid-1980s saw a gradual consolidation of power by the 'centrist' Social Democratic Party (PSD), led by Anibal Cavaco Silva. The PSD finally achieved single party majority rule in 1987, on the basis of a reformist programme with an emphasis on market-oriented policies and extensive privatisation. The political dominance of the PDS ended in October 1995 with the election of the Socialist Party. The position of this minority government was strengthened in January 1996 with the election of a socialist president – Mr Jorge Sampaio. This new left of centre administration has not introduced any major changes in economic policy and, like the previous administration, is strongly committed to implementing policies to achieve the targets of the Maastricht Treaty.

12.2 MAIN ECONOMIC CHARACTERISTICS

12.2.1 Population and labour force

The resident population of Portugal numbers some 10 million persons, approximately half a million of which live on the two off-lying island

groups of Madeira and Azores. The level of urbanisation is low – around 30% – with the main concentrations of urban population in the areas around Lisbon, Sintra, and Setubal in the mid-west of the country, and Oporto in the north. Population statistics are complicated by the fact that about four million nationals are resident outside the country, which gives rise to significant migration flows; historically the country has experienced net emigration, but this was dramatically reversed in the mid-1970s when, as a consequence of colonial independence, the domestic population increased by 8% in two years. Approximately one million Portuguese live and work in other EU countries, France being the principal destination of migrant workers. Income reparations from expatriates amount to some 10% of GDP and contribute significantly to Portugal's balance of payments (equivalent to 20% of current receipts).

12.2.2 Employment and labour market

The sectoral employment pattern diverges quite markedly from the EU norm; however, the last decade has witnessed a rapid decline in agricultural employment and a sustained expansion of the service sector. Currently 12% of the civilian labour force are employed in agriculture, 33% in industry and 55% in services; this contrasts with 1985, where 25% of the workforce were in agriculture and 42%; in service employment (see Table G19 & OECD Survey, 1995).

Current unemployment levels are low in comparison with other EU countries; while unemployment averaged 7–8% in the early to mid-1980s, the level fell to 4–5% in the late 1980s and early 1990s, rising to the 7% level in the recession of the mid 1990s. Because of high levels of underemployment in agriculture and some parts of the public sector, the absolute level of unemployment is not a good indicator of labour market disequilibrium. The unemployment figures do not take account of those on temporary contracts or short-time working, if these figures were to be included Portugal's unemployment would be closer to the EU average. Both male and female participation rates are low; in part, this may be a consequence of the extended 'black economy' and the limited coverage of unemployment insurance schemes. During the 1990s there has been a significant increase in self-employment as a proportion of total employment (30% in 1995). This would appear to be part of a move by some enterprises to reduce payroll costs by moving from permanent employment contracts to out-sourcing.

OECD estimates suggest that the levels of real wage flexibility are high, responding rapidly to changing demand conditions. This combines with a high level of employment rigidity, resulting from legislative restriction on dismissal. Consequently, labour market adjustment is initially via wage movement while employment response is subject to a significant lag. Overall, wages are sensitive to cyclical conditions; this means that wages, rather than employment, tend to adjust in the face of changing demand conditions. Labour costs are low, about one third of Spain's and a quarter of the EU average. However, the high rates of long-term unemployment (37%) and youth unemployment (15%), suggests a short-fall of industrial skills and the need for sustained investment to enhance the level of human capital (see OECD Survey, 1995).

12.2.3 Output and inflation

Portugal remains a poor country by EU standards; per capita GNP is 70% of the EUR15 (Table G24). However, apart from the disruptive years of 1983–84, when external shocks com-

Table 12.1 GDP growth at constant prices

GDP (ann.% 1990 prices)	1986–90	1991	1992	1993	1994	1995	1996
Portugal	5.1	2.1	1.1	−1.2	1.0	2.5	2.3
EUR15	3.3	1.4	1.0	−.6	2.8	2.5	1.5

Source: Tables G1 & G13.

bined with internal instability, and the recession of 1993–94, the country has experienced sustained growth in real GDP. As may be seen from Table 12.1, this has produced some measure of real income convergence. Portugal's average GDP growth over the past decade has been almost double that of Greece; this has resulted in a significant change in their positions in the relative wealth league (see Table G24).

The major problem during this extended period of adjustment was the initial inability to contain the inflationary pressures which frequently characterise a modernising economy with an under-developed financial sector. As can be seen from the graph below, for much of this period the Portuguese inflation rate has been substantially above the average for the EU economies. Although both exhibit a declining trend during the 1980s, Portugal experienced sharp and erratic price movements. The price movements in the 1990s suggest that the government has established tighter control over the macroeconomy (see Figure 12.1).

During the twenty-year period 1971–90 inflation averaged 17% per annum, which was well above the EU average. Following IMF-inspired

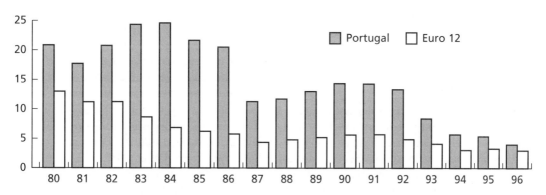

Figure 12.1 Comparative inflation (GDP deflator), Eurostat, Tables G1 and G13

stabilisation programmes in the early 1980s and EC membership in 1986, the inflation record has improved somewhat and there is evidence that, following a series of reforms of the financial sector (see below), the government has gained a measure of control over domestic monetary aggregates. Government commitment to price stability was reinforced by the decision to replace the crawling-peg exchange rate system, which had accommodated the inflationary pressures, with participation in the European Exchange Rate Mechanism (ERM) in 1992. Reinforcing the above, the recent all-party commitment to entry into the European single currency has resulted in a tight fiscal and monetary policy which has achieved significant reductions in both inflation and government deficits; inflation is forecast to drop from 3.6% in 1996 to 2.5% in 1997 – a level close to the EU average.

12.2.4 Consumption, savings and investment

Private consumption has traced a somewhat erratic path over the last decade. The late 1970s and early 1980s were characterised by a very high savings ratio and low and sometimes negative growth in private consumption. Following EC entry, falling tariffs and rising real incomes combined to produce an aura of confidence which produced a sustained consumer boom, with the savings ratio falling from a high of 28% in 1985 to 22% in 1990, returning to 25% in 1993. Private consumption has grown on average by 4–5% per annum in the early 1990s, fuelled by the strong growth in real wages. However, consumption growth stagnated in 1993–94, as a result of the contraction in aggregate demand and restricted wage growth in the public sector.

In spite of high real interest rates, there has been a sustained high level of fixed investment since 1985 (Table 12.2). This reflects the pressing need to both enlarge and modernise the capital stock. Much of the investment has been in the form of capital-widening projects in infrastructure and services which has had a positive impact on employment. However, the continuing need for capital-deepening to enhance

Table 12.2 Gross fixed capital formation

	1986–90	1991	1992	1993	1994	1995	1996
GFCF as % of GDP (current prices)	26.9	26.7	26.7	25.1	25.5	25.4	25.9

Source: Eurostat, Table G13.

industrial productivity is beginning to produce increasing amounts of labour displacement. Investment volumes have been substantially boosted by the rapid growth of foreign direct investment (see Section 12.5.2).

12.2.5 Agriculture

Agriculture represents one of the key problem areas of the Portuguese economy. The sector provides shelter for extensive underemployment, supported by a generous government subsidy of producer prices. These subsidies are being progressively phased out, which means that efficiency must improve substantially if farm incomes are not to fall sharply. In 1987 average labour productivity in agriculture was only 16% of EC average and crop yields varied from 37% to 71% of European averages. Part of the problem derives from the land tenure system which has produced excessive division into non-viable small land holdings in the north, and equally inefficient large cooperative farms in the south. Some 50% of all farms have less than one hectare of land and 94% have less than 20 hectares. In addition, the sector suffers from low infrastructure investment, an inefficient distribution system, poor education levels (45% of farmers are said to be illiterate) and inadequate agricultural extension services.

Significant progress has been made in the last decade, employment in agriculture has fallen from 24% of the working population in 1985 to 12% in 1994 while agricultural output as a percentage of GDP remained constant at about 7% (Barclays Bank, 1996). However, these figures remain at about twice the EU average.

In spite of the large areas of agricultural land and favourable climatic conditions, Portugal cannot meet its domestic food requirements, half of which is met by imports. A land reform initiative has started the process of the progressive privatisation of the large cooperative farms and capital investment has been raised significantly through EC structural support programmes. As yet this has produced only modest results and in spite of improvement in labour productivity and crop yields, these remain well below the EU average. A continuing policy of structural reform is required to convert the sector from subsistence to commercial agriculture.

An exception to the above is forestry, an important sub-sector of agricultural activity. Forestry and the associated process industry have expanded rapidly in the last decade. Portugal is the world's largest exporter of cork (harvested from the cork oak) and a significant net exporter of pulp products. The total area under forest cultivation is 3.7 million hectares, and, although cork oak plantations are the dominant crop, there has been a rapid expansion of eucalyptus tree plantations which are becoming an increasingly important source of raw material for the paper product industry.

12.2.6 Industry

The industrial sector of the economy is quite large; the manufacturing share of both gross value-added and civilian employment are marginally above the EU average (see Tables G19–25). Including energy and construction, industry accounts for 32% of employment, 39% of GNP and 90% of exports (1994).

The sector is, however, characterised by a fundamentally dualistic structure. The major source of employment is in traditional small-scale labour-intensive manufacturing industries dominated by textiles, clothing and footwear, a legacy of the pre-revolution period. This stands in contrast to a rapidly growing sub-sector of large capital-intensive manufacturing and processing firms which are either state-owned or, increasingly, local subsidiaries of multinational corporations. An important and expanding sector is paper and pulp processing, which is dominated by four large, vertically integrated,

conglomerates. Over half the annual output of 800 000 tonnes of pulp is produced by Portucel, a state-owned corporation, while the remaining production is controlled by British and Swedish multinationals.

The heavy industrial sector is still dominated by state-owned and foreign-owned firms: in 1986, ten of the top twenty-five companies were state-owned, eight were foreign-owned and seven were private. Multinationals such as Rio Tinto Zinc, Stora and BAT have focused on resource processing (paper and pulp), while others, such as Ford/VW, are developing component sourcing activities. The balance between private and public ownership has been changing during the 1990s, as the government privatisation programme is implemented (see Section 12.3.2).

Textiles appear as the most exposed and vulnerable sector of manufacturing industry. It is also a very important element of the country's industrial base, providing 28% of manufacturing employment and contributing 30% of the country's exports earnings. The industry is characterised by low technology, low value-added products which compete in the highly competitive end of the world market. The market in the 1990s is characterised by a continued expansion of supply capacity fed by the low-cost producers from the Far East and east Europe. The Portugese industry must modernise if it is to survive in this market environment.

Heavy investment is required to raise capital intensity and maintain competitiveness in the spinning and weaving sub-sectors, while modernisation in the final product sectors is required to improve quality and move products up-market. The sector is already experiencing considerable employment contraction and is the focus of EU-financed industrial restructuring. The difficulties of structural adjustment and contraction are exacerbated by the high level of geographical concentration, with most of the industry in the north and central regions.

12.2.7 The informal economy

As in many transitional developing economies the informal or 'black' economy represents an important element of economic life. As these activities are undeclared – and thus untaxed, they are by their nature very difficult to quantify. In the rich economies of the EU the unmeasured black economy is variously estimated to be between 5 and 8% of GDP; in Portugal some commentators put the figure in the region of 15–20% of GDP. The construction industry is a major source of unmeasured economic activity, as is tourism and the craft manufacture of tourist artifacts. The plethora of regulations and controls which have traditionally circumscribed legitimate business processes, together with an eccentric and inequitable system of income taxation, have, in the past, provided strong incentives for the expansion of unrecorded economic activity. The government is making great efforts to extend tax coverage and limit tax evasion, forcing the informal sector to contribute to government revenue.

12.3 GOVERNMENT INVOLVEMENT IN THE ECONOMY

In spite of strong growth in the private sector in recent years, the legacy of the 'nationalisation experiment' of the mid-1970s has meant that the state continues to account for nearly 40% of GDP. In certain sectors such as metals and heavy engineering, its weight is overwhelming. Even in the private sector, legislative and bureaucratic controls on the economy remain extensive and contribute to an unnecessarily high level of transaction costs for business firms. The government took an important step toward the rationalisation of bureaucratic regulation with the establishment of a new *Commercial Code* in 1987, but much still remains to be done.

12.3.1 Government revenue and tax reform

Traditionally tax revenues, excluding social security payments, have represented a small but growing proportion of government revenue, rising from 16% in 1987 to 24% in 1994. Initially,

the narrow tax base had been insufficient to support growing government expenditure and since 1974 the country has experienced continuous budget deficits. The Public Debt/GDP ratio quadrupled between 1974 and 1988 when it reached a peak of 74%, the ratio currently stands at 70% (1995) but this is forecast to decline, with the aim of reaching the Maastricht target of 60% by the end of the decade.

In an effort to improve fiscal efficiency and control the inflationary tendency of public finance, the country has embarked upon a far-reaching programme of tax reform. The aim has been to widen the tax base and to reduce the opportunities for tax avoidance. The introduction of VAT in 1986, followed by income tax reforms in 1989, combined to provide a stronger fiscal multiplier and to increase the horizontal equity of the system. A gradual reduction in marginal tax rates by between 8 and 14 percentage points is being implemented progressively over the period 1994–98 with the object of increasing work incentives. A 'green' element in taxation is represented by the recent decision to impose excise duties on electricity and fossil fuel use. In 1995 the government raised the rate of VAT from 16 to 17% and used this to finance a reduction in the rate of employers' contributions to social security – thus reducing the burden of indirect labour costs.

The general easing of the financing constraint enabled the government to advance reform of the financial markets, including a deregulation of interest rates. The combination of improved revenue structures and sustained growth of GDP has produced a modest decline in the budget deficit – equivalent to 5% of GDP (1995). The budget forecast for 1997 aims at a figure close to the Maastricht target of 3%.

Government spending has exhibited strong growth in the last decade – rising from 38% of GDP in 1989 to 45% in 1996. This, however, remains below the EU average of 50% (Table G32). Spending on the social security budget is likely to remain a major burden, but privatisation offers prospects of reducing the level of subsidy to the loss-making public sector industries.

12.3.2 Privatisation

The process of privatising the very large public sector depended on the mobilisation of substantial political support to amend the 1976 Constitution which explicitly outlawed the sale of public assets. Amendments to the Constitution in 1988 and 1989 allowed first for partial privatisation (private/public partnership) and finally for full privatisation. The main activity to date has been in the financial services sector where some banks and insurance companies have been sold to the private sector. In addition, there has been successful privatisation of the brewery sector and some progress toward restructuring the heavy industrial sector in preparation for a return to private ownership – notably cement, petro-chemicals and steel. Sale of public assets, which had progressed rapidly in the early 1990s, slowed down somewhat in the recession of 1993–94; however, the revenue equivalent to 9% of GDP has been raised since the privatisation programme began in 1989. Current projected sales of public enterprises such as the pulp and paper group *Portucel* and the cement groups *Secil* and *Cimpor* are expected to raise $2.5 billion by the end of this decade – making a significant contribution to government debt reduction.

12.3.3 Structural reform

Following EC entry in 1986, there was a general recognition of the need to modernise and adapt agriculture, industry and commerce to face the increased competition resulting from the 1992 Single Market. The backbone of the far-reaching programme of industrial restructuring is the *Specific Programme for Industrial Development in Portugal (PEDIP)*. This programme is funded from private investors, the Portuguese government and the EU – the latter funding coming from community structural and regional funds. Between 1988 and 1992 $2 billion was channelled through PEDIP for industrial modernisation. Key areas of funding have included: infrastructure investment, professional training, capital investment and advisory support services

for improving productivity and product quality. Advisory support services are provided by specially created 'centres of competence' which are providing international expertise in areas such as information technology, manufacturing logistics and financial management for both established firms and new business projects. The second community support framework (CSF) covers the period 1994–99 and envisages grants of 3250 billion escudos. This is equivalent to 25% of the 1993 GDP and the aim is to use these funds to target improvements in human capital, infrastructure and organisational know-how to support the SME sector (OECD Survey 1994–95).

Active labour market policies are being implemented as part of the modernisation process. The main thrust of these policies is towards occupational training and subsidies for job creation. With an illiteracy rate variously estimated at between 15 and 20%, raising the general level of education and the occupational skill profile of the work-force is a key ingredient of the government's modernisation strategy. Substantial disbursements from the European Social Fund have been earmarked for adult training and the general development of human resources.

A new competition law was passed in 1994 which widened the spread of previous legislation and increased the scope for acting against the abuse of market power. The law can be applied to both the public and private sector but enterprises such as utilities, which are subject to special legislation, are exempt.

12.3.4 Policies for prices and wages

National minimum wage legislation was introduced in 1974 as part of a general policy of improving conditions for the least-favoured groups of the labour force. Currently, only about 3% of the work-force are directly affected by statutory wage provision. The majority, about 80%, are subject to collective agreements or civil service statutory regulation, thus leaving a not insignificant group without collective wage regulation.

The government has developed a non-statutory prices and incomes policy based upon the

Economic and Social Agreement (*acordo economico e social*). The process involves a negotiated pact between employers, trade unions and the government which set pay targets for wage negotiations in the public and private sectors. In 1992 the collectively agreed pay limit was 9.75%, with a government pay target of 8%. This was wrapped up in a package which included improvements in the minimum wage, income and mortgage tax relief. There were no national wage agreements in 1994 and 1995 and the net result of this was that real wages stagnated and reduced the upward pressure on unit labour costs which have shown a relative decline in comparison to the experience of other EU countries (see Table G27).

12.3.5 Regional policy

Regional divisions between the north and south are a long-established feature of the country. The 1974 revolution reflected and reinforced these differences; the more highly politicised south moved down the path of nationalisation and collectivisation, while ownership structures in the north – family firms and peasant landholdings – remained largely untouched. Present regional policy is administered by the Ministry of Planning and Terratorial Co-ordination and is targeted on improving communication linkages between the north and south. Considerable emphasis is placed on the Lisbon–Oporto coastal axis, to the neglect of the underdeveloped eastern interior. The continuing processes of structural adjustment will impact differentially on the regions, creating a need for more focused regional policy in the future. The existing structures of centralised administration are likely to face increasing demands for regional devolution as economic imbalances become more marked.

The autonomous island regions of Madeira and Azores present particular development problems due to their size and location. The strategy has been to negotiate free trade zone status within Portugal and the EU. Madeira has already used this status to advance its position as an offshore financial centre, capitalising on its traditional role as a link between Europe and South America.

12.4 FINANCIAL SYSTEM

Following the 1974 revolution the stock exchanges of Lisbon and Oporto were closed and almost the whole of the financial sector was nationalised – commercial banks, saving banks, insurance companies and agricultural credit institutions. The only significant exceptions were the four foreign-owned banks.

Government control was exercised via a network of direct controls, the only financial instruments available to the private sector were bank and saving deposits which were mobilised to provide funding for the government and state enterprises. In essence the whole of the private and public sectors were financed by the banking sector; in 1984 99% of households' financial assets consisted of sight or term deposits with the banking system. Since the mid-1980s there has been a major effort to revitalise and modernise the financial system, to create a competitive market environment with the flexibility necessary to underpin the processes of economic development. In 1987 banks were authorised to issue marketable certificates of deposit and subsequently there has been a progressive deregulation of interest rates on credits and deposits. The removal of credit ceilings and administered interest rates are aimed at the establishment of market discipline and the price rationing of credit for both the private and public sector. In the past, credit ceilings not only subsidised government borrowing but also protected the inefficient state-owned banks, which now face a much more threatening competitive environment. There has been a partial privatisation of some of the state institutions and the formation of a number of new private banks. This, together with the increasing presence of foreign banks, has radically increased competition and stimulated reform within those institutions remaining in state ownership.

The Stock Exchanges of Lisbon and Oporto were re-opened in 1982, but until 1990 the market remained small, with the shares of only 30 companies being continuously traded. Market activity has been dominated by trade in government bonds and securities, which were introduced in 1986 and now finance a substantial proportion of government debt. Some progress is being made to widen the market by improving the administrative structures and reducing transaction costs of market activity. More recently the securities market has expanded as a result of 'privatisation placements' and the capitalisation of the Lisbon Exchange increased by 35% between 1990 and 1995.

12.4.1 Monetary and exchange rate policy

The various measures of liberalisation and marketisation of financial markets and institutions have created new problems of money market management. The increased liquidity, following the removal of quantitative restrictions, was partly absorbed by sales of government securities, but in spite of this there was significant liquidity growth in 1991–92. Interest rates, both real and nominal, rose in the early 1990s, which contributed to capital inflows and a tendency for currency appreciation. The decline in interest rates since 1992 is a reflection of both improved inflation outlook and financial liberalisation. Monetary growth in the mid 1990s has decreased from 14% p.a. in 1990–92 to 6.5% in 1995–96.

The authorities decided to abandon the crawling-peg system of currency management in 1990, first shadowing and then joining the ERM in April 1992. In addition to the inflation discipline which this action imposed, membership of the ERM offered substantial benefits from reduced exchange rate variability, especially for a country whose currency is not used extensively in international trade and where the financial sector is underdeveloped. However, the continuing high level of domestic inflation, albeit declining relative to other Community countries, led to a substantial real appreciation of the escudo in terms of unit labour costs. The currency turmoil in September 1992 which resulted in the withdrawal of sterling and the lira from the ERM led to a further deterioration in competitiveness; when, in November, Spain devalued within the ERM and Portugal was obliged to follow the Spanish move. Since then the escudo's central rate against the deutschmark has depreciated by

some 15% and resulted in a currency realignment in 1995. The recent improvement in Portugal's inflation performance has resulted in currency stability and allowed the monetary authorities to institute a policy of interest rate reduction – nominal short term rates falling from 11.1% in 1994 to 7.5% in 1996. A consequence of this is that interest rate differentials relative to Germany have narrowed significantly.

Given the current level of underdevelopment of the Portugese economy, the decision to opt for a non-accommodating exchange rate regime has introduced a valuable dimension of financial discipline. However, it has also simultaneously removed an element of policy flexibility for a country facing the continuing burdens of structural adjustment.

12.5 INTERNATIONAL RELATIONS

12.5.1 Trade and the balance of payments

The geographical pattern of Portugal's trade has changed radically over the last 30 years. This is particularly noticeable with reference to the destination of exports. Traditionally, Portuguese exports had been oriented toward its colonial territories, but the 'end of empire' in the 1970s and EC membership in the 1980s have combined to switch trade into EU markets. The proportion of intra-EU trade has risen from 63% in 1985 to 75% in 1995 and the share of imports sourced from the EU has risen from 48 to 73%. Germany is the most important single market for Portuguese exports, followed by Spain, France and the UK. Of particular importance has been the growth of trade with Spain, which has expanded rapidly over the last decade. Following many years of separate development, EU membership appears to have stimulated a process of Iberian integration; however, tensions still remain, stimulated by the persistence of a strong bilateral trade imbalance in favour of Spain, and high levels of Spanish corporate investment in the Portugese market.

In spite of substantial growth of exports, the sustained growth in domestic demand has resulted in rapid import growth and a continuous trade deficit throughout the 1980s and early 1990s. The 'services' account has consistently provided a positive net balance: this derives from high earnings from tourism and emigrants remittances (the latter representing the equivalent of some 10% of GDP). The current account deficit, which averaged 3.5% of GDP in the 1980s, narrowed to below 2% of GDP in the first half of the 1990s (see Table G37). This is expected to move into rough balance by 1988, as new investment comes on stream (in particular, the Ford/Volkswagen car assembly plant) boosting merchandise exports.

12.5.2 Foreign direct investment

This has made a major contribution to the country's economic development since the mid-1980s. Over recent years FDI flows have averaged between 3 and 4% of GDP. The combination of low labour costs, EU investment incentives and a favourable local tax regime provide an attractive environment for foreign investment. This activity seeks to capitalise on the high rates of return obtainable in the domestic market where there is a dearth of local competition, as well as to establish export-oriented production platforms. With the exception of Belgium–Luxembourg, Portugal has the highest level of FDI/GDP of any EU country; foreign firms are now operating in most sectors of the economy and are particularly well represented in finance, vehicles, real estate and business services (OECD Survey, 1992, p. 34, Table 9). Since 1992 there has been a contraction in FDI flows which is in part a consequence of the distortion caused by the heavy investment associated with the Ford/Volkswagen project. FDI represents a vital means for achieving economic modernisation: it is an important channel for knowledge transfer, a source of much needed financial capital and a competitive stimulus for domestic firms. The government believes the Portuguese membership of the EMU will increase the attractiveness of the country as a location for further overseas investment.

Foreign debt has virtually doubled in recent years, rising from $29 billion in 1991 to $59 billion in 1995 (Barclays Bank, 1996). While a significant proportion of this debt is in the private sector, the internationalisation of the Lisbon capital market has, in recent years, facilitated the international funding of government debt.

12.6 IMPACT OF EUROPEAN INTEGRATION AND FUTURE PROSPECTS

Portugal's entry to the EC followed nearly two centuries of virtual isolation from European affairs. Since 1977, when the country first made application to join the EC, there has been a radical shift towards west European values and socio-political structures. This has been followed by sustained structural adjustment in the economy but there remains a long way to go if significant economic convergence is to be achieved. Net resource transfers via EU structural funds seem set to continue through the 1990s but pressures on key sectors of the economy, notably agriculture, will increase as full EU integration is completed. The real challenge facing the economy in the remaining years of the 20th century derives from the competitive pressures generated from the simultaneous completion of the single market and end of the transition period for EU accession.

The country's commitment to the European Union is illustrated by the determination of both main political parties to participate in the first stage of monetary union in 1999. The Prime Minister, Antonio Guterres, believes that the Maastricht targets can be achieved within the next two years and forecasts that the public debt/GDP ratio will fall to 63% by 1998 (*Financial Times*, 15/10/96). The economy's recent performance, in terms of both inflation and debt reduction, raises the prospect that Portugal will be closer to qualifying than will Spain or its other southern neighbours. If Portugal was to enter the EMU on its own, there would be a significant risk of exposure to disruptive competitive pressure from those outside the system. Successful integration will depend upon the country's ability to sustain 'supply-side' improvements, notably: continuing privatisation, financial liberalisation, increased flexibility of the labour market and extended administrative reform. The continuing high levels of financial transfers – in 1993 the net public transfer from the European Union to Portugal was 456.4 billion escudos – will be crucial in funding these structural changes.

While progress is being made in most of the above areas, reform of the bureaucracy is a central problem which remains to be addressed. Portuguese public administration is rule-bound, inefficient and extensively overmanned. Public administration employment, excluding health and education, is 6.6% of the working population, compared to 5% in the UK and 4.5% in west Germany. The public bureaucracy grew rapidly in the 1970s, and in part, provided a means of absorbing the large numbers of returning colonial administrators.

An essential requirement for the transformation to a modern market economy is the elimination of the overload of regulation and restriction which has accumulated over the long period of pre-democratic dictatorship, together with the associated bureaucratic structures and attitudes. Improvements in attitude and efficiency of the civil service require the creation of a meritocratic system of promotion, proper training and rational pay structures. The 1990s has seen a concerted effort to reduce levels of administration and improve efficiency but much remains to be done and represents a real challenge in the last years of the 20th century.

12.7 BIBLIOGRAPHY

Barclays Bank (1996): *Economic Report – Portugal*

Bliss, C., de Macedo, J.B. (eds) (1990): *Unity with diversity in the European Economy: The community's southern frontier*

Corkill, D. (1993): *The Portuguese Economy since 1974*, Edinburgh University Press

Council of the European Community (1996): *Annual Economic Report*

OECD (1988–95): *Economic Surveys Portugal*

Economic Intelligence Unit (1992): *'Portugal' in the European Community: Economic structure and analysis* (Regional Reference Series)

Hudson (1989): *Portugal to 1993, Investing in a European Future*, E.I.U. Special Report No.1157

EU15: Accession of Nordic countries and Austria

PART E EU15: ACCESSION OF THE NORDIC COUNTRIES AND AUSTRIA

The end of the cold war in the early 1990s removed one of the last obstacles for the Austrian, Swedish and Finnish membership. In order to preserve their neutrality these countries could not be firmly linked to a group of countries all belonging to Western organisations such as NATO and the EU. The dissolution of the former communist block has ended this situation. The integration of Austria (Chapter 13), Sweden (Chapter 14) and Finland (Chapter 15) into the EU can also be regarded as a kind of merger between the EU and the largest part of EFTA, creating one large trading block of 370 million people in the western and southern parts of Europe.

EFTA was established in 1960, mainly consisting of countries which could not or would not commit themselves to the more far-reaching integration aimed for by the recently founded EEC. When the most important country and initiator of EFTA, the UK, entered into the EC, EFTA lost most of its significance. For that reason, a more intensified cooperation was sought with the EC, resulting in the establishment of the European Economic Area (EEA) in 1994. This agreement extended the internal EU Market to the EFTA countries by realising the 'four freedoms' for the whole EU-EFTA block: the free movement of goods, services, capital and people. One of the EFTA members, Switzerland, rejected this agreement by referendum. For four others, Sweden, Finland, Austria and Norway, the difference with full Membership, seemed only marginal. It would mainly bring the right to participate in EU decision-making. With the ending of the Cold War, neutrality was not an issue any more, so the road was open to full Membership for Austria, Sweden and Finland. Their applications were accepted by the EU, leading to the joining of these countries as of 1 January 1995. The Norwegians, however, rejected Membership by referendum.

It is not certain whether the remaining EFTA countries, Switzerland, Norway and Liechtenstein will definitely stay out; one day they might apply again.

CHAPTER 13

Austria

Franz Hackl
Friedrich Schneider

13.1 INSTITUTIONAL AND HISTORICAL CONTEXT

13.1.1 The historical background

Austria in its present form emerged following the dissolution of the Habsburg empire in 1918. From being part of a trade area incorporating more than 50 million people at the beginning of this century, Austria represents today a small country, centrally located within Europe, with 8 million inhabitants. Before the First World War, production in what is now the Federal Republic of Austria comprised mainly services and industrial goods, with raw materials and in particular food being 'imported' from other parts of the empire. After the empire was carved up, serious questions were raised as to whether, as a small independent country, Austria would be in the position to survive without its own raw materials and other basic goods. This uncertainty over the viability of Austria and the adverse macroeconomic conditions of the inter-war period, contributed to political instability and economic weakness which culminated in occupation by Germany in 1938. This experience has given strong encouragement to the building up of stable political and economic institutions since 1945. This framework of political and economic institutions has been a major contributor to the above-average economic performance of Austria in the post-war period (see Section 13.7 on the Austrian Social Partnership).

During the seven years in which Austria was annexed to Germany (1938–45) several economic changes took place which influenced the Austrian industrial and economic structure significantly:

- Before the Second World War Austria specialised in producing consumer goods. Driven by military demand industrial production of basic materials (e.g. steel) and the construction sector were significantly expanded.
- A number of large efficiently operated companies were established during that time (e.g. the VOEST steel works).
- Because of the trade orientation towards eastern European countries before the Second World War the economic activity was concentrated in the eastern part of Austria. Annexation was accompanied by a reorientation of trade and economic activity towards western states with the main emphasis on Germany.

After the Second World War, Austria was an occupied but still autonomous country. Its territory was divided into four occupation zones. The eastern part of the country was under Russian control, the rest was divided between France, Great Britain and the United States. The period since 1945 can be roughly divided into four phases. Initially, during 1945–55, the goals of economic policy were directed at reconstructing and re-establishing Austria's political and economic independence. Following this period of rebuilding, Austria experienced a relatively stable period of economic growth which was brought to an end by the oil price shocks of 1973–74. This ensued a period when the economy exhibited rising rates of inflation and unemployment and, in comparison to the second phase, low growth rates. Entry into the European Union has ushered in a new phase. While the former three periods were characterised by the pursuit of social and economic welfare objectives as a neutral and independent country with an autonomous economic and security policy, the accession to the European Union has given rise to a re-examination of the values and concepts which have applied throughout the period since 1945. The intended membership in the Monetary Union, the debate over abolishing the 'everlasting neutrality', which was one important prerequisite for Austria's independence in 1955, as well as the government pronouncements about possible membership of NATO, are examples for the noticeable long term reorientation of Austria's economic and political attitudes.

13.1.2 The political framework in Austria

Austria is a federal parliamentary democracy with nine provinces. At present (the next elections are scheduled for 1999) there are five parties in the Federal Parliament. Apart from the two traditionally large and influential parties – the Social Democratic Party (71 seats) and the Austrian People's Party (conservative, 53 seats) – the legislative authority also consists of three smaller groups – the Freedom Party (nationalist, 40 seats), the Liberal Forum (10 seats) and the Greens (9 seats), with the Freedom Party receiving a fresh impetus in the last 10 years. From 1945 until 1966 the governments of Austria were formed by grand coalitions between the Social Democratic Party and the Austrian People's Party. Whereas the Austrian People's Party held the absolute majority from 1967 to 1970, the Social Democratic Party formed the governments during 1971–83. After a short period of coalition government between the Social Democratic Party and the Freedom Party (1984–86) Austria has since been governed again by a grand coalition of Social Democrats and Conservatives.

Austria has thus been ruled by grand coalitions for more than half the period since the Second World War, which implies that most of the decisions have been based on a broad societal consensus. The disadvantages arising from that kind of decision-making are addressed in Section 13.7 on the Austrian Social Partnership.

13.2 MAIN ECONOMIC CHARACTERISTICS

13.2.1 Gross domestic product

The period before the oil price shock of 1973–74 was characterised by high real growth rates around 5% which were in line with the international experience. In spite of an appreciable worsening of the national economic climate and a sharp rise in national savings induced by the oil price shock, high levels of discretionary government spending ensured that Austria avoided a sharp recession during the 1970s and early 1980s (average growth rate 2.2%; see Table G12 and Figure 13.1). It is remarkable that Austria implemented demand management policies during the late 1970s and early 1980s when most other European countries started with supply-side-orientated policies. However, efforts were undertaken to consolidate the Austrian federal budget and to cut public expenditures. From an ex-post point of view these attempts predominantly took place in times with relatively low growth rates, which resulted in a pro-cyclical pattern of government spending during that period. Even though the pronounced government spending did not lead to a serious problem of inflation due to the moderate income policy (see Section 13.2.3 on wages and prices), the demand-side-orientated policy of the 1970s and early 1980s is certainly one reason for the potential structural problems in Austria (see Section 13.2.4 on economic structure and sector shares). However, at the latest in 1985 the period of intense discretionary government spending came to an end.

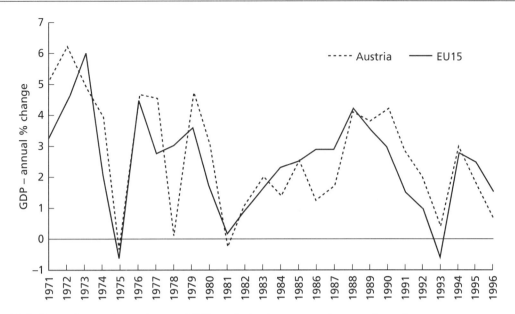

Figure 13.1 Gross domestic product at 1990 market prices: annual percentage change

Source: Eurostat, Table G23.

Expanded export credits, increasing transfer payments to the population and subsidies to a large number of big companies to protect them from bankruptcy (e.g. the VOEST) led to high government budget deficits. Subsequent attempts at severer budget consolidation reduced the rate of economic growth. A new stimulus to growth, however, was once again triggered by foreign trade in 1983–84. The expanding American economy provided the basis for increasing Austrian exports which initiated a new upswing. This period of growth was, however, associated with high levels of unemployment, although not of the same magnitude as in other OECD countries.

The international recession in the early 1990s was, in Austria, partly offset by a boom in the construction industry and rising exports to eastern European countries. A decline in overall exports and non-construction investment subsequently produced a moderate economic downturn which by 1993 saw the growth rate decline to 0.4%. It was at that point that the Austrian government decided again to use discretionary counter-cyclical fiscal measures.

Buoyant exports to the reunified Germany and – unusual for Austria – growing private investment, strengthened the recovery with growth rates of 3.0% and 1.8% in 1994 and 1995, respectively. But meeting the Maastricht convergence targets again requires the Austrian government to reduce its large budget deficit, and spending cuts planned for 1996 and 1997 have reduced GDP growth rate expectations (e.g. 0.7% for 1996).

13.2.2 Employment

From the time of the initial oil price shocks until 1985 the Austrian economy had successfully detached itself from international trends in unemployment rates. Whereas the average unemployment rate of the European Union was about 6.5% during the period of oil crises, the unemployment rate in Austria amounted to only 2.5%. For this reason Austria was sometimes called the 'island of the blessed'. The policy mix, which was seen as being responsible for this disengagement from the international business cycle, was later termed 'Austro-Keynesianism'.

The main objective of this policy bundle lay in achieving full employment by discretionary government intervention. Moreover, the hard currency policy, institutional arrangements as well as a moderate income policy, were instruments of this particular conception of economic policy. However, because of problems with rising budget deficits and also the way in which excessive government spending can operate to inhibit the economy from making desirable structural adjustments (see also Section 13.2.4 on economic structure and sector shares), the application of the concept of Austro-Keynesianism could not be sustained at the same level of intensity. Nevertheless, as can be seen from Figure 13.2, Austria has been very successful in maintaining relatively low unemployment. With an estimated unemployment rate of 4.6% for 1996, Austria stands well below the EU average, although the Austrian labour market displays the characteristic of a marked unemployment persistence, varying little over time. These low and relatively stable unemployment rates can be attributed to a high real wage flexibility (see also Section 13.2.3 on wages and

prices) which is the product of the special institutional features found in Austria.

One special characteristic of Austria's labour statistic is that the official registered unemployment rate, as measured by the labour office (7.3% in 1996; this rate comprises mainly those who declare themselves unemployed in order to get the unemployment benefits and information about job opportunities), is substantially higher than the survey-based unemployment figure (4.6%), which means that the number of people receiving benefits is substantially higher than the number actually looking for a job. This difference is one of the largest in the OECD and can be explained mainly by high seasonal unemployment in the tourism and the construction industries.

Second, the low unemployment rate is not associated with a correspondingly high employment rate. This is because in Austria, important segments of the labour force have relatively low participation rates. Due to generous regulation in relation to early retirement and invalidity pension, there is a relatively low retirement age in Austria. In addition, a shortage of part-time work

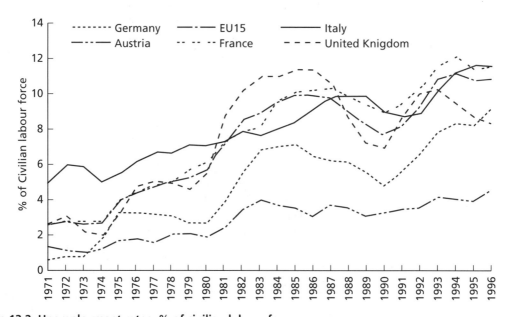

Figure 13.2 Unemployment rates: % of civilian labour force

Source: Eurostat, Table G20.

has given rise to a comparatively low female labour force participation rate.

13.2.3 Wages and prices

Austria's performance in relation to inflation has been very similar to the EU average (see Table G31). Due to the intense Keynesian government spending and the lack of competition in a number of sectors, Austria is confronted with a rather stubborn inflation pressure. On average, the consumer price inflation rate in Austria is about one percentage point higher than in Germany. However, with expected inflation for 1996 of below 2%, it cannot be argued that inflation is a serious problem.

The Austrian approach to achieving price stability has two main elements: (1) The use of a moderate income policy. To avoid wage-push inflation, agreements are made within the framework of the Social Partnership such that wage increases are closely related to the rate of inflation, the rise in productivity, as well as the actual situation of the economy according to the growth rate of the sectoral GDPs. (2) The second instrument for achieving price stability is exchange rate policy. By keeping Austria's foreign exchange rate high imported inflation is minimised (the so-called 'hard currency policy').

Austrian wages are determined rather by institutional agreements within the Social Partnership than by competitive markets. Although comparable countries, in which institu-

tions determine the wages as well, are characterised by a high degree of wage rigidity, the opposite is true for Austria, with real wages being relatively flexible despite the significant influence of interest groups. Two arguments can be given for that feature:

● Following Olson (1985) the damage caused by lobbyists is serious, especially when interest groups are powerful enough to exert influence on the economy but small enough to avoid experiencing the negative economic consequences of their behaviour themselves. In the special case of Austria the size of the interest groups with their high degree of organisation and their substantial dependence on the macroeconomic performance of the country exceeds this critical mass, such that they would suffer from the negative consequences of too high wage levels in periods of low growth rates. Therefore, the actual GDP growth has a considerable influence on the Austrian wage bargaining process.

● In other countries wage rigidity often results if income policy is used as an instrument for redistribution. In Austria there was always the attempt to redistribute through the size of the public sector by either providing public goods (e.g. free access to the educational system) or paying high transfers to the households (e.g. family allowances). Therefore, income policy

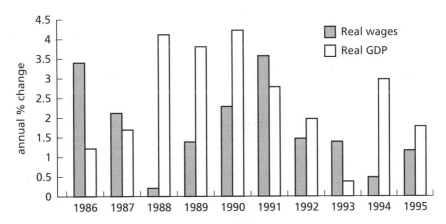

Figure 13.3 Changes of the real standard wages and the real GDP

Source: OeNB, *Statistische Monatshefte*, March 1996.

and especially wage determination is not seen as a primary instrument of redistribution, a fact that guarantees room for a relatively high real wage flexibility.

To illustrate this flexibility Figure 13.3 shows growth rates of the real GDP and changes of the real standard wages between 1986 and 1995. The comparison of these two time series indicates that changes in real standard wages follow quite well the movement of the real GDP growth rate even though the reaction of the real wages lags behind by at least one year which results from the annual wage bargaining process within the Austrian Social Partnership.

13.2.4 Economic structure and sector shares

Partly for historical reasons, reaching back to the period of occupation by Germany, Austria has the largest industrial sector of all EU countries. With 44% of gross value-added in industry (including construction), Austria lies substantially beyond the EU15 average of about 35% (see Table G25). The most important branch of industry (measured by number of employees) is machinery and steel/metal production, followed by electrical engineering and chemicals. The primary sector, 3.4% of Austria's gross value-added, is also above the EU average (although the figures for agriculture show a continuous trend for it to shrink, and decreasing agricultural producer prices resulting from accession to the EU suggests a continuation of this trend is likely). The tertiary sector, with a share of 53% of the gross value-added, is well below the EU15 average of 62%. Austria is a major centre for tourism within Europe and accounts for 8% of the Austrian GDP and employment. While Austria's share of OECD GDP is only 1%, receipts from tourism amount to 5.5% of the OECD total.

In spite of Austria's generally sound economic performance, with low inflation and unemployment rates as well as a satisfying overall trend in relation to labour productivity, there are a number of structural problems which can be identified:

- The country has achieved only a slow rate of job creation and productivity growth in the service sector is weak.
- The prevalence of risk aversion among Austrian people is widely attributed as responsible for the low level of new firm creation.
- High levels of government spending have allowed inefficient companies to survive and failed to encourage such firms to exploit economies of scale and scope.
- The small size of the domestic market combined with the lack of competition in protected sectors are also structural weaknesses within the Austrian economy. A prominent example is the heavily regulated telecommunications sector (e.g. the telephone monopoly), which critics argue has hampered attempts to develop the infrastructure necessary or an information-based economy.
- Although there are signs of change, the focus of industrial production in Austria is still on basic industries, with a lack of knowhow in high-technology sectors.

The strong competition from both East European and EU producers as well as the budget cuts necessary to achieve the Maastricht convergence criteria are strong incentives to overcome these problems and to release deregulation in the protected sectors. Time will tell whether current efforts to deal with structural weaknesses are sufficient to achieve an economic structure which meets the requirements of a modern welfare state. Evidence from the past experience suggests that Austria will be sufficiently flexible to cope with these new challenges.

13.3 GOVERNMENT INVOLVEMENT IN THE ECONOMY

13.3.1 Structure and size of the public sector

As far as the actual size of the public sector is concerned, a glance at the total expenditures and total current receipts of the general government (see Tables G32 and G33) shows that Austria is lying somewhere above the EU15 average.

Austria is a federal republic, with the government's responsibilities being shared between the federal government (Bund), the nine provinces (Länder) and the municipalities (Gemeinden). Whereas the Bund is responsible for the most important national agenda such as defence, foreign policy and macro-economic policy, the provinces are in charge of tasks of regional and local importance. In spite of this federal structure of Austria's public sector, the central government claims 74% of the gross revenues (including social security contributions), which is by far the highest ratio among federal countries (which otherwise ranges from 60% in Germany down to 50% in Canada). Within the scope of the financial redistribution process (*Finanzausgleich*) between the Bund and the Länder, parts of these revenues have to be paid to the provinces, which means that the Länder are financed for their tasks from the federal government. This results in a loose connection between the political responsibilities of spending and taxing which has contributed to the expansion of the public sector. The federal tax revenue share indicates the dominance of the central state in Austria, which is also reflected in the share of gross public expenditures (Austria 78% compared with the United States 65% and Canada 50%).

The structure of the public sector in Austria corresponds to a country with a highly developed social welfare system which gives priority to equalising the standards of living among the people and reducing inter-regional differences. In line with other European countries, Austria has experienced a significant increase in the public expenditure proportion of GDP since the 1970s, with spending on social security (especially contributions to the pension fund) and the servicing of the public debt being of major importance. Along with these 'official' budget developments there has been a rapid growth of public investment transacted by special semi-public finance companies outside the conventional budget frame (e.g. the ASFINAG, which is responsible for freeway construction). In the 1980s this extra-budgetary investment volume increased from 20% to 45% of the budget-effective public investment.

As regards to the income side of the public sector, Austria has a relatively low rate of direct taxes on income and wealth as compared to other OECD countries. However, the rates of indirect taxes and social security contributions (for health, accident, pension and unemployment insurance) are significantly higher, in particular social security contributions have risen markedly in recent years.

13.3.2 Budget deficit

The 1980s were characterised by a chronic deficit in Austria's budget, linked to excessive levels of government spending. At the point when it appeared that the attempts during the early 1990s to reduce the deficit were working, economic stagnation in 1993 produced a government response which once more pushed up central government net borrowing to more than 4% of GDP in 1993 and 1994. The introduction of a new system of federal nursing care assistance and reduced public revenues arising out of the second phase of a general tax reform were also factors contributing to the increase in the public deficit. Furthermore, contributions to the EU budget created an additional fiscal burden. Overall, these developments led to a net borrowing requirement equivalent to over 6% of GDP in 1995, while the national debt increased to 70% of GDP (compare Table G12 and Figure 13.4).

Since both of these indicative figures are outside the acceptable levels defined in the convergence criteria of the Maastricht Treaty – the prerequisite for the membership to European Monetary Union – the Austrian government introduced a drastic fiscal consolidation programme for the years 1996 and 1997. Public expenditures have been reduced by reductions in public consumption through virtually freezing nominal salaries and reducing the number of public employees by 11 000. In addition, social security contributions by farmers and entrepreneurs have been increased, and there have been reductions in government contributions to public utilities and in subsidies to the mortgage loan system. On the revenue side, the programme includes the ending of some

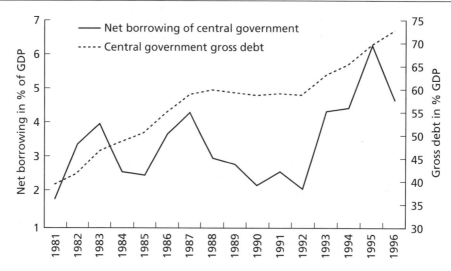

Figure 13.4 Net borrowings and gross debt of the central government (% of GDP)

Source: Eurostat, Tables G34 and G12.280

exemptions from wage and personal income taxation, an increase in the minimum level of corporate income taxation and the introduction of an energy tax on electricity and natural gas.

With this far-reaching consolidation programme, the deficit of the central government is projected to come down to 2.7% of the GDP in 1997. Allowing for a deficit of 0.3% of GDP for the provinces and the communities, Austria is expected to reach the Maastricht public deficit criterion. As far as the national debt figure is concerned, Austria is not, within the allotted timescale, going to be in a position to reduce its cumulated deficits to less than 60% of GDP, but privatisation of public enterprises should indicate a distinct change in the trend of public debt.

13.3.3 Public ownership in the economy

Compared to other European countries public ownership plays an important role in Austria. In 1990 state-owned industry was responsible for 18% of gross production, over 20% of investment and 13% of employment. It should be stressed that these enterprises do not fulfil any allocative function of providing public or merit goods but rather produce private goods which are traded in highly competitive markets. The

government's primary economic goal in the 1970s was full employment, which led to the maintenance of the highest possible level of employment in the nationalised industries, even in situations when rationalisation measures were required. The lack of incentives for profit maximisation and cost efficiency, and the neglect of cost accounting and auditing entailed a loss of international competitiveness which was reflected in huge deficits for a number of public-owned enterprises. Substantial subsidies were necessary to protect these inefficient large firms from bankruptcy (e.g. the largest Austrian enterprise, the VOEST steel company). This kind of economic policy, that protected employment in public owned industries by covering the deficits through subsidies, is certainly one important structural weakness within the large industrial sector with its emphasis on heavy machinery, chemical and basic industries.

Granting high subsidies with the associated lack of incentives for profit maximisation and the resulting budgetary problems led to a debate within Austria on the nature and the size of the public sector. This led to a reorientation in economic policy involving a reduction in the size of the public sector. The VOEST steel company, to take a prominent example, was severely (and successfully) restructured. More than 50% of the OMV, the national oil and gas company, has been sold-off. Among others the mechanical engineering firm VA Technologies, formerly part of the VOEST steel company, has been successfully floated on the stock exchange. In the context of the Maastricht convergence criteria, privatisation is primarily seen in Austria today as a means by which the government can raise revenue rather than as a means of improving efficiency. The expected sale of the Creditanstalt-Bankverein (Austria's largest bank), the Federal Tobacco Company and important provinces-owned holdings in the housing and energy supply sectors should also be seen in that overall context.

13.4 FINANCIAL SYSTEM

13.4.1 Financial markets

While the Austrian bond market has developed since 1980 more or less in line with the nominal GDP, the Vienna stock market has risen dramatically. Moreover, the Austrian futures and options market, which was established in 1991 and has developed rapidly, represents a new feature in the Austrian financial system. With these developments, Austria's financial system has managed to achieve standards near to those of other western European countries, although the country plays no important role within the capital markets. Two reasons can be given for this modest Austrian performance:

- Usually the capital markets for fixed-interest-bearing securities (e.g. markets for bonds, loans or investment certificates) are an important source for the direct financing of the private non-banking sector. The contrary is true in Austria where the public sector and the banking sector issue 91% of the papers in these fixed-interest-bearing markets (1992 data). Thus only 9% of the market remains for private enterprises, which means that private firms are financed by means of bank credits in the first place as opposed to other European countries, in which many enterprises go

directly to the capital markets and issue their own securities.
- Austria's existing pension system does not encourage the formation of private pension funds, which is a major impulse for the development of the capital markets in other countries.

13.4.2 Monetary policy

Actual monetary policy, in the sense of influencing inflation and interest rates by manipulating the money supply, plays an insignificant role in Austria. The monetary policy of Austria is mainly determined by the hard currency policy. As part of this policy, the attempt is made to hold the foreign exchange rate constant and, in particular, to keep the Austrian schilling–German mark relationship constant. Devaluation is not used as an instrument to encourage exports. The hard currency policy has worked very well. On the one hand, stable conditions for decision-making are achieved in foreign trade (especially that with the largest export and import market, Germany); on the other hand, imported inflation is damped. Since there is no serious domestic pressure for a change, this policy has acquired a large degree of international credibility. Due to the strong orientation of the Austrian currency to the German mark, the patterns of long- and short-term nominal interest rates of both countries are quite similar (see Tables G35 and G36), the slightly higher rates in Austria being a reflection of the difference in inflation rates between the two countries.

13.5 INTERNATIONAL RELATIONS

13.5.1 Geographic orientation and composition of trade

Austria has always sought to dismantle protectionist foreign trade and to establish an open, international economic structure. However, the State Treaty of 1955 (*Staatsvertrag*) forbade Austria to join the European Economic Community at its inception in 1958. In particular the State Treaty of 1955 includes the obligation of the 'everlasting neutrality' which prohibited Austria from entering any formal integration arrangements with Germany. Further attempts to reinterpret this State Treaty (e.g. in the 1960s) were frustrated by the Soviet Union, which raised political objections against an Austrian EU accession[1]. However, Austria entered the European Free Trade Association (EFTA) in 1959. Although this has substantially diverted trade flows towards the member states of EFTA, most of Austria's trade is still with EU member states. Considering the geographical distances to the important EFTA member states – which are located mainly in the north of Europe – this situation is not surprising. The country's pronounced trade orientation towards the European Union was a strong argument in favour of EU accession.

In 1994 EU states accounted for 63% of Austria's total exports and 66% of total imports. Germany is the most important trading partner (38% of total exports and 40% of imports) followed at some distance by Italy (8% of total exports and 9% of imports). Moreover, due to its geographical location between the western industrialised countries and the eastern European countries, Austria has benefited substantially from the opening of the former Eastern Bloc. Exports to eastern Europe account for 14% of Austrian's exports and 8% of its imports.

With an export share of around 37% (exports of goods and services relative to GDP) Austria has one of the highest levels of foreign trade involvement among OECD countries. However, in comparison to OECD average, Austria exports a smaller proportion of high-tech goods and a larger share of labour and resource intensive products; another indicator of the structural weakness of Austria's industry.

13.5.2 Balance of payments

Traditionally, Austria's trade balance has shown a chronic deficit of about 5% of GDP, which is usually counter-balanced by a surplus in the balance of services. Tourism, especially, has been the major source of funds for financing the large

trade deficits. That is why the current account was more or less balanced over the run of years. Since 1992, however, a persistent deficit in the current account statistic has been noticeable. This is due to a structural crisis in the tourism sector. A relatively high price level associated with the 'strong' Austrian schilling, changing tastes in favour of long-distance journeys, a high dependence on German tourists whose demand for holidays in Austria has fallen and a high regional and seasonal over-concentration with associated negative consequences are the reasons for the decline in tourism.

Since the early 1970s the capital account has shown a surplus in most of the years – a fact that can be attributed to a strong foreign demand for long-run fixed-interest-bearing securities. The capital account surplus and the current account deficit have resulted in a settled balance of payment with a small surplus such that no deviation from the hard currency policy is anticipated in the foreseeable future.

13.6 IMPACT OF EUROPEAN INTEGRATION

In 1994 the Austrian Institute of Economic Research (WIFO) estimated that EU membership (as opposed to merely belonging to the European Economic Area) would, over the period 1995–2000, lead to a cumulative increase in growth (2.8%) and employment (1.3%) but a cumulative decrease of retail inflation (3.3%). When a decisive majority (two thirds) voted in favour of an EU membership in June 1994, the Austrian population had high expectations about welfare effects through the EU accession.

Today, two years after the EU accession of Austria, the short-term effects of joining the EU are ambiguous and less than spectacular:

- Apart from a significant fall in prices for agricultural products, the inflation rate in 1995 has not fallen to the extent anticipated. Although the price increases for manufacturing products have came to a standstill, the prices in the service sector have been persistently moving upwards. Restricted competition in some sec-

---

[1] From a political point of view only the breakdown of the Soviet Union made the Austrian EU membership in 1995 possible.

tors, the market power of foreign producers and the fact that several price reductions have not been passed on to consumers are considered responsible for the disappointing performance in relation to inflation. At the time of writing, however, there are signs of a faster decrease in the inflation rate due to delayed repercussions of the accession to the EU.

- Existing price differentials relating to a number of consumer goods has made cross-border shopping in Italy and Germany very popular. The depreciation of the Italian lira and the lower VAT in Germany have encouraged many people to take advantage of opportunities to make purchases in the 'single market without frontiers' to the disadvantage of the domestic business sector.

These rather disappointing short-run effects of EU accession, in the context of initially inflated expectations of the population, has resulted in a degree of scepticism towards the EU on the part of the Austrian populace. The fact that Austria is a net contributor to the European Union and that the home population is currently dealing with major budget cuts introduced to achieve the Maastricht criteria has merely compounded this general feeling.

The over-optimistic short-run expectations of the Austrian population concerning the welfare effects of EU accession are to a large extent attributed to a political polarisation associated with the referendum and with the subsequent parliamentary elections in 1995. Politicians made exaggerated claims when describing the positive effects of EU membership and economists, the majority of whom argued for EU accession, failed to stress the long-run perspective of joining the EU. Opinion polls taken during 1996 suggests that, if a new referendum were held, the voters would probably reject EU membership. Politicians are faced with the need to convince Austrians of the overall value of membership by making clear how the country can benefit in the long-term.

13.7 SPECIAL ISSUES: THE AUSTRIAN SOCIAL PARTNERSHIP

This section deals with an institutional characteristic – the Social Partnership – that influences Austria's economic policy to a large extent. The motivation for this kind of economic cooperation dates back to the period between the First and the Second World Wars when the failure to establish a stable economic framework led to a civil war. With regard to this bad experience the Austrian politicians decided to create an institutionalised form of cooperation to create stable economic and political conditions. Practically speaking, the Austrian Social Partnership arose from the five price wage agreements between 1947 and 1951 which were very successful in avoiding wage push inflation in the era of reconstruction and which were supported by a broad consensus of representatives of both workers and employers.

Roughly speaking, this partnership is a kind of institutionalised cooperation under which basic economic policy is not determined by the prevailing economic circumstances but rather through key economic actors getting together round a table. A committee consisting of representatives from the government and important interest groups takes decisions on social and economic policy on the basis of minimising conflicts. To understand the working of this form of decision-making some of the country's features need to be highlighted:

- The strong centralisation of trade unions and the compulsory system of chambers leads to a small number of decision-makers, which makes close cooperation easier. On the one hand there are the interest groups which have legal status and receive public funding (*Kammern*): for the employers there is the Federal Chamber of Industry and Commerce (*Bundeskammer der gewerblichen Wirtschaft*) and for the employees, the Chamber of Workers (*Arbeiterkammer*). Another important organisation is the Chamber of Agriculture (*Landwirtschaftskammer*). On the other hand, other influential pressure groups exist which are characterised by voluntary membership: the employees are represented by the trade unions (*Gewerkschaftsbund*) and the employers by the confederation of business owners (*Industriellenvereinigung*). All of these organisations are centrally organised, whereby the basic guidelines are set by the central office.

- The historical and political development and the stability of the country since 1945 is characterised by long periods of grand coalition governments.
- The advisory function for the parliament is carried out by experts from political parties or from the interest groups, through which they have a great influence on the decision-making process.
- Traditionally in Austria there has always been a marked interdependence among the personnel, with employees in political offices also having functions in the interest groups, as well as decision-makers also working for trust funds and commissions; the implementation of the decisions taken is thus guaranteed.

13.7.1 The parity commission

The core of the Social Partnership is the parity commission for prices and incomes, which is based on voluntary cooperation. It is composed of members of the government, representatives of the Federal Chamber of Industry and Commerce, the Chamber of Agriculture, the Confederation of Trade Unions and the Chamber of Workers. Alongside informal contact between its members, this committee meets regularly to discuss and reach decisions on important questions of economic policy. Decisions must be taken unanimously making compromise obligatory. The meetings provide a forum for an early solution to a conflict or for a softening of differing opinions.

The parity commission is the main body to which three further sub-committees report: the sub-committee for prices, the sub-committee for incomes and the advisory board on economic and social questions.

13.7.2 Advisory board on economic and social questions

This sub-committee of the parity commission prepares reports and makes recommendations on general economic questions for the parity commission. In its current form, the social partnership goes far beyond questions of prices and incomes. Their recommendations do not represent completely independent expert opinion, but rather reflect the fact that a part of the discussion (and thus potential for conflict) has already been dealt with. Differences in opinions between politicians and experts on current matters of policy are very rare (unlike in Germany, where the body of expert consultants, *Sachverständigenrat*, is often at odds with the government). Almost all recommendations are made on the basis of a broad consensus, and this contributes to a general framework of political and economic stability. It is not uncommon for collective bargaining solutions to be achieved because the social partners are used to working in close cooperation in a wide range of economic issues. Parliament often merely ratifies important economic policy recommendations from the parity commission.

13.7.3 Prices sub-committee

Because of the small size of the economic area and the fact that in Austria the law on cartels is based on the principle of misuse rather than prohibition, close attention has to be given to the maintenance of competitive prices. This is guaranteed via two mechanisms: first, some prices are determined by the authorities; second, a large number of goods are subject to price control through the prices sub-committee. This does not entail controlling prices in the sense of a fixed price, but rather an administrative instrument to influence price trends in Austria. Due to the fact that a growing number of goods and services have been put outside of this kind of price control in recent years, the prices sub-committee's influence on economic performance has diminished.

13.7.4 Incomes sub-committee

In principle, all interest groups (or 'tariff partners') in the industrial sectors negotiate a guideline on the wage rate within their industries on the basis of a collective agreement. The tariff partners are obliged, however, not to start their individual negotiations until the basic bargaining position has been agreed upon in the incomes sub-committee of the parity commission. Thus a double 'filter' is built into wage negotiations in the form of the umbrella organisation for the interest groups, and through the discussion within the Social Partnership. This system ensures that the wage negotiations are in line with the general economic situation. Particular consideration is also given to the timing of the wage negotiations with the intention of achieving some continuity in the income policy. As a rule, this system ensures wage negotiations which are concluded swiftly and without resort to extreme measures.

13.7.5 The problems with the Austrian Social Partnership

It is undisputed that this kind of decision-making and problem-solving has brought considerable benefits in the form of stable economic conditions for Austria. Due to the breadth of involvement through the partnership, there are ample opportunities for compromise and bargaining which would not exist if the room for manoeuvre in negotiations was very limited. Nevertheless, the Austrian Social Partnership has been criticised on a number of counts:

- Not all groups which take part in the economic process are sufficiently involved in the system of the economic and social partnership. Thus the interests and preferences of groups which are inadequately represented receive too little consideration in the Austrian economic structure which is dominated by the Social Partnership. On the other hand, it is possible that influential groups which are not included in the partnership can operate, to some degree, as free riders and achieve advantages, without considering the implications for the economy as a whole.
- The powerful administrative network and the 'all-pervasiveness' of the social partners in the economy gives rise to the possibility that some groups may pursue self-interest under the guise of a Social Partnership. The danger of bribery, corruption and 'mutual self-interest' is great.

- Because of the centralised organisation and the relatively large influence of a small and closed group of experts, there is the danger of a lack of innovation and of insufficient flexibility in recognising new tasks and problems. The Social Partnership is accused, for example, of being unable to cope with the structural change in the economy. In that sense the Austrian Social Partnership is another reason for the structural problems discussed in Section 13.2.4 on economic structure and sector shares.

All things considered, the institution of the Social Partnership can be judged as having a positive impact within Austria. It has undoubtedly contributed to the economic and political stability which Austria has experienced.

13.8 BIBLIOGRAPHY

Abele, H., Nowotny, E., Schleicher, S., Winckler, G. (eds) (1989): *Handbuch der österreichischen Wirtschaftspolitik*, (3rd edn), Manz Verlag, Vienna

Butschek, F. (1985): *Die österreichische Wirtschaft im 20. Jahrhundert*, Austrian Institute of Economic Research, Gustav Fischer Verlag, Vienna, 1985

Hackl, F., Schneider, F. (1995): 'Austrian economic policy since 1945: an exploratory analysis', *Journal des Economistes et des Etudes Humaines*, **VI**(2, 3), July/September

Handler, H., E. Hochreiter (1996): *The Austrian Economy in the European Union: A First Assessment*, WIFO Working Paper Nr. 88, 1996

Neck, R. (1990): 'Was bleibt vom Austro-Keynesianismus?', in Beigewum and Memorandumsgruppe (eds), *Steuerungsprobleme der Wirtschaftspolitik*, Vienna and Bremen, pp. 159–60

Nowotny, E. (1982): 'Nationalized industries as an instrument of stabilization policy', *Annalen der Gemeinwirtschaft*, **51** (1), pp. 41–57

Nowotny, E., (1978): *Das System der 'Sozial- und Wirtschaftspartnerschaft' in Österreichgesamtwirtschaftliche und einzelbetriebliche Formen und Effekte*, Die Betriebswirtschaft (DBW) 38/2: pp. 273–285

Nowotny, E., Winkler, G. (eds) (1994): *Grundzüge der Wirtschaftspolitik Österreichs*, Manz Verlag, Vienna, 1994

OECD (1994, 1995): *Economic Surveys*, Austria, Paris

OECD (1995): *Economic Outlook,* **58**, Paris

Olson, M. (1985): *Aufstieg und Niedergang von Nationen*, J.C.B. Mohr, Tübingen (Paul Siebeck), Tübingen

Rosner, P. (1987): 'Sozialpartnerschaft – eine Revision', *Wirtschaftspolitische Blätter*, 4(87), 515–28

Schnabel, C. (1992): 'Korporatismus und gesamtwirtschaftliche Entwicklung', *IW-Trends*, **19**, 91–102

Winckler, G. (1988): 'Der AustroKeynesianismus und sein Ende', *Österreichische Zeitschrift für Politikwissenschaft*, **3**, 221–30

CHAPTER 14

Sweden

Jan-Evert Nilsson

14.1 INSTITUTIONAL AND HISTORICAL CONTEXT

Sweden has long been characterised by unusual political stability. The Social Democrats were in power uninterruptedly for 40 years until 1976, and during much of that time they enjoyed a majority in Parliament. This stability reflects both great cohesion in the electorate (people voted according to class membership) and an electoral system that favoured a large party that was in power.

During the post-war period, voting along class lines has diminished in extent. Today's Swedish voters have a far greater propensity to switch parties between two elections. In addition, the Constitution has been rewritten. The old bicameral system has been abandoned in favour of a unicameral system in which all parties that receive at least 4% of the votes cast in a parliamentary election are represented in parliament. The size of this representation is directly proportional to each party's share of the votes cast. In the previous electoral system there was a built-in over-representation of the largest party, which contributed to facilitating the possibilities of building a majority government.

The result of these two changes has been an intensification of the struggle to gain power. Since 1976 the Social Democrats have been in power for 11 years, while Sweden has been led by non-Socialist coalition governments for 9 years. For the past 15 years, the country has been led by minority governments. One effect of this change in the political system has been both sharpening the contention for power and shortening the time perspective in politics.

Sweden's economic development during the 1950s and 1960s, as was also true of most other European countries, was distinguished by large and steady economic growth. Recessions were weak and short-lived. There was full employment. Many viewed this favourable economic development as a result of a successful economic policy. Confidence in the possibility of using Keynesian theory to assure full employment grew dramatically in all political parties. This is an important explanation for Sweden's main strategy to parry the effects of the oil crisis of 1973–74, the aim of which was to stimulate consumption in order to guarantee a domestic demand that could counteract the demand-dampening effects of the rise in oil prices. The change in government in 1976 led to an intensification of efforts to carry on the policy that the Social Democrats had so successfully pursued during the 1960s. The non-Socialist parties wanted to convince the voters of their own ability to sustain full employment. The government therefore chose to conduct an expansive financial policy that helped maintain the demand for manpower even as the labour market situation was helping to drive up Swedish wage and salary levels, which in turn entailed a deterioration in the international competitiveness of Swedish industry. The growth in exports was arrested and the balance-of-trade deficit increased. The resulting situation was dealt with by repeated devaluations of the Swedish currency. Altogether, the Swedish krona was devalued by one third between 1977 and 1982.

Hence this economic policy was based on recurrent devaluations that helped to temporarily bolster the international competitiveness of the Swedish business sector. The strategy was partially successful. Devaluations during recessions provided the business sector with the prerequisites, in terms of costs, for increasing production and profitability during the following economic upswing. During those upswings, however, the gains registered by devaluation were regularly devoured. Large salary increases meant that the cost situation in relation to that in competing countries deteriorated once again, as the rate of inflation was pushed up. The economic slumps were accompanied by an expansive financial policy that assured high domestic demand. Full employment could be maintained despite a weak international market.

However, the successes in the area of employment also meant that economic slumps were followed by repeated cost crises. The level of activity in the segments of the business sector competing on the foreign market declined dramatically, and workers were laid off. These segments were forced to bear the entire burden of economic downturns which combined decline in international demand with rising salary costs per unit produced. This resulted in strong pressure to reduce industrial employment. During the 1970s, the government sought to counteract this by giving extensive support to particularly vulnerable businesses. These measures, however, could not prevent the gradual shrinkage of Sweden's industrial base. The balance-of-payments deficit became chronic.

The combination of weak economic growth, full employment and a permanent balance-of-payments deficit could not be sustained in the long run. It would be necessary to dampen domestic demand and accept higher unemployment in order to eliminate the balance-of-payments deficit. The Social Democratic regime then in power decided to take that step in the fall of 1990. The changeover in economic policy was simultaneously successful and devastating. The success consisted of a dramatic downturn in infla-

tion. Interest rates did not decline correspondingly, however, and so real rates of interest rose dramatically, which created a serious real estate and financial crisis. An unfavourable cost situation combined with high real interest rates also contributed to a major decrease in industrial production. The priority given by the government to inflation meant that this time it did not confront the slump in production and employment with an expansive financial policy. The Bank of Sweden, meanwhile, stood firm with its exchange rate commitments in relation to the ECU. Devaluation was no longer perceived as a legitimate solution.

The cost crisis gradually developed into a general economic crisis that was to have impact on every sector of the Swedish economy. The setback was the worst since the depression years of 1931–32. The gross domestic product (GDP) fell three years in a row, an event never previously experienced in the 20th century. From 1991 through 1993, the gross national product (GNP) fell by 4.7%, gross investments went down by 36%, private consumption by 3.6% and public consumption by 0.5%. The number of people employed shrank by 11% while unemployment, including people supported by labour market policy measures, rose from 3.3% to 9.8%. This increase primarily reflected a drastic slump in employment in Swedish industry, where the number of people employed went down by 22.6% during this period. Sweden's unemployment had thus risen to European levels, and no means to achieve rapid improvement could be discerned. The changes on the labour market were the primary reason why the government's borrowing requirement increased from 1.1% to 12% of GDP (Table G15).

14.2 MAIN ECONOMIC CHARACTERISTICS

Sweden is a country large in area and small in population. Its 450 000 km² accounts for 14% of total EU territory, while its population of 8.9 million comprises only 2.4% of the population of the EU. Since 1971, the population has gone up by 877 000, or 10.8% (Table G17). Population increase in Sweden is 4.8% below the average for EU countries. The Swedish labour force (people both employed and unemployed) has increased by 564 000 (14%) during this same period. This increase is the result of rising numbers of women gainfully employed outside the home. During this period, women's share of the labour force has grown from 35% to 49% (Table G18).

14.2.1 GDP and output growth

Sweden, Japan and Finland are the countries who experienced the largest economic growth between 1870 and 1970. Since 1970, economic development in Sweden has been weak, not only as compared with earlier times but also in comparison with other countries. During the period 1971–93, the average annual real rate of GDP growth was 1.6%, a rate of growth significantly lower than the rates in EUR 15 (2.4%), the USA (2.6%) and Japan (3.7%) (Table G23). One characteristic of developments in Sweden is that the slowdown in growth during the 1970s was greater than in other European countries. From 1961 to 1970, the GDP rose at an average of 4.6% annually. During the next 10 years, growth declined to an annual average of 2% and Sweden, along with the UK, presented the lowest rate of growth among the industrialised nations. Unlike the other countries in EUR 15, except for the UK and Luxembourg, the growth rate in Sweden did not slow down further in the 1980s, which helped reduce the gap in growth in relation to EUR 15 (Table G23).

The severe economic depression in the early 1990s meant that the picture changed again. Between 1991 and 1995, Swedish growth averaged 0.3% annually, which was by far the lowest figure throughout the EU. The average growth for EUR 15 during the same period was 1.3%, which was nevertheless only about half that for the USA.

This weak growth since 1970 has resulted in Sweden's falling behind in welfare development. In 1970, Sweden's per capita GDP exceeded that of EUR 15 by 22%, and she could boast the highest per capita GDP of those 15 countries except for Luxembourg. Twenty-five years later GDP per capita in EUR 15 exceeds that of Sweden by 3%.

Based on GDP per capita nine of the fifteen countries in the EU have higher material welfare than Sweden (Table G24).

14.2.2 Unemployment, productivity and wages

One particular feature of Sweden's economic development was the country's long success in combining economic growth with full employment. Swedish employment rose by almost 10% from 1974 to 1985. Most of this increase occurred in the public sector, whereas industrial employment decreased. During this period, employment remained unchanged in the EU.

During this same period, unemployment in Sweden ranged between 1.6% and 3.9% (see Figure 14.1). The growth in employment increased during the second half of the 1980s, even though it was below the average for the EU. The increase in employment in the public sector slowed substantially, while there was an increase in growth in the non-industrial private sector. Industrial employment continued to decline. The combined effect was that unemployment was reduced from 3% in 1985 to 1.8% in 1990. The country's politicians were proud of having so successfully prevented the emergence of mass unemployment of the kind that was common for most of Europe.

Most economists pointed out that this success demanded a price in the form of a continuing worsening of the international competitiveness of Swedish industry. Low unemployment led to relatively rapid increases in wages. During the period 1971–90, costs for wages and salaries in the business sector rose by an annual average of 9.3%. This rise during this period exceeded that in Sweden's major trade partners by 26%.

The increase in productivity was significantly lower during the same period, on average only 2.7%, which implies that the overall increase in productivity fell short of that in major trade partners by 15%. The gap between rises in salaries and wages and increased productivity meant that costs per unit produced in Sweden rose faster than in competing countries. During this period, 1971–90, the relative unit labour cost in national

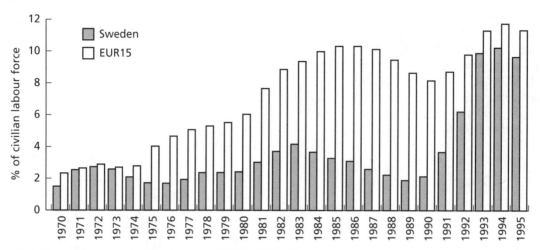

Figure 14.1 Unemployment in Sweden and EUR15, 1970–95
Source: Eurostat, Table G20.

currency for the Swedish business sector rose by 49%. The negative effects of this rise in costs were somewhat neutralised by the repeated depreciations of the Swedish crown, which amounted to 37% altogether.

⌐ The economic downturn and the restructuring of economic policy in the fall of 1990 have meant an appreciable improvement in the competitive situation of Swedish business. Between 1991 and 1995, labour cost increases have lagged behind those in competing countries by 3% while increase in production has exceeded theirs by 12%. As the value of Swedish currency simultaneously fell by 23%, the beginning of the 1990s signalled an improvement by 32% in the international competitiveness of the business sector, expressed as unit labour cost. This advance has contributed to a rapid increase of Swedish exports.

Cost developments during this period recall what happened from 1980 to 1982, when the picture of relative unit labor costs as reflected in common currencies improved by 24%. At that time, the change was of only a temporary character. During the subsequent years up to 1990, the business sector lost all of the cost advantage it enjoyed between 1980 and 1982. The question is whether the recently improved cost situation similarly represents only a temporary upswing, or if a lasting change in the pattern of develop-

ment is truly in place. There is one main difference which may indicate that the options for a lasting change this time is greater. In the beginning of the 1980s unemployment was just about 3%, now it exceeds 9%.

Simultaneously, as has already been mentioned, the political reorganisations of 1990 entailed a serious rise in unemployment. The combination of a restrictive fiscal policy, a firm currency exchange policy, a tight money policy and an emerging economic slowdown resulted in a decrease in GNP and employment, and a rise in unemployment, from 1991 to 1993. Employment went down in all of the major segments of the economy. Since 1993, a small increase in employment has been registered, primarily in manufacturing industries, but unemployment has only marginally decreased.

14.2.3 Inflation

The inflation rate also rose in Sweden in connection with the 1973–74 oil crisis. It doubled from 1973 to 1975, from 7.0% to 14.5% (Figure 14.2). The inflation impulses arrived in Sweden somewhat later than in other EU countries, but in return the increase was larger. Although Sweden, unlike most other EU countries, had managed to prevent a large increase in unemployment during the 1970s, inflation was no

Figure 14.2 Inflation: price deflator for private consumption
Source: Eurostat, Table G31.

higher than the EU average throughout that period (Table G31). Thus accumulated price rises in Sweden in the second half of the 1970s amounted to 54%, as compared with 59% for EUR 15. Inflation began to fall throughout the entire EU area after 1980.

The 1982 devaluation of the Swedish krona by 16% broke this downward trend. Between 1982 and 1983, inflation in Sweden rose from 8.3% to 10.1% while dropping from 10.4% to 8.4% in EUR 15. After 1983, inflation in Sweden, as throughout the EU, went down gradually until 1987, when the inflation rate went up once again. Whereas the increase in EUR 15 was moderate – from 4.1% in 1987 to 5.4% in 1990 – the corresponding increase in Sweden was significantly larger – from 4.8% to 8.8%. This vigorous rise in the inflation rate was a major reason why the Swedish government tightened its fiscal policy during the fall of 1990. This austerity policy resulted in a drastic decrease in inflation, so that by 1992 it was only 1%. Thus during the 1990s, the Swedish inflation rate corresponds well with the average of that in the EU.

14.2.4 Consumption and investment

The share of the Swedish GNP represented by private consumption has gradually declined since 1960. At that time, it was 59.2%. During the 1960s, it sank to 56%. This decline continued during the 1970s to 52.8%, and during the 1980s to 51.8% (Table G28). This decline primarily reflects a continuing increase in public consumption. The private consumption share of the GNP is lower in Sweden than in the other EU countries, even though Denmark, in recent years, has reached the Swedish level.

As in other EU countries, gross fixed capital formation in Sweden has gradually declined since the mid-1960s, and since the 1970s has been under the EU average (see Table G30). The private business sector accounts for approximately 70% of total investments, which is why changes in gross fixed capital formation are strongly influenced by the investments of the business sector. The first half of the 1970s was characterised by a comparatively high level of investments by the business sector, while there was a decrease in investments by the housing and public sectors. After the oil crisis, business sector investment activity stagnated, but to some extent this was compensated for by increased investments by the housing and public sectors. The long upward economic trend during the second half of the 1980s supported an impressive increase in the total volume of investments, which rose by 31% between 1985 and 1990. The restructuring of economic policy in the fall of 1991, with the simultaneous rise in interest rates, contributed to a notable reduction in the investment volume. Investments by the business sector fell by 29%, and investments in housing by 70%, between 1990 and 1994.

14.3 GOVERNMENT INVOLVEMENT IN THE ECONOMY

A rough indicator of the extent of government involvement in the economy is provided by the ratio between public expenditures and GDP. In Sweden, in 1950, it was 24.7%. Thereafter, it has gradually risen to the beginning of the 1990s. In 1993, it reached its highest level thus far – 72.8% – a value that exceeds those of other countries by a wide margin. Evaluated by this indicator, the Swedish government is far more involved in the economy than that of any other EU country. By way of comparison, it can be observed that the corresponding 1993 figure for the UK was 43.6%, for Germany 49.6%, for France 55.0%, for the Netherlands 55.3% and for Denmark, 63.8%.

That the ratio has risen depends – during different periods of time – on rapid increases in public expenditures, whereas the increase during other periods reflects the slow growth in GDP. During the 1950s and 1960s, public consumption grew by an annual average of almost 6% annually, while the GDP rose by an annual average of only 4%. During the 1970s, the increase in public consumption was reduced by nearly half, but at the same time public transfer payments doubled and the GDP increase fell by 50%, which meant that the ratio between public outlays and GDP continued to rise. The rate of increase in public consumption dropped by half once again during the 1980s, simultaneously as the increase in public transfer payments dropped by 75%. The reduction in growth of GDP was less this time, which explains why the ratio went from 62% in 1980 to 61% in 1990. During the first half of the 1990s, public expenditures have by and large stabilised at the 1990 level, and transfer payments have risen by only 18%. Despite all this, the weak economic growth

during this period has resulted in a continued increase in the ratio.

14.3.1 Public expenditure

Of the public outlays (see Figure 14.3), over half consist of transfers, about a quarter of municipal and over one-tenth of state consumption. In fixed prices, the extent of the transfers has increased by 240% since 1970. During the 1970s, transfers to the business sector rose by 261% as a result of the government's ambitions to counteract the structural transformation that followed in the wake of the 1973–74 oil crisis. Vulnerable businesses like the shipbuilding, steel, forestry and textile and clothing industries received state support to help them survive in the new competitive situation. During the same period, housing policy transfers rose by 312% because a higher inflation rate required larger rent subsidies to prevent increases in housing costs. Swedish policy during the 1970s was based on the notion that the current economic problems were of a transitory nature, hence the state stepped in to compensate groups afflicted by the new economic situation.

Confidence in this economic policy flagged over time. There was a growing awareness that the enervated economic growth represented more far-reaching changes than those associated with an ordinary recession. The governmental changeover in 1982, when a Social Democratic minority government succeeded a non-Socialist

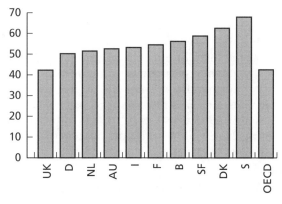

Figure 14.3 Public expenditure, 1995 (% of GDP)
Source: Eurostat, Table G32.

coalition, meant a reorganisation of economic policy. The government pointed to the need for restraint in public expenditures. However, public expenditures continued to grow. The protracted international economic prosperity meant that restraint was limited to reducing the rate of increase in public expenditures. The major intervention was made in state consumption, which rose by only 0.8% during the 1980s; during that time, municipal consumption rose by 21% and transfer payments by 33%. The picture is somewhat different during the first half of the 1990s. Municipal consumption is declining, while state consumption has risen by 10% and public transfers by 18%.

One important difference is concealed behind the increase in public transfers during the 1980s and 1990s as compared with the situation in the 1970s, when the increase was partly the result of larger transfers to the business sector. These continued to rise until 1993, and then the increase stopped. Thus the transfers to the business sector in 1995 exceed the corresponding transfers in 1983 by only 5.5%. During the same period, on the other hand, public transfers to households rose by 37%. The greatest increase occurred in housing policy transfers, which went up by 78%. In absolute numbers, the greatest increase transpired in transfers to retired people, which rose by 33%. In addition, payments to unemployed people and recipients of social benefits increased dramatically during the 1990s as a result of rising unemployment. The fact that transfers are now rising as a consequence of increased transfers to households implies greater difficulties in winning political support for further efforts to reduce expenditures. This probably indicates that the government's interest in creating leeway for higher taxes will increase. The alternative is that the rate of growth increases so that the need for transfers declines at the same time as the government's tax revenues go up. The problem is that European experiences indicate that there is at present no public policy which offers such a happy future in the short term.

14.3.2 Revenue sources

The increase in public expenditures has largely been counterbalanced by increases in public revenues. Public revenues as a share of GDP have also gradually risen from 23.7% in 1950 to 47.6% in 1970 and to 59.5% in 1995 (Table G29). Most of these revenues come from taxes. The tax burden, measured as tax revenues as a percentage of GDP, has hence risen from 20.6% in 1950 to 40.5% in 1970 and to 50.4% in 1995. This means that the Swedish tax burden is significantly higher than in other EU countries, with the exception of Denmark.

The distribution among different types of taxes has changed over time. At the outset, the construction of the welfare state was financed by higher income taxes. An extremely progressive income tax was introduced, and income taxes thereafter continued to rise by gradual stages. In 1960, an average of 18% of the total income was paid in taxes. Ten years later that share had risen to 29.6%. During the 1980s it rose further, to 34.2%, before a new tax system with only two classes of taxes was introduced in 1991. This tax reform was aimed at making it more profitable to work, save and invest for the future. Hopes were great that the tax reorganisation would have dynamic effects in the form of increased economic growth. The new tax system has resulted in the reduction of tax as a percentage of income to 29.5%. The reason this tax reform was instituted was that there was a broad political consensus that the old tax system with its extremely progressive income tax was impeding economic growth. In 1950, direct taxes contributed 53% of total tax revenues, a share which had declined to 43% by 1995.

During the 1960s and 1970s, payroll taxes, together with social contributions, both legislated and regulated by negotiations, rose from 3.4% of the income of industrial workers in 1960 to 37.8% in 1980. In 1995, this share was 38.9%. In 1950, payroll taxes accounted for 12% of total tax revenues, a share which rose to 27% by 1995.

The third important tax resource is sales taxes. In 1960 a general sales tax was introduced at the end of the process – i.e. involving sales to the consumer. Originally, this implied a price increase of 4.2%, but it was later raised to 10% or 10% of the product's price including the value-added tax (VAT). In 1969 the general sales tax was replaced by a VAT, which implied that taxes were levied on the increasing value accrued by a product during its process from raw material to the consumer. When the new tax was introduced, the tax rate was 11.1%, but it was gradually raised until, by 1995, it was 25%. Simultaneously, the base for the tax levy has been expanded on several occasions. When, on 1 January 1995, Sweden joined the EU as a member the VAT system was changed. The tax rate became differentiated for different types of goods and services. For most goods and services it was still 25%. On food the tax was reduced to 12%, while a VAT on newspaper of 6% was introduced.

During recent years, political attention has been addressed to the possibilities of taxing environmentally hazardous wastes. Discussions of the advantages and disadvantages of 'tax shifting' between payroll taxes and environmental taxes have been carried on. The first step in this direction was taken in 1991 through the introduction of a tax on carbon dioxide emissions. At the end of 1996 the tax rate is SEK 0.09 per kilogram carbon dioxide emissions for manufacturing industry and SEK 0.36 per kilogram emissions in other sectors (transportation, heating etc.)

14.3.3 The PSBR and the national debt

The public sector borrowing requirement (PSBR) rose from less than 2% of the GDP in the late 1970s to 13% in 1982, until increasing growth helped to bring it down. In 1988 and 1989, the borrowing requirement was negative. Table G34 shows that Sweden's borrowing requirement between 1981 and 1990 amounted to an annual average of 0.8%, which was appreciably lower than the 4.1% average annual increase recorded by EUR 14. This great difference is explained by Sweden's having a negative PSBR during 1987–90. This major improvement in PSBR was made possible by an increase in growth, which brought about a large increase in public revenues. The state's revenues

as share of GDP went up from 61% in 1985 to 64.9% in 1990 (Table G33).

The economic downturn at the beginning of the 1990s took a major toll on public finances. The negative growth entailed lower tax revenues, while growing unemployment contributed to painful increases in public transfers to households. The PSBR rose rapidly. Within three years, a negative borrowing requirement of 4.2% of GDP was transformed to a PSBR that corresponded to 12.3% of GDP. Between 1991 and 1995, Sweden's borrowing requirement exceeded that of EUR 15 by 50%. This dramatic worsening of public finances forced the Swedish government repeatedly to impose austerity measures. The non-Socialist government that was in power when the deficit developed offered a number of proposals for savings. Their policies were hampered by the fact that the four parties who constituted the government disagreed as to how the economies should be carried out, as well as by the fact that the opposition was opposed to cuts in public expenditures. The Parliamentary elections of 1994 replaced the centre-right coalition with the Social Democrats. When they assumed power, they chose to continue with the non-Socialist austerity policies. One difference can be noted between the strategies of the two governments. The Social Democrats have shown a greater inclination to improve state finances through raising taxes.

The large public sector borrowing requirement during the 1990s meant that Sweden's national debt increased by 135% between 1990 and 1995. This in turn means that in 1995, the national debt amounted to 83.8% of GDP. The Swedish national debt has been rising since the end of the 1960s. In 1970, it corresponded to 17.9% of GDP; by 1980, it had risen to 36.2%. Five years later, it had nearly doubled again, to 64.6%. In 1995, only Belgium, Italy, Greece and Ireland had larger national debts.

14.3.4 Industrial policy

The first political reaction to the structural problems that afflicted some segments of Swedish industry during the second half of the 1970s was to use state funds to support the threatened businesses. Between 1975 and 1982, the state's net costs in fixed prices for this industrial policy rose by 730%. A significant part of this help took the form of non-recurring support for vulnerable businesses, primarily shipbuilding and steel, and for state-owned companies. This policy was gradually phased out during the 1980s, and a new policy was aimed at creating a business climate with incentives that encouraged renewal and growth.

The government has assigned three roles to economic policy. One role is to create efficiency by designing an institutional framework within which companies must operate. One important prerequisite for exploiting the potential for growth in the economy is that the markets for products, resources and capital function efficiently. The government therefore sees it as its task to eliminate unnecessary regulations, obstructions to setting up businesses and competitive distortions, while supporting such institutions that contribute to the efficient functioning of the markets. The deregulations in such areas as air traffic, telecommunications, postal services and public transportation are examples of state efforts aimed at enhancing efficiency in the Swedish economy. It has been emphasised by the business sector that efficiency would be fostered by a modernisation of labour legislation. The union movement's opposition to such changes, however, has led the government to forgo them.

Economic policy also has a supportive role, which includes promoting the establishment of new businesses and stimulating growth in small and medium companies. One activity here was the establishment in 1994 of 24 regional corporations with 51% state ownership; their task is to support small and medium companies with financing and advice. Among other things, they are to strengthen the competence of company management and initiate proficient performance by the boards of directors of small companies.

Finally, economic policy has been assigned an instigatory role. This means that the state has a responsibility to support research and technical development. Traditionally, Swedish state support of industrial R&D has mainly been funnelled through research at universities. The weakness in this approach has been the great uncertainty about the extent to which these investments culminate in commercially interesting results. In the prevailing labour market situation, the government has intensified its efforts to increase the commercial value of state R&D investments. In 1993, Parliament adopted a program, suggested by the centre-right government, to stimulate technological development in the business sector by establishing a competitive R&D environment in Sweden. This is to come about with the help of 19 independent foundations, which were beyond the range for public policy, that were given a nonrecurring governmental appropriation of SEK 20 billion to promote research, innovation and the dissemination of technology. The succeeding labour government has changed the research foundations in order to gain influence on the foundations' allocation of research money.

14.3.5 Regional policy

Swedish regional policy was established in the mid-1960s in response to major depopulation of rural areas in the northern parts of the country. Structural rationalisations in forestry and agriculture meant that people were forced to move to coastal cities and to the south where expanding industries were in need of an expanding work-force. With the passage of time, there was growing resistance to moving. Regional policy was presented as a means of industrialising the vulnerable regions and thus increasing the demand for a work-force in those areas of Sweden as well. On a superficial level, this policy was successful. During the 1970s, emigration from the targeted regional support area ceased as industrial employment rose. In this sense, regional policy had achieved what it had been intended to achieve. Furthermore, the structural rationalisations in forestry and agriculture had now gone so far that the numbers of people active in these businesses were relatively few. Hence this structural rationalisation no longer constituted a major motivation for the population shifts in this region.

The structural problems in industry during the 1970s and 1980s contributed to a partial redirection of regional policy. Industrial regions with structural problems were identified as new areas to be given priority. The area to be supported by regional policy was expanded. Industrial regions in central and southern Sweden were added to the old regional policy support area in northern Sweden. Regional policy in these new areas sought to ease the industrial adjustments and contribute to the modernisation of the business sector. The support of companies through regional policy has primarily cushioned the full blow of the structural transformations in these regions. The rate of transformation has thus been adapted to the conditions prevailing in the regions. At the same time, this implies that some of the investments are being made in the businesses that constitute a part of the regional problem. To some extent the policy support the established industrial structure in the designated areas.

The rise in unemployment at the beginning of the 1990s altered the prerequisites for regional policy. In a full-employment economy, unemployment constituted an acceptable indicator of the occurrence of regional problems. Unemployment in the areas supported by regional policy was higher than the national average. Unemployment was a regional/local problem. The rise in unemployment meant that this (previously) regional problem was transformed into a national problem. The regional differences in unemployment dwindled simultaneously as the level of unemployment rose dramatically. The current situation has stimulated debate as to which regions actually suffer regional problems. In parts of the major metropolitan regions – Stockholm, Göteborg and Malmö – the unemployment problem is greater than in many of the areas prioritised by regional policy.

This discussion is abetted by the fact that Sweden, as a new member of the EU, also has access to the EU Structural Funds. The geographical target areas in Sweden – Objectives 2, 5b and 6 – are characterised by embracing the entire national support area plus certain segments that lie outside it. At the same time, the Swedish government hopes that the Structural Funds money from the EU can be treated as an addendum to the country's regional policy. This would mean that the areas supported by regional policy would receive a large increase in the resources set aside for regions. In all probability, the future will show that access to relevant projects and the supply of supplementary financial sources are inadequate to enable the areas identified for support to take advantage of the economic resources allotted to them.

14.4 FINANCIAL SYSTEM

In 1992 the Swedish banking system was verging on collapse. Several factors contributed to the enormous growth both in Sweden's lending portfolios during the latter half of the 1980s and in the increased element of risk in the investments of both banks and other credit institutions. Deregulation of the financial market resulted in a great increase in lending portfolios. At the same time, the Swedish economy was enjoying a period of great growth. Lending was also encouraged by a high rate of inflation and expectations of continued inflation. High marginal taxes and generous deductions for interest payments by individual taxpayers also contributed to an increasing demand for credit. Finally, the increasingly intensive competition for market shares led to imprudent credit approvals. The effect of this was that the overall lending by credit institutions rose very dramatically. Between 1985 and 1990, the increase was from a little over 90% to nearly 150% of GDP.

At the beginning of the 1990s there were changes in economic policy that radically altered the prerequisites for banks and other credit institutions. The tax system was reformed so that marginal taxes on income were lowered to maximum 50% and deduction possibilities on income taxes were reduced. Subsidies to the housing sector were decreased. The rapid reduction in inflation in Sweden also had an impact on the credit institutions. And then there was the general business slowdown both in Sweden and internationally.

The changes mentioned above led to falling real estate prices. Due to the previous system of regulations, Swedish banks had more real estate-related loans than their counterparts in other countries. That meant that most Swedish banks were hit very hard by falling real estate prices and the collapse of real estate firms. Credits for housing had been extended during the late 1980s in the expectation that real estate prices would continue to rise. The banks were also hit by the fact that lending levels which they themselves did not accept were often approved by credit companies that were customers or subsidiaries of the banks.

The credit companies were the first to be hurt by the financial crisis. Since they had earlier been favoured by liberal legislation, the field was flooded by the end of the 1980s, which forced margins down. Some companies chose to expand their lending in order to safeguard profit levels. The result was a marked deterioration in the quality of their assets. Then, when real estate prices fell and the real rate of interest soared, the financial crisis was a fact in the fall of 1990. Credit companies were hit hard. Their numbers fell by more than half as compared with the top year of 1988, and credit company share of total lending to the public sank to about 6%.

The crisis reached the banks in 1991, when the banking sector as a whole showed negative results. The banks were then affected by the general liquidity crisis caused by the increasing difficulty of borrowing from abroad and by the steadily shrinking time for repayment of loans to Swedish banks. They received lower ratings from international audit evaluation organisations, which upped their borrowing costs. In that situation the government, in the fall of 1992, elected to guarantee the liabilities of Swedish banks and certain other credit institutions to depositors and other creditors.

Now, five years later, the Swedish banks have survived the crisis. Profitability has been revived and credit losses have contracted to the point where, in most cases, they are less than 1% of the banks' credit portfolios. The banks' capital ratios have again risen to satisfactory levels.

In certain respects the crisis has helped to strengthen the Swedish banks. The big credit losses forced them to cut back on personnel and reduce the number of branch offices, which makes them appear now to be cost effective. This can be a good thing now that the market is weak, lending is still less than before the bank crisis, and the competitive situation has become more acute.

Many leading European and American banks have established operations in Stockholm offering corporate and investment banking services. The realisation of the European Monetary Union will probably heighten the foreign competition in the field. Deregulation has also entailed the dissolving of the old distinction among banking, insurance and savings institutions. Insurance companies, mortgage banks and retail chains have opened niche banks that communicate with their customers through the telephone system, backed by advanced technology.

14.5 INTERNATIONAL RELATIONS

Sweden is an open economy with exports of goods and services that on average amount to 33.2% (1991–95). The EU is its most important market. Nearly two thirds of Swedish exports go to member states. The single most important export market is Germany, which received 13.3% of Sweden's total exports in 1994, followed by Great Britain (10.2%), Norway (8.1%) and the USA. (8.0%). In recent years, exports to the Far East have particularly increased. Countries there absorb 10% of Swedish exports, which makes that part of the world a more important market than North America. The significance of central and eastern Europe as export markets for Swedish production has also increased during the 1990s, even though their share of the total consumption of Swedish goods is still low. In 1994, countries in central and eastern Europe accounted for only 3% of the total value of Swedish exports.

Natural resources still play an important economic role in Sweden. Forest based products – wood, pulp and paper – form the single most important group of export products with 17% of the Swedish export, followed by machinery (16.5%) and vehicles (14%).

Since the mid-1960s, Sweden has had a deficit in its balance on current transactions. Between 1965 and 1995, the country has shown a positive balance for only 6 years. In this period the total foreign gross debt has grown from zero to SEK 1 300 000 000. Reduced by Swedish assets in foreign countries the total debts amount to SEK 600 000 000.

During the last few years, the deficit has been turned into a surplus. This has primarily resulted from the growing surplus in the balance of trade following a major increase in exports, which was inspired by a strong surge in the international economic situation and the lasting effects of Sweden's improved competitiveness resulting from the depreciation of the krona in 1992. At the same time, the small increase in disposable income meant that imports rose much less than exports. Unlike the trade balance, the service balance shows a deficit, which has nevertheless decreased significantly since 1992 thanks to a reduction in the deficit in the net foreign exchange. The weakening of the Swedish currency has resulted in an increased interest in tourism in Sweden.

14.6 SPECIAL ISSUES

14.6.1 Internationalisation

The Swedish economy is heavily dependent on international companies, i.e. companies that have subsidiaries in other countries. The number of employees in Swedish companies abroad is significantly higher than the numbers employed by foreign-owned companies in Sweden. In 1993, Swedish companies employed over 535 000 people abroad, while only 210 000 people in Sweden were employed by foreign-owned companies in Sweden. The former figure implies that the number of employees in Swedish companies abroad amounts to 73% of the people employed by those companies in Sweden. That share has risen continuously since the 1970s. If this development continues, it will not be long before the Swedish business sector is larger abroad than at home.

In recent years the number of people employed abroad by the largest Swedish compa-

nies' has gone down, no doubt as a consequence of those companies' foreign acquisitions during the late 1980s. Such purchases are probably followed by structural rationalisations involving the disposal of irrelevant enterprises. Among smaller companies, however, in this context those with fewer than 1 000 employees, the number of people employed abroad continues to increase.

14.6.2 Research and development

Among OECD countries, Sweden has the largest R&D investments in the business sector. These investments amount to 2.2% of GDP, a share that can be compared with 1.9% for the USA and Japan and 1.5% for Germany.

R&D activities in Sweden are carried out mainly in manufacturing industries and universities. Industrial R&D is concentrated in a few large concerns. Six engineering industries – Ericsson, Volvo, Saab, Scania, ABB and Sandvik – accounted for 51% of industrial R&D outlays in 1991. Large pharmaceutical concerns – Astra, Pharmacia, Perstorp and Nobel Industries – accounted for a further 18%. Hence these ten concerns accounted for three quarters of all industrial R&D in Sweden in 1991.

Even in terms of kinds of business, R&D is strongly concentrated. The transportation and telecommunications industries account for nearly two thirds of annual R&D operations. Pharmaceutical and machinery industries together answer for an additional quarter.

In relation to the average for other OECD countries, Swedish industry is technologically concentrated – as measured in R&D expenditures per capita of people of working age – on telecommunications products (Ericsson), pharmaceuticals (Astra, Pharmacia), road vehicles (Volvo, Scania, Saab), machinery (excluding computers – ABB), and paper (MoDo, Stora, SCA, Assidomän). R&D expenditures in the metal and metal products industries are on about the same level as the OECD average, while in other industrial areas Sweden lies under the OECD average.

Between 1991 and 1993, industrial R&D expenditures rose by 11% in fixed prices, which can be compared with a total increase of just under 6% during the entire 1987–93 period. The number of R&D annual operations has grown appreciably slower than R&D expenditures. There were actually fewer industrial R&D operations in 1993 than in 1987. Developments have varied among different industries. Telecommunications and pharmaceuticals have increased their R&D activities significantly faster than the industrial average.

Large international companies based in Sweden constitute a resource for the entire business sector. As companies become ever more internationalised, their flexibility also increases. Companies with enterprises in many countries, and extensive international networks, can much more easily and rapidly than before reallocate resources from one place to another. The national environment for industrial development in Sweden is decisively influenced by where the Sweden-based international companies decide to locate their R&D activities. Large R&D activities represent an important resource for industrial innovations, which may transform into new production in Sweden.

14.7 EUROPEAN POLICIES

The Swedish membership in EU has mainly influenced policies in three areas.

The Union's economic criteria for member countries which aspire to join the EMU has exerted a strong influence on economic policy, in spite of the fact that the Swedish government has not yet decided if Sweden will join EMU in 1999. The government has announced that such a decision will be made in autumn 1997. At present the likely decision is that the Swedish entrance into the EMU will be postponed beyond 1999.

The membership has also implied a step backward, from an economic point of view, in agricultural policy. Since the 1980s forceful national efforts have been made to reduce the amount of subsidy to Swedish agriculture. As members of the EU the framework for agricultural policy was changed. Many new regulations on agricultural production have been introduced and

the amount of public money transferred to Swedish agriculture has grown significantly.

Finally, the membership has also, as a result of the fact that Structural Funds money was treated as an addendum to the old national regional policy, contributed to a significant increase in the the the amount of money allocated to regional policy.

14.8 FUTURE PROSPECTS

The future development of the Swedish economy depends on the power in three different growth engines.

In the short run Sweden's large corporations are the most important growth engine. Their growth will play a decisive role for economic growth in Sweden during the next 3–5 years. Most large Swedish corporations have their roots in market areas which were dynamic and growing fast before the Second World War. The long-term growth of these corporations depends on their ability to continually adjust their products and production processes to changing external conditions. Ericsson's success in mobile telephone systems is an important showcase for other large Swedish corporations illustrating the potential benefit of such an adjustment.

In the medium-term perspective small- and medium-sized corporations represent an important source for growth. Swedish economy has for many decades suffered from a serious lack of fast growing small- and medium-sized corporations. Each decade has only produced one corporation with a turnover exceeding SEK 1 000 000 000. In order to increase the Swedish growth rate it is necessary to raise the number of fast growing small- and medium-sized corporations. There are signs indicating the existence of a growing number of such companies.

In the long run, 15–20 years, newly established companies play an important role as growth engine. Normally such companies are characterised by their ability to use new technology in innovative ways satisfying new demands and creating new fast growing markets. At present many new established corporations are based on IT-applications, multi-media and consulting.

As a small country located on top of Europe Sweden has to import ideas and innovations from abroad in order to safeguard a dynamic economic development. About 98% of all new knowledge is produced outside Sweden. Historically the Swedish business community has shown an astonishing ability to learn from abroad. The upgrading and maintenance of this ability will have critical importance for the long-term economic development in Sweden.

14.9 BIBLIOGRAPHY

National administration for industrial and technology policy (NUTEK), (1996), *Swedish industry and industrial policy*, Stockholm

Nilsson, J.-E. (1995): *Sverige i förändringens Europa. En industrinations uppgång och fall*, Malmö, Liber Hermods

CHAPTER 15

Finland

Markku Kotilainen

15.1 INSTITUTIONAL AND HISTORICAL CONTEXT

Finland is a country located in northern Europe with somewhat more than 5 million inhabitants. The country is sparsely populated, considering its size; the geographic area is 338 145 km², which is more than in Italy and only slightly less than in Germany. The neighbours are Sweden in the west, Norway in the north, Russia in the east and Estonia (behind the Baltic sea) in the south. The official languages are Finnish and Swedish, with Finnish being the main language and about 6% of the population speaking Swedish as their mother tongue (*Statistical Yearbook of Finland*.)

Finland became independent in 1917 after being a part of Sweden until the early 19th century, and an autonomous part of Russia after that until independence. Politically Finland is a constitutional republic. The highest political power belongs to the one-chambered parliament, which is elected every four years. The cabinet has to have the confidence of the parliament. Because of the rather fragmented political system, cabinets are based on coalitions of several parties. The fragmentation is due to the proportional election system as well as due to the historically based channelling of interests through different parties rather than through factions inside large parties. The cabinet has the main executive power. The head of state is the president, whose responsibilities lie mainly in the area of foreign policy. The president is elected directly by the people.

The greatest parties are the Social Democratic Party with 63 seats in the parliament after the 1994 election, the Centre Party with 44 seats, the National Coalition Party (conservatives) with 39 seats, and the Left Wing Alliance with 22 seats. The number of seats is 200 all together. The cabinet coalitions change over time. Currently the cabinet is formed by the so-called 'rainbow coalition' consisting of the Social Democrats, the conservatives, the Left Wing Alliance, the Swedish People's Party in Finland, and of the Green League.

In foreign policy Finland has followed a neutral stance. This policy was followed during the cold war era. Finland did not want to interfere in the conflict between the superpowers, one of which, the Soviet Union, was her neighbour. After the end of the cold war neutrality is not of as much importance as before. In the definition of the international position of the country 'military non-alignment' is, however, still an important concept.

Finland has wanted to be identified as a Nordic democratic welfare state. Cooperation with the other Nordic countries Sweden, Norway, Denmark and Iceland has been close in various areas. In foreign trade policy Finland's aim has been to reduce trade barriers through GATT negotiations as well as through regional trade arrangements. Finland became associated with EFTA in 1961, and became a full member in 1986. The real difference between these forms of membership was negligible. In 1973 Finland arranged her trade relations to the EEC with a free trade agreement. When the single market programme ('EC 1992') started in the late 1980s, it became evident that Finland and the other EFTA countries had to deepen their cooperation with the EC. A free trade agreement did not cover the abolition of non-tariff barriers, which was the crucial aim of the '1992 program'.

The first reaction to the deepening of the EC integration was the European Economic Area (EEA) agreement between the EC and EFTA. The agreement entered into force on the 1 January 1994. The agreement widened the internal market programme to cover EFTA countries also. It meant abolishing barriers to trade, capital and labour. The main problem with the EEA was the subordinate role of the EEA rules to EC legislation. The EC was able to change its own legislation, and the EFTA countries either agreed or were left out of that part of activity. The EEA suffered thus from a democracy deficit. Membership in the planned Economic and Monetary Union (EMU) was also outside the EEA agreement.

There was already a widespread movement in the EFTA countries towards EU membership before the EEA agreement formally entered into force. Austria applied for EU membership in 1989, Sweden in 1991, Finland, Switzerland and Norway in 1992. The membership of Austria, Finland and Sweden was realised on the 1 January 1995. In Norway and in Switzerland membership was not accepted by the population even if the political leaders were in favour of it.

15.2 MAIN ECONOMIC CHARACTERISTICS

In Finland the gross domestic product has been growing somewhat more than in the current 15 EU countries on average during the past 26 years. In Finland the average annual growth rate in 1970–95 was 2.7% whereas in the EUR15 it was 2.5%. In Finland the average growth rate was reduced drastically by the recession of the early 1990s (see Figure 15.1 and Table G23). The GDP declined from the level of the year 1990 cumulatively by 12% during the three following years. In 1994 and 1995 the annual growth rate was already more than 4%.

The reasons for the severe recession were numerous. The immediate reason was the current account deficit, which prevailed and increased in the late 1980s (Figure 15.2). The current account deficit was due to a decline in exports to the Soviet Union (because of reduced export possibilities under the bilateral clearing arrangement due to the collapse in oil prices in early 1986) as well as due to booming domestic demand, which was to a large extent caused by the liberalisation of financial markets. The deterioration of cost-competitiveness was also one reason for the export problems although the deterioration was not large. Increases in labour costs (in domestic currencies) contributed clearly negatively to competitiveness. The high increase in productivity compensated for this

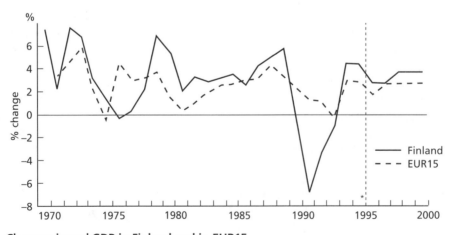

Figure 15.1 Changes in real GDP in Finland and in EUR15.
Source: Eurostat, Table G23.

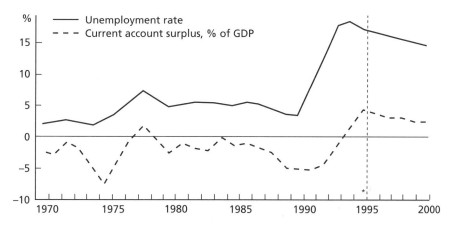

Figure 15.2 Economic inbalances

Source: Eurostat, Tables G20 and G37.

partly. The exchange rate was kept strong to avoid inflation and to signal to the market a 'hard nosed' exchange rate and monetary policy.

The increased foreign debt finally led to an increase in the interest rates through market reactions and to a tightening of economic policies. The indebtedness of the households and firms also led to a decline in consumption, in demand for houses and in investments. The collapse of the Soviet Union reduced Finnish exports to the east further. An attempt was made to restore the cost competitiveness by a general wage freeze, but this did not succeed well enough, and the initiative came too late. The competitiveness of the Finnish industry was improved by a devaluation of the markka in November 1991, and by letting the markka float freely in September 1992.

Unemployment was low in Finland by European standards until the recession of the early 1990s, when it exploded. The recession led to a drastic cut in the number of firms, especially in those producing for the home market. The restored competitiveness through the weakening of the markka led to an increase in exports. The Finnish economy is now recovering and the growth rate of the GDP will be clearly higher than in the EUR15 on average. ETLA's forecast for the average annual GDP growth rate for 1996–2000 is 3% for Finland and 2.5% for the EU as a whole (Research Institute of the Finnish Economy, 1996a). Unemployment is coming

down gradually, but it will take several years before even the EU average, now about 10.5%, is achieved. The current account is running a clear surplus and the foreign debt is declining. Domestic demand is, however, recovering slowly. The high unemployment rate slows down the increase in private consumption. The negative experience of the households regarding high indebtedness in turn slow down the increase in the demand for dwellings.

In Finland the investment ratio has been high when compared to the average of the EU countries. The share of gross fixed capital formation was 25% in Finland in 1970–94, whereas in the EUR15 it was 21% (Table G29). This is at least partly due to the capital intensiveness of the forest industry, which is an important branch of industry. It has also been argued that it reflects inefficiency of investments (Pohjola, 1996). The share of private consumption has accordingly been lower. During the same period it was 55% in Finland and 60% in the EUR15 (Table G28). During the recession of the early 1990s investments dropped drastically, and so did their share of GDP. Private consumption maintained its relative share.

The share of government consumption was on average half a percentage point higher in Finland than in the EUR15. This reflects differences in the organisation of welfare services. In Finland as well as in the other Nordic countries these are provided more through public organisations than in western Europe.

Finland is somewhat more open than the EUR15 average. The average share of exports was 28% in Finland in 1970–94 and 27% in EUR15. This share fell in the late 1980s and achieved 22% in 1991. The poor performance of exports led to a large current account deficit. During the recession, and after the depreciation of the markka, the share of exports increased to more than 35% relative to GDP in 1994. At the same time the EUR15 average was 27.5%. Domestic demand is currently recovering and this leads gradually to a decline in the GDP share of exports. As a small country Finland will, however, also in the future rely on international specialisation, more than the large EU countries.

Finland has traditionally had a higher rate of inflation than the western European countries. The situation changed, however, during the recession of the early 1990s (Table G31). Inflation is currently clearly lower than in the EUR15 on average. In 1995 consumer prices increased by 1% in Finland and by 3% in the EUR15. Inflation will increase somewhat during the next few years, but at least the domestic causes for it are under control until the end of 1997. The labour unions and employer organisations achieved in 1995 a modest centralised two-year wage agreement. Also during the coming years the increased international competition, the high unemployment, participation in the EMU process and increased responsibility of the labour unions are supposed to keep the inflation rate low.

In manufacturing the largest branch is that of metal products and engineering (see Table 15.1). Inside this the electrical and electronics industries account for almost a half of the production. Telecommunication equipment and mobile phones are the most important articles in these branches. Nokia is the largest firm in this area. In machinery production Finnish companies have special know-how in building paper machines.

The expertise in paper machines is connected to the large Finnish paper industry, which makes a clear difference when compared to the average of the EUR15. The share of the paper industry in the whole manufacturing production in Finland in 1990 was 21%, whereas it was only 4.4% in

Table 15.1 Finland's production structure in manufacturing when compared to that of the average of EU and EFTA in 1990, % shares of different product groups[1]

Groups of products	Finland	EU+EFTA
Food, beverages and tobacco	12.70	12.40
Textiles, apparel and leather	3.50	4.80
Wood products and furniture	7.80	3.50
Paper, paper products and printing	21.20	7.70
Chemical products	12.70	18.40
Non-metallic mineral products	4.80	4.20

[1]Portugal in 1987 and Spain in 1988.
Sources: OECD, *Industrial Structure Statistics*, 1992; *Bank of Finland Monthly Bulletin* (exchange rates).

Germany. In the paper industry Finnish companies are important exporters on a European scale. The biggest companies are UPM-Kymmene, Enso-Gutzeit and the Metsäliitto Group. The high share of paper production is due to the big geographic area of the country and to the amount of forests. Inside the industry Finnish companies have specialised in high quality paper, whose demand is growing the fastest. (For more about the Finnish economic 'clusters', see Hernesniemi, *et al*. 1996.)

In manufacturing the production in the metal products and engineering industries is growing the fastest. ETLA's forecast for the average growth rate in 1996–2000 is 8% (Research Institute of the Finnish Economy, 1996a). Growth rates are especially high in the electrical equipment and electronics industries. In the paper industry the average growth rate of production is forecast to be about 3%. The metal product and engineering industries are thus becoming more dominant in the Finnish economy. The position of the forest industry remains, however, strong when compared to the position of this branch of industry in other EU countries. The forest industry is also more important in exports than in production. The combined share of the paper and wood industries in exports was 35% in 1995, and the share of the metal industry was 47%. Because the forest industry uses mainly domestic inputs, the importance of this branch as an earner of net export revenues is greater than the gross export figures show. In 1985 the share of the forest industry in total net exports was 36% and the corresponding share of the metal industry was 29%. The share of industry was 83% while the rest consisted of services (Ahde, 1990, p. 119).

The manufacturing industry accounts for about 30% of total GDP, the share of services is 55% (Table G25). The rest consists of construction, agriculture, forestry and mining. One third of services is produced by the public sector. The production of private services is forecast to grow on average by 3% annually in 1996–2000. The clear current account surplus forecast for the next five years gives room for the growth in home market services. The service sector and construction are crucial in providing new jobs in the coming years. Reducing the tax wedge by lowering income taxes and side costs of employing people would create additional demand for private services and construction work, especially in households. Production of public services grows by only 2% per year, because of the fiscal restraint caused by the indebtedness of the public sector – associated with the EMU convergence requirements.

One of the long-term strengths of the Finnish economy is the educated labour force, which made it possible to develop high-tech production in electronics but also in other branches of industry. The know-how base of the country has thus grown cumulatively. Because of the relatively high cost level of the country, the comparative advantage of Finland lies also in the future in producing high-quality products rather than in competing with low-cost countries in the production of standard products (Figure 15.3).

The vast forest resources also give a basis for an extensive forest industry. This branch has developed its production in the direction of high-quality goods. The technical know-how has been used in developing products as well as machinery and methods of production.

One of the weaknesses is the small size of the country. This implies a small domestic market and narrows the production base of the country. Modern technology and flexible ways of organising production give, however, better chances than before to shift from branch to branch if necessary. The negative effects of the small domestic market are partly compensated for by the deepening European integration and by the growth and opening up of the eastern European market. The geographic location of Finland beside the large and growing Russian market will be a benefit in the future.

The current high unemployment is a weakness at the moment, and weakening of the vocational skills of those who are unemployed for a long time can lead to long-term problems, too. Because of the demographic structure of the population, unemployment will, however, diminish clearly in a couple of decades.

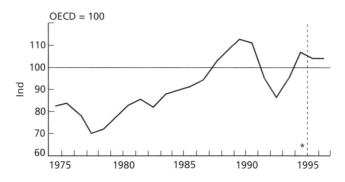

Figure 15.3 Labour cost level in Finnish manufacturing industry compared to OECD countries on average (14 OECD countries' labour costs in a common currency, weighted by Finland's export shares)
The cost concept: hourly compensation for production workers in manufacturing

Source: US Department of Labour, Bureau of Labor Statistics.

The indebtedness of the government is due to the severe recession of the early 1990s. The debt will be gradually reduced by keeping the growth of public expenditure in control. In the longer run the relative size of the public sector must be diminished to give more room for private activity and to lower the currently high income taxation. The high income taxes together with high indirect costs of employing people leads to a high tax wedge, which in turn worsens employment possibilities.

15.3 GOVERNMENT INVOLVEMENT IN THE ECONOMY

Government consumption constitutes a higher share of GDP in Finland than in the EUR15 on average. During 1970–94 the average share of government consumption of GDP was 19% in Finland and 18.5% in EUR15. The share has, however, been rather stable in the EU, but has increased clearly in Finland. In 1994 the GDP share of government consumption was over 22% in Finland and 18.5% in EUR15. The size of government investment was 2.5% of GDP in Finland in 1995.

The GDP share of government expenditure has increased due to the drastic increase in unemployment, which has led to an increase in transfers to households (Table G32). At the same time government incomes have increased slowly. The central government deficit has accordingly ballooned (Figure 15.4). The central government deficit was about 10% of GDP in 1995. Because of the surplus of the local government and especially of the social security funds, the general government (EMU) deficit was 5.5% of GDP. The central government deficit is declining due to the spending cuts agreed upon for the next years. According to the forecast of ETLA, the EMU deficit will be 2.2% in 1997, which is the year used when choosing EMU members in spring 1998 (Research Institute of the Finnish Economy, 1996b). This forecast includes a 2.5% GDP growth for 1996 and a growth of 3.5% for 1997. The central government will still have a deficit amounting to 5% of GDP, but the surplus of the social security funds partly compensates for this in the aggregate. The municipality's finances are about in balance.

The tax burden of households has increased during the recession. There is already some room in the government finances to cut income taxes during the next five years. Cutting taxes means, however, that the increase in public expenditure must be kept under control.

The growth in the GDP increases tax revenues. The gradual but slow reduction in unemployment in turn reduces unemployment benefit payments. Although the Finnish benefit system is

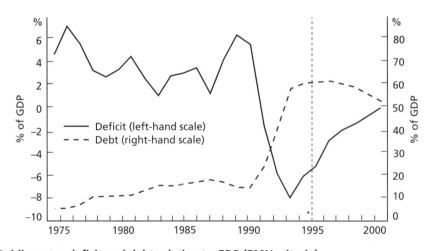

Figure 15.4 Public sector deficit and debt relative to GDP (EMU criteria).
Source: ETLA, The Finnish Economy 2/1996 and 4/1996.

not among the most generous in Europe, the general aim of the government is to make the benefit system cheaper. The benefits as well as other welfare systems are also to be developed in such a way that they will create more incentives for individuals to search for a job.

In addition to transfers to the households the government provides services in education and health care. The schools and universities are mainly public. The general health care is also provided by governmental health clinics and hospitals. In addition to these, also private medical centres and hospitals exist. In dentistry private care is more common than in other medical care. Even when using private health care, the governmental sickness insurance pays a part of the costs.

The number of state enterprises has been small in Finland. Some state-owned firms have existed in the mining and energy sectors. The state has also owned some paper industry firms and a shipyard. Nowadays the state is selling parts or whole companies to private owners. Previously the motivation for state ownership was the size of risks involved in building large-scale production in rural areas, for example in Lapland, and the externalities in energy production. The railway system and the postal service are still owned by the state, but these activities are taken care of by independent firms, which operate almost according to the same principles as private companies.

Finland is a highly unionised country. The share of organised workers among the working population in Finland was 71% in 1988, whereas in the OECD, Europe, the corresponding figure was 38% (OECD, 1991). Only in Sweden and in Denmark is the unionisation higher. In Sweden the rate was 85% and in Denmark 73%. The high rate of unionisation in turn has led to a governmental interest in wage negotiations.

The government has participated in some form or another in the wage negotiations since the late 1960s. The tripartite cooperation between the state, the labour unions and the employer organisations (complemented with the farmers' central organisation) has sometimes led to a formal incomes policy agreement. It has included also some commitments from the side of the government in terms of tax and transfer policy as well as in terms of some labour market legislation. The centralism has been dominant in the Finnish wage negotiations, but sometimes the negotiations have been decentralised to the branch union level. Also in the case of central agreements the acceptance of branch unions is required, which has led to wage-drift at the union and firm levels. For this reason the centralism has been criticised by the employer organisations.

In the future many things which previously were decided in a centralised way will be agreed upon at the firm level. One reason for this is the possible membership in the Economic and Monetary Union (EMU), which requires more flexibility at the firm and branch level. The high unionisation rate, however, will obviously keep the Finnish negotiation system rather centralised also in the near future. The strength of the unions gives them the possibility to press the government, which in turn keeps the government as a labour market participant in one way or another.

15.4 FINANCIAL SYSTEM

In Finland financial markets were regulated until the mid-1980s as in many other European countries. The liberalisation started in 1983 by diminishing the control of the average rate on bank lending. The lifting of these controls continued in 1983 and 1984. In August 1986 the Bank of Finland removed all regulation of the average lending rate. Upper limits on bank lending were also removed in 1986 A real interbank market thus emerged in 1986 (Aaltonen, *et al.* 1994).

Dismantling of foreign exchange controls occurred at about the same time as the internal liberalisation. One of the motivations for liberalisation was the fact that controls had lost their significance because of the internal liberalisation and because of the development of new financial instruments. The other motivation was to ensure that Finnish banks and companies had the same opportunities for competing as foreign entities and to improve the efficiency of the financial markets (Aaltonen, *et al.,* 21). The liberalisation started by allowing foreign exchange banks to use currency options in 1985 and by allowing industrial enterprises and shipping companies to take out long-term loans abroad in 1986. A year later long-term borrowing of other corporations was deregulated. In 1990 households were permitted to invest abroad. The liberalisation process ended in 1991 by deregulating short-term capital movements and by allowing households to borrow money abroad.

The liberalisation was motivated by structural and efficiency reasons. When occurring during a rather short period of time it had, however, negative cyclical side-effects. Together with the collapse of energy prices in 1986, liberalisation contributed to an essential increase in the purchasing power of households and firms. This led to an overheating of the economy – to a consumption, investment, and housing demand boom. The boom increased asset prices and contributed to the increase in the current account deficit, which in turn contributed to the severe recession of the early 1990s.

After the collapse of the Bretton Woods system Finland had a currency basket exchange rate regime with foreign trade shares as weights. In June 1991 Finland decided to peg the Finnish markka to the ECU index. The pegging was realised at an unchanged exchange rate. It soon appeared, however, that the rate was considered by the market as overvalued, and the markka was forced to be devalued in November the same year. The pressure on the markka was not ended by this and in September 1992 the markka was allowed to float freely.

The Finnish government has declared that Finland aims to enter the Economic and Monetary Union among the first countries by the beginning of 1999. To be on the safe side Finland joined the Exchange Rate Mechanism (ERM) on the 14 October in 1996. The government and the Bank of Finland were not very eager to peg the markka, because of the danger for speculative attacks, which are possible in fixed but adjustable exchange rate regimes. This risk is, however, currently small. Prospects for the Finnish economy seem favourable in the

near future and the cost competitiveness of the Finnish industry is good.

The main aim in the monetary policy of the central bank is price stability. The Bank of Finland is already a rather independent central bank. The independence will be further increased by the new monetary legislation, which will increase the power of the board of governors and reduces the power of the parliamentary supervisory board.

The banking sector has traditionally been rather centralised and powerful – because of the high leverage of Finnish companies. This feature has recently strengthened, because the number of banks has been reduced. On the other hand, firms have increased the share of their own resources in financing investments, and international competition in financial intermediation is increasing.

Two big banking groups have disappeared. The savings banks organised around Skopbank went bankrupt because of bad loans and the recession. The two largest private banks, Kansallis and the Union Bank of Finland, merged because of financial difficulties of the aforementioned bank. The new Merita Bank has a two thirds market share in financing of firms. It has a large market share in household financing, too. In addition to Merita there are two other large banking groups, the cooperative Okobank group and the state-owned Postipankki. Some small savings banks (which did not fail with Skopbank) survived during the crisis. They have, however, a small market share in the whole country.

Finnish companies have internationalised during the past ten years. Nokia, even if it is firmly located in and led from Finland, is 60% owned by foreigners. The foreign ownership is widely distributed, for example to different mutual funds. Internationalised companies have also listed themselves, in addition to the Helsinki Stock Exchange, on the financial centres of London and New York.

Finland has suffered from lack of breadth and depth in the long-term securities market. Currently the financing needs of the central government (due to the large deficit) have developed the long-term end of the market. This phenomenon is, however, not long-lasting, and other means must be developed. There are plans for creating new channels for long-term housing loans in the form of some kind of housing fund. These kinds of securities could in principle develop the long end of the securities market. These plans have, however, not been realised because of differences in opinions between banks, government officials and political interest groups.

15.5 INTERNATIONAL RELATIONS

Finland has actively worked for free trade through GATT, EFTA, OECD and now the EU. Previously free trade concerned only trade in industrial goods. Nowadays services and agricultural goods are included, especially through membership in the EU.

In 1995 more than 57% of exports were directed to other EU countries, 11% to the rest of Europe, almost 12% to developing countries, 6.5% to the USA and 2.5% to Japan (National Board of Customs, 1995). Among individual countries Germany had the largest export share, 13.5%. The second largest were Sweden and the UK with almost the same share of more than 10%. The export share of Russia was about 5%. This is clearly less than in the time of the Soviet Union, when about 20% of exports were directed there. The near geographic proximity and the complementarity of production structures will certainly increase the share of exports to Russia. Obviously the share will remain, however, smaller than in the days of the Soviet Union, when high energy prices, large volumes of energy imports and the clearing trade system kept the trade at a high level.

During recent years Finnish companies have increased their exports to the rapidly growing Asian countries. The export share of the Asian countries (excluding Japan) was more than 10% in 1995. Finnish firms are interested in trade and foreign direct investments to the Baltic states, which are located near Finland. Because of the small size of these countries, the overall scale of the activities remains, however, modest.

Capital movements, from Finland as well as to Finland, have been liberalised. Finnish firms have traditionally invested mainly in Sweden. During the past ten years direct investments to other countries have increased, too. Germany, the UK, Belgium (especially Brussels) and the United States, in addition to Sweden, are among the most important target countries for Finnish investors. In direct investments from abroad to Finland companies from Sweden and the USA dominate (Bank of Finland, 1996).

Direct investments from Finland have been greater than those to Finland. This reflects the strength of large Finnish enterprises, which follow a global strategy in their investment policy. On the in-flow side direct investments were restricted until the early 1980s, which might still have lagged effects on foreign investments to Finland. The remote location of the country, a rather small domestic market and the high cost level are additional reasons for the relatively small foreign investments in Finland.

15.6 IMPACT OF EUROPEAN INTEGRATION

One of the main motivations for Finnish EU membership when compared to the EEA agreement was the possibility to participate in decision-making. Finland has now participated in decision-making at different levels and gathered experiences from it. The adjustment to full exploitation of the possibilities will still take some time.

In 1995 Finland's budget payments to the EU were somewhat less than the receipts from the EU. The net outcome was positive because of payments for Finnish agriculture during a transition period. In the long run Finland will be clearly a net payer. Even if the severe recession has led to a drastic decline in the GDP per capita, Finland belongs to the rather wealthy nations of the EU (Table G24).

One of the clearest impacts of Finnish EU membership was the decline in food prices by more than 10%. Finnish food prices before membership were clearly higher than those in the EU on average, mainly because of the Nordic location of the farming land and because of protection of domestic production. Opening the Finnish agriculture to EU competition has reduced the producer prices of farmers. The compensation for it is paid as a direct income subsidy. In addition to EU payments, Finland is able to pay transitional subsidies to farmers for some years.

In addition to payments for agriculture Finland obtains receipts from the structural funds. It obtains funds on the basis of different objectives as other EU countries, too. The criterion for objective 1 (assisting less developed areas) is, however, not met by rural areas of Finland, Sweden and Austria. The criterion requires the GDP to be less than 75% of the EU average. For these countries a new objective 6 was established to take into account the special difficulties of areas with a low density of population. This objective is defined on the basis of the special circumstances of these countries; in fact it replaces objective 1. In Finland the areas which fulfil the criteria of objective 6 are located in the northern and eastern parts of the country.

A clear impact of EU membership is seen in competition policy. The EU Commission rejected in November 1996 the merger of two large Finnish wholesale firms Kesko and Tuko on the basis that the company would have a dominant market position in Finland. Strict competition policy together with the small Finnish domestic market creates some obstacles for the growth of Finnish home-market-orientated firms. In the future they will evidently have to find possibilities for widening their business abroad.

One of the greatest challenges in EU policy for Finland as for many other countries will be membership of the EMU. The aim of the Finnish government is membership among the first countries entering the third stage of the EMU. The main benefits from it are an increase in the credibility of economic policies and a decline in interest rates. A common currency leads also to savings in transaction costs as well as to more competition and efficiency in the financial market. The problems and costs are related to the fact that the Finnish production structure and accordingly variations in output differ from those of the EU average. The northern EU coun-

tries resemble Finland the most in these respects, the southern ones are the most different (Kotilainen 1996).

Membership of the EMU requires an increase in the flexibility in the labour market. The wage system, especially in the tradables sector, might have to be developed in such a way that a part of the compensation for employees is paid as bonuses, the size of which depends on the success of the firm or branch. Flexibility is needed especially in the forest industry, the size and importance of which is greater for Finland than for the average of the EU. More efficiency and flexibility is needed also in fiscal policy to minimise the effects of asymmetric shocks.

Finland has good possibilities to fulfil the EMU criteria. Inflation is under control, which is reflected in the long-term interest rates. The general government deficit will be clearly below 3% in relation to GDP in 1997. The gross public debt will evidently meet the 60% criterion, too. The Finnish markka remained quite stable even before joining the ERM on 14 October 1996.

15.7 FUTURE PROSPECTS

The Finnish economy experienced a severe recession during 1990–93. The economy has been recovering since then. The growth rate of the GDP is forecast to exceed that of the EU average during the next five years. ETLA forecasts an annual growth of 3% on average in 1996–2000 (Research Institute of the Finnish Economy, 1996a). The corresponding forecast of the Ministry of Finance is 3.5% (Ministry of Finance, 1996). The current account is running a surplus and is forecast to remain so for several years. The net foreign debt is accordingly diminishing. There is thus room for an increase in domestic demand.

Unemployment will still remain the greatest problem in Finland for several years. The tools of traditional economic policy as well as structural reforms, which affect the functioning of the labour market, are needed to bring down the unemployment rate currently at 16.5%. Assuming that the current policies are continued, the unemployment rate will fall according to ETLA's forecast to 14% by the year 2000. According to the more optimistic forecast of the Ministry of Finance the corresponding rate is 11%.

The decision on EMU membership is one of the most important questions in Finnish EU policy during the next five years. If the membership is realised, various sectors of the economy must be prepared for it and the flexibility of the economy must be increased.

15.8 BIBLIOGRAPHY AND SOURCES OF INFORMATION

Aaltonen, A., Aurikko, E. and Kontulainen, J. (1994): *Monetary Policy in Finland*, Bank of Finland A:92

Ahde, P. (1990): *The Role of Imports in Finnish Economy and Exports*, The Research Institute of the Finnish Economy (ETLA), B 64 (in Finnish with an English summary)

Bank of Finland: *Direct investment capital flows in Finland's balance of payments* (various issues)

Hernesniemi, H., Lammi, M. and Ylä-Anttila, P. (1996): *Advantage Finland – The Future of Finnish Industries*, The Research Institute of the Finnish Economy, B 113

Kotilainen, M. (1996): 'Is the EU an optimum currency area and is Finland a part of it?', in Alho, K., Erkkilä, M., Kotilainen, M. (eds) *The Economics and Policies of Integration – A Finnish Perspective*, Kluwer Academic Publishers

Ministry of Finance (1996): *Talouspolitiikan linja*, Helsinki (in Finnish)

National Board of Customs (1995): *Foreign Trade*, 12/1995

OECD (1991): *Employment Outlook*, Paris.

Pohjola, M. (1996): *Tehoton pääoma (Inefficient Capital)*, Werner Söderström (WSOY), Helsinki (in Finnish)

Research Institute of the Finnish Economy (ETLA) (1996a): *The Finnish Economy*, 2/1996

Research Institute of the Finnish Economy (ETLA) (1996b): *The Finnish Economy*, 4/1996

Statistical Yearbook of Finland 1995, Statistics Finland

International comparisons

CHAPTER 16

International comparisons

Frans Somers

16.1 INTRODUCTION

This final chapter is concerned with international comparisons. There are both remarkable similarities and clear distinctions in the developments occurring in the fifteen European countries.

Section 16.2 deals with the way in which the role of government has been reduced in almost all the member states. All fifteen show a movement towards market-oriented policies. This development is obviously in line with the overall market orientation of the Union policies. But there are also clear differences. Changes in Italy have not been as profound as in the UK, for instance, with most of the other countries somewhere between these two nations in terms of the extent to which they have increased their market orientation. The possibility of disparities in policies within the framework of the emerging economic and monetary union is also reviewed.

Sections 16.3 and 16.4 deal with the output, growth and international competitiveness of the fifteen countries. Portugal and Ireland in particular demonstrated impressive growth rates in recent decades; while growth in the UK (except for the last decade) has been lagging behind. Furthermore, it will be shown that there are substantial differences between the various countries in terms of competitiveness.

Section 16.5 outlines the marked differences in the financial systems within the EU, especially in the field of finance for industry. The UK especially, and to a minor extent the Netherlands and Belgium, occupy a rather special position in this area, in that their firms are mainly financed through the stock markets. The differences in monetary policies are also discussed.

In Section 16.6 a speculative attempt is made to identify possible fields of national specialisation within the framework of the ongoing reallocation of factors of production within the Union. The final Section (16.7) draws some conclusions from the comparative study, including the potential shift of relative importance from national states to regions in the future European Union, leaving the significance of national states, nevertheless, for the greater part unimpaired.

16.2 THE REDUCED ROLE OF GOVERNMENT

16.2.1 The return of free-market ideologies

The economic crisis of the 1970s and the early 1980s marked a turning point in views on the role of government in the mixed economies of the western World. The general consensus on state interventionist policies in the Keynesian welfare state broke down.

After the Second World War social tensions in Europe were reduced considerably by the reaching of a kind of 'historical compromise' between labour and business management. Private enterprise and the freedom of the market were accepted by labour, in return for collective bargaining, social security, income redistribution and full employment policies and demand management. For business management this arrangement meant harmonious labour relations, political stability, assured demand and motivated workers. The welfare state enjoyed wide political support from both conservative and progressive parties. Naturally, there were differences in political opinions and aims, but in most west European countries these differences tended to be fairly small. Parties on both the extreme left and extreme right generally attracted a limited number of voters. Only in France and Italy did the communist parties remain significant, though even in these countries they were unable to gain power. The main exceptions were Spain and Portugal, both ruled by right-wing dictatorships, and both with highly regulated, centralised and autarchic economies with protected interests for vested business groups.

Income and production in western Europe increased very rapidly in the decades following the Second World War. Average GDP real growth rates of around 5% were achieved and unemployment was reduced to minimal levels. The Keynesian welfare state seemed to enjoy a measure of success in generating prosperity, employment, social security and harmonious industrial relations. Among theorists, a certain degree of consensus emerged, with a majority believing that a regulated market economy would lead to optimal results.

Within this 'mixed economy' framework, the degree of regulation, however, remained a subject of extensive debate. In Germany, for instance, the idea of planning in any form was widely rejected. France on the other hand adopted a system of 'indicative planning', intended to establish a state-controlled framework for the market economy. There remained also differences of opinion on the issues of nationalisation of key industries, the extension of social security systems and the size of the public sector in the various west European countries. But the extremes of, on the one hand, a free market economy and, on the other hand, a centrally planned economy were almost completely abandoned as realistic options; instead a convergence of economic policies along the lines of Keynesian theories took place.

The break-down of the general post-war consensus on economic policies which took place from the early 1970s has two main causes: the economic crises of that period and the internationalisation of the economy.

1. The economic crises began in the early 1970s. The rapid economic growth of the post-war decades started to slow down, mainly because of increasing labour costs, saturation of output markets, surplus capacity and environmental constraints. The economy experienced serious difficulties after the first oil-shock in 1973; and after some recovery, further serious problems accompanied the second oil price hike in 1979. Both oil shocks resulted in rapidly increasing input prices for industry, putting strong upward pressure on inflation. This process was reinforced by a rapid expansion of the money supply, resulting in a situation of 'stagflation': a situation of inflation and stagnation combined. The welfare state proved unable to deal with mass unemployment and stagnating economic growth, because these phenomena put a heavy pressure on government expenditure while simultaneously reducing revenue. The social safety net of the welfare state was built for individual cases, not for mass unemployment. Thus, the 1970s was marked by increasing government expenditure, deficits and rising taxes, adding an increased tax burden to already depressed business profitability. Reduced profits meant a deepening of the crisis and gave rise to a vicious circle via lower investment and shut-down of firms. Keynesian demand policies were generally not effective in face of this crisis, because the problems were essentially located on the supply side: rising costs of inputs of energy and labour.

2. The internationalisation of the economy resulted, among other things, in a intensification of competition. Domestic industries became more exposed to the world economy. Companies were forced to lower costs to compete in world market, demanding improvement of efficiency and putting downward pressure on wages and labour.

In order to support their industries, governments were inclined to decrease taxes and reduce social security contributions and to relax labour protection. Another consequence of the increasing internationalisation was the reduced ability of national governments to implement stabilisation policies. To be effective, such policies should be carried out more and more on a global scale, via a supranational authority, as yet not in existence.

The above developments paved the way for what could be called a new paradigm in economic theory and practice. Many economists and politicians blame the problems of the 1970s and early 1980s on government involvement in the economy. The welfare state, it is argued, created too heavy a burden for business and resulted in rigidities in many markets, particularly the labour market. Prices were distorted by taxes and subsidies, resulting in misallocation of production factors; profits were squeezed. And on top of that, governments were inclined to cover their deficits by monetary financing, fuelling inflation in the process.

Whatever the truth of the matter, it is a fact that from the 1970s on there has been a strong preference among economists and most governments of the western World in favour of a return to the principles of the free market. This tendency has been reinforced by the events in eastern Europe, where the failure of the planned economy became clear.

In practice, free-market principles have not been wholly dominant. It can be argued that an undoubted advocate of the free market like Ronald Reagan, President of the United States from 1980 to 1988, combined supply-side measures with Keynesian demand policies. In Europe, pollution and other urgent environmental problems called for new regulations. But the general tendency of the last decade is clear. Most western governments, whether led by Christian or Social Democrats, by Socialists, Liberals or by others, have been in favour of 'more market and less state' ideologies. To a certain degree this is in line with the Union policies in Europe which, as we have seen in Part A, are largely founded on free-market principles. But substantial differences, nevertheless, exist in the approach to the role of government by the various countries in the EU. These distinctions could become important barriers for a further integration, particularly to the Economic and Monetary Union.

16.2.2 Policy shifts in the major EU countries

United Kingdom: sweeping reforms

Arguably it is the *United Kingdom* that has made the most pronounced changes towards creating a more liberal economy. These changes were set in motion when the Thatcher administration came to power in 1979. What has been said above about breaking an existing consensus is especially applicable to the UK. 'Thatcherism' has come to be synonomous with the abandonment of Keynesian demand management, deregulation of labour and capital markets, denationalisation of state enterprises, withdrawal of subsidies to industries, dismantling of labour union power, reduction of government expenditure and taxes and the eradication of the budget deficit. The only goal which eluded the government was that of controlling the money supply.

The Thatcher government was able to carry out such sweeping shifts in policy because the British political system normally guarantees that one party will be in power. The replacement of Mrs Thatcher by Mr Major as prime minister in 1990 merely meant a continuation of the same policies, albeit that some of them were softened to a certain degree. Even if a Labour government is returned to power in the 1997 elections, no radical changes of these policies are anticipated.

Federal Republic of Germany: moderate changes

In comparison with the UK, reforms in the *Federal Republic of Germany* have been moderate. While tax reforms, reductions in the growth of government expenditure, the elimination of the budget deficit, deregulation and some privatisation have been carried through, alongside the UK, changes since the beginning of the 1980s have been more tentative and gradual. A tight monetary policy and an anti-inflationary stance have been constant factors in German political attitudes ever since the war. The *Bundesrepublic* never experimented with forms of economic planning and established few large state enterprises. Public sector ownership is mainly limited to the holding of private sector company assets by the federal government or the states.

Arguably, the biggest change has been the shift from short-run stabilisation and full employment to long-run growth policies. Demand management was renounced in favour of supply-side policies. These policies included measures to reduce labour and other costs (for instance, by lowering the tax burden), deregulation (e.g. in the field of telecommunication, transport and housing) and privatisation (in the form of selling of government assets).

The German unification in 1990 called for intensified state intervention. Government expenditure was raised considerably and taxes went up. However, the bulk of the money was used to improve the East German infrastructure, clean up the environment, restructure the East German industry and to create an appropriate institutional framework for a market economy. In other words, although there are areas where government intervention has increased, this is only temporary and meant to establish the right conditions for a free market economy. It is in line with the long-term supply-side approach dominating German policy since the early 1980s.

France: role of government still significant

The last decade has also witnessed a remarkable policy shift in *France*. Though France can be considered as a market economy, it has a long tradition of state interventionism, which goes back as far as the mercantilist policies of the 17th-century statesman Colbert (see Chapter 3). Changes took place only after a fruitless attempt during the early 1980s to combat the crises with intensified state intervention. In 1982, which can be regarded as a watershed year in French politics, the ruling socialist government became converted to supply-side politics. To a certain extent it was forced to do so, because the French membership of the EMS effectively prevented the depreciation of the French franc, needed in order to restore competitiveness and reduce the trade deficit. In essence, the free market principles of the Union influenced an individual Member State to act according to common principles in relation to a matter which would normally be regarded as one of national sovereignty.

A whole range of measures to strengthen the supply side were implemented, from austerity policies to denationalisation and deregulation. The famous French system of 'indicative planning' was partly dismantled and the country's rigid financial markets liberalised (in 1984). Industrial policy shifted from supporting specific industries and enterprises to provision of a favourable overall business environment. Nevertheless, state intervention has not altogether vanished in France. The role of government remains significant when compared with most other Community countries. Privatisation has been limited in extent and large state enterprises still exist.

Attempts to abolish altogether the planning process were not successful either. The 11th plan, launched in 1993 by the incoming right-wing Balladur government defines (in line with its predecessors) a range of targets, some of which require a substantial government involvement; compared to the past, however, the content of this plan is more macroeconomic in its orientation. Nevertheless, this approach to economic policy is noticeably different from the British one, and also, though to a lesser extent, from the German one.

Spain: liberalisation led by state

For different reasons *Spain* is also moving in the direction of a freer market economy. This is mainly caused by Spain's efforts towards integration into the world economy in general and the European economy in particular. This integration represents a distinct break with the practices of the Franco era. The early Franco period was characterised by extensive and wide-ranging public intervention, the existence of large dominant industrial groups, the complete absence of social consultation and high external trade barriers. The year 1959 marked a turning point: Spain became a member of the OEEC (the predecessor of the OECD) and started a liberalisation process by removing controls and relaxing import restrictions. This development gathered momentum after Franco's death in 1975 and particularly after Spain's entry into the European Community in 1986.

The Civil War and the first period of Franco's dictatorship (1939–1959) are crucial to understanding why Spain still lags so far behind in western Europe. The international isolation, monopolistic structure and rigid state intervention were responsible for a long period of stagnation in the Spanish economy; since their relaxation in 1959, Spain has been liberalising its highly centralised economy and is aiming to convert it eventually into a market-dominated system. Full exposure of the Spanish economy to the international competition within the framework of the future EMU requires continued modernisation of the industry, enhancement of competitiveness and an increase in productivity. It is quite remarkable, however, to observe that the restructuring of the Spanish economy along market-oriented lines has not only been performed by relaxation of controls and regulations, but also in large measure by state intervention. The state has sought, for instance, to revitalize traditional manufacturing sectors, to stimulate technological innovation, to build a social security system and to remove rigidities in the labour market.

The restructuring measures have met with considerable success since Spain is catching up with the rest of the EU. Compared with other advanced market economies, however, the involvement of the government in industry is still very large. Total financial support for the business sector in the middle of the reconstruction process (in the mid-1980s) rose to over 5% of GDP, the highest percentage within the EU next to Italy. A large part of these transfers and subsidies went to public enterprises and they have been only partly reduced since, preventing market-determined structural adjustments. Despite a vigorous privatisation programme in the 1980s and 1990s, Spanish state-owned businesses still account for around 8% of GDP at present. On the other hand, the provision of public services (e.g. health care, public education and transportation) is still underdeveloped, with the potential to become an important constraint on continuing growth. Generally, a sufficient level of these services is considered to be a necessary condition for the functioning of the market; that is why the Spanish government, despite a tight budget policy, is intending to give public investment a high priority in the near future.

Italy: still a high degree of state intervention

Of all EU countries, *Italy* is probably least affected by the reinvigorated neo-liberal free market ideology of the 1980s. Like France it has a long tradition of state intervention. Central government is still responsible for a substantial part of total investment in Italy; direct investment by the public sector in a broad sense (including state enterprises and public and semi-public enterprises in which the State has a large stake) accounted in the 1980s for around 6% of GDP. Italy devoted a larger part of its GDP to aiding industry than any other European country in the early 1980s. A substantial proportion of this aid was destined for (not very successful) development programmes in the south and the support of ailing industries. Public expenditure increased considerably in the last decade, mainly due to transfers to families and companies and interest payments to service the rising national debt.

Nevertheless, a movement towards the free market can also be observed. There has been a shift in industrial policy towards favouring the more advanced and strategic sectors, encouraging R&D expenditure and stimulating export performance. The financial system has been deregulated and capital can move more freely, especially since 1990 when the Community Directive relating to this came into force.

A start has also been made on a programme of privatising state enterprises. The main aims of this policy are the reduction of public debt and strengthening the role of the market. Public enterprises and the public service sector in general are notorious for their inefficiency; the discipline of the market is expected to reduce costs and to increase productivity.

As yet, however, this denationalization process has not gone as far as in the UK, or even France. A large state enterprise sector remains a distinctive characteristic of the Italian economy, accounting for about one third of GDP (as in France). The three major state companies (IRI, ENI and EFIM) employ 550 000 people.

One of the main reasons why major policy shifts have not been carried out thus far is the nature of the Italian political system itself. Radical political solutions and economic measures are ruled out by fragmented political power and the necessity to form coalition governments, as Fineschi points out in Chapter 4. This is a major contrast to the situation in (for example) the UK, where the stable political system facilitated significant changes. Political reforms, which started in 1993, have not really changed this situation so far.

16.2.3 Policy shifts in the smaller European countries

The year 1982 appears to be a watershed year in European politics, at least for the smaller European countries. Leftist or centrist left (coalition) governments were replaced by centrist right (coalition) governments in *The Netherlands*, *Belgium* and *Denmark*. These governments – in line with the general trend of the 1980s – shifted their approach away from public intervention, the welfare state and Keynesian demand management policies to tight fiscal and monetary policies, wage moderation, inflation

reduction, improvement of competitiveness, strengthening of the supply side and other market-orientated policies. Since the mid-1980s governments in *Portugal* (led by 'centrist' social democrats) adopted similar policies, especially focusing on privatisation. Even the replacement of right-wing parties by more leftist ones in later years in some of the countries mentioned above did not really change this trend. Despite the efforts to reach a freer market economy, government influence remained important in these countries; in Denmark and the Netherlands the public sector was reduced only to a limited extent, while Portugal is still characterised by a very large state enterprise sector, accounting for nearly 40% of GDP.

The major exception in the 1980s was *Greece*, which was, from 1981–90, ruled by a socialist-led government, which put heavy stress on nationalisation, subsidies, licensing and price and income controls. The result was excessive inflation and public deficits, declining investment and a stagnating economy. In 1990, however, the socialist government was replaced by a conservative one, which launched a programme aimed at reducing the size of the public sector, bringing down inflation and liberalising the economy. Though the socialists returned to power in 1993 (re-elected in 1996), they did not substantially change the policies initiated by the conservatives. This has finally brought Greek economic policies more in line with European ones.

Traditionally, government involvement in the Nordic welfare states *Sweden* and *Finland* used to be comparatively high. Public expenditure (as a percentage of GDP) is – together with Denmark – the highest in the world, the labour market is strongly regulated and expansive fiscal policies were frequently implemented to fight recessions, with a strongly negative effect on costs and competitiveness. The deep recession of the early 1990s finally led to a fundamental change in both countries, with austerity and strong currency policies being prioritised. Deregulation and improving the flexibility of markets (especially the labour market) are also high on the political agenda.

Austria, finally, appears to be least affected by the return-to-the-market philosophies so far; the country has been ruled most of the time since the war by a grand coalition which puts strong emphasis on social consensus and consultation with workers and employers (the Social Partnership). Nevertheless, a start has been made with the privatisation of some large state companies and with a reduction of public expenditure recently.

16.2.4 European integration and government involvement in the economy

Does the completion of the internal market and the coming of the EMU require a further convergence in economic policies (e.g. fiscal policies)? To a certain extent, this is inevitable. Large inflation, wage and productivity differentials between EU countries can no longer be offset by national use of the exchange rate mechanism. Large and sustained budget deficits can result in inflationary pressures, which in turn can threaten the common monetary policy of the Community (to be implemented by the future European Central Bank). Fiscal discipline is therefore supposed to be a crucial component of EMU.

With regard to fiscal policies, (more) convergence for indirect taxation and capital income taxation is certainly needed, because these taxes relate to free-moving goods and capital. According to an EC report of 1990 on the EMU, however, there is no case for an overall harmonisation of the tax systems; Member States would remain free to choose their taxing and spending levels. Tax differentials, especially of income taxes and social security contributions, do not necessarily cause individual citizens to move if higher tax levels are matched by higher public welfare provisions and vice versa. This raises the question of the cost of public goods and services. First, there is the issue of efficiency. An inefficient public sector, as in Italy, will result in higher costs, to be financed by higher taxes. Second, countries with high debts have to devote a relatively large proportion of their budgets to servicing their debts. This means that (again, as in Italy) their public good provisions will be low compared with their tax levels. So, a mismatch of taxing and levels of public provi-

sions can be a reason for citizens moving from one country to another in order to maximise their benefits and minimise spending. Moreover, benefits and costs of public goods can spill over from one country to another, in areas such as transportation and telecommunication provisions and a clean environment.

Finally, diverging redistributive policies can cause spill-over effects if persons with higher incomes are allowed to migrate to countries with low tax regimes and if those entitled to social benefits also have some freedom of choice in selecting a country of residence (e.g. after leaving the work-force).

It may be that a complete harmonisation of fiscal policies is not needed. But there are clear limits to the extent to which disparities may occur. In the emerging Economic and Monetary Union, the levels of taxation and public goods will be prominent elements in the increasing rivalry between national states. Governments want to offer favourable conditions for business; hence it is most likely that there will be downward pressure on taxes.

For public goods and services the question is more complicated. On the one hand, a high level of public provision will strengthen national competitiveness; on the other, financial constraints (because of lower taxes) and the possibility of cross-frontier spill-over effects will have a negative impact on government spending.

This inclination to lower public provision may be offset partly by common regulations, which will involve long and complicated negotiations. But the fact remains that the intensified competition of the Single Market, together with the loss of national autonomy, tend to a further reduction in the role of government in the EU. This tendency may be reinforced if competition increases due to an economic recession, similar to that of the early 1990s. The traditional instrument of protection cannot be used; hence governments will be inclined to reduce tax burdens in order to enhance competitiveness.

State aid to industry is also under threat. This aid distorts free competition and is one of the obstacles to be (at least partly) removed in order to achieve a barrier-free internal market after

1992. It is likely therefore that despite vigorous opposition from countries like France and Italy, EU limits to state aid will be tightened in the near future.

For all these reasons it seems likely that the trend towards a free market economy, which started in the 1970s, will be furthered by the process of European unification.

16.3 OUTPUT AND GROWTH

16.3.1 The overall picture

Following the world-wide recession of the early 1980s, the period of 1984 to 1990 constituted a period of considerable growth for the countries now forming the European Union; the average real growth rate amounted to around 3% (EUR15). This upturn was, however, followed by a deep recession in the early 1990s, leading to negative growth of 0.6% in 1993, more severe than in most other OECD countries. Important explanations for this recession were the overheating of the European economy in the late 1980s and the problems related to German unification.

Since this recession the European economy has shown only a moderate recovery. This seems quite remarkable, since the underlying economic fundamentals are very favourable (*European Economy*, 1996, no. 61). The world economy is growing rapidly, inflation and interest rates have been reduced to historically low levels, unit labour costs have strongly decreased and capital profitability is as high as in the 'golden age' of the 1960s. Since 1995 most European currencies depreciated against the dollar and the yen, leading to increased price competitiveness, and budget deficits have been reduced. The basic conditions for sound long-term economic growth seem to be realised. Impediments to this growth materialising, however, are the repeated turmoils on currency markets and the lack of confidence among consumers and producers. The latter is strongly related to moderate growth of incomes, high unemployment levels and the lack of job security – factors having a strongly negative effect on (expected) demand. The instability of currency markets may be sharply reduced once the Euro has been introduced.

It is obvious that in the last decade European growth rates have lagged considerably behind the rates of other industrialised countries, like the USA and Japan (see Table 16.1). Nevertheless, although an international trend can be recognised, there are quite noticeable differences between the various European countries.

Table 16.1 Real growth rates, 1960–96: (a) The five major European countries, USA and Japan; (b) The smaller European countries

	Germany[2]	France	Italy	UK	Spain	EU15[2]	USA	Japan
1961–96[1]	2.8	3.3	3.5	2.3	4.1	3.1	2.9	5.6
1961–80	3.5	4.4	4.7	2.4	5.4	3.9	3.2	7.5
1981–90	2.2	2.4	2.2	2.6	3.0	2.4	2.7	4.1
1991–96[1]	1.9[3]	1.1	1.2	1.4	1.5	1.4	2.2	1.6

	Netherlands	Belgium	Austria	Sweden	Denmark	Finland	Portugal	Greece	Ireland	Luxembourg
1961–96	3.1	3.0	3.2	2.4	2.7	3.1	4.1	4.1	4.3	3.1
1961–80	4.0	4.0	4.1	3.3	3.3	4.1	5.5	6.1	4.4	3.0
1981–90	2.2	1.9	2.1	2.0	2.0	3.1	3.0	1.6	3.6	3.6
1991–96	1.9	1.3	1.8	0.3	1.9	−0.2	1.3	1.3	5.0	2.3

[1] 1996: estimates
[2] Excluding eastern Germany
[3] Whole Germany
Source: Table G23 / *Eurostat*.

16.3.2 The major EU countries

Germany: moderate growth

Since the years of the *Wirtschaftswunder* in the 1950s economic growth in the *Federal Republic of Germany* has been very moderate. Between 1961 and 1996 the real average growth rate was only 2.8% versus the EU average of 3.1%. Only the UK, Sweden and Finland showed a worse performance. Forecasts for the near future are not very optimistic: recovery from the recession in the early 1990s had already stagnated by 1995. Until 1990 the expansion of the German economy, however, had been very solid and stable and had been achieved without many imbalances. Inflation rates and the budget deficit had been very modest, unemployment was low and the current account mostly showed a strong surplus. The economy seemed to be 'shock-proof' more than any other, mainly because of its solid character and basically sound structure.

However, there are three major concerns for the German economy. The first is the high level of costs, such as labour costs, cost of social safety, environmental protection, energy and taxes. This problem has been sharply reinforced by the increase in the real effective exchange rate of the Deutsch Mark in the last decades. The high cost level can only be maintained if Germany manages to achieve a sustained increase in productivity. The competitive advantage of the German economy lies in its ability to develop quality products with a high-tech content, not in its cost level. If it wants to keep up with its main rivals, the USA and Japan, it needs to continue to devote a large proportion of its GDP to investment and research and development. In reality, R&D spending in recent years has declined and the ratio of R&D spending to GDP in Germany is lower than in the USA and Japan at present.

The second concern has to do with the German economic system, which is organised as a social market economy. On the positive side it can be argued that this system is one of the main causes of German economic and political stability. However, it is also characterised by many fixed arrangements and institutions, defended by well-organised interest groups. This has led to many rigidities in the form of labour market and industry regulations, working and closing hours, entrance requirements, competition rules and bureaucracy in general. The social security system, which is one of the reasons for the high labour costs, is very generous compared to international standards. Because of these rigidities, costs are driven up and flexibility and international competitiveness are undermined. Increasing international competition has put the system under strain.

The third concern is related to German unification, which took place in October 1990. The integration of the former GDR, resulting, among other things, in large-scale bankruptcies, increasing unemployment and the revelation of enormous environmental problems, put a heavy burden on Germany as a whole. The transformation process is requiring far more money and time than originally expected, resulting in increased taxes and persistent upward pressure on inflation, the budget deficit and interest rates. The high unification cost is one of the major reasons why it will be difficult for Germany to bring its public deficit below the Maastricht norm of less than 3%. The biggest fear with respect to the unification is that a permanent dual economy will arise, causing similar problems to those in Italy. A successful integration, on the other hand, may possibly raise the German long-term growth trend. Because of a catch-up process, east German growth could take off at a later stage and then eventually surpass west German growth, increasing the combined figure.

Obviously, the problems mentioned above are strongly interrelated; taken together they lead to a number of structural weaknesses in the German economy. If these problems are not addressed, the prospects for the German economy remain gloomy.

France: potential not fully realised

The French economy has been an average performer in the long-run, with the long-term growth rate of 3.3% slightly above the average EU rate of 3.1%. In the last decade (especially in the 1990s), however, the French economy has been growing at a slower pace than the European average. This is fairly remarkable since the market-orientated reforms, which were implemented since the early 1980s, have resulted in a fundamentally sound economy. Inflation and interest rates are comparatively low, the currency is stable, the current account mostly shows surpluses, wage increases are only moderate, profitability of the private sector is high and the international competitiveness of French firms has sharply improved. Nevertheless, France was more severely hit by the recession in the early 1990s than almost all other EU economies (except for Finland and Sweden), while the public deficit, which seemed to be under control in the second half of the 1980s, sharply rose to levels far above the Maastricht norm.

The main long-term weakness of the economy, which is putting a drag on economic growth, is unemployment. After reaching a peak in the middle of the 1980s of well over 10%, unemployment has proved to be rather persistent, even in times of output expansion. In 1994 unemployment soared again to a new record of around 12%. Rigidities in the labour market seem to be the major reason for this development. The insufficient educational system is another reason. The high institutional minimum wage has probably contributed to high unemployment among low-skilled workers and a capital-deepening investment trend. Another matter of concern is the high value of the French franc, caused by the nominal exchange rate adjustments of some important trading partners (notably the UK, Italy and Spain) in recent years. This has eroded French competitiveness, while the policy of stable exchange rate relationship with the deutschmark also limited the room for interest reductions, which could be useful in pulling the country out of recession.

In general terms, however, the overall picture for France looks pretty sound. In a favourable international environment the French economy should be capable of realising its full potential and reaching more than average growth rates.

Italy: growth slowing down

For Italy growth in the last 36 years has been satisfactory; with an average rate of 3.5%, it is well above the EUR15 average and surpasses most other European countries, including Germany. But growth has markedly slowed down in the last decade, mainly because the Italian economy lacks balance in a number of respects.

First, there is an immense regional problem, with marked regional disparities between centre–north on the one hand and the south (*Mezzogiorno*) and Islands on the other hand. It could be argued that these disparities constitute an impediment to the further development of the more prosperous parts of Italy. Support for local industries, development plans and unemployment benefits put large claims on the budget already in deficit. Second, servicing the rising national debt and transfers to families and companies are crowding out urgently required public investments in infrastructure and public services. Third, public services in Italy are very inefficient and ill-suited to an advanced economy, such as in the north and central area. Public education, too, should be upgraded to meet the growing demand for well-trained management. Fourth, inflation rates are significantly higher than European average, undermining Italian competitiveness.

Many of the above disequilibria are interrelated with political problems. The highly fragmented and discredited political system existing until 1993 can be held in part responsible for a number of the problems indicated above; for instance, for the mismanagement of the public sector. It is to be hoped that the political reforms which have been subsequently set in motion will result in radical changes. The present Italian government (led by Prodi), for instance, is very determined to reduce the public deficit. It is not clear, however, how long it will remain in power.

The high inflation rates and loss of competitiveness forced Italy to leave the ERM in 1992. Since then, the lira lost around 40% of its value over two-and-a-half years. This triggered a sharp upsurge of exports and GDP growth, followed by a partial recovery of the lira. In November 1996 the lira returned into the ERM.

On the positive side, the private sector, especially the small- and medium-sized industrial enterprises, has proved itself a strong feature of the Italian economy, and has shown itself capable of adapting to changing conditions. Italian entrepreneurship has proved to be very vibrant and innovative. A substantial reduction of the disequilibria would strongly improve the effectiveness and the overall performance of the Italian economy. The first steps in this direction have been made, but the necessary adjustment measures might have a negative impact on growth rates in the mid-term.

United Kingdom: return to higher growth rates not assured

Long-term growth in the UK has been the lowest of the fifteen countries under consideration: only 2.3% from 1960 to 1996. This is basically due to the poor performance of the UK economy in the period preceding the last upswing in the international economy in the 1980s.

Since then, the country has succeeded in keeping pace with the average trend within Europe. The conservative Thatcher government claimed the credit for this recovery, ascribing it to the return to the market and monetarist and supply-side politics. The British service industry – and especially the financial sector – has expanded sharply in the last decade. The economy has been strongly deregulated, labour costs are among the lowest in Europe and productivity has been increased, leading to a strong upsurge in the economy in the late 1980s.

In the early 1990s, however, the British economy was hit again by a deep, albeit short, recession. The downturn in the business cycle hit Britain first and more severely than most other European countries. Unemployment and the budget deficit increased again to high levels. During the subsequent recovery these imbalances were only partly offset, revealing that the British economy still exhibits important structural weaknesses.

First, saving and investment (especially in R&D) remain comparatively low. Despite the strong depreciation of the pound in 1992–93, the current account still shows large deficits. Underlying the latter is the lack of competitiveness of British industry, and the manufacturing sector in particular. There is a tendency for UK manufacturing to concentrate on lower-value products, as Stone explains in Chapter 7. A positive element, however, is the high level of direct foreign investment in the UK, Japanese in particular. This development could contribute substantially to a revitalisation and modernisation of British manufacturing, for example in the fields of (electrical) engineering, office machines and vehicles.

Second, the example of the UK clearly highlights the negative aspects of rigorously implemented monetarist and other market orientated policies. Public investment in infrastructure has been neglected, with serious consequences for public transport, education, training, the level of R&D and regional disparities. A satisfying level of public provision is arguably a necessary condition for a flourishing private sector. The current insufficient level of public good provision is one of the explanations for the deterioration of the competitiveness of British industry.

In conclusion: although there clearly have been positive developments in the UK economy in the last decade, it is far from guaranteed that UK growth rates will reach a significantly higher level in the mid-term. Some policy adjustments in order to secure long-term growth may be necessary.

Spain: high, but unbalanced growth

Apart from short cyclical disturbances, Spain has shown very high growth rates ever since it began to liberalise its economy by the end of the 1950s. The average real growth rate over the last 36 years was 4.1%, the highest (together with Portugal and Greece) of the 15 countries of the present EU. For all that, Spain has been confronted with very serious imbalances, in respect of high unemployment and inflation rates, large trade deficits and substantial regional disparities. Its infrastructure and social security system are improving, but still underdeveloped. Despite the progress made, Spanish per capita income is still only three quarters of EC15 average.

By the mid-1990s, some of the disequilibria (e.g. inflation and the current account balance deficit) have been successfully addressed, providing a sounder basis for sustained growth. Employment has been rising in recent years, but the labour market remains a major concern. However, a reduction of unemployment should not lead to substantial wage increases. For Spain in particular, with its economy still on an intermediate level, it will be of vital importance to increase productivity while controlling labour costs. The key factor for the Spanish economy is to enhance competitiveness and to keep real unit labour costs at an acceptable level in order to withstand strongly increasing European competition.

16.3.3 The smaller European countries

The Netherlands

The Netherlands is an average performer in terms of output, with a long-term growth rate in line with the average EU15 rate. Of all EU countries, the Netherlands was most hit by the economic crisis of the early 1980s. The most important problems for the country are the high levels of labour costs and taxation, mainly caused by high social security expenditure. Particularly in the 1970s and early 1980s these costs squeezed profits and hence depressed investment, while other factors negatively influencing output are labour market rigidities and the low level of labour participation. Since the early 1980s economic policy has aimed to redress these problems; and although further progress would be desirable, substantial achievements can be observed.

The Dutch economy has also some remarkable strong points, however. Inflation rates are among the lowest in the world, the currency is very strong and closely pegged to the German mark, competitiveness has been sharply increased, the current account shows persistent surpluses and the budget deficit has been reduced to acceptable levels. The Dutch economy was hardly hit by the recession in the early 1990s and employment has been strongly rising for more than a decade. In combination with the strong international orientation and favourable central location of the country, the Netherlands

appears to be well prepared for further European integration and internationalisation of the economy.

Belgium

Belgium is also a moderate performer with respect to output growth, with a long-term growth rate close to average. It is an extremely open economy (the most open within the EU, apart from Luxembourg), which is why it is forced to perform well in terms of competitiveness, currency stability and inflation. However, the country is characterised by major imbalances as well, such as a tremendous national debt, high public deficits, high labour costs, a large tax wedge, and – last but not least – regional disputes and disparities.

Servicing the gross debt of general government (around 130% of GDP in 1996), mainly created in the 1970s and 1980s, puts a heavy burden on the government budget, causing an upward pressure on taxes and depressing government investment in infrastructure. Furthermore, labour market disequilibria put a constraint on future economic growth. Recent governments gave priority to plans aimed at reducing labour costs, increasing international competitiveness and stimulating employment. The central location of Belgium (like the Netherlands) and its international orientation will be a clear advantage for the country in the near future.

Austria

GDP growth in Austria has been in line with the European average since 1960. It is noteworthy that recessions in Austria have been relatively mild in recent decades. For the recession of the early 1980s this can be largely attributed to the demand management policies applied by the Austrian government in departing from the prevailing supply-side policies in other EU countries. Inflationary pressures were prevented at the same time by a policy aimed at moderating wages. Nonetheless, it is assumed that the counter-cyclical policies have had an impact on structural problems in the Austrian economy. The recession in the early 1990s was partly offset by a boom in the construction industry and by increased exports to eastern Europe. The outlook in the mid-term appears to be moderate; inflation is under control and the currency stable, but the public deficit is far too high and the current account shows substantial deficits, mainly due to a crisis in the tourist industry. If Austria – as a small open economy – wants to realise high growth rates, international competitiveness should be improved.

Sweden

In the 1960s Swedish per capita incomes were (after Luxembourg) the highest in Europe. Since 1970 Swedish real growth rates have been (together with the UK) the lowest of the present EU countries. The most dramatic events took place in the early 1990s, when Sweden faced the severest economic crisis since the 1930s, with three years of negative growth in a row. In the same period unemployment and the public and current account deficits sharply increased and the currency strongly depreciated. The main explanations for these developments are the deterioration of international competitiveness due to the high costs of maintaining the welfare state and full employment. The depreciation of the Swedish krona, anti-inflationary and tight fiscal policies, together with an upswing of the international economy, have led to a recovery of the economy in the mid-1990s, although Swedish per capita incomes had dropped to 9th place in the EU by 1996.

Denmark

Mainly because of weak growth rates in the 1960s and 1970s, until recently Denmark used to be a poor performer in terms of output growth. This can be explained in part because of the high starting level in the 1950s. Another reason appears to have been the slow growth in productivity, caused by the high levels of public sector expenditure and non-market services

employment. Within the EU, Denmark has by far the largest public sector (in terms of both revenue and expenditure as a percentage of GDP), which has had a negative effect on the development of the private sector. Another constraint on growth is rigidities in the labour market, which are caused in part by the (extended) social security system and the compressed wage structure.

On the positive side, cost-competitiveness and the international character of Danish industry need to be mentioned. In 1990, the current account went into surplus for the first time in 25 years and has shown substantial surpluses since then. The integrating European economy will provide an opportunity for the Danish economy. On top of that, austerity policies, structural reforms and a more favourable international environment (in the mid-1990s) have clearly had positive effects on the economy. Inflation, interest rates and the public deficit have been considerably reduced. As a result, Danish growth rates sharply picked up and unemployment decreased in the mid-1990s, while profitability went up and the currency gained strength. Further structural reforms of the public sector and the labour market may be necessary to secure higher growth rates in the future.

Finland

The Finnish economy was doing fairly well until 1990, with growth rates generally above the EU15 average. In the early 1990s Finland experienced the deepest economic recession since the 1930s, with a cumulative decrease in GDP of 12% in three years. GDP per head dropped to less then 90% of the EU15 average. The major factors contributing to this development were the sudden collapse of trade with the former Soviet Union, the overheated economy in the late 1980s, the deterioration of international cost competitiveness and the unfavourable international economic climate. The recession resulted in a number of imbalances, notably public and current account deficits and unemployment. Austerity measures, tight monetary policies, wage moderation and a sharp depreciation of the Finnish markka led to a marked recovery with growth rates well above the European average by the mid-1990s. Unemployment and the public deficit remain the main matters of concern.

Greece

The exceptional Greek long-term output growth rate of 4.1% mainly came about due to fast growth in the 1960s and 1970s. Since then, growth performance has been relatively poor, in spite of the Greek entrance into the EU in 1981 and substantial aid from EU regional funds. The most important problems for Greece are fiscal imbalances, public sector inefficiency, high inflation rates, lack of competitiveness and the underdeveloped infrastructure. Since a liberal–conservative party came into power in 1991, successive Greek governments (including subsequent socialist ones) have tried to address these problems, mainly by market-oriented structural reforms and austerity policies. Without a successful completion of this programme real GDP growth performance will probably remain weak.

Portugal

Together with Ireland, Spain and Greece, Portuguese growth rates are among the highest over the last four decades, averaging 4.1%, although the underdevelopment of the country in the 1950s at the periphery of a developed continent offered plenty of room for growth. The entrance of Portugal into the EU in 1986 turned out to be quite beneficial for the country to date, though Portugal was more seriously hit by the recession in the early 1990s than most other EU countries. Between 1986 and 1996 growth rates remained far above the EU average. Restructuring policies, which aimed to convert the highly regulated and protected economy into a market-orientated one, have proved rather successful. The country received large amounts of money from EU structural funds and special status until the end of 1992. Successful real (and nominal) convergence in the future will crucially depend on supply-side improvements like industrial restructuring, privatisation, financial liberalisation and administrative reform. Effective improvements will ensure that the country remains attractive for foreign capital as well, which can make a vital contribution to the development of the country.

Ireland

Ireland managed to realise impressive growth rates in both the long run and the recent past. Real convergence appears to be under way: per capita GDP increased from around 60% of the EU average in the early 1970s to around 94% in 1996! The country was furthermore very successful in redressing a number of imbalances in the 1980s, such as high inflation rates and huge budget and current account deficits; since 1991 the latter has even shown large surpluses. Since the mid-1970s the government pursued an intensive industrialisation programme, based among other things on attracting direct inward investment. The economy's orientation shifted from predominantly agriculture to services and manufacturing.

The major remaining imbalance is unemployment; Ireland has, together with Spain, the worst record within the EU. The high unemployment rates are in part explained by the excessive growth of the labour force and in part by other factors such as the Irish development strategy. The industrialisation programmes failed to attract labour-intensive industries and to integrate the successful foreign-based sectors with the indigenous sectors. The recent buoyancy of domestic demand, however, has had a very favourable effect on the more labour-intensive indigenous industries, contributing also to a substantial increase in employment.

The outlook for the Irish economy is very positive. Wage moderation and a stable currency will contribute to low inflation rates, providing the basis for a continuation of stable and high growth rates.

Luxembourg

The long-term growth rates of Luxembourg are roughly average over the last 36 years. In the 1960s and 1970s Luxembourg was an underperformer, mainly because of declining manufacturing industries. In the 1980s and 1990s, however, the country outpaced all other EU countries except Ireland. It has become a major international financial centre and is engaged in many international service activities. It has an outstanding record in almost every macroeconomic field, while per capita income is the highest in Europe. Future growth prospects look very favourable.

16.3.4 Real convergence in the Union?

For a successful economic integration to be achieved, a certain degree of nominal and real convergence is needed. Nominal convergence was discussed in Chapter 1 (Section 1.2.2, Table 1.1). This section addresses itself to real convergence. Has the Union witnessed a reduction in real income disparities in recent decades? Generally, the per capita incomes in purchasing power standards are taken as the most important indicator to evaluate this question. Real GDP growth is corrected for population increase in this case. In Figure 16.1 the development of real per capita GDP from 1975–96 of a number of selected countries is shown.

Of the four least developed countries (Greece, Portugal, Spain and Ireland) Portugal, Spain and

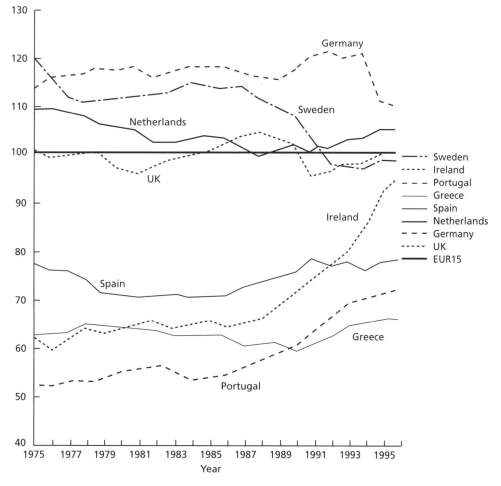

Figure 16.1 GDP per head at current prices for selected countries, 1975–96 (PPS: EUR15 average = 100) (1995, 1996 including east Germany = 100)

Source: Eurostat, Table G24.

especially Ireland made remarkable progress from 1986 onwards. This was also the year Portugal and Spain entered the Union. The efforts of these four countries to catch up to the average standard of living were supported by the Union's structural funds and national restructuring policies. Average income in Ireland had already been in an upward trend since 1973 (the year of entry of that country into the EU) and are close to the EU average at present. So far, EU membership appears to have beneficial for these three countries. Nevertheless, for Spain and Portugal there is still a long way to go before they meet the average living standard. For Greece it is a different story. Since its entry into the Union in 1981 the situation has hardly improved, despite heavy support from structural EU funds.

From Figure 16.1 some trends in the more advanced countries can also be identified. The most marked decline can be observed in Sweden, which used to be one of the richest countries in Europe, but is ranking at present even below the average level. The high costs of maintaining the welfare state are an important factor to explain this development. Dutch per capita income too showed, until 1990, a clear downward trend. This is due to the combination of average real income growth and an above average population increase. Since 1990 some improvement has been made, mainly caused by augmented labour participation rates and the relative mildness of the latest recession. Figure 16.1 also indicates that the German position has been deteriorating in recent years, although it should be taken into consideration that the figures of 1995 and 1996 include the poorer eastern part as well. The UK curve reflects the very moderate increase in real GDP; only in the late 1980s was a sharp improvement realised, which has been offset again during the deep recession of the early 1990s. Italy (not in the figure) made indisputable progress, particularly around 1980, and has surpassed both the UK and the Netherlands. Luxembourg (not in the figure) is nowadays by far the richest country in Europe, with a per capita income of around 165% of the EU average, clearly reflecting the country's success story.

Taken all together, it can be stated that real convergence indeed has taken place in the EU. Per capita income in virtually all countries (apart from tiny Luxembourg) has been tending towards the EU15 average in recent times. It appears that economic integration clearly favours this development. Some countries, notably Greece and Portugal, still have a long way to go, however.

16.4 PRODUCTIVITY AND COMPETITIVENESS

16.4.1 The overall picture

National competitiveness is affected by inflation, unit labour costs and productivity growth in relation to exchange rates. It is usual to consider these factors as they relate to tradable goods and services. The competitiveness of the European economy as a whole improved strongly in the 1990s, even relative to Japan and the USA. In the case of Japan, this is largely explained by the continuous appreciation of the yen, which only came to an end in 1994. By the mid-1980s the US dollar had increased very strongly in value, which had a very negative impact on US competitiveness. From 1986 onwards the dollar depreciated dramatically to reach, in 1992, an even lower level than a decade earlier. Since then, the dollar has slightly recovered, which has had a negative impact on American competitiveness in the following years.

Considerable progress has thus been made, also due to very moderate wage increases and sharp rises in productivity in the EU as a whole (see Table G1). The modest wage development can be attributed (at least partly) to a Phillips curve effect: unemployment and the unfavourable economic conditions at the beginning of the 1990s considerably reduced the bargaining power of the trade unions and hence resulted in limited wage demands. Labour productivity rose because of the lay-off of workers in company rationalisation measures and the capital-deepening investment policies implemented by employers in response to the economic crisis in the early

1990s. As a result the real unit labour costs of the whole European economy decreased by 5% between 1991 and 1996, compared to 1% in the USA and 0% in Japan (see Table G27). The real labour costs reduction contributed significantly to the improvement of company profits, which by the mid-1990s surpassed even the level of the prosperous 1960s (see Table G1).

More relevant for the degree of international competitiveness, however, are the unit labour costs of exported goods and services. If we take the double weighted[1] nominal unit labour costs of the total economy in a common currency (relative to six industrial non-member countries) as a standard, then the competitiveness of the EUR15 countries as a whole rose by 7% between 1991 and 1996; at the same time American competitiveness slightly decreased (–2%) while Japanese sharply fell (–20%). Considered in the long term, European competitiveness is at present about the same level as it used to be in the 1960s; in the late 1970s it was decisively lower.

16.4.2 The major EU countries

For individual European countries, their national degree of competitiveness is much more important, however, especially since almost 60% (on average) of their exports are going to other Member States of the Union. If we look at the nominal unit labour costs figures (in a common currency) of the five major European countries, striking differences can be observed (see Figure 16.2[2]).

Competitiveness in Germany (and France, to a lesser extent) clearly deteriorated between 1991 and 1996. The main explanation for these developments is the strong currencies of these countries, which appreciated against those of most of their competitors. Nominal unit labour costs measured in the national currency rose in Germany only slightly more than the European average and for France they increased considerably less in the same period. Before the depreciations of 1992–93, France had made substantial progress in improving competitiveness (see Figure 16.2). This was mainly due to successful policies of wage moderation in the 1980s.

The other three major countries in the EU – Italy, the UK and Spain – sharply improved their competitive position in the early 1990s. By far the most important cause for this improvement

[1] Weighted for geographical orientation and basket composition.

[2] For an overview of the relevant data (inflation, wages, unit labour costs etc.), per country, see Tables G2–16.

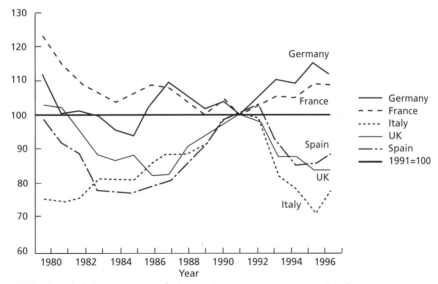

Figure 16.2 Nominal unit labour costs of the major European countries in a common currency (US$), 1980–92: total economy. Relative to 19 industrial countries; double export weights

Source: Eurostat, European Economy, No. 62

was the repeated depreciation of the currencies of these countries. In 1992, the UK pulled out of the ERM and Italy suspended its membership. Spain continued its participation, but was confronted with repeated devaluations. Between 1992 and 1995 the Italian lire lost more than 40% of its value vis-à-vis the German mark and the French franc before increasing, the British pound and the Spanish peseta around 20%.

Other factors played a role as well, however. In the early 1980s, the UK sharply improved its position, but fell back in the second half mainly due to inflationary pressures. The growth of annual earnings was quite considerable in the UK in that period and was not fully compensated by productivity growth. The deterioration of competitiveness came to an end only in the early 1990s, mainly because of the slowdown of wage increases due to the recession and the above-mentioned depreciation of sterling in 1992. Again it explains Britain's hesitation to participate in the EMS (and the European integration process in general), because the UK's membership will largely rule out use of the exchange rate instrument.

The development of Spain's competitiveness shows a similar pattern to that of the UK. After initial improvements in the early 1980s, the situation was reversed. This was mainly due to inflationary pressures in the country in the late 1980s caused by the demand side. Buoyant demand in an economy operating near capacity resulted in a gradual overheating and hence in a tendency for inflation to rise. The weakening of demand resulted in a substantial reduction of inflation, but only after a time lag. This is the main reason why nominal unit labour costs in terms of pesetas have risen more strongly than the European average, despite the very limited (cumulative) wage increase in the early 1990s. The gain in international competitiveness was realised only because of the depreciations of the peseta. Since stabilisation of the exchange rate has taken place, a deterioration of the Spanish position can be observed.

Italy's experience is quite different. Its steep deterioration in competitiveness in the 1980s compared to other European countries appears to be fairly dramatic; it only came to a halt after the sharp depreciation of the lira, which was in turn triggered by Italy's lack of international competitiveness. Especially in the 1980s, for the Italian economy as a whole, wage increases were higher than improvements in productivity. After a marked diminution of pay rises at the beginning of the decade, provoked by the unfavourable economic circumstances, wage inflation picked up again in the second half of the 1980s. This can be explained by the regained strength of trade unions, the continuing rise of social security transfers and the relative overall high level of inflation in Italy. Since the economic recession in the early 1990s the situation has changed radically, however. From 1991 onwards, nominal unit labour cost development (measured in national currencies) has been more or less in line with the European average. This increase in competitiveness is almost entirely attributable to the depreciation of the currency. One of the problems of the country is that Italy should perhaps, in this respect, not be treated as one country. While wage negotiations are centralised and on a national level, productivity improvements are certainly not. There are marked disparities between the northern and central parts on the one hand and the south on the other hand. So the increase in labour unit costs in the south has been much more dramatic than in the centre–north. But there are other reasons why concern over Italian competitiveness is justified. Italian industry is not particularly strong in those sectors which will benefit most from the completion of the internal market (i.e. the advanced sectors). The removal of internal barriers will also sharpen rivalry in the more mature and labour-intensive sectors which are still of great importance for Italy (and for the south in particular). Decentralisation of wage negotiations, an industrial policy encouraging R&D expenditure and the promotion of education and skills might be the spearheads in a medium-term policy to reverse the negative trend in Italian competitiveness. If Italy participates in the EMU, competitive devaluations will be no longer be an escape route.

16.4.3 The smaller EU countries

The currency crisis of 1992–93 was also one of the major determinants of the international competitiveness of the smaller countries. Countries with strong currencies, linked to the Deutschmark, generally saw their competitive strength decreasing – at least temporarily. This applies in particular to Austria, the Netherlands, Belgium and Denmark. Nonetheless, marked differences between these countries can be observed. The Netherlands, Belgium and, in particular, Denmark, were more successful in controlling inflation and moderating wage increases in the 1990s than Austria. This is reflected in the nominal unit labour costs in terms of national currencies, which increased considerably less in the first three countries than in Austria. Part of the loss of international competitiveness caused by higher exchange rates in the 1990s was compensated for by a better performance in terms of moderation of (nominal) wages, especially in the Netherlands and Denmark (See Figure 16.3).

In the 1980s, *the Netherlands* was very successful in increasing their competitiveness by means of successful government policies aimed at wage moderation, reduction of government expenditure and the budget deficit, and a decrease in inflation. To safeguard jobs, trade unions also refrained from excessive wage demands. The impact of the steadily increasing exchange rate of the guilder in those years was exceeded by far by the effect of modest real wage increases, causing unit labour costs to go down. In *Belgium*, too, wage increases have been constrained by government policies. In the early 1980s wage indexation and free wage negotiations were suspended and pay rises in the public sector were limited. In 1989, legislation was adopted giving the government ultimate authority to impose wage controls if Belgian competitiveness deteriorated. In 1994 a real wage freeze (covering 1994–96) was introduced to reduce the cost of labour.

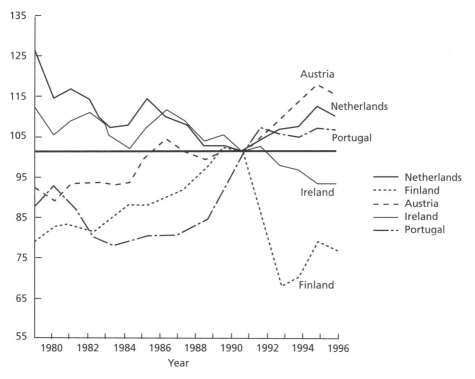

Figure 16.3 Nominal unit labour costs for a selected number of smaller European countries in a common currency (US$), 1980–92: total economy. Relative to 19 industrial countries; double export weights

The conservative-led coalition government, which came into power in *Denmark* in 1982, also put heavy stress on the reduction of the public sector, the cutback of direct taxes, the containment of wage increases and the recovery of Danish competitiveness. As a result, Danish competitiveness initially improved considerably in the 1980s; but it deteriorated again in the second half of the 1980s due to the hard currency policy of the government in combination with persistent inflation differentials. Since 1990 some good progress has been made again, however; productivity has risen more strongly than (real) wages.

Despite moderate wage development Austria's international competitiveness has been decreasing since the early 1970s. It appears that – especially in the 1980s – productivity growth has not been high enough to offset the effects of the steadily appreciating exchange rate. Monetary stability in Europe might improve the Austrian position.

Portugal was characterised by very high inflation rates in the 1980s. During most of the decade these inflation rates were more than offset by frequent depreciations of the escudo, preventing competitiveness deteriorating. This development was reversed, however, when Portugal started to pursue an anti-inflationary hard currency policy in the late 1980s, culminating in the membership of the escudo in the exchange rate mechanism of the EMS in 1992. During this period, Portugal's competitiveness deteriorated very rapidly (see Figure 16.3), due to strong rises in real wages, mainly caused by the tight situation on the labour market and time lags with respect to the falling rate of inflation. The decrease of Portugal's international competitiveness came to an end because of the repeated devaluations of the escudo in the period 1992–95 (immediately after its entrance into the ERM). It appears that Portugal is on its way to getting inflationary pressures under control.

Although wages and prices in *Greece* have been soaring since the end of the 1970s, competitiveness has, nevertheless, not been worsened in that decade. This can be explained by the continuous fall of the Greek drachma, which never participated in the ERM. Between 1980 and 1992 the double weighted nominal effective exchange rate of the drachma has fallen by almost 80% (!), largely offsetting the average yearly increase in nominal compensation per employee of 20% during the last decade. Since 1993 Greece's competitiveness has been reduced, however, mainly because of increased wage pressures and the sharply reduced pace of depreciation of the currency.

The improvement of *Irish* competitiveness in the second half of the 1980s was mainly due to very low inflation rates and moderate wage development in relation to productivity. The latter can be explained by the existing social consensus, and the high unemployment rate (Phillips curve effect). The Irish position was further strengthened after the devaluations of the Irish currency (the punt) in 1993, when the punt had to follow the depreciation of the British pound. The outlook for Ireland is very favourable: high productivity growth, low inflation and moderate wage increases. Strongly increasing international competitiveness provides another explanation for the country's successes in recent years.

The developments in *Sweden* and *Finland* showed some strong similarities. The international competitiveness of both countries fell sharply in the 1980s, mainly because of rapidly rising wage costs not matched by productivity increases. These developments resulted for both countries in substantial deficits on their external balances, causing in turn a dramatic fall of their currencies in the years 1991–92. The cheaper currencies had an immediate effect on competitiveness, which sharply improved. Unit labour costs in a common currency considerably decreased (for Finland: see Figure 16.3). It is uncertain what will happen with competitiveness once the currencies have been stabilised; both countries are likely to opt for EMU membership. It appears to be that by the mid-1990s Finland has managed to bring inflationary pressures under control.

16.5 FINANCIAL SYSTEM

16.5.1 The European financial markets

Financial markets and financial intermediation play an important role in the economy. They provide, for instance, the following services:

- gathering financial surpluses (savings) and channelling these funds to investment opportunities (real and financial);
- allocation of financial resources to the most efficient users;
- spread of risks.

The financial sector is also quite important in terms of output and employment. In 1993 it accounted for approximately 8% of total value-added of the Union and for some 4% of total employment. An efficient financial system will obviously enhance economic welfare. The total amount of saving and investment will rise, new business formation will be encouraged and factors of production will be better allocated, increasing their productivity. That is why the Union is aiming to improve the European financial system by establishing a common European financial area. Distinct national banking regulation, high establishment costs for new banks, restrictions on foreign acquisitions or participations in indigenous banks, limitations in cross-frontier activities, exchange controls and other regulatory barriers have segmented European financial markets and hence prevented their efficient operation until recently.

In line with most other Union policies, the creation of a common financial market is mainly sought via deregulation, removal of barriers and harmonisation of standards and banking licences and, last but not least, in strengthening of the monetary system. Considerable progress has been made in the adoption by the European Council in 1988 of the directive on the complete liberalisation of capital movements, which came into effect on 1 July 1990. From that moment on all restrictions on monetary or quasi-monetary transactions (financial loans and credits, current account, deposit account and stock market operations)

were abolished. For Member States facing balance of payments difficulties because of this capital liberalisation, the medium-term financial support facility (MTFS) was created, a regulation granting them medium-term loans. On top of that some countries (notably Spain, Greece and Ireland) got temporary derogations. With the completion of the first stage of the EMU by the end of 1994 (see also Chapter 1, Section 1.2.2), free movement of capital has been realised and all temporary derogations have expired. Nevertheless, some obstacles are still in place, such as differences in tax arrangements applied to certain financial investments. It is intended to harmonise these arrangements as well in the near future.

Notwithstanding this trend towards integration of the financial system within the Community, marked discrepancies in financial attitudes and practices can still be observed at present in Europe. Examples can be found in the field of:

1. the financing of firms (see Section 16.5.2);
2. monetary policies and the stances and responsibilities of central banks (see Section 16.5.3).

16.5.2 Financing of firms

The financing of firms is dominated by the banks (and special credit institutions) in Germany, Spain, France and Italy. Of the EU countries, only in the UK, the Netherlands and Belgium, is the stock market of major importance. Financing of companies through the stock market is also more widespread in the USA and especially in Japan (see Table 16.2).

Table 16.2 Stock market capitalisation, end 1992

	billion ECU	*% of GDP*
UK	651	81
Netherlands	134	54
France	280	27
FR Germany	320	20
Spain	76	17
Italy	133	14
Japan	1768	62
USA	3663	81

In both Spain and Italy, the stock market has been very underdeveloped until now. This is less the case in Germany and France, where it is of growing importance. The method of company financing is of particular relevance in affecting management attitudes towards risks and profits. On the one hand, financing through stock markets has the advantage of spreading business risks more widely. This can encourage investment involving high risks, because banks are generally reluctant to engage in this kind of business. Another advantage of market-based financing is that the financial vulnerability of companies will be reduced because equity is higher. Furthermore, public information on business will be more widely available because of legal disclosure requirements for firms issuing stocks and bonds. This will enhance transparency of the capital markets. Against this, it is recognised that security-based finance can result in a preoccupation of management with short-term profits and dividend goals as Stone explains in Chapter 7. Focusing on short-term objectives may have a negative influence on long-term development and performance. Most shareholders (including institutional investors) are not concerned with the running of companies, while banks generally supply expertise if they are financially involved in a company.

If we apply the foregoing remarks to company financing in Europe, we reach the following conclusions. Spain, Italy and, arguably, Germany: stock markets should play a more prominent role. Well-developed, risk capital markets are missing in these countries, frustrating new business formation and new venture initiatives. In the UK, by contrast, the dominance of stock market financing prevents business management from achieving long-term goals and objectives, essential for survival and long-term profitability of the companies involved. The best solution may be a convergence of the two extreme positions; the UK shifting to long-term finance through banks and the other countries to a more security-based financing. There are clear signs that this is happening.

16.5.3 Central banks and monetary policies

The stance and responsibilities of central banks vary greatly in the Community. At the one extreme is the German central bank. The *Deutsche Bundesbank* is almost completely independent from the German Treasury. Its main goal is to support price stability and the value of the deutschmark. Furthermore, it is supposed to support the economic policy of the Federal Government, but only in so far that this policy does not interfere with its main task. This arrangement reflects the German preoccupation with inflation, originating from Germany's traumatic pre-war experiences. In general, it has proved to be very successful.

In Italy, too, the central bank is relatively independent of central government. Since 1982 it has no longer been obliged to act as 'buyer of last resort' of public debt bonds. This 'divorce from the Treasury' was mainly effected in order to ensure a more solid stance of monetary authorities towards inflation, government itself being at the mercy of unstable political relations and interests. In the Netherlands, the central bank is formally subordinate to the Treasury. In practice, however, it is largely independent. It normally adapts to the policies of the German *Bundesbank*.

The German, Italian and Dutch system used to be in sharp contrast to those of the British, Spanish and French. In France for example, the *Banque de France* was closely related to the centralised French state and played an even more important role in state-induced credit distribution in the past. In the UK, the *Bank of England* is a public sector body which acts under the (ultimate) authority of the Treasury, so the Bank of England can be considered a policy instrument of the British government. In Spain, too, there are close links between the banking sector and government; besides the central bank (*Banco de Espana*) many banks are state-owned.

What does this mean with respect to monetary policy? For the *Bundesbank*, fighting inflation is the first and utmost priority. The control of the money supply and interest rates principally serves this goal. Other objectives, like demand management, prevention or smoothing of recessions, attraction of foreign capital and stabilisation of exchange rates are subordinate. Spain, Italy, Portugal, however, also used interest rates to support their currency or to attract foreign capital. Even more important is the utilisation of interest rates as a major weapon against recession, even if this may cause inflation or a downward pressure on exchange rates, as the UK, Spain and Italy did in the recent past. That is also one of the major reasons why disturbances occurred on the currency markets in 1992–93. Basically, these events were caused by differences in monetary objectives of the countries involved, in part due to different stances and responsibilities of their central banks.

Clearly, nominal interest rate differentials cannot be maintained, once monetary unification occurs. This means that the goals and implementation of monetary policy should be agreed upon internationally. The problem, however, is that apart from convergence problems, the setting of short-term monetary objectives may be influenced by differences in the phases of the business cycle applying to the various countries as well. This was clearly the case in 1992 when the UK found itself in the middle of a recession while the economy in Germany was just peaking.

Nevertheless, it has been decided (by the Treaty of Maastricht) that Europe's EMU will have a system of central banks (ESCB), coordinated by an *independent* European Central Bank (ECB), the main objective of which will be price stability. The main task of the national central banks will be the implementation of the supranational policies set by the ECB. For that reason, they should also receive autonomous status and no longer be subordinate to their governments, before EMU can start. Germany is an avowed proponent of this set-up. For many other countries the establishment of the ECSB and ECB means a radical change in approach to monetary policies and in the position of their central banks. For all Member States it will mean another substantial loss of national sovereignty. That is one of the reasons why the UK is very reluctant to participate in EMU. Other countries,

notably France and Spain, have recently given their central banks an autonomous status, as was agreed to be realised in the second stage of the EMU treaty (see Section 1.2.2).

16.6 NATIONAL SPECIALISATION WITHIN THE UNION

The establishment of the large internal market, which came into effect in January 1993, will almost certainly induce a reallocation of factors of production and economic activities, according to each country's specific competitive advantages. This will be the case because most artificial barriers, protecting inefficient industries, have been removed. This raises the question of what the distribution of industries will look like in the future Europe. Obviously, nothing can be said for sure, but a tentative attempt can be made to identify some future industry patterns in Europe. A higher degree of specialisation can be expected in the field of tradeable goods and services along the lines of a country's or region's strong and weak points.

This raises the question, first of all, by which conditions are comparative advantages of nations determined? It may be clear that this question is not simple to answer. According to Michael Porter, international successes of a particular (branch of) industry in a certain country is dependent on four determinants:

1. the costs and availability of factors of production;
2. demand conditions;
3. the presence of related and supporting industries;
4. firm strategy, industry structure and rivalry.

These determinants are strongly interrelated and form a kind of mutually reinforcing system (called a 'diamond' in Porter's terminology). Additional variables, influencing the national system, are government and chance. Without relying completely on Porter's system, one can appreciate that competitiveness is dependent on a whole range of conditions. A large and demanding domestic market, vigorous competition, sufficient scale, favourable physical conditions, a high concentration of related industries, a good infrastructure, entrepreneurship, starting positions and government support play a prominent role. With this in mind we will try to ascertain some possible fields of specialisation for the EU countries (Table 16.3). The list, which does not pretend to be complete, is principally based on existing dominant positions and future perspectives.

Table 16.3 Possible fields of specialisation within the European Community

Major EC countries:

Germany

Services:
- construction services

Manufacturing:
- electrical engineering (electric motors, generators, transformers, household appliances, telecommunications)
- mechanical and instrument engineering (machineries, machine tools and equipment, plant for mines, iron, steel)
- motor vehicles and motor vehicles parts and accessories
- metal goods
- chemicals
- environment protection equipment and know-how
- energy-efficient machinery and tools

France

Services:
- tourism
- engineering

Manufacturing:
- data processing, office machinery
- motor vehicles, parts and accessories
- aerospace
- nuclear power and hydroelectricity
- electrical equipment
- food
- drink (wine, brewing and malting, soft drinks, water)
- pharmaceutical products
- wool

Agriculture:
- dairy, livestock produce, fruit and vegetables

Italy

Services:
- tourism
- design services, fashion

Manufacturing:
- motor vehicle parts and accessories, motorcycles
- textile and leather, footwear and clothing
- furnishing
- jewellery
- machinery, machine tools
- electrical household appliances
- insulated wires and cables
- food industry (manufactured pasta, wine)

United Kingdom

Services:
- financial services (banking, insurance, financial intermediation)
- business services (advertising, management consulting, accounting, engineering)
- trading services

Manufacturing:
- chemicals (basic, industrial, agricultural)
- pharmaceuticals
- aircraft, aircraft parts and engines
- office machinery, computers and computer parts, software
- printing and publishing
- telecommunication equipment
- electrical plant and machinery and other equipment
- brewing, soft drinks

Energy:
- oil products

Spain

Services:
- tourism

Manufacturing:
- motor vehicles
- oil refinery
- electrical household appliances
- insulated wires and cables
- food and drink products
- footwear, household textiles, clothing
- rubber goods, ceramics
- wine, olive, oil

Agriculture:
- fruit and vegetables

Smaller countries:

Netherlands

Services:
- transport and communication
- trading services
- business services

Manufacturing:
- basic industrial chemicals
- telecommunications equipment

- electronic appliances, radio, TV
- food processing
- shipbuilding

Agriculture:
- dairy products
- horticulture

Belgium

Services
- (international) administration
- transport and distribution
- financial services (banking and insurance)

Manufacturing
- basic industrial chemicals
- food and drink (brewing, malting, water, soft drinks, chocolate)
- car assembly
- wool and cotton, carpets, household textiles
- glass and glassware

Austria

Services
- tourism

Manufacturing
- machinery
- steel and metal products
- electrical engineering
- chemicals

Sweden

Services:
- business services (consulting, engineering)

Manufacturing
- iron and steel (steel powders, high carbon steel, blades, tips for tools)
- machinery (paper mill machinery, agricultural machinery)
- bearings (ball, roller bearings)
- aircraft
- marine engines
- gas welders
- mechanical handling equipment and power hand tools
- telecommunication equipment
- electrical transformers
- builders woodwork, prefabricated

Denmark

Services:
- transport and distribution
- trading services

Manufacturing:
- pharmaceuticals
- machinery

- medical and surgical equipment
- shipbuilding
- processing of plastics

Agriculture:
- fishing

Finland

Services:
- engineering services, consulting
- telecommunications services
- tourism

Manufacturing
- paper
- paper industry
- telecommunications equipment
- electrical machinery for industrial use
- energy technology

Portugal

Services:
- tourism

Manufacturing
- textiles, clothing, footwear
- fish and other seafood, wine
- ceramics
- insulated wires and cables
- paper and pulp

Greece

Services:
- shipping
- tourism

Manufacturing:
- cement
- clothing and footwear
- household textiles
- wool and knitting industry

Ireland

Manufacturing:
- office and data-processing
- telecommunications equipment
- medical and surgical equipment
- pharmaceuticals
- dairy products
- insulated wires and cables

Luxembourg

Services:
- financial services (banking and insurance)
- trading and business services

Specialisation within a particular country in a certain field of industry in this list does not mean that other countries will retreat from this kind of activity; it merely indicates that this country has or will possibly develop a leading position in (branches of) this industry. Moreover, dominant positions can be shared with other countries. Apart from these specialisations, many industries will continue to exist in virtually every country, simply because these industries are hardly able to serve more than local markets (e.g. construction and most services).

The table shows that – in broad terms – it is to be expected that of the major EU countries Germany will remain the industrial workshop of Europe, the UK the financial heart, Italy the designing and fashion centre. Similar striking national specialisations can not so easily be identified in France or Spain; only in tourism do these countries occupy rather dominant positions. The scope of activities in both countries is fairly broad; France, having clear-cut comparative advantages in capital and R & D intensive sectors, is engaged in industrial activities at a more advanced level and Spain still at an intermediate level.

The key to German success is a high level of productivity, quality, reliability. Maintaining and strengthening of the German position, which is now under threat, will crucially depend on R&D, education, social stability, improvement of the labour market and restriction of labour costs increases. German competitiveness in international services (except for construction services) is rather weak. The UK has a leading position in this field. The City of London has become the third financial centre of the world, directly after New York and Tokyo, with technical innovations and deregulation contributing to the reinforcement of its dominant position. London is confronted more and more, however, with competition from its continental rivals in, for example, Frankfurt and Paris. Commitment to Europe is a essential condition for London to maintain its position.

The use of English as a major language of communication may be one of the explanations of the strong presence of the UK in the international business service market.

Italy's powerful place in the area of design, fashion, apparel and related industries can be attributed to the sophisticated demand of the domestic market and the possibility performing this kind of activity in small- and medium-sized companies, which are typical of the Italian private sector.

The strength of the French nuclear power and defence industry is partly due to favourable government procurement and state intervention policies and the independent attitude with regard to national defence of consecutive French governments.

Of the smaller economies Belgium, the Netherlands and Denmark occupy strong positions in the service industry, especially in distribution, transport, communication and trading services. Belgium leads in the intra-EU sea transport market and the Netherlands in the intra-EU road transport market. The central location of these countries clearly offers them a comparative advantage in this field. In addition, Belgium and Luxembourg have solid positions in the financial service industry; both countries also accommodate the seats of numerous international organisations and companies.

Due to their favourable climate and attractive coasts Portugal and Greece are well placed for tourism. Because of their low wages both countries also have a comparative advantage in labour-intensive manufacturing sectors (such as clothing and footwear). These sectors, however, are characterised by low demand growth and are facing increased competition from developing countries. Without substantial restructuring Greece, Portugal (and also Spain) will lose their competitive advantage in this field, Spain and Portugal being well on their way to doing so. Modernisation of the traditional industries should possibly be combined with an improvement of product quality (upgrading), in order to develop non-cost competitive factors. Italy can serve as an example in the implementation of such a policy.

Although wages in Ireland are modest as well, the country has a rather weak position in labour-intensive industries. It does hold a strong position in high-tech manufacturing sectors, however, due to the presence of many multinationals.

Of the new EU members Finland is very strong in paper and paper industry; the acquired competitive advantage in this field is originally based on abundant natural resources (wood) in this country. The country also developed an advanced telecommunications industry. Sweden traditionally has a competitive advantage in industries (originally) based on iron and steel, like machineries and engines; furthermore, it holds a strong position in the field of advanced industries like aircraft and telecommunications equipment. Austria, finally, has a notable manufacturing tradition as well, especially in machinery and metal and metal production and electrical engineering. In order to keep its advantage, however, innovation and a shift towards more high-technology sectors might be required.

A dominant position, once established, tends to reinforce itself. The removal of administrative barriers can act as a catalyst in addition. So, the completion of the internal market will probably have a positive effect on national specialisation.

16.7 FINAL CONCLUSIONS

In concluding this book, we will return to the subject of the importance of national states within the emerging European Economic and Monetary Union.

The completion of the EMU before the end of this millennium will mean that monetary and budgetary policies will be carried out chiefly by a central authority, backed up by centrally controlled policies in the field of infrastructure, education, R&D, environment, regional policy and competition.

Important responsibilities left to national governments are expected to be the supply of public goods (those without cross-frontier effects), income transfers and redistribution and fiscal policies (in part).

This transfer of power from national to supranational level means a considerable reduction of national sovereignty and will lead to a loss of

significance of the national states as independent entities.

This development notwithstanding, there will remain substantial geographical differences within the Union. These differences are determined by distinct industry patterns, inequalities in economic development and performance, variations in mentalities, tastes and culture, and will even be reinforced by an eventual higher degree of local specialisation.

With the national states losing influence as economic and political entities, however, regions probably will become relatively more important. Barriers between neighbouring regions will be broken down and cross-frontier contacts intensified.

Regions within nations will possibly be of increasing importance as well. This can apply to differences between rural and urban areas, but also to differences between one agglomeration and another.

New opportunities and increased competition caused by the integrated market may emphasize not only local specialisation, but also disparities and unequal developments between nations. National instruments to adjust these developments will partly be dismantled or transferred to the Union level. The size, effectiveness and degree of differentiation of the Union policy is not yet clear. But despite of this expected shift in relative importance from the national to the regional level, national differences will probably remain of great interest, even in a United Europe.

16.8 BIBLIOGRAPHY

Commission of the European Communities, *European Economy* (four issues a year) plus Supplement A: Economic Trends (eleven issues per year)

OECD (annually): *Country surveys*

The Economist Intelligence Unit, *Country Reports* (four issues per year)

Jacqemin, A., Wright, D. (eds), *The European Challenges Post-1992, Shaping Factors, Shaping Actors,* Edward Elgar Publishing Ltd., 1993

PART G

Statistical information

LIST OF TABLES

Main economic indicators, 1961–96

G1   EUR15+
G2   Belgium
G3   Denmark
G4   Germany
G5   Greece
G6   Spain
G7   France
G8   Ireland
G9   Italy
G10 Luxembourg
G11 Netherlands
G12 Austria
G13 Portugal
G14 Finland
G15 Sweden
G16 UK

Population

G17 Total population in thousands

Labour force and employment

G18 Working population and employment – 1993
G19 Civilian employment by main sectors of economic activity – 1993 (in thousands)
G20 Unemployment rate (percentage of civilian labour force)

Gross domestic product

G21 GDP at current market prices (ECU;mrd)
G22 GDP at current market prices (PPS)
G23 GDP at 1990 market prices (percentage change)
G24 GDP at current market prices per head of population (PPS; EUR15=100)

G25 Gross value-added at market prices by branch (as a percentage) – 1992
G26 Use of gross domestic product at market prices (as a percentage) – 1993

Wages and productivity

G27 Real unit labour costs – total economy

Consumption, saving, investment

G28 Private consumption at current prices (ESA) (percentage of GDP at market prices)
G29 Gross fixed capital formation at current prices; total economy (percentage of GDP at market prices)
G30 Gross fixed capital formation at 1990 prices; total economy (annual percentage change)

Prices

G31 Price deflator GDP at market prices (national currency; annual percentage change)

Government

G32 Total expenditure by general government (percentage of GDP at market prices)
G33 Total current receipts; general government (percentage of GDP at market prices)
G34 Net lending or net borrowing of general government (percentage of GDP at market prices)

Finance

G35 Nominal short-term interest rates
G36 Nominal long-term interest rates

International relations

G37 Balance on current account with the rest of the world (ESA) percentage of GDP at market prices)

G38 Structure of EU exports by country and region, 1958 and 1994

G39 Structure of EU imports by country and region, 1958 and 1994

G40 Balance of payments by main heading – 1993 (MioECU)

G41 Exchange rates (annual average, national currency units per ECU)

G42 Nominal effective exchange rates. Performance relative to 19 industrial countries, double export weights.

FIGURES

GF1 GDP per head, volume (PPS)[1]

GF2 Civilian employment – 1993

SOURCES

All data are derived from official EU publications.

Statistical Annex of European Economy, June 1996: Tables G1–17, G20–24, G27–39, G41–42

Eurostat: Basic Statistics of the European Union, 32nd edition, 1995: Tables G18–19, G25–26, G40, Figures GF 1–2.

1995 and 1996 figures are estimates and forecasts made by Commission staff using the definitions and latest figures available from national sources and based on data up to 15 May 1996.

Reproduced by kind permission of the European Communities.

SYMBOLS AND ABBREVIATIONS USED

B	Belgium
DK	Denmark
D	Federal Republic of Germany
GR	Greece
E	Spain
F	France
IRL	Ireland
I	Italy
L	Luxembourg
NL	Netherlands
A	Austria
P	Portugal
SF	Finland
S	Sweden
UK	United Kingdom
EUR15	Total of Member States of the EU (15); 1960–90: incl. West Germany; 1991–96 including the whole of Germany (unless otherwise stated).
EUR12	EU before latest enlargement with Sweden, Austria and Finland
–	nil
:	not available
Mio	Million
ECU	European Currency Unit
PPS	Purchasing Power Standard
GDP	Gross Domestic Product

Table G1 EUR15+[1]: Main economic indicators 1961–96 (annual percentage change, unless otherwise stated)

	1961–73	*1974–85*	*1986–90*	*1991–95*	*1991*	*1992*	*1993*	*1994*	*1995*	*1996*
1 Gross domestic product[2]										
At current market prices	10.2	12.8	8.3	5.4	7.1	5.5	3.1	5.5	5.5	4.1
At 1990 market prices	4.7	2.0	3.3	1.4	1.5	1.0	–0.6	2.8	2.5	1.5
2 Gross fixed capital formation at 1990 prices[2]										
Total	5.7	–0.1	5.7	–0.4	–0.3	–0.9	–6.5	2.5	3.5	2.2
Construction	:	–1.2	4.8	0.1	–0.4	–0.9	–3.3	2.1	1.5	0.9
Equipment	:	–1.9	6.9	–1.0	–0.4	–3.3	–10.8	3.2	6.3	4.0
3 Gross fixed capital formation at current prices (% of GDP)[3]										
Total	23.4	21.3	20.3	19.5	20.9	20.2	18.9	18.7	18.9	18.9
General government	:	3.2	2.8	2.8	3.0	3.0	2.8	2.7	2.6	2.5
Other sectors	:	18.0	17.4	16.7	18.0	17.2	16.1	16.0	16.4	16.5
4 Final national uses incl. stocks[4]										
At 1990 prices	4.5	1.6	3.6	0.8	1.2	0.6	–2.1	2.5	2.1	1.3
Relative against 6 other OECD countries	–0.8	–0.9	0.2	–0.8	0.9	–0.5	–3.9	–0.6	0.0	–0.9
5 Inflation[2]										
Price deflator private consumption	4.7	10.7	4.2	4.1	5.6	4.7	4.1	3.2	3.0	2.6
Price deflator GDP	5.2	10.5	4.9	3.9	5.5	4.5	3.7	2.7	3.0	2.6
6 Compensation per employee[2]										
Nominal	9.9	12.4	6.2	4.9	7.0	6.8	4.0	3.2	3.5	3.4
Real, deflator private consumption	5.0	1.5	1.9	0.8	1.3	2.0	0.0	0.0	0.5	0.8
Real, deflator GDP	4.5	1.7	1.2	1.0	1.4	2.1	0.3	0.5	0.5	0.7
7 GDP at 1990 market prices per person employed[2]	4.4	2.0	1.9	2.0	1.3	2.4	1.3	3.1	1.9	1.2
8 Real unit labour costs[4]										
1961–73 = 100	100.0	103.6	97.9	95.9	97.7	97.7	96.7	94.3	93.2	93.0
Annual % change	0.2	–0.1	–0.5	–0.9	0.3	0.0	–1.0	–2.5	–1.1	–0.3
9 Relative unit labour costs in common currency[4] Against 9 other OCED countries										
1961–73 = 100	100.0	101.0	97.3	98.5	103.9	107.8	94.5	91.5	94.9	97.3
Annual % change	0.9	–1.9	5.4	–2.4	–3.0	3.8	–12.4	–3.1	3.7	2.6
10 Employment[2]	0.3	0.0	1.3	–0.6	0.1	–1.4	–1.9	–0.3	0.6	0.2
11 Unemployment rate (% of civilian labour force)[3]	2.3	6.4	9.0	10.2	8.3	9.4	10.9	11.3	10.9	11.0
12 Current balance (% of GDP)[3]	0.3	–0.3	0.1	–0.4	–1.3	–1.2	0.0	0.1	0.5	0.5
13 Net lending (+) or net borrowing (–) of general government (% of GDP)[3]	–0.5	–3.9	–3.4	–5.3	–4.3	–5.1	–6.3	–5.5	–5.1	–4.4
14 General government gross debt[3] (end of period; % of GDP)	:	53.7	55.3	71.2	56.1	60.4	66.2	68.2	71.2	74.1
15 Interest payments by general government (% of GDP)[3]	:	3.2	4.7	5.3	4.9	5.3	5.4	5.3	5.4	5.4
16 Money supply (end of year)[3] [5]	12.6	12.8	10.2	:	6.4	5.6	6.6	2.5	:	:
17 Long-term interest rate (%)[3]	7.0	11.8	9.8	8.9	10.3	9.8	7.8	8.2	8.6	7.6
18 Profitability (1961–73 = 100)[4]	100.0	73.6	88.6	93.8	90.3	91.3	90.1	97.4	100.0	101.5

[1] incl. West Germany, unless otherwise stated.
[2] 1961–91: incl. West Germany.
[3] 1961–90: incl. West Germany.
[4] 1961–94: incl. West Germany.
[5] Broad money supply M2 or M3 according to country.

Table G2 Denmark: Main economic indicators 1961–96 (annual percentage change, unless otherwise stated)

	1961–73	1974–85	1986–90	1991–95	1991	1992	1993	1994	1995	1996
1 Gross domestic product										
At current market prices	11.7	11.2	5.4	3.9	3.6	3.4	2.2	6.1	4.4	3.3
At 1990 market prices	4.3	2.0	1.4	2.0	1.3	0.2	1.5	4.4	2.6	1.3
2 Gross fixed capital formation at 1990 prices										
Total	6.5	−0.9	0.9	−0.3	−5.7	−4.2	−4.7	3.0	11.0	3.8
Constuction	:	−3.4	0.0	−1.9	−11.2	0.3	−8.8	3.2	8.3	4.2
Equipment	:	3.5	1.6	1.4	0.5	−8.3	−0.9	3.2	13.5	3.5
3 Gross fixed capital formation at current prices (% of GDP)										
Total	24.0	19.6	18.8	15.6	16.5	15.6	15.0	14.8	16.1	16.5
General government	:	3.2	2.1	2.0	1.6	2.3	2.2	2.1	2.0	1.9
Other sectors	:	16.4	16.7	13.6	14.9	13.3	12.8	12.7	14.1	14.6
4 Final national uses incl. stocks										
At 1990 prices	4.6	1.3	0.4	2.1	−0.4	−0.1	0.8	5.8	4.5	1.1
Relative against 19 competitors	0.2	−0.6	−2.9	1.0	−1.1	−0.7	1.7	3.0	2.4	−0.6
Relative against other member countries	0.3	−0.3	−3.1	1.4	−1.4	−0.4	3.2	3.3	2.5	−0.3
5 Inflation										
Price deflator private consumption	6.6	9.6	3.7	1.6	2.4	2.0	0.3	1.7	1.8	1.8
Price deflator GDP	7.0	9.0	3.9	1.9	2.2	3.2	0.7	1.7	1.7	2.0
6 Compensation per employee										
Nominal	10.7	10.1	5.1	3.3	4.3	3.8	1.6	3.6	3.3	3.9
Real, deflator private consumption	3.8	0.5	1.4	1.7	1.8	1.7	1.4	1.8	1.5	2.1
Real, deflator GDP	3.4	1.0	1.2	1.4	2.1	0.6	0.9	1.8	1.6	1.9
7 GDP at 1990 market prices per person employed	3.2	1.5	1.2	2.4	2.9	0.9	2.5	5.0	1.1	1.3
8 Real unit labour costs										
1961–73 = 100	100.0	100.0	94.4	90.9	92.9	92.7	91.3	88.5	89.0	89.5
Annual % change	0.2	−0.4	0.0	−1.0	−0.8	−0.3	−1.5	−3.0	0.5	0.6
9 Relative unit labour costs in common currency										
Against 19 other competitors										
1961–73 = 100	100.0	110.0	107.4	106.4	104.1	106.9	106.1	104.5	110.6	110.2
Annual % change	2.1	−1.3	2.7	0.2	−5.0	2.6	−0.7	−1.5	5.8	−0.3
Against other member countries										
1961–73 = 100	100.0	109.4	107.8	106.0	101.9	103.5	107.1	106.2	111.2	110.0
Annual % change	1.9	−0.8	1.0	0.8	−4.5	1.6	3.4	−0.8	4.7	−1.1
10 Employment	1.1	0.5	0.3	−0.4	−1.5	−0.6	−1.0	−0.6	1.5	0.0
11 Unemployment rate (% of civilian labour force)	1.1	6.4	6.4	8.5	8.4	9.2	10.1	8.2	6.8	6.1
12 Current balance (% of GDP)	−2.0	−3.5	−2.1	1.6	1.1	2.3	2.9	1.4	0.4	0.6
13 Net lending (+) or net borrowing (−) of general government (% of GDP)	2.2	−2.8	0.9	−2.8	−2.1	−2.9	−3.9	−3.5	−1.4	−0.9
14 General government gross debt (end of period; % of GDP)	8.8	72.0	59.6	71.9	64.6	68.7	80.1	76.0	71.9	71.0
15 Interest payments by general government (% of GDP)	:	4.5	8.0	7.2	7.4	6.8	7.8	7.1	6.7	6.4
16 Money supply (end of year)[1]	10.6	13.5	6.3	3.7	6.4	−0.7	14.6	−5.6	3.9	:
17 Long-term interest rate (%)	9.0	16.0	10.8	8.7	10.1	10.1	7.2	7.9	8.3	7.4
18 Profitability (1961–73 = 100)	100.0	76.6	86.9	76.2	69.4	70.9	72.6	83.0	84.9	84.3

[1] M2.

Table G3 Belgium: Main economic indicators 1961–96 (annual percentage change, unless otherwise stated)

	1961–73	1974–85	1986–90	1991–95	1991	1992	1993	1994	1995	1996
1 Gross domestic product										
At current market prices	9.2	8.6	6.2	4.3	4.9	5.4	2.4	4.9	3.9	3.2
At 1990 market prices	4.9	1.8	3.0	1.3	2.2	1.8	−1.6	2.2	1.9	1.1
2 Gross fixed capital formation at 1990 prices										
Total	5.1	−0.7	9.5	−1.0	−1.5	0.2	−6.7	0.5	2.7	3.8
Constuction	:	−2.9	7.6	1.7	2.3	5.5	−2.1	1.4	1.8	2.9
Equipment	:	2.4	11.7	−4.2	−5.1	−6.1	−12.4	−0.8	4.0	4.9
3 Gross fixed capital formation at current prices (% of GDP)										
Total	21.8	19.6	17.8	18.3	19.5	19.1	17.8	17.4	17.5	18.0
General government	3.4	3.3	1.7	1.4	1.4	1.5	1.5	1.5	1.3	1.3
Other sectors	18.4	16.3	16.1	16.8	18.0	17.6	16.3	15.9	16.2	16.7
4 Final national uses incl. stocks										
At 1990 prices	4.8	1.2	3.8	1.1	2.0	2.2	−1.8	1.4	1.6	1.4
Relative against 19 competitors	−0.1	−0.6	0.2	−0.1	0.7	1.4	−0.6	−1.3	−0.4	0.0
Relative against other member countries	0.0	−0.4	0.2	0.1	0.5	1.5	0.2	−1.1	−0.4	0.2
5 Inflation										
Price deflator private consumption	3.7	7.5	2.3	2.4	2.5	2.0	3.1	3.0	1.5	2.0
Price deflator GDP	4.1	6.7	3.1	3.0	2.7	3.5	4.1	2.6	2.0	2.1
6 Compensation per employee										
Nominal	9.0	9.4	3.8	4.8	7.9	6.0	3.3	4.8	1.9	1.7
Real, deflator private consumption	5.1	1.8	1.5	2.3	5.3	4.0	0.2	1.8	0.4	−0.3
Real, deflator GDP	4.7	2.5	0.6	1.8	5.1	2.4	−0.8	2.1	0.0	−0.4
7 GDP at 1990 market prices per person employed	4.3	2.1	1.9	1.7	2.1	2.3	−0.4	2.9	1.6	1.2
8 Real unit labour costs										
1961–73 = 100	100.0	111.3	104.1	104.4	105.2	105.3	104.9	104.2	102.6	100.9
Annual % change	0.4	0.4	−1.2	0.1	3.0	0.1	−0.4	−0.7	−1.5	−1.6
9 Relative unit labour costs in common currency										
Against 19 other competitors										
1961–73 = 100	100.0	104.3	92.7	100.3	94.9	97.3	99.6	103.2	106.4	103.2
Annual % change	−0.3	−1.1	1.3	2.5	0.8	2.5	2.3	3.7	3.1	−3.1
Against other member countries										
1961–73 = 100	100.0	103.1	92.7	100.1	93.7	95.3	100.1	104.5	106.8	103.2
Annual % change	−0.7	−0.7	0.1	3.0	1.5	1.7	5.1	4.4	2.3	−3.4
10 Employment	0.6	−0.3	1.1	−0.4	0.1	−0.4	−1.2	−0.6	0.4	−0.1
11 Unemployment rate (% of civilian labour force)	2.0	7.7	8.7	8.5	6.6	7.3	8.9	10.0	9.9	10.1
12 Current balance (% of GDP)	1.0	−1.6	1.4	3.4	1.7	2.1	3.9	4.3	5.0	4.6
13 Net lending (+) or net borrowing (−) of general government (% of GDP)	−2.6	−8.0	−7.2	−6.0	−6.7	−7.1	−6.7	−5.3	−4.5	−3.2
14 General government gross debt (end of period: % of GDP)	60.8	123.1	130.9	133.7	130.3	131.5	137.9	136.0	133.7	132.2
15 Interest payments by general government (% of GDP)	3.1	6.5	10.7	10.2	10.3	10.7	10.5	10.2	9.2	8.4
16 Money supply (end of year)[1]	10.1	9.4	9.7	4.5	5.8	7.8	13.7	−5.0	0.2	:
17 Long-term interest rate (%)	6.5	10.6	8.5	8.1	9.3	8.6	7.2	7.8	7.5	6.7
18 Profitability (1961–73 = 100)	100.0	67.2	82.8	81.6	81.2	80.4	79.5	81.9	84.8	86.7

[1]M3H.

Table G4 Germany: Main economic indicators 1961–96 (annual percentage change, unless otherwise stated)

	1961–73	1974–85	1986–90	1991–95	1991	1992	1993	1994	1995	1996
1 Gross domestic product[1]										
At current market prices	8.9	5.9	5.9	5.8	9.1	7.8	2.6	5.2	4.2	1.9
At 1990 market prices	4.3	1.7	3.4	2.2	5.0	2.2	–1.2	2.9	1.9	0.5
2 Gross fixed capital formation at 1990 prices[1]										
Total	3.9	–0.3	4.8	1.9	6.0	3.5	–5.6	4.3	1.5	–1.7
Construction	3.4	–1.4	3.1	4.5	2.7	9.7	0.9	7.8	1.2	–3.1
Equipment	4.9	1.6	7.2	–1.3	10.0	–3.5	–14.1	–1.2	2.0	0.5
3 Gross fixed capital formation at current prices (% of GDP)[2]										
Total	24.9	20.8	19.9	22.3	23.0	23.1	21.8	22.0	21.7	21.1
General government	4.2	3.2	2.4	2.6	2.6	2.8	2.7	2.6	2.5	2.4
Other sectors	20.8	17.6	17.5	19.7	20.4	20.2	19.1	19.4	19.2	18.8
4 Final national uses incl. stocks[3]										
At 1990 prices	4.5	1.3	3.5	1.4	4.8	1.1	–2.5	2.1	1.7	0.3
Relative against 19 competitors	–0.5	–0.6	–0.1	0.3	4.5	0.4	–1.9	–0.8	–0.6	–1.4
Relative against other member countries	–0.3	–0.4	–0.2	0.6	4.5	0.6	0.6	–0.7	–0.6	–1.3
5 Inflation[1]										
Price deflator private consumption	3.5	4.3	1.5	3.5	3.9	4.8	3.9	2.7	2.0	1.6
Price deflator GDP	4.4	4.1	2.4	3.5	3.9	5.5	3.8	2.3	2.2	1.4
6 Compensation per employee[1]										
Nominal	9.1	5.8	3.5	5.5	5.9	10.5	4.3	3.2	3.8	2.6
Real, deflator private consumption	5.4	1.4	2.0	2.0	1.9	5.5	0.3	0.5	1.7	1.0
Real, deflator GDP	4.5	1.6	1.0	1.9	1.9	4.8	0.5	0.9	1.5	1.2
7 GDP at 1990 market prices per person employed[1]	4.0	1.9	1.9	2.6	2.5	4.1	0.6	3.6	2.2	1.3
8 Real unit labour costs[3]										
1961–73 = 100	100.0	103.7	98.4	94.7	95.5	96.0	96.0	93.3	92.7	92.6
Annual % change	0.5	–0.3	–0.8	–0.7	–0.6	0.5	0.0	–2.8	–0.7	–0.1
9 Relative unit labour costs in common currency[3]										
Against 19 competitors										
1961–73 = 100	100.0	107.0	103.0	106.0	98.8	104.0	107.9	106.7	112.6	109.2
Annual % change	2.3	–2.2	1.9	2.0	–2.9	5.3	3.7	–1.2	5.6	–3.0
Against other member countries										
1961–73 = 100	100.0	107.3	104.1	107.0	96.9	101.2	110.7	110.6	115.8	111.2
Annual % change	2.2	–1.7	0.0	3.2	–2.2	4.4	9.4	–0.1	4.8	–4.0
10 Employment[1]	0.3	–0.2	1.5	–0.4	2.5	–1.8	–1.8	–0.7	–0.3	–0.8
11 Unemployment rate[2] (% of civilian labour force)	0.7	4.2	5.9	7.4	5.6	6.6	7.9	8.4	8.3	9.3
12 Current balance (% of GDP)[2]	0.7	0.8	4.2	–1.0	–1.0	–1.0	–0.9	–1.3	–1.0	–0.9
13 Net lending (+) or net borrowing (–) of general government (% of GDP)[2]	0.4	–2.8	–1.5	–3.1	–3.3	–2.8	–3.5	–2.5	–3.5	–3.9
14 General government gross debt[2] (end of period: % of GDP)	18.3	41.7	43.8	58.1	41.5	44.1	48.2	50.4	58.1	61.5
15 Interest payments by general government (% of GDP)[2]	0.9	2.1	2.8	3.3	2.7	3.3	3.3	3.4	3.8	3.9
16 Money supply (M3: end of year)[2]	10.9	7.5	5.8	6.0	6.3	7.6	10.9	1.6	3.6	:
17 Long-term interest rate (%)[2]	7.2	8.0	6.8	7.3	8.6	8.0	6.4	6.9	6.8	6.4
18 Profitability (1961–73 = 100)[3]	100.0	73.3	80.6	89.4	90.0	88.1	83.8	91.6	93.4	92.0

[1]1961–91: incl. West Germany
[2]1961–90: incl. West Germany
[3]1961–94: incl. West Germany

Table G5 Greece: Main economic indicators 1961–96 (annual percentage change, unless otherwise stated)

	1961–73	1974–85	1986–90	1991–95	1991	1992	1993	1994	1995	1996
1 Gross domestic product										
At current market prices	12.5	20.7	18.6	15.0	23.5	15.1	13.0	12.6	11.5	10.4
At 1990 market prices	7.7	2.5	1.9	1.2	3.1	0.4	–1.0	1.5	2.0	2.0
2 Gross fixed capital formation at 1990 prices										
Total	10.0	–1.6	1.7	1.4	4.8	–1.4	–2.8	0.5	6.3	7.8
Construction	8.8	–3.2	1.7	–1.8	3.2	–6.0	–5.1	–3.0	2.1	8.5
Equipment	12.7	0.7	2.7	6.8	7.9	7.5	1.1	6.3	11.5	7.8
3 Gross fixed capital formation at current prices (% of GDP)										
Total	27.9	26.8	22.2	21.0	22.5	21.6	20.7	19.9	20.2	20.9
General government	:	:	3.1	2.9	3.0	3.1	2.8	2.7	2.8	2.8
Other sectors	:	:	19.0	18.1	19.5	18.6	17.8	17.2	17.4	18.1
4 Final national uses incl. stocks										
At 1990 prices	7.9	2.0	2.5	1.6	3.7	0.3	–0.7	1.2	3.3	2.9
Relative against 19 competitors	3.0	0.1	–1.0	0.4	2.3	–0.6	0.5	–1.4	1.3	1.4
Relative against other member countries	3.1	0.3	–1.1	0.6	2.0	–0.4	1.6	–1.2	1.3	1.7
5 Inflation										
Price deflator private consumption	3.5	17.5	17.0	13.7	19.7	15.0	15.7	10.8	9.3	8.3
Price deflator GDP	4.5	17.7	16.5	13.7	19.8	14.6	14.1	10.9	9.3	8.3
6 Compensation per employee										
Nominal	10.1	21.6	17.9	11.4	14.3	8.2	10.1	11.9	12.5	11.1
Real, deflator private consumption	6.4	3.5	0.7	–2.0	–4.5	–5.9	–3.2	1.0	3.0	2.6
Real, deflator GDP	5.4	3.3	1.2	–2.0	–4.6	–5.6	–3.6	0.9	3.0	2.6
7 GDP at 1990 market prices per person employed	8.1	1.6	1.0	0.3	4.9	–1.0	–3.2	–0.4	1.1	0.9
8 Real unit labour costs										
1961–73 = 100	100.0	97.0	100.9	93.6	96.6	92.2	91.8	93.0	94.7	96.7
Annual % change	–2.5	1.8	0.2	–2.3	–9.0	–4.6	–0.4	1.3	1.9	1.6
9 Relative unit labour costs in common currency										
Against 19 competitors										
1961–73 = 100	100.0	77.0	68.4	72.6	71.6	69.8	70.2	73.3	78.1	82.5
Annual % change	–4.2	0.3	0.6	0.1	–8.0	–2.5	0.6	4.4	6.5	5.7
Against other member countries										
1961–73 = 100	100.0	76.5	69.2	73.2	71.2	68.8	71.5	75.3	79.4	83.5
Annual % change	–4.6	1.0	–0.8	0.7	–7.3	–3.4	4.1	5.2	5.5	5.2
10 Employment	–0.5	1.0	0.9	0.9	–1.8	1.4	2.2	1.9	0.9	1.0
11 Unemployment rate (% of civilian labour force)	4.5	3.8	6.6	8.3	7.0	7.9	8.6	8.9	9.1	9.1
12 Current balance (% of GDP)	–2.4	–2.4	–3.5	–2.5	–3.8	–3.2	–1.7	–1.0	–2.7	–2.8
13 Net lending (+) or net borrowing (–) of general government (% of GDP)	:	:	–12.4	–11.9	–11.5	–12.3	–14.2	–12.1	–9.2	–8.1
14 General government gross debt (end of period: % of GDP)	16.1	51.6	90.1	111.7	92.3	99.2	111.8	110.4	111.7	112.0
15 Interest payments by general government (% of GDP)	:	2.2	7.2	12.2	9.4	11.7	12.8	14.2	12.9	12.4
16 Money supply (end of year)[1]	18.2	25.5	21.1	12.2	12.3	14.4	15.0	8.9	10.5	:
17 Long-term interest rate (%)	:	13.6	:	:	:	:	:	:	:	:
18 Profitability (1961–73 = 100)	100.0	66.3	48.6	61.3	57.5	62.9	62.4	62.0	61.5	60.4

[1] M3.

Table G6 Spain: Main economic indicators 1961–96 (annual percentage change, unless otherwise stated)

	1961–73	1974–85	1986–90	1991–95	1991	1992	1993	1994	1995	1996
1 Gross domestic product										
At current market prices	14.9	17.2	12.2	6.8	9.5	7.6	3.1	6.1	7.9	6.0
At 1990 market prices	7.2	1.9	4.5	1.4	2.3	0.7	−1.2	2.1	3.0	2.0
2 Gross fixed capital formation at 1990 prices										
Total	10.5	−0.9	11.6	−0.9	1.6	−4.2	−10.6	1.4	8.4	4.7
Construction	:	−1.5	10.9	0.1	3.9	−4.3	−6.6	1.2	7.0	2.6
Equipment	:	−0.5	13.0	−2.8	−2.5	−4.0	−18.1	1.7	11.0	8.3
3 Gross fixed capital formation at current prices (% of GDP)										
Total	24.4	22.6	22.3	21.2	23.8	21.9	19.9	19.8	20.8	21.3
General government	:	2.4	3.9	4.0	4.8	4.0	4.1	3.7	3.2	2.8
Other sectors	:	20.3	18.4	17.3	19.0	17.8	15.8	16.1	17.6	18.6
4 Final national uses incl. stocks										
At 1990 prices	7.7	1.3	6.6	0.7	2.9	1.0	−4.2	1.1	3.2	2.2
Relative against 19 competitors	2.8	−0.6	2.9	−0.4	1.8	0.0	−3.5	−1.6	1.2	0.6
Relative against other member countries	2.9	−0.3	2.8	−0.2	1.5	0.3	−2.3	−1.4	1.2	0.8
5 Inflation										
Price deflator private consumption	6.5	15.4	6.6	5.6	6.4	6.4	5.5	4.9	4.6	3.6
Price deflator GDP	7.2	15.0	7.4	5.4	7.1	6.8	4.3	3.9	4.8	3.9
6 Compensation per employee										
Nominal	14.6	18.0	7.7	6.0	8.6	9.7	6.5	3.1	2.4	3.8
Real, deflator private consumption	7.6	2.3	1.0	0.4	2.0	3.1	0.9	−1.7	−2.2	0.2
Real, deflator GDP	7.0	2.6	0.3	0.6	1.4	2.7	2.1	−0.8	−2.3	−0.1
7 GDP at 1990 market prices per person employed	6.5	3.4	1.2	1.8	1.3	2.2	2.6	2.7	0.3	0.5
8 Real unit labour costs										
1961–73 = 100	100.0	101.6	88.9	87.0	88.6	89.0	88.5	85.5	83.3	82.7
Annual % change	0.5	−0.8	−0.9	−1.2	−0.1	0.5	−0.5	−3.4	−2.6	−0.7
9 Relative unit labour costs in common currency										
Against 19 competitors										
1961–73 = 100	100.0	114.8	113.2	120.2	130.5	133.2	117.5	109.7	110.1	113.6
Annual % change	1.7	−0.6	5.0	−3.0	1.8	2.1	−11.8	−6.6	−0.3	3.2
Against other member countries										
1961–73 = 100	100.0	111.7	112.0	118.1	126.7	127.9	117.0	110.1	109.1	112.1
Annual % change	1.2	0.1	3.2	−2.4	2.6	1.0	−8.5	−5.9	−0.9	2.8
10 Employment	0.7	−1.4	3.3	−0.4	1.0	−1.5	−3.7	−0.6	2.7	1.4
11 Unemployment rate (% of civilian labour force)	2.6	11.3	18.9	20.9	16.4	18.5	22.8	24.1	22.9	22.5
12 Current balance (% of GDP)	−0.7	−1.4	−1.3	−1.8	−3.6	−3.6	1.0	−1.2	0.3	0.0
13 Net lending (+) or net borrowing (−) of general government (% of GDP)	:	−2.8	−3.8	−5.9	−4.9	−4.1	−7.5	−6.9	−6.2	−4.8
14 General government gross debt (end of period: % of GDP)	13.1	43.7	45.1	65.7	45.8	48.4	60.5	63.1	65.7	67.8
15 Interest payments by general government (% of GDP)	:	1.0	3.6	4.7	3.9	4.2	5.2	5.1	5.4	5.4
16 Money supply (end of year)[1]	:	17.6	14.5	7.8	10.0	5.0	7.7	7.6	8.8	:
17 Long-term interest rate (%)	:	:	12.9	11.2	12.4	12.2	10.1	10.1	11.3	9.3
18 Profitability (1961–73 = 100)	100.0	81.0	130.1	136.5	136.3	135.3	128.4	137.3	145.0	145.0

[1] ALP: Liquid assets held by the public.

Table G7 France: Main economic indicators 1961–96 (annual percentage change, unless otherwise stated)

	1961–73	1974–85	1986–90	1991–95	1991	1992	1993	1994	1995	1996
1 Gross domestic product										
At current market prices	10.7	12.6	6.7	3.3	4.1	3.5	1.0	4.1	3.9	2.8
At 1990 market prices	5.4	2.2	3.2	1.1	0.8	1.3	−1.5	2.7	2.2	1.0
2 Gross fixed capital formation at 1990 prices										
Total	7.7	−0.2	5.9	1.0	0.0	−3.1	−5.8	1.1	2.8	1.5
Construction	:	−0.8	5.3	−1.5	0.2	−2.5	−5.9	0.2	0.5	0.9
Equipment	:	1.0	6.9	−0.3	0.2	−4.1	−5.8	2.3	6.2	2.4
3 Gross fixed capital formation at current prices (% of GDP)										
Total	24.0	22.2	20.5	19.2	21.2	20.0	18.6	18.1	18.1	18.1
General government	:	3.2	3.2	3.4	3.4	3.5	3.4	3.4	3.2	3.1
Other sectors	:	19.0	17.3	15.8	17.8	16.5	15.2	14.7	14.8	14.9
4 Final national uses incl. stocks										
At 1990 prices	5.6	1.8	3.8	0.7	0.6	0.4	−2.3	2.9	2.0	1.2
Relative against 19 competitors	0.7	−0.1	0.2	−0.5	−0.7	−0.6	−1.4	0.4	−0.1	−0.4
Relative against other member countries	1.0	0.2	0.1	−0.2	−1.1	−0.4	−0.2	0.6	−0.1	−0.2
5 Inflation										
Price deflator private consumption	4.8	10.5	2.9	2.2	3.2	2.4	2.2	1.8	1.6	1.8
Price deflator GDP	5.0	10.2	3.4	2.2	3.3	2.1	2.5	1.4	1.6	1.7
6 Compensation per employee										
Nominal	9.9	12.9	4.2	3.0	4.3	4.3	2.2	2.1	2.4	2.3
Real, deflator private consumption	4.9	2.2	1.3	0.8	1.1	1.9	−0.1	0.3	0.7	0.5
Real, deflator GDP	4.6	2.5	0.8	0.8	0.9	2.1	−0.4	0.6	0.7	0.5
7 GDP at 1990 market prices per person employed	4.7	2.1	2.4	1.2	0.7	2.1	−0.4	2.6	1.0	1.0
8 Real unit labour costs										
1961–73 = 100	100.0	105.5	97.1	94.9	95.6	95.6	95.7	93.9	93.6	93.1
Annual % change	−0.1	0.4	−1.6	−0.4	0.3	0.1	0.1	−1.9	−0.3	−0.5
9 Relative unit labour costs in common currency										
Against 19 competitors										
1961–73 = 100	100.0	92.1	84.3	83.6	80.6	82.3	84.2	84.0	86.8	86.6
Annual % change	−0.8	−0.6	−0.3	0.7	−3.6	2.0	2.3	−0.2	3.4	−0.2
Against other member countries										
1961–73 = 100	100.0	92.1	85.6	84.4	79.9	80.6	86.0	86.7	88.7	88.0
Annual % change	−1.2	0.1	−2.1	1.5	−2.9	0.9	6.7	0.8	2.3	−0.8
10 Employment	0.7	0.1	0.8	−0.1	0.1	−0.7	−1.1	0.1	1.2	0.0
11 Unemployment rate (% of civilian labour force)	2.0	6.4	9.8	11.1	9.5	10.4	11.7	12.3	11.5	11.7
12 Current balance (% of GDP)	0.4	−0.3	−0.3	0.7	−0.5	0.1	1.0	1.1	1.6	1.6
13 Net lending (+) or net borrowing (−) of general government (% of GDP)	0.4	−1.7	−1.8	−4.5	−2.2	−3.9	−5.9	−5.8	−5.0	−4.2
14 General government gross debt (end of period: % of GDP)	:	31.0	35.4	52.4	35.8	39.7	45.4	48.4	52.4	56.1
15 Interest payments by general government (% of GDP)	:	1.7	2.8	3.4	3.1	3.2	3.4	3.6	3.7	3.7
16 Money supply (end of year)[1]	13.7	12.3	8.9	2.3	2.0	5.1	−3.0	1.8	5.3	:
17 Long-term interest rate (%)	6.9	12.2	9.1	7.8	9.0	8.6	6.7	7.3	7.5	6.5
18 Profitability (1961–73 = 100)	100.0	73.0	90.0	94.6	91.8	92.4	91.2	97.5	100.0	100.7

[1] M3.

Table G8 Ireland: Main economic indicators 1961–96 (annual percentage change, unless otherwise stated)

	1961–73	1974–85	1986–90	1991–95	1991	1992	1993	1994	1995	1996
1 Gross domestic product										
At current market prices	11.8	17.0	7.9	7.0	4.0	6.0	7.3	8.0	9.9	7.8
At 1990 market prices	4.4	3.8	4.6	4.9	2.2	3.9	3.1	6.7	8.6	5.6
2 Gross fixed capital formation at 1990 prices										
Total	9.9	0.7	4.0	1.5	−7.1	−3.1	−0.8	7.3	12.2	8.3
Constuction	:	0.6	2.6	4.1	1.3	0.3	−3.7	9.9	13.6	9.0
Equipment	:	1.6	5.6	−2.2	−17.5	−8.2	4.0	3.3	10.0	7.0
3 Gross fixed capital formation at current prices (% of GDP)										
Total	20.9	24.4	16.9	15.7	16.6	15.6	14.9	15.1	16.2	16.8
General government	:	4.8	2.4	2.3	2.2	2.1	2.3	2.3	2.4	2.4
Other sectors	:	19.6	14.5	13.4	14.4	13.5	12.6	12.8	13.8	14.4
4 Final national uses incl. stocks										
At 1990 prices	5.1	2.1	3.3	1.9	−0.1	−1.2	0.8	4.2	5.9	4.5
Relative against 19 competitors	1.2	0.4	−0.2	0.7	−0.4	−2.0	1.1	1.4	3.9	2.8
Relative against other member countries	1.3	0.7	−0.4	1.0	−0.6	−1.8	2.1	1.5	3.9	3.0
5 Inflation										
Price deflator private consumption	6.3	13.8	3.2	2.5	2.8	2.5	1.7	2.7	2.5	2.3
Price deflator GDP	7.2	12.8	3.2	2.0	1.7	2.0	4.1	1.2	1.2	2.1
6 Compensation per employee										
Nominal	11.3	16.6	6.0	3.8	4.4	5.8	5.5	1.8	1.8	4.0
Real, deflator private consumption	4.7	2.5	2.7	1.3	1.5	3.3	3.7	−0.9	−0.7	1.7
Real, deflator GDP	3.9	3.4	2.7	1.8	2.6	3.8	1.3	0.6	0.6	1.9
7 GDP at 1990 market prices per person employed	4.3	3.7	3.6	3.1	2.2	3.5	2.5	3.5	4.0	3.2
8 Real unit labour costs										
1961–73 = 100	100.0	99.6	91.2	88.2	90.2	90.5	89.4	86.9	84.0	83.0
Annual % change	−0.4	−0.2	−0.8	−1.3	0.4	0.3	−1.1	−2.8	−3.3	−1.2
9 Relative unit labour costs in common currency										
Against 19 competitors										
1961–73 = 100	100.0	95.9	98.0	88.5	91.2	92.7	88.1	86.8	83.7	83.9
Annual % change	0.4	−0.3	−0.6	−2.5	−4.1	1.7	−5.0	−1.5	−3.6	0.3
Against other member countries										
1961–73 = 100	100.0	94.9	97.4	87.2	88.7	89.4	87.8	86.9	83.0	83.0
Annual % change	0.1	0.2	−2.1	−2.0	−3.6	0.7	−1.8	−0.9	−4.6	0.1
10 Employment	0.1	0.1	1.0	1.7	0.0	0.4	0.6	3.1	4.4	2.3
11 Unemployment rate (% of civilian labour force)	5.6	10.6	15.5	15.0	14.8	15.4	15.7	14.7	14.4	13.5
12 Current balance (% of GDP)	−2.4	−7.7	−1.2	4.4	2.0	3.3	4.9	5.1	6.6	6.3
13 Net lending (+) or net borrowing (−) of general government (% of GDP)	−3.8	−10.5	−5.5	−2.3	−2.2	−2.4	−2.4	−2.0	−2.4	−2.0
14 General government gross debt (end of period: % of GDP)	42.5	103.3	96.5	85.5	96.7	94.4	97.5	91.1	85.5	81.3
15 Interest payments by general government (% of GDP)	:	6.6	8.5	6.5	7.6	7.1	6.7	5.9	5.2	4.9
16 Money supply (end of year)[1]	12.1	15.7	7.3	11.8	3.1	9.1	23.3	9.7	14.1	:
17 Long-term interest rate (%)	:	14.6	10.2	8.5	9.2	9.1	7.8	8.1	8.3	7.5
18 Profitability (1961–73 = 100)	100.0	82.0	115.4	134.2	120.5	121.1	128.0	143.4	158.1	165.3

[1] M3.

Table G9 Italy: Main economic indicators 1961–96 (annual percentage change, unless otherwise stated)

	1961–73	*1974–85*	*1986–90*	*1991–95*	*1991*	*1992*	*1993*	*1994*	*1995*	*1996*
1 Gross domestic product	11.0	19.4	10.1	6.2	8.9	5.2	3.2	5.7	8.1	6.3
At current market prices	5.3	2.8	3.0	1.1	1.1	0.6	–1.2	2.1	3.0	1.8
At 1990 market prices										
2 Gross fixed capital formation at 1990 prices										
Total	4.7	0.5	4.4	–1.7	0.8	–1.8	–12.8	0.2	5.9	4.2
Constuction	:	–1.3	2.1	–2.6	1.4	–2.4	–6.3	–5.8	0.5	2.8
Equipment	:	3.2	6.9	–0.9	0.2	–1.2	–19.5	7.5	11.5	5.6
3 Gross fixed capital formation at current prices (% of GDP)										
Total	24.5	23.1	20.0	17.9	19.8	19.2	16.9	16.6	17.0	17.4
General government	:	3.3	3.4	2.7	3.3	3.0	2.7	2.3	2.3	2.2
Other sectors	:	19.9	16.6	15.2	16.5	16.2	14.3	14.3	14.7	15.3
4 Final national uses incl. stocks										
At 1990 prices	5.3	2.4	3.6	0.1	1.8	0.7	–5.1	1.3	2.0	1.8
Relative against 19 competitors	0.4	0.5	0.0	–1.2	0.6	–0.2	–4.6	–1.5	–0.1	0.3
Relative against other member countries	0.6	0.9	–0.1	–0.9	0.3	0.0	–3.5	–1.3	–0.1	0.6
5 Inflation										
Price deflator private consumption	4.9	16.0	5.9	5.7	6.9	5.6	5.4	4.6	5.8	4.1
Price deflator GDP	5.5	16.2	6.9	5.0	7.7	4.7	4.4	3.5	5.0	4.4
6 Compensation per employee										
Nominal	11.5	18.2	8.8	5.3	8.7	5.8	3.7	3.0	5.2	5.4
Real, deflator private consumption	6.3	1.9	2.7	–0.4	1.6	0.2	–1.6	–1.6	0.6	1.2
Real, deflator GDP	5.7	1.8	1.8	0.2	0.9	1.1	–0.6	–0.5	0.2	0.9
7 GDP at 1990 market prices per person employed	5.5	1.8	2.4	2.2	0.3	1.6	1.8	3.7	3.4	1.6
8 Real unit labour costs										
1961–73 = 100	100.0	103.7	98.3	95.3	99.3	98.7	96.4	92.5	89.7	89.1
Annual % change	0.1	–0.1	–0.6	–1.9	0.6	–0.5	–2.4	–4.0	–3.1	–0.7
9 Relative unit labour costs in common currency										
Against 19 competitors										
1961–73 = 100	100.0	89.6	107.1	101.1	118.8	116.4	96.3	91.0	82.9	91.6
Annual % change	–0.3	0.2	4.0	–6.6	1.7	–2.0	–17.2	–5.6	–8.9	10.5
Against other member countries										
1961–73 = 100	100.0	89.2	108.5	101.4	118.1	114.1	97.9	93.2	83.5	92.1
Annual % change	–0.7	1.0	2.2	–6.2	2.7	–3.4	–14.2	–4.8	–10.4	10.4
10 Employment	–0.2	0.9	0.6	–1.0	0.8	–1.0	–2.9	–1.5	–0.4	0.2
11 Unemployment rate (% of civilian labour force)	5.0	7.0	9.6	10.3	8.8	9.0	10.3	11.4	11.8	11.8
12 Current balance (% of GDP)	1.4	–0.7	–0.7	0.1	–2.1	–2.4	1.0	1.5	2.4	2.5
13 Net lending (+) or net borrowing (–) of general government (% of GDP)	–3.1	–9.6	–10.8	–9.1	–10.2	–9.5	–9.6	–9.0	–7.1	–6.3
14 General government gross debt (end of period: % of GDP)	51.3	82.4	98.0	124.8	101.4	108.5	119.4	125.6	124.8	124.5
15 Interest payments by general government (% of GDP)	:	5.6	8.6	11.1	10.2	11.4	12.1	10.7	11.2	10.3
16 Money supply (end of year)[1]	15.4	16.8	8.7	5.3	9.1	4.7	8.1	1.7	2.6	:
17 Long-term interest rate (%)	7.0	15.1	12.3	12.0	13.0	13.7	11.1	10.4	11.9	9.7
18 Profitability (1961–73 = 100)	100.0	67.5	87.9	95.5	88.1	87.9	89.9	101.0	110.6	112.6

[1] M2.

Table G10 Luxembourg: Main economic indicators 1961–96 (annual percentage change, unless otherwise stated)

	1961–73	*1974–85*	*1986–90*	*1991–93*	*1994–96*	*1991*	*1992*	*1993*	*1994*	*1995*	*1996*
1 Gross domestic product											
At current market prices	8.7	8.5	8.8	8.2	6.3	7.7	6.9	10.0	7.0	7.4	4.7
At 1990 market prices	4.0	1.8	4.6	1.6	3.0	3.1	1.9	0.0	3.3	3.2	2.6
2 Gross fixed capital formation at 1990 prices											
Total	4.9	–2.7	13.9	3.7	5.0	9.8	–2.1	3.9	2.4	6.0	6.5
Construction	:	–2.8	10.2	:	:	8.7	:	:	:	5.1	6.2
Equipment	:	–2.6	20.4	:	:	11.2	:	:	:	7.3	7.0
3 Gross fixed capital formation at current prices (% of GDP)											
Total	23.9	21.7	22.7	24.5	21.7	25.9	23.4	24.0	21.3	21.5	22.4
General government	:	5.5	:	:	5.2	:	:	:	5.0	5.1	5.4
Other sectors	:	16.2	:	:	16.5	:	:	:	16.2	16.4	17.0
4 Final national uses incl. stocks											
At 1990 prices	4.1	1.5	5.5	2.7	2.8	7.7	0.8	–0.3	2.3	3.2	3.0
Relative against 19 competitors	:	:	:	:	:	:	:	:	:	:	:
Relative against other member countries	:	:	:	:	:	:	:	:	:	:	:
5 Inflation											
Price deflator private consumption	3.0	7.4	3.5	3.7	2.0	2.6	1.6	7.0	2.4	2.0	1.7
Price deflator GDP	4.4	6.7	4.0	6.5	3.2	4.5	5.0	10.0	3.6	4.1	2.0
6 Compensation per employee											
Nominal	7.4	9.2	5.2	5.7	3.6	6.4	5.5	5.2	3.4	3.9	3.5
Real, deflator private consumption	4.2	1.7	1.7	1.9	1.6	3.7	3.8	–1.6	1.0	1.9	1.8
Real, deflator GDP	2.8	2.4	1.2	–0.7	0.4	1.8	0.5	–4.3	–0.1	–0.2	1.5
7 GDP at 1990 market prices per person employed	3.0	1.2	1.5	–1.1	0.8	–1.0	–0.6	–1.7	0.8	0.7	0.8
8 Real unit labour costs											
1961–73 = 100	100.0	115.4	106.4	110.2	107.3	110.3	111.5	108.6	107.6	106.8	107.4
Annual % change	–0.2	1.1	–0.3	0.4	–0.4	2.8	1.1	–2.6	–0.9	–0.8	0.6
9 Relative unit labour costs in common currency											
Against 19 competitors											
1961–73 = 100	:	:	:	:	:	:	:	:	:	:	:
Annual % change	:	:	:	:	:	:	:	:	:	:	:
Against other member countries											
1961–73 = 100	:	:	:	:	:	:	:	:	:	:	:
Annual % change	:	:	:	:	:	:	:	:	:	:	:
10 Employment	1.1	0.5	3.1	2.8	2.2	4.1	2.5	1.8	2.5	2.5	1.7
11 Unemployment rate (% of civilian labour force)	0.0	1.7	2.1	2.2	3.0	1.7	2.1	2.7	3.2	2.9	3.0
12 Current balance (% of GDP)	6.3	24.4	28.1	21.6	16.5	25.2	24.5	15.2	15.9	17.5	16.3
13 Net lending (+) or net borrowing (–) of general government (% of GDP)	1.9	1.9	:	1.5	1.1	1.9	0.8	1.8	2.2	0.3	0.7
14 General government gross debt (end of period: % of GDP)	18.5	12.9	4.7	6.2	6.2	4.2	5.2	6.2	5.9	5.9	6.2
15 Interest payments by general government (% of GDP)	0.9	1.0	0.2	0.4	0.4	0.4	0.4	0.4	0.4	0.3	0.4
16 Money supply (end of year)	:	:	:	:	:	:	:	:	:	:	:
17 Long-term interest rate (%)	:	8.1	8.0	7.7	5.9	8.2	7.9	6.9	6.4	6.1	5.4
18 Profitability (1961–73 = 100)	100.0	68.6	105.2	94.5	116.9	92.3	91.2	99.9	115.9	120.1	114.8

Table G11 Netherlands: Main economic indicators 1961–96 (annual percentage change, unless otherwise stated)

	1961–73	*1974–85*	*1986–90*	*1991–95*	*1991*	*1992*	*1993*	*1994*	*1995*	*1996*
1 Gross domestic product										
At current market prices	11.2	7.5	4.0	4.2	5.0	4.3	2.3	5.1	4.5	3.4
At 1990 market prices	4.8	1.9	3.1	1.9	2.3	2.0	0.2	2.7	2.4	1.8
2 Gross fixed capital formation at 1990 prices										
Total	5.3	−0.1	3.7	1.1	0.2	0.6	−3.1	3.0	5.0	2.4
Constuction	:	−1.7	3.8	1.5	0.0	2.6	−1.6	4.6	2.0	1.4
Equipment	:	2.8	3.6	0.5	0.6	−1.5	−5.3	0.3	9.0	3.7
3 Gross fixed capital formation at current prices (% of GDP)										
Total	25.7	20.5	21.0	19.7	20.4	20.0	19.3	19.3	19.6	19.7
General government	:	3.4	2.6	2.7	2.7	2.8	2.7	2.7	2.7	2.8
Other sectors	:	17.1	18.4	17.0	17.7	17.2	16.6	16.5	16.9	17.0
4 Final national uses incl. stocks										
At 1990 prices	4.9	1.6	3.0	1.6	1.9	1.6	−1.2	3.3	2.5	1.3
Relative against 19 competitors	0.2	−0.2	−0.6	0.5	0.4	0.7	0.1	0.7	0.5	−0.1
Relative against other member countries	0.3	0.0	−0.7	0.7	0.1	0.8	0.9	0.9	0.5	0.1
5 Inflation										
Price deflator private consumption	5.0	5.8	0.9	2.4	3.2	3.1	2.3	2.4	1.1	1.9
Price deflator GDP	6.0	5.5	0.8	2.3	2.7	2.3	2.0	2.3	2.1	1.6
6 Compensation per employee										
Nominal	11.4	6.6	1.7	3.5	4.5	4.7	3.1	2.3	3.0	1.9
Real, deflator private consumption	6.0	0.8	0.8	1.1	1.2	1.5	0.8	0.0	1.9	0.0
Real, deflator GDP	5.0	1.1	0.8	1.2	1.7	2.3	1.1	0.0	0.9	0.3
7 GDP at 1990 market prices per person employed	3.9	2.0	1.2	1.2	0.9	1.0	0.4	2.6	1.0	0.7
8 Real unit labour costs										
1961–73 = 100	100.0	102.6	94.1	92.7	92.4	93.6	94.2	91.8	91.7	91.4
Annual % change	1.0	−0.9	−0.3	0.0	0.8	1.4	0.6	−2.5	−0.1	−0.4
9 Relative unit labour costs in common currency										
Against 19 competitors										
1961–73 = 100	100.0	116.1	101.2	100.4	95.6	98.0	101.2	101.2	106.1	103.7
Annual % change	2.9	−1.5	0.1	1.7	−1.9	2.5	3.4	0.0	4.8	−2.3
Against other member countries										
1961–73 = 100	100.0	115.7	101.8	100.5	94.6	96.3	102.1	102.7	106.8	104.0
Annual % change	2.7	−1.1	−1.0	2.1	−1.4	1.7	6.0	0.6	4.0	−2.6
10 Employment	0.9	−0.1	1.9	0.7	1.3	1.0	−0.2	0.1	1.4	1.0
11 Unemployment rate (% of civilian labour force)	1.1	7.1	7.4	6.5	5.8	5.6	6.6	7.2	7.3	7.2
12 Current balance (% of GDP)	0.5	1.9	3.0	4.0	3.4	3.1	4.4	4.4	4.8	5.0
13 Net lending (+) or net borrowing (−) of general government (% of GDP)	−0.7	−3.6	−5.1	−3.3	−2.9	−3.9	−3.2	−3.2	−3.4	−3.5
14 General government gross debt (end of period: % of GDP)	:	71.5	78.8	79.0	78.8	79.4	81.1	77.6	79.0	79.4
15 Interest payments by general government (% of GDP)	:	4.2	6.2	6.1	6.2	6.3	6.4	6.1	5.8	5.7
16 Money supply (end of year)[1]	10.3	8.4	8.1	4.6	5.2	6.3	7.7	−0.5	4.4	:
17 Long-term interest rate (%)	5.9	9.4	7.1	7.4	8.7	8.1	6.3	6.9	6.9	6.3
18 Profitability (1961–73 = 100)	100.0	79.3	88.8	92.1	93.7	90.9	87.5	93.5	94.8	95.0

[1] M3.

Table G12 Austria: Main economic indicators 1961–96 (annual percentage change, unless otherwise stated)

	1961–73	1974–85	1986–90	1991–95	1991	1992	1993	1994	1995	1996
1 Gross domestic product										
At current market prices	9.7	7.9	6.0	5.5	7.0	6.3	3.8	6.5	4.0	2.6
At 1990 market prices	4.9	2.2	3.0	2.0	2.8	2.0	0.4	3.0	1.8	0.7
2 Gross fixed capital formation at 1990 prices										
Total	6.5	0.5	4.9	3.1	6.3	1.7	−1.6	6.8	2.4	0.3
Constuction	7.2	−0.7	5.0	4.0	6.2	5.6	2.9	5.5	−0.2	−1.5
Equipment	5.5	2.6	4.9	1.7	6.5	−3.6	−8.2	8.8	6.1	2.7
3 Gross fixed capital formation at current prices (% of GDP)										
Total	26.9	25.0	23.7	24.8	25.4	25.1	24.3	24.8	24.8	24.6
General government	4.7	4.3	3.4	3.1	3.3	3.3	3.1	3.0	2.9	3.0
Other sectors	22.2	20.7	20.3	21.7	22.1	21.8	21.1	21.7	21.8	21.6
4 Final national uses incl. stocks										
At 1990 prices	4.9	1.9	3.4	2.7	2.8	2.2	−0.2	5.9	3.0	0.5
Relative against 19 competitors	0.0	0.1	−0.2	1.7	1.2	1.6	1.3	3.3	0.9	−0.9
Relative against other member countries	0.1	0.3	−0.2	1.8	0.9	1.6	2.3	3.5	0.9	−0.7
5 Inflation										
Price deflator private consumption	4.1	5.9	2.1	3.2	3.4	3.9	3.4	3.0	2.2	2.1
Price deflator GDP	4.6	5.5	2.9	3.4	4.0	4.1	3.4	3.4	2.1	1.9
6 Compensation per employee										
Nominal	9.6	7.9	4.4	4.7	6.4	5.9	4.6	3.1	3.8	3.0
Real. deflator private consumption	5.3	1.9	2.3	1.5	2.9	1.9	1.1	0.1	1.5	0.8
Real. deflator GDP	4.8	2.2	1.5	1.3	2.3	1.6	1.1	−0.3	1.6	1.1
7 GDP at 1990 market prices per person employed	5.0	1.6	2.2	0.9	1.1	1.5	0.8	−0.8	1.9	1.8
8 Real unit labour costs										
1961–73 = 100	100.0	105.1	104.1	103.9	103.4	103.5	103.8	104.4	104.1	103.4
Annual % change	−0.2	0.7	−0.7	0.4	1.2	0.1	0.3	0.6	−0.3	−0.7
9 Relative unit labour costs in common currency										
Against 19 competitors										
1961–73 = 100	100.0	110.8	122.1	130.7	121.3	125.2	130.2	135.4	141.2	138.1
Annual % change	0.1	0.9	1.6	3.0	−0.4	3.2	4.0	4.0	4.3	−2.2
Against other member countries										
1961–73 = 100	100.0	112.7	126.7	135.9	124.1	127.0	136.5	143.5	148.6	144.2
Annual % change	−0.1	1.6	0.4	3.7	0.4	2.4	7.5	5.1	3.6	−2.9
10 Employment	−0.1	0.7	0.7	1.1	1.7	0.5	−0.4	3.9	−0.1	−1.1
11 Unemployment rate (% of civilian labour force)	1.8	2.5	3.4	3.9	3.5	3.6	4.2	4.1	4.0	4.6
12 Current balance (% of GDP)	0.1	−1.0	0.2	−0.7	0.1	−0.1	−0.4	−1.0	−2.0	−1.6
13 Net lending (+) or net borrowing (−) of general government (% of GDP)	0.8	−2.4	−3.2	−3.9	−2.6	−2.1	−4.3	−4.4	−6.2	−4.6
14 General government gross debt (end of period: % of GDP)	17.5	50.5	58.3	69.4	58.7	58.3	62.8	65.0	69.4	72.4
15 Interest payments by general government (% of GDP)	0.9	2.4	3.9	4.3	4.3	4.3	4.3	4.1	4.3	4.6
16 Money supply (end of year)[1]	11.7	10.2	7.2	5.5	8.0	4.2	4.0	5.3	5.7	:
17 Long-term interest rate (%)	:	8.9	7.4	7.5	8.6	8.3	6.6	6.7	7.2	6.5
18 Profitability (1961–73 = 100)	100.0	83.0	77.5	76.6	79.3	78.2	75.5	75.2	74.9	73.8

[1] M3.

Table G13 Portugal: Main economic indicators 1961–96 (annual percentage change, unless otherwise stated)

	1961–73	1974–85	1986–90	1991–95	1991	1992	1993	1994	1995	1996
1 Gross domestic product										
At current market prices	11.1	23.4	19.1	10.3	16.7	14.7	6.2	6.5	7.7	6.2
At 1990 market prices	6.9	2.2	5.1	1.1	2.1	1.1	−1.2	1.0	2.5	2.3
2 Gross fixed capital formation at 1990 prices										
Total	7.9	−1.3	9.9	2.1	2.4	5.4	−4.8	3.5	4.0	4.8
Construction	:	:	6.4	3.1	4.7	5.4	−1.0	1.0	5.5	5.0
Equipment	:	:	13.2	0.7	−0.1	5.4	−9.2	5.4	3.0	4.6
3 Gross fixed capital formation at current prices (% of GDP)										
Total	26.6	29.7	26.9	25.9	26.7	26.7	25.1	25.5	25.4	25.9
General government	:	:	3.4	4.0	3.8	4.1	4.2	3.8	4.2	4.5
Other sectors	:	:	23.5	21.9	22.9	22.6	20.9	21.7	21.2	21.4
4 Final national uses incl. stocks										
At 1990 prices	7.3	1.1	7.6	2.4	4.3	4.3	−0.9	1.8	2.5	2.7
Relative against 19 competitors	2.6	−0.6	3.9	1.3	3.4	3.6	0.3	−0.9	0.3	1.2
Relative against other member countries	2.8	−0.4	3.7	1.5	3.1	3.8	1.2	−0.7	0.3	1.3
5 Inflation										
Price deflator private consumption	3.9	22.2	11.7	8.0	12.6	11.1	7.1	5.2	4.2	3.1
Price deflator GDP	3.9	20.8	13.3	9.1	14.2	13.5	7.4	5.4	5.1	3.8
6 Compensation per employee										
Nominal	10.9	24.1	16.4	8.6	14.7	9.4	9.1	5.4	4.6	4.6
Real, deflator private consumption	6.7	1.6	4.2	0.5	1.8	−1.5	1.9	0.2	0.4	1.5
Real, deflator GDP	6.7	2.8	2.7	−0.4	0.4	−3.6	1.6	0.0	−0.5	0.8
7 GDP at 1990 market prices per person employed	6.6	2.6	3.9	1.5	−0.6	2.9	0.7	1.2	3.1	2.4
8 Real unit labour costs										
1961–73 = 100	100.0	117.4	97.2	93.2	98.9	92.6	93.4	92.2	89.0	87.6
Annual % change	0.1	0.1	−1.2	−1.9	1.0	−6.4	0.8	−1.2	−3.5	−1.5
9 Relative unit labour costs in common currency										
Against 19 competitors										
1961–73 = 100	100.0	98.3	83.9	105.5	101.4	107.9	105.8	105.0	107.2	106.9
Annual % change	−0.6	−1.9	2.8	3.2	10.7	6.4	−1.9	−0.8	2.1	−0.3
Against other member countries										
1961–73 = 100	100.0	96.6	83.3	104.2	99.2	104.7	105.4	105.2	106.5	105.8
Annual % change	−1.0	−1.5	1.5	3.6	11.2	5.6	0.7	−0.2	1.2	−0.6
10 Employment	0.3	−0.4	1.1	−0.4	2.8	−1.8	−1.9	−0.2	−0.6	−0.1
11 Unemployment rate (% of civilian labour force)	2.5	6.9	6.1	5.6	4.0	4.2	5.7	7.0	7.2	7.4
12 Current balance (% of GDP)	0.4	−5.8	−0.5	−1.5	−1.9	−1.9	−2.1	−1.2	−0.4	−1.1
13 Net lending (+) or net borrowing (−) of general government (% of GDP)	0.5	:	−4.7	−5.6	−6.4	−3.3	−7.1	−5.8	−5.4	−4.4
14 General government gross debt (end of period: % of GDP)	15.5	62.3	68.6	71.6	70.2	62.4	67.2	70.0	71.6	72.2
15 Interest payments by general government (% of GDP)	0.5	3.4	7.8	6.9	8.5	7.7	6.7	5.8	5.8	5.1
16 Money supply (end of year)[1]	:	22.3	17.0	11.1	18.3	13.3	6.2	9.4	8.2	:
17 Long-term interest rate (%)	:	:	17.1	13.0	18.3	15.4	9.5	10.4	11.5	9.1
18 Profitability (1961–73 = 100)	100.0	42.2	58.2	63.5	58.9	65.9	63.4	62.9	66.4	66.6

[1] L–: Liquid assets of the residents.

Table G14 Finland: Main economic indicators 1961–96 (annual percentage change, unless otherwise stated)

	1961–73	1974–85	1986–90	1991–95	1991	1992	1993	1994	1995	1996
1 Gross domestic product										
At current market prices	12.1	13.7	9.2	1.4	−4.8	−2.9	1.2	5.5	8.4	5.0
At 1990 market prices	5.0	2.7	3.4	−0.7	−7.1	−3.6	−1.2	4.4	4.4	3.0
2 Gross fixed capital formation at 1990 prices										
Total	4.8	1.1	4.8	−10.2	−20.3	−16.9	−19.2	−0.3	9.4	11.0
Construction	5.1	0.7	4.0	−11.3	−14.5	−17.3	−18.8	−5.6	1.3	4.7
Equipment	4.7	1.8	6.2	−9.8	−30.2	−16.0	−20.0	4.9	21.4	21.0
3 Gross fixed capital formation at current prices (% of GDP)										
Total	26.3	26.1	25.5	17.2	22.4	18.4	14.8	14.6	15.5	17.0
General government	4.2	3.7	3.5	3.1	3.7	3.5	2.8	2.8	2.7	2.6
Other sectors	22.1	22.4	22.0	14.1	18.7	15.0	12.0	11.8	12.9	14.3
4 Final national uses incl. stocks										
At 1990 prices	5.0	2.5	4.0	−2.8	−9.2	−6.4	−6.4	3.7	5.1	4.1
Relative against 19 competitors	0.4	0.6	0.6	−3.9	−10.0	−7.1	−5.6	1.0	2.9	2.4
Relative against other member countries	0.6	0.9	0.5	−3.6	−10.2	−6.9	−4.4	1.1	3.0	2.8
5 Inflation										
Price deflator private consumption	5.7	10.8	4.5	3.3	5.6	4.1	4.2	1.4	1.1	1.0
Price deflator GDP	6.8	10.7	5.6	2.1	2.5	0.7	2.4	1.1	3.8	2.0
6 Compensation per employee										
Nominal	11.2	13.4	8.8	3.3	5.7	1.9	1.0	2.7	5.3	4.0
Real, deflator private consumption	5.2	2.4	4.1	0.0	0.0	−2.2	−3.0	1.3	4.2	2.9
Real, deflator GDP	4.1	2.5	3.0	1.2	3.1	1.2	−1.3	1.6	1.5	2.0
7 GDP at 1990 market prices per person employed	4.5	2.4	3.2	3.0	−2.0	3.7	5.7	5.7	2.2	1.3
8 Real unit labour costs										
1961–73 = 100	100.0	99.8	96.1	94.2	101.7	99.2	92.6	89.0	88.4	89.0
Annual % change	−0.4	0.1	−0.2	−1.8	5.2	−2.5	−6.6	−3.9	−0.7	0.7
9 Relative unit labour costs in common currency										
Against 19 competitors										
1961–73 = 100	100.0	99.2	110.4	94.1	118.6	98.7	78.8	82.0	92.2	89.2
Annual % change	−1.2	1.3	2.9	−5.2	−1.5	−16.8	−20.1	4.0	12.4	−3.2
Against other member countries										
1961–73 = 100	100.0	99.9	112.9	95.5	118.6	97.4	81.2	85.4	94.9	90.9
Annual % change	−1.4	2.0	1.3	−4.5	−0.6	−17.9	−16.7	5.1	11.1	−4.2
10 Employment	0.5	0.3	0.2	−3.6	−5.2	−7.0	−6.5	−1.3	2.2	1.7
11 Unemployment rate (% of civilian labour force)	2.1	5.3	4.7	14.8	7.6	13.1	17.9	18.4	17.2	16.3
12 Current balance (% of GDP)	−1.4	−2.0	−3.2	−1.3	−5.4	−4.6	−1.3	1.3	3.4	2.5
13 Net lending (+) or net borrowing (−) of general government (% of GDP)	3.0	3.7	4.0	−5.4	−1.5	5.9	−8.0	−6.3	−5.6	−3.3
14 General government gross debt (end of period: % of GDP)	10.5	16.5	14.5	59.4	23.0	41.5	57.3	59.5	59.4	62.5
15 Interest payments by general government (% of GDP)	0.9	1.1	1.6	3.9	1.9	2.6	4.6	5.1	5.4	5.6
16 Money supply (end of year)[1]	12.0	14.7	13.5	2.6	6.8	−0.1	5.8	1.9	0.4	:
17 Long-term interest rate (%)	8.0	11.2	11.7	9.8	11.7	12.0	8.2	8.4	8.8	7.4
18 Profitability (1961–73 = 100)	100.0	74.2	82.2	74.8	55.1	59.9	76.1	87.7	95.2	95.4

[1] Till 1983: MI from 1984: M3.

Table G15 Sweden: Main economic indicators 1961–96 (annual percentage change, unless otherwise stated)

	1961–73	1974–85	1986–90	1991–95	1991	1992	1993	1994	1995	1996
1 Gross domestic product										
At current market prices	9.2	11.7	9.4	3.7	6.4	−0.4	0.3	5.4	7.2	3.2
At 1990 market prices	4.1	1.8	2.3	0.1	−1.1	−1.4	−2.2	2.6	3.0	1.2
2 Gross fixed capital formation at 1990 prices										
Total	4.4	0.6	5.4	−5.7	−8.4	−10.8	−17.2	−0.2	10.6	10.1
Construction	:	−1.1	3.9	−9.5	−5.2	−7.7	−19.2	−11.5	−3.1	7.8
Equipment	:	3.2	6.9	−0.9	−11.9	−16.0	−14.7	18.1	28.5	12.4
3 Gross fixed capital formation at current prices (% of GDP)										
Total	23.4	19.7	20.3	15.7	19.4	17.0	14.2	13.6	14.5	15.8
General government	:	4.0	2.9	3.1	3.0	2.9	3.1	3.3	3.3	3.3
Other sectors	:	15.8	17.4	12.6	16.4	14.0	11.1	10.2	11.3	12.4
4 Final national uses incl. stocks										
At 1990 prices	3.7	1.5	2.9	−1.2	−2.1	−1.8	−5.2	1.8	1.6	1.2
Relative against 19 competitors	−1.0	−0.5	−0.3	−2.4	−2.6	−2.5	−4.9	−1.3	−0.7	−0.6
Relative against other member countries	−0.8	−0.1	−0.6	−2.0	−2.9	−2.2	−3.5	−1.0	−0.7	−0.2
5 Inflation										
Price deflator private consumption	4.8	10.2	6.5	4.7	10.2	2.2	5.7	3.1	2.7	1.7
Price deflator GDP	4.9	9.8	7.0	3.6	7.6	1.0	2.6	2.8	4.1	2.0
6 Compensation per employee										
Nominal	8.4	10.7	9.2	4.7	6.8	3.9	4.4	5.4	3.0	5.2
Real, deflator private consumption	3.5	0.4	2.5	0.0	−3.0	1.7	−1.2	2.2	0.3	3.5
Real, deflator GDP	3.4	0.8	2.0	1.1	−0.8	2.9	1.7	2.5	−1.0	3.2
7 GDP at 1990 market prices per person employed	3.5	1.0	1.2	2.3	0.4	3.2	3.2	3.6	1.4	0.6
8 Real unit labour costs										
1961–73 = 100	100.0	101.3	95.7	95.3	97.2	96.9	95.5	94.5	92.2	94.5
Annual % change	−0.2	−0.1	0.8	−1.3	−1.1	−0.3	−1.4	−1.1	−2.4	2.5
9 Relative unit labour costs in common currency										
Against 19 competitors										
1961–73 = 100	100.0	92.6	86.9	84.7	96.4	95.6	76.9	77.3	77.1	86.5
Annual % change	−0.3	−1.3	3.5	−4.1	1.3	−0.8	−19.6	0.5	−0.2	12.2
Against other member countries										
1961–73 = 100	100.0	91.8	85.9	82.3	92.9	91.0	75.7	76.5	75.3	84.4
Annual % change	−0.5	−0.8	1.5	−3.8	1.9	−2.1	−16.8	1.2	−1.6	12.1
10 Employment	0.6	0.8	1.0	−2.2	−1.5	−4.4	−5.2	−1.0	1.6	0.6
11 Unemployment rate (% of civilian labour force)	1.9	2.5	2.1	7.5	3.3	5.8	9.5	9.8	9.2	8.8
12 Current balance (% of GDP)	0.2	−1.7	−1.6	−1.0	−2.1	−3.1	−1.4	−0.7	2.0	1.5
13 Net lending (+) or net borrowing (−) of general government (% of GDP)	:	−1.7	3.2	−8.0	−1.1	−7.8	−12.3	−10.8	−8.1	−5.2
14 General government gross debt (end of period: % of GDP)	29.7	63.8	43.5	79.9	53.0	67.1	76.0	79.3	79.9	80.8
15 Interest payments by general government (% of GDP)	:	4.5	6.0	6.1	5.1	5.4	6.2	6.8	7.1	7.5
16 Money supply (end of year)[1]	:	9.7	8.3	2.8	4.0	3.2	4.0	0.3	2.7	:
17 Long-term interest rate (%)	6.3	11.0	11.7	10.0	11.8	10.0	8.6	9.5	10.2	8.5
18 Profitability (1961–73 = 100)	100.0	84.1	102.1	102.6	94.8	95.6	95.6	107.3	119.7	113.3

[1] M3.

Table G16 United Kingdom: Main economic indicators 1961–96 (annual percentage change, unless otherwise stated)

	1961–73	1974–85	1986–90	1991–95	1991	1992	1993	1994	1995	1996
1 Gross domestic product										
At current market prices	8.4	14.0	9.1	4.9	4.4	3.8	5.6	6.0	4.8	5.1
At 1990 market prices	3.1	1.4	3.3	1.2	–2.0	–0.5	2.2	3.8	2.4	2.4
2 Gross fixed capital formation at 1990 prices										
Total	4.6	0.7	5.7	–1.6	–9.5	–1.5	0.6	3.7	–0.7	4.2
Construction	:	–0.4	6.2	–1.6	–8.4	0.3	0.1	2.1	–1.7	3.8
Equipment	:	2.1	5.3	–1.5	–10.8	–3.8	1.2	5.8	0.6	4.6
3 Gross fixed capital formation at current prices (% of GDP)										
Total	18.5	18.0	18.9	15.9	17.0	15.7	15.1	15.0	15.0	15.4
General government	:	2.9	1.9	1.9	2.1	2.1	1.8	1.9	1.7	1.6
Other sectors	:	15.1	17.0	13.6	14.9	13.6	13.2	13.1	13.2	13.7
4 Final national uses incl. stocks										
At 1990 prices	3.2	1.2	4.0	0.8	–3.1	0.2	2.1	3.3	1.6	2.3
Relative against 19 competitors	–1.9	–0.8	0.6	–0.5	–4.3	–0.8	2.8	0.6	–0.6	0.6
Relative against other member countries	–1.8	–0.4	0.4	–0.1	–5.1	–0.5	4.9	0.9	–0.6	1.0
5 Inflation										
Price deflator private consumption	4.8	12.0	5.0	4.1	7.4	4.7	3.5	2.5	2.6	2.7
Price deflator GDP	5.1	12.4	5.5	3.7	6.5	4.4	3.2	2.1	2.4	2.7
6 Compensation per employee										
Nominal	8.3	13.9	8.3	4.9	8.6	5.2	4.3	3.5	3.1	3.6
Real, deflator private consumption	3.3	1.7	3.2	0.8	1.1	0.5	0.8	1.0	0.5	0.9
Real, deflator GDP	3.0	1.3	2.6	1.2	2.0	0.8	1.0	1.3	0.7	0.9
7 GDP at 1990 market prices per person employed	2.9	1.6	1.5	2.4	1.1	1.4	3.7	3.8	1.8	1.5
8 Real unit labour costs										
1961–73 = 100	100.0	101.4	99.1	100.6	103.8	103.2	100.5	98.1	97.1	96.5
Annual % change	0.1	–0.3	1.0	–1.2	0.9	–0.6	–2.6	–2.4	–1.0	–0.6
9 Relative unit labour costs in common currency										
Against 19 competitors										
1961–73 = 100	100.0	92.2	95.9	97.8	108.1	104.8	93.8	93.4	89.2	88.9
Annual % change	–1.9	1.1	1.9	–3.1	3.4	–3.0	–10.5	–0.4	–4.5	–0.3
Against other member countries										
1961–73 = 100	100.0	90.0	94.4	95.4	104.1	99.1	92.9	93.5	87.3	86.6
Annual % change	–2.8	2.2	–0.6	–2.6	4.8	–4.9	–6.2	0.7	–6.6	–0.8
10 Employment	0.3	–0.2	1.8	–1.2	–3.1	–1.9	–1.5	0.1	0.6	0.9
11 Unemployment rate (% of civilian labour force)	1.9	6.9	9.0	9.5	8.8	10.1	10.4	9.6	8.8	8.4
12 Current balance (% of GDP)	–0.1	–0.1	–3.8	–2.4	–2.7	–2.6	–2.5	–2.1	–2.3	–2.3
13 Net lending (+) or net borrowing (–) of general government (% of GDP)	–0.8	–3.7	–1.1	–5.9	–2.6	–6.3	–7.8	–6.8	–6.0	–4.4
14 General government gross debt (end of period: % of GDP)	66.3	53.8	35.3	54.1	35.7	41.9	48.5	50.3	54.1	55.6
15 Interest payments by general government (% of GDP)	:	4.5	3.9	3.2	3.0	2.9	2.9	3.3	3.7	3.7
16 Money supply (end of year)[1]	:	13.9	16.3	5.5	5.6	3.1	5.1	3.5	10.1	:
17 Long-term interest rate (%)	7.6	13.0	9.9	8.5	9.9	9.1	7.3	8.1	8.2	8.0
18 Profitability (1961–73 = 100)	100.0	76.5	91.5	97.4	81.7	89.3	99.6	108.3	107.9	109.1

[1] M4.

Table G17 Total population in thousands

	B	DK	D¹	GR	E	F	IRL	I²	L	NL	A	P	SF	S	UK	EUR15³	USA	J
1960	9119	4581	55433	8327	30470	45684	2834	48967	314.9	11483	7048	8682	4430	7480	52372	297224	180671	94118
1970	9638	4929	60651	8793	33831	50772	2950	52771	339.2	13032	7467	8692	4606	8043	55632	322146	205052	104674
1971	9673	4963	61284	8769	34190	51251	2978	53124	342.4	13194	7500	8644	4612	8098	55928	324550	207661	105713
1972	9709	4992	61672	8889	34498	51701	3024	53499	346.9	13330	7544	8631	4640	8122	56097	326694	209896	107156
1973	9738	5022	61976	8929	34810	52118	3073	53882	350.5	13438	7586	8634	4666	8137	56223	328583	211909	108660
1974	9768	5045	62054	8962	35147	52460	3124	54390	355.1	13543	7599	8755	4691	8161	56236	330290	213854	110160
1975	9795	5060	61829	9046	35515	52699	3177	54764	359.0	13660	7579	9094	4712	8192	56226	331706	215973	111520
1976	9811	5073	61531	9167	35937	52909	3228	55070	360.7	13773	7566	9356	4726	8222	56216	332945	218035	112770
1977	9822	5088	61400	9309	36367	53145	3272	55266	361.3	13856	7568	9456	4739	8251	56190	334090	220239	113880
1978	9830	5104	61326	9430	36778	53376	3314	55446	362.0	13939	7562	9559	4753	8275	56178	335231	222585	114920
1979	9837	5117	61359	9548	37108	53606	3368	55602	362.9	14034	7549	9662	4765	8294	56240	336452	225056	115880
1980	9847	5123	61566	9642	37386	53880	3401	55657	364.2	14148	7549	9767	4780	8311	56330	337750	227225	116800
1981	9854	5122	61682	9730	37741	54182	3443	55774	365.3	14247	7564	9835	4800	8320	56352	339012	230138	117650
1982	9863	5119	61638	9790	37943	54493	3480	55995	365.5	14312	7571	9864	4827	8325	56318	339903	232520	118450
1983	9867	5114	61423	9847	38121	54772	3505	56228	365.5	14368	7552	9885	4856	8329	56377	340609	234799	119260
1984	9871	5112	61175	9896	38273	55026	3529	56344	365.9	14423	7553	9898	4882	8337	56506	341192	237001	120020
1985	9879	5114	61024	9934	38408	55284	3540	56498	366.7	14488	7558	9905	4902	8350	56685	341935	239279	120750
1986	9888	5121	61066	9964	38519	55547	3541	56576	368.4	14567	7566	9904	4918	8370	56852	342765	241625	121490
1987	9901	5127	61077	9984	38609	55824	3547	56664	370.6	14664	7576	9900	4932	8398	57009	343582	243942	122090
1988	9915	5130	61449	10005	38691	56118	3531	56763	373.3	14760	7596	9886	4947	8436	57158	344759	246307	122610
1989	9932	5132	62063	10038	38768	56423	3510	56837	376.7	14846	7624	9884	4964	8493	57358	346248	248781	123120
1990	9961	5141	63253	10089	38836	56735	3506	56737	380.2	14947	7718	9869	4986	8591	57561	348310	249924	123540
1991	10001	5154	79984	10200	38916	57055	3526	56760	384.5	15068	7823	9861	5029	8644	57808	366214	252137	123920
1992	10045	5171	80595	10314	39006	57374	3549	56859	389.8	15182	7884	9833	5042	8692	58007	367942	255078	124320
1993	10084	5189	81180	10368	39083	57655	3563	57070	395.3	15290	7945	9840	5066	8745	58191	369664	257908	124670
1994	10116	5205	81423	10426	39143	57903	3571	57181	401.0	15381	7983	9840	5088	8807	58366	370834	260427	124960
1995	10155	5226	81610	10478	39234	58147	3582	57284	406.9	15458	8015	9846	5108	8885	58480	371915	262833	125249
1996	10194	5247	81825	10530	39312	58388	3584	57370	411.0	15534	8046	9856	5126	8920	58680	373023	265265	125351

(1) 1960–1990: WD
(2) Break in 1989/90
(3) 1960–1990: incl. WD; 1991–1996: incl. D

Table G18 Working population and employment – 1993

Country	Civilian working population		Civilian employment	
	Thousands	As a percentage of total population	Thousands	Percentage of females
EUR 12	153 941	45.0	137 576	41.0
1 Belgium	4 073	41.0	3 744	40.0
2 Denmark	2 875	56.0	2 567	47.0
3 Germany	39 113	49.0	36 111	42.0
4 Greece	4 101	41.0	3 715	35.0
5 Spain	15 263	39.0	11 868	34.0
6 France	24 718	44.0	21 908	44.0
7 Ireland	1 352	39.0	1 149	35.0
8 Italy	22 235	40.0	19 898	35.0
9 Luxembourg	169	43.0	165	36.0
10 Netherlands	7 085	47.0	6 640	40.0
11 Portugal	4 714	48.0	4 464	44.0
12 United Kingdom	28 244	49.0	25 348	45.0
13 Austria	3 728	47.0	3 570	42.0
14 Finland	2 474	49.0	2 030	49.0
15 Sweden	4 286	49.0	3 912	49.0
16 USA	128 040	50.0	119 306	46.0
17 Japan	66 149	53.0	64 495	40.0

Table G19 Civilian employment by main sectors of economic activity – 1993 (in thousands)

Country	Agriculture	Industry	Services	Total
EUR 12	7 644	43 330	86 280	137 945
1 Belgium	99	1 103	2 542	3 744
2 Denmark	131	667	1 757	2 567
3 Germany	1 272	13 702	21 138	36 111
4 Greece	791	899	2 026	3 715
5 Spain	1 212	3 658	6 998	11 868
6 France	1 195	6 023	14 658	21 908
7 Ireland	157	322	667	1 149
8 Italy	1 488	6 576	12 203	20 267
9 Luxembourg	5	43	115	165
10 Netherlands	256	1 472	4 421	6 640
11 Portugal	516	1 467	2 481	4 464
12 United Kingdom	522	7 399	17 274	25 348
13 Austria	245	1 250	2 074	3 570
14 Finland	174	548	1 308	2 030
15 Sweden	139	992	2 780	3 912
16 USA	3 262	28 694	87 335	119 306
17 Japan	3 832	22 122	38 542	64 495

Table G20 Unemployment rate (percentage of civilian labour force)

	B	DK	D[2]	GR	E	F	IRL	I	L	NL	A[3]	P	SF	S	UK	EUR15[4]	USA[3]	J[4]
1960	3.4	2.0	1.0	6.1	2.4	1.5	5.8	5.7	0.0	0.7	2.6	1.8	1.5	1.7	1.4	2.4	5.5	1.7
1970	1.8	0.6	0.5	4.2	2.6	2.4	6.3	5.1	0.0	1.0	1.6	2.6	1.9	1.5	2.2	2.3	4.9	1.1
1961–70	2.0	1.2	0.7	5.1	2.5	1.8	5.4	4.8	0.0	0.9	2.0	2.5	2.0	1.7	1.7	2.2	4.7	1.2
1971	1.7	0.9	0.6	3.1	3.4	2.7	6.0	5.1	0.0	1.3	1.3	2.5	2.3	2.5	2.7	2.6	5.9	1.2
1972	2.2	0.8	0.8	2.1	2.9	2.8	6.7	6.0	0.0	2.3	1.1	2.5	2.5	2.7	3.1	2.8	5.6	1.4
1973	2.2	0.7	0.8	2.0	2.6	2.7	6.2	5.9	0.0	2.4	1.0	2.6	2.3	2.5	2.2	2.6	4.9	1.3
1974	2.3	2.8	1.8	2.1	3.1	2.8	5.8	5.0	0.0	2.9	1.2	1.7	1.7	2.0	2.0	2.7	5.6	1.4
1975	4.2	3.9	3.3	2.3	4.5	4.0	7.9	5.5	0.0	5.5	1.7	4.4	2.3	1.6	3.2	3.9	8.5	1.9
1976	5.5	5.1	3.3	1.9	4.9	4.4	9.8	6.2	0.0	5.8	1.8	6.2	4.1	1.6	4.8	4.5	7.7	2.0
1977	6.3	5.9	3.2	1.7	5.3	4.9	9.7	6.7	0.0	5.6	1.6	7.3	6.2	1.8	5.1	4.9	7.1	2.0
1978	6.8	6.7	3.1	1.8	7.1	5.1	9.0	6.7	1.2	5.6	2.1	7.9	7.6	2.2	5.0	5.1	6.1	2.2
1979	7.0	4.8	2.7	1.9	8.8	5.8	7.8	7.2	2.4	5.7	2.1	7.9	6.4	2.2	4.6	5.3	5.8	2.1
1980	7.4	5.2	2.7	2.7	11.6	6.2	8.0	7.1	2.4	6.4	1.9	7.6	5.2	2.2	5.6	5.8	7.1	2.0
1971–80	4.6	3.7	2.2	2.2	5.4	4.1	7.7	6.1	0.6	4.4	1.6	5.1	4.1	2.1	3.8	4.0	6.4	1.8
1981	9.5	8.3	3.9	4.0	14.4	7.3	10.8	7.4	2.4	8.9	2.5	7.3	5.6	2.8	8.9	7.4	7.6	2.2
1982	11.2	8.9	5.6	5.8	16.3	8.0	12.5	8.0	2.4	11.9	3.5	7.2	6.2	3.5	10.3	8.6	9.7	2.4
1983	11.1	9.0	6.9	7.1	17.5	8.2	14.0	7.7	3.5	9.7	4.1	7.8	6.3	3.9	11.1	9.1	9.6	2.6
1984	11.1	8.5	7.1	7.2	20.3	9.8	15.5	8.1	3.1	9.3	3.8	8.5	6.2	3.4	11.1	9.7	7.5	2.7
1985	10.3	7.1	7.2	7.0	21.6	10.2	16.9	8.5	2.9	8.3	3.6	8.7	6.3	3.0	11.5	10.0	7.2	2.6
1986	10.3	5.4	6.5	6.6	21.2	10.3	16.8	9.2	2.6	8.3	3.1	8.4	6.9	2.8	11.5	10.0	7.0	2.8
1987	10.0	5.4	6.3	6.7	20.5	10.4	16.6	9.9	2.5	8.0	3.8	6.9	5.1	2.3	10.6	9.8	6.2	2.8
1988	8.9	6.1	6.2	6.8	19.5	9.9	16.1	10.0	2.0	7.5	3.6	5.5	4.5	1.9	8.7	9.1	5.5	2.5
1989	7.5	7.4	5.6	6.7	17.2	9.4	14.7	10.0	1.8	6.9	3.1	4.9	3.5	1.6	7.3	8.3	5.3	2.3
1990	6.7	7.7	4.8	6.4	16.2	9.0	13.4	9.1	1.7	6.2	3.2	4.6	3.4	1.8	7.0	7.8	5.5	2.1
1981–90	9.7	7.4	6.0	6.4	18.5	9.3	14.7	8.8	2.5	8.5	3.4	7.0	5.4	2.7	9.8	9.0	7.1	2.5
1991	6.6	8.4	5.6	7.0	16.4	9.5	14.8	8.8	1.7	5.8	3.5	4.0	7.6	3.3	8.8	8.3	6.7	2.1
1992	7.3	9.2	6.6	7.9	18.5	10.4	15.4	9.0	2.1	5.6	3.6	4.2	13.1	5.8	10.1	9.4	7.4	2.2
1993	8.9	10.1	7.9	8.6	22.8	11.7	15.7	10.3	2.7	6.6	4.2	5.7	17.9	9.5	10.4	10.9	6.8	2.5
1994	10.0	8.2	8.4	8.9	24.1	12.3	14.7	11.4	3.2	7.2	4.1	7.0	18.4	9.8	9.6	11.3	6.1	2.9
1995	9.9	6.8	8.3	9.1	22.9	11.5	14.4	11.8	2.9	7.3	4.0	7.2	17.2	9.2	8.8	10.9	5.6	3.2
1996	10.1	6.1	9.3	9.1	22.5	11.7	13.5	11.8	3.0	7.2	4.6	7.4	16.3	8.8	8.4	11.0	5.6	3.1

(1) Definition *Eurostat*
(2) 1960–90: WD
(3) OECD
(4) 1960–90: incl. WD; 1991–96: incl. D.

Table G21 Gross domestic product at current market prices (ECU; mrd)

	B	DK	D¹	GR	E	F	IRL	I	L	NL	A	P	SF	S	UK	EUR15²	USA	J
1960	10.5	5.6	68.2	4.0	10.9	57.7	1.7	37.5	0.5	11.2	5.9	2.7	4.8	13.3	68.5	303.3	487.3	42.1
1970	24.7	15.5	180.5	11.8	36.9	139.8	4.0	105.0	1.2	33.2	14.1	6.9	10.7	32.9	121.2	738.3	989.6	199.3
1971	27.2	16.9	205.7	12.7	40.9	153.2	4.5	112.6	1.2	37.9	16.0	7.6	11.5	35.1	134.4	817.3	1048.1	221.8
1972	31.3	19.4	230.1	13.6	48.4	174.6	5.2	121.9	1.4	43.5	18.5	8.6	12.6	38.6	143.6	911.3	1076.8	272.0
1973	36.7	23.3	280.0	15.9	58.5	206.6	5.6	134.9	1.8	52.1	22.5	10.6	15.2	42.6	147.5	1053.7	1096.4	337.7
1974	44.8	26.9	318.8	19.1	74.7	229.6	6.1	154.2	2.3	63.9	27.5	12.9	19.9	48.5	163.0	1212.1	1215.0	395.2
1975	49.8	30.4	336.7	20.4	85.9	276.0	7.0	171.1	2.1	71.2	30.5	13.6	22.6	59.2	188.6	1364.9	1279.5	411.2
1976	59.7	37.2	398.0	24.4	97.2	318.2	7.8	187.8	2.6	86.5	36.2	15.9	27.1	70.1	201.1	1570.2	1583.4	502.9
1977	68.1	40.7	451.3	27.7	106.2	342.1	9.1	212.7	2.8	99.6	42.3	16.3	28.0	73.1	222.8	1742.8	1731.1	607.0
1978	74.6	44.4	502.2	30.1	115.8	380.3	10.6	234.5	3.1	109.1	45.6	16.0	27.2	72.6	253.3	1919.1	1749.9	765.3
1979	79.4	48.1	552.9	34.1	143.5	425.6	12.3	271.9	3.4	116.4	50.2	16.9	31.1	79.6	306.1	2171.5	1813.9	737.4
1980	85.0	47.8	583.2	34.9	152.1	478.5	14.4	325.6	3.6	123.8	55.4	20.5	37.0	90.3	386.4	2438.5	1945.1	762.4
1981	86.7	51.5	610.6	40.3	166.0	524.0	17.1	367.0	3.8	129.1	59.6	24.9	45.2	103.2	459.7	2688.7	2719.2	1051.3
1982	87.0	56.9	668.4	47.7	183.4	563.8	20.2	411.4	3.9	142.7	67.9	27.0	51.7	103.5	496.5	2932.1	3217.8	1111.1
1983	90.8	63.0	734.9	47.8	176.7	591.7	21.6	468.7	4.2	152.7	75.2	26.5	54.9	104.4	517.1	3130.3	3812.9	1333.2
1984	97.6	69.4	782.3	52.1	201.6	634.8	23.6	524.8	4.7	160.8	81.1	27.7	64.5	122.5	550.0	3397.5	4769.7	1606.4
1985	105.7	76.7	818.9	52.9	218.4	691.7	26.0	559.2	5.0	169.5	86.2	30.8	70.6	132.9	604.7	3649.2	5263.7	1774.6
1986	114.0	84.0	904.7	48.6	235.2	745.5	26.9	614.9	5.7	182.4	95.1	34.2	71.3	135.4	571.3	3869.0	4298.8	2028.0
1987	121.1	88.8	960.9	48.6	254.2	770.2	27.2	657.4	6.0	188.9	101.7	36.2	76.4	140.0	598.8	4076.3	3895.0	2091.4
1988	128.1	92.1	1010.4	54.7	291.8	815.1	29.3	709.5	6.6	196.0	107.4	40.6	87.9	153.9	707.0	4430.4	4104.9	2452.3
1989	138.9	95.3	1074.5	60.9	345.4	877.0	32.7	789.3	7.5	207.7	114.8	46.9	103.1	173.6	763.8	4831.5	4723.9	2607.6
1990	151.2	101.7	1182.2	65.3	387.5	941.5	35.4	861.2	8.1	223.4	124.7	52.9	106.2	180.8	769.6	5191.8	4310.9	2311.5
1991	159.5	104.7	1391.5	72.1	427.6	971.7	36.8	931.1	8.8	234.8	133.5	62.6	98.1	193.5	818.2	5644.4	4564.7	2710.6
1992	170.7	109.6	1522.3	75.6	445.8	1023.7	39.4	941.7	9.6	248.9	144.0	73.4	82.1	191.4	807.1	5885.2	4573.8	2820.2
1993	179.6	115.2	1629.3	78.6	408.4	1067.7	40.2	842.0	10.8	266.2	155.9	72.3	72.0	158.5	805.6	5902.5	5345.8	3580.4
1994	192.3	123.1	1725.3	82.5	406.6	1120.5	43.8	855.6	11.8	281.9	167.1	73.7	82.2	166.4	858.6	6191.4	5568.7	3867.0
1995	205.6	132.2	1846.4	87.4	427.7	1174.4	46.8	831.4	13.1	303.0	178.5	79.7	96.6	175.1	842.6	6440.5	5293.9	3834.2
1996	208.8	136.0	1850.0	94.8	463.7	1217.4	51.3	952.8	13.4	308.4	180.1	84.6	98.0	197.4	885.1	6742.0	5785.0	3664.2

(1) 1960–1990: WD.
(2) 1960–90: incl. WD; 1991–96: incl. D.

Table G22 Gross domestic product at current market prices (PPS)

	B	DK	D¹	GR	E	F	IRL	I	L	NL	A	P	SF	S	UK	EUR15²	USA	J
1960	9.0	5.3	68.3	3.6	17.6	48.5	1.7	43.5	0.6	13.0	6.8	3.4	3.9	9.3	64.7	299.2	328.0	51.2
1970	22.1	12.6	160.3	11.3	54.2	126.9	3.9	115.3	1.2	32.5	16.3	9.8	9.5	22.2	130.5	728.6	726.2	210.6
1971	24.6	13.9	177.4	13.0	61.0	142.8	4.4	125.9	1.3	36.4	18.5	11.2	10.5	24.0	142.9	807.7	802.2	235.9
1972	27.7	15.6	197.6	15.2	70.5	159.4	5.0	138.1	1.4	40.1	20.9	12.9	12.0	26.3	158.1	900.8	897.5	272.8
1973	31.9	17.6	225.8	17.7	82.8	183.2	5.7	161.3	1.8	45.8	24.0	15.7	14.0	29.8	184.0	1041.1	1028.4	320.1
1974	37.3	19.6	254.2	19.2	98.3	212.3	6.7	191.1	2.2	53.5	28.0	17.8	16.2	34.5	203.9	1194.9	1147.4	357.5
1975	41.6	22.0	283.9	23.0	111.8	239.5	8.0	210.4	2.1	60.5	31.5	19.3	18.5	40.0	230.5	1342.8	1285.3	416.0
1976	48.2	25.7	327.8	26.8	126.6	273.6	8.9	245.8	2.4	69.7	36.1	22.6	20.2	44.3	258.3	1537.0	1476.5	475.1
1977	52.4	28.3	365.1	30.1	141.0	305.8	10.4	275.2	2.5	77.2	40.9	25.8	22.0	47.3	285.7	1709.6	1671.3	538.8
1978	57.8	30.9	404.1	34.5	153.7	339.7	11.9	306.6	2.8	85.0	44.0	28.5	24.1	51.7	318.1	1893.6	1883.3	607.3
1979	64.7	35.0	461.1	39.1	168.4	383.9	13.5	355.8	3.1	95.1	50.5	33.0	28.2	58.8	357.8	2148.0	2113.0	701.6
1980	74.7	38.5	515.1	44.1	188.7	431.6	15.4	410.3	3.5	106.5	57.4	38.2	32.9	66.1	389.3	2412.2	2328.3	804.4
1981	81.3	42.0	566.5	48.4	207.0	479.8	17.4	453.2	3.8	116.4	62.9	42.6	36.8	72.6	422.2	2653.0	2614.3	915.4
1982	89.3	46.8	607.8	52.7	227.7	532.9	19.3	492.0	4.2	124.6	68.9	47.2	41.2	79.4	464.4	2898.4	2770.6	1022.8
1983	94.4	50.5	650.5	55.6	244.7	564.4	20.3	522.4	4.5	133.3	73.9	49.5	44.5	85.0	505.7	3099.1	3018.7	1104.7
1984	101.9	55.7	706.6	60.4	262.4	604.1	22.3	566.8	4.9	145.4	79.1	51.3	48.4	93.4	547.6	3350.4	3401.8	1217.0
1985	107.6	60.8	755.0	65.2	281.9	644.5	24.1	609.0	5.4	157.0	84.9	55.3	52.4	99.7	593.7	3596.5	3674.6	1337.9
1986	112.5	65.0	797.1	68.4	300.1	681.6	25.0	646.5	5.9	166.4	88.6	59.4	55.3	105.3	639.4	3816.5	3896.0	1416.4
1987	117.5	66.8	828.1	69.7	324.6	713.5	26.7	682.7	6.0	172.8	92.2	64.2	59.0	111.1	685.8	4020.6	4111.7	1509.7
1988	128.3	70.3	894.4	75.8	355.5	776.4	29.0	739.8	6.8	184.6	99.9	70.7	64.4	118.3	749.7	4363.9	4450.2	1669.6
1989	139.4	74.3	974.1	82.7	391.3	850.8	32.4	800.4	7.6	203.1	109.1	78.6	71.5	127.3	805.2	4748.0	4805.1	1837.7
1990	150.7	78.8	1076.6	86.5	424.5	911.9	36.5	854.7	8.1	221.1	118.9	85.6	74.8	135.0	845.1	5108.7	5086.1	2013.9
1991	161.8	84.9	1282.9	94.8	468.2	979.6	39.9	918.5	8.9	233.8	127.9	95.7	71.4	137.0	850.1	5555.6	5246.3	2189.5
1992	173.6	86.5	1375.7	101.5	475.7	1009.3	43.4	951.8	9.5	244.9	135.3	102.6	69.3	136.0	893.3	5808.4	5500.1	2292.8
1993	180.6	92.2	1390.2	106.1	482.7	998.7	45.3	936.8	10.2	251.4	142.0	108.0	73.5	136.3	913.7	5867.7	5799.3	2356.9
1994	202.1	105.4	1585.5	119.6	526.3	1100.5	53.8	1055.9	11.6	283.0	160.7	121.4	81.8	152.2	1019.8	6579.8	6556.8	2565.7
1995	230.3	120.8	1807.3	136.5	605.9	1257.7	65.3	1215.6	13.6	324.1	182.9	139.1	95.5	175.3	1167.7	7537.7	7479.8	2893.0
1996	230.0	120.9	1794.5	137.5	610.3	1255.2	68.1	1222.0	13.8	325.7	181.9	140.5	97.2	175.3	1180.4	7553.3	7546.3	2939.6

(1) 1960–90: WD.
(2) 1960–90: incl. WD; 1991–96: incl. D.

Table G23   Gross domestic product at 1990 market prices (% change)

	B	DK	D¹	GR	E	F	IRL	I	L	NL	A	P	SF	S	UK	EUR15²	USA	J
1961	5.0	6.4	4.6	11.1	11.8	5.5	5.0	8.2	3.8	3.1	5.3	5.2	7.6	5.7	3.3	5.6	2.7	12.0
1970	6.4	2.0	5.0	8.0	4.2	5.7	2.7	5.3	1.7	5.7	7.1	7.6	7.5	6.5	2.3	4.8	-0.3	10.7
1961–70	4.9	4.5	4.4	7.6	7.3	5.6	4.2	5.7	3.5	5.1	4.7	6.4	4.8	4.6	2.9	4.8	3.8	10.5
1971	3.7	2.7	3.1	7.1	4.6	4.8	3.5	1.6	2.7	4.2	5.1	6.6	2.1	0.9	2.0	3.2	2.8	4.3
1972	5.3	5.3	4.3	8.9	8.1	4.4	6.5	2.7	6.6	3.3	6.2	8.0	7.6	2.3	3.5	4.4	4.7	8.2
1973	5.9	3.6	4.8	7.3	7.8	5.4	4.7	7.1	8.3	4.7	4.9	11.2	6.7	4.0	6.7	6.0	5.1	7.6
1974	4.1	-0.9	0.2	-3.6	5.6	3.1	4.3	5.4	4.2	4.0	3.9	1.1	3.0	3.2	-1.4	2.1	-0.7	-0.6
1975	-1.5	-0.7	-1.3	6.1	0.5	-0.3	5.7	-2.7	-6.6	-0.1	-0.4	-4.3	1.2	2.6	-0.1	-0.6	-1.0	2.9
1976	5.6	6.5	5.3	6.4	3.3	4.2	1.3	6.6	2.5	5.1	4.6	6.9	-0.4	1.1	2.2	4.4	4.8	4.2
1977	0.5	1.6	2.8	3.4	2.8	3.2	8.1	3.4	1.6	2.3	4.5	5.5	0.2	-1.6	2.2	2.7	4.5	4.7
1978	2.7	1.5	3.0	6.7	1.5	3.4	7.1	3.7	4.1	2.4	0.1	2.8	2.1	1.8	3.6	3.0	4.8	4.9
1979	2.1	3.5	4.2	3.7	0.0	3.2	3.1	6.0	2.3	2.2	4.7	5.6	7.0	3.8	2.8	3.6	2.5	5.5
1980	4.3	-0.4	1.0	1.8	1.3	1.6	3.1	4.2	0.8	1.2	2.9	4.6	5.3	1.7	-1.6	1.5	-0.4	3.6
1971–80	3.2	2.2	2.7	4.7	3.5	3.3	4.7	3.8	2.6	2.9	3.6	4.7	3.4	2.0	2.0	3.0	2.7	4.5
1981	-1.0	-0.9	0.1	0.1	-0.2	1.2	3.3	0.6	-0.6	-0.5	-0.3	1.6	1.9	0.0	-1.3	0.1	2.2	3.6
1982	1.5	3.0	-0.9	0.4	1.6	2.5	2.3	0.2	1.1	-1.2	1.1	2.1	3.2	1.0	1.5	0.9	-2.2	3.2
1983	0.5	2.5	1.8	0.4	2.2	0.7	-0.2	1.0	3.0	1.7	2.0	-0.2	2.7	1.8	3.6	1.7	3.6	2.7
1984	2.2	4.4	2.8	2.8	1.5	1.3	4.3	2.7	6.2	3.3	1.4	-1.9	3.0	4.0	2.5	2.3	6.7	4.3
1985	0.8	4.3	2.0	3.1	2.6	1.9	3.1	2.6	2.9	3.1	2.5	2.8	3.4	1.9	3.5	2.5	3.1	5.0
1986	1.4	3.6	2.3	1.6	3.2	2.5	0.3	2.9	4.8	2.8	1.2	4.1	2.4	2.3	4.4	2.9	2.8	2.6
1987	2.0	0.3	1.5	-0.5	5.6	2.3	4.7	3.1	2.9	1.4	1.7	5.5	4.1	3.1	4.8	2.9	3.1	4.1
1988	4.9	1.2	3.7	4.5	5.2	4.5	4.3	4.1	5.7	2.6	4.1	5.8	4.9	2.3	5.0	4.2	3.9	6.2
1989	3.4	0.6	3.6	3.8	4.7	4.3	6.1	2.9	6.7	4.7	3.8	5.7	5.7	2.4	2.2	3.5	2.7	4.7
1990	3.4	1.4	5.7	0.0	3.7	2.5	7.8	2.1	3.2	4.1	4.2	4.3	0.0	1.4	0.4	2.9	1.2	4.8
1981–90	1.9	2.0	2.2	1.6	3.0	2.4	3.6	2.2	3.6	2.2	2.1	3.0	3.1	2.0	2.6	2.4	2.7	4.1
1992	1.8	0.2	2.2	0.4	0.7	1.3	3.9	0.6	1.9	2.0	2.0	1.1	-3.6	-1.4	-0.5	1.0	2.5	1.1
1993	-1.6	1.5	-1.2	-1.0	-1.2	-1.5	3.1	-1.2	0.0	0.2	0.4	-1.2	-1.2	-2.2	2.2	-0.6	3.4	-0.2
1994	2.2	4.4	2.9	1.5	2.1	2.7	6.7	2.1	3.3	2.7	3.0	1.0	4.4	2.6	3.8	2.8	3.5	0.5
1995	1.9	2.6	1.9	2.0	3.0	2.2	8.6	3.0	3.2	2.4	1.8	2.5	4.4	3.0	2.4	2.5	2.0	0.9
1996	1.1	1.3	0.5	2.0	2.0	1.0	5.6	1.8	2.6	1.8	0.7	2.3	3.0	1.2	2.4	1.5	2.1	2.9

(1) 1961–90: WD.
(2) 1961–90: incl. WD; 1992–96: incl. D.
Aggregates: PPS weighted.

Table G24 Gross domestic product at current market prices per head of population (PPS; EUR15 = 100)

	B	DK	D¹	GR	E	F	IRL	I	L	NL	A	P	SF	S	UK	EUR15²	USA	J
1960	97.8	115.7	122.4	42.6	57.2	105.5	60.3	88.3	177.6	112.8	95.6	39.4	88.0	123.0	122.8	100.0	108.4	54.1
1970	101.3	112.7	116.8	56.9	70.9	110.5	59.1	96.6	160.0	110.2	96.8	49.8	91.6	121.8	103.7	100.0	156.6	89.0
1971	102.1	112.2	116.3	59.7	71.7	112.0	59.2	95.2	148.5	110.8	98.9	52.1	91.2	119.2	102.7	100.0	155.2	89.7
1972	103.3	113.2	116.2	61.8	74.1	111.8	59.8	93.6	151.1	109.2	100.7	54.4	94.0	117.2	102.2	100.0	155.1	92.3
1973	103.5	110.7	115.0	62.7	75.1	110.9	58.5	94.5	161.6	107.6	99.6	57.3	94.7	115.4	103.3	100.0	153.2	93.0
1974	105.7	107.4	113.2	59.2	77.3	111.8	59.1	97.1	172.9	109.3	101.8	56.3	95.5	116.9	100.2	100.0	148.3	89.7
1975	105.0	107.6	113.4	62.9	77.8	112.3	62.0	94.9	143.5	109.4	102.8	52.4	97.2	120.7	101.3	100.0	147.0	92.1
1976	106.3	109.8	115.4	63.4	76.3	112.0	59.5	96.7	143.2	109.6	103.5	52.3	92.8	116.8	99.5	100.0	146.7	91.3
1977	104.3	108.7	116.2	63.1	75.8	112.5	62.0	97.3	133.6	108.9	105.7	53.4	90.6	111.9	99.4	100.0	148.3	92.5
1978	104.2	107.1	116.7	64.8	74.0	112.7	63.8	97.9	136.5	107.9	103.0	52.9	89.8	110.6	100.2	100.0	149.8	93.6
1979	103.0	107.1	117.7	64.2	71.1	112.2	62.7	100.2	134.7	106.1	104.7	53.5	92.8	110.0	99.7	100.0	147.1	94.8
1980	106.2	105.3	117.1	64.0	70.7	112.2	63.3	103.2	134.1	105.4	106.5	54.8	96.4	111.3	96.8	100.0	143.1	96.4
1981	105.4	104.7	117.4	63.6	70.1	113.2	64.7	103.8	132.9	104.4	106.3	55.4	98.0	111.5	95.7	100.0	145.2	99.4
1982	106.2	107.3	115.6	63.1	70.4	114.7	65.1	103.0	135.0	102.1	106.7	56.1	100.0	111.9	96.7	100.0	139.7	101.3
1983	105.1	108.5	116.4	62.1	70.6	113.2	63.5	102.1	134.8	101.9	107.5	55.1	100.6	112.2	98.6	100.0	141.3	101.8
1984	105.1	110.9	117.6	62.1	69.8	111.8	64.5	102.4	137.2	102.7	106.7	52.8	101.0	114.1	98.7	100.0	146.2	103.3
1985	103.6	113.0	117.6	62.4	69.8	110.8	64.8	102.5	138.9	103.0	106.8	53.1	101.6	113.6	99.6	100.0	146.0	105.3
1986	102.2	114.0	117.2	61.6	70.0	110.2	63.3	102.6	143.5	102.6	105.2	53.8	101.0	112.9	101.0	100.0	144.8	104.7
1987	101.4	111.3	115.9	59.6	71.8	109.2	64.4	103.0	139.5	100.7	104.0	55.4	102.2	113.1	102.8	100.0	144.0	105.7
1988	102.3	108.3	115.0	59.8	72.6	109.3	65.0	103.0	142.9	98.8	103.9	56.5	102.9	113.1	103.6	100.0	142.7	107.6
1989	102.4	105.6	114.5	60.1	73.6	110.0	67.3	102.7	147.3	99.8	104.3	58.0	105.1	110.8	102.4	100.0	140.9	108.8
1990	103.1	104.5	116.0	58.4	74.5	109.6	71.0	102.7	144.8	100.9	105.0	59.2	102.3	107.1	100.1	100.0	138.8	111.1
1991	106.7	108.6	105.7	61.2	79.3	113.2	74.6	106.7	152.2	102.3	107.8	64.0	93.6	104.5	96.9	100.0	137.2	116.5
1992	109.5	105.9	108.1	62.3	77.3	111.4	77.5	106.0	153.8	102.2	108.7	66.1	87.1	99.1	97.6	100.0	136.6	116.8
1993	112.8	112.0	107.9	64.5	77.8	109.1	80.2	103.4	163.3	103.6	112.6	69.1	91.3	98.2	98.9	100.0	141.7	119.1
1994	112.6	114.1	109.7	64.7	75.8	107.1	84.9	104.1	162.7	103.7	113.4	69.6	90.7	97.4	98.5	100.0	141.9	115.7
1995	111.9	114.1	109.3	64.3	76.2	106.7	89.9	104.7	165.2	103.5	112.6	69.7	92.3	97.3	98.5	100.0	104.4	114.0
1996	111.4	113.8	108.3	64.5	76.7	106.2	93.8	105.2	165.8	103.6	111.7	70.4	93.6	97.0	99.3	100.0	140.5	115.8

(1) 1960-90: WD.
(2) 1960-90: incl. WD; 1991-96: incl. D.

Table G25 Gross value-added at market prices by branch (as a percentage) – 1992

Country	Agriculture, forestry and fishing	Industry (incl. construction)	Services and general government	Gross value-added at market prices
EUR 12	2.6	33.1	64.3	100.0
1 Belgium	1.8	31.4	66.7	100.0
2 Denmark	3.6	27.2	69.2	100.0
3 Germany	1.2	39.4	59.3	100.0
4 Greece	17.0	27.3	55.6	100.0
5 Spain	3.8	34.0	62.2	100.0
6 France	3.1	30.9	66.0	100.0
7 Ireland	7.6	38.0	54.4	100.0
8 Italy	3.3	33.5	63.2	100.0
9 Luxembourg	1.7	35.8	62.5	100.0
10 Netherlands	4.0	30.9	65.1	100.0
11 Portugal	6.3	39.0	54.7	100.0
12 United Kingdom	1.5	34.5	64.0	100.0
13 Austria	3.4	43.9	52.7	100.0
14 Finland	6.7	38.0	55.3	100.0
15 Sweden[1]	3.1	40.4	56.5	100.0
16 USA[2]	2.3	32.7	65.0	100.0
17 Japan	2.4	43.8	53.8	100.0

[1] 1991.
[2] 1987.

Table G26 Use of gross domestic product at market prices (as a percentage) – 1993

Country	National private consumption	Collective consumption of general government	Gross fixed capital formation	Change in stocks	Balance of exports and imports of goods and services	Gross domestic product at market prices
EUR 12	63.1	17.1	19.1	−0.4	1.0	99.9
1 Belgium	62.0	15.3	17.8	−0.2	5.1	100.0
2 Denmark	52.6	25.9	14.8	−1.1	7.8	100.0
3 Germany	64.8	12.9	22.2	−0.2	0.3	100.0
4 Greece	76.7	15.4	20.9	−0.3	−12.6	100.1
5 Spain	63.3	17.5	19.8	0.1	−0.7	100.0
6 France	61.5	19.5	19.1	−1.4	1.4	100.1
7 Ireland	56.0	16.0	14.9	−0.6	13.7	100.0
8 Italy	61.9	17.7	17.1	−0.2	3.5	100.0
9 Luxembourg	54.7	12.7	24.4	2.1	6.1	100.0
10 Netherlands	60.9	14.6	19.7	−0.2	5.0	100.0
11 Portugal	67.6	17.7	25.8	0.7	−11.8	100.0
12 United Kingdom	64.2	22.0	15.1	0.0	−1.3	100.0
13 Austria	55.2	19.2	24.1	0.4	1.1	100.0
14 Finland	56.8	23.4	14.9	−0.6	5.5	100.0
15 Sweden	54.9	28.0	14.3	−0.8	3.6	100.0
16 USA	67.6	17.1	16.2	0.3	1.2	100.0
17 Japan	57.8	9.6	30.1	0.2	2.3	100.0

Table G27 Real unit labour costs – total economy (1991=100)[1]

	B	DK	D	GR	E	F	IRL	I	L	NL	A	P	SF	S	UK	EUR15	USA	J
1960	93.9	103.2	101.8	122.6	108.0	104.4	112.2	101.3	87.8	98.6	96.4	102.4	99.6	101.0	95.6	107.2	99.4	106.7
1971	95.7	110.6	106.6	96.5	113.7	104.5	111.3	103.4	92.2	112.6	95.1	108.0	97.0	103.3	95.8	107.8	99.5	99.5
1972	97.5	106.1	106.8	95.4	114.4	103.5	107.0	104.0	92.2	111.5	93.0	107.4	96.2	102.7	96.6	107.8	99.5	99.7
1973	98.4	105.9	108.4	88.1	114.6	103.2	106.8	103.1	86.1	112.8	94.5	103.5	95.2	98.9	97.4	107.7	99.4	101.4
1974	100.7	111.6	111.2	90.3	114.2	106.3	115.5	102.1	89.2	115.2	95.4	115.4	93.9	100.9	102.7	110.1	101.0	106.3
1975	104.7	112.4	111.0	91.3	117.2	111.1	116.4	108.8	109.5	117.8	100.9	138.1	103.8	102.4	106.4	114.1	99.1	111.5
1976	106.3	110.0	108.9	92.7	118.9	110.9	112.5	105.9	105.6	113.9	99.9	137.8	105.9	107.0	102.3	112.3	98.9	111.2
1977	106.9	109.4	108.0	97.6	118.0	111.3	107.3	105.4	112.9	113.5	100.1	128.6	102.8	110.5	97.2	110.9	98.6	111.2
1978	107.0	108.3	108.0	100.2	118.2	110.4	107.1	104.3	108.6	113.6	103.6	119.5	97.6	110.4	96.1	109.7	98.9	109.6
1979	107.0	107.7	107.4	100.5	118.2	109.7	112.0	103.9	107.0	114.4	101.8	116.1	95.5	108.2	95.6	108.8	99.6	108.3
1980	108.3	109.4	109.8	98.4	116.9	117.7	115.8	102.8	108.1	113.7	100.9	114.9	96.2	106.9	97.7	109.4	100.8	107.1
1981	109.1	108.1	110.2	104.8	116.9	112.5	111.7	105.3	110.1	110.7	103.3	117.5	98.1	106.8	97.3	109.8	99.3	107.0
1982	106.7	106.7	109.8	105.6	113.7	112.1	108.3	104.7	104.9	109.7	105.5	113.7	96.6	103.5	94.7	108.1	101.4	106.8
1983	105.6	104.9	106.7	108.4	112.8	111.3	108.3	105.2	101.6	106.9	103.6	110.0	95.7	99.9	93.2	106.4	99.9	106.4
1984	104.7	102.1	105.3	106.0	106.9	109.6	106.1	103.0	98.7	102.5	102.4	107.4	94.7	97.3	94.8	104.5	98.5	103.9
1985	103.1	100.7	104.9	108.7	104.6	107.9	103.7	102.5	98.7	100.8	102.4	105.1	96.1	97.3	94.1	103.4	98.5	100.9
1986	102.8	99.6	104.3	103.0	101.3	104.6	103.6	100.0	96.5	102.1	102.7	99.1	96.0	97.3	94.3	101.7	98.9	100.6
1987	101.1	103.2	104.9	101.0	101.0	103.2	102.7	99.4	99.2	104.6	102.5	98.9	95.4	97.1	93.9	101.3	99.5	100.5
1988	98.4	103.0	103.4	101.7	100.6	100.9	102.1	98.2	95.4	103.3	100.2	97.5	93.3	97.3	94.0	100.0	99.8	99.3
1989	95.3	101.4	101.7	106.4	98.8	99.3	97.6	97.8	93.5	100.0	99.4	96.9	92.5	99.3	96.1	99.1	98.6	99.3
1990	97.1	100.8	100.6	109.9	99.9	99.7	99.6	99.4	97.3	99.2	98.8	99.0	95.1	101.2	99.1	99.9	99.5	99.6
1991	100.0	100.0	100.0	100.0	100.0	100.0	100.0	100.0	100.0	100.0	100.0	100.0	100.0	100.0	100.0	100.0	100.0	100.0
1992	100.1	99.7	100.7	95.4	100.5	100.1	100.3	99.5	101.1	101.4	100.1	93.6	97.5	99.7	99.4	99.8	100.1	100.0
1993	99.8	98.2	100.5	95.0	100.0	100.1	99.1	97.1	98.4	102.0	100.4	94.4	91.1	98.3	96.8	98.7	100.1	100.6
1994	99.1	95.3	97.9	96.2	96.6	98.2	96.3	93.2	97.5	99.4	101.0	93.3	87.5	97.3	94.5	96.3	99.4	101.7
1995	97.5	95.7	97.3	98.0	94.1	97.9	93.1	90.3	96.8	99.3	100.7	90.0	86.9	94.9	93.5	95.0	99.5	102.4
1996	96.0	96.3	97.2	99.6	93.4	97.5	92.0	89.8	97.3	98.9	100.1	88.6	87.5	97.3	93.0	94.5	98.6	100.2

Aggregates: PPS weighted.
[1] Nominal unit labour costs deflated by the GDP price deflator.

Table G28 Private consumption at current prices (ESA) (percentage of gross domestic product at market prices)

	B	DK	D	GR	E	F	IRL	I	L	NL	A	P	SF	S	UK	EUR15	USA	J
1960	69.2	62.0	59.4	83.6	69.2	59.7	78.6	59.5	60.2	58.6	59.6	72.4	60.8	59.1	65.5	62.1	63.7	58.7
1961–70	64.3	59.8	59.4	75.9	67.4	59.3	73.8	59.4	62.9	59.5	58.2	68.0	60.2	56.0	63.6	61.0	62.4	56.5
1971	60.3	55.8	58.7	70.8	64.9	57.8	69.8	59.7	61.1	58.0	54.8	67.7	55.9	53.1	61.7	59.4	62.7	53.6
1972	60.2	53.4	59.4	68.4	64.5	57.7	66.7	59.9	59.7	57.5	54.2	63.6	56.4	53.4	62.3	59.5	62.5	54.0
1973	60.6	54.5	58.8	66.1	64.2	57.1	66.0	60.3	54.5	56.9	53.7	64.3	55.0	52.9	62.0	59.1	61.7	53.6
1974	59.8	54.3	59.7	70.5	64.8	57.5	70.2	60.1	51.4	56.9	53.4	72.0	53.1	53.4	63.3	59.7	62.3	54.3
1975	61.2	55.5	62.9	70.4	64.9	58.7	65.8	61.9	64.4	58.8	56.1	76.5	55.7	51.9	61.7	61.0	63.3	57.1
1976	60.9	56.6	62.5	68.5	66.3	58.4	66.2	60.7	63.1	58.9	56.6	74.4	56.3	53.0	60.6	60.6	63.3	57.5
1977	61.9	56.9	63.1	68.6	65.6	58.2	65.8	60.1	66.3	59.9	57.4	71.3	56.5	53.5	59.5	60.6	63.1	57.7
1978	61.6	56.2	62.6	67.9	64.4	57.9	65.4	59.3	64.5	60.6	55.7	67.4	56.5	53.1	59.4	60.2	62.3	57.7
1979	62.8	56.4	62.3	66.0	65.0	58.1	67.0	59.6	64.4	61.1	55.7	66.9	55.2	52.4	59.9	60.3	62.2	58.7
1980	62.9	55.9	63.1	67.3	65.9	58.9	67.5	60.9	65.4	60.8	55.5	66.7	54.1	51.5	59.6	60.7	63.1	58.8
1971–80	61.2	55.5	61.3	68.5	65.0	58.0	67.0	60.2	61.5	58.9	55.3	69.1	55.5	52.8	61.0	61.0	62.6	56.3
1981	65.2	56.0	64.0	70.3	66.3	60.3	67.6	61.0	67.8	59.9	56.5	69.0	54.1	52.5	60.3	61.5	62.2	58.1
1982	65.5	55.0	64.1	70.2	65.6	60.7	61.4	61.4	67.2	60.1	56.5	68.9	55.1	53.5	60.5	61.6	64.0	59.4
1983	65.1	54.6	63.8	69.5	64.8	60.8	61.3	61.0	66.4	60.1	57.8	68.7	55.1	51.9	60.8	61.5	64.9	60.2
1984	64.8	54.5	63.6	67.4	63.9	60.8	60.5	60.9	64.8	59.2	57.4	70.1	54.2	50.6	60.8	61.2	63.8	59.4
1985	65.4	54.8	63.4	68.3	64.1	61.1	61.3	61.3	65.4	59.4	57.5	67.3	54.5	51.2	60.6	61.2	64.7	58.9
1986	64.1	55.0	61.9	70.3	63.2	60.4	61.6	61.2	62.6	59.4	56.5	64.5	54.7	51.4	62.5	61.0	65.3	58.6
1987	64.4	54.0	62.2	72.4	63.2	60.9	61.0	61.5	64.3	60.8	56.6	64.0	54.7	52.5	62.5	61.3	65.8	58.7
1988	63.0	53.1	61.8	70.9	62.7	60.1	61.4	61.3	62.4	59.4	56.4	64.2	53.5	52.4	63.4	61.0	65.9	57.9
1989	62.6	52.6	61.1	71.8	63.0	59.6	60.6	61.9	59.8	58.7	55.9	63.1	52.3	51.3	63.3	60.7	65.7	57.7
1990	62.5	51.9	60.6	73.3	62.4	59.6	58.5	61.3	62.1	58.7	55.4	64.0	52.3	50.9	62.9	60.4	66.4	57.4
1981–90	64.3	54.2	62.6	70.4	63.9	60.4	61.5	61.3	64.3	59.6	56.7	66.4	54.1	51.8	61.8	61.1	64.9	58.6
1991	62.9	52.0	63.8	73.0	62.4	59.9	59.0	61.8	63.0	59.4	55.1	64.8	56.0	53.3	63.3	61.6	66.8	56.5
1992	62.5	52.2	64.2	74.3	63.0	60.0	58.7	62.8	60.9	60.2	55.4	65.1	57.1	53.9	63.8	62.1	67.3	57.2
1993	62.5	52.4	65.1	74.9	63.1	60.9	56.4	62.0	58.7	60.8	55.6	65.8	57.1	55.1	64.2	62.6	67.7	58.1
1994	62.2	53.6	64.5	74.8	62.9	60.4	56.0	62.0	57.5	60.5	55.1	65.0	55.8	54.3	63.9	62.2	67.5	59.2
1995	61.6	53.5	64.3	74.5	62.1	60.1	54.0	61.4	56.0	59.7	55.2	64.0	54.5	52.2	64.0	61.8	67.6	59.7
1996	61.6	53.7	64.9	74.5	61.5	60.4	53.1	61.3	55.6	60.0	55.5	63.5	54.5	52.0	64.4	62.0	67.3	59.3

Table G29 Gross fixed capital formation at current prices; total economy (percentage of gross domestic product at market prices)

	B	DK	D	GR	E	F	IRL	I	L	NL	A	P	SF	S	UK	EUR15	USA	J
1960	19.3	21.6	24.3	23.4	20.4	20.9	14.2	26.0	19.0	24.7	25.0	25.6	28.3	22.6	16.4	21.7	18.0	29.0
1961–70	21.9	23.8	24.9	26.3	24.2	23.8	20.0	24.6	23.6	26.0	26.3	25.9	25.7	23.8	18.3	23.2	18.3	32.2
1971	22.1	24.2	26.2	31.1	23.8	24.7	23.3	24.0	25.7	26.0	27.9	27.3	27.5	21.8	18.9	24.0	18.5	34.2
1972	21.3	24.6	25.4	34.2	24.9	24.7	23.4	23.2	25.2	24.2	30.2	29.9	27.9	22.0	18.5	23.8	19.2	34.1
1973	21.4	24.8	23.9	34.5	26.4	25.2	24.9	24.9	24.7	23.6	28.5	29.6	28.8	21.7	19.9	24.1	19.5	36.4
1974	22.7	24.0	21.6	27.4	27.9	25.8	24.3	26.0	22.3	22.5	28.4	28.7	29.8	21.3	20.9	23.8	18.9	34.8
1975	22.5	21.1	20.4	25.6	26.4	24.1	22.4	25.0	25.1	21.6	26.7	28.6	31.5	20.8	19.9	22.7	17.6	32.5
1976	22.1	23.0	20.1	26.1	24.9	23.9	22.9	23.9	22.6	19.9	26.0	27.6	28.1	21.0	19.6	22.2	17.9	31.2
1977	21.6	22.1	20.3	28.3	23.9	22.9	23.8	23.5	22.7	21.6	26.7	29.2	27.2	20.9	18.6	21.9	19.3	30.2
1978	21.7	21.7	20.6	29.5	22.6	22.4	26.5	22.8	21.8	21.8	25.6	30.8	24.1	19.3	18.5	21.6	20.7	30.4
1979	20.7	20.9	21.7	31.8	21.5	22.4	26.5	22.9	22.1	21.4	25.3	29.3	23.3	19.7	18.7	21.8	21.3	31.7
1980	21.1	18.8	22.6	29.8	22.2	23.0	27.9	24.3	24.6	21.4	25.7	31.5	25.4	20.0	18.0	22.2	20.2	31.6
1971–80	21.7	22.5	22.3	29.8	24.4	23.9	25.0	24.0	23.7	22.4	27.1	29.2	27.4	20.9	19.1	22.8	19.3	32.7
1981	18.0	15.6	21.6	27.4	21.9	22.1	28.3	23.9	23.0	19.6	25.4	34.0	25.3	18.8	16.2	21.1	19.9	30.6
1982	17.3	16.1	20.4	24.6	21.6	21.4	25.3	22.4	22.7	18.6	23.2	34.3	25.3	18.6	16.1	20.3	18.7	29.5
1983	16.2	16.0	20.4	25.0	20.8	20.2	22.1	21.3	19.3	18.6	22.4	32.2	25.6	18.6	16.0	19.8	18.5	28.0
1984	16.0	17.2	20.0	22.8	18.7	19.3	20.5	21.1	18.2	19.1	22.2	26.0	24.0	18.7	17.0	19.4	19.3	27.7
1985	15.6	18.7	19.5	23.5	19.2	19.3	18.2	20.7	16.0	19.7	22.6	24.0	23.9	19.3	17.0	19.3	19.5	27.5
1986	15.7	20.8	19.4	22.7	19.5	19.8	17.5	19.8	19.6	20.4	22.8	24.4	23.4	18.5	17.0	19.2	19.1	27.3
1987	16.0	19.7	19.4	21.1	20.8	19.8	16.4	19.8	22.3	20.8	23.1	27.0	23.9	19.3	17.8	19.6	18.5	28.5
1988	17.7	18.1	19.6	21.4	22.6	20.7	15.7	20.1	24.3	21.3	23.7	28.2	25.2	20.2	19.5	20.4	18.3	29.9
1989	19.1	18.1	20.2	22.5	24.1	21.3	16.9	20.2	23.1	21.5	24.3	27.5	28.0	22.0	20.5	21.1	17.7	31.0
1990	20.3	17.4	20.9	23.0	24.5	21.4	18.0	20.3	24.1	20.9	24.6	27.3	27.0	21.5	19.6	21.2	16.9	32.2
1981–90	17.2	17.8	20.1	23.4	21.4	20.5	19.9	20.9	21.3	20.0	23.4	28.5	25.2	19.5	17.7	20.1	18.6	29.2
1991	19.5	16.5	23.0	22.5	23.8	21.2	16.6	19.8	25.9	20.4	25.4	26.7	22.4	19.4	17.0	20.9	15.6	31.8
1992	19.1	15.6	23.1	21.6	21.9	20.0	15.6	19.2	23.4	20.0	25.1	26.7	18.4	17.0	15.7	20.2	15.6	30.7
1993	17.8	15.0	21.8	20.7	19.9	18.6	14.9	16.9	24.0	19.3	24.3	25.1	14.8	14.2	15.1	18.9	16.2	29.8
1994	17.4	14.8	22.0	19.9	19.8	18.1	15.1	16.6	21.3	19.3	24.8	25.5	14.6	13.6	15.0	18.7	16.8	28.6
1995	17.5	16.1	21.7	20.2	20.8	18.1	16.2	17.0	21.5	19.6	24.8	25.4	15.5	14.5	15.0	18.9	17.2	28.3
1996	18.0	16.5	21.1	20.9	21.3	18.1	16.8	17.4	22.4	19.7	24.6	25.9	17.0	15.8	15.4	18.9	17.5	29.2

Table G30 Gross fixed capital formation at 1990 prices; total economy (annual percentage change)

	B	DK	D	GR	E	F	IRL	I	L	NL	A	P	SF	S	UK	EUR15	USA	J
1961	12.4	13.9	6.5	8.1	17.9	10.9	16.9	11.6	9.0	6.0	12.6	6.7	9.2	8.0	9.8	9.8	1.3	23.4
1961–70	5.8	7.0	4.2	9.3	11.3	7.8	9.6	5.1	3.4	6.7	5.9	6.9	4.4	5.1	5.2	6.0	3.9	15.7
1971	-1.9	1.9	5.9	14.0	-3.0	7.3	8.9	0.2	10.7	1.5	13.8	10.2	3.8	-0.6	1.8	3.6	5.4	4.4
1972	3.4	9.3	2.7	15.4	14.2	6.0	7.8	1.3	7.0	-2.3	12.1	14.0	6.5	4.2	-0.2	4.3	8.9	9.7
1973	7.0	3.5	-0.3	7.7	13.0	8.5	16.2	8.8	11.8	4.2	0.3	10.3	8.5	2.7	6.5	5.9	7.0	11.6
1974	6.9	-8.9	-9.7	-25.6	6.2	1.3	-11.6	2.0	-7.0	-4.0	4.0	-6.1	3.5	-3.0	-2.4	-2.2	-6.0	-8.3
1975	-1.9	-12.4	-5.4	0.2	-4.5	-6.4	-3.6	-7.3	-7.4	-4.4	-5.0	-10.6	5.9	3.1	-2.0	-4.9	-10.9	-1.0
1976	4.0	17.1	3.6	6.8	-0.8	3.3	10.1	0.0	-4.2	-2.2	3.8	1.3	-8.8	1.9	1.7	2.0	7.4	2.7
1977	0.0	-2.4	3.6	7.8	-0.9	-1.8	4.8	1.8	-0.1	9.7	5.1	11.5	-2.7	-2.9	-1.8	1.1	12.1	2.8
1978	2.8	1.1	4.1	6.0	-2.7	2.1	18.3	0.6	1.1	2.4	-4.1	6.2	-7.2	-6.8	3.0	1.7	9.3	7.8
1979	-2.7	-0.4	6.7	8.8	-4.4	3.1	14.5	5.7	3.8	-1.5	3.5	-1.3	2.6	4.5	2.8	3.3	4.2	6.2
1980	4.6	-12.6	2.2	-6.5	0.7	2.6	-3.7	8.7	12.7	-0.2	3.0	8.5	11.0	3.5	-5.4	2.0	-6.7	0.0
1971–80	2.2	-0.8	1.2	2.8	1.6	2.5	5.7	2.1	2.6	0.2	3.5	4.1	2.1	0.6	0.4	1.6	2.8	3.4
1981	-16.1	-19.2	-5.0	-7.5	-2.5	-1.9	7.3	-3.1	-7.4	-9.9	-1.4	5.5	1.3	-6.0	-9.6	-4.8	0.6	2.4
1982	-1.7	7.1	-5.4	-1.9	2.1	-1.4	-3.4	-4.7	-0.5	-4.2	-8.2	2.3	5.1	-0.4	5.4	-1.8	-7.2	-0.1
1983	-4.4	1.9	3.1	-1.3	-2.4	-3.6	-9.0	-0.6	-11.8	2.5	-0.6	-7.1	3.7	1.7	5.0	0.1	5.8	-1.0
1984	1.7	12.9	0.1	-5.7	-6.9	-2.6	-2.7	3.6	0.1	5.8	2.1	-17.4	-2.1	7.2	8.9	0.9	14.7	4.7
1985	0.7	12.6	-0.5	5.2	6.1	3.2	-7.8	0.6	-9.5	7.0	5.0	-3.5	2.2	6.1	4.2	2.5	5.5	5.3
1986	4.4	17.1	3.3	-6.2	9.9	4.5	0.0	2.2	31.2	6.9	3.7	10.9	-0.4	1.0	2.6	4.0	0.6	4.8
1987	5.6	-3.8	1.8	-5.1	14.0	4.8	-2.3	5.0	14.7	0.9	3.1	16.8	4.9	7.9	10.3	5.5	1.0	9.6
1988	15.4	-6.6	4.4	8.9	13.9	9.6	-1.6	6.9	14.1	4.5	6.0	11.2	9.8	6.0	13.9	8.5	3.7	11.9
1989	12.3	1.0	6.3	7.1	13.6	7.9	13.8	4.3	8.9	4.9	6.2	4.3	14.8	11.7	6.0	7.2	1.4	9.3
1990	10.1	-1.7	8.5	5.0	6.6	2.8	11.1	3.8	2.5	1.6	5.7	6.8	-4.1	0.7	-3.5	3.5	-0.6	8.8
1981–90	2.4	1.6	1.6	-0.3	5.2	2.3	0.3	1.7	3.5	1.9	2.1	2.5	3.4	3.5	4.1	2.5	2.4	5.5
1992	0.2	-4.2	3.5	-1.4	-4.2	-3.1	-3.1	-1.8	-2.1	0.6	1.7	5.4	-16.9	-10.8	-1.5	-0.9	5.8	-1.1
1993	-6.7	-4.7	-5.6	-2.8	-10.6	-5.8	-0.8	-12.8	3.9	-3.1	-1.6	-4.8	-19.2	-17.2	0.6	-6.5	11.9	-1.8
1994	0.5	3.0	4.3	0.5	1.4	1.1	7.3	0.2	2.4	3.0	6.8	3.5	-0.3	-0.2	3.7	2.5	7.9	-2.4
1995	2.7	11.0	1.5	6.3	8.4	2.8	12.2	5.9	6.0	5.0	2.4	4.0	9.4	10.6	-0.7	3.5	5.4	0.5
1996	3.8	3.8	-1.7	7.8	4.7	1.5	8.3	4.2	6.5	2.4	0.3	4.8	11.0	10.1	4.2	2.2	5.0	5.7

Aggregates: PPS weighted.

Table G31 Price deflator gross domestic product at market prices (national currency; annual percentage change)

	B	DK	D	GR	E	F	IRL	I	L	NL	A	P	SF	S	UK	EUR15	USA	J
1961	1.3	4.3	4.7	1.5	1.8	3.4	2.5	2.8	-3.7	2.4	5.4	2.3	5.3	2.9	2.7	3.3	0.9	7.8
1961–70	3.4	6.4	3.8	3.1	6.5	4.4	5.5	4.5	4.1	5.2	3.8	2.9	5.9	4.3	4.2	4.4	3.0	5.4
1971	5.6	7.7	7.7	3.2	7.8	6.3	10.5	6.9	-0.8	8.1	6.2	5.1	7.6	7.1	9.4	7.5	5.6	5.5
1972	6.2	9.2	5.3	5.0	8.5	7.0	13.4	6.5	5.8	9.4	7.6	7.8	8.4	7.0	8.1	7.0	5.0	5.8
1973	7.2	10.7	6.4	19.4	11.8	8.5	15.3	13.2	12.2	9.0	8.0	9.4	14.1	7.0	7.6	9.2	6.4	13.1
1974	12.6	13.1	7.1	20.9	16.0	11.8	6.1	19.8	17.0	9.2	9.5	18.9	22.5	9.5	14.6	13.1	8.9	20.1
1975	12.1	12.4	5.7	12.3	16.8	13.0	20.1	16.5	-0.9	10.2	6.5	16.2	13.3	14.5	26.3	14.4	9.8	7.4
1976	7.6	9.1	3.6	15.4	16.5	11.1	21.0	18.4	12.2	9.0	5.6	16.3	13.5	11.9	15.8	11.8	6.4	7.8
1977	7.5	9.4	3.7	13.0	23.4	9.3	13.3	18.6	1.2	6.7	5.1	26.5	9.9	10.5	14.1	11.7	6.7	6.4
1978	4.4	9.9	4.3	12.9	20.6	10.1	10.7	14.1	5.1	5.3	5.7	22.3	8.4	9.5	11.5	10.3	7.7	5.0
1979	4.5	7.6	3.8	18.6	16.9	10.1	13.8	15.3	6.4	4.1	4.1	19.4	8.8	7.9	14.5	10.5	8.8	2.7
1980	3.8	8.2	5.0	17.7	13.4	11.4	14.8	20.0	7.9	5.5	5.2	20.9	9.7	11.7	18.8	12.4	9.4	4.6
1971–80	7.1	9.7	5.2	13.7	15.1	9.8	13.8	14.8	6.5	7.6	6.3	16.1	11.5	9.6	13.9	10.8	7.5	7.7
1981	4.7	10.1	4.2	19.8	12.6	11.4	17.5	19.0	7.2	5.4	6.5	17.6	11.1	9.5	11.4	10.9	9.7	3.7
1982	7.1	10.6	4.4	25.1	13.9	11.7	15.2	17.2	10.8	5.4	6.2	20.7	8.9	8.3	7.8	10.4	6.1	1.7
1983	5.6	7.6	3.2	19.1	11.8	9.7	10.8	15.1	6.8	2.1	3.9	24.6	8.6	10.1	5.3	8.5	3.9	1.4
1984	5.2	5.7	2.1	20.3	11.6	7.5	6.4	11.6	4.4	1.4	4.9	24.7	8.9	7.6	4.4	6.9	4.0	2.3
1985	6.1	4.3	2.1	17.7	7.7	5.8	5.3	8.9	3.0	1.8	3.1	21.7	5.3	6.6	5.9	5.9	3.5	1.6
1986	3.8	4.6	3.2	17.5	11.1	5.2	5.8	7.9	5.9	0.1	4.3	20.5	4.6	6.9	3.2	5.6	2.5	1.8
1987	2.3	4.7	1.9	14.3	5.8	3.0	2.2	6.0	0.4	-0.7	2.4	11.1	4.7	4.8	5.0	4.1	3.1	0.0
1988	1.8	3.4	1.5	15.6	5.7	2.8	3.4	6.6	4.8	1.2	1.6	10.9	7.0	6.5	6.1	4.4	3.9	0.4
1989	4.8	4.2	2.4	14.4	7.1	3.0	5.4	6.2	6.6	1.2	2.9	11.4	6.1	8.0	7.1	5.0	4.4	1.9
1990	3.0	2.7	3.2	20.6	7.3	3.1	-0.8	7.6	2.4	2.3	3.3	12.9	5.8	8.8	6.4	5.4	4.2	2.2
1981–90	4.4	5.8	2.8	18.4	9.4	6.3	7.0	10.5	5.2	2.0	3.9	17.5	7.1	7.7	6.2	6.7	4.5	1.7
1992	3.5	3.2	5.5	14.6	6.8	2.1	2.0	4.7	5.0	2.3	4.1	13.5	0.7	1.0	4.4	4.5	2.4	1.5
1993	4.1	0.7	3.8	14.1	4.3	2.5	4.1	4.4	10.0	2.0	3.4	7.4	2.4	2.6	3.2	3.7	2.0	0.8
1994	2.6	1.7	2.3	10.9	3.9	1.4	1.2	3.5	3.6	2.3	3.4	5.4	1.1	2.8	2.1	2.7	2.3	0.2
1995	2.0	1.7	2.2	9.3	4.8	1.6	1.2	5.0	4.1	2.1	2.1	5.1	3.8	4.1	2.4	3.0	2.5	-0.3
1996	2.1	2.0	1.4	8.3	3.9	1.7	2.1	4.4	2.0	1.6	1.9	3.8	2.0	2.0	2.7	2.6	3.2	0.7

Aggregates: PPS weighted.

Table G32 Total expenditure by general government (percentage of gross domestic product at market prices)

	B	DK	D	GR	E	F	IRL	I	L	NL	A	P[1]	SF	S[1]	UK	EUR11[2]	EUR14[3]	EUR15[3]
1970	41.5	42.0	38.5	:	21.6	38.1	36.0	32.1	30.1	41.8	39.1	20.4	30.5	43.2	37.3	36.9	:	:
1971	43.3	42.9	39.9	:	23.1	38.0	36.8	34.4	33.6	43.3	39.7	20.2	32.0	45.3	36.7	37.9	:	:
1972	44.6	42.5	40.7	:	22.7	38.3	35.5	36.4	34.0	43.8	39.8	21.5	32.4	46.1	37.9	38.7	:	:
1973	45.0	40.8	41.3	:	22.4	38.3	35.4	35.1	32.9	44.0	41.3	20.5	31.0	44.6	38.9	38.8	:	:
1974	45.2	44.8	44.3	:	22.8	39.4	43.3	34.4	32.6	45.9	41.9	23.2	32.0	47.9	43.1	40.7	:	:
1975	50.8	47.0	48.6	:	24.6	43.8	45.1	39.1	44.1	50.8	46.0	28.0	38.4	48.8	44.7	44.3	:	:
1976	51.7	46.4	47.7	:	25.8	44.3	44.8	37.8	44.7	50.9	46.8	32.2	39.6	51.6	44.4	44.3	:	:
1977	53.5	47.2	47.7	:	27.3	44.1	42.6	37.7	47.1	51.1	46.7	30.7	41.5	57.4	41.9	44.4	:	:
1978	54.9	48.7	47.2	:	29.1	45.2	43.1	40.4	46.7	52.8	49.6	31.9	40.9	59.1	41.5	45.2	:	:
1979	56.7	51.4	47.2	27.2	30.3	45.6	44.2	39.7	47.7	54.7	48.8	31.8	39.9	60.5	41.0	45.2	44.8	44.8
1980	57.9	54.8	48.0	27.3	32.9	46.6	48.4	42.0	50.3	56.7	48.8	:	39.4	61.6	43.2	46.6	46.0	46.0
1981	63.1	58.6	48.9	32.2	35.5	49.2	50.0	45.8	53.7	58.5	50.3	38.5	40.5	64.1	45.7	48.9	48.4	48.4
1982	63.0	60.0	49.3	32.7	37.2	50.9	52.4	47.4	51.4	60.7	50.9	37.8	42.0	66.3	45.1	49.7	49.2	49.2
1983	63.0	60.4	48.0	34.5	38.3	52.0	52.2	48.6	50.7	60.8	51.1	42.1	43.6	66.1	44.8	49.9	49.5	49.5
1984	61.7	58.8	47.6	36.6	38.7	52.5	50.9	49.4	47.6	59.7	50.8	39.0	43.4	63.5	45.3	49.9	49.5	49.5
1985	61.2	58.1	47.2	39.8	42.2	52.7	51.5	51.0	46.1	58.0	51.7	38.1	45.0	64.9	44.1	50.0	49.7	49.7
1986	60.6	54.3	46.5	39.3	41.9	52.2	51.4	50.8	44.7	57.9	52.4	40.8	45.9	63.1	42.9	49.5	49.7	49.7
1987	58.9	55.7	46.9	39.3	40.8	51.7	49.4	50.3	47.4	59.5	52.6	39.2	46.3	59.3	40.8	48.9	49.2	49.2
1988	56.6	58.0	46.4	42.2	41.0	50.8	46.1	50.4	:	57.7	50.9	38.5	45.3	59.5	38.9	48.0	48.6	:
1989	54.7	58.4	45.0	43.6	42.3	49.9	39.7	51.4	:	54.8	49.6	37.3	43.3	60.0	38.7	47.4	47.7	:
1990	54.4	57.4	45.3	48.2	43.6	50.5	40.0	53.4	:	55.0	49.3	41.3	46.8	60.7	40.3	48.4	47.2	:
1991	55.4	57.9	48.1	44.4	45.1	51.1	40.6	53.7	:	55.6	50.4	43.2	55.5	62.7	40.9	49.5	49.5	:
1992	55.7	59.8	48.8	46.0	46.3	52.7	41.3	53.8	:	56.1	51.1	42.2	60.7	68.6	43.3	50.8	50.8	:
1993	56.3	62.2	50.0	48.5	49.5	55.2	41.3	57.0	42.9	56.3	53.7	43.4	61.9	72.6	43.7	52.5	52.5	52.4
1994	55.6	62.3	49.3	48.0	47.9	55.2	41.6	54.2	42.4	54.1	52.4	43.8	60.9	70.2	43.3	51.5	51.5	51.4
1995	54.4	59.7	49.8	46.0	46.0	54.3	39.7	51.8	41.3	51.9	53.1	44.8	58.2	67.6	43.6	50.8	50.8	50.8
1996	53.7	60.0	50.0	45.5	45.2	54.6	38.6	52.0	40.9	51.3	52.7	44.7	57.0	66.7	42.4	50.7	50.6	50.6

(1) Breaks: in 1985–86 for P; in 1979–80 for S

(2) EUR15 excl. GR L P SF

(3) EUR15 excl. L

Table G33 Total current receipts; general government (percentage of gross domestic product at market prices)

	B	DK	D	GR	E	F	IRL	I	L	NL	A	P¹	SF	S¹	UK	EUR11²	EUR14³	EUR15
1970	39.3	46.1	38.7	:	22.3	39.0	31.9	28.8	33.0	40.6	40.3	22.8	34.8	47.6	39.8	37.3	:	:
1971	40.0	46.8	39.8	:	22.6	38.6	32.8	29.5	35.9	42.3	41.2	22.2	36.5	50.4	38.1	37.6	:	:
1972	40.1	46.4	40.1	:	23.0	38.9	31.6	29.4	36.0	43.3	41.8	22.3	36.2	50.5	36.0	37.5	:	:
1973	41.2	46.0	42.5	:	23.5	39.0	31.0	28.6	36.4	44.7	42.5	21.9	36.8	48.7	35.4	38.1	:	:
1974	42.3	47.9	43.1	22.1	23.0	39.7	35.4	28.0	37.3	45.7	43.1	22.0	36.6	49.9	39.3	39.0	38.6	38.6
1975	45.8	45.7	43.1	22.4	24.6	41.4	33.1	28.6	45.1	48.0	43.5	24.4	43.1	51.5	40.0	39.9	39.6	39.6
1976	46.0	46.1	44.3	24.1	25.5	43.5	36.5	29.8	46.5	48.3	43.0	27.0	46.8	56.1	39.4	41.3	41.0	41.0
1977	47.7	46.6	45.3	24.4	26.7	43.2	35.3	30.7	50.1	50.3	44.4	26.6	47.1	59.0	38.5	41.9	41.5	41.5
1978	48.6	48.4	44.8	24.7	27.4	43.1	33.7	31.9	51.2	50.5	46.9	25.8	44.1	58.6	37.1	41.8	41.4	41.4
1979	49.6	49.8	44.6	25.1	28.7	44.7	33.2	31.4	48.3	51.7	46.4	26.3	42.6	57.6	37.8	42.0	41.6	41.6
1980	49.0	51.5	45.1	24.9	30.3	46.5	36.2	33.4	49.8	52.4	47.1	27.5	42.8	57.6	39.7	43.0	42.7	42.7
1981	50.0	51.7	45.3	23.8	31.6	47.3	37.2	34.4	50.5	53.1	48.5	29.2	45.0	58.9	41.7	43.9	43.4	43.5
1982	51.9	50.9	46.0	26.4	31.6	48.2	39.1	36.1	50.4	54.1	47.5	31.1	44.5	59.4	42.2	44.5	44.1	44.1
1983	51.4	53.2	45.4	27.4	33.6	48.8	40.9	38.0	52.8	55.0	47.1	33.2	44.6	61.1	41.5	44.9	44.6	44.6
1984	52.3	54.7	45.6	28.3	33.3	49.8	41.5	37.8	51.0	54.2	48.2	32.8	46.1	60.6	41.4	45.1	44.8	44.8
1985	52.2	56.0	46.0	28.3	35.2	49.9	40.7	38.4	52.6	54.4	49.2	31.6	48.0	61.0	41.3	45.5	45.2	45.2
1986	51.2	57.7	45.2	29.0	35.9	49.4	40.8	39.1	49.3	52.8	48.7	34.4	49.3	61.9	40.1	45.2	44.9	45.0
1987	51.3	58.1	45.0	29.7	37.7	49.8	41.0	39.3	50.3	53.6	48.4	33.6	47.3	63.6	39.4	45.3	45.0	45.0
1988	49.9	58.6	44.2	30.6	37.7	49.2	41.7	39.7	:	53.1	47.8	34.9	49.3	63.0	39.1	44.7	44.6	45.0
1989	48.2	57.9	45.1	29.2	39.5	48.7	37.9	41.4	:	50.1	46.8	35.0	49.6	65.3	38.6	45.0	44.8	:
1990	48.6	55.9	43.3	32.1	39.5	49.0	37.7	42.4	:	49.9	47.1	35.8	52.1	64.9	38.8	44.8	44.7	:
1991	48.8	55.8	44.8	32.9	40.2	48.9	38.4	43.4	:	52.7	47.8	36.8	54.0	61.6	38.3	45.3	45.2	:
1992	48.7	57.0	46.0	33.7	42.2	48.8	38.8	44.3	:	52.1	49.0	38.9	54.9	60.9	37.0	45.7	45.6	:
1993	49.6	58.3	46.5	34.4	42.0	49.3	38.9	47.4	44.7	53.1	49.4	36.3	53.8	60.3	35.9	46.4	46.2	46.2
1994	50.4	58.8	46.8	35.8	41.0	49.4	39.5	45.2	44.6	50.8	48.0	38.0	54.6	59.4	36.4	46.1	45.9	45.9
1995	49.9	58.3	46.3	36.8	39.9	49.3	37.3	44.8	41.6	48.6	46.9	39.4	52.6	59.5	37.6	45.8	45.7	45.7
1996	50.5	59.1	46.0	37.4	40.4	50.4	36.6	45.7	41.5	47.9	48.1	40.3	53.8	61.6	38.1	46.3	46.2	46.2

(1) Breaks: in 1985–86 for P; in 1979–80 for S
(2) EUR15 excl. GR L P SF
(3) EUR15 excl. L

Table G34 Net lending (+) or net borrowing (−) of general government (percentage of gross domestic product at market prices)

	B[1]	DK	D[2]	GR[3]	E[3]	F	IRL	I	L[4]	NL[3]	A	P[1]	SF	S[1]	UK	EUR11[2]	EUR14[3]	EUR15
1970	-2.2	4.1	0.2	:	0.7	0.9	-4.1	-3.3	2.9	-1.2	1.2	2.5	4.3	4.4	2.5	0.4	:	:
1971	-3.2	3.9	-0.2	:	-0.6	0.6	-4.0	-4.8	2.3	-1.0	1.5	2.0	4.5	5.1	1.3	-0.3	:	:
1972	-4.5	3.9	-0.5	:	0.3	0.6	-4.0	-7.0	2.1	-0.4	2.0	0.8	3.9	4.4	-1.8	-1.2	:	:
1973	-3.8	5.2	1.2	:	1.1	0.6	-4.4	-6.5	3.5	0.7	1.3	1.4	5.7	4.0	-3.5	-0.7	:	:
1974	-2.9	3.1	-1.3	:	0.2	0.3	-7.8	-6.4	4.8	-0.2	1.3	-1.3	4.6	1.9	-3.8	-1.6	:	:
1975	-5.0	-1.4	-5.6	:	0.0	-2.4	-12.1	-10.6	1.0	-2.8	-2.5	-3.6	4.6	2.7	-4.7	-4.4	:	:
1976	-5.7	-0.3	-3.4	:	-0.3	-0.7	-8.2	-8.1	1.9	-2.6	-3.7	-5.2	7.2	4.5	-4.9	-3.1	:	:
1977	-5.9	-0.6	-2.4	:	-0.6	-0.8	-7.3	-7.1	3.0	-0.8	-2.4	-4.1	5.6	1.7	-3.4	-2.6	:	:
1978	-6.3	-0.4	-2.4	:	-1.7	-2.1	-9.3	-8.5	4.5	-2.3	-2.8	-6.1	3.2	-0.5	-4.4	-3.4	:	:
1979	-7.1	-1.7	-2.6	-2.1	-1.6	-0.8	-11.0	-8.3	0.7	-3.0	-2.4	-5.5	2.7	-2.9	-3.3	-3.2	-3.1	-3.1
1980	-8.9	-3.3	-2.9	-2.4	-2.6	0.0	-12.2	-8.6	-0.5	-4.2	-1.7	:	3.4	-4.0	-3.5	-3.6	-3.4	-3.4
1981	-13.1	-6.9	-3.7	-8.4	-3.9	-1.9	-12.9	-11.4	-3.2	-5.4	-1.8	-9.3	4.5	-5.3	-4.0	-5.0	-5.0	-5.0
1982	-11.1	-9.1	-3.3	-6.3	-5.6	-2.8	-13.2	-11.3	-1.0	-6.6	-3.4	-6.7	2.5	-7.0	-2.9	-5.2	-5.1	-5.1
1983	-11.6	-7.2	-2.6	-7.1	-4.7	-3.2	-11.3	-10.6	2.1	-5.8	-4.0	-8.9	1.0	-5.0	-3.4	-4.9	-4.9	-4.9
1984	-9.4	-4.1	-1.9	-8.3	-5.4	-2.8	-9.4	-11.6	3.4	-5.5	-2.6	-6.2	2.8	-2.9	-3.9	-4.8	-4.7	-4.7
1985	-9.0	-2.0	-1.2	-11.6	-6.9	-2.9	-10.7	-12.6	6.5	-3.6	-2.5	-6.5	2.9	-3.8	-2.8	-4.6	-4.5	-4.5
1986	-9.4	3.4	-1.3	-10.3	-6.0	-2.7	-10.6	-11.6	4.6	-5.1	-3.7	-6.5	3.4	-1.2	-2.9	-4.3	-4.2	-4.2
1987	-7.6	2.4	-1.9	-9.6	-3.1	-1.9	-8.5	-11.0	2.9	-5.9	-4.3	-5.6	1.0	4.2	-1.4	-3.6	-3.6	-3.6
1988	-6.8	0.6	-2.2	-11.5	-3.3	-1.7	-4.4	-10.7	:	-4.6	-3.0	-3.6	4.1	3.5	0.1	-3.2	-3.2	:
1989	-6.5	-0.5	0.1	-11.5	-2.8	-1.2	-1.8	-9.9	:	-4.7	-2.8	-2.3	6.3	5.4	-0.1	-2.4	-2.4	:
1990	-5.8	-1.5	-2.1	-16.1	-4.1	-1.6	-2.3	-11.0	5.0	-5.1	-2.2	-5.5	5.4	4.2	-1.5	-3.6	-3.6	-3.6
1991	-6.7	-2.1	-3.3	-11.5	-4.9	-2.2	-2.2	-10.2	1.9	-2.9	-2.6	-6.4	-1.5	-1.1	-2.6	-4.3	-4.3	-4.3
1992	-7.1	-2.9	-2.8	-12.3	-4.1	-3.9	-2.4	-9.5	0.8	-3.9	-2.1	-3.3	-5.9	-7.8	-6.3	-5.1	-5.1	-5.1
1993	-6.7	-3.9	-3.5	-14.2	-7.5	-5.9	-2.4	-9.6	1.8	-3.2	-4.3	-7.1	-8.0	-12.3	-7.8	-6.1	-6.3	-6.2
1994	-5.3	-3.5	-2.5	-12.1	-6.9	-5.8	-2.0	-9.0	2.2	-3.2	-4.4	-5.8	-6.3	-10.8	-6.8	-5.4	-5.5	-5.5
1995	-4.5	-1.4	-3.5	-9.2	-6.2	-5.0	-2.4	-7.1	0.3	-3.4	-6.2	-5.4	-5.6	-8.1	-6.0	-5.0	-5.1	-5.0
1996	-3.2	-0.9	-3.9	-8.1	-4.8	-4.2	-2.0	-6.3	0.7	-3.5	-4.6	-4.4	-3.3	-5.2	-4.4	-4.4	-4.4	-4.4

(1) 1993–94 include proceeds from the sale participations, amounts involved are 32.2 and 12.7 bn BFR.
(2) Not including unification-related debt and asset assumptions by the federal government in 1995 (Treu-and, eastern housing companies and Deutsche Kreditbank), equal to DM 229 bn.
(3) Breaks: in 1987–88 for GR; in 1979–80 and 1984–85 for E; in 1976–77 for NL.
(4) 1990–92; excessive deficit procedure figures.

Table G35 Nominal short-term interest rates (%)

	B	DK	D	GR	E	F	IRL	I	NL	A	P	SF	S	UK	EUR7¹	EUR15	USA	J
1960	..	..	5.1	..	..	4.1	..	3.5	2.1	..	..	..	..	..	..	..	..	..
1961–70	5.2	6.8	5.0	..	..	5.4	..	3.7	3.8	..	..	..	..	6.3	5.1	..	4.3	..
1971	5.4	7.6	7.1	..	..	6.0	6.6	5.7	4.5	4.4	4.3	8.1	..	6.2	6.2	..	4.3	6.5
1972	4.2	7.3	5.7	..	..	5.3	7.1	5.2	2.7	5.2	4.4	7.8	..	6.8	5.6	..	4.2	5.2
1973	6.6	7.6	12.2	..	..	9.3	12.2	7.0	7.5	6.9	4.4	9.3	..	11.8	9.9	..	7.2	8.3
1974	10.6	10.0	9.8	..	..	13.0	14.6	14.9	10.4	7.3	5.3	10.4	..	13.4	12.3	..	7.9	14.7
1975	7.0	8.0	4.9	..	..	7.6	10.9	10.4	5.4	5.5	6.8	11.7	..	10.6	7.9	..	5.8	10.1
1976	10.1	8.9	4.3	..	..	8.7	11.7	16.0	7.4	4.7	8.4	12.4	..	11.6	9.5	..	5.0	7.3
1977	7.3	14.5	4.3	..	15.5	9.1	8.4	14.0	4.8	7.5	11.1	11.8	..	8.0	8.3	..	5.3	6.4
1978	7.3	15.4	3.7	..	17.6	7.8	9.9	11.5	7.0	6.4	15.5	8.6	..	9.4	7.9	..	7.4	5.1
1979	10.9	12.5	6.9	..	15.5	9.7	16.0	12.0	9.6	5.6	16.1	8.5	..	13.9	10.3	..	10.1	5.9
1980	14.2	16.9	9.5	16.4	16.5	12.0	16.2	16.9	10.6	10.3	16.3	13.8	..	16.8	13.4	..	11.6	10.7
1971–80	8.4	10.9	6.9	..	..	8.8	11.4	11.3	7.0	6.4	9.3	10.2	..	10.8	9.1	..	6.9	8.0
1981	15.6	14.9	12.4	16.8	16.2	15.3	16.7	19.3	11.8	11.4	16.0	12.7	..	14.1	14.9	..	14.0	7.4
1982	14.1	16.4	8.8	18.9	16.3	14.6	17.5	19.9	8.2	8.8	16.8	13.7	13.3	12.2	13.3	13.6	10.6	6.9
1983	10.5	12.0	5.8	16.6	20.1	12.5	14.0	18.3	5.7	5.4	20.9	14.2	11.4	10.1	11.0	11.8	8.7	6.5
1984	11.5	11.5	6.0	15.7	14.9	11.7	13.2	17.3	6.1	6.6	22.5	15.8	11.9	10.0	10.6	11.3	9.5	6.3
1985	9.6	10.0	5.4	17.0	12.2	10.0	12.0	15.0	6.3	6.2	21.0	12.8	14.2	12.2	10.0	10.6	7.5	6.5
1986	8.1	9.1	4.6	19.8	11.7	7.7	12.4	12.8	5.7	5.3	15.6	11.7	9.8	10.9	8.5	9.1	6.0	5.0
1987	7.1	9.9	4.0	14.9	15.8	8.3	11.1	11.4	5.4	4.4	13.9	10.0	9.7	9.7	7.9	8.8	5.9	3.9
1988	6.7	8.3	4.3	15.9	11.6	7.9	8.1	11.3	4.8	4.6	13.0	10.0	10.2	10.3	8.0	8.5	6.9	4.0
1989	8.7	9.6	7.1	18.7	15.0	9.4	9.8	12.7	7.4	7.5	15.1	12.6	11.6	13.9	10.3	10.9	8.4	5.4
1990	9.8	10.9	8.4	19.9	15.2	10.3	11.4	12.3	8.7	8.5	16.9	14.0	13.8	14.8	11.0	11.7	7.8	7.8
1981–90	10.2	11.3	6.7	17.4	14.9	10.8	12.6	15.0	7.0	6.9	17.2	12.7	..	11.8	10.6	..	8.5	6.0
1991	9.4	9.7	9.2	22.7	13.2	9.6	10.4	12.2	9.3	9.1	17.7	13.1	11.8	11.5	10.3	11.0	5.5	7.4
1992	9.4	11.0	9.5	23.5	13.3	10.4	12.4	14.0	9.4	9.3	16.2	13.3	13.5	9.6	10.6	11.2	3.5	4.4
1993	8.2	10.4	7.2	23.5	11.7	8.6	9.3	10.2	6.9	7.2	13.3	7.8	8.8	5.9	7.9	8.6	3.1	3.0
1994	5.7	6.2	5.3	24.6	8.0	5.9	5.9	8.5	5.2	5.0	11.1	5.3	7.6	5.5	6.1	6.7	4.7	2.3
1995	4.7	6.1	4.5	16.4	9.4	6.6	6.3	10.3	4.4	4.5	9.8	5.8	8.9	6.7	6.5	7.0	6.0	1.2

Aggregates: PPS weighted.
(1) B DK D F I NL UK.

Table G36 Nominal long-term interest rates (%)

	B	DK	D	GR	E	F	IRL	I	L	NL	A	P	SF	S	UK	EUR9[1]	EUR15	USA	J
1960	..	..	6.3	..	..	5.7	..	5.3	..	4.2	..	..	..	5.2	5.4	..	..	..	..
1961–70	6.3	8.3	6.8	..	..	6.5	..	6.7	..	5.6	..	..	7.9	6.0	7.0	6.7	..	4.8	..
1971	7.3	11.0	8.0	..	..	8.4	9.2	8.3	..	7.1	7.7	..	8.1	7.2	8.9	8.3	..	5.7	..
1972	7.0	11.0	7.9	..	..	8.0	9.1	7.5	..	6.7	7.4	..	8.0	7.3	9.0	8.0	..	5.6	6.9
1973	7.5	12.6	9.3	9.3	..	9.0	10.7	7.4	6.8	7.3	8.3	..	8.3	7.4	10.8	9.0	..	6.3	7.0
1974	8.8	15.9	10.4	10.5	..	11.0	14.6	9.9	7.3	10.7	9.7	..	8.8	7.8	15.0	11.3	..	7.0	8.1
1975	8.5	12.7	8.5	9.4	..	10.3	14.0	11.5	6.7	9.2	9.6	..	8.8	8.8	14.5	10.8	..	7.0	8.4
1976	9.1	14.9	7.8	10.2	..	10.5	14.6	13.1	7.2	9.2	8.8	..	10.2	9.3	14.6	11.0	..	6.8	8.2
1977	8.8	16.2	6.2	9.5	..	11.0	12.9	14.6	7.0	8.5	8.7	..	10.8	9.7	12.5	10.6	..	7.1	7.4
1978	8.5	16.8	5.7	10.0	..	10.6	12.8	13.7	6.6	8.1	8.2	..	9.8	10.1	12.6	10.2	..	7.9	6.3
1979	9.7	16.7	7.4	11.2	13.3	10.9	15.1	14.1	6.8	9.2	8.0	..	9.5	10.5	13.0	11.0	11.1	8.7	8.3
1980	12.2	18.7	8.5	17.1	16.0	13.1	15.4	16.1	7.4	10.7	9.3	..	11.6	11.7	13.9	12.5	12.8	10.8	8.9
1971–80	8.7	14.6	8.0	..	..	10.3	12.8	11.6	..	8.7	8.6	..	9.5	9.0	12.5	10.3	..	7.3	..
1981	13.8	19.3	10.4	17.7	15.8	15.9	17.3	20.6	8.7	12.2	10.6	..	12.4	13.5	14.8	14.8	14.9	12.9	8.4
1982	13.5	20.5	9.0	15.4	16.0	15.7	17.0	20.9	10.4	10.5	9.9	..	12.4	13.0	12.7	14.0	14.1	12.2	8.3
1983	11.8	14.4	7.9	18.2	16.9	13.6	13.9	18.0	9.8	8.8	8.2	..	13.1	12.3	10.8	12.1	12.5	10.8	7.8
1984	12.0	14.0	7.8	18.5	16.5	12.5	14.6	15.0	10.3	8.6	8.0	27.7	14.0	12.3	10.7	11.3	11.8	12.0	7.3
1985	10.6	11.6	6.9	15.8	13.4	10.9	12.7	14.3	9.5	7.3	7.8	19.5	12.7	13.0	10.6	10.4	10.9	10.8	6.5
1986	7.9	10.6	5.9	15.8	11.4	8.4	11.1	11.7	8.7	6.4	7.3	16.8	11.7	10.3	9.8	8.7	9.2	8.1	5.2
1987	7.8	11.9	5.8	17.4	12.8	9.4	11.3	11.3	8.0	6.4	7.0	15.5	11.2	11.7	9.5	8.9	9.4	8.7	4.7
1988	7.9	10.6	6.1	16.6	11.7	9.0	9.4	12.1	7.1	6.3	6.7	16.9	10.6	11.4	9.3	8.9	9.3	9.0	4.7
1989	8.7	10.2	7.0	..	13.7	8.8	8.9	12.9	7.7	7.2	7.1	16.8	12.1	11.2	9.6	9.4	9.8	8.5	5.2
1990	10.7	11.0	8.9	..	14.7	9.9	10.1	13.4	8.6	9.0	8.7	..	13.2	14.2	11.1	10.7	11.1	8.6	7.5
1981–90	10.4	13.4	7.6	..	14.3	11.4	12.6	15.0	8.9	8.3	8.1	..	12.3	12.3	10.9	10.9	11.3	10.2	6.6
1991	9.3	10.1	8.6	..	12.4	9.0	9.2	13.0	8.2	8.7	8.6	18.3	11.7	11.8	9.9	10.0	10.3	8.1	6.7
1992	8.6	10.1	8.0	..	12.2	8.6	9.1	13.7	7.9	8.1	8.3	15.4	12.0	10.0	9.1	9.6	9.8	7.7	5.3
1993	7.2	7.2	6.4	..	10.1	6.7	7.8	11.1	6.9	6.3	6.6	9.5	8.2	8.6	7.3	7.6	7.8	5.8	4.0
1994	7.8	7.9	6.9	..	10.1	7.3	8.1	10.4	6.4	6.9	6.7	10.4	8.4	9.5	8.1	8.0	8.2	7.1	4.2
1995	7.5	8.3	6.8	..	11.3	7.5	8.3	11.9	6.1	6.9	7.2	11.5	8.8	10.2	8.2	8.3	8.6	6.6	3.3

Aggregates: PPS weighted.
[1] B DK D F I NL UK S SF.

Table G37 Balance on current account with the rest of the world (ESA) (percentage of gross domestic product at market prices)

	B	DK	D	GR	E	F	IRL	I	L	NL	A	P	SF	S	UK	EUR15	USA	J
1960	0.1	-1.1	1.6	-2.4	3.4	1.5	-0.1	0.7	11.3	2.8	-1.1	-3.5	-0.9	-0.6	-1.0	0.6	0.6	0.5
1961–70	0.6	-2.1	0.7	-2.6	-1.3	0.2	-2.2	1.6	5.1	0.0	0.1	0.5	-1.3	-0.2	-0.1	0.2	0.6	0.2
1971	2.1	-2.4	0.4	-1.2	2.2	0.9	-3.7	1.4	6.0	-0.3	0.5	2.2	-2.8	1.0	1.8	0.9	0.1	2.5
1972	3.5	-0.4	0.6	-1.0	1.5	1.0	-2.1	1.6	9.6	2.8	0.1	4.8	-0.9	1.3	0.1	1.0	-0.3	2.2
1973	2.0	-1.7	1.5	-3.2	0.9	0.6	-3.3	-1.6	14.9	3.8	-0.3	2.7	-1.9	2.7	-1.9	0.4	0.6	0.0
1974	0.3	-3.1	2.7	-2.3	-3.5	-1.3	-9.5	-4.2	24.0	3.1	-1.0	-5.4	-4.9	-0.9	-4.5	-1.0	0.5	-1.0
1975	-0.2	-1.5	1.2	-3.0	-2.9	0.8	-1.5	-0.2	15.4	2.5	-0.1	-4.9	-7.6	-0.5	-2.0	-0.2	1.3	-0.1
1976	0.2	-4.9	0.8	-1.6	-3.9	-0.9	-1.5	-1.2	19.5	2.9	-2.3	-7.1	-3.7	-2.1	-1.6	-0.8	0.5	0.7
1977	-1.2	-4.0	0.8	-1.7	-1.7	0.1	-5.1	1.1	19.6	0.9	-3.6	-8.2	-0.3	-2.6	0.0	-0.2	-0.5	1.5
1978	-1.3	-2.7	1.4	-1.6	1.0	1.4	-5.2	2.2	17.8	-0.7	-0.7	-5.0	1.9	0.0	0.5	0.8	-0.5	1.7
1979	-2.9	-4.7	-0.5	-1.5	0.5	0.9	-12.8	1.7	19.7	-1.1	-1.0	-1.5	-0.3	-2.2	0.2	-0.1	0.0	-0.9
1980	-4.4	-3.7	-1.7	0.4	-2.4	-0.6	-11.3	-2.2	17.2	-1.3	-2.7	-5.2	-2.7	-3.4	1.5	-1.3	0.4	-1.0
1971–80	-0.2	-2.9	0.7	-1.6	-0.8	0.3	-6.1	-0.1	16.4	1.2	-1.1	-2.8	-2.3	-0.7	-0.6	-0.1	0.2	0.6
1981	-3.9	-3.0	-0.6	-0.6	-2.7	-0.8	-14.2	-2.2	19.3	2.2	-2.0	-10.7	-1.0	-2.5	2.5	-0.7	0.3	0.5
1982	-3.8	-4.2	0.8	-3.6	-2.6	-2.1	-10.1	-1.5	31.2	3.3	1.1	-11.9	-1.9	-3.4	1.5	-0.7	-0.1	0.7
1983	-0.9	-2.6	0.9	-4.2	-1.8	-0.8	-6.6	0.3	35.7	3.2	0.7	-7.3	-2.3	-1.1	0.8	0.0	-1.0	1.8
1984	-0.7	-3.3	1.4	-3.3	1.2	0.0	-5.6	-0.6	35.4	4.3	-0.3	-3.0	0.0	0.3	-0.3	0.3	-2.5	2.8
1985	0.1	-4.6	2.4	-6.7	1.4	0.1	-3.8	-0.9	37.6	4.3	-0.2	0.3	-1.4	-1.7	0.3	0.5	-2.9	3.6
1986	1.9	-5.4	4.3	-4.4	1.6	0.5	-3.3	0.5	33.5	3.1	0.3	2.7	-1.0	0.2	-1.1	1.2	-3.3	4.3
1987	1.2	-2.9	4.1	-2.5	0.1	-0.2	-0.2	-0.2	27.0	1.9	-0.2	0.6	-2.0	-0.6	-1.1	0.6	-3.4	3.6
1988	1.7	-1.3	4.3	-1.8	-1.1	-0.3	0.0	-0.7	25.6	2.8	-0.2	-3.4	-2.6	-1.1	-4.9	0.0	-2.4	2.8
1989	1.6	-1.5	4.8	-4.3	-3.2	-0.5	-1.7	-1.3	26.6	3.5	0.2	-0.9	-5.1	-2.7	-5.6	-0.4	-1.7	2.0
1990	0.6	0.5	3.5	-4.7	-3.7	-1.0	-0.7	-1.6	27.6	3.8	0.8	-1.8	-5.1	-3.6	-4.9	-0.7	-1.4	1.3
1981–90	-0.2	-2.8	2.6	-3.6	-1.1	-0.5	-4.6	-0.8	29.9	3.2	0.0	-3.5	-2.3	-1.6	-1.4	0.0	-1.9	2.4
1991	1.7	1.1	-1.0	-3.8	-3.6	-0.5	2.0	-2.1	25.2	3.4	0.1	-1.9	-5.4	-2.1	-2.7	-1.3	0.1	2.5
1992	2.1	2.3	-0.9	-3.2	-3.6	0.1	3.3	-2.4	24.5	3.1	-0.1	-1.9	-4.6	-3.1	-2.6	-1.2	-1.0	3.3
1993	3.9	2.9	-0.9	-1.7	-1.0	1.0	4.9	1.0	15.2	4.4	-0.4	-2.1	-1.3	-1.4	-2.5	0.1	-1.5	3.2
1994	4.3	1.4	-1.3	-1.0	-1.2	1.1	5.1	1.5	15.9	4.4	-1.0	-1.2	1.3	-0.7	-2.1	0.1	-1.5	2.7
1995	5.0	0.4	-1.0	-2.7	0.3	1.6	6.6	2.4	17.5	4.8	-2.0	-0.4	3.4	2.0	-2.3	0.5	-2.1	2.2
1996	4.6	0.6	-0.9	-2.8	0.0	1.6	6.3	2.5	16.3	5.0	-1.6	-1.1	2.5	1.5	-2.3	0.5	-1.8	1.9

Table G38 Structure of EU exports by country and region, 1958 and 1994 (percentage of total exports)

Export of to	B/L 1958	B/L 1994	DK 1958	DK 1994	D 1958	D 1994	GR 1958	GR 1994	E 1958	E 1994	F 1958	F 1994	IRL 1958	IRL 1994	I 1958	I 1994	NL 1958	NL 1994	P 1958	P 1994	UK 1958	UK 1994	EUR12 1958	EUR12 1994
B/L	—	—	1.2	1.9	6.6	6.7	1.0	1.6	2.1	2.8	6.3	8.5	0.8	3.9	2.2	3.0	15.0	13.9	3.7	3.7	1.9	5.5	4.8	6.0
DK	1.6	0.9	—	—	3.0	1.8	0.2	0.8	1.7	0.6	0.7	0.9	0.1	1.1	0.8	0.8	2.6	1.6	1.2	2.3	2.4	1.4	2.0	1.3
D	11.6	20.8	20.0	23.0	—	—	20.5	21.1	10.2	13.4	10.4	17.7	2.2	14.1	14.1	19.0	19.0	28.6	7.7	18.7	4.2	12.9	7.6	13.6
GR	0.8	0.6	0.3	0.7	—	0.8	—	—	0.1	0.9	0.6	0.7	0.1	0.5	1.9	1.8	0.6	1.0	0.6	0.5	0.7	0.7	0.8	0.9
E	0.7	2.9	0.8	1.8	1.2	3.2	0.2	2.2	—	—	1.6	6.9	0.8	2.3	0.7	4.6	0.8	2.5	0.7	14.3	0.8	3.8	1.0	3.8
F	10.6	19.3	3.0	5.6	7.6	12.0	12.8	5.4	10.1	19.0	—	—	0.8	9.2	5.3	13.1	4.9	10.6	6.6	14.7	2.4	10.2	4.7	10.6
IRL	0.3	0.4	0.3	0.5	0.3	0.5	0.4	0.3	0.3	—	0.2	0.6	—	—	0.1	0.3	0.4	0.6	0.6	0.5	3.5	5.4	1.1	1.1
I	2.3	5.2	5.3	4.0	5.0	7.6	6.0	13.9	2.7	8.7	3.4	9.8	0.4	3.9	—	—	2.7	5.5	4.3	3.3	2.1	5.1	3.1	6.1
NL	20.7	13.0	2.2	4.3	8.1	7.5	2.0	2.5	3.2	3.6	2.0	4.5	0.5	5.5	2.0	2.9	—	—	2.5	5.2	3.2	7.1	5.3	5.7
P	1.1	0.8	0.3	0.5	0.9	0.9	0.3	0.4	0.4	7.4	0.8	1.4	0.1	0.4	0.7	1.3	0.4	0.8	—	—	0.4	1.0	0.8	1.3
UK	5.7	8.3	25.9	8.8	3.9	8.0	7.6	5.9	4.9	7.6	4.9	9.8	76.8	27.5	6.8	6.5	11.9	9.6	11.3	11.7	—	—	5.9	7.7
Total intra-EC trade	55.4	72.1	59.3	51.2	37.9	48.9	50.9	54.2	46.8	64.5	30.9	60.7	82.4	70.0	34.5	53.4	58.3	74.7	38.9	75.1	21.7	54.1	37.2	58.4
Other European OECD countries	8.7	5.8	16.6	22.2	22.7	16.9	10.3	8.1	12.4	5.8	9.0	7.8	0.9	6.9	18.9	11.3	11.9	6.7	5.1	8.1	9.1	8.2	13.7	10.7
USA	9.4	4.9	9.3	5.5	7.3	7.9	13.6	4.8	10.1	4.6	5.9	7.0	5.7	8.1	9.9	7.8	5.6	4.0	8.3	5.3	8.8	12.0	7.9	7.3
Canada	1.1	0.4	0.7	0.5	1.2	0.6	0.3	0.5	1.3	0.5	0.8	0.7	0.7	0.9	1.2	0.9	0.8	0.4	1.1	0.7	5.8	1.4	2.3	0.7
Japan	0.6	1.3	0.2	4.0	0.9	2.6	1.4	1.0	1.7	1.1	0.3	1.9	0.0	3.1	0.3	2.1	0.4	1.0	0.5	0.8	0.6	2.3	0.6	2.1
Australia	0.5	0.3	0.3	0.6	1.0	0.7	0.1	0.4	0.3	0.4	0.5	0.4	0.1	0.6	0.8	0.7	0.7	0.4	0.6	0.3	7.2	1.4	2.4	0.7
Developing countries of which:	18.0	11.3	9.3	10.9	20.9	12.7	7.2	17.2	18.4	20.7	46.9	18.0	1.6	6.7	26.2	17.1	17.6	8.3	42.3	7.9	33.6	16.4	27.4	14.2
OPEC	3.3	1.7	2.3	1.8	4.8	2.6	0.9	4.0	2.6	3.0	21.3	3.7	0.2	1.4	7.5	3.8	4.5	1.8	2.0	0.8	7.0	3.6	7.6	2.9
Other developing countries	14.7	9.6	7.0	9.1	16.1	10.1	6.3	13.2	15.8	17.7	25.6	14.3	1.4	5.3	18.7	13.3	13.1	6.5	40.3	7.1	26.6	12.8	19.8	11.3
Rest of the world and unspecified	6.3	3.9	4.3	5.1	8.1	9.7	16.2	13.8	9.0	2.4	5.7	3.5	8.6	3.7	8.2	6.7	4.7	4.5	3.2	1.8	13.2	4.2	8.5	5.9
World (excl. EU)	44.6	27.9	40.7	48.8	62.1	51.1	49.1	45.8	53.2	35.5	69.1	39.3	17.6	30.0	65.5	46.6	41.7	25.3	61.1	24.9	78.3	45.9	62.8	41.6
World (incl. EU)	100	100	100	100	100	100	100	100	100	100	100	100	100	100	100	100	100	100	100	100	100	100	100	100

Table G39 Structure of EU imports by country and region, 1958 and 1994 (percentage of total imports)

Import of from	B/L 1958	B/L 1994	DK 1958	DK 1994	D 1958	D 1994	GR 1958	GR 1994	E 1958	E 1994	F 1958	F 1994	IRL 1958	IRL 1994	I 1958	I 1994	NL 1958	NL 1994	P 1958	P 1994	UK 1958	UK 1994	EUR12 1958	EUR12 1994
B/L	–	–	3.8	3.7	4.5	7.1	3.3	3.8	1.8	3.9	5.4	10.3	1.8	1.6	2.0	4.7	17.8	10.7	7.3	3.5	1.6	4.6	4.4	6.2
DK	0.5	0.6	–	–	3.4	1.9	0.7	1.5	1.3	0.8	0.6	1.0	0.7	0.7	2.2	1.0	0.7	1.1	0.8	0.8	3.1	1.4	2.0	1.2
D	17.2	18.9	19.9	21.8	–	–	20.3	16.4	8.7	15.3	11.6	20.4	4.0	7.0	12.0	19.2	19.5	20.9	17.6	14.0	3.6	14.2	8.7	13.4
GR	0.1	0.1	0.0	0.2	0.7	0.5	–	–	–	0.3	0.6	0.2	0.2	0.1	0.4	0.8	0.2	0.1	0.1	0.1	0.2	0.2	0.4	0.3
E	0.5	1.6	0.7	1.2	1.6	2.8	0.1	3.1	–	–	1.2	6.0	0.2	0.9	0.4	3.8	0.4	1.6	0.4	19.8	1.0	2.4	0.9	3.2
F	11.6	15.2	3.4	5.4	7.6	11.3	5.4	8.1	6.8	18.0	–	–	1.6	3.4	4.8	13.6	2.8	6.9	7.7	12.7	2.7	9.8	4.4	9.5
IRL	0.1	1.0	0.0	0.8	0.1	1.1	0.0	0.9	0.6	0.9	0.0	–	–	–	0.0	0.9	0.0	1.1	0.1	0.7	2.9	4.7	0.9	1.5
I	2.1	4.1	1.7	4.2	5.5	8.4	8.8	16.7	1.8	8.9	2.4	9.9	0.8	2.0	–	–	1.8	3.4	3.7	8.5	2.1	4.9	2.7	6.2
NL	15.7	17.0	7.3	6.9	8.1	10.5	4.8	7.5	2.6	4.5	2.5	6.5	2.9	3.3	2.6	5.7	–	–	2.9	4.4	4.2	6.5	5.2	7.5
P	0.4	0.5	0.3	1.3	0.4	0.9	0.3	0.4	0.3	2.8	0.4	1.1	0.2	0.3	0.4	0.8	0.2	0.5	–	–	0.4	0.8	0.3	0.9
UK	7.4	9.1	22.8	6.7	4.3	6.3	9.9	6.2	7.8	8.0	3.5	8.2	56.3	41.2	5.5	6.1	7.4	8.5	12.9	6.7	–	–	5.4	6.8
Total intra-EU trade	55.5	68.1	60.0	52.1	36.3	50.7	53.7	64.4	31.8	63.5	28.3	65.0	68.9	63.3	30.2	56.2	50.7	54.8	53.4	71.4	21.8	49.9	35.2	57.0
Other European OECD countries	7.7	6.8	18.6	25.5	15.2	16.5	11.5	6.6	8.4	5.5	6.7	7.6	3.4	4.8	13.1	11.6	7.2	9.0	8.6	6.0	8.7	10.8	10.1	11.1
USA	9.9	5.9	9.1	4.3	13.6	5.9	13.7	3.2	21.6	6.2	10.0	7.3	7.0	16.9	16.4	4.6	11.3	8.7	7.0	3.6	9.4	12.8	11.4	7.4
Canada	1.4	0.7	0.2	0.4	3.1	0.6	0.8	0.3	0.5	0.4	1.0	0.6	3.0	0.6	1.5	0.9	1.4	0.7	0.5	0.3	8.2	1.2	3.6	0.7
Japan	0.6	2.7	1.5	3.1	0.6	4.8	2.0	3.8	0.7	2.8	0.2	2.5	1.1	4.3	0.4	2.4	0.8	4.4	0.0	2.8	0.9	5.9	0.7	3.9
Australia	1.7	0.3	0.0	0.2	1.2	0.2	0.3	0.0	0.8	0.3	2.4	0.3	1.2	0.1	3.0	0.5	0.2	0.4	0.9	0.1	5.4	0.7	2.6	0.4
Developing countries of which:	19.2	10.0	5.9	8.3	23.9	11.0	9.6	13.6	32.0	17.0	45.6	12.6	9.3	7.3	29.4	14.2	24.4	17.3	27.6	13.3	34.7	13.2	29.5	12.8
OPEC	5.7	1.4	0.3	0.7	6.7	2.1	1.7	5.3	17.7	6.1	19.7	3.8	0.7	0.3	13.9	5.3	11.5	5.3	6.3	5.8	11.3	2.4	10.8	3.2
Other developing countries	13.5	8.6	5.6	7.6	17.2	8.9	7.9	8.3	14.3	10.9	25.9	8.8	8.6	7.0	15.5	8.9	12.9	12.0	21.3	7.5	23.4	10.8	18.7	9.6
Rest of the world and unspecified	4.0	5.5	4.7	6.1	6.1	10.3	8.4	8.1	4.2	4.3	5.8	4.1	6.1	2.7	6.0	9.6	4.0	4.7	2.0	2.5	10.9	5.5	6.9	6.7
World (excl. EU)	44.5	31.9	40.0	47.9	63.7	49.3	46.3	35.6	68.2	36.5	71.7	35.0	31.1	36.7	69.8	43.8	49.3	45.2	46.6	28.6	78.2	50.1	64.8	43.0
World (incl. EU)	100	100	100	100	100	100	100	100	100	100	100	100	100	100	100	100	100	100	100	100	100	100	100	100

Table G40 Balance of payments by main heading – 1993 (Mio ECU)

Country	Goods (fob)	Transport	Travel	Other services	Investment income	Labour income	Govern-mental transactions	Unrequited transfers	Current balance	Direct investment	Other long-term capital	Portfolio investment	Reserves	Errors and omissions
EUR12	54 197	-4 972	-892	11 391	-21 228	-3 132	7 348	-32 550	10 161	-15 211	43 475	109 747	22 353	-17 676
1 Belgium	3 156	1 369	-1 958	3 923	2 554	-333	3 198	-2 243	9 667	5 650	17 886	-6 931	1 831	-536
2 Denmark	6 675	477	-144	1 530	-4 092	:	16	-440	4 022	274	5 459	10 855	397	1 050
3 Germany	38 545	-4 210	-23 067	-13 091	7 690	-2 472	6 592	-26 702	-16 715	-10 222	4 417	102 149	18 520	-12 362
4 Greece	-9 017	-255	2 002	2 563	-1 264	39	-232	5 541	-624	835	3 753	0	-2 638	-528
5 Spain	-13 702	209	12 489	-2 026	-5 161	-1	-873	3 900	-5 165	4 026	7 429	21 659	3 967	-856
6 France	6 027	-950	9 044	7 552	-6 702	-280	-594	-5 253	8 844	-38	-6 146	3 217	8 024	2 252
7 Ireland	6 031	493	316	-1 409	-4 830	:	105	2 373	3 080	75	-1 418	1 983	-2 238	642
8 Italy	27 767	-3 052	6 834	-3 546	-13 874	-60	289	-4 613	9 746	-3 024	-5 713	61 095	-1 212	-15 556
9 Luxembourg	:	:	:	:	:	:	:	:	:	:	:	:	:	:
10 Netherlands	11 065	2 480	-3 607	2 218	691	-102	89	-4 389	8 445	-3 994	-1 358	1 592	-5 783	7 571
11 Portugal	-5 854	-532	1 994	-374	-42	67	-145	5 724	837	977	414	-512	2 408	-134
12 United Kingdom	-17 132	-724	-4 566	13 118	2 146	:	-1 150	-6 700	-15 009	-9 599	18 817	-55 508	-923	4 510
13 Austria	-6 680	848	4 389	1 953	-893	174	235	-786	-759	-536	-1 243	7 515	-1 916	-705
14 Finland	5 471	-20	-312	-1 154	-4 254	7	-74	-469	-805	-1 070	2 160	4 875	-214	823
15 Sweden	6 579	590	-1 550	267	-5 972	-123	156	-1 497	-1 549	323	12 043	963	-1 678	-4 142
16 USA	-113 583	3 248	14 583	29 320	3 338	-983	2 375	-27 513	-89 215	-31 113	3 600	-6 606	-1 209	17 730
17 Japan	120 968	-8 913	-19 922	-11 062	35 231	-685	1 843	-5 204	112 256	-11 644	-1 953	-56 387	-23 337	-560

Table G41 Exchange rates (annual average, national currency units per ECU)

	BFR	DKR	DM	100 DR	100 PTA	FF	IRL	100 LIT	LFR	HFL	OS	100 ESC	FMK	SKR	UKL	USD	100 YEN
1960	52.810	7.2954	4.4361	0.3169	0.6337	5.2145	0.37722	0.6601	52.810	4.0136	27.461	0.3037	3.3799	5.4640	0.37722	1.0562	3.8023
1971	50.866	7.7526	3.6457	0.3143	0.7257	5.7721	0.42858	0.6474	50.866	3.6575	26.179	0.2964	4.3842	5.3707	0.42858	1.0478	3.6383
1972	49.361	7.7891	3.5768	0.3365	0.7200	5.6572	0.44894	0.6543	49.361	3.5999	25.930	0.3048	4.6512	5.3424	0.44894	1.1218	3.3972
1973	47.801	7.4160	3.2764	0.3695	0.7181	5.4678	0.50232	0.7165	47.801	3.4285	24.117	0.3027	4.7067	5.3792	0.50232	1.2317	3.3317
1974	45.912	7.1932	3.0867	0.3578	0.6884	5.6745	0.51350	0.7917	45.912	3.1714	22.471	0.2993	4.5365	5.3367	0.51350	1.2021	3.3968
1975	45.569	7.1227	3.0494	0.3999	0.7027	5.3192	0.55981	0.8095	45.569	3.1349	21.547	0.3144	4.5640	5.1413	0.56003	1.2408	3.6073
1976	43.166	6.7618	2.8155	0.4088	0.7474	5.3449	0.62192	0.9302	43.166	2.9552	20.035	0.3362	4.3112	4.8666	0.62158	1.1180	3.3121
1977	40.883	6.8557	2.6483	0.4216	0.8682	5.6061	0.65370	1.0068	40.883	2.8001	18.842	0.4362	4.5934	5.1193	0.65370	1.1411	3.0581
1978	40.061	7.0195	2.5561	0.4680	0.9742	5.7398	0.66389	1.0802	40.061	2.7541	18.464	0.5587	5.2385	5.7494	0.66391	1.2741	2.6708
1979	40.165	7.2079	2.5110	0.5076	0.9197	5.8298	0.66945	1.1384	40.165	2.7488	18.310	0.6701	5.3220	5.8717	0.64630	1.3705	3.0046
1980	40.598	7.8274	2.5242	0.5942	0.9970	5.8690	0.67600	1.1892	40.598	2.7603	17.969	0.6955	5.1722	5.8810	0.59849	1.3923	3.1504
1981	41.295	7.9226	2.5139	0.6162	1.0268	6.0399	0.69102	1.2632	41.295	2.7751	17.715	0.6849	4.7930	5.6347	0.55311	1.1164	2.4538
1982	44.712	8.1569	2.3760	0.6534	1.0756	6.4312	0.68961	1.3238	44.712	2.6139	16.699	0.7801	4.7072	6.1434	0.56046	0.9797	2.4355
1983	45.438	8.1319	2.2705	0.7809	1.2750	6.7708	0.71496	1.3499	45.438	2.5372	15.969	0.9869	4.9482	6.8212	0.58701	0.8902	2.1135
1984	45.442	8.1465	2.2381	0.8842	1.2657	6.8717	0.72594	1.3814	45.442	2.5234	15.735	1.1568	4.7241	6.5110	0.59063	0.7890	1.8709
1985	44.914	8.0188	2.2263	1.0574	1.2913	6.7950	0.71517	1.4480	44.914	2.5110	15.643	1.3025	4.6942	6.5213	0.58898	0.7631	1.8056
1986	43.798	7.9357	2.1282	1.3742	1.3746	6.7998	0.73353	1.4619	43.798	2.4009	14.964	1.4709	4.9797	6.9957	0.67154	0.9842	1.6500
1987	43.041	7.8847	2.0715	1.5627	1.4216	6.9291	0.77545	1.4949	43.041	2.3342	14.571	1.6262	5.0652	7.3100	0.70457	1.1544	1.6660
1988	43.429	7.9515	2.0744	1.6758	1.3760	7.0364	0.77567	1.5373	43.429	2.3348	14.586	1.7006	4.9436	7.2419	0.66443	1.1825	1.5146
1989	43.381	8.0493	2.0702	1.7884	1.3041	7.0239	0.77682	1.5105	43.381	2.3353	14.570	1.7341	4.7230	7.0994	0.67330	1.1017	1.5194
1990	42.426	7.8565	2.0521	2.0141	1.2941	6.9141	0.76777	1.5220	42.426	2.3121	14.440	1.8111	4.8550	7.5205	0.71385	1.2734	1.8366
1991	42.223	7.9086	2.0508	2.2522	1.2847	6.9733	0.76781	1.5332	42.223	2.3110	14.431	1.7861	5.0021	7.4793	0.70101	1.2392	1.6649
1992	41.593	7.8093	2.0203	2.4703	1.3253	6.8484	0.76072	1.5955	41.593	2.2748	14.217	1.7471	5.8070	7.5330	0.73765	1.2981	1.6422
1993	40.471	7.5936	1.9364	2.6857	1.4912	6.6337	0.79995	1.8412	40.471	2.1752	13.624	1.8837	6.6963	9.1215	0.77999	1.1710	1.3015
1994	39.657	7.5433	1.9245	2.8803	1.5892	6.5826	0.79362	1.9151	39.657	2.1583	13.540	1.9690	6.1908	9.1631	0.77590	1.1895	1.2132
1995	38.552	7.3280	1.8738	3.0299	1.6300	6.5251	0.81553	2.1301	38.552	2.0989	13.182	1.9610	5.7086	9.3319	0.82879	1.3080	1.2301

Table G42 Nominal effective exchange rates. Performance relative to 19 industrial countries; double export weights (1991=100)

	B	DK	D[(1)]	GR	E	F	IRL	I	NL
1960	89.4	108.7	42.8	797.3	202.2	148.3	172.7	271.9	64.3
1971	89.9	101.3	52.5	779.2	175.0	127.6	161.0	268.4	67.6
1972	92.5	102.0	53.9	729.5	178.3	130.7	157.7	266.5	68.6
1973	93.8	108.2	59.5	671.4	181.1	135.0	146.8	239.3	70.8
1974	95.1	108.7	62.7	673.1	186.4	126.0	143.2	216.0	74.5
1975	96.5	112.4	63.8	607.2	181.7	138.3	135.0	207.1	76.3
1976	98.7	114.9	67.4	574.2	166.9	133.2	121.3	171.7	78.3
1977	104.4	114.3	72.8	557.4	146.1	126.8	117.0	158.0	82.5
1978	107.4	114.2	77.1	506.6	132.1	125.2	117.7	148.2	84.5
1979	108.7	113.3	80.7	478.2	144.4	126.0	117.9	143.2	85.7
1980	108.2	104.4	81.1	413.9	134.4	126.6	115.4	138.1	85.9
1981	101.9	96.6	76.5	371.8	121.5	115.4	105.4	121.0	82.2
1982	92.5	92.4	80.3	342.1	114.2	105.8	104.2	112.6	86.3
1983	89.9	91.8	83.6	280.2	94.5	98.3	99.9	108.4	88.1
1984	88.0	88.4	82.2	240.0	92.2	93.5	95.7	102.0	86.7
1985	88.7	89.5	82.5	201.9	90.1	94.5	96.8	96.8	86.9
1986	93.6	95.2	91.3	158.9	88.8	98.8	100.4	100.4	93.6
1987	97.4	99.2	97.6	143.3	88.9	99.8	98.3	101.5	98.4
1988	96.1	97.3	96.9	132.9	91.7	97.5	96.9	97.9	97.9
1989	95.3	94.7	95.7	122.9	95.5	96.3	95.7	98.3	97.0
1990	100.3	101.9	101.1	113.0	100.3	102.2	101.3	102.0	100.7
1991	100.0	100.0	100.0	100.0	100.0	100.0	100.0	100.0	100.0
1992	102.3	102.8	103.3	92.8	98.2	103.6	102.8	97.3	102.4
1993	103.1	104.9	106.1	83.4	85.3	105.5	96.7	80.8	105.5
1994	104.8	105.0	106.3	77.5	79.6	106.1	97.0	77.1	106.0
1995	109.4	110.4	112.3	75.3	79.5	110.0	97.0	70.2	110.5
1996	107.3	109.1	109.3	73.5	80.8	110.2	98.2	75.8	108.5

Aggregates: PPS weighted.
[(1)] 1960–94: WD.

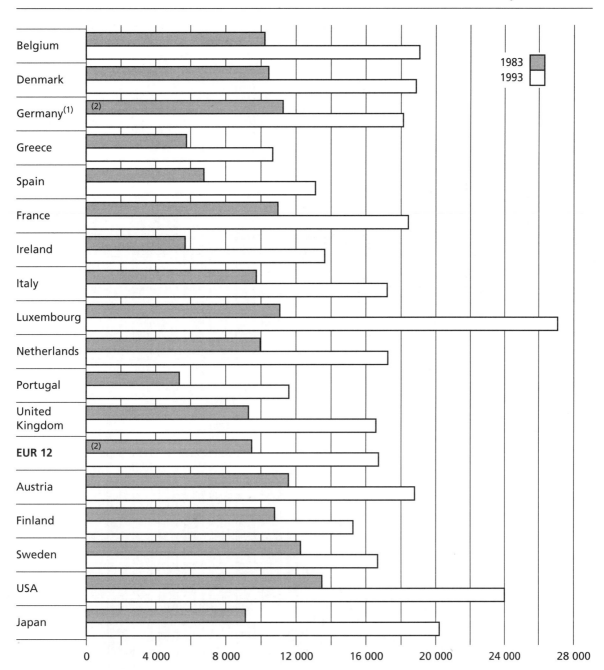

Figure G1 Gross domestic product per head, volume (PPS)

[1] Break in series owing to the unification of 3.10.1990.
[2] Except the new Länder.
PPS = Purchasing Power Standards.

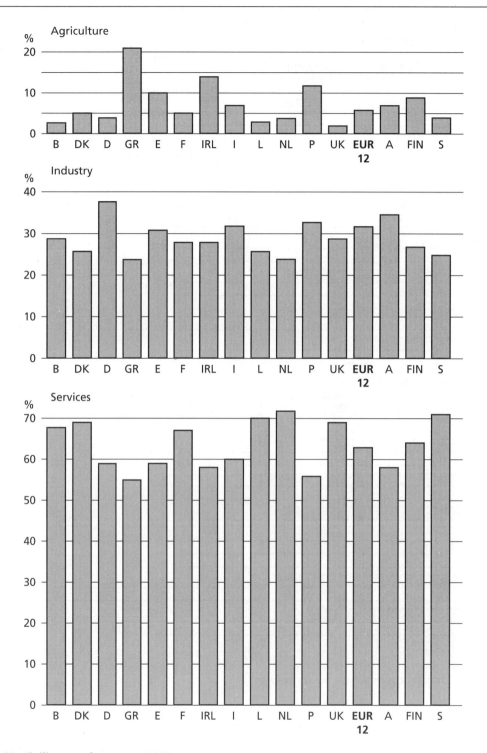

Figure G2 Civilian employment – 1993

GLOSSARY OF ABBREVIATIONS AND FOREIGN TERMS

Germany

AG (Aktiengesellschaft)	Joint stock company
Aufsichtsrat	Board of a company
Berufsgenossenschaften	Insurance scheme covering occupational health risks (all firms are compulsory members)
Beschäftigungsgesellschaften	Companies offering job and training opportunities in the new states
Betriebsträte	Councils of elected representatives of employees in firms
Betriebsverfassungsgesetz	Law granting employees and their elected representatives comprehensive rights of information and consultation
BDA (Bundesvereinigung der Deutschen Arbeitgeberverbände) BDI (Bundesverband der Deutschen Industrie)	} Umbrella organisations of German employers' associations (having their headquarters in Cologne)
BMWI (Bundesministerium für Wirtschaft)	Federal Department of Commerce
Bundeskartellamt	Cartel authority (in Berlin)
Bundesländer	German states
Bundesaufsichtsamt für das Kreditwesen	Regulatory authority with respect to banking activities
Bundesregierung	Central government
Bundesstaat	Federal state
Deutsche Bundesbank	Central bank in Germany
Deutsche Bundespost	Former German PTT (now split up into three separate activities: Telecommunication, Postal Services, Banking)
DGB (Deutsche Gewerkschaftsbund)	Umbrella organisation for the German labour unions
DIHT (Deutsche Industrie und Handelstag) Deutsche Handwerkskammertag	} Umbrella organisations of regional chambers of commerce

Erblastenfonds	Treuhandanstalt debt transferred to federal government
Gemeinden	Local authorities
Gewerbekapitalsteuer	Local trade on business capital
GG (Grundgesetz)	German constitution (of 1949)
Gesetz über die Deutsche Bundesbank	Law regulating the position, tasks and instruments of the German central bank (1957)
GmbH (Gesellschaft mit beschränkter Haftung)	Limited liability company
Günstigkeitsprinzip	Principle stating that individual labour contracts may only deviate from collective agreements if such a deviation is to the advantage of the employee
GWB (Gesetz gegen Wettbewerbsbeschränkungen)	Competition law
Handwerksordnung	Craft codes
Industrie und Handelskammer Handwerkskammer	} Regional chambers of commerce
Kombinate	State enterprises in the former GDR
Landwirtschaftliche Produktionsgenossenschaften (LPG)	Agricultural co-operatives in the former GDR
Langzeitarbeitslose	Long-term unemployed (over one year)
Marktbeherrschende Unternehmen	Market dominating companies
Meisterprüfung	Formal qualification for craftsmen (second degree)
Mitbestimmungsgesetz	Law granting substantial rights of consultation, information and co-determination to employees of corporations with more than 2,000 employees
Monopolkommission	Federal commission reviewing concentration processes and providing expertise in merger cases
Pflegeversicherung	Possible insurance scheme for the nursing of the old
Solidaritätszuschlag	A surcharge in taxation to meet costs of unification
Soziale Marktwirtschaft	Social market economy
Sozialleistungsquote	Social security expenditure as a proportion of GDP

Sozialplan	Social plan to be negotiated between management and employees in cases of mass lay-offs (of more than 10% of a firm's employees)
Statistisches Bundesamt	Central Statistics Agency
Subsidiaritätsprinzip	Principle of subsidiarity: principle whereby decision-making is delegated to the lowest possible authority
Tarifverträge	Collective labour agreements
Treuhandanstalt	Public agency concerned with the privatisation of East German state enterprises
Wellblechkonjunktur	Continuous expansion with only minor fluctuations in growth rates
Zinsabschlagsteuer	Tax on capital income

France

ANPE (Agence Nationale pour l'Emploi	Employment Office
Banque de France	Central bank
CAC (Cotation Assistée en Continu)	Stock exchange quotation system
CCI (Chambre de Commerce et d'Industrie)	Chamber of Commerce
CFDT (Confédération Française Démocratique du Travail)	Trade union (left-wing)
CGT (Confédération Générale du Travail)	Trade union (communist)
COFACE (Compagnie Française d'Assurance pour le Commerce Extérieur)	Foreign trade insurance company
CNPF (Confédération Nationale du Patronat Français)	Employers' federation
DATAR (Délégation à l'Aménagement du Territoire)	Industrial Development Board
EDF (Electricité de France)	National electricity company
FO (Force Ouvrière)	Trade union (socialist)
GEN (Grandes Entreprises Nationales)	Nationalised enterprises
Grande Ecole	Specialised university level educational establishments
INSEE (Institut National des Statistiques et des Etudes Economiques)	National Statistical Office

MATIF (Marché à Terme d'Instruments Financiers)	Financial futures market
OPA (Offre Public d'Achat)	Take-over bid
PME (Petites et Moyennes Entreprises)	Small and medium businesses
RMI (Revenu Minimum d'Insertion)	Basic social security income
SA (Société Anonyme)	Public limited company
SARL (Société à Responsabilité Limitée)	Private limited company
SICAV (Société d'Investissement à Capital Variable)	Unit trusts
SME (Système Monétaire Européen)	European monetary system
SMIC (Salaire Minimum Interprofessional de Croissance)	Minimum salary
TGV (Train à Grande Vitesse)	High speed train
TVA (Taxe sur la Valeur Ajoutée)	Value added tax
VRP (Voyageurs, Représentant Placier)	Salaried commercial salesmen

Italy

AUSL (Azienda Unità Sanitarie Locali)	Local centres of the national health service
Autorità garante della concorrenza e del mercato	Instituion with general responsibility for ensuring market competition
Autorità garante per l'editoria	Institution with specific responsibility for ensuring competition and controlling ownership concentration in the mass-media sector
Cassa depositi e prestiti	State institution for financing local administrations using deposits collected by Italian Post Office
Cassa integrazione guadagni	Wage-related unemployment benefit scheme
CGIL (Confederazione Generale Italiana del Lavoro)	Left-wing workers' trade union
CISL (Confederazione Italiana Sindacati Lavoratori)	Trade union whose members are, generally, supporters of the centre
Comit (Banca Commerciale Italiana)	Bank of national interest recently privatised
Confindustria	The most relevant organisation of the Italian entrepreneurs
Credit (Istituto di Credito Italiano)	Bank of national interest recently privatised
EFIM (Ente partecipazione e Finanziamento Industrie Manifatturiere)	State-owned industrial group

ENEL (Ente Nazionale per l'Energia Elettrica)	State-owned industrial group (joint stock company) for power supply
ENI (Ente Nazionale Idrocarburi)	State-owned (joint stock company) industrial group partially privatised, basically involved in chemical and oil sectors
Ferruzzi	Private-owned industrial group in the agricultural sector
Fininvest	The biggest private-owned group for radio and television
IMI (Istituto Mobiliare Italiano)	State agency established in 1931 to grant medium and long-term loans to the industry, recently privatised
INAIL (Istituto Nazionale di Assicurazione per gli Infortuni sul Lavoro)	State insurance institution for workers in case of accidents
INPS (Istituto Nazionale per la Previdenza Sociale)	State insurance institution for paying pensions to the workers
IRI (Istituto per la Ricostruzione Industriale)	The most relevant state-owned industrial group
ISCO (Istituto per lo Studio della Congiuntura)	Institution for studying economic cycles
Istituti speciali di credito	Financial institutions specialised for medium- and long-term loans
ISTAT (Istituo Centrale di Statistica)	State central statistical office
Montedison	The most relevant private chemical group in Italy
Olivetti	Private-owned industrial group in the telecommunications sector (mobile telephony)
RAI (Radio Televisione Italiana)	State-owned group for radio and television
Scala mobile	Wage-indexation scale introduced in 1975, later abolished by public referendum
SIM (Società di intermadiazione mobiliare)	Stock brokerage companies dealing in listed securities in the Stock Exchange Market
Stet	State-holding group for telecommunications
SVIMEZ (associazone per lo sviluppo dell'industria nel Mezzogiorno)	Institution for the study of the industrialisation of the south of the country
UIL (Unione Italiana del Lavoro)	Trade union of centre-left wing workers

The Netherlands

ABN AMRO ING RABO	} Three largest banks
Benelux	Customs Union of Belgium, The Netherlands and Luxembourg

CDA (Christen Democratisch)	Christian Democratic Party (centrist party)
D'66 (Democraten '66)	(Liberal) Democratic Party
DNB (De Nederlandsche Bank)	Dutch Central Bank
NMP (Nationaal Milieubeleidsplan)	National Environmental Policy Plan; introduced in 1989
PvdA (Partij van de Arbeid)	Labour Party
SER (Sociaal Economisch Raad)	Social Economic Council; Advisory Board to the government
VVD (Volkspartij voor Vrijheid and Democratie)	Right-wing liberal party

Belgium and Luxembourg

B-Franc	Belgian Franc
Bank Nationale de Belgique	Central bank of Belgium (50% state-owned)
BENELUX	Treaty of Economic Union between Belgium, Luxembourg and The Netherlands enforced in 1948
BLEU	Belgium and Luxembourg Economic Union
Generale Bank	Largest bank in Belgium
GIMV	Flemish Investment Company, assists business with investment
IMEC	Inter-University Micro-Electronics Centre (Flemish)
NATO	North Atlantic Treaty Organisation
SRIW	Walloon Regional Investment Company

United Kingdom

'Chunnel'	Channel Tunnel
'Big Bang'	Deregulation of the Stock Exchange (1986)
EER	Effective Exchange Rate
EFTA	European Free Trade Association
EMU	Economic and Monetary Union
ERDF	European Regional Development Fund
ERM	Exchange Rate Mechanism
G7	The seven largest western industrialised economies (USA, Japan, Germany, France, Italy, United Kingdom, Canada)

GDFCF	Gross Domestic Fixed Capital Formation
GDP	Gross Domestic Product
ILO	International Labour Organisation
MMC	Mergers and Monopolies Commission
MTFS	Medium-Term Financial Strategy
MU	Monetary Union
NBFI	Non-Banking Financial Institution
NVQ	National Vocational Qualification
Ofgas	Office of Gas (Regulatory Body)
Oftel	Office of Telecommunications (Regulatory Body)
PSBR	Public Sector Borrowing Requirement
PSDR	Public Sector Debt Repayment
RPI	Retail Price Index
SE	International (formerly London) Stock Exchange
SMEs	Small and Medium Enterprises
TECs	Training and Enterprise Councils

Denmark

CO Industri	Industrial trade union cartel
Dansk Industri	Employers' organisation
Nationalbank	Central bank of Denmark

Greece

PASOK	Panhellenic Socialist Movement
ND	New Democracy
QUANGO	Quasi-Autonomous Non-Governmental Organisation
Ecu	European Currency Unit

Spain

ALP	The Spanish abbreviation for liquid assets
Banco de Bilbao (nowadays, Banco Bilbao-Vizcaya)	Bank of Bilbao (one of the major Spanish banks)
Banco de España	Bank of Spain (the central bank of Spain)
Cajas de Ahorros	Savings banks (owned by local authorities, which have evolved from their ancient savings bank

	financial activity to their present fully banking business)
Comunidades Autónomas	Autonomous communities (the official name of Spanish regions)
Consejo General de la Formación Profesional	General Council of Occupational Training (a body composed of representatives of workers, employers and the administration responsible for designing general objectives in the area of occupational training)
Cooperativas de Crédito	Credit co-operatives (private financial institutions, operating locally, and initially created for aiding regional development and presently running as banks)
Corporación Bancaria	Banking Corporation (a banking institution created in the 1980s jointly owned by the private banks and the Banco de España, which took control over some failing banks in order to sell them after re-establishing their profitability)
Direccion General de Aduanas	General Customs Direction
Estatuto de los Trabajadores	Workers' Statute (the legal document which sets out the workers' rights recognised by the Constitution)
Impuesto de Compensación de Gravámenes Interiores (ICGI)	Tax to compensate for home taxation (theoretically introduced in Spain in the 1960s to tax imported products as home products, but in practice meant a protection level of 2–3%)
Instituto de Crédito Oficial (ICO)	Official Credit Institute (which comprises several (state-owned) banking institutions, each one specialised in financial transactions for specific economic activities such as industry, shipbuilding, agriculture, etc.)
Instituto Español de Emigración	Spanish Institute for Emigration (the public institution responsible for emigration issues)
Mercado de Títulos de Deuda Pública Anotados en Cuenta	Treasury bill market (where there are not 'physical' transfers of titles but accounting records on books of the institutions involved)
Pagarés and Letras del Tesoro	Short-term treasury bills
Zonas de Urgent Reindustrialización (ZUR)	Areas of urgent re-industrialisation (areas set up in the late 1980s in an attempt to counteract the effects of the industrial restructuring process)

Portugal

Acordo economico e social	Non-statutory prices and incomes policy
PEDIP	Specific Programme for Industrial Development in Portugal

Austria

Arbeiterkammer	Chamber of workers
Arbeitsamt	Labour office
ASFINAG	State-owned company responsible for freeway construction
Beirat für Wirtschafts- und Sozialfragen	Advisory board on economic and social questions
Bund	Federal government
Bundeskammer der gewerblichen Wirtschaft	Federal chamber of industry and commerce
Bundesland	Province
Finanzausgleich	Financial redistribution process between the federal government, the provinces, and the municipalitites
Gemeinden	Municipalities
Gewerkschaftsbund	Federation of labour unions
Industriellenvereinigung	Confederation of business owners
Landwirtschaftskammer	Chamber of agriculture
Lohnunterausschuß	Income sub-committee
Paritätische Kommission	Parity commission
Preisunterausschuß	Prices sub-committee
Sozialpartnerschaft	Social partnership
VOEST (Vereinigte Österreichische Eisen und Stahlwerke)	Austria's largest steel company, reorganised in 1993, today more than 50% private ownership
WIFO	Austrian institute of economic research

Finland

Bank of Finland	Central bank
Supervisory Board	Supervises the activities of the Bank of Finland, appointed by the parliament; its power will be reduced in the new central bank law

Board of Governors	Consists of the Director General and of four members of the Board (Directors), the power of the Board will increase in the new legislation at the cost of the Supervisory Board
Clearing trade agreement	Arrangement through which payments in trade between Finland and the Soviet Union were kept in balance in 1945–90; bilateral trade with some flexibility in balancing accounts
Currency basket exchange rate regime	Exchange rate regime used in Finland in 1973–1991/6; the Finnish markka was pegged to a trade-weighted basket of foreign currencies
EEA (European Economic Area)	System through which most EFTA countries were integrated into the internal market programme of the EC; Finland participated in it for only one year (1994) before membership in the EU
Enso-Gutzeit	The second largest forest industry company in Finland and the fifth largest in Europe
ETLA (Elinkeinoelämän tutkimuslaitos)	Research Institute of the Finnish Economy (ETLA), largest private Finnish economic research institute
Kansallis Bank	Major Finnish private bank, merged with Union Bank of Finland (name of the new bank: Merita Bank)
Kesko	The largest Finnish wholesale firm
Merita Bank	The largest commercial bank in Finland, originated in 1996 as a result of the merger of Kansallis Bank and Union Bank of Finland
Metsäliitto-Group	The third largest Finnish forest industry company
Nokia	The largest Finnish (internationalised) firm, concentrated in electronics, mainly in telecommunications equipment
Okobank	Cooperative private bank
Postipankki	State-owned bank
Tax wedge	Difference between the labour costs paid by the employer and the net wage of the employee
Tuko	Large Finnish wholesale firm
Union Bank of Finland	Major Finnish commercial bank, merged in 1996 with Kansallis Bank into Merita Bank
UPM-Kymmene	The largest forest industry company in Finland and in Europe

General

CAP	Common Agricultural Policy
GATT	General Agreements on Tariffs and Trade
NIC	Newly Industrialised Countries
OECD	Organisation for Economic Co-operation and Development
OPEC	Organisation of Petroleum Exporting Countries
R&D	Research and Development
USA	United States of America
VAT	Value Added Tax

INDEX